Transliteration Table

Arabic		Example	Arabic		Example
فتحة+ا	a	about	ن	n	nurse
	a	c<u>a</u>t	و	oo	pool
ع	AA	say "a" twice distinctly with an open mouth	أ	o	on
ب	b	box	ق	q	queen ("k" sound made in back of throat)
د	d	door	ر	r	rabbit (Rolled "r" sound, similar to Spanish "r")
ض	<u>d</u>	heavy "d" sound (Open jaw but keep lips slightly round i.e: duh)	ش	sh	ship
ي	ee	feet	س	s	sea
ف	f	fish	ص	s	heavy "s" sound (Open jaw but keep lips slightly round)
غ	gh	the sound you make when gurgling (Touch very back of tongue to very back of mouth)	ت	t	tan
ه	h	hat	ط	t	heavy "t" sound (Open jaw but keep lips slightly round)
ح	<u>h</u>	heavy "h" sound (Drop back of tongue to open back of throat, then force air out for "h")	ث	th	think
كسرة+ا	i	ink	ذ	<u>th</u>	the
ج	j	jar	ظ	<u>*th*</u>	"th" sound as in "the", but heavier (Open jaw but keep lips slightly round)
ك	k	kit	ضمة	u	put
خ	kh	gravely "h" sound (Touch back of tongue to roof of mouth and force air out)	و	w	water
ل	l	look	ا+ع	/	pronounce the letter before but cut it short by stopping suddenly
م	m	man	ي	y	yarn
Bold letters are silent i.e w: **w**rite			ز	z	zebra
			(-) is to make some words easier to read		

<u>**CONTENTS**</u>

**[Against the Qur'aanic Chapter No. in every line below are: the Chapter name &
no. of Verses in it in ()]**

<u>Chapter 1</u>. **Al-Fatiha (7)**

<u>Chapter 2</u>. **Al-Baqarah (286)**

<u>Chapter 3</u>. **Aale-Imran (200)**

<u>Chapter 4</u>. **An-Nisa (176)**

In the Name of Allah, the Gracious, the Merciful

****

Study the Qur'aan in Qur'aanic light to understand Islam in its pristine simplicity, clarity, beauty, and purity

****

QUR'AANIC STUDIES – A Modern Tafsir

Manzil I

by
Mohammad Shafi

PREFACE

Below the Arabic text of every Verse of the Qur'aan in this book, its transliteration, followed by translation and Chapter Notes, if any, essentially based on the Qur'aan itself, is given. Please remember that the Arabic text is divine and, therefore, sacrosanct, but the transliteration, translation and the Notes are human and, therefore, subject to correction. Please also remember that the human-made Notes cannot, and do not, explain the divine Verses. They seek to explain the human translation only and/or to relate the Verse to present circumstances or to divine explanations given in other Verses of the Qur'aan.

I have adopted the transliteration method employed by the Muslim Students' Association (MSA) of the University of Southern California. And, in this regard, I may usefully quote from their site:

> "MSA-USC would like to thank muslimnet.net for making their transliteration of the Qur'an publicly available.
>
> 'We would like to emphasize that this [transliteration] text is not a substitute for the original Arabic Qur'an. It is only an attempt to help those who are trying to learn to read the Arabic text, since it is as close to the written text as possible.
>
> It is important to practice pronouncing the letters as directed in the transliteration table, especially the underlined letters, before starting to read. It will be helpful if an Arabic speaker can help you.
>
> This work is free for use to everyone as long as no changes that might distort it are done to it. We request from those who benefit from it to pray for us. We pray to Almighty Allah to help you learn to read the Holy Qur'an, and to do every good thing.'"

I present this humble work in the earnest hope that it will prompt my Readers to try and understand the divine Message in its original Arabic text. They should remember that no translation however meticulously done can ever equal the original Arabic text in its divine grandeur and pristine clarity.

One may wonder why this yet another addition to the existing plethora of Translations and Commentaries! The answer to this question lies in the beauty of the fact that the divine Message of the Qur'aan remains valid for all times and ages since its revelation until the Last Day. The Message therefore needs to be studied from time to time in the changing perspectives of the changing times. It would be wrong to confine this universal Message for mankind to the circumstances and situations of a period in the past. Unfortunately, however, most of the commentators so far have based their understanding of the Qur'aan in the strict perspective of the circumstances and situations prevailing at the time of its revelation way back in 7th century A.D. The Muslim mindset generally has thus got stagnated and therefore unable to cope with the changing situations of the changing times. This humble attempt of mine is to help Muslims generally to come out, Allah willing, of that crippling stagnation.

This Part (Manzil I) of my Qur'aanic Studies relates to Chapters 1 to 4 of the Qur'aan.

Mohammad Shafi
Mumbai, INDIA,
15th December 2018.

Chapter 1: Al-Fatiha (The Opening)

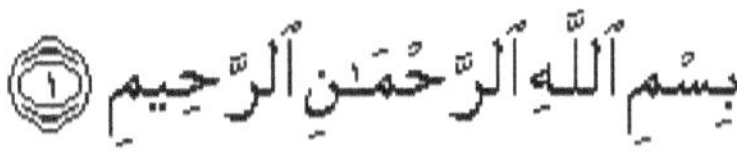

1. Bismi Allahi alrrahmani alrraheemI

1:1. In the name of Allah[1], the Gracious[2], the Merciful[2].

Chapter Notes:

1. I have retained here the original Arabic word. The English near-equivalent God does not convey the same significance or uniqueness that the word implies. Non-Muslim readers are requested not to get the wrong impression that Muslims have a separate god called Allah. Allah is the sole Creator and Sustainer of the entire Universe and of all things, animate or inanimate, therein.

2. Root letters for both the Arabic words, in the original text, are the same: *ra, ha, ma*. The root word denotes compassion, mercy, or, more comprehensively, grace. It is by Allah's grace that we receive from Him even unmerited favours. The epithet *Rahmaan* signifies possession of grace, and the epithet *Raheem*, active manifestation of that grace upon all Creation. Allah not only possesses grace, but actively bestows it upon His creatures. Both these words are prefixed by the definite article *al* (the). It signifies that it is Allah who is the real possessor of grace and the real one who bestows it on others. It is only the reflection of this divine quality that we see in His creatures.

2. Alhamdu lillahi rabbi alAAalameena

1:2. The praise[3] is for Allah, Lord[4] of the worlds[5],

3. Prefix of the definite article here, too, is significant. It is only Allah, who is praiseworthy. When we praise a person for his/her beauty, intelligence, work etc., our praise is, in fact, misdirected! We should really be praising the Creator who made the person beautiful or intelligent or gave him the capacity to produce the good work. That is why Muslims, whenever they see anything praiseworthy, utter this phrase in Arabic, *alhamdulillah!*

4. The original Arabic word is *Rabb.* It is a very comprehensive word, covering the meanings of Master, Owner, Nourisher, Developer, Guide, Provider et al. For want of a befitting corresponding word in English, the word "Lord" is used, although it does not convey the same comprehensive meaning. For this translation, therefore, "Lord" is redefined to have the comprehensive meaning of the Arabic word *Rabb.*

5. This is the dictionary meaning of the Arabic word *aalameen.* It is in plural: worlds, and not world. In most of the places where this word has been used in the Qur'aan, it is accompanied by the word *Rabb,* as in this place. But there are a few places where it isn't, as in Verses 2:47, 3:97, 6:86, 6:90, 21:107 and 29:6. A close study of these latter Verses would show that the word is used in the same sense as in the sentence, "My world is different from yours." Every individual life is one's own individual world in the sense that his/her environment, conditions of living, circle of contacts etc. are different from others'. One's own world is, in other words, one's own individual life. It is to these millions of individual worlds that the Qur'aan refers to as *aalameen.* Allah thus declares that He is the *Rabb* of <u>every</u> individual life. If every individual would but submit completely to His will and obey His commands as given in the Qur'aan, the Lord will surely nourish and lead the individual's life to Success and Salvation! In the phrase *Rabbulaalameen,* however, *Aalameen* would include jinn, angels, all living things (besides human) and all inanimate things in the entire universe as well. Refer in this context Moses' reply to Pharaoh in Verses 24, 26 and 28 of Chapter 32 (Manzil V). *Rabbulaalameen* could as well be translated as the Lord of the Universe.

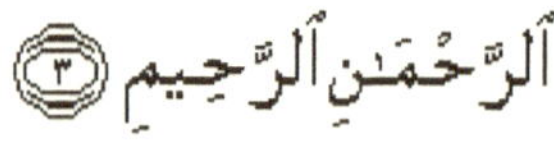

3. Alrrahmani alrraheemi

1:3. The Gracious, the Merciful,

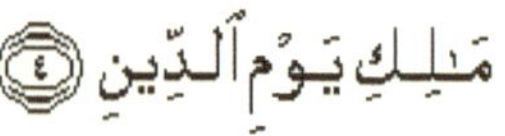

4. Maliki yawmi alddeeni

1:4. Master of the Judgement Day[6]!

6. Judgement Day mentioned here has been described in the Qur'aan as, "The Day when no person shall be able to do anything for another. And the Authority, that Day, shall be with Allah!" [82:19] The Day obviously will not be any day of this world in which we are living now. It has got to be of another world, after our deaths! That Day, Allah will judge every person, strictly on merit. No influence, no recommendation!

5. Iyyaka naAAbudu wa-iyyaka nastaAAeenu

1:5. You, we worship, and, You, we ask for help.

أَهْدِنَا الصِّرَاطَ الْمُسْتَقِيمَ ۝

6. Ihdina alssirata almustaqeema

1:6. Guide us to the Straight Path –

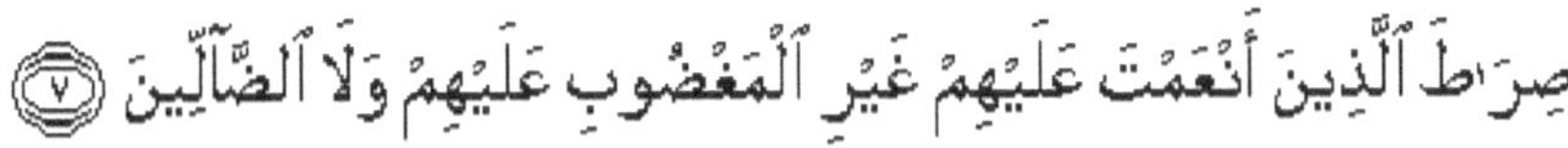

7. Sirata allatheena anAAamta AAalayhim ghayri almaghdoobi AAalayhim wala alddalleena

1:7. Path of those upon whom You have bestowed favours[7], not of those who have incurred Your wrath[8], nor of those who have gone astray[9]!

7. The Qur'aan elsewhere declares, "And whoever obeys Allah and the Messenger, shall be with those on whom Allah has bestowed favours - the Prophets, the truthful, the martyrs, the reformers and doers of good. And good, indeed, are such companions!" [4:69]

8. Explaining why or how people incurred Allah's wrath, the Qur'aan says, "...That was because they disobeyed and exceeded all limits!" [2:61] and [3:112]

9.. The Qur'aan says elsewhere, "Surely, in the matter of those who have suppressed the Truth after attaining to belief therein, and who have gone on to suppress it further, their repentance shall not be accepted. And those are the ones who have gone astray!" [3:90]

This Chapter is obviously in the form of a prayer from mankind. The rest of the Qur'aan is Allah's response thereto.

Chapter 2: Al-Baqarah (The Cow)

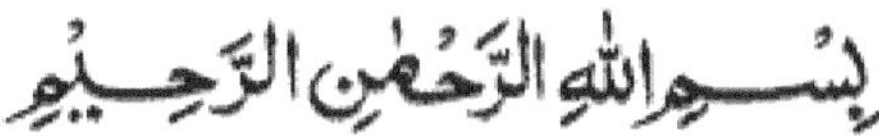

In the Name of Allah, the Gracious, the Merciful

1. Alif-lam-meem

2:1. Alif-lam-meem.[1]

---

1. These are three of the letters of the Arabic alphabet. Such letters appear at the beginning of some other Chapters too. Their meaning or significance, however, is a mystery. The All-knowing Allah has placed them there, perhaps, as tokens of the many mysteries of Creation mankind is still unaware of.

---

2. Thalika alkitabu la rayba feehi hudan lilmuttaqeena

2:2. There, no doubt, is the (divine) Record[1a] wherein is guidance for the pious, the Allah-fearing[2] –

Manzil I: 2: Baqarah

1a. Allah Almighty has not abandoned mankind – after creating them – to fend for themselves. HE has recorded all necessary guidance for them. The Qur'aan – so also every other divine Scripture – was downloaded from that Record with Him.

2. The original Arabic word '*al-muttaqeen*' has been translated here as 'the pious, the Allah-fearing', but hereafter in this translation of the Qur'aan the Arabic word will be referred to as 'the pious', for brevity. It should always however be construed to mean what its divine definition, given in the succeeding Verses 3 and 4, says.

ٱلَّذِينَ يُؤْمِنُونَ بِٱلْغَيْبِ وَيُقِيمُونَ ٱلصَّلَوٰةَ وَمِمَّا رَزَقْنَٰهُمْ يُنفِقُونَ

3. Alla<u>th</u>eena yu/minoona bialghaybi wayuqeemoona al<u>ss</u>al<u>a</u>ta wamimm<u>a</u> razaqn<u>a</u>hum yunfiqoon<u>a</u>

2:3. (For) those who believe in the Unseen[3], establish the Prayer[4] and spend[5] out of what We have provided for them,

3. Belief in the Unseen, non-apparent or unknown things ('Al-Ghayb' in the original Arabic text) is fundamental to Islam, as it is to many other Religions. Without this belief, words like Allah, angels, life after death, paradise, hell etc. shall carry no meaning. This belief is nothing, but recognition of the very apparent fact that human knowledge does not encompass everything. Things, which we are not physically aware of, do exist. The Qur'aan declares elsewhere, "...None in the heavens, or on the earth, knows the Unseen, except Allah..." [27:65]. It means that no being, even if it is an angel, other than Allah can be aware of everything. Knowing the Unseen is therefore the exclusive prerogative of Allah.

4. "...and be attentive at every place of worship and invoke Him alone to make the Religion exclusive for Him..." [7:29] "...invoke Him in fear and in hope..." [7:56] "And remember your Lord within yourself humbly and without being loud..." [7:205] "And woe unto the prayer-offerers who are neglectful of their prayers!" [107:5] - these and some other Verses of the Qur'aan tell us how to establish the Prayer. (See Chapter Note 108 also.)

5. The Qur'aan says elsewhere: "...And they ask you as to what they should spend. Say: what you can spare..." [2:219] "...Whatever you spend of good must be for the parents and the kindred and the orphans and the poor and the wayfarer..." [2:215] "...And you spend not, but to seek Allah's pleasure..." [2:272]

10

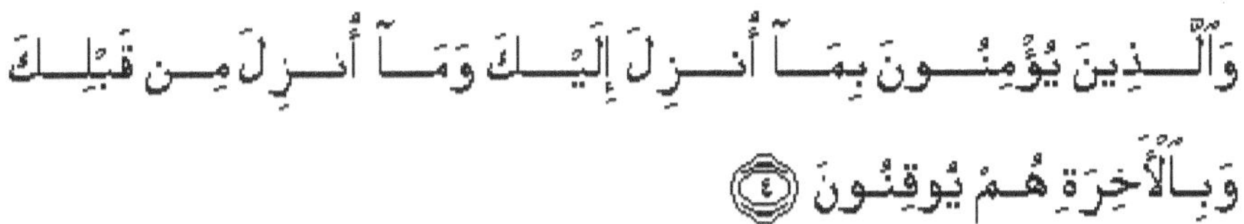

4. Waallatheena yu/minoona bima onzila ilayka wama onzila min qablika wabial-akhirati hum yooqinoona

---

2:4. And those who believe in what has been bestowed upon you[6] and in what had been bestowed before you[6], and who are certain of the Hereafter[7].

---

6. In the original Arabic text, the pronoun used is 'ka', the 2nd person singular equivalent to the English 'Thou'. Since the usage of 'Thou' has now become archaic, I have used 'You' instead, which stands for both singular and plural. In the Qur'aanic context, the Arabic 'ka' is used when the divine address is directed personally to Prophet Muhammed (peace and Allah's blessings be upon him).

7. "And the life of this world is nothing but play and amusement, but the abode in the Hereafter is better for the pious! Won't you understand?" [6:32] This Qur'aanic Verse clearly indicates that the Hereafter is a world beyond this one. Humans, after their deaths in this world, will obviously be resurrected for another life in that other world, the Hereafter!

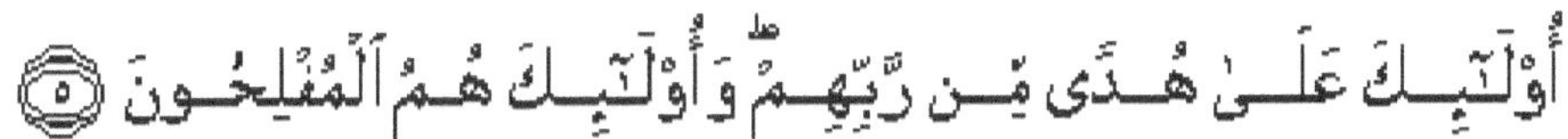

5. Ola-ika AAala hudan min rabbihim waola-ika humu almuflihoona

---

2:5. Those are on guidance from their Lord, and those are the ones who are successful!

إِنَّ ٱلَّذِينَ كَفَرُواْ سَوَآءٌ عَلَيْهِمْ ءَأَنذَرْتَهُمْ أَمْ لَمْ تُنذِرْهُمْ

لَا يُؤْمِنُونَ ۝

6. Inna allatheena kafaroo sawaon AAalayhim aanthartahum am lam tunthirhum la yu/minoona

---

2:6. [8]For those, indeed, who suppress the Truth[9], it is all the same whether you warn them, or you do not: they shall believe not!

---

8. The preceding Verses of this Qur'aanic Chapter describe the persons who would get guidance from the divine Book. This Verse, and the Verses that immediately follow, describe those persons, who would not get the guidance!

9. In the original Arabic text, the word used is 'kafaru'. The root word is 'kafara'. It is equivalent, phonetically as well as in meaning, to the English word 'cover'. So, the Arabic 'kafara' literally means to cover, to hide, or to suppress. And what does one cover, hide or suppress? Obviously, the obvious, the fact, the naked truth! Later, in Verse 18 below and in Verse 171 of this Qur'aanic Chapter, such persons are described as deaf, dumb and blind. They are so described as they suppress the truth they hear and see, and do not speak out the truth they know of. 'Kafaru' is therefore translated here as 'who suppress the Truth'.

خَتَمَ ٱللَّهُ عَلَىٰ قُلُوبِهِمْ وَعَلَىٰ سَمْعِهِمْ وَعَلَىٰٓ أَبْصَٰرِهِمْ

غِشَٰوَةٌ وَلَهُمْ عَذَابٌ عَظِيمٌ ۝

7. Khatama Allahu AAala quloobihim waAAala samAAihim waAAala absarihim ghishawatun walahum AAathabun AAatheemun

---

2:7. Allah has set a seal on their minds and on their sense of hearing. And in their discernment, is a blind. And for them, a severe punishment!

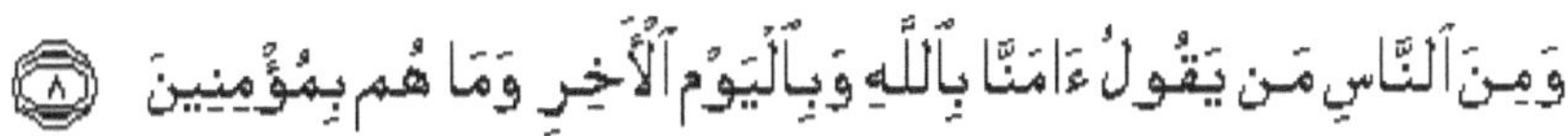

8. Wamina alnnasi man yaqoolu amanna biAllahi wabialyawmi al-akhiri wama hum bimu/mineena

2:8. And among mankind there are some who say, "We believe in Allah and in the Last Day." And yet they believe not! [10]

10. Alas! An overwhelming majority of the so-called believers in today's world, I am afraid, fall in the category of people described in this Verse, and in the few Verses that follow this Verse. They declare themselves as Muslims (believers), but their deeds betray the hollowness of their belief. Their attitude towards observance of divine commands regarding praying, fasting etc. is, at best, indifferent. And the general conduct of their worldly affairs does not reflect any concern at all that they would have to account for these before the Lord in the Hereafter. They delude themselves under the deception that this worldly life is the be-all and end-all of their existence! Allah Almighty describes their mental attitude as a disease, which He worsens if they continue indulging in their falsehoods.

Such a mental attitude inculcates in them a tendency to grab what they can, by hook or by crook, here and now! And then the Satan steps in and lures them to the temptations of this world. While in the grips of such a temptation, if they are told not to indulge in any mischief, they protest and say that they are only trying to improve their conditions!

And when someone points out to them that they are not so strict in following the tenets of Islam as some other Muslims are even at the expense of material or business interests, they say - at least, to themselves - that they are not fools like the others!

On the other hand, if social compulsions make them go through, albeit reluctantly, some religious duties like performing prayers etc., when they meet with their own ilk they dismiss their religious acts as mere delusion.

Allah Almighty compares them to blinded people unable to see the light around them - the light of the Qur'aan, which they hardly ever read with a view to get any guidance there from. Like people caught in a rainstorm putting their fingers into their ears to shut out the thunderbolts, they are ever afraid of death, which could put an abrupt end to their illusory life on this earth! It is only because of Allah's grace and mercy that they can carry on with whatever lives they could enjoy on this earth. Allah could, if He so willed, deprive them of the little earthly enjoyment too! Allah can indeed do - or undo - whatever He wills!

يُخَـٰدِعُونَ ٱللَّـهَ وَٱلَّـذِينَ ءَامَنُـوا۟ وَمَـا يَخْـدَعُونَ إِلَّآ أَنفُسَـهُمْ وَمَـا يَشْعُرُونَ ۝

9. YukhadiAAoona Allaha waallatheena amanoo wama yakhdaAAoona illa anfusahum wama yashAAuroona

2:9. They are trying to deceive Allah and those who believe, and they deceive none but themselves but perceive it not!

فِى قُلُوبِهِم مَّرَضٌ فَزَادَهُمُ ٱللَّـهُ مَرَضًا ۖ وَلَهُمْ عَذَابٌ أَلِيمٌۢ بِمَا كَانُوا۟ يَكْذِبُونَ ۝

10. Fee quloobihim maradun fazadahumu Allahu maradan walahum AAathabun aleemun bima kanoo yakthiboona

2:10. In their minds is a disease, and Allah has increased the disease for them. And for them, a painful punishment as they have been lying!

وَإِذَا قِيلَ لَهُمْ لَا تُفْسِدُوا۟ فِى ٱلْأَرْضِ قَالُوٓا۟ إِنَّمَا نَحْنُ مُصْلِحُونَ ۝

11. Wa-itha qeela lahum la tufsidoo fee al-ardi qaloo innama nahnu muslihoona

2:11. And when they are told, "Make no mischief on the earth," they say, "We are but trying to improve things."

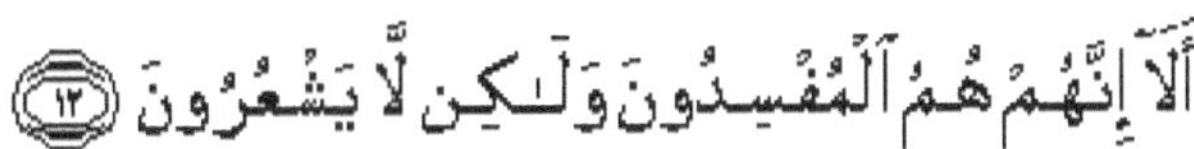

12. Al<u>a</u> innahum humu almufsidoona wal<u>a</u>kin l<u>a</u> yashAAuroon<u>a</u>

2:12. Nay! In fact, they are the ones who make mischief, but they perceive it not!

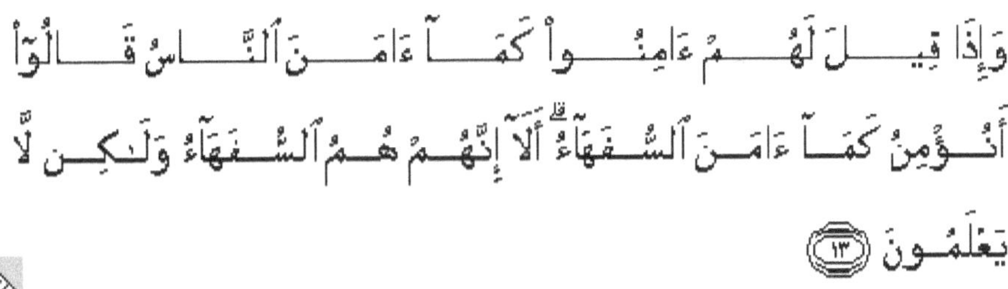

13. Wa-i<u>tha</u> qeela lahum <u>a</u>minoo kam<u>a</u> <u>a</u>mana alnn<u>a</u>su q<u>a</u>loo anu/minu kam<u>a</u> <u>a</u>mana alssufah<u>a</u>o al<u>a</u> innahum humu alssufah<u>a</u>o wal<u>a</u>kin l<u>a</u> yaAAlamoon<u>a</u>

2:13. And when they are told, "Believe like those who believe," they say, "Shall we believe as the fools did?" Nay! In fact, they are the ones who are the fools, but they know not!

---

14. Wa-i<u>tha</u> laqoo alla<u>th</u>eena <u>a</u>manoo q<u>a</u>loo <u>a</u>mann<u>a</u> wa-i<u>tha</u> khalaw il<u>a</u> shay<u>a</u>teenihim q<u>a</u>loo inn<u>a</u> maAAakum innam<u>a</u> na<u>h</u>nu mustahzi-oon<u>a</u>

2:14. And when they meet those who believe, they say, "We believe," and when they are closeted with their own satanic folk, they say, "We surely are with you! We have been but mocking."

15. Allahu yastahzi-o bihim wayamudduhum fee tughyanihim yaAAmahoona

2:15. Allah mocks at them and leaves them to lose their way committing their excesses.

16. Ola-ika allatheena ishtarawoo alddalalata bialhuda fama rabihat tijaratuhum wama kanoo muhtadeena

2:16. These are the people who bartered away right guidance for straying away there from. But their barter deal benefited them not, and they failed to become guided!

17. Mathaluhum kamathali allathee istawqada naran falamma adaat ma hawlahu thahaba Allahu binoorihim watarakahum fee thulumatin la yubsiroona

2:17. Their situation is as the situation in which someone kindled a fire. But when it lighted up its environs, Allah snatched away their light and left them, in manifold darkness, unable to see!

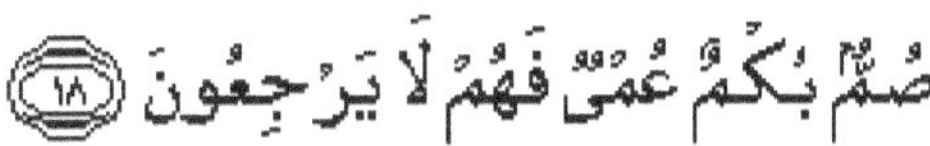

18. <u>S</u>ummun bukmun AAumyun fahum l<u>a</u> yarjiAAoon<u>a</u>

2:18. Being deaf, dumb and blind, they return not!

19. Aw ka<u>s</u>ayyibin mina alssam<u>a</u>-i feehi _th_ulum<u>a</u>tun waraAAdun wabarqun yajAAaloona a<u>s</u>abiAAahum fee <u>ath</u>anihim mina al<u>ss</u>aw<u>a</u>AAiqi <u>h</u>a<u>th</u>ara almawti waAll<u>a</u>hu mu<u>h</u>ee<u>t</u>un bialk<u>a</u>fireen<u>a</u>

2:19. Or, [11]their situation is as in a rainstorm from the sky, that is accompanied by manifold darkness and thunder and lightning! They thrust their fingers in their ears to keep out the thunderbolts, fearing death. And Allah encompasses the suppressors of Truth!

11. In the original Arabic text, the equivalent of "their situation is" is understood and not actually expressed. The understood expression is expressed in the translation to render the meaning clearer in the context of the English language syntax and idiom.

يَكَادُ ٱلْبَرْقُ يَخْطَفُ أَبْصَـٰرَهُمْ كُلَّمَآ أَضَآءَ لَهُم مَّشَوْاْ فِيهِ وَإِذَآ أَظْلَمَ عَلَيْهِمْ قَامُواْ وَلَوْ شَآءَ ٱللَّهُ لَذَهَبَ بِسَمْعِهِمْ وَأَبْصَـٰرِهِمْ إِنَّ ٱللَّهَ عَلَىٰ كُلِّ شَىْءٍ قَدِيرٌ ۝

20. Yak<u>a</u>du albarqu yakh<u>t</u>afu ab<u>s</u>arahum kullam<u>a</u> a<u>da</u>a lahum mashaw feehi wa-i<u>tha</u> a<u>th</u>lama AAalayhim qamoo walaw sh<u>a</u>a All<u>a</u>hu lathahaba bisamAAihim waab<u>s</u>arihim inna All<u>a</u>ha AAal<u>a</u> kulli shay-in qadeer**un**

2:20. The lightning almost snatches their sights away! Whenever it flashes for them, they move forward in its light, and, when darkness falls on them, they stop. And, had Allah so willed, He could indeed have taken away their hearing and their sights. Allah certainly has power over everything!

يَـٰٓأَيُّهَا ٱلنَّاسُ ٱعْبُدُواْ رَبَّكُمُ ٱلَّذِى خَلَقَكُمْ وَٱلَّذِينَ مِن قَبْلِكُمْ لَعَلَّكُمْ تَتَّقُونَ ۝

21. Y<u>a</u> ayyuh<u>a</u> alnnasu oAAbudoo rabbakumu alla<u>th</u>ee khalaqakum wa<u>a</u>lla<u>th</u>eena min qablikum laAAallakum tattaqoona

---

2:21. [12]O mankind! Worship[13] your Lord, Who created you, as well as those before you, so that you become pious -

---

12. **Readers may recall that during the first 5 Verses of this Qur'aanic Chapter, it is stated that the pious will get guidance from the divine Book. In the next fifteen Verses, following the first 5, those other people are described who will not get the guidance there from. Having thus categorised mankind into 2 distinct sections, the Qur'aan advises them all, in this 21st Verse, as to how to belong to the category of the pious to get the guidance and attain salvation. Readers may also take note, here, that the Qur'aanic Message is addressed to the entire mankind, and not to any regional or racial group.**

13.   To worship is to adore someone as divine. The root of the Arabic word used in the original text is 'abada', which also means to be a slave to. So, in the Qur'aanic concept of worship, the worshipper submits himself completely to the divine as a slave would to an absolute master! At another place in the Qur'aan, Allah exhorts His Messenger (peace and Allah's blessings be upon him), 'Say: I have been forbidden to worship those whom you invoke besides Allah, since there have come to me evidences from my Lord; and I am commanded to submit to the Lord of the worlds.' [40:66]

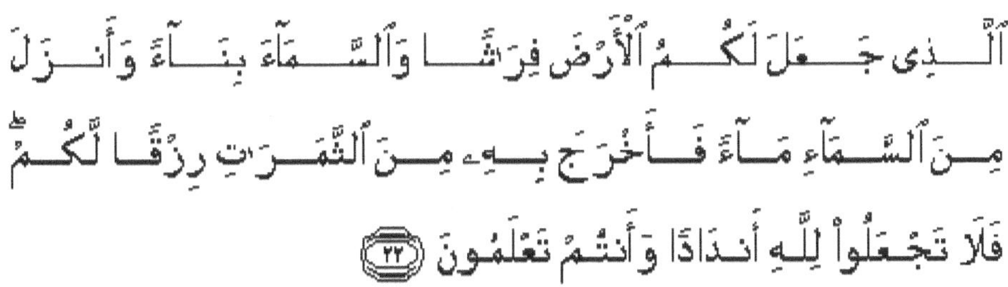

22. Allathee jaAAala lakumu al-arda firashan waalssamaa binaan waanzala mina alssama-i maan faakhraja bihi mina alththamarati rizqan lakum fala tajAAaloo lillahi andadan waantum taAAlamoona

2:22. The Lord Who made the earth a habitable place[14] for you, and the sky, a generator of means to provide sustenance[15]! And He sent down water from the sky. Then He brought out therewith – from the produce – sustenance for you. Do not then knowingly instal false rivals to Allah.

14.   'Farasha' is the root of the corresponding Arabic word used in the original divine text. One of its varied meanings is 'to render easy, convenient and commodious; to furnish a house'. Science is witness to the fact that the earth is so placed in a mathematically precise and correct position in the Universe as to make it habitable by human beings, as also by an innumerable variety of other living creatures. The original Arabic word used is therefore rendered as 'habitable place' in the translation.

15. The root of the original Arabic word used here has the meanings, inter alia, to build, construct, raise, strengthen and assist by benefits. Read with these meanings, the role of the sky, as described subsequently in this very Verse, provides the obvious contextual meaning - viz., a generator of means to provide sustenance - of the original Arabic word used.

19

وَإِن كُنتُمْ فِى رَيْبٍ مِّمَّا نَزَّلْنَا عَلَىٰ عَبْدِنَا فَأْتُوا۟ بِسُورَةٍ مِّن مِّثْلِهِۦ وَادْعُوا۟ شُهَدَآءَكُم مِّن دُونِ اللَّهِ إِن كُنتُمْ صَـٰدِقِينَ ۝

23. Wa-in kuntum fee raybin mimma nazzalna AAala AAabdina fa/too bisooratin min mithlihi waodAAoo shuhadaakum min dooni Allahi in kuntum sadiqeena

---

2:23. And if you are in doubt concerning what We have sent down unto Our Devotee, then come up with a Chapter like one thereof[16] and call your witnesses – other than Allah – for your aid, if you are truthful.

---

16.   This is an open divine challenge for those who entertain doubts in the divine authorship of the Qur'aan. The Book elsewhere gives a hint of what the challenge means. "Do they not then ponder over the Qur'aan? Had it been from someone other than Allah, they would surely have found therein many a contradiction." [Q: 4:82]

فَإِن لَّمْ تَفْعَلُوا۟ وَلَن تَفْعَلُوا۟ فَاتَّقُوا۟ النَّارَ الَّتِى وَقُودُهَا النَّاسُ وَالْحِجَارَةُ أُعِدَّتْ لِلْكَـٰفِرِينَ ۝

24. Fa-in lam tafAAaloo walan tafAAaloo faittaqoo alnnara allatee waqooduha alnnasu waalhijaratu oAAiddat lilkafireena

---

2:24. But, if you do it not – and you can never do it – then fear the Fire fuelled by humans and stones and kept ready for suppressors of the Truth.

وَبَشِّرِ ٱلَّذِينَ ءَامَنُوا۟ وَعَمِلُوا۟ ٱلصَّٰلِحَٰتِ أَنَّ لَهُمْ جَنَّٰتٍ تَجْرِى مِن تَحْتِهَا ٱلْأَنْهَٰرُ ۖ كُلَّمَا رُزِقُوا۟ مِنْهَا مِن ثَمَرَةٍ رِّزْقًا ۙ قَالُوا۟ هَٰذَا ٱلَّذِى رُزِقْنَا مِن قَبْلُ ۖ وَأُتُوا۟ بِهِۦ مُتَشَٰبِهًا ۖ وَلَهُمْ فِيهَآ أَزْوَٰجٌ مُّطَهَّرَةٌ ۖ وَهُمْ فِيهَا خَٰلِدُونَ ۝٢٥

25. Wabashshiri alla<u>th</u>eena <u>a</u>manoo waAAamiloo al<u>ss</u>ali<u>h</u>ati anna lahum jann<u>a</u>tin tajree min ta<u>h</u>ti<u>h</u>a al-anh<u>a</u>ru kullam<u>a</u> ruziqoo minh<u>a</u> min thamaratin rizqan q<u>a</u>loo h<u>atha</u> alla<u>th</u>ee ruziqn<u>a</u> min qablu waotoo bihi mutash<u>a</u>bihan walahum feeh<u>a</u> azw<u>a</u>jun mu<u>t</u>ahharatun wahum feeh<u>a</u> kh<u>a</u>lidoon<u>a</u>

2:25. And gladden the minds of those who believe and do good deeds, with prophesy that there would certainly be for them gardens underneath which the rivers flow. Every time they are served there with the food of a fruit, they will say, "This is what we had been served with before," and they will be given things resembling one another[17]. And for them therein will be mates purified. And therein will they have lives eternal!

---

17. In Verse 3:7, the Qur'aan says, "It is He (Allah) Who has sent down the Book. In it are Verses that are entirely clear - these form the fundamentals of the Book - and others, not entirely clear. Then as for those in whose minds there is proneness for deviation, they follow the Verse that is not entirely clear, to find fault and to seek its hidden meaning. And none but Allah knows its hidden meaning. And those who are firmly grounded in knowledge say, 'We believe in it; every Verse is from our Lord.' And none remember it except for the people of deep understanding." This Verse of Chapter 2, currently under our study, describing a scene in Paradise, and the preceding Verse (No. 24), stating that human beings would be the fuel of Hell Fire, are among those unclear Verses spoken of in Verse 3:7. The intelligence endowed to humans in this world, is not capable of comprehending how, for example, humans would be used as fuel of the Fire and yet go on living to suffer continuously therein. We have but to believe in such unclear Verses verbatim, as described in the Qur'aan. It is a test of our belief in Allah and in the Unseen!

إِنَّ ٱللَّهَ لَا يَسْتَحْىِ أَن يَضْرِبَ مَثَلًا مَّا بَعُوضَةً فَمَا فَوْقَهَا فَأَمَّا ٱلَّذِينَ ءَامَنُوا۟ فَيَعْلَمُونَ أَنَّهُ ٱلْحَقُّ مِن رَّبِّهِمْ وَأَمَّا ٱلَّذِينَ كَفَرُوا۟ فَيَقُولُونَ مَاذَآ أَرَادَ ٱللَّهُ بِهَـٰذَا مَثَلًا يُضِلُّ بِهِۦ كَثِيرًا وَيَهْدِى بِهِۦ كَثِيرًا وَمَا يُضِلُّ بِهِۦٓ إِلَّا ٱلْفَـٰسِقِينَ ﴿٢٦﴾

26. Inna Allaha la yastahyee an yadriba mathalan ma baAAoodatan fama fawqaha faamma allatheena amanoo fayaAAlamoona annahu alhaqqu min rabbihim waamma allatheena kafaroo fayaqooloona matha arada Allahu bihatha mathalan yudillu bihi katheeran wayahdee bihi katheeran wama yudillu bihi illa alfasiqeena

---

2:26. Indeed, Allah blushes not at quoting an example of even a fly or of anything tinier. Those, then, who believe, know this to be nothing but the Truth from their Lord. And those who suppress the Truth, question, "What is Allah's intention in giving such an example?" By it, He sends many astray; and, by it, He guides many to the Right Path. And He sends astray none by it, but the wicked!

ٱلَّذِينَ يَنقُضُونَ عَهْدَ ٱللَّهِ مِنۢ بَعْدِ مِيثَـٰقِهِۦ وَيَقْطَعُونَ مَآ أَمَرَ ٱللَّهُ بِهِۦٓ أَن يُوصَلَ وَيُفْسِدُونَ فِى ٱلْأَرْضِ أُو۟لَـٰٓئِكَ هُمُ ٱلْخَـٰسِرُونَ ﴿٢٧﴾

27. Allatheena yanqudoona AAahda Allahi min baAAdi meethaqihi wayaqtaAAoona ma amara Allahu bihi an yoosala wayufsidoona fee al-ardi ola-ika humu alkhasiroona

---

2:27. They (the wicked) are those who go back on their declaration, recognizing Allah as their Lord, after it (the declaration) was solemnly affirmed[18]. And they cut asunder what Allah has commanded to be adhered to[19]. And they spread corruption on the earth. Those are the people, doomed!

---

18. The Qur'aan tells us elsewhere: "And when your Lord brought forth from Adam's children - from their loins - their offspring, He asked them to testify upon the evidence of their own selves, 'Am I not your Lord?' and they said, 'Yes, we do testify!' Lest you should say on the Day of Resurrection, 'We were indeed unaware of this.' Or, lest you should say, 'Our forefathers had indeed assigned partners to You before, and we were but the offspring following them. Would You then destroy us for what those others indulging in falsehood did?' And thus, do We explain the Verses/signs in detail, and so that they revert." [Q: 7:172 to 174] And in Verse 4:107, the Qur'aan says, "And argue not on behalf of those who deceive themselves. Allah indeed loves not those who sinfully betray their trust." From these divine Verses it should be abundantly clear that the truth about the existence of the Almighty Creator is ingrained in what we call the conscience of every human being at his/her very birth!

19. Allah has commanded adherence to a life of piety for mankind to enable it to get guidance from the Qur'aan and to attain to salvation [2:2 to 2:5]. The wicked wilfully keep themselves away from leading such a life.

كَيْفَ تَكْفُرُونَ بِاللَّهِ وَكُنْتُمْ أَمْوَٰتًا فَأَحْيَاكُمْ ثُمَّ يُمِيتُكُمْ

ثُمَّ يُحْيِيكُمْ ثُمَّ إِلَيْهِ تُرْجَعُونَ ﴿٢٨﴾

28. Kayfa takfuroona biAllahi wakuntum amwatan faahyakum thumma yumeetukum thumma yuhyeekum thumma ilayhi turjaAAoona

---

2:28. How can you suppress the Truth about Allah!? It was He Who gave you life when you were but dead. He will then make you die and raise you up again to life. And to Him you will then return!

هُوَ ٱلَّذِى خَلَقَ لَكُم مَّا فِى ٱلْأَرْضِ جَمِيعًا ثُمَّ ٱسْتَوَىٰ إِلَى ٱلسَّمَآءِ

فَسَوَّىٰهُنَّ سَبْعَ سَمَٰوَٰتٍ وَهُوَ بِكُلِّ شَىْءٍ عَلِيمٌ ﴿٢٩﴾

29. Huwa allathee khalaqa lakum ma fee al-ardi jameeAAan thumma istawa ila alssama-i fasawwahunna sabAAa samawatin wahuwa bikulli shay-in AAaleemun

---

2:29. He it is Who created for you all that is on the earth. He then rose over towards the atmosphere and outer space and set them right, into seven spheres and skies[20 & 21]. And He does have knowledge of all things.

---

20. It is interesting to note in this context that, as per recent discoveries, the atmosphere immediately surrounding the earth has seven layers, one over another. They are: Troposphere, Tropopause, Stratosphere, Stratopause, Mesosphere, Mesopause and Thermosphere. These layers, inter alia, shield the earth from the ultraviolet rays radiating from the Sun. The Troposphere provides oxygen and the water recycling facility for sustenance of life on earth. And Allah says in Verse Q: 21:32, "And We have made the atmosphere safe and well guarded..." In Verse 67:3, the Qur'aan speaks of the Blessed Lord, "Who has created the seven layers of the atmosphere, one over another..." And in Verse 40:13, it speaks of Allah, "Who... sends down provisions for you from the atmosphere..."

21. But from some other Verses it is apparent that the Arabic word *Samaa* (plural: *Samaawaat)* has been used in the Qur'aan both for earth's atmosphere as well as outer space. It is so indicated in Verse 65:12: "It is Allah Who has created seven skies and of the earth the like thereof..." In the divine terminology, the sky nearest to the earth includes its (earth's) atmosphere. While mankind has come to know of the seven layers of earth's atmosphere, the six layers of the outer space, beyond the lowest which is studded with the stars [Q: 41:12], appear to be still beyond human knowledge and comprehension.

وَإِذْ قَالَ رَبُّكَ لِلْمَلَآئِكَةِ إِنِّى جَاعِلٌ فِى الْأَرْضِ خَلِيفَةً قَالُوٓاْ أَتَجْعَلُ فِيهَا مَن يُفْسِدُ فِيهَا وَيَسْفِكُ الدِّمَآءَ وَنَحْنُ نُسَبِّحُ بِحَمْدِكَ وَنُقَدِّسُ لَكَ قَالَ إِنِّىٓ أَعْلَمُ مَا لَا تَعْلَمُونَ ﴿٣٠﴾

30. Wa-ith qala rabbuka lilmala-ikati innee jaAAilun fee al-ardi khaleefatan qaloo atajAAalu feeha man yufsidu feeha wayasfiku alddimaa wanahnu nusabbihu bihamdika wanuqaddisu laka qala innee aAAlamu ma la taAAlamoona

---

2:30. And when your Lord said to the angels, "I am indeed going to establish a vicegerent[22 to 25] on the earth", they said, "Will You establish therein those who would spread discord therein and shed blood? And we glorify You with praises and sanctify You!" He (Allah) said, "I know that which you do not know."

---

22. *Khalifa* is the word used in the original Arabic text and it is important to understand the divine meaning thereof. One of the dictionary meanings of this word is 'successor', but this meaning cannot be applied in the context here. Allah obviously wanted to make the first human, Adam, a *Khalifa* on the earth and so there is no question of his being a 'successor' there. Earlier to Adam being sent to the earth, Allah's was the only, and complete, sway over there, and it would be preposterous to think that Almighty Allah would appoint any 'successor' to Him, Himself!

23. It would therefore be most appropriate to take the other meaning viz. 'vicegerent' or, so to say, a viceroy acting as the Absolute Sovereign's deputy ruler in a specific region of the Sovereign's vast dominion and exercising some of His delegated powers to a limited extent.

24. And in Verse 35:39, the Qur'aan speaks of the entire mankind being made the *Khalaif*, or the vicegerents (in plural, that is), on the earth. This Verse and other Verses like 6:165, 7:74, 7:69 etc. go to show that it is not Adam only who had been made the *Khalifa*, but that human beings that came through his progeny to inhabit this earth so far and that would come in future, are all the *Khalaif* or *Khulafa* on this earth. In some translations, this plural word has been wrongly interpreted as 'successors'. All human beings are Allah's vicegerents on this earth. They are, in other words, His deputies, everyone having control over his/her respective little world (*aalam*).

25. But these little deputies tend to forget their real position and status. They forget that they are only deputies of their common Sovereign, the real Nourisher and Sustainer of all their little worlds (*Rabb-il-aalameen*). They forget that Allah is, as do Verses 6:165 and 10:14 explain, only testing them by the limited delegation of some of His powers to them. Allah is testing whether His deputies are exercising their delegated powers justly and fairly for constructive creation within the spheres of their little worlds, remembering all the while that they are answerable to their Sovereign for all their acts of omission and commission.

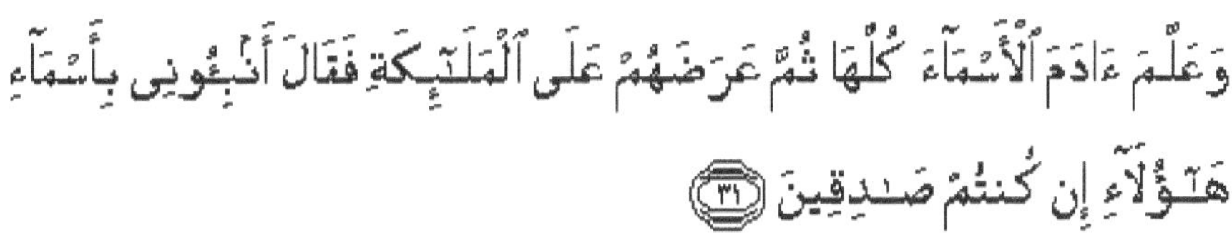

31. WaAAallama adama al-asmaa kullaha thumma AAaradahum AAala almala-ikati faqala anbi-oonee bi-asma-i haola-i in kuntum sadiqeena

---

2:31. And He taught Adam all the names[26] of certain things. Then He placed those before the angels. And He said to them, "Describe to me names of these, if you do really know the truth."

---

26. "And to Allah belong the best Names; so, call Him by those..." is how the Verse 7:180 begins. Speaking of the idols worshipped by the pagan Arabs, the Qur'aan says, "They are but names which you have given – you and your fathers – for which Allah has sent no authority..." [53:23] In the light of these

and similar other Verses, we may safely infer that the names (*asma*), in the context of the Verse (2:31) presently under study, are but the genuine characteristics or real attributes of things.

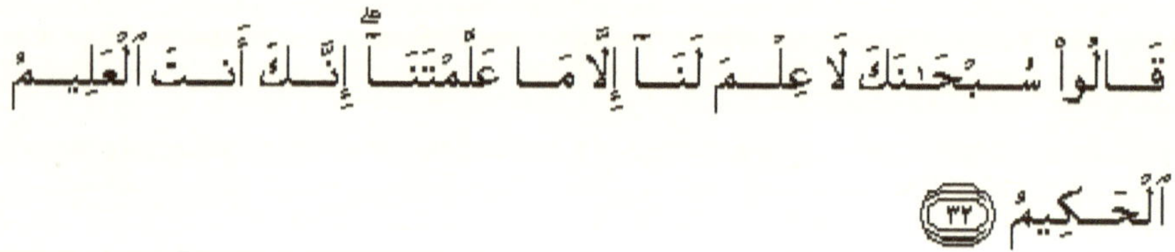

32. Qaloo subhanaka la AAilma lana illa ma AAallamtana innaka anta alAAaleemu alhakeemu

2:32. They said, "Glory to You! We do have no knowledge other than what You have taught us. You indeed are the One having knowledge of everything and the One possessing all wisdom!"

33. Qala ya adamu anbi/hum bi-asma-ihim falamma anbaahum bi-asma-ihim qala alam aqul lakum innee aAAlamu ghayba alssamawati waal-ardi waaAAlamu ma tubdoona wama kuntum taktumoona

2:33. Said He, "O Adam! Describe to them the names of these things." And when he described to them the names thereof, He said, "Did I not tell you that I know the secrets of the atmosphere and skies beyond and of the earth, and that I know what you declare and what you have been concealing?"

$$\text{وَإِذْ قُلْنَا لِلْمَلَـٰئِكَةِ ٱسْجُدُوا۟ لِـَٔادَمَ فَسَجَدُوٓا۟ إِلَّآ إِبْلِيسَ أَبَىٰ وَٱسْتَكْبَرَ وَكَانَ مِنَ ٱلْكَـٰفِرِينَ ۝}$$

34. Wa-ith qulna lilmala-ikati osjudoo li-adama fasajadoo illa ibleesa aba waistakbara wakana mina alkafireena

---

2:34. And when We asked the angels to prostrate[27 & 28] before Adam, prostrated they all except for Iblees[29]. He (Iblees) refused and was proud[30] and became one of the suppressors of Truth!

---

27. One may think that it is the prerogative of Allah to be bowed or prostrated to. And Allah does say, "...Prostrate not to the sun or to the moon, but prostrate to Allah Who created them, if it is He Whom you worship." [Q: 41:37] But here, in Verse 2:34, Allah Himself asked the angels to prostrate to Adam who was but a creature of Allah. To understand properly the truth behind this apparent contradiction, one must remember that to worship is to obey completely and unquestioningly. When Allah Himself asked the angels to prostrate to Adam, He was just testing their absolute obedience to Him.

28. There is another instance mentioned in the Qur'aan of a man, Prophet Yusuf (may peace be upon him), being prostrated to by his brothers and parents [Q: 12:100]. That was an involuntary act in divine fulfilment of the inerpretation of a dream seen by Yusuf in his childhood. Neither this instance, nor that of the angels prostrating before Adam at the express order of the Almighty Creator, should be taken as a precedent for us humans to prostrate before any created thing. For us, the standing divine command, as given in Verse 41:37 quoted above in the preceding Note, is to prostrate only to Allah!

29. In Verse 18.50, Iblees has been described as Jinn.

30. Justifying his pride, Iblees is quoted, in Verse 7:12, as saying, "I am better than him (Adam). You created me from fire, and him You created from clay."

$$\text{وَقُلْنَا يَـٰٓـَٔادَمُ ٱسْكُنْ أَنتَ وَزَوْجُكَ ٱلْجَنَّةَ وَكُلَا مِنْهَا رَغَدًا حَيْثُ شِئْتُمَا وَلَا تَقْرَبَا هَـٰذِهِ ٱلشَّجَرَةَ فَتَكُونَا مِنَ ٱلظَّـٰلِمِينَ ۝}$$

35. Waqulna ya adamu oskun anta wazawjuka aljannata wakula minha raghadan haythu shi/tuma wala taqraba hathihi alshshajarata fatakoona mina alththalimeena

2:35. And We said, "O Adam! Dwell you and your wife in the Garden[31]. And eat and live therein, both of you, in ease and affluence, whatever and wherever you wish. But come not near this tree; for, then, you both will be among the wicked! [32]"

31. The Garden (*Al-Jannah*) has been described elsewhere in the Qur'aan as follows, "...in it are rivers of water the colour, taste and smell of which are not changed, rivers of milk of which the taste never changes, rivers of wine delicious to the drinkers and rivers of purified honey; therein for them is every kind of fruit, and forgiveness from their Lord..." [47:15]; "...its provision is eternal and so is its shade..." [13:35]; "...they will have therein all that they wish..." [16:31]; "...their provision therein will be without limit." [40.40]; entry therein will be in happiness [43:70]; it will be a place of bliss [56:12].

32. This was obviously the first test humans were put to. Allah, the Absolute Creator, could have, if He wanted to, so made Adam and Eve that they would by nature avoid going to the tree in question. But He left the freedom of choice – of conscious disobedience – to the first humans. And He has likewise left that freedom to their progeny. Deep down in every human mind is ingrained the fact of the existence of the Absolute Creator and the distinction between right and wrong, just as Adam and Eve were aware of the fact and of the distinction. But, like Adam and Eve, every human being is prone to suppress the promptings of his/her conscience and thus land himself/herself in trouble!

فَأَزَلَّهُمَا ٱلشَّيْطَٰنُ عَنْهَا فَأَخْرَجَهُمَا مِمَّا كَانَا فِيهِ وَقُلْنَا ٱهْبِطُوا۟ بَعْضُكُمْ لِبَعْضٍ عَدُوٌّ وَلَكُمْ فِى ٱلْأَرْضِ مُسْتَقَرٌّ وَمَتَٰعٌ إِلَىٰ حِينٍ

36. Faazallahuma alshshaytanu AAanha faakhrajahuma mimma kana feehi waqulna ihbitoo baAAdukum libaAAdin AAaduwwun walakum fee al-ardi mustaqarrun wamataAAun ila heenin

2:36. Then the Satan[33 & 34] made them slip there from and got them out from where they were. And We said, "Down you go, in reciprocal enmity[35]. And on the earth, for a while, will there be board and lodging for you."

33. The root of the Arabic word *Shaitaan* is *shatan* which means 'to oppose/hinder' or 'to be distant'. In the context of Verse No. 34 of this same Chapter Al-Baqarah, 'the *Shaitaan*' mentioned here is obviously with reference to *Iblis*, who, in his ill-conceived pride, refused to obey Allah's command to prostrate before Adam. He (the Satan) thus distanced himself from Allah and His mercy. He also vowed to hinder mankind from following Allah's path [Q: 7:16 & 17]. *Iblis* has therefore been addressed as 'the Shaitaan' here.

34. But, as has already been seen earlier in Verse 2:14, the Qur'aan refers to *shayaateen* (plural of *Shaitaan*) also. And in Verse 6:112, it refers to *shayaateen* of both mankind and jinn. Therefore, *shayaateen* are all those humans and jinn of rebellious nature, who distance themselves away from Allah's Straight Path and try to seduce others from that Path.

35. The Qur'aan repeatedly informs us (in Verses 2:168, 43:62, for example,) that the Satan is our open enemy. So primarily, in the context of the situation depicted in this Verse, the mutual enmity Allah refers to is between Adam and Eve on the one hand, and the Satan on the other. This mutual enmity with the Satan would extend to the entire human race as the latter would multiply on the earth. But, since the Satan would have a following among humans also, the mutual enmity would as well be between the followers of Satan and the others, among human beings themselves.

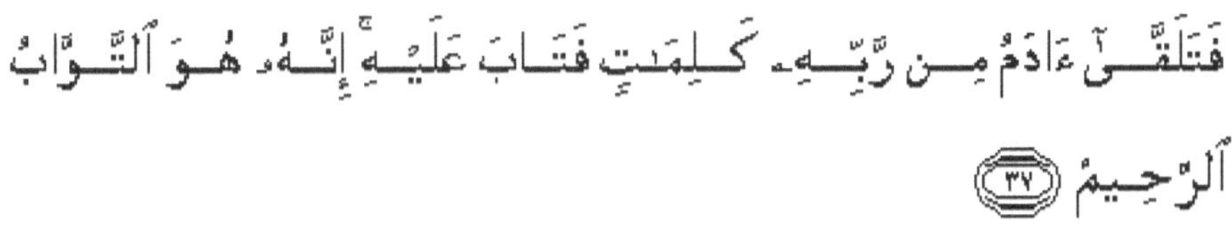

37. Fatalaqqa adamu min rabbihi kalimatin fataba AAalayhi innahu huwa alttawwabu alrraheemu

---

2:37. Adam thereupon learned/received Words[36] from his Lord, Who then pardoned him. Surely, He is the One Who forgives, the One Merciful!

---

36. In the context of the divine words that follow immediately, it appears that the 'Words' Adam learned from his Lord were the words of prayer mentioned in Verse Q: 7:23. That is the prayer Adam made to his Lord for the forgiveness of his and Eve's disobedience of the divine injunction against approaching the tree in the Garden. The 'Words' could also be the highly important message contained in the succeeding Verses 38 and 39 of this very Chapter 2. Or the 'Words' could be any other divine message that the first human received from his Lord for the proper conduct of the lives of the first human inhabitants of the earth. It was important for Adam to know then exactly what those words were, but it is not so for us, now. What is important and necessary for us now is to know exactly what the Qur'aan contains!

قُلْنَا اهْبِطُوا مِنْهَا جَمِيعًا فَإِمَّا يَأْتِيَنَّكُم مِّنِّى هُدًى فَمَن تَبِعَ هُدَاىَ فَلَا خَوْفٌ عَلَيْهِمْ وَلَا هُمْ يَحْزَنُونَ ﴿٣٨﴾

38. Qulna ihbitoo minha jameeAAan fa-imma ya/tiyannakum minnee hudan faman tabiAAa hudaya fala khawfun AAalayhim wala hum yahzanoona

2:38. We said, "Down you go all from this place! Then whenever Guidance comes to you from Me, all those who follow My Guidance shall have no fear, nor shall they grieve."

وَالَّذِينَ كَفَرُوا وَكَذَّبُوا بِآيَاتِنَا أُولَٰئِكَ أَصْحَابُ النَّارِ هُمْ فِيهَا خَالِدُونَ ﴿٣٩﴾

39. Waallatheena kafaroo wakaththaboo bi-ayatina ola-ika as-habu alnnari hum feeha khalidoona

2:39. "And those who suppress the Truth, and belie Our Verses/signs, those will be dwellers of the Fire, therein to remain, forever! [37]"

37. And this - the divine message contained in these two Verses 38 and 39 - is what is vitally important and necessary for us now to know and always remember. This is the divine mantra for the ultimate salvation of any individual among mankind. The individual ought to remember that it is only the purely divine - and not any other - guidance that will get him/her the salvation. The individual also ought to remember that if he/she suppresses or in any way whatsoever belies the truth behind any piece of the divine guidance, he/she would certainly be doomed! [For a comprehensive meaning of aayaat (translated here as Verses/Signs), please see this Chapter Notes 150 & 151 of these Studies.]

يَـٰبَنِىٓ إِسْرَٰٓءِيلَ ٱذْكُرُواْ نِعْمَتِىَ ٱلَّتِىٓ أَنْعَمْتُ عَلَيْكُمْ وَأَوْفُواْ بِعَهْدِىٓ

أُوفِ بِعَهْدِكُمْ وَإِيَّـٰىَ فَٱرْهَبُونِ ۝

40. Ya banee isra-eela o<u>th</u>kuroo niAAmatiya allatee anAAamtu AAalaykum waawfoo biAAahdee oofi biAAahdikum wa-iyy<u>a</u>ya fa<u>i</u>rhabooni

---

2:40. O Children of Israel[38 & 39]! Remember My favour[40] which I bestowed upon you and fulfil your terms[41] of the Covenant with Me and I will fulfil my terms[42]. And <u>Me</u>, then, you hold in awe!

---

38. The earliest people, so addressed (*Bani Israel*, in original Arabic) in the Qur'aan, were the ethnic group among whom Prophet Moses (peace be upon him) was born. Pharaoh, the ruler of ancient Egypt, had then subjected those people to harassment and persecution. Moses was sent by Allah to Pharaoh to ask him to "let Children of Israel come with me." [Q: 7:105]

39. The bulk of the descendents of those people of Moses (also known as Jews, Hebrews or Israelites) are now brought together in the present State of Israel. This bringing together is a prediction of the Qur'aan [17:104] that has come true! Also come true is the indirect prophecy and warning that the nominal followers of the Qur'aan today would be following the behavioural pattern of the Children of Israel. This latter prophecy is inherent in the frequent references made in the Qur'aan to various aspects of Jewish history.

40. Glimpses of the divine favour bestowed upon the Children of Israel are shown in Verses 47 to 64 of this very Chapter (Al-Baqarah) of the Qur'aan.

41. The terms to be fulfilled by the Children of Israel are enumerated in Verses 83 and 84 of this Chapter.

42. And Allah promises - to all those who believe in Him and fear Him and obediently do His bidding - the good both of this world and of the Hereafter! [Q: 10:64]

وَءَامِنُواْ بِمَآ أَنزَلْتُ مُصَدِّقًا لِّمَا مَعَكُمْ وَلَا تَكُونُوٓاْ أَوَّلَ كَافِرٍۭ بِهِۦ

وَلَا تَشْتَرُواْ بِـَٔايَـٰتِى ثَمَنًا قَلِيلًا وَإِيَّـٰىَ فَٱتَّقُونِ ۝

41. Waaminoo bima anzaltu musaddiqan lima maAAakum wala takoonoo awwala kafirin bihi wala tashtaroo bi-ayatee thamanan qaleelan wa-iyyaya faittaqooni

2:41. And believe in what[43] I have sent down in confirmation of that which is with you. And be not the first to suppress it. And do not trade my Verses/signs for a little benefit[44]. And <u>Me</u>, then, you fear!

43. What is referred to here is obviously the Qur'aan. Verse 46:12 makes this further clear. The basic message of all the preceding divine books had been the same as that of the Qur'aan.

44. In Qur'aanic Verses 3:187 and 5:44, we find similar expressions – on trading divine Verses for a little gain – made with reference to the people on whom earlier divine books were bestowed. A study of these Verses, as also of the Verses 41 and 42 currently under our study here, would make it clear that the expression means knowingly suppressing, hiding or twisting the meanings of the divine Verses for gaining temporal benefits. The benefit or price mentioned here should not be confused with price tags attached to copies and translations of the Qur'aan and to commentaries thereon, made available in the market or on the Net. When we buy a copy of the Qur'aan, for example, from the market, we do not, and cannot, buy the invaluable divine Verses as such. We pay only for the human effort put in, in making a printed copy of the Qur'aan made conveniently available to us. [For a comprehensive meaning of *aayaat* (translated here as Verses/signs), see <u>notes 2:150 & 2:151</u> of these Studies.]

42. Wala talbisoo alhaqqa bialbatili wataktumoo alhaqqa waantum taAAlamoona

2:42. And confound not the truth with the falsehood and thus knowingly conceal the truth!

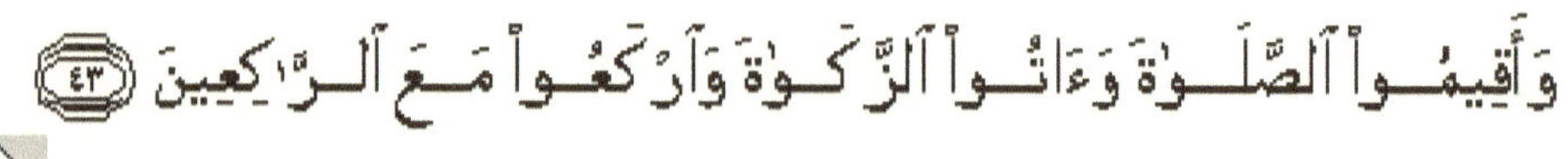

43. Waaqeemoo alssalata waatoo alzzakata wairkaAAoo maAAa alrrakiAAeena

2:43. And say the prayer properly[45] and give in charity[46]. And bow with those who bow[47]!

45. Please refer <u>study note 2:4</u>.

46. In Qur'aanic Verse 30:39, the charity (*az-zakaat*, in Arabic) is defined as that which is given away to seek just the pleasure or approval of Allah.

47. Bowing – bowing before Allah – forms an essential part of the Islamic prayer. This act symbolises, as nothing else does, complete and utter submission to Allah's will and command! In asking the Children of Israel to bow with those who bow, Allah is inviting them to join the Muslims in complete submission to their One and Only Lord.

۞ أَتَأْمُرُونَ ٱلنَّاسَ بِٱلْبِرِّ وَتَنسَوْنَ أَنفُسَكُمْ وَأَنتُمْ تَتْلُونَ ٱلْكِتَـٰبَ أَفَلَا تَعْقِلُونَ ﴿٤٤﴾

44. Ata/muroona alnnasa bialbirri watansawna anfusakum waantum tatloona alkitaba afala taAAqiloona

2:44. You tell people to be good and you forget your own selves? And you read the Book! Do you not then understand!?

وَٱسْتَعِينُواْ بِٱلصَّبْرِ وَٱلصَّلَوٰةِ ۚ وَإِنَّهَا لَكَبِيرَةٌ إِلَّا عَلَى ٱلْخَـٰشِعِينَ ﴿٤٥﴾

45. WaistaAAeenoo bialssabri waalssalati wa-innaha lakabeeratun illa AAala alkhashiAAena

2:45. And seek divine help[48] with the patience[49] and the proper prayer[45]! And this indeed is the hard thing except for those who dread -

48. The Arabic *Wastaeenu* has been rendered as 'And seek divine help' in the light of Verse 1:5.

49. 'The patience' that mankind is repeatedly exhorted, in the Qur'aan, to aspire to, along with 'the proper prayer', is that referred to in the exquisitely appropriate anecdote related in Verses 18:65 to 18:82. Please go through that anecdote. It is too long for me to repeat here. Man is wont to get exasperated, as Prophet Moses was in that anecdote, by the apparent inscrutability of the happenings in this world. He should have unshakable faith in Allah and be patient. The inscrutable happenings would turn out to be for the good, in the end.

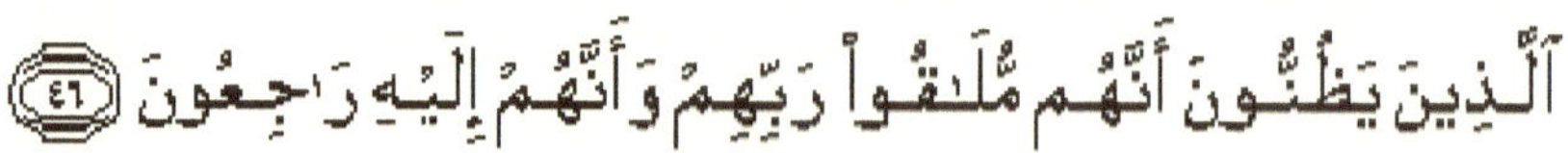

46. Alla*th*eena ya*th*unnoona annahum mulaqoo rabbihim waannahum ilayhi rajiAAoona

2:46. - Those, who think that they certainly shall meet their Lord and that unto Him they certainly shall return! [50]

50. The addressees of this divine address (Verses 2.40 to 2.46), covered in this section of these Qur'aanic Studies, could as well have been the Muslims of today, besides the Children of Israel! And I have no doubt in my mind that the modern-day Muslims too are the indirect addressees here. The All-knowing Allah knew that, in the future, the bulk of the Muslims would be treading the path of the Children of Israel! That is why, as already noted in note 39 above, the Qur'aan makes frequent references to the Jews.

47. Y*a* banee isr*a*-eela o*th*kuroo niAAmatiya allatee anAAamtu AAalaykum waannee fa*dd*altukum AAal*a* alAAalameena

2:47. O Children of Israel! Remember My Favour which I bestowed upon you. And remember that I gave you preference over the Worlds.[51 & 52]

51. Glimpses of "My Favour" that Allah spoke of earlier in <u>Verse 40 above</u>, are being mentioned, one by one, from this Verse. The first, mentioned here, is the divine preference given to the Children of Israel, in granting them the divine Favour, over all the worlds. [As for 'worlds' (*aalameen*), please see <u>note 5</u> under Chapter 1 above]. And as for the reason for that preference, Allah says in Verse 7.137, "...And the fair Word of your Lord was fulfilled upon the Children of Israel because of their patience..." That was the patience they displayed, while suffering at the hands of the despotic Pharaoh and his people. Refer <u>Verse 49 below</u>.

52. And in this recounting of the exemplary patience displayed in the face of terrible torment, there is a hint for the Muslims of today to exercise similar patience in the adverse circumstances the latter find them themselves surrounded with now. The Muslims however, it is sad to note, are resorting to manifest acts of impatience, thus (and otherwise, as well) betraying lack of faith in Allah and His Message! No wonder therefore that they (the Muslims) merit no favour from Allah and end up as the favourite 'whipping boy', for all and sundry, around the world today.

وَٱتَّقُواْ يَوْمًا لَّا تَجْزِى نَفْسٌ عَن نَّفْسٍ شَيْئًا وَلَا يُقْبَلُ مِنْهَا شَفَٰعَةٌ وَلَا
يُؤْخَذُ مِنْهَا عَدْلٌ وَلَا هُمْ يُنصَرُونَ ۝

48. Waittaqoo yawman la tajzee nafsun AAan nafsin shay-an wala yuqbalu minha shafaAAatun wala yu/khathu minha AAadlun wala hum yunsaroona

2:48. And fear that Day when none can be of any avail on anything to another, when no intercession will be accepted from anyone nor any ransom taken, and when they will be given no help![53]

53. This is a divine statement, made quite categorically. In defiance thereof, however, almost the entire Christendom and many Muslims cling to their futile fond hopes that Jesus and Muhammad (may peace be upon them both) shall ransom their sinning souls out, with their – the two Messengers' – respective powers(?) of intercession!

وَإِذْ نَجَّيْنَاكُم مِّنْ ءَالِ فِرْعَوْنَ يَسُومُونَكُمْ سُوٓءَ ٱلْعَذَابِ يُذَبِّحُونَ أَبْنَاءَكُمْ وَيَسْتَحْيُونَ نِسَاءَكُمْ وَفِى ذَٰلِكُم بَلَآءٌ مِّن رَّبِّكُمْ عَظِيمٌ ﴿٤٩﴾

49. Wa-ith najjaynakum min ali firAAawna yasoomoonakum soo-a alAAathabi yuthabbihoona abnaakum wayastahyoona nisaakum wafee thalikum balaon min rabbikum AAatheemun

---

2:49. And there was that time when We delivered you from Pharaoh's people! They were inflicting on you a terrible torment: they were slaughtering your sons and sparing the lives of your womenfolk. And therein was a mighty trial from your Lord!

وَإِذْ فَرَقْنَا بِكُمُ ٱلْبَحْرَ فَأَنجَيْنَاكُمْ وَأَغْرَقْنَآ ءَالَ فِرْعَوْنَ وَأَنتُمْ تَنظُرُونَ ﴿٥٠﴾

50. Wa-ith faraqna bikumu albahra faanjaynakum waaghraqna ala firAAawna waantum tanthuroona

---

2:50. And the time when We split the sea for you! We then saved you. And We drowned Pharaoh's people. And you had been watching!

وَإِذْ وَاعَدْنَا مُوسَىٰٓ أَرْبَعِينَ لَيْلَةً ثُمَّ ٱتَّخَذْتُمُ ٱلْعِجْلَ مِنۢ بَعْدِهِ وَأَنتُمْ ظَٰلِمُونَ ﴿٥١﴾

51. Wa-ith waAAadna moosa arbaAAeena laylatan thumma ittakhathtumu alAAijla min baAAdihi waantum thalimoona

2:51. And the time when We gave an appointment to Moses of forty nights! You then took to the calf after he left. And you were indulging in wickedness!

52. Thumma AAafawna AAankum min baAAdi thalika laAAallakum tashkuroona

2:52. Then, after that, We forgave you that you might express gratefulness![54]

54. The episode mentioned in Verses 51 and 52 above, is explained in greater details in Verses 7:142 to 7:154. The divine appointment was to give Moses written Tablets containing "admonition and details on everything". For the appointment with Allah, Moses had to go away from his people, the Children of Israel, for forty nights. It was during this period of Moses' absence from them that the Children of Israel took to the abomination of worshipping a calf-like object made from ornaments.

53. Wa-ith atayna moosa alkitaba waalfurqana laAAallakum tahtadoona

2:53. [55]And there was that time when We gave to Moses the Book[56], and the standard by which to distinguish between right and wrong[57], so that you might be guided.

55. The Qur'aan continues here from the preceding Verses to reminisce the history of the Jewish people to them.

56. Verse 3:65 makes it clear that the divine Book Torah was not revealed till after Prophet Abraham. And in Verse 5:46, it is made clear that the divine Book Gospel (*Injeel*) was revealed to Prophet Jesus,

and that the Torah was revealed before the time of Jesus. Again, in Verse 5:43 it is mentioned that the Jews have the Torah. These circumstantial evidences from the Qur'aan leave no room for any doubt that the divine Book revealed to Moses <u>was</u> the Torah.

57. The Arabic word used in the original revelation is *al-furqaan*. *Furqaan* is a thing that distinguishes between good and evil, between right and wrong. In Verse 8:29, the Qur'aan tells the believers, "...If you fear Allah, He effects *furqaan* for you..." The word is used in that Verse without the prefix *al*, and the quoted part of the Verse obviously means that Allah enables the believers, who fear Him, to distinguish between good and evil, right and wrong. In this Verse 53, which we are currently studying, as also in Verse 21:48, the word with the prefix *al* is used as a synonym for the Torah. In other words, the Torah is described as a criterion, or a standard, by which to distinguish between good and evil, right and wrong. In Verses 3:4 and 25:1, the Qur'aan is also described as *al-furqaan*.

وَإِذْ قَالَ مُوسَىٰ لِقَوْمِهِۦ يَٰقَوْمِ إِنَّكُمْ ظَلَمْتُمْ أَنفُسَكُم بِٱتِّخَاذِكُمُ ٱلْعِجْلَ فَتُوبُوٓاْ إِلَىٰ بَارِئِكُمْ فَٱقْتُلُوٓاْ أَنفُسَكُمْ ذَٰلِكُمْ خَيْرٌ لَّكُمْ عِندَ بَارِئِكُمْ فَتَابَ عَلَيْكُمْ إِنَّهُۥ هُوَ ٱلتَّوَّابُ ٱلرَّحِيمُ ۞

54. Wa-*ith* qala moosa liqawmihi ya qawmi innakum *th*alamtum anfusakum biittikha*th*ikumu alAAijla fatooboo ila bari-ikum faoqtuloo anfusakum *th*alikum khayrun lakum AAinda bari-ikum fataba AAalaykum innahu huwa alttawwabu alrra*h*eemu

2:54. And that time when Moses said to his people, "O my people! You did indeed wrong your own selves by taking to the worship of the calf. So, turn in repentance to your Creator and kill those selves[58] of yours! That will be better for you with your Creator." Allah then accepted your repentance. Truly, He is the One to accept repentance, the One Merciful!

58. The original Arabic word, which I have translated as 'those selves of yours' or as 'your own selves' earlier in the same Verse, is *anfusakum*, literally, 'your souls'. So, when Moses urged his people to kill '*anfusakum*', he did not urge them to kill one another <u>physically</u>, as is wrongly depicted in some English translations. He urged them to annihilate their inner tendencies to polytheism. He urged them to change their 'nature'. The use of this very word in Verses 16:72, 30:21 and 42:11 in that sense, corroborates this interpretation. In those Verses, it is pointed out to mankind that Allah has made for them mates, *min anfusikum* ('of your nature').

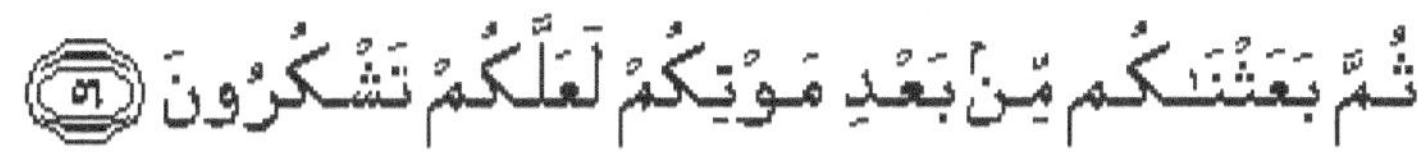

55. Wa-i_th_ qultum y_a_ moos_a_ lan nu/mina laka _h_att_a_ nar_a_ All_a_ha jahratan faakha_th_atkumu al_ss_aAAiqatu waantum tan_th_uroona

---

2:55. And that time when you said, "O Moses! We won't believe you until we see Allah with our own eyes." The thunderbolt then struck you as you were watching! [59]

---

59. In Verse 7:143, the Qur'aan also speaks of Moses himself individually expressing his desire to his Lord to see Him. But this expression of desire was not the result of any intransigence - it was just his curiosity. Moses became unconscious when he tried to see Him. Allah thus made Moses understand the absurdity of a finite creature like a human being, in the circumstances of his/her earthly existence, attempting to see the Infinite Being! This incongruity is also highlighted in Verse 42:51: "It is not for any human being that Allah would speak to him except ... from behind a veil ... " In Verse 25:21, Allah condemns those who ask why they do not see Allah, as being driven by self-conceit and utter arrogance! The Children of Israel were, similarly, driven by their intransigence in what they told Moses as recorded in this Verse under our study presently. It was obviously by way of divine punishment for this intransigence that the thunderbolt struck them!

---

56. Thumma baAAa_th_n_a_kum min baAAdi mawtikum laAAallakum tashkuroona

---

2:56. We then raised you up after your death[60], so you might be grateful!

---

60. Death (*Maut* in Arabic) is the irreversible ending of the present worldly life on this earth, especially so far as human beings are concerned. The Qur'aan corroborates when it says that Allah withholds the souls of those on whom He has passed the decree of death [39:42]. But nothing is impossible for Allah! And to illustrate, the Qur'aan speaks of a person whom Allah caused to die for a hundred years and then raised him up again [2:259]. The Verse under our study presently is another instance wherein Allah raised up the Children of Israel to life, after their death from the thunderbolt that struck them. We do

hear of some medical cases in our present times also, when persons, after having been declared clinically dead, regained life.

وَظَلَّلْنَا عَلَيْكُمُ الْغَمَامَ وَأَنزَلْنَا عَلَيْكُمُ الْمَنَّ وَالسَّلْوَىٰ كُلُوا۟ مِن طَيِّبَـٰتِ مَا رَزَقْنَـٰكُمْ وَمَا ظَلَمُونَا وَلَـٰكِن كَانُوٓا۟ أَنفُسَهُمْ يَظْلِمُونَ ﴿٥٧﴾

57. Wa*th*allalna AAalaykumu alghamama waanzalna AAalaykumu almanna waalssalwa kuloo min tayyibati ma razaqnakum wama *th*alamoona walakin kanoo anfusahum ya*th*limoona

2:57. We caused the clouds to provide you with shade. And We sent down the manna and the quail: "Eat of the good, lawful and pure things We have provided for you." They could do no wrong to Us, but they were doing wrong to themselves! [61]

61. Down in this same Qur'aanic Chapter, in Verse 61, we are informed as to why the Children of Israel thus gained the displeasure of Allah. They told Moses that they could not endure one kind of food – the manna and the quail, the superior sources of food divinely provided to them. They wanted to have inferior agricultural products like herbs, onions, lentils etc.

وَإِذْ قُلْنَا ٱدْخُلُوا۟ هَـٰذِهِ ٱلْقَرْيَةَ فَكُلُوا۟ مِنْهَا حَيْثُ شِئْتُمْ رَغَدًا وَٱدْخُلُوا۟ ٱلْبَابَ سُجَّدًا وَقُولُوا۟ حِطَّةٌ نَّغْفِرْ لَكُمْ خَطَـٰيَـٰكُمْ وَسَنَزِيدُ ٱلْمُحْسِنِينَ ﴿٥٨﴾

58. Wa-i*th* qulna odkhuloo ha*th*ihi alqaryata fakuloo minha haythu shi/tum raghadan waodkhuloo albaba sujjadan waqooloo *h*ittatun naghfir lakum khatayakum wasanazeedu almu*h*sineena

2:58. And the time when We said, "Enter this place and eat and live therein, in ease and affluence, wherever you wish. And enter the gate, prostrating and praying for forgiveness (*hittatun*). We shall forgive you your sins and grant much more, of our mercy, to the good people."

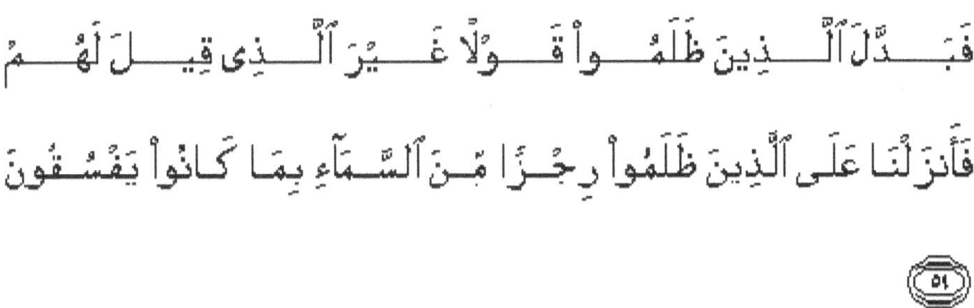

59. Fabaddala alla<u>th</u>eena <u>th</u>alamoo qawlan ghayra alla<u>th</u>ee qeela lahum faanzaln<u>a</u> AAal<u>a</u> alla<u>th</u>eena <u>th</u>alamoo rijzan mina alssam<u>a</u>-i bim<u>a</u> k<u>a</u>noo yafsuqoon<u>a</u>

2:59. But then the wicked people changed the word to one other than what they were asked to utter! We thereupon sent down upon those wicked people a disgraceful calamity from the sky because they had been transgressing.[62]

62. In Verses 7:161 and 7:162, the same episode (narrated here in Verses 58 and 59 of this Qur'aanic Chapter presently under our study) is repeated in almost identical words and with no further details. What is of relevance to us now from this episode is that the Almighty Allah expects believers to obey His commands in letter and spirit! The Jews in that episode were punished because of their mischievous change of the word *hittatun* they were ordered to utter. Earlier, our first fore parents, Adam and Eve, were banished from Paradise because they had gone near the tree, although Allah had prohibited them from doing so! Likewise, in our present-day world, Muslims are facing ignominious situations all over the world because of their negligence of, disregard for and/or open disobedience to the divine commands in the Qur'aan!

۞ وَإِذِ ٱسْتَسْقَىٰ مُوسَىٰ لِقَوْمِهِۦ فَقُلْنَا ٱضْرِب بِّعَصَاكَ ٱلْحَجَرَ ۖ فَٱنفَجَرَتْ مِنْهُ ٱثْنَتَا عَشْرَةَ عَيْنًا ۖ قَدْ عَلِمَ كُلُّ أُنَاسٍ مَّشْرَبَهُمْ ۖ كُلُوا۟ وَٱشْرَبُوا۟ مِن رِّزْقِ ٱللَّهِ وَلَا تَعْثَوْا۟ فِى ٱلْأَرْضِ مُفْسِدِينَ ۝

60. Wa-ithi istasqa moosa liqawmihi faqulna idrib biAAasaka alhajara fainfajarat minhu ithnata AAashrata AAaynan qad AAalima kullu onasin mashrabahum kuloo walshraboo min rizqi Allahi wala taAAthaw fee al-ardi mufsideena

---

2:60. And when Moses asked for water for his people, We said, "Strike the stone with your stick." Sprang forth there from, then, twelve[63] springs. Everyone knew one's own place for water. "Eat and drink of that which Allah has provided and do not act wickedly[64] on the earth spreading corruption."

---

63. In Verse 7:160 we are informed that Moses' people were divided into twelve tribes. The twelve springs of water were obviously for those twelve tribes, one for every tribe.

64. This divine command was ostensibly addressed to Moses' people here, but it is a universal command for all mankind. Man is generally not content with what Allah has provided for him. He is ever greedy for more! As Allah says, "You are obsessed with the greed to have more and more, until you are lowered into the graves." [Q: 102:1 & 2] So obsessed is he that he tries to get more by hook or by crook. Means no longer matter to him. If he does not get it fast by fair means, he has no compunction in resorting to foul means. He loses patience. He loses faith in his Creator. Thus, is wickedness and corruption spread on earth. It may well be noted here in this context that what Allah has provided for us is what we get by fair means!

وَإِذْ قُلْتُمْ يَٰمُوسَىٰ لَن نَّصْبِرَ عَلَىٰ طَعَامٍ وَٰحِدٍ فَٱدْعُ لَنَا رَبَّكَ يُخْرِجْ لَنَا مِمَّا تُنۢبِتُ ٱلْأَرْضُ مِنۢ بَقْلِهَا وَقِثَّآئِهَا وَفُومِهَا وَعَدَسِهَا وَبَصَلِهَا قَالَ أَتَسْتَبْدِلُونَ ٱلَّذِى هُوَ أَدْنَىٰ بِٱلَّذِى هُوَ خَيْرٌ ٱهْبِطُوا۟ مِصْرًا فَإِنَّ لَكُم مَّا سَأَلْتُمْ وَضُرِبَتْ عَلَيْهِمُ ٱلذِّلَّةُ وَٱلْمَسْكَنَةُ وَبَآءُو بِغَضَبٍ مِّنَ ٱللَّهِ ذَٰلِكَ بِأَنَّهُمْ كَانُوا۟ يَكْفُرُونَ بِـَٔايَٰتِ ٱللَّهِ وَيَقْتُلُونَ ٱلنَّبِيِّۦنَ بِغَيْرِ ٱلْحَقِّ ذَٰلِكَ بِمَا عَصَوا۟ وَّكَانُوا۟ يَعْتَدُونَ ۝

61. Wa-ith qultum ya moosa lan nasbira AAala taAAamin wahidin faodAAu lana rabbaka yukhrij lana mimma tunbitu al-ardu min baqliha waqiththa-iha wafoomiha waAAadasiha wabasaliha qala atastabdiloona allathee huwa adna biallathee huwa khayrun ihbitoo misran fa-inna lakum ma saaltum waduribat AAalayhimu alththillatu waalmaskanatu wabaoo bighadabin mina Allahi thalika bi-annahum kanoo yakfuroona bi-ayati Allahi wayaqtuloona alnnabiyyeena bighayri alhaqqi thalika bima AAasaw wakanoo yaAAtadoona

---

2:61. And when you said, "O Moses! We cannot indeed endure but one kind of food. So, invoke your Lord on our behalf to bring forth for us agricultural products like herbs, cucumbers, garlic, lentils and onions." He said, "Would you change what is better for what is worse? Go you down to a town! You will certainly get there what you want!" And they were hit by the ignominy and the poverty, and they incurred Allah's wrath. That was because they were suppressing Allah's signs/Verses and they were killing the Prophets wrongfully. That was because they disobeyed, and they were crossing the limits.[65 & 66]

---

65. Living ignominiously in this very world could well be the lot of those who exceed Allah-set limits in their disobedience of divine commands. It was the lot of the Jews for the same crime in the pre-Qur'aanic times, as this Verse under our study presently informs us. For the same crime besides, Verse 5:78 informs us, they incurred the curse of Prophets David and Jesus. Verse 3:112, read with Verse 3:110, informs us further that the said crime could bring about the same fate (of living ignominiously in this very world) on *ahl-ul-kitaab* (people of the Book). Muslims of the present-day world, being one of the peoples of the Book, are afflicted with the same fate, for the same crime – the crime of persistent disobedience of Qur'aanic commands!

66. Living ignominiously, yes – but still living! There's a ray of hope therein, nevertheless, from the Merciful Lord! It is as though He is warning us – through the ignominy we Muslims are facing – to mend our ways! To revert to obedience of His commands, in letter and in spirit, before it is too late! Before we

are finally lowered into our graves! [For a comprehensive meaning of *aayaat* (translated here as signs/Verses), please see Chapter Notes 150 & 151 of these Studies.]

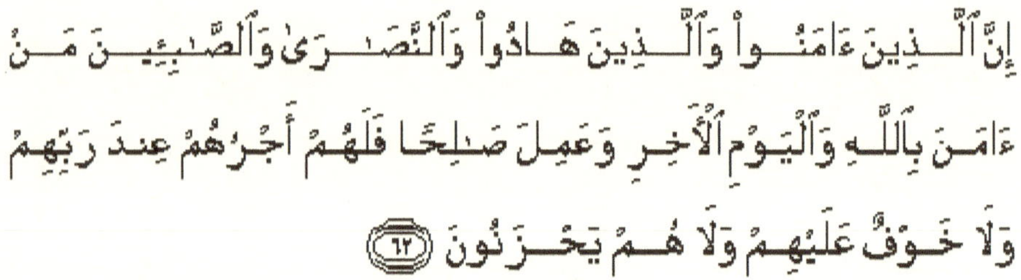

62. Inna allatheena amanoo waallatheena hadoo waalnnasara waalssabi-eena man amana biAllahi waalyawmi al-akhiri waAAamila salihan falahum ajruhum AAinda rabbihim wala khawfun AAalayhim wala hum yahzanoona

2:62. Indeed, those who believe and those who are Jews, the Christians and the *Saabieen*[67] – whosoever believed in Allah and in the Last Day, and acted righteously[68] – for them then, of course, is their reward with their Lord. And fear shall overpower them not; nor shall they grieve! [69]

67. In two other Verses of the Qur'aan namely, 5:69 and 22:17, are these people (the *Saabieen* or the *Saabioon*) mentioned. While Verse 5:69 is almost a replica of Verse 2:62 we are presently studying, Verse 22:17 informs us that on the Day of Resurrection, Allah will judge between all the groups of people mentioned here (in Verse 2:62) along with the polytheists. That is all! So, while we find plenty of information about the Jews and the Christians elsewhere in the Qur'aan, there isn't much therein about the *Saabieen*. Obviously, our Lord did not consider it necessary to give us more information about them. As the Qur'aan says, "... And they will not encompass anything of His knowledge except that which He wills. ..." [2:255].

68. In Verse 8:29, the Qur'aan informs the believers that Allah creates for them the *furqaan*, the ability to distinguish between right and wrong, if they are pious! Even a thief, when he steals, knows in his heart of hearts that he is doing something wrong! But he suppresses this call of his conscience. And with its repeated suppressions, his conscience so to say dies much before his physical death! A pious, Allah-fearing man, on the other hand, does not suppress his conscience - his *furqaan*! The Qur'aan guides us further in this regard by explaining, in Verses 2:44, 2:177 and 2:189, what *Al-Birr* (good, righteous conduct or behaviour) ought to be!

69. From Adam to Muhammad (peace be upon them all), all the Prophets have preached but one Religion - the Religion of Islam! And the fundamentals of this Religion have always been: belief in Allah, belief in the Hereafter and performance of righteous deeds. So no eyebrows need be raised when this Verse 2:62 informs us that even the Jews and the Christians shall attain to salvation if they only satisfied the three conditions mentioned. And no dichotomy be sought between this Verse here and Verse 3:85, wherein Allah informs us that no religion other than Islam shall be accepted! The moot question that

now arises is whether the present-day Christians and the present-day Jews – with all their notions about Trinity, and about each being the chosen people of God with guaranteed divine visas to Paradise, and with their outright rejection of Muhammad and of the Qur'aan as the last Prophet and the last divine Testament - do thus satisfy the three fundamental conditions to be entitled to Salvation. And the moot question also is whether the present-day Muslims - with their neglect and ignorance of, and therefore with their fundamental deviations from, divine commands laid down in the Qur'aan - do thus satisfy the three fundamental conditions to be entitled to Salvation.

63. Wa-ith akhathna meethaqakum warafaAAna fawqakumu alttoora khuthoo ma ataynakum biquwwatin waothkuroo ma feehi laAAallakum tattaqoona

2:63. And that time when We took your pledge and raised the Mountain over you! [70] "Hold on to what We have given you steadfastly! And do repeatedly refer to and remember its contents in order that you become pious!"[71]

70. We get further explanation on this episode, in the history of the Children of Israel, in Verse 7:171. The mountain was so raised over them (i.e. Moses' people) that they thought it was about to fall on them. Allah thus used even coercion to make the recalcitrant Jews abide by the Book of Allah given to Moses. HE does that even now to the so-called Muslims to make them abide by the Qur'aan. HE coerces them by involving them in some or the other calamity or ignominy every now and then. And we are very much the witnesses thereto! But alas! The Muslims of today generally are as recalcitrant as the Jews had been during Moses' time.

71. This divine command was ostensibly given to the Jews. But it is as if Allah is telling the Muslims of today: 'Hold on to the Qur'aan steadfastly! And do repeatedly refer to and remember its contents in order that you become pious!' Are there any amongst us, listening to the divine Whisper, my fellow Muslims?

$$ \text{ثُمَّ تَوَلَّيْتُم مِّنۢ بَعْدِ ذَٰلِكَ ۖ فَلَوْلَا فَضْلُ ٱللَّهِ عَلَيْكُمْ وَرَحْمَتُهُۥ لَكُنتُم مِّنَ ٱلْخَٰسِرِينَ ﴿٦٤﴾} $$

64. Thumma tawallaytum min baAAdi thalika falawla fadlu Allahi AAalaykum warahmatuhu lakuntum mina alkhasireena

2:64. You then turned away, thereafter! Had it not been for Allah's Grace upon you and His Mercy, you would certainly have been among the doomed! [72]

72. This divine statement too is ostensibly addressed to the Jews, but it is no less applicable to the Muslims of today!

$$ \text{وَلَقَدْ عَلِمْتُمُ ٱلَّذِينَ ٱعْتَدَوْا۟ مِنكُمْ فِى ٱلسَّبْتِ فَقُلْنَا لَهُمْ كُونُوا۟ قِرَدَةً خَٰسِـِٔينَ ﴿٦٥﴾} $$

65. Walaqad AAalimtumu allatheena iAAtadaw minkum fee alssabti faqulna lahum koonoo qiradatan khasi-eena

2:65. And you did indeed know those of you who committed transgression on Sabbath[73]. So, We told them, "Be you monkeys, despised!"

73. The dictionary informs us that Sabbath is the religious day of rest kept by Christians on Sunday and by Jews on Saturday. The Qur'aan informs us, in Verse 4:154, that the Jews were specifically commanded not to transgress the strict observance of their Sabbath. That is, they were asked to take an obligatory rest from usual pursuits for earning worldly wealth. In Verse 7:163, the Qur'aan further informs us how a township of Jewish fishermen was put to a test, by making the fish in the sea more easily available, for catching, on the day they observed Sabbath, than on other days! The fishermen failed in the trial and committed transgression. It is this transgression that is alluded to here.

فَجَعَلۡنَٰهَا نَكَٰلًا لِّمَا بَيۡنَ يَدَيۡهَا وَمَا خَلۡفَهَا وَمَوۡعِظَةً لِّلۡمُتَّقِينَ ۝

66. FajaAAalnaha nakalan lima bayna yadayha wama khalfaha wamawAAithatan lilmuttaqeena

2:66. We set it then as an exemplary punishment for those present at that time and for those who lived thereafter.[74] And We made it a lesson for the pious![75 & 76]

74. We have seen earlier, in <u>Verse 63</u> of this Chapter, that Allah raised the Mountain over Moses' people to coerce them into abiding by the Book of Allah given to Moses. Here is another method adopted by Allah to coerce the recalcitrant Jews. The punishment meted out to the fishermen breaking the Sabbath Law was made an example of, to warn off the other Jews against breaking any divine commandment.

75. During the pre-historic times before the advent of the Last Prophet (peace and Allah's blessings be upon him), Allah sent direct signs for the people to recognise prophets sent to them. HE also gave direct signs to warn them against disobedience of divine Law. This is what we learn from various anecdotes mentioned in the Qur'aan. The direct signs were given obviously to compensate those people for the lack of means to acquisition of knowledge that Mankind now enjoys. We cannot but marvel at the tremendous divine sense of justice in this! So we do not witness those direct divine signs now. But we do witness indirect signs of warnings. Like the ignominious state of Muslims all over the world at present. It's a divine sign warning us against our neglect and disobedience of the divine commands contained in the Qur'aan (see also <u>study note 70</u> above). And in the Qur'aan itself, the caring hand of our Caretaker can be seen, as here in this Verse, asking the pious to take a lesson from history.

76. The pious amongst the present-day Muslims do have to take a lesson from this episode in Jewish history. For, the Qur'aan too prescribes abstaining from our worldly affairs for a short period on Fridays. In Verses 62:9 and 62:10, Allah commands the Believers to leave off business from the time the *Muazzin* gives the call for the Friday noon prayers till the end of the prayers. If we flout this command, Allah may not now turn us into apes, but our *aakhira* is bound to be ruined! And, despised like apes we already are; we may further be despised in this very world!

وَإِذۡ قَالَ مُوسَىٰ لِقَوۡمِهِۦٓ إِنَّ ٱللَّهَ يَأۡمُرُكُمۡ أَن تَذۡبَحُواْ بَقَرَةً ۖ قَالُوٓاْ أَتَتَّخِذُنَا هُزُوًا ۖ قَالَ أَعُوذُ بِٱللَّهِ أَنۡ أَكُونَ مِنَ ٱلۡجَٰهِلِينَ ۝

67. Wa-ith qala moosa liqawmihi inna Allaha ya/murukum an tathbahoo baqaratan qaloo atattakhithuna huzuwan qala aAAoothu biAllahi an akoona mina aljahileena

---

2:67. [77]And that time when Moses told his people, "Allah does command you to sacrifice a cow[78]"! They said, "Are you teasing us?" He said, "I seek refuge with Allah from being among the ignorant!"[79 & 80]

---

77. The Qur'aan here continues with reminiscences from the history of the Jews.

78. It is the mention here of the word 'cow' that this Qur'aanic Chapter (*Surah*) gets its title from. An in-depth study of Verses 2:67 to 2:71 reveals that the title is not just a random pick-up of a word mentioned in the *Surah*. The title epitomizes a matter of deeper significance. It symbolises a human trait highlighted in the episode described in these five Verses. A trait, which has often landed mankind in trouble *vis-a-vis* its Creator!

79. From these very initial words of the episode here, it is apparent that his people were not taking Moses – their Prophet – seriously! Their Prophet, who had come to Pharaoh, their erstwhile oppressive ruler in Egypt, with clear signs of his Prophethood! Their Prophet, who had rescued them, with Allah's help, from that ruler's torments! When this man – whom they thus very well knew as the Prophet of Allah – informs them of the command from Allah, they thought he was just jesting!!

80. It is such casual approach to commands divine, that Allah abhors! HE expects His express orders to be obeyed unquestioningly, in letter and in spirit! Remember how Adam had to lose Paradise for disobeying Allah's order not to go near a particular tree. This propensity to blatant disobedience is innate to human nature. Observe a child deliberately disobeying any elder's order to him unless the child is made aware that he would be punished if he disobeys. This innate nature is evident in the Muslims of today who casually treat Allah's express order to them to leave off business the moment they hear the call to Friday prayers! (See note 76 above.) There are many who completely ignore the call to prayer and continue with their businesses. And there are many who delay their departure for the Masjid till it is time for the actual cogregational prayer to start! Compare this casual approach to a divine order, with the immediate compliance to the bugle sounded for soldiers in a military camp to come out to the ground for the early morning parade! No soldier can dare disobey the bugle call for fear of being immediately punished by the Corporal!

قَالُوا۟ ٱدْعُ لَنَا رَبَّكَ يُبَيِّن لَّنَا مَا هِىَ قَالَ إِنَّهُۥ يَقُولُ إِنَّهَا بَقَرَةٌ

لَّا فَارِضٌ وَلَا بِكْرٌ عَوَانٌۢ بَيْنَ ذَٰلِكَ فَٱفْعَلُوا۟ مَا تُؤْمَرُونَ ۝

68. Qaloo odAAu lana rabbaka yubayyin lana ma hiya qala innahu yaqoolu innaha baqaratun la faridun wala bikrun AAawanun bayna thalika faifAAaloo ma tu/maroona

---

2:68. They said, "Invoke your Lord for us to make clear to us what she is to be like." Said he, "HE does say that the cow should be neither old, nor young, but of an age in between. Now carry out what you have been commanded to do! [81]"

---

81. There is a hint here of divine displeasure at Moses' people asking for details of the cow to be sacrificed.

قَالُواْ ٱدْعُ لَنَا رَبَّكَ يُبَيِّن لَّنَا مَا لَوْنُهَا قَالَ إِنَّهُۥ يَقُولُ إِنَّهَا بَقَرَةٌ صَفْرَآءُ فَاقِعٌ لَّوْنُهَا تَسُرُّ ٱلنَّٰظِرِينَ ۝

69. Qaloo odAAu lana rabbaka yubayyin lana ma lawnuha qala innahu yaqoolu innaha baqaratun safrao faqiAAun lawnuha tasurru alnna_th_ireena

---

2:69. They said, "Invoke, for us, your Lord to make clear to us of what colour she is to be!" He said, "HE does say that the cow should be yellow – bright in colour, pleasing to the beholders."

قَـالُواْ ٱدْعُ لَنَا رَبَّـكَ يُبَيِّـن لَّنَا مَا هِـىَ إِنَّ ٱلْبَقَرَ تَشَـٰبَهَ عَلَيْنَا وَإِنَّا إِن شَآءَ ٱللَّهُ لَمُهْتَدُونَ ۝

70. Qaloo odAAu lana rabbaka yubayyin lana ma hiya inna albaqara tashabaha AAalayna wa-inna in shaa Allahu lamuhtadoona

---

2:70. They said, "Invoke, for us, your Lord to make clear to us what she is to be like; for, all cows look alike to us! And now, Allah willing, we shall indeed be guided!"

قَالَ إِنَّهُۥ يَقُولُ إِنَّهَا بَقَرَةٌ لَّا ذَلُولٌ تُثِيرُ ٱلْأَرْضَ وَلَا تَسْقِى ٱلْحَرْثَ مُسَلَّمَةٌ لَّا شِيَةَ فِيهَا قَالُوا۟ ٱلْـَٰٔنَ جِئْتَ بِٱلْحَقِّ فَذَبَحُوهَا وَمَا كَادُوا۟ يَفْعَلُونَ

71. Qala innahu yaqoolu innaha baqaratun la thaloolun tutheeru al-arda wala tasqee alhartha musallamatun la shiyata feeha qaloo al-ana ji/ta bialhaqqi fathabahooha wama kadoo yafAAaloona

---

2:71. He said, "HE does say that the cow should be one that is not trained to till the earth or water the field. It should be sound in body, with no scar or blemish in her." They said, "You have now come with the Truth!" They sacrificed her then; and they were not keen on doing it! [82 to 84]

---

82. And here's confirmation of the divine displeasure! The Jews, as usual, loathed carrying out the divine command. It was this loathing or reluctance that had prompted them to seek clarifications about the cow to be sacrificed. Their inquisitiveness only helped in making the divine command more complicated, and difficult to implement. Had they been content with the initial order given in Verse 67, they could have sacrificed any cow easily available to them. The choice was very wide, and therefore the command, easy to implement. But their persistent inquisitiveness narrowed the choice, and thus made the command more difficult to implement.

83. I would like to invite attention in this context to Qur'aanic Verses 5:101 and 5:102. The believers are forbidden therein from being more inquisitive about things revealed in the Qur'aan, which, if further clarified, might cause hardship to them. The believers are further informed that people who lived earlier had come to suppressing the Truth, because of such inquisitiveness. The reference there is obviously to this persistent questioning of the Jews regarding the cow to be sacrificed!

84. And we Muslims of the present day, faithfully follow the Jews in almost every wrong thing they did! We are not content with the perfect divine Islamic law enunciated to us, in sufficient details, in the perfect, incorruptible and clear Verses of the Qur'aan! We seek further explanations for and interpretations of those perfect Verses elsewhere! Some of our religious leaders tell us that we cannot claim to know Islam perfectly unless we make ourselves conversant with thousands and thousands of _ahaadeeth_, besides the Qur'aan! (Please also go through study notes 96 to 98 below, in this context.) We have thus rendered our perfect, easy and simple Religion, difficult and complicated. No wonder therefore that the Muslims, today, have come to suppress the Truth, as did the other people mentioned in Verse 5:102!

وَإِذْ قَتَلْتُمْ نَفْسًا فَٱدَّارَٰتُمْ فِيهَا وَٱللَّهُ مُخْرِجٌ مَّا كُنتُمْ تَكْتُمُونَ ۝

72. Wa-ith qataltum nafsan faiddara/tum feeha waAllahu mukhrijun makuntum taktumoona

---

2:72. [85]And when you killed a person! You then quarrelled therein. And Allah is the One Who would bring out what you were hiding.

---

85. This is in continuation of reminiscences from the history of the Jews.

فَقُلْنَا ٱضْرِبُوهُ بِبَعْضِهَا كَذَٰلِكَ يُحْيِ ٱللَّهُ ٱلْمَوْتَىٰ وَيُرِيكُمْ ءَايَٰتِهِ لَعَلَّكُمْ تَعْقِلُونَ ۝

73. Faqulna idriboohu bibaAAdiha kathalika yuhyee Allahu almawta wayureekum ayatihi laAAallakum taAAqiloona

---

2:73. So We asked them to raise him up[86] from something thereof[87 to 89]. Thus, does Allah give life to the dead[90 & 91], and show you His signs so that you understand[92].

---

86. Among the various meanings in which the Arabic root word *zaraba* is used in the Qur'aan, one is 'to set up' or 'to raise'. It is in this meaning that this word, with its grammatical variation, is used in Verse 57:13. It is used therein to connote 'setting up' or 'raising' a wall between the believers and the hypocrites, in the Hereafter. And the pronoun *hu* obviously refers to the murdered person mentioned in the preceding Verse 2:72. Since the pronoun is masculine, it is obvious that the murdered person was a man. And in the context of the reference made to Allah giving life to the dead, further down in this very Verse (2:73), it is obvious that the killed man was brought to life again to disclose to the people as to who had killed him.

87. Here, the pronoun used is the feminine *ha*. This has led some of the commentators of the Qur'aan to link it to the slaughtered cow referred to in Verse 2:71. But this linkage is unwarranted. For, in the immediately preceding Verse 2:72, mention is made of a murdered man, and his dead body (the Arabic word for which is feminine in gender) is already referred to therein as *ha*. We should remember that the All-knowing Allah could make no mistakes!

88. The fact, that His choice of words is perfect, is well illustrated in the use of the masculine pronoun *hu* just before, in this very Verse 2:73. Had the Jews been told to hit or strike at the dead body of the murdered man, the pronoun used would have been *ha* and not *hu*. The use of *hu* there conclusively proves that the Jews were told to raise a living man, and not to strike at a dead body.

89. So, the Jews were asked to raise the murdered man to life from or with something or some part of the dead body. It needs no mentioning that in this act of raising the living from the dead, Allah was the sole Architect and the people were just the instruments! Just like: a man and a woman are merely the instruments with which Allah brings a new human being into this world.

90. And in this divine statement lies the divine confirmation of the conclusions drawn in the foregoing notes! The reference here, obviously, is mainly to the Resurrection of mankind in the Hereafter. Allah says that He <u>thus</u> gives life to the dead. That is, just as He had given life to the murdered man (of the episode narrated in these two Verses) from some part or remnant of his dead body. Allah has thus disclosed to us that on the Resurrection Day, He will give life to every human that ever lived on this earth and died, <u>from any remnant of that human</u>. And the good earth contains distinctive remnants aplenty of every such individual! A tiny bit of a bone, a tooth, or even hair from any dead person, mixed with the earth, serves as a good enough remnant for the Almighty Allah to resurrect that person from!

91. Modern knowledge has enabled us to have an insight into these wonderfully meaningful divine Verses. Any bit of a remnant from the dead person contains microcells. And every such cell contains a DNA map distinctive to that person! So even a man now can come to know, by conducting a proper DNA test, as to which person that remnant belongs to. So, we can now understand how the Almighty Creator can have no problems at all in distinguishing the remnants, one from another.

92. In the pre-historic age – the setting for this episode described here in these two Verses under our study – the extent of human knowledge was limited. The All-knowing Allah had compensated the people living then with seemingly miraculous signs to make them understand the Reality of, inter alia, the Hereafter. The seemingly miraculous bringing of a murdered person back to life in the episode, described here in these two Verses, was one such sign. But now, with the considerable advance in human knowledge, the divine signs about the Reality are implanted in that advanced knowledge itself. A few years back, with such knowledge, man succeeded, for the first time, in making a surrogate mother sheep give birth to a lamb that was genetically identical – a clone – to another sheep! The lamb was made to be conceived in the surrogate mother's womb <u>asexually</u> by implanting the nucleus of a cell taken from the body of the other sheep into an unfertilised egg of the mother sheep! This human effort of course involved a very complicated and uncertain procedure, the success rate of which is said to be very, very low! But it did give the unmistakable sign that the Resurrection is a distinct possibility!

ثُمَّ قَسَتْ قُلُوبُكُم مِّنۢ بَعْدِ ذَٰلِكَ فَهِىَ كَٱلْحِجَارَةِ أَوْ أَشَدُّ قَسْوَةً وَإِنَّ مِنَ ٱلْحِجَارَةِ لَمَا يَتَفَجَّرُ مِنْهُ ٱلْأَنْهَٰرُ وَإِنَّ مِنْهَا لَمَا يَشَّقَّقُ فَيَخْرُجُ مِنْهُ ٱلْمَآءُ وَإِنَّ مِنْهَا لَمَا يَهْبِطُ مِنْ خَشْيَةِ ٱللَّهِ وَمَا ٱللَّهُ بِغَٰفِلٍ عَمَّا تَعْمَلُونَ

74. Thumma qasat quloobukum min baAAdi thalika fahiya kaalhijarati aw ashaddu qaswatan wa-inna mina alhijarati lama yatafajjaru minhu al-anharu wa-inna minha lama yashshaqqaqu fayakhruju minhu almao wa-inna minha lama yahbitu min khashyati Allahi wama Allahu bighafilin AAamma taAAmaloona

2:74. Then, thereafter[93], your minds became as hard as stones or harder still! And, indeed, through some of the stones, do the rivers flow. And some, indeed, break; and the water springs out there from. And some stones, indeed, fall for fear of Allah.[94] And Allah is not unaware of what you do!

93. After, that is, the numerous favours – recounted in the foregoing Verses of this Qur'aanic Chapter - Allah had bestowed upon the Children of Israel.

94. Despite the divine favours bestowed upon them, the Children of Israel remained adamant and unyielding; they wouldn't yield to the pleas of their Prophets to submit themselves completely to the will of Allah and to abide by every command of His. Their unyielding nature is compared to the hardness of the stones. Even the stones do submissively obey the laws of Nature, or, in other words, the divine laws. Loosened stones at top of the mountains roll down the slopes in obedience to the divine force of gravitation. The same divine force compels other stones to make way, through them, for streams of water gushing down from melting snow. The divine law, by which water seeks its own level, forces stones embedded deep down in the earth to break and allow spring water to come up through them. Thus, do even hard stones obey divine commands of Nature; but the recalcitrant Children of Israel wouldn't obey the divine commands given to them! And the moot question that arises in my mind is whether the Muslims of today are any better than the Jews. The Muslims too, generally, do openly disobey the divine commands given to them through the Qur'aan! And Allah is not unaware of what we do!!

۞ أَفَتَطْمَعُونَ أَن يُؤْمِنُواْ لَكُمْ وَقَدْ كَانَ فَرِيقٌ مِّنْهُمْ يَسْمَعُونَ كَلَـٰمَ ٱللَّهِ ثُمَّ يُحَرِّفُونَهُۥ مِنۢ بَعْدِ مَا عَقَلُوهُ وَهُمْ يَعْلَمُونَ ﴿٧٥﴾

75. AfatatmaAAoona an yu/minoo lakum waqad kana fareequn minhum yasmaAAoona kalama Allahi thumma yuharrifoonahu min baAAdi ma AAaqaloohu wahum yaAAlamoona

---

2:75. Are you confident then that they will believe now, for your sake!?[95] And a section of them had already been listening to Allah's Word; and then, after understanding it, they had perverted what they had understood - knowingly! [96 to 98]

---

95. Allah thus hints at the unlikelihood of the Jews, generally, ever accepting Islam.

96. Here's yet another wrong that the Jews committed, and the Muslims have been faithfully following them in committing the same sort of wrong! Unlike the Torah, however, the Qur'aan cannot be changed; the preservation of the latter is divinely guaranteed [Q: 15:9]. Even so, a section of the Muslims, claiming to be learned in religious matters, are found perverting the simple, easy and clear meanings of some of the Words of Allah! Take, for example, Verse 2.2 which we have already studied. The Qur'aan unambiguously and categorically tells us therein that the pious (*muttaqi*) would certainly get guidance from the divine Book. It prescribes no other condition to enable mankind to get the guidance. A pious, Allah-fearing man will of course take all necessary steps to enable him to understand the original Qur'aanic text in Arabic. He doesn't need this to be specifically told him.

97. But our self-proclaimed religious leaders think otherwise. They think (*nauzubillah*) they are wiser than Allah! They say it is not enough to be a *muttaqi*. They impose additional conditions: one should be a qualified *Aalim*, well Versed in Arabic as a language, well conversant with thousands and thousands of *ahaadeeth* and well read in the numerous works of the *fuqha*!

98. They (the religious leaders) have thus unwarrantedly rendered the understanding of the universal divine Message for the entire mankind, as the prerogative of the privileged few like themselves!

وَإِذَا لَقُواْ ٱلَّذِينَ ءَامَنُواْ قَالُواْ ءَامَنَّا وَإِذَا خَلَا بَعْضُهُمْ إِلَىٰ بَعْضٍ قَالُواْ أَتُحَدِّثُونَهُم بِمَا فَتَحَ ٱللَّهُ عَلَيْكُمْ لِيُحَاجُّوكُم بِهِۦ عِندَ رَبِّكُمْ أَفَلَا تَعْقِلُونَ ۝

76. Wa-itha laqoo allatheena amanoo qaloo amanna wa-itha khala baAAduhum ila baAAdin qaloo atuhaddithoonahum bima fataha Allahu AAalaykum liyuhajjookum bihi AAinda rabbikum afala taAAqiloona

---

2:76. And when they[99] meet those who believe, they say, "We do believe."[100] And when they are alone, one with another, they say, "Do you tell them what Allah has opened to you, to enable them to quarrel with you therewith, before your Lord? Have you no sense?"[101]

---

99. This is in continuation of the Jewish history. 'They' here therefore connotes 'the Jews'.

100. The same clause in Arabic has been used in <u>Verse 2:14</u>, as we have already seen in these Studies. There, the hypocrites in general are referred to; and here, the hypocrites from among the Jews!

101. Verse 2:14 informs us that the hypocrites' declaration of faith was only a mockery. Here, in Verse 2:76, we get the further information that the Jews were worried about the hypocrites from among them divulging things divinely revealed – exclusively for them, as they thought – in the Torah, to the believers! Later, in Verse 3:119, we are informed of the acute state of ill will and anger that raged in the hypocrites' minds against the believers, despite their (the hypocrites') outward show of belief!

أَوَلَا يَعْلَمُونَ أَنَّ ٱللَّهَ يَعْلَمُ مَا يُسِرُّونَ وَمَا يُعْلِنُونَ ۝

77. Awa la yaAAlamoona anna Allaha yaAAlamu ma yusirroona wama yuAAlinoona

---

2:77. Do they not know that Allah is aware of what they conceal and what they declare?

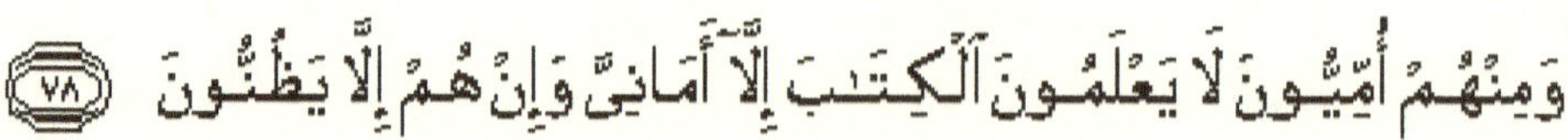

78. Waminhum ommiyyoona la yaAAlamoona alkitaba illa amaniyya wa-in hum illa yathunnoona

---

2:78. And among them are illiterates who know nothing of the Book - they know nothing but their own desires/fancies. And they do not but guess! [102 & 103]

---

102. Even at the risk of sounding repetitive, I wish to reiterate the fact that the All-knowing Allah hasn't given us these glimpses of Jewish history just to remember these for answering questions in a written test. HE knew beforehand that a substantial majority of those who profess to follow the Qur'aan, would in fact be following the footsteps of the Jews, in their behaviour and attitude towards divine Guidance! HE has given these glimpses at some length, and even sometimes repeatedly, to warn us against following those faulty footsteps.

103. The illiteracy among the professed followers of the Qur'aan, now, may not be as high as among the Jews at the time of the revelation of the Qur'aan. But we have a sort of neo-illiterates now! These neo-illiterates do know how to read the Qur'aan, and do read it, in original Arabic, but they do not know – nor do they deem it necessary to know – what the Arabic text means!! These neo-illiterates, like the illiterate Jews before them, know nothing of the Book; they do but know their own false desires, and they do not but guess!!!

---

79. Fawaylun lillatheena yaktuboona alkitaba bi-aydeehim thumma yaqooloona hatha min AAindi Allahi liyashtaroo bihi thamanan qaleelan fawaylun lahum mimma katabat aydeehim wawaylun lahum mimma yaksiboona

---

2:79. Woe then[104] unto those who write the book with their own hands but claim it to be from Allah to trade it for a little gain! Woe then unto them for what their hands wrote, and woe unto them for what they earn.[105]

104. There is obvious connection here to the earlier <u>Verse 77</u> wherein people are reminded that Allah knows all that they reveal and all that they conceal. This 79th Verse has relevance too to the immediately preceding <u>Verse 78</u>, the unlettered people spoken of wherein could easily be led astray by man-written books falsely publicised as divine.

105. The divine condemnation contained in this Verse should not be misconstrued – as some people seem to do – as condemnation of all those who write books on religious topics and market them for a price. What is condemned here is <u>knowingly</u> passing off a personal opinion or view falsely as a divine edict, without adequate evidence therefor from a truly and purely divine source, uncontaminated by human interpolations. The Qur'aan is the only such source available to us now! It is the only source, moreover, enjoying divine guarantee of protection [Q: 15:9].

وَقَالُواْ لَن تَمَسَّنَا ٱلنَّارُ إِلَّا أَيَّامًا مَّعْدُودَةً قُلْ أَتَّخَذْتُمْ عِندَ ٱللَّهِ عَهْدًا فَلَن يُخْلِفَ ٱللَّهُ عَهْدَهُۥٓ أَمْ تَقُولُونَ عَلَى ٱللَّهِ مَا لَا تَعْلَمُونَ ۝

80. Waqaloo lan tamassana alnnaru illa ayyaman maAAdoodatan qul attakhathtum AAinda Allahi AAahdan falan yukhlifa Allahu AAahdahu am taqooloona AAala Allahi ma la taAAlamoona

2:80. And they say, "The Fire shall not touch us, but for a few days." Say, "Have you taken from Allah a pledge, which He would not breach? Or is it that you say of Allah what you know not?!"[106]

106. It may be remembered that this is a continuation of a narrative about the Jews. And it was the Jews who were the original authors of the arrogant statement that the Fire would not touch them, but for a few days if at all! But now, the Jews are not alone in this arrogance! The Christians are sure that, whatever be their sins, their belief in the divinity of Jesus (peace be upon him) will fetch them the passport to Paradise. And the Muslims! Well, most of them are sure that, whatever be their sins, Muhammad (peace be upon him) will intercede on their behalf to get them into Paradise.

بَلَىٰ مَن كَسَبَ سَيِّئَةً وَأَحَـٰطَتْ بِهِۦ خَطِيٓئَتُهُۥ فَأُوْلَـٰٓئِكَ أَصْحَـٰبُ ٱلنَّارِ هُمْ فِيهَا خَـٰلِدُونَ ﴿٨١﴾

81. Bala man kasaba sayyi-atan waahatat bihi khatee-atuhu faola-ika as-habu alnnari hum feeha khalidoona

2:81. Yes, indeed, whosoever earns evil, and his wrong has engulfed him, he would be among dwellers of the Fire, therein to abide!

وَٱلَّذِينَ ءَامَنُواْ وَعَمِلُواْ ٱلصَّـٰلِحَـٰتِ أُوْلَـٰٓئِكَ أَصْحَـٰبُ ٱلْجَنَّةِ هُمْ فِيهَا خَـٰلِدُونَ ﴿٨٢﴾

82. Waallatheena amanoo waAAamiloo alssalihati ola-ika as-habu aljannati hum feeha khalidoona

2:82. And those who believe and do righteous deeds! Those shall be the dwellers of Paradise, therein to abide! [107]

107. In Verse 81, Allah categorically denies the arrogant claim – be it from the Jews, the Christians, the nominal Muslims or any other community – made in Verse 80. HE lays down the criteria, in Verses 81 and 82, for anyone to be welcomed into Paradise, or to be thrown into Hell-fire!

وَإِذْ أَخَذْنَا مِيثَـٰقَ بَنِى إِسْرَٰٓءِيلَ لَا تَعْبُدُونَ إِلَّا ٱللَّهَ وَبِٱلْوَٰلِدَيْنِ إِحْسَانًا وَذِى ٱلْقُرْبَىٰ وَٱلْيَتَـٰمَىٰ وَٱلْمَسَـٰكِينِ وَقُولُوا۟ لِلنَّاسِ حُسْنًا وَأَقِيمُوا۟ ٱلصَّلَوٰةَ وَءَاتُوا۟ ٱلزَّكَوٰةَ ثُمَّ تَوَلَّيْتُمْ إِلَّا قَلِيلًا مِّنكُمْ وَأَنتُم مُّعْرِضُونَ ۞ ﴿٨٣﴾

83. Wa-ith akhathna meethaqa banee isra-eela la taAAbudoona illa Allaha wabialwalidayni ihsanan wathee alqurba waalyatama waalmasakeeni waqooloo lilnnasi husnan waaqeemoo alssalata waatoo alzzakata thumma tawallaytum illa qaleelan minkum waantum muAAridoona

---

2:83. And when We made a covenant with Children of Israel that they shall not worship anyone but Allah and shall be good to parents, near ones, the orphans and the poor, that they shall speak to the people nicely, establish proper prayer[108] & [109] and give the *Zakaat*[110]! You then – except for a few of you – went back on your promises. And you are people, wont to slide back to bad habits!

---

108. Please see Chapter Note 4 in this context. We have seen there, in Qur'aanic light, what establishing the Prayer would mean. Besides the Verses quoted in that Note, other Qur'aanic Verses command us to be devout (2:238), humble (23:2) and constant (70:23) in our prayers. We are instructed to offer our prayers at fixed times (4:103) and to be neither too loud nor muted while saying the prayers (17:110). Allah categorically tells us to establish the Prayer solely for His remembrance (20:14). HE asks us to guard our prayers (2:238, 23:9) obviously against satanic deviations from these divine instructions and commands, and against saying the prayers in divinely abhorred manners described in Verses 4:142, 8:35 and 9:54.

109. Although the divine instructions mentioned in the foregoing Note, for proper conduct of prayers, are from the Qur'aan, the instructions in the Torah, for Children of Israel, ought to be essentially similar as both the Books are by the same Author. And the later divine Book confirms the earlier.

110. In Verse 30:39, the Qur'aan defines *Zakaat* as anything given away, seeking only Allah's pleasure.

وَإِذْ أَخَذْنَا مِيثَٰقَكُمْ لَا تَسْفِكُونَ دِمَآءَكُمْ وَلَا تُخْرِجُونَ أَنفُسَكُم مِّن دِيَٰرِكُمْ ثُمَّ أَقْرَرْتُمْ وَأَنتُمْ تَشْهَدُونَ ۝

84. Wa-ith akhathna meethaqakum la tasfikoona dimaakum wala tukhrijoona anfusakum min diyarikum thumma aqrartum waantum tashhadoona

---

2:84. And when We made a covenant with you that you shall not shed your blood and shall not drive your own people out of your homes! You then affirmed. And you did bear witness!

ثُمَّ أَنتُمْ هَٰٓؤُلَآءِ تَقْتُلُونَ أَنفُسَكُمْ وَتُخْرِجُونَ فَرِيقًا مِّنكُم مِّن دِيَٰرِهِمْ تَظَٰهَرُونَ عَلَيْهِم بِالْإِثْمِ وَالْعُدْوَٰنِ وَإِن يَأْتُوكُمْ أُسَٰرَىٰ تُفَٰدُوهُمْ وَهُوَ مُحَرَّمٌ عَلَيْكُمْ إِخْرَاجُهُمْ أَفَتُؤْمِنُونَ بِبَعْضِ الْكِتَٰبِ وَتَكْفُرُونَ بِبَعْضٍ فَمَا جَزَآءُ مَن يَفْعَلُ ذَٰلِكَ مِنكُمْ إِلَّا خِزْيٌ فِى الْحَيَوٰةِ الدُّنْيَا وَيَوْمَ الْقِيَٰمَةِ يُرَدُّونَ إِلَىٰ أَشَدِّ الْعَذَابِ وَمَا اللَّهُ بِغَٰفِلٍ عَمَّا تَعْمَلُونَ ۝

85. Thumma antum haola-i taqtuloona anfusakum watukhrijoona fareeqan minkum min diyarihim tathaharoona AAalayhim bial-ithmi waalAAudwani wa-in ya/tookum osara tufadoohum wahuwa muharramun AAalaykum ikhrajuhum afatu/minoona bibaAAdi alkitabi watakfuroona bibaAAdin fama jazao man yafAAalu thalika minkum illa khizyun fee alhayati alddunya wayawma alqiyamati yuraddoona ila ashaddi alAAathabi wama Allahu bighafilin AAamma taAAmaloona

---

2:85. Yet, it is you who kill your own people and drive a section from among you out of their homes, aiding and abetting in sin and hostility against them. And if they come to you as captives, you ransom them, and it is, in the first place, unlawful for you to drive them out! Do you then believe in part of the Scripture while you suppress another part thereof? Recompense to whoever does so amongst you, is nothing but ignominy in this world. And on Resurrection Day, they will be condemned to intense torment. And Allah is not unaware of what they do[111 & 112].

111. Here's another indirect divine warning for us Muslims, the nominal followers of the Qur'aan! We swear by the Qur'aan, as the Jews swear by the Torah. And like the Jews' suppressing parts of the Torah, we do ignore and blatantly act, knowingly or unknowingly, against divine commands in the Qur'aan. There are examples galore; but, here, I would like to throw light on just one - a glaring one.

112. In Verse 17.110, as pointed out in note 108 above, Allah Ta'ala instructs us not to be too loud in our prayers. But here, in my part of the world, I do often hear Masaajid loudspeakers broadcasting even the prayers, besides the *Azaan*! Not only are the non-Muslims around disturbed by this, but it disturbs even the Muslims praying in nearby Masjid. This apart, what is more disturbing, inscrutable and universal is the blatant disobedience of the other part of the divine edict. This other part ordains that the prayers should neither be muted nor of too low and feeble sound. Even so, it's a great mystery as to why we say parts of our prayers, like those of *Zuhr* and *Asr*, in absolute silence! No wonder then, that ignominy has hit us – and hit us badly, all around the world.

أُوْلَـٰٓئِكَ ٱلَّذِينَ ٱشْتَرَوُاْ ٱلْحَيَوٰةَ ٱلدُّنْيَا بِٱلْآخِرَةِ ۖ فَلَا يُخَفَّفُ عَنْهُمُ ٱلْعَذَابُ وَلَا هُمْ يُنصَرُونَ ﴿٨١﴾

86. Ola-ika allatheena ishtarawoo alhayata alddunya bial-akhirati fala yukhaffafu AAanhumu alAAathabu wala hum yunsaroona

2:86. Those are the people who have purchased the life of this world for the Hereafter! So, then the severity of the punishment shall not be lessened for them; nor shall they be helped.

وَلَقَدْ ءَاتَيْنَا مُوسَى ٱلْكِتَـٰبَ وَقَفَّيْنَا مِنۢ بَعْدِهِۦ بِٱلرُّسُلِ وَءَاتَيْنَا عِيسَى
ٱبْنَ مَرْيَمَ ٱلْبَيِّنَـٰتِ وَأَيَّدْنَـٰهُ بِرُوحِ ٱلْقُدُسِ أَفَكُلَّمَا جَآءَكُمْ رَسُولٌۢ بِمَا لَا
تَهْوَىٰٓ أَنفُسُكُمُ ٱسْتَكْبَرْتُمْ فَفَرِيقًا كَذَّبْتُمْ وَفَرِيقًا تَقْتُلُونَ ﴿٨٧﴾

87. Walaqad atayna moosa alkitaba waqaffayna min baAAdihi bialrrusuli waatayna AAeesa ibna maryama albayyinati waayyadnahu biroohi alqudusi afakullama jaakum rasoolun bima la tahwa anfusukumu istakbartum fafareeqan kaththabtum wafareeqan taqtuloona

---

2:87. And We did give Moses the Book; and, after him, We caused a succession of Messengers to follow him in his track. And We gave Jesus, son of Mary, clear signs and fortified him with the Holy Spirit[113-116]. Didn't you become arrogant and behave haughtily whenever a Messenger came to you with what wasn't in accord with your carnal desires? You then accused some of being false; and some, you killed!

---

113. In Verses 2:253 and 5:110 too, it is similarly stated that Jesus was fortified with the Holy Spirit. And in Verse 16:102, it is stated that the Holy Spirit (*Roohul Qudus*) brought the Qur'aan down from the Lord in Truth. In Verses 26:192-194, the Trustworthy Spirit (*Roohul Ameen*) is stated to have brought the Qur'aan down upon Prophet Muhammad's mind/consciousness. In Verse 58:22, it is stated that the Believers too are fortified with the Spirit (*Rooh*) from Him.

114. In Verses 59:23 and 62:1, one of Allah's attributes mentioned is *Quddoos* (Holy). Besides, the Qur'aan states: (i) when Allah fashioned Adam from clay, He breathed into it His Spirit (15:29 & 38:71-72), (ii) when He fashioned Adam's progeny from 'contemptible water', He breathed into it from His Spirit (32:9), (iii) "We sent to her (Mary) Our Spirit", who appeared before her as a real man (19:17), whereafter, miraculously, without the agency of a man, Mary gave birth to Jesus, who was Allah's Word and a Spirit from Him (4:171), (iv) the Angels and the Spirit ascend to Him in a period of time, the measure whereof is fifty thousand years (70:4); and they (the Spirit and the Angels) would stand in attention, in rows, on the Resurrections Day (78:38), (v) the Spirit is one of Allah's Commands, and mankind has been given but little knowledge (17:85)!

115. From the Qur'aan thus, what we know, for certain, is that the Spirit or the Holy Spirit is an entity very close to Allah – so close that He calls it My or Our Spirit. This Spirit it is with which are all human lives kindled. Prophet Jesus (peace upon him) was especially fortified with it so that he could talk to people even while in his cradle and perform many miraculous deeds. All believers are also additionally fortified with it so that they keep to the right path. It was through this Spirit that Allah revealed the Qur'aan to Prophet Muhammad (peace and Allah's blessings be upon him). The Spirit nevertheless is subservient to Allah and would be standing in respectful attention, on the Resurrection Day, before Him!

116. We should be content with the info that the Qur'aan gives us on the *Rooh*, the *Roohul Qudus* or the *Roohul Ameen*. These Qur'aanic terms are beyond the scope of our human understanding

(*mutashabihaat*). We should not therefore speculate over their meanings further with our own human opinions. See Verse 3:7 and study note 2:17, in this context.

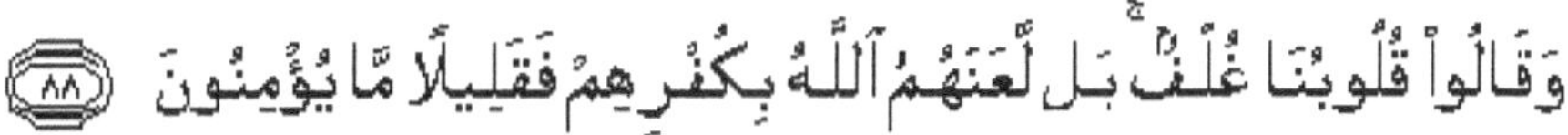

88. Waqaloo quloobuna ghulfun bal laAAanahumu Allahu bikufrihim faqaleelan ma yu/minoona

---

2:88. And they say, "Our minds[117] are closed." Nay! Allah has cursed[118] them because of their suppression of the Truth. Few then are those who do believe!

---

117. It has been the practice in almost all the languages, which I know of, (Arabic and English, both included) to attribute the functions of the mind to the heart! It may be a human error, continued by default, from days of ignorance. But Allah can make no mistakes. I have therefore preferred 'minds' in the translation over 'hearts', both of which figure among the meanings, of the Arabic word *qulub*, given in the dictionary.

118. The divine curse is unlike one human being cursing another. The divine curse could constitute just the withdrawal of Allah's hand of mercy and guidance, without which no human being can ever tread the Right Path. It was such divine curse that rendered the minds of the Children of Israel closed to Allah's messages that came to them through His Messengers.

---

89. Walamma jaahum kitabun min AAindi Allahi musaddiqun lima maAAahum wakanoo min qablu yastaftihoona AAala allatheena kafaroo falamma jaahum ma AAarafoo kafaroo bihi falaAAnatu Allahi AAala alkafireena

---

2:89. And when there came to them a Book from Allah confirming that which is with them – and they had earlier been praying for victory over those who suppressed the Truth – and when there came to them that which they recognised[119], they suppressed it! So, Allah's curse is on those who suppress the Truth.

---

119. This is divine confirmation that the Jews, at the time of the revelation of this Verse, knew in their consciences that the Qur'aan is divine.

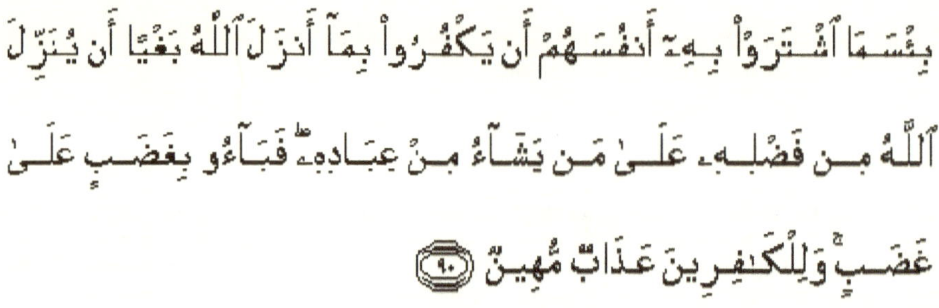

90. Bi/sama ishtaraw bihi anfusahum an yakfuroo bima anzala Allahu baghyan an yunazzila Allahu min fadlihi AAala man yashao min AAibadihi fabaoo bighadabin AAala ghadabin walilkafireena AAathabun muheenun

---

2:90. Disgusting is what they[120] sell their own selves for! They suppress the truth about Allah's revelations, rebelliously, just because Allah, in His Grace, bestows His revelations upon whomsoever He wills among His worshippers[121]. They have thus incurred wrath upon wrath[122]. And for the suppressors of Truth is a disgraceful punishment!

---

120. I.e. the Jews. This Verse is in continuation of the immediately preceding ones.

121. In Verse 5:18, we are informed that both Jews and Christians boasted, "We are the children of Allah and His loved ones." The Jews were obviously irked therefore that the Qur'aan was revealed on an outsider! Their arrogance was akin to that of Iblees when he rebelliously disobeyed Allah's order to prostrate before Adam. See study notes 27 to 30.

122. The Jews incurred the double wrath obviously for (i) their rebellious rejection of the Truth in the Qur'aan and (ii) their lie against Allah that they are a special race among mankind, deserving His Love and Patronage exclusively for themselves.

وَإِذَا قِيلَ لَهُمْ ءَامِنُواْ بِمَآ أَنزَلَ ٱللَّهُ قَالُواْ نُؤْمِنُ بِمَآ أُنزِلَ عَلَيْنَا وَيَكْفُرُونَ بِمَا وَرَآءَهُۥ وَهُوَ ٱلْحَقُّ مُصَدِّقًا لِّمَا مَعَهُمْ قُلْ فَلِمَ تَقْتُلُونَ أَنۢبِيَآءَ ٱللَّهِ مِن قَبْلُ إِن كُنتُم مُّؤْمِنِينَ ۝

91. Wa-itha qeela lahum aminoo bima anzala Allahu qaloo nu/minu bima onzila AAalayna wayakfuroona bima waraahu wahuwa alhaqqu musaddiqan lima maAAahum qul falima taqtuloona anbiyaa Allahi min qablu in kuntum mu/mineena

2:91. And when it is said to them, "Believe in what Allah has sent down," they say, "We believe in that which has been sent down upon us." And they suppress the Truth in what has been sent down thereafter. And what has been sent down thereafter is the Truth, confirming what is with them! Say, "Why then did you kill Allah's Prophets afore, if you indeed were believers?"[123]

123. The Jews had – as we have already seen in Verse [2:84] – solemnized a covenant with Allah that they would not resort to bloodshed among themselves. Allah here exposes the hollowness of the Jews' claim that they believed in what was sent down to them. Had they really believed in their own scriptures, they wouldn't have killed the Jewish Prophets – their own people!

۞ وَلَقَدْ جَآءَكُم مُّوسَىٰ بِٱلْبَيِّنَـٰتِ ثُمَّ ٱتَّخَذْتُمُ ٱلْعِجْلَ مِنۢ بَعْدِهِۦ وَأَنتُمْ ظَـٰلِمُونَ ۝

92. Walaqad jaakum moosa bialbayyinati thumma ittakhathtumu alAAijla min baAAdihi waantum thalimoona

2:92. And indeed did Moses come to you with clear signs; then you took to the Calf[124 & 125] thereafter! And you were wicked.

124. This episode about the Calf, in Jewish history, is also mentioned, as we have already seen, in Verses 51 and 54 of this Qur'aanic Chapter (refer also to study note 54 in this context). It has been mentioned again in Verses 7:148 and 7:152. This repeated reference to the same episode – as to many other episodes also – should not be misconstrued as unnecessary. There is nothing unnecessary or redundant in things divine; those who ponder shall discover the divine purpose. Repetition helps in creating a more lasting impression on the human mind. And, in the Qur'aan, repetitions are often accompanied by elaborations and explanations in varied ways.

125. In Verse 7:152, for example, while making a repeated mention of this episode, Allah tells us, in no uncertain terms, that those who invent lies like that of the Calf shall incur Allah's wrath and may suffer humiliation in this world itself. Allah knew beforehand that the so-called Muslims in today's world would have their own 'Calves' in the shapes of shrines built over graves of dead persons, whom they call upon for redressal of their individual sufferings or for fulfilment of their individual worldly dreams! No wonder then that the Muslims, generally, all around the world, are suffering humiliation now, in this world itself. It's a prophecy come true.

وَإِذْ أَخَذْنَا مِيثَاقَكُمْ وَرَفَعْنَا فَوْقَكُمُ ٱلطُّورَ خُذُوا۟ مَا ءَاتَيْنَاكُم بِقُوَّةٍ وَٱسْمَعُوا۟ قَالُوا۟ سَمِعْنَا وَعَصَيْنَا وَأُشْرِبُوا۟ فِى قُلُوبِهِمُ ٱلْعِجْلَ بِكُفْرِهِمْ قُلْ بِئْسَمَا يَأْمُرُكُم بِهِۦٓ إِيمَٰنُكُمْ إِن كُنتُم مُّؤْمِنِينَ ﴿٩٣﴾

93. Wa-ith akhathna meethaqakum warafaAAna fawqakumu alttoora khuthoo ma ataynakum biquwwatin waismaAAoo qaloo samiAAna waAAasayna waoshriboo fee quloobihimu alAAijla bikufrihim qul bi/sama ya/murukum bihi eemanukum in kuntum mu/mineena

2:93. And when We made a Covenant with you and raised the Mount over you, "Hold fast to that which We have given you and listen!"[126], they said, "We hear; and we obey not!" Their minds were drunk with the thought of the Calf because of their suppression of the Truth. Say, "What you order therewith is harming your belief, if you do indeed believe!"[127]

126. Refer Verse 2:63 and Chapter Note 70 in this context.

127. Just as the Calf did harm the belief of the Jews, the Shrines built by the Muslims on graves of some dead persons whom they invoke besides Allah, is now harming the belief of the Muslims.

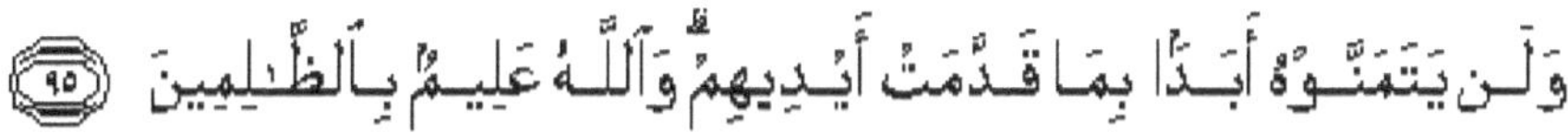

94. Qul in kanat lakumu alddaru al-akhiratu AAinda Allahi khalisatan min dooni alnnasi fatamannawoo almawta in kuntum sadiqeena

2:94. Say, "Were the abode in the Hereafter, close to Allah, exclusively for you among all Mankind, pine you for death if you truly believe so!"

95. Walan yatamannawhu abadan bima qaddamat aydeehim waAllahu AAaleemun bialththalimeena

2:95. And they shall never do that because of the deeds they have sent ahead. And Allah is fully aware of the wicked people! [128]

128. Muslims today need to do a deep introspection whether, like the Jews, they too are not indulging in the wishful thinking that they (Muslims) would be the ones close to Allah in the Hereafter. They need to examine critically whether the deeds they send ahead are such that Allah may, in His mercy, be pleased to grant them that enviable position.

وَلَتَجِدَنَّهُمْ أَحْرَصَ النَّاسِ عَلَىٰ حَيَوٰةٍ وَمِنَ ٱلَّذِينَ أَشْرَكُوٓا۟ يَوَدُّ أَحَدُهُمْ لَوْ يُعَمَّرُ أَلْفَ سَنَةٍ وَمَا هُوَ بِمُزَحْزِحِهِۦ مِنَ ٱلْعَذَابِ أَن يُعَمَّرَ وَٱللَّهُ بَصِيرٌۢ بِمَا يَعْمَلُونَ ۝٩١

96. Walatajidannahum ahrasa alnnasi AAala hayatin wamina allatheena ashrakoo yawaddu ahaduhum law yuAAammaru alfa sanatin wama huwa bimuzahzihihi mina alAAathabi an yuAAammara waAllahu baseerun bima yaAAmaloona

---

2:96. And you will indeed find them[129] to be persons greedy for life – more so even than the polytheists! Every one of them longs for a life of a thousand years. But no long life can serve as a saviour for him/her from the punishment. And Allah is vigilant over all they do.[130]

---

129. This Qur'aanic Verse is in continuation of a narrative about the Jews. The pronoun 'them' here therefore stands for the Jews.

130. Here's some more food for thought for the Muslims of today. Aren't we ourselves, likewise, greedy for long lives? We do pray to Allah to grant us long lives. But for what purpose? If we search our minds honestly, we may find that the purpose is mostly mundane in nature – to gain and enjoy some worldly benefits! We tend to forget that our Creator has granted us a fixed span of life in this world. We tend to forget the Hereafter. We tend to forget that the life in this world is only a test, a trial. It's a test to see if we are worthy of happiness in the Hereafter. And if our desire for longer life is only for enjoying some illusory fruits of this world, chances are, we may end up worsening our prospects for the everlasting Hereafter!

قُلْ مَن كَانَ عَدُوًّا لِّجِبْرِيلَ فَإِنَّهُۥ نَزَّلَهُۥ عَلَىٰ قَلْبِكَ بِإِذْنِ ٱللَّهِ مُصَدِّقًا لِّمَا بَيْنَ يَدَيْهِ وَهُدًى وَبُشْرَىٰ لِلْمُؤْمِنِينَ ۝٩٧

97. Qul man kana AAaduwwan lijibreela fa-innahu nazzalahu AAala qalbika bi-ithni Allahi musaddiqan lima bayna yadayhi wahudan wabushra lilmu/mineena

2:97. Say, "Whoever is an enemy of Gabriel," - He indeed it is who brings down upon your mind, with Allah's permission, this that confirms what preceded it, and which is guidance and harbinger of good tidings for the believers[131] -

---

131. By comparing this parenthetic statement in this Verse with Verses 16:102 and 26:192-194, it is apparent that *Jibreel* (Gabriel), *Roohul Qudus* and *Roohul Ameen* are, all three, one and the same entity. (Refer also to Chapter notes 113 to 116 in this context).

مَن كَانَ عَدُوًّا لِّلَّهِ وَمَلَـٰٓئِكَتِهِۦ وَرُسُلِهِۦ وَجِبْرِيلَ وَمِيكَىٰلَ فَإِنَّ ٱللَّهَ عَدُوٌّ لِّلْكَـٰفِرِينَ ﴿٩٨﴾

98. Man kana AAaduwwan lillahi wamala-ikatihi warusulihi wajibreela wameekala fa-inna Allaha AAaduwwun lilkafireena

---

2:98. [132]"Whoever is an enemy of Allah, of His Angels, of His Messengers, of Gabriel and of Michael[133], Allah is certainly then enemy of the suppressors of Truth!"[134]

---

132. The quote, interrupted with the parenthetic explanation about Gabriel in the preceding Verse, is completed here in this Verse.

133. The All-knowing Allah has obviously considered it unnecessary to give any fuller details about this Unseen Being in the Qur'aan. What He is pleased to disclose by implication is that this Being is one of those close to Allah, like Gabriel and the Angels.

134. As this address of the Prophet to the Jews was begun initially – in the preceding Verse – with the specific mention of Gabriel, it is apparent that the Jews had been harbouring some grouse and enmity especially towards this Being close to Allah.

وَلَقَدْ أَنزَلْنَآ إِلَيْكَ ءَايَـٰتِۭ بَيِّنَـٰتٍ ۖ وَمَا يَكْفُرُ بِهَآ إِلَّا ٱلْفَـٰسِقُونَ

99. Walaqad anzalna ilayka ayatin bayyinatin wama yakfuru biha illa alfasiqoona

---

2:99. And indeed have We sent down to you clear Verses. And none do suppress the Truth thereof, except the rebels.[135]

---

135. Allah thus reassures the Prophet of the clarity and truthfulness of the Verses sent down to him, whatever may be the Jews' opinion thereof. The clarity of its Verses is reiterated at several places throughout the Qur'aan (refer also Chapter Note 17). It is unfortunate for the Muslim *Ummah* that even so, many of their own members harbour doubts about some of the Qur'aanic Verses being clear! They therefore seek clarification and explanation therefor in man-influenced *ahaadeeth* and in man-made *fatwas*! And in terms of this Verse presently under our study, non-belief in the clarity of such Qur'aanic Verses is *kufr*, and persons indulging in such *kufr* are rebels! [For a comprehensive meaning of *aayaat* (translated here as Verses), please see Chapter Notes 150 and 151.]

أَوَكُلَّمَا عَـٰهَدُوا۟ عَهْدًا نَّبَذَهُ فَرِيقٌ مِّنْهُم ۚ بَلْ أَكْثَرُهُمْ لَا يُؤْمِنُونَ

100. Awa kullama AAahadoo AAahdan nabathahu fareequn minhum bal aktharuhum la yu/minoona

---

2:100. Every time they made a covenant, didn't a section among them throw it over? Nay! Believe they not - do many of them!![136]

---

136. This Verse is in continuation of the divine narration of a brief history of the Children of Israel. The narration started at Verse 40 of this Qur'aanic Chapter. The brief history highlights, in ample measure,

the perfidious nature of those people at Prophet Moses' time. This Verse (2.100) encapsulates that nature. It also provides the *raison d'être* for anyone or any group of people having such a nature. The *raison d'être* is lack of Faith – primarily in Allah and in the Hereafter.

وَلَمَّا جَآءَهُمْ رَسُولٌ مِّنْ عِندِ ٱللَّهِ مُصَدِّقٌ لِّمَا مَعَهُمْ نَبَذَ فَرِيقٌ مِّنَ ٱلَّذِينَ أُوتُواْ ٱلْكِتَـٰبَ كِتَـٰبَ ٱللَّهِ وَرَآءَ ظُهُورِهِمْ كَأَنَّهُمْ لَا يَعْلَمُونَ ۞

101. Walamma jaahum rasoolun min AAindi Allahi musaddiqun lima maAAahum nabatha fareequn mina allatheena ootoo alkitaba kitaba Allahi waraa thuhoorihim kaannahum la yaAAlamoona

2:101. And when there came to them a Messenger from Allah, confirming what is with them, a section of those, who were given the Book, threw Allah's Book behind their backs[137, 138] as if they knew nothing!

137. The meaning of this metaphoric phrase 'threw Allah's Book behind their backs' is evident in what follows: 'as if they knew nothing!' Obviously, the Jews feigned ignorance about the divine Book revealed for them (i.e. the Torah) containing the same Truths as are revealed in the Qur'aan.

138. It is interesting – nay, saddening – to take note how we, the present-day Muslims, only literally follow the implied Qur'aanic injunction against 'throwing the Book behind our backs'! In any congregational, ritual reading of the Qur'aan (mostly without understanding the contents, of course), we take abundant care to see that we are not reading the Holy Book behind anybody's back!! And we remain blissfully ignorant that we're woefully and blatantly throwing the Qur'aan behind our backs when it comes to implementing the divine commands contained in the Book!!!

وَٱتَّبَعُواْ مَا تَتْلُواْ ٱلشَّيَـٰطِينُ عَلَىٰ مُلْكِ سُلَيْمَـٰنَ وَمَا كَفَرَ سُلَيْمَـٰنُ وَلَـٰكِنَّ ٱلشَّيَـٰطِينَ كَفَرُواْ يُعَلِّمُونَ ٱلنَّاسَ ٱلسِّحْرَ وَمَآ أُنزِلَ عَلَى ٱلْمَلَكَيْنِ بِبَابِلَ هَـٰرُوتَ وَمَـٰرُوتَ وَمَا يُعَلِّمَانِ مِنْ أَحَدٍ حَتَّىٰ يَقُولَآ إِنَّمَا نَحْنُ فِتْنَةٌ فَلَا تَكْفُرْ فَيَتَعَلَّمُونَ مِنْهُمَا مَا يُفَرِّقُونَ بِهِۦ بَيْنَ ٱلْمَرْءِ وَزَوْجِهِۦ وَمَا هُم بِضَآرِّينَ بِهِۦ مِنْ أَحَدٍ إِلَّا بِإِذْنِ ٱللَّهِ وَيَتَعَلَّمُونَ مَا يَضُرُّهُمْ وَلَا يَنفَعُهُمْ وَلَقَدْ عَلِمُواْ لَمَنِ ٱشْتَرَىٰهُ مَا لَهُۥ فِى ٱلْأَخِرَةِ مِنْ خَلَـٰقٍ وَلَبِئْسَ مَا شَرَوْاْ بِهِۦٓ أَنفُسَهُمْ لَوْ كَانُواْ يَعْلَمُونَ ۞ ﴿١٠٢﴾

102. WaittabaAAoo ma tatloo alshshayateenu AAala mulki sulaymana wama kafara sulaymanu walakinna alshshayateena kafaroo yuAAallimoona alnnasa alssihra wama onzila AAala almalakayni bibabila haroota wamaroota wama yuAAallimani min ahadin hatta yaqoola innama nahnu fitnatun fala takfur fayataAAallamoona minhuma ma yufarriqoona bihi bayna almar-i wazawjihi wama hum bidarreena bihi min ahadin illa bi-ithni Allahi wayataAAallamoona ma yadurruhum wala yanfaAAuhum walaqad AAalimoo lamani ishtarahu ma lahu fee al-akhirati min khalaqin walabi'sa ma sharaw bihi anfusahum law kanoo yaAAlamoona

2:102. And, during the reign of Solomon[139], they followed what the satanic folk[140] recited to them. And Solomon did not suppress the Truth, but the satanic folk did. They taught the people sorcery and what came down at Babylon upon the two Angels, Haaroot and Maaroot. And the two did not teach it to anyone till they informed him/her, "We are but a test for you. Do not then suppress the Truth." Even then, people learnt from the two that with which they could bring about separation between man and his wife - and they could not harm anyone therewith except by Allah's leave[141] - and they learnt what harmed, and not what benefited, them. And they did know that whoever bought it, would have no share of happiness in the Hereafter. And vile indeed was what they traded their own selves for, if only they knew!

139. The Qur'aan informs us that Solomon (*Sulaiman*) was one of the great Prophets upon whom Allah had sent His revelations (4:163). He was the heir to David, another great Prophet-king, and had been taught the language of birds (27:16). Allah had granted him wisdom and knowledge (21:79). HE had made even the wind subservient to him and had made Jinns work for him (34:12)!

140. Refer <u>Chapter notes 33 and 34</u> **for a more detailed explanation of the Arabic term** *shayaateen*.

141. It's a general universal truth for all times, that Allah declares here. No malafide act of anyone against any other, can affect the latter unless Allah so wills. It is important that we understand this truth correctly and carefully. Allah is much too exalted and sublime to will any harm to come to any of His creatures unjustly. If any human being is afflicted at any time, it may be for either of two reasons. One, Allah may be putting him/her through a test for eligibility to award of better things by His grace. Two, He may be giving the person a punishment, in this world itself, for some past sin/sins committed, so that the person and/or others take heed and man-generated crimes do not cross safety limits.

103. Walaw annahum amanoo waittaqaw lamathoobatun min AAindi Allahi khayrun law kanoo yaAAlamoona

2:103. And had they indeed believed and observed piety, better surely would be their lot with Allah - if only they knew! [142, 143]

142. But alas! The satanic folk, during Solomon's time, refused to know what would really benefit them – and so do, most of us, in the present age. We refuse to believe in the One and Only Creator of the entire Universe that includes mankind. We refuse to believe that He has granted us our present lives on this earth, only as a long-drawn-out test. We refuse to believe that He would resurrect us, after our deaths, to stand before Him in trial for what we did here. We refuse to believe that He would punish us severely then for our acts of omission and commission, on this earth, in disobedience to His commands.

143. So we continue to indulge in the sort of things the satanic folk did, during Solomon's time. We get satanic pleasure in harming others, even when the others did nothing to harm us! A topical example: the cyber-crime of spreading computer viruses and of spamming. I have myself also fallen a victim, moreover, to the cyber-theft of my email ID to spread around, in my name, political views which I do not subscribe to! (In fact, I have not written any political article.) Such satanic folk of our time fail to realise that the Creator is watching them closely and constantly. Oh! If only they knew – knew that they are proceeding, inexorably, towards their own doom!!

يَـٰٓأَيُّهَا ٱلَّذِينَ ءَامَنُوا۟ لَا تَقُولُوا۟ رَٰعِنَا وَقُولُوا۟ ٱنظُرْنَا وَٱسْمَعُوا۟ وَلِلْكَـٰفِرِينَ عَذَابٌ أَلِيمٌ ۝

104. Ya ayyuha allatheena amanoo la taqooloo raAAina waqooloo onthurna waismaAAoo walilkafireena AAathabun aleemun

---

2:104. O you who believe! Say not, "*Raayinaa*"[144], but say, "*Anzurnaa*"[144] and listen. And for those who suppress the Truth[145]: a grievous punishment!

---

144. The Arabic root word *Ra'aa* means 'to take care of', 'to attend to' or 'to listen to'. The believers, obviously, did use it in this sense to draw the Prophet's attention to them when they said '*Raayinaa*' (listen to us). But the root word also means 'to graze cattle'. And in Verse 4:46, the Qur'aan informs us that the Jews, during the time of Prophet Muhammad (peace and Allah's blessings be upon him), took a word out of its context and used to say the word *Raayinaa* twisting their tongues to imply a taunt on the Religion of Islam! Allah therefore admonishes the believers to use the alternative word Anzurnaa (look at us).

145. It is obviously implied here that the people who used the word *Raayinaa* just to taunt at the Religion of Islam, were among those who suppressed the Truth!

مَّا يَوَدُّ ٱلَّذِينَ كَفَرُوا۟ مِنْ أَهْلِ ٱلْكِتَـٰبِ وَلَا ٱلْمُشْرِكِينَ أَن يُنَزَّلَ عَلَيْكُم مِّنْ خَيْرٍ مِّن رَّبِّكُمْ وَٱللَّهُ يَخْتَصُّ بِرَحْمَتِهِۦ مَن يَشَآءُ وَٱللَّهُ ذُو ٱلْفَضْلِ ٱلْعَظِيمِ ۝

105. Ma yawaddu allatheena kafaroo min ahli alkitabi wala almushrikeena an yunazzala AAalaykum min khayrin min rabbikum waAllahu yakhtassu birahmatihi man yashao waAllahu thoo alfadli alAAatheemi

---

2:105. Neither do those who suppress the Truth among the people of the Book[146, 147], nor do the polytheists wish for any good to come down upon you[148] from your Lord. And

Allah graces whomsoever He wishes with His Favours.[149] And Allah is the Benefactor, Supreme!

---

146. People of the Book are the groups of people generally known to be following divinely revealed Books. Of such Books, those that are most often mentioned in the Qur'aan are: the Qur'aan itself, the Torah (*Tauraat*) and the Gospel (*Injeel*). The Psalms (*Zabur*), revealed upon Prophet David, is also mentioned, but rarely (Q: 4:163 & 21:105) – and any separate group of people, following the Psalms only, is not well known. The People known to be following the Qur'aan, the Torah and the Gospel are of course the Muslims, the Jews and the Christians respectively. Those nominal (hypocritical) Muslims, Jews and Christians, who do not believe in and do not follow their respective Books, as originally revealed, are described here in this Verse as those 'who suppress the Truth among people of the Book' (*alladheena kafaru min ahl-il-kitaabi*).

147. We should however remember in this context that Allah had sent His Messenger to every nation (Q: 10:47). Some of the Messengers are mentioned in the Qur'aan, and some are not (Q: 4:164). But all the Messengers had of course received divine revelations. It may therefore be safely inferred that there could have been other divinely revealed Books - other than those specifically mentioned in the Qur'aan.

148. We should remember that the addressees of these two divine Verses, taken for our study here, are the believers (see the beginning of the preceding Verse 104). The pronoun 'you' here therefore connotes 'the believers', and not just the Prophet.

149. Allah here negates the fond assumptions of every group, be they Muslims, Christians, Jews or any other religious/ethnic group, that their own respective group alone is Allah's favourite. Refer Verse 2:111 in this context.

۞ مَا نَنسَخْ مِنْ ءَايَةٍ أَوْ نُنسِهَا نَأْتِ بِخَيْرٍ مِّنْهَا أَوْ مِثْلِهَا أَلَمْ تَعْلَمْ أَنَّ ٱللَّهَ عَلَىٰ كُلِّ شَيْءٍ قَدِيرٌ ﴿١٠٦﴾

106. Ma nansakh min ayatin aw nunsiha na/ti bikhayrin minha aw mithliha alam taAAlam anna Allaha AAala kulli shay-in qadeerun

---

2:106. Against that which do We abrogate of a Verse[150, 151], or do We cause it to be forgotten, We bring forth a better one or one that is similar to it![152, 153] Are you not aware that, certainly, Allah is in control of everything?

---

150. Proper understanding of the meaning of the Qur'aanic word *aayat* (plural: *aayaat*) used, is necessary for the proper understanding of the divine statement made in this Verse 106. The Arabic word is translated here as 'Verse', following a long-standing tradition in this regard. However, our understandings of the English word 'Verses' are the short, numbered divisions of the Qur'aan, *a la* the Bible. Consequently, we have generally come to understand *aayaat* to mean <u>only</u> the short, numbered divisions of the Qur'aan, just as this *aayat* 106 is one of the over 6000 such *aayaat* constituting the entire divine Book.

151. But *aayat/aayaat* has been given a much wider meaning in the Qur'aan. The word is used at over 200 places throughout therein. In our on-going Studies of the Qur'aan, so far, we have come across this word in Verses <u>2:39</u>, <u>2:41</u>, <u>2:61</u> and <u>2:99</u>. And we have seen that the word *aayaat* is used therein to denote the Verses of not only the Qur'aan, but also the earlier divine Messages. The meaning of the word is not restricted to divisions of the divine Messages either. As can be seen from Verse <u>2:164</u>, the word covers natural phenomena like the heavens and the earth, the alternation of night and day, the ship sailing on the sea, the rains, the winds etc., also. It covers miraculous signs like those with which Prophet Moses was sent to Pharaoh (7:103), and it (in its singular form) covers the entire divine Message (20:47) as well. In short, it covers the numbered divisions of any divine Message, any divine Message itself, any natural phenomenon, any miraculous sign and any other offering from Allah that is meant to help His human creatures understand the Reality - the Reality of His existence and of the Hereafter!

152. Under the influence of the restricted meaning of *aayat* as one of the short, numbered divisions <u>only</u> of the Qur'aan, some people think that there were some abrogated Qur'aanic Verses which find no place in the Qur'aan, as we find it today. And some others think that the Qur'aan, as we find it today, does contain some abrogated Verses also. Were either of these two presumptions correct, it would lead us to an absurd conclusion that the All-knowing and Almighty Allah, like the authors among His human creatures, needs drafting, correcting and redrafting before finalising His Book of guidance to these creatures!

153. If, on the other hand, we consider the broad meaning of *aayat*, as delineated in Note 151 above in Qur'aanic light, the meaning of the Verse becomes clear. The context, in which the word is used here, itself suggests its meaning to be a divine Message, like the Torah or the *Injeel*, given in an earlier age to a particular community, or to be a particular divine Law given in those earlier Books. All divine Messages were essentially the same, but Allah did give different commands (for implementing the same basic principles of religion) to different people at different points of time to suit the different conditions they were in. And at the threshold of the world becoming virtually a global village, so to say, He issued His final commands, in the form of the Qur'aan, <u>for the entire mankind</u>. It is this change, effected from time to time, in the divine commands for implementation of the same basic principles, that is hinted at here when Allah says He abrogates or causes to be forgotten *min aayat* (of a Verse). '*min aayat*' may well be translated, in Qur'aanic light (see Note 151 above), as 'of a divine Message sent to people earlier'. This interpretation squarely fits into the context of the immediately preceding <u>Verse 105</u> mentioning the people (Jews and Christians) of the Book disliking any good (in the form of a better or superceding divine Message) coming to people other than them themselves.

أَلَمْ تَعْلَمْ أَنَّ ٱللَّهَ لَهُۥ مُلْكُ ٱلسَّمَٰوَٰتِ وَٱلْأَرْضِ وَمَا لَكُم مِّن دُونِ ٱللَّهِ

مِن وَلِيٍّ وَلَا نَصِيرٍ ﴿١٠٧﴾

107. Alam taAAlam anna Allaha lahu mulku alssamawati waal-ardi wama lakum min dooni Allahi min waliyyin wala naseerin

---

2:107. Are you not aware that, certainly, it is Allah who has absolute sovereignty over the heavens and the earth? And none is there for you, other than Allah, as a *wali*[154] nor anyone who can help! [155]

---

154. I find it difficult to find an appropriate English word for this Qur'aanic word, *wali* (plural: *awliya*). Some translators have rendered it as 'guardian' or 'protector'. But in Verse 10:62, the Qur'aan has called some good human beings as *awliya* of Allah. Surely it would be preposterous to call human beings as 'guardians' or 'protectors' of Allah! Let us therefore go to the literal meaning of the three-letter Arabic root word *wali*, which is to be close or near. It is used in the Qur'aan in that very sense. So, when the Qur'aan says that good, Allah-fearing persons are *awliya* of Allah, it means that Allah is so pleased with such persons that He has kept them spiritually close to Himself. In Verse 2:257, we are told that Allah is the *wali* of the believers. In other words, Allah is so very close to the believers that He protects and guides them at every step they take in their worldly lives. In Verse 60:9, Allah forbids the believers from being close to (*tawallaw*) only those who fight with them on religion, etc. It is in this sense that in Verse 5:51, Allah asks believers not to take Jews and Christians as *awliya*. Otherwise, Allah makes it clear in Verse 60:8, that He does not forbid the believers to have normal good relations with them if they do not fight with them (the believers) in religious matters, etc.

155. In the Qur'aanic light delineated in the preceding Note, the obvious meaning of the latter part of this Verse is that if anyone were not to accept Allah as his/her *wali*, there could be no one else who could be that person's *wali* or helper. If one accepts, without any reservations whatsoever, Allah as one's *wali*, then there could be one's other *awliya* among living believers, by way of being one's confidants, advisors and helpers in worldly and spiritual matters. But there could be no question of any person, dead or martyred – or of any unseen being (*jinn*) – becoming a *wali* or helper of a living person. If one takes such a being as one's *wali* or helper, besides Allah, one is committing the sin of *shirk* (polytheism). Alas! A majority among the Muslims today are openly indulging in this <u>unpardonable</u> sin. Allah asks, "Do then those who suppress the Truth think that, other than Me, they can take My worshippers as *awliya*? ..." [Q: 18:102]

أَمْ تُرِيدُونَ أَن تَسْـَٔلُوا۟ رَسُولَكُمْ كَمَا سُئِلَ مُوسَىٰ مِن قَبْلُ ۗ وَمَن يَتَبَدَّلِ ٱلْكُفْرَ بِٱلْإِيمَـٰنِ فَقَدْ ضَلَّ سَوَآءَ ٱلسَّبِيلِ ۝

108. Am tureedoona an tas-aloo rasoolakum kama su-ila moosa min qablu waman yatabaddali alkufra bial-eemani faqad dalla sawaa alssabeeli

---

2:108. Or[156], do you want to question your Messenger just as was Moses questioned[157] before? And the one, who exchanges Faith for suppression of the Truth, has indeed gone astray from the Right Path.[158]

---

156. This conjunction obviously connects this Verse to the preceding ones. In the preceding Verses, mention is made of the 'people of the Book' and of the thinking of the Muslims influenced by those people.

157. In this context refer to Verses 55, 61, and to Verses 67 to 71 of this Qur'aanic Chapter. You may also go through Chapter Notes 78 to 84. The questions that the Children of Israel bothered their Prophet Moses with were prompted more out of mischief than by any genuine desire to acquire knowledge.

158. And we have seen, in our on-going Qur'aanic Studies so far, the divine condemnation Moses' people received for their mischievous questionings. Their questions betrayed their lack of Faith. The modern-day Muslim has a lesson to learn there from. His seeking of spiritual guidance from sources other than, and at variance with, the Qur'aan, betrays his lack of Faith in the divine Book.

وَدَّ كَثِيرٌ مِّنْ أَهْلِ ٱلْكِتَٰبِ لَوْ يَرُدُّونَكُم مِّنۢ بَعْدِ إِيمَٰنِكُمْ كُفَّارًا حَسَدًا مِّنْ عِندِ أَنفُسِهِم مِّنۢ بَعْدِ مَا تَبَيَّنَ لَهُمُ ٱلْحَقُّ فَٱعْفُوا۟ وَٱصْفَحُوا۟ حَتَّىٰ يَأْتِىَ ٱللَّهُ بِأَمْرِهِ إِنَّ ٱللَّهَ عَلَىٰ كُلِّ شَىْءٍ قَدِيرٌ ﴿١٠٩﴾

109. Wadda katheerun min ahli alkitabi law yaruddoonakum min baAAdi eemanikum kuffaran hasadan min AAindi anfusihim min baAAdi ma tabayyana lahumu alhaqqu faoAAfoo waisfahoo hatta ya/tiya Allahu bi-amrihi inna Allaha AAala kulli shay-in qadeerun

---

2:109. Many among the people of the Book[159], after what rendered the Truth manifest unto them, would wish, out of their own jealousy, that if only they could turn you back after your attaining to Faith![160] Forgive and forget for now, until further orders from Allah[161 & 162]. Surely, Allah is in control of everything[163].

---

159. Please see Notes 146 and 147 above for a comprehensive understanding of what the term 'people of the Book' (*ahl-il-kitaab*) means.

160. Reflected here is the mentality of a group of people fully aware of the Truth being on the other side. But they would not admit this fact, out of sheer jealousy! This sort of mentality is one of the major causes of friction and conflict in this world, often leading to unnecessary bloodshed.

161. Some commentators say that Verse 9:29 has abrogated this provision of this Verse. We shall, *inshaAllah*, consider the provision under Verse 9.29 when we come to study that Verse. But here, the moot question for our consideration is whether any existing Verse of the Qur'aan can be considered as abrogated! The Qur'aan that is divinely authored! The Qur'aan that is divinely protected!! The Qur'aan that is divinely claimed to contain no contradictions!!! To impute that such a Book could contain, by mistake, an abrogated Verse would be nothing less than blasphemy. No human being can have the authority to declare any divine Verse as abrogated. Today one person may declare one Verse as abrogated. Tomorrow another person may say the same thing about another Verse. In fact, the person who says this betrays his/her lack of faith in the Book being divine.

162. Just the existence of the Verse in the divinely protected Qur'aan is proof enough that it is not abrogated! Its provisions are still relevant. Let us analyse why and how. You see, it is Allah, with His absolute knowledge of the secret intentions in the minds of the *ahl-il-kitaab* at the time of the revelation of the Qur'aan, Who is informing the Believers here of those secret intentions. The secret intentions were yet to be translated into actual acts of any offence against the believers. It was in such a situation that Allah asked the believers to forgive and forget. This divine instruction is valid even now. It wouldn't be right for any group of persons to take any overt or covert offensive action against any other group just on the suspicion that the latter had bad intentions against the former. [You may also go through Chapter Notes 150 to 153 regarding Verse 106, above]

163. And Allah thus reassures the believers that they need not be unduly perturbed about the *ahl-il-kitaab* harbouring bad intentions against them. HE is in control of everything and the believers should be rest assured that He will give them the protection as and when needed. The immediately following Verse 110 of this Qur'aanic Chapter is in continuation of this divine reassurance to the believers. If only they (the believers) would perform their duties assigned to them by their Lord, they need have no fear. HE will assuredly take due care of them! [For a proper understanding of what is meant by 'the establishment of proper prayer' and by 'the *Zakaat*' mentioned in Verse 110, please refer Chapter Notes 4, 108 and 110]

وَأَقِيمُواْ ٱلصَّلَوٰةَ وَءَاتُواْ ٱلزَّكَوٰةَ وَمَا تُقَدِّمُواْ لِأَنفُسِكُم مِّنْ خَيْرٍ تَجِدُوهُ

عِندَ ٱللَّهِ إِنَّ ٱللَّهَ بِمَا تَعْمَلُونَ بَصِيرٌ ﴿١١٠﴾

110. Waaqeemoo alssalata waatoo alzzakata wama tuqaddimoo li-anfusikum min khayrin tajidoohu AAinda Allahi inna Allaha bima taAAmaloona baseerun

---

2:110. And establish the proper prayer and give the *Zakaat*! And whatever good you send forth for your own selves, you'll find it with Allah. Surely, Allah is aware of what you do!

وَقَالُوا لَن يَدْخُلَ الْجَنَّةَ إِلَّا مَن كَانَ هُودًا أَوْ نَصَـٰرَىٰ تِلْكَ أَمَانِيُّهُمْ قُلْ هَاتُوا بُرْهَـٰنَكُمْ إِن كُنتُمْ صَـٰدِقِينَ ۞

111. Waqaloo lan yadkhula aljannata illa man kana hoodan aw nasara tilka amaniyyuhum qul hatoo burhanakum in kuntum sadiqeena

2:111. And they[164] say, "None shall enter the Paradise except for one who has been a Jew/Christian!" That is what they just desire. Say, "Produce your evidence, if you are truthful!"

164. From their statement, that follows, it is obvious that the pronoun 'they' here stands for the Jews or the Christians.

بَلَىٰ مَنْ أَسْلَمَ وَجْهَهُ لِلَّهِ وَهُوَ مُحْسِنٌ فَلَهُ أَجْرُهُ عِندَ رَبِّهِ وَلَا خَوْفٌ عَلَيْهِمْ وَلَا هُمْ يَحْزَنُونَ ۞

112. Bala man aslama wajhahu lillahi wahuwa muhsinun falahu ajruhu AAinda rabbihi wala khawfun AAalayhim wala hum yahzanoona

2:112. Yes, indeed! Anyone who surrenders one's self for Allah and is a doer of righteous deeds[165] besides – for such a one is one's reward with one's Lord. And no fear shall such people have, nor shall they grieve!

165. If we compare this Verse (2:112) with <u>Verse 2:62</u> conveying almost the same divine message, we see that in place of the Arabic term *amila saalihan* there (in Verse 2:62) the word used here is *muhsin*. In keeping with its way of explaining things variously, the Qur'aan here thus gives the meaning of *muhsin* to

be one who has acted righteously (*amila saalihan*). And to understand what constitutes righteous acts in the Qur'aanic light, please see Note 68 above.

وَقَالَتِ ٱلْيَهُودُ لَيْسَتِ ٱلنَّصَٰرَىٰ عَلَىٰ شَىْءٍ وَقَالَتِ ٱلنَّصَٰرَىٰ لَيْسَتِ ٱلْيَهُودُ عَلَىٰ شَىْءٍ وَهُمْ يَتْلُونَ ٱلْكِتَٰبَ كَذَٰلِكَ قَالَ ٱلَّذِينَ لَا يَعْلَمُونَ مِثْلَ قَوْلِهِمْ فَٱللَّهُ يَحْكُمُ بَيْنَهُمْ يَوْمَ ٱلْقِيَٰمَةِ فِيمَا كَانُوا۟ فِيهِ يَخْتَلِفُونَ

113. Waqalati alyahoodu laysati alnnasara AAala shay-in waqalati alnnasara laysati alyahoodu AAala shay-in wahum yatloona alkitaba kathalika qala allatheena la yaAAlamoona mithla qawlihim faAllahu yahkumu baynahum yawma alqiyamati feema kanoo feehi yakhtalifoona

---

2:113. And say the Jews, "Not on any base are the Christians!" And say the Christians, "Not on any base are the Jews!" And they do recite the Book!! Thus – in statements like theirs – did those, who knew not, speak.[166] Then, on the Day of Resurrection, shall Allah judge between them in matters in which they differed.

---

166. And alas! In statements like theirs, the bulk of the so-called Muslims today speak. And they do read the Qur'aan, but without understanding – without even trying to understand! They are therefore more like those who know not! They know not that by merely calling themselves Muslims – without fulfilling the criterion divinely laid down in Verse 112 herein above read with Verse 2:62 – is of no value for attainment of salvation.

وَمَنْ أَظْلَمُ مِمَّن مَّنَعَ مَسَٰجِدَ ٱللَّهِ أَن يُذْكَرَ فِيهَا ٱسْمُهُۥ وَسَعَىٰ فِى خَرَابِهَآ أُو۟لَٰٓئِكَ مَا كَانَ لَهُمْ أَن يَدْخُلُوهَآ إِلَّا خَآئِفِينَ لَهُمْ فِى ٱلدُّنْيَا خِزْىٌ وَلَهُمْ فِى ٱلْءَاخِرَةِ عَذَابٌ عَظِيمٌ

114. Waman a*th*lamu mimman manaAAa mas*a*jida All*a*hi an yu*th*kara feeh*a* ismuhu wasaAA*a* fee khar*a*bih*a* ol*a*-ika m*a* k*a*na lahum an yadkhuloob*a* ill*a* kh*a*-ifeena lahum fee aldduny*a* khizyun walahum fee al-*a*khirati AAa*th*abun AAa*th*eemun

2:114. And who can do a greater wrong than one who forbids anyone, in places for prostrating to Allah[167], from eulogizing His Name therein, and who works for their ruin/desertion? Those places! They ought not to have entered those places, except in awe!! For them, in this world, disgrace; and for them, in the Hereafter, severe punishment!!!

167. In Verse 22:40, monastries, churches and synagogues are mentioned, besides *masaajids,* **wherein Allah's Name is remembered frequently. This Verse (2:114), we are presently studying, is therefore applicable to all places where Allah is eulogised, albeit under different Names (like, for example, God). This divine command and** <u>grave</u> **warning, here, are equally applicable to anyone (including a Muslim) who may work for the devastation of places of worship of other religions, as those are applicable to anyone working for the devastation of the** *masaajids.*

وَلِلَّهِ ٱلْمَشْرِقُ وَٱلْمَغْرِبُ فَأَيْنَمَا تُوَلُّواْ فَثَمَّ وَجْهُ ٱللَّهِ إِنَّ ٱللَّهَ وَٰسِعٌ عَلِيمٌ ۝

115. Walill*a*hi almashriqu waalmaghribu faaynam*a* tuwalloo fathamma wajhu All*a*hi inna All*a*ha wasiAAun AAaleemun

2:115. And for Allah are the East and the West. So, whichever way you turn, there the divine Face of Allah[168]! Allah is indeed all encompassing, all knowing!

168. The Arabic term used is *wajhu-Allah.* **We find similar terms used in Verses 2:272 & 76:9 (***wajhi-Allah***), 30:38 & 30:39 (***wajha-Allah***). In all those four Verses, the term is, obviously in the context of the contents of those Verses, used in the meaning of 'pleasure/approval of Allah'. But, obviously again, the same rendering would not quite fit into the context of this Verse 2:115. Resorting therefore to the literal meanings of** *wajha,* **we find 'face', 'front', 'aspect', 'prominent personage' 'style' to be among those meanings. In the context of this word being used as an attribute of the One and Only Divine Being, I have rendered** *wajhu-Allah* **as 'divine Face of Allah'. Whatever any human being does, whatever lifestyle he/she adopts, there is no escape route for him/her from being closely observed by Allah. The divine Face would always be towards him/her.**

116. Waqaloo itakha<u>th</u>a All<u>a</u>hu waladan sub<u>h</u>anahu bal lahu m<u>a</u> fee alssam<u>a</u>w<u>a</u>ti waal-ar<u>d</u>i kullun lahu q<u>a</u>nitoona

2:116. And they[169] say, "Allah has a son!" HE is much too glorified to have one!! HIS, on the other hand, is everything that is in the heavens and the earth!!! All are obedient to Him.

169. In Verse 9:30, the Qur'aan informs us that the Jews and the Christians say so. And we know of other religious groups too, who have this purely man-conceived concept of their Creator having a family, *a la* **a human being!**

117. Badee<u>A</u>u alssam<u>a</u>w<u>a</u>ti waal-ar<u>d</u>i wa-i<u>th</u>a qa<u>da</u> amran fa-innam<u>a</u> yaqoolu lahu kun fayakoonu

2:117. Originator of the heavens and the earth! And when He decides to accomplish anything, He just tells it, "Be!" And, it is!![170]

170. And thus, in these two divine Verses (2:116 and 2:117), does the Creator logically demolish that man-conceived concept!! Everything in the heavens and the earth is His creation. He just has to say, "Be", and anything, He wishes, comes into existence. Why would He then come down to the level of His creatures to beget a son?! A human being may need a son to support him when he becomes weak in his old age, or to inherit and look after his worldly property when he is no more. But that obviously is not

the case with Allah! There is no question of He ever becoming weak or being 'no more'!! The idea of a 'divine son' is therefore nothing but a figment of man's imagination. This idea places him on an entirely false, and therefore wrong, footing that would inevitably lead him astray in this world and make him completely lost in the next!

وَقَالَ ٱلَّذِينَ لَا يَعْلَمُونَ لَوْلَا يُكَلِّمُنَا ٱللَّهُ أَوْ تَأْتِينَا ءَايَةٌ كَذَٰلِكَ قَالَ ٱلَّذِينَ مِن قَبْلِهِم مِّثْلَ قَوْلِهِمْ تَشَٰبَهَتْ قُلُوبُهُمْ قَدْ بَيَّنَّا ٱلْأَيَٰتِ لِقَوْمٍ يُوقِنُونَ ۝١١٨

118. Waqala allatheena la yaAAlamoona lawla yukallimuna Allahu aw ta/teena ayatun kathalika qala allatheena min qablihim mithla qawlihim tashabahat quloobuhum qad bayyanna al-ayati liqawmin yooqinoona

---

2:118. And those, who know not, said, "If only Allah would talk to us, or a sign would come to us!"[171] Likewise did those, who lived earlier to them, say things like what these people said. Their mind-sets are alike. WE have certainly made the signs clear to the people who have been firm in their Faith.

---

171. This was the condition put forth by the ignorant, for their belief in Allah! How stupid of them!! This stupidity flew from their ignorance of the grand divine purpose for creating mankind. Unlike other creations, mankind was given freedom of choice. The divine purpose is to test human beings whether they would come to recognise and submit unto the One and Only Creator, without seeing or speaking to Him. About the signs to help mankind come to an unshakeable Belief in His existence, there are a good many – a galore – in and around every human being. But unfortunately, under satanic influence, most of mankind ignore these signs or wilfully suppress their existence – to their own ultimate doom!

إِنَّا أَرْسَلْنَٰكَ بِٱلْحَقِّ بَشِيرًا وَنَذِيرًا وَلَا تُسْـَٔلُ عَنْ أَصْحَٰبِ ٱلْجَحِيمِ ۝١١٩

119. Inna arsalnaka bialhaqqi basheeran wanatheeran wala tus-alu Aaan as-habi aljaheemi

2:119. WE have indeed sent you, in Truth, to give glad tidings, and to warn! And you will not be subjected to any inquisition about the dwellers of the blazing Fire.[172]

172. The addressee, of this divine speech, is obviously the Prophet (may peace and Allah's blessings be upon him!) The divine address was by way of a reassurance to the Prophet. He was reassured that despite the disbelief shown to him by certain sections of people, he is no doubt the accredited Messenger of Allah! He should therefore continue, unmindful, in his given task of giving the glad tidings of Paradise to those who abide by the divine Message, and of warning those who do not, of Hell Fire! The Prophet perhaps worried about people who, despite his best efforts to convince them, did still not believe. He worried that such people would go to Hell. Allah therefore absolves him of any responsibility for the dwellers of the Fire. The Prophet's responsibility was to warn them; and the Prophet had very well fulfilled that responsibility!

وَلَن تَرْضَىٰ عَنكَ ٱلْيَهُودُ وَلَا ٱلنَّصَارَىٰ حَتَّىٰ تَتَّبِعَ مِلَّتَهُمْ قُلْ إِنَّ هُدَى ٱللَّهِ هُوَ ٱلْهُدَىٰ وَلَئِنِ ٱتَّبَعْتَ أَهْوَآءَهُم بَعْدَ ٱلَّذِى جَآءَكَ مِنَ ٱلْعِلْمِ مَا لَكَ مِنَ ٱللَّهِ مِن وَلِيٍّ وَلَا نَصِيرٍ ۝

120. Walan tarda AAanka alyahoodu wala alnnasara hatta tattabiAAa millatahum qul inna huda Allahi huwa alhuda wala-ini ittabaAAta ahwaahum baAAda allathee jaaka mina alAAilmi ma laka mina Allahi min waliyyin wala naseerin

2:120. And the Jews shall not be pleased with you, and nor shall the Christians, till you follow their creed.[173] Say, "Allah's guidance – it is the[174] Guidance!"[175] And, if you were to follow their desires, after what has come to you of knowledge, shall there be none to patronise you, nor anyone to help you, against Allah.

173. Although the addressee here is the Prophet (peace and Allah's blessings be upon him), the divine statement has connotations for all followers of Islam in general. And history is witness to this divine prophecy in general terms. The long-drawn-out Crusades of the middle ages and the recent Arab-Israeli conflicts are evidences enough.

174. Please take note of the emphasis placed on Guidance by the definite article 'the' (*al* in Arabic). This is divine reiteration of the fact that Allah is the Sole Source of all guidance for mankind. And logically so! HE is, after all, the Sole Creator of everything. And, logically too, it follows that His Book of Guidance, the Qur'aan, epitomises that Sole Source. And the Qur'aan contains the divine confirmation: "... We have neglected nothing in the Book ..." [Q: 6:38] The golden rule, therefore, for us to follow in the conduct of our worldly lives is that we should reject anything that is contrary to the Qur'aanic guidance.

175. And in the context in which the Prophet was asked to say this to the Jews and the Christians, those two groups of people were thus plainly told that the Prophet would not be following their guidance. He (the Prophet) would be following the only real guidance – the divine Guidance – that came to him! All other guidance, at variance with the divine Guidance, is misleading because it emanates from personal desires/bias of persons giving that guidance.

ٱلَّذِينَ ءَاتَيْنَٰهُمُ ٱلْكِتَٰبَ يَتْلُونَهُۥ حَقَّ تِلَاوَتِهِۦٓ أُوْلَٰٓئِكَ يُؤْمِنُونَ بِهِۦ ۗ وَمَن يَكْفُرْ بِهِۦ فَأُوْلَٰٓئِكَ هُمُ ٱلْخَٰسِرُونَ ﴿١٢١﴾

121. Alla*th*eena *ataynah*umu alkit*a*ba yatloonahu *h*aqqa til*a*watihi ol*a*-ika yu/minoona bihi waman yakfur bihi faol*a*-ika humu alkh*a*siroon*a*

2:121. Those upon whom We have bestowed the Book, recite and follow it as it ought to be recited and followed[176]. Those are the ones who believe therein! And those who wantonly suppress and deny the Truth thereof[177] – those are the ones doomed!

176. In the original Arabic text, the word used is *tilaawat*. This Arabic word is commonly understood to mean 'reading' or 'reciting'. But when I say that I have read a novel, I mean that I have read and understood it. Nobody reads a novel just for the sake of reading and not for understanding the gripping story that runs through it. Unfortunately, however, we, modern-day Muslims, assume that just reading the Qur'aan, without taking the trouble of understanding what we read, fetches us enough *thawaab* (reward) from Allah Ta'ala. We are under a grievous misconception that has contributed a lot to our downfall. In this Qur'aanic Verse, Allah pricks that balloon of our false assumptions. The word *tilaawat* also connotes 'meditation'; and the root word *ta la wa* means 'to follow'. And it needs no great intelligence to know what the right way of *tilaawat* of the Qur'aan (*haqqa tilaawatihi*) is. We must ponder over what we read in order to understand it, and then to follow the instructions scrupulously.

177. As a Muslim, I ought to follow all Qur'aanic instructions applicable to me. And if I do (*nauzubillah*) wantonly not follow any such instruction, I do thereby be among those who suppress and/or deny the Truth thereof (*yakfur bihi*). I'm sure to be doomed then! I pray Allah to save me, and save all my Muslim brothers/sisters, from this certain doom! Amen!!

$$\text{يَٰبَنِىٓ إِسْرَٰٓءِيلَ ٱذْكُرُوا۟ نِعْمَتِىَ ٱلَّتِىٓ أَنْعَمْتُ عَلَيْكُمْ وَأَنِّى فَضَّلْتُكُمْ عَلَى ٱلْعَٰلَمِينَ ﴿١٢٢﴾}$$

122. Ya banee isra-eela othkuroo niAAmatiya allatee anAAamtu AAalaykum waannee faddaltukum AAala alAAalameena

---

2:122. O Children of Israel! Remember My Favour that I bestowed upon you. And remember that I gave you preference over the Worlds.

$$\text{وَٱتَّقُوا۟ يَوْمًا لَّا تَجْزِى نَفْسٌ عَن نَّفْسٍ شَيْـًٔا وَلَا يُقْبَلُ مِنْهَا عَدْلٌ وَلَا تَنفَعُهَا شَفَٰعَةٌ وَلَا هُمْ يُنصَرُونَ ﴿١٢٣﴾}$$

123. Waittaqoo yawman la tajzee nafsun AAan nafsin shay-an wala yuqbalu minha AAadlun wala tanfaAAuha shafaAAatun wala hum yunsaroona

---

2:123. And fear the Day when none can be of any avail on anything to another, nor any ransom, from anyone, accepted. And no intercession shall benefit anyone; nor shall they be helped! [178]

---

178. These two Verses (2:122 & 2:123) are almost the same as Verses 2:47 & 2:48. **Please go through** Chapter Notes 51 to 53 **thereon. About the question as to why this repetition, please see** Chapter Note 124. **And, moreover, what follows in the next Verse, provides the immediate justification for the repetition.**

وَإِذِ ٱبْتَلَىٰٓ إِبْرَٰهِۦمَ رَبُّهُۥ بِكَلِمَٰتٍ فَأَتَمَّهُنَّ قَالَ إِنِّى جَاعِلُكَ لِلنَّاسِ إِمَامًا ۖ قَالَ وَمِن ذُرِّيَّتِى ۖ قَالَ لَا يَنَالُ عَهْدِى ٱلظَّٰلِمِينَ ﴿١٢٤﴾

124. Wa-ithi ibtala ibraheema rabbuhu bikalimatin faatammahunna qala innee jaAAiluka lilnnasi imaman qala wamin thurriyyatee qala la yanalu AAahdee alththalimeena

2:124. And when his Lord put Abraham to trial with Commands, and he fulfilled those Commands, He said, "I am going to make you a leader for mankind." He (Abraham) said, "And from among my offspring?" HE said, "MY word (of promise) extends not to the wicked!"[179]

179. The implication of the divine reply to Abraham (peace and Allah's blessings be upon him), obviously, is that Allah-approved leadership among human beings would not be bestowed upon the progeny of Abraham if the progeny go against divinely laid down law. In the context of the earlier Verse, addressed to the Children of Israel (a progeny of Abraham), this progeny is thus being told, in unmistakable terms that merely being the progeny of a Prophet would not help them get leadership of mankind. Nor shall that fact by itself get them salvation in the Hereafter! No intercession – not even of Abraham – would help them, if they go against divine law. Herein is a lesson also for us, Muslims of today. But alas! We won't take heed. We insist on treading the trodden path of *Bani Israel*!! [Please also refer Chapter Note 181 below about Abraham.]

وَإِذْ جَعَلْنَا ٱلْبَيْتَ مَثَابَةً لِّلنَّاسِ وَأَمْنًا وَٱتَّخِذُوا۟ مِن مَّقَامِ إِبْرَٰهِۦمَ مُصَلًّى ۖ وَعَهِدْنَآ إِلَىٰٓ إِبْرَٰهِۦمَ وَإِسْمَٰعِيلَ أَن طَهِّرَا بَيْتِىَ لِلطَّآئِفِينَ وَٱلْعَٰكِفِينَ وَٱلرُّكَّعِ ٱلسُّجُودِ ﴿١٢٥﴾

125. Wa-ith jaAAalna albayta mathabatan lilnnasi waamnan waittakhithoo min maqami ibraheema musallan waAAahidna ila ibraheema wa-ismaAAeela an tahhira baytiya liltta-ifeena waalAAakifeena waalrrukkaAAi alssujoodi

2:125. And behold! WE made the House[180] a secure place of assembly for mankind. – And take the place where Abraham[181] stood[182] as a place of worship! – And We bade Abraham and Ishmael[183] to cleanse My[184] House for those who would go around it and spend some time there in devotion, and who would bow and prostrate.

---

180. In Verse 3:96, the Qur'aan informs us that the first House set up for mankind is the one at *Bakkah* (Makkah). Pilgrimage thereto is a duty unto Allah, for those who can undertake the journey (3:97). It is described as *al-Baital-haraam* (the sacred House) in Verses 5:2 and 5:97, and as *al-Baitil-ateeq* (the ancient House) in 22:29 and 22:33. From Verse 14:37, we learn that Abraham had settled some of his offspring in the uncultivable terrain near Allah's sacred House and had prayed for their provision. And from Verse 22:26, we learn that it was Allah who guided Abraham to the site of His sacred House. In some other Verses of the Qur'aan, like in Verse 2:144, the House has been also called as *al-Masjidil-haraam.*

181. We have already seen this Prophet and Messenger of Allah mentioned as a leader of men, in Verse 2:124. In Verse 2:127, we are informed that it was he, along with his son, who had raised the foundation of the House of Allah. He has been described as a *haneef* (an upright man, one who professes the true religion) whom Allah has taken as a *khaleel* (a beloved one), and whose religion believers are commanded to follow [4:125]. And Allah Ta'ala speaks highly of him at many other places throughout in the Qur'aan!

182. In Verse 3:97, we are informed that one of the clear signs in the House of Allah is the place where Abraham stood.

183. We learn from Verse 14:39 that Ishmael was one of the two sons Allah gave Abraham in his old age. He too was a Messenger, a Prophet (19:54).

184. Those who would wonder as to why this sudden change in the same sentence from the plural We to the singular My, may well reflect that the conveyance of the divine command might have been made through the angels. So, the plural 'We' was used. But the House was for devotion to Allah exclusively. Hence, the singular 'My'.

وَإِذْ قَالَ إِبْرَاهِيمُ رَبِّ اجْعَلْ هَٰذَا بَلَدًا ءَامِنًا وَارْزُقْ أَهْلَهُ مِنَ الثَّمَرَاتِ مَنْ ءَامَنَ مِنْهُم بِاللَّهِ وَالْيَوْمِ الْآخِرِ قَالَ وَمَن كَفَرَ فَأُمَتِّعُهُ قَلِيلًا ثُمَّ أَضْطَرُّهُ إِلَىٰ عَذَابِ النَّارِ وَبِئْسَ الْمَصِيرُ ﴿١٢٦﴾

126. Wa-ith qala ibraheemu rabbi ijAAal hatha baladan aminan waorzuq ahlahu mina aththamarati man amana minhum biAllahi waalyawmi al-akhiri qala waman kafara faomattiAAuhu qaleelan thumma adtarruhu ila AAathabi alnnari wabi/sa almaseeru

2:126. And when Abraham prayed "O my Lord! Make this land[185] safe, secure and peaceful, and make provisions for its residents from its produce – for those who believe in Allah and in the Hereafter", Allah replied, "And, for a while, I shall keep contented the one who suppresses the Truth and then shall draw him/her to punishment by the Fire![186] And how vile a destination!!"

185. In some translations, the Arabic word *balad* is rendered as City. But, obviously, during Abraham's time there was no city around the House of Allah. It would therefore be illogical for Abraham to call the place near the House, a City. The place was uncultivable, and few other settlers could have been there at that time besides a part of Abraham's family, whom Allah had led thereto. It might have been the open arid state of the land which prompted Abraham to make the prayer.

186. Please note that Abraham had prayed for the safety and well-being of those future residents of the land who believed in Allah and in the Hereafter. But Allah would allow suppressors of Truth to enjoy life for a while, before giving them the ultimate punishment! Believers should therefore not allow themselves to be led astray by the apparent lives of prosperity that some suppressors of Truth lead in this world!

وَإِذْ يَرْفَعُ إِبْرَاهِيمُ الْقَوَاعِدَ مِنَ الْبَيْتِ وَإِسْمَاعِيلُ رَبَّنَا تَقَبَّلْ مِنَّا إِنَّكَ أَنتَ السَّمِيعُ الْعَلِيمُ ﴿١٢٧﴾

127. Wa-ith yarfaAAu ibraheemu alqawaAAida mina albayti wa-ismaAAeelu rabbana taqabbal minna innaka anta alssameeAAu alAAaleemu

2:127. And while raising the foundations of the House, Abraham and Ishmael prayed, "O our Lord! May You accept this[187] from us. Surely, You are the One Who listens, the One Who knows!

187. Accept what? Accept the service rendered by father and son in raising the foundations of the House? Or, accept the prayer that they are about to make? The context of the divine Name *As-Sameeoo* (the One Unseen who listens to His creatures' prayers) clearly suggests that it was their ensuing prayers that the two were entreating Allah to accept.

رَبَّنَا وَاجْعَلْنَا مُسْلِمَيْنِ لَكَ وَمِن ذُرِّيَّتِنَآ أُمَّةً مُّسْلِمَةً لَّكَ وَأَرِنَا مَنَاسِكَنَا وَتُبْ عَلَيْنَآ إِنَّكَ أَنتَ ٱلتَّوَّابُ ٱلرَّحِيمُ ۝

128. Rabbana waijAAalna muslimayni laka wamin thurriyyatina ommatan muslimatan laka waarina manasikana watub AAalayna innaka anta alttawwabu alrraheemu

---

2:128. "O our Lord! Turn us into persons who submit unto You; [188] and out of our progeny, make a community that would submit unto You. And show us the rites that would symbolise our submitting to You.[189] And accept our repentance.[190] Surely, You are the One to accept repentance, the One Merciful!

---

188. Submitting to the One Lord – the Creator – is the solid base on which a true Muslim – a Muslim not only in name, but in deed also – firmly stands. Like Abraham, he observes the innumerable Signs that his Lord has furnished to him. Like Abraham, he uses his Allah-given intelligence to recognise that these are unmistakable Signs of His existence. The true Muslim does not allow the limited powers of his intelligence to go to his head and make him think erroneously that he is the lord of all he surveys. Abraham did truly symbolise a true Muslim! That's why, perhaps, the Lord preserved the place where he once stood in the House (the *Kaaba*) – literally, his footsteps – as a manifest Sign for all true Muslims to follow (3:97). That's why the Lord ordered us, in <u>Verse 2:125</u>, to take *maqaam-e-Ibrahim* as a *musalla* for us.

189. We observe fasts during the month of *Ramadaan*, primarily because Allah has asked us to do so. We have similarly to observe all other religious rites, divinely prescribed in the Qur'aan, without any reservations whatsoever! If we do not observe them, we are not, *nauzubillah*, submitters to Allah then – we are not Muslims. That's as simply clear as that! So, our observations of Allah-prescribed religious rites – our *manaasik* – are, so to say, symbols of our complete submitting to Allah, our Lord!

190. Yes, we ought to observe all our *manaasik*, strictly and without exception. But human beings are weak. They are vulnerable to satanic temptations. And, despite our best intentions, we fail sometimes to observe our *manaasik*. We should therefore follow the leader. We should follow Abraham in constantly seeking Allah's indulgence, His merciful forbearance of our shortcomings.

رَبَّنَا وَابْعَثْ فِيهِمْ رَسُولًا مِّنْهُمْ يَتْلُوا۟ عَلَيْهِمْ ءَايَـٰتِكَ وَيُعَلِّمُهُمُ ٱلْكِتَـٰبَ وَٱلْحِكْمَةَ وَيُزَكِّيهِمْ إِنَّكَ أَنتَ ٱلْعَزِيزُ ٱلْحَكِيمُ ۝

129. Rabbana waibAAath feehim rasoolan minhum yatloo AAalayhim ayatika wayuAAallimuhumu alkitaba waalhikmata wayuzakkeehim innaka anta alAAazeezu alhakeemu

2:129. "O our Lord! Raise among them[191] a Messenger from amongst them, to recite to them Your Verses, to teach to them the Book and the Wisdom, and to purify them.[192] Indeed, You are the One Omnipotent, the One Wise!"

191. In the context of the preceding Verse, 'them' here obviously stands for the progeny of Abraham through his son Ishmael. And their progeny around the *Kaaba* are obviously the Arab people.

192. And we are aware that this prayer was heard and responded to by the Wise and Almighty Allah several centuries later! HE did raise Prophet Muhammad (peace and Allah's blessings be upon him) for the very task Abraham and Ishmael had prayed for. During the intervening centuries, the Arab people had come to forget what their great forefather and Allah's *Khaleel*, Abraham, had stood for. They had fallen back to idol-worship, which Abraham had valiantly and steadfastly fought against! By Allah's grace, Prophet Muhammad recited His Verses to his people. He taught them the Book of the divine Verses, the Qur'aan, for 23 long years through numerous trials and tribulations. He thus convinced them of the wisdom of abiding by the divine commands contained in those Verses. He thus, through Allah's grace, purified a non-descript and utterly backward people into the most potent force that shook the entire world and brought about an ideological, moral and intellectual renaissance therein!

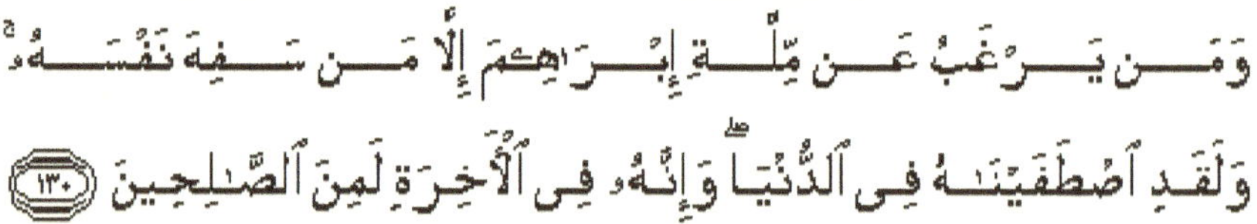

130. Waman yarghabu AAan millati ibraheema illa man safiha nafsahu walaqadi istafaynahu fee alddunya wa-innahu fee al-akhirati lamina alssaliheena

2:130. And who would turn away from Abraham's creed, but one who has made a fool of oneself? And We did indeed select him in this world. And, of course, in the Hereafter, he shall be among the righteous! [193]

193. It would indeed be foolish of anyone to be averse to a lifestyle that the Creator approved of and that got the one leading such a lifestyle an assured place of honour in the Hereafter. Doomed indeed would be the one who does not follow, or does not at least try to follow, Abraham's lifestyle!

إِذْ قَالَ لَهُۥ رَبُّهُۥٓ أَسْلِمْ قَالَ أَسْلَمْتُ لِرَبِّ ٱلْعَٰلَمِينَ ﴿١٣١﴾

131. I<u>th</u> qala lahu rabbuhu aslim qala aslamtu lirabbi alAA<u>a</u>lameen**a**

2:131. When his Lord told him, "Submit", he obeyed: "I submit to the Lord of the worlds!"[194]

194. And that was Abraham's lifestyle! It is indeed the essence of the Allah-approved Religion of Islam. Complete submission to His Will! Let us take note of the Name, Allah made Abraham choose here, from among His various Names: _Rabbil aalameen_. Lord of the worlds! (Please refer to <u>Note 1:5</u> **above to understand the comprehensive Qur'aanic meaning of the term** _aalameen_.**) Every person is a** _khalifa_ **(representative) of Allah to his/her individual world, where he/she has to take his/her own decisions. It is the nature of these decisions that make or mar that person. If he/she is deluded into thinking that he/she is the lord of all he/she surveys and makes his/her decisions accordingly, then he/she is doomed. If, on the other hand, he/she realises that Allah is the real** _Rabb_ **(see** <u>Note 1:4</u>**) of his own world as well as of all other individual worlds, makes his/her decisions fearing Allah, and submits completely to the results that follow as being from Allah, he/she would be the one to get befitting reward from the Lord.**

وَوَصَّىٰ بِهَآ إِبْرَٰهِۦمُ بَنِيهِ وَيَعْقُوبُ يَٰبَنِيَّ إِنَّ ٱللَّهَ ٱصْطَفَىٰ لَكُمُ ٱلدِّينَ فَلَا تَمُوتُنَّ إِلَّا وَأَنتُم مُّسْلِمُونَ ﴿١٣٢﴾

132. Wawa<u>ss</u>a bih<u>a</u> ibr<u>a</u>heemu baneehi wayaAAqoobu y<u>a</u> baniyya inna All<u>a</u>ha i<u>s</u>taf<u>a</u> lakumu alddeena fal<u>a</u> tamootunna ill<u>a</u> waantum muslimoon**a**

2:132. And Abraham did advise his sons in this regard[195], and so did Jacob[196], "O my sons! Indeed, Allah has chosen the Religion for you. Die you not then except in the state of complete surrender unto Him!"[197]

195. Regarding, that is, Allah's command and Abraham's obedience thereof, mentioned in the preceding Verse <u>2:131</u>**.**

196. From Verse 11:71, we learn that Jacob (*Yaqoub*) was a progeny of Abraham, the glad tidings of whom the Angels gave to Abraham's old wife. Jacob was promised to her as one who would come after her son, Isaac. And from Verse 12:68, we gather that Jacob was the father of Prophet Joseph.

197. And since death is subject to the sweet wishes of no man, however big or well-placed, and is liable to occur at any time, the advice to the sons could only mean that they should never ever allow themselves to deviate from Islam, the Religion of Abraham.

أَمْ كُنتُمْ شُهَدَآءَ إِذْ حَضَرَ يَعْقُوبَ ٱلْمَوْتُ إِذْ قَالَ لِبَنِيهِ مَا

تَعْبُدُونَ مِنْ بَعْدِى قَالُواْ نَعْبُدُ إِلَـٰهَكَ وَإِلَـٰهَ ءَابَآئِكَ إِبْرَٰهِـۧمَ

وَإِسْمَٰعِيلَ وَإِسْحَٰقَ إِلَـٰهًا وَٰحِدًا وَنَحْنُ لَهُۥ مُسْلِمُونَ ﴿١٣٣﴾

133. Am kuntum shuhadaa ith hadara yaAAqooba almawtu ith qala libaneehi ma taAAbudoona min baAAdee qaloo naAAbudu ilahaka wa-ilaha aba-ika ibraheema wa-ismaAAeela wa-ishaqa ilahan wahidan wanahnu lahu muslimoona

---

2:133. Or[198], were you the witnesses when death approached Jacob and he asked his sons, "Whom will you worship after I am gone?" They said, "We shall worship the One, you have worshipped and your forefathers, Abraham, Ishmael and Isaac, had worshipped – the One and only, deserving to be worshipped – and we do indeed submit unto That One!"

---

198. This word connects the various episodes concerning the lives of Abraham and his progeny, described in all the Verses right from Verse 2:124. These anecdotes are connected for the divine statement that follows in Verse 2:134. The obvious implication is that the people for whom these Qur'aanic Verses were revealed did not exist when those episodes occurred, and therefore were unaware thereof. Allah is the One aware of all things, past, present and future. And He it is Who supplies us the necessary information, out of His infinite knowledge, for our guidance.

تِلْكَ أُمَّةٌ قَدْ خَلَتْ لَهَا مَا كَسَبَتْ وَلَكُم مَّا كَسَبْتُمْ وَلَا تُسْـَٔلُونَ عَمَّا كَانُوا۟ يَعْمَلُونَ ۝١٣٤

134. Tilka ommatun qad khalat laha ma kasabat walakum ma kasabtum wala tus-aloona AAamma kano yaAAamaloona

---

2:134. That was a community, now dead and gone! To it what it earned, and to you what you have earned. And you shall not be questioned on what they did! [199]

---

199. Important implications of this divine statement are:

- **Divine assessment of people would not be based on the performance of their forefathers, but on what they themselves do individually.**

- **No one can claim to be one of God's chosen people, and hence exempt from assessment of one's own performance.**

- **We need not just ape what the Islamic religious scholars in the past said and did! For, we shall not be questioned on what they said or did. But we shall certainly be questioned on what we do in compliance of the divine commands contained in the divinely preserved Qur'aan.**

وَقَالُوا۟ كُونُوا۟ هُودًا أَوْ نَصَٰرَىٰ تَهْتَدُوا۟ قُلْ بَلْ مِلَّةَ إِبْرَٰهِـۧمَ حَنِيفًا وَمَا كَانَ مِنَ ٱلْمُشْرِكِينَ ۝١٣٥

135. Waqaloo koonoo hoodan aw nasara tahtadoo qul bal millata ibraheema haneefan wama kana mina almushrikeena

---

2:135. And they[200] say, "Be a Jew, or a Christian, to be rightly guided." Say, "Nay! Be of Abraham's Creed, devoutly.[201] And he was not one from among the polytheists[202]."

---

200. In the context of the quote that immediately follows, it is obvious that 'they' here stands for either the Jews or the Christians.

201. Let us re-read in this context Verse 2:130, wherein anyone turning away from Abraham's creed is virtually called a fool. Let us also again go through Verse 2:131, which informs us of the essence of Abraham's creed.

202. Allah thus indirectly tells the Jews and the Christians, of that period at the revelation of the Qur'aan, that they have both strayed away from the pure Abrahamic creed and fallen into polytheism. Are the Jews and the Christians – or the Muslims, for that matter, of the present time generally – any better than those Jews and Christians addressed in this Verse?

قُولُوٓاْ ءَامَنَّا بِٱللَّهِ وَمَآ أُنزِلَ إِلَيْنَا وَمَآ أُنزِلَ إِلَىٰٓ إِبْرَٰهِـۧمَ وَإِسْمَٰعِيلَ وَإِسْحَٰقَ وَيَعْقُوبَ وَٱلْأَسْبَاطِ وَمَآ أُوتِىَ مُوسَىٰ وَعِيسَىٰ وَمَآ أُوتِىَ ٱلنَّبِيُّونَ مِن رَّبِّهِمْ لَا نُفَرِّقُ بَيْنَ أَحَدٍ مِّنْهُمْ وَنَحْنُ لَهُۥ مُسْلِمُونَ ﴿١٣٦﴾

136. Qooloo amanna biAllahi wama onzila ilayna wama onzila ila ibraheema wa-ismaAAeela wa-ishaqa wayaAAqooba waal-asbati wama ootiya moosa waAAeesa wama ootiya alnnabiyyoona min rabbihim la nufarriqu bayna ahadin minhum wanahnu lahu muslimoona

---

2:136. You say[203], "We do believe in Allah. And we do believe in what has been sent down to us, and in what had been sent down upon Abraham, Ishmael, Isaac, Jacob and the descendent Tribes. And we do believe in what had been given to Moses and Jesus, and to the Prophets from their Lord. We differentiate not between any of them. And we do submit unto Him."[204]

---

203. Since the verb used here is in the plural form, the addressees of this divine command are obviously all the believers.

204. This divinely dictated Declaration of Faith, that every believer has solemnly to make, categorically proclaims the Unity of Faith. We are made to declare specifically that we do not hold any of the Prophets above the others. And yet, in practice, we do just the opposite! We hold our Prophet above the other Prophets. Just like the Jews, the Christians and the others hold their own Prophets above the others. They, of course, go to the extent of deifying their Prophets. But, alas, we are not lagging far behind them!

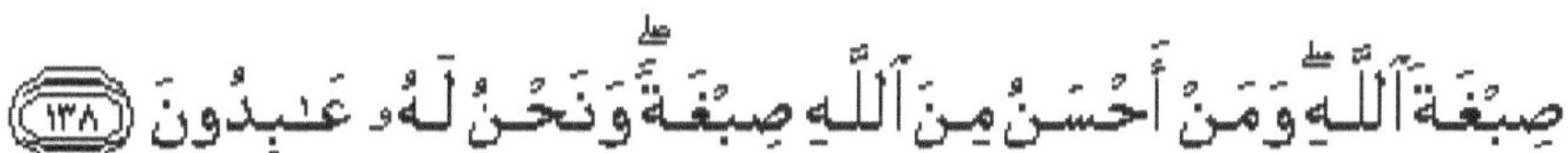

137. Fa-in amanoo bimithli ma amantum bihi faqadi ihtadaw wa-in tawallaw fa-innama hum fee shiqaqin fasayakfeekahumu Allahu wahuwa alssameeAAu alAAaleemu

2:137. If they[205] then believe in what, and in the way, you have believed[206], they certainly are on right guidance. And if they turn away, then they indeed are on the other side of the divide. Allah will suffice you against them. And He is the One Who hears all, the One Who knows all! [207]

205. That is those who wanted the believers to be Jews or Christians to be on the right path [ref: Verse 2:135].

206. Refer Verse 2:136.

207. Allah thus reassures the believers of His help in the event of any hostility on the part of those who do not believe as the believers do. We should however remember that the divine help is contingent on our strictly adhering to and abiding by the Declaration of Faith dictated to us by Allah in Verse 2:136.

138. Sibghata Allahi waman ahsanu mina Allahi sibghatan wanahnu lahu AAabidoona

2:138. Allah has done the painting! [208] And who could be better than Allah in painting? And worship Him, we[209] do!

208. Allah has done – and is, in fact, continuously re-doing – the painting on His infinitely vast canvas stretching the entire Universe. We, the creatures, are of course unable to see the full picture. But whatever parts of it we can see make us marvel at the exquisite mingling of colours to produce the breath-takingly beautiful pictures of natural sceneries. No human artist can ever hope to come even remotely near the perfection divinely executed. Our heads ought to automatically bow in recognition of and in utter submission to the Great, Inimitable Artist.

209. And who could the pronoun 'we' here, stand for? The context of this Verse and the preceding one, suggests that it is the Angels conveying the Qur'aanic Verses that 'we' refers to here. It is the Angels, moreover, who can have a better view of the infinitely large divine Painting than we, humans, and therefore can appreciate its grandeur, better. It is this better appreciation that makes them sincerely worship Allah.

139. Qul atuhajjoonana fee Allahi wahuwa rabbuna warabbukum walana aAAmaluna walakum aAAmalukum wanahnu lahu mukhlisoona

2:139. Say[210], "Do you quarrel on Allah with us? And He is our Lord as well as yours! And to us, our deeds; and to you, yours. And we do sincerely submit to Him!"

210. The context makes it obvious that this is a divine command to the Prophet to confront the Jews and the Christians with the reasoned argument that follows. It is with such cogent arguments throughout, appealing to human reason, that the Qur'aan presents the Reality to humans at large!

140. Am taqooloona inna ibraheema wa-ismaAAeela wa-ishaqa wayaAAqooba waal-asbata kanoo hoodan aw nasara qul aantum aAAlamu ami Allahu waman athlamu mimman katama shahadatan AAindahu mina Allahi wama Allahu bighafilin AAamma taAAmaloona

2:140. [211]"Or say you that Abraham, Ishmael, Isaac, Jacob and the Tribes were but Jews or Christians?" Say, "Is it you who know or is it Allah Who knows? And who can be wicked other than the one who suppresses the evidence, from Allah, that is with him?! And Allah is not unaware of what you do."[212]

211. This is in continuation of the address, to the Jews and Christians, that Allah commanded the Prophet to give (see the preceding Verse).

212. Allah nails the lie, of both the Jews and the Christians, of Abraham having been a Jew/Christian, by pointing out in Verse 3:65 that the Torah (for the Jews) and the Gospel (for the Christians) were not revealed till after he (Abraham) had passed away! And in Verse 3:67 it is reiterated that Abraham was neither a Jew nor a Christian. Like Abraham, all those others mentioned in this Verse (2:140) too had passed away before the revelation of the said divine Books. The Jews and the Christians were suppressing these facts. They were also suppressing the mention of Prophet Muhammad (peace and Allah's blessings be upon him) in their own Books, the Torah and the Gospel [Q: 7:157]!

تِلْكَ أُمَّةٌ قَدْ خَلَتْ لَهَا مَا كَسَبَتْ وَلَكُم مَّا كَسَبْتُمْ وَلَا تُسْـَٔلُونَ عَمَّا كَانُوا۟ يَعْمَلُونَ ﴿١٤١﴾

141. Tilka ommatun qad khalat laha ma kasabat walakum ma kasabtum wala tus-aloona AAamma kanoo yaAAmaloona

2:141. That was a community, now dead and gone! To it, what it earned and to you what you have earned. And you shall not be questioned on what they did! [213]

213. The contents of this Verse (2:141) could well be part of the Prophet's address to the Jews and the Christians started in Verse 2:139 and continued in Verse 2:140. But this Verse (2:141) is verbatim the same as Verse 2:134. Since Verse 2:134 is obviously addressed to the believers in the Qur'aan, the addressees of this Verse (2:141) are, no doubt, the believers as well. Please refer to Chapter Note 199 above in this regard.

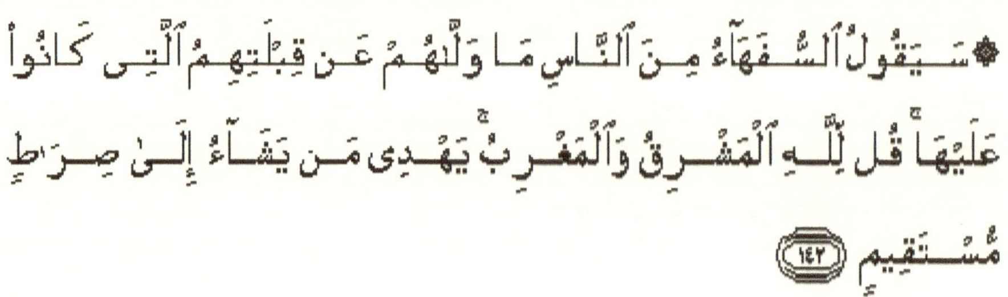

142. Sayaqoolu alssufahao mina alnnasi ma wallahum AAan qiblatihimu allatee kanoo AAalayha qul lillahi almashriqu waalmaghribu yahdee man yashao ila siratin mustaqeemin

2:142. The fools among the people will say, "What turned them from their Qiblah[214], which they had been facing?" Say, "The East and the West are all Allah's[215]. HE guides whom He wills to the Straight Path[216]!"

214. I have retained this original Arabic word in the translation, for brevity. For, there is no equivalent single word in English. Qiblah connotes a specific place on earth in the direction of which people located anywhere on the earth, are required to face while performing the formal prayers to their Creator. In Verse 2:144, *Al-Masjidil Haraam* (the Sacred Place of Worship at Makkah, the Kaabah) has been divinely designated as the Qiblah for the believers. It should be clearly and carefully understood that the Qiblah does not symbolise the Creator, the way the polytheists consider man-made idols as symbols of their gods and goddesses. The Qiblah symbolises, if anything, the unity of the entire mankind. It symbolises the common centre of the innumerable concentric circles in which the believers pray around the world to their one common Creator!

215. It is like 'the East' and 'the West' divide we speak about in politics, or even in common day-to-day talk. This division encompasses all places in the world, including those in the North and in the South. The obvious implication of this divine statement is that all places on the earth are Allah's, and He can choose any of these places as the Qiblah. It is foolish indeed of the mere creatures to question this divine right of their Creator!

216. The Straight Path is to worship Allah, the One Lord of all (Verses 3:51, 19:36). To worship Him is to obey, unquestioningly, all His commands and directions. The fools who do not obey Him, in the matter of Qiblah or in any other matter, are obviously not those whom He has guided to the Straight Path – the Path of those upon whom He has bestowed favours (refer Verse 1:7).

وَكَذَلِكَ جَعَلْنَـٰكُمْ أُمَّةً وَسَطًا لِّتَكُونُوا۟ شُهَدَآءَ عَلَى ٱلنَّاسِ وَيَكُونَ ٱلرَّسُولُ عَلَيْكُمْ شَهِيدًا وَمَا جَعَلْنَا ٱلْقِبْلَةَ ٱلَّتِى كُنتَ عَلَيْهَآ إِلَّا لِنَعْلَمَ مَن يَتَّبِعُ ٱلرَّسُولَ مِمَّن يَنقَلِبُ عَلَىٰ عَقِبَيْهِ وَإِن كَانَتْ لَكَبِيرَةً إِلَّا عَلَى ٱلَّذِينَ هَدَى ٱللَّهُ وَمَا كَانَ ٱللَّهُ لِيُضِيعَ إِيمَٰنَكُمْ إِنَّ ٱللَّهَ بِٱلنَّاسِ لَرَءُوفٌ رَّحِيمٌ ﴿١٤٣﴾

143. Waka_th_alika jaAAalna_kum ommatan wasa_t_an litakoonoo shuhada_a AAal_a_ alnn_a_si wayakoona alrrasoolu AAalaykum shaheedan wama_ jaAAaln_a_ alqiblata allatee kunta AAalayh_a_ ill_a_ linaAAlama man yattabiAAu alrrasoola mimman yanqalibu AAal_a_ AAaqibayhi wa-in kanat lakabeeratan ill_a_ AAal_a_ alla_th_eena hada_ Alla_h_u wama_ kana Alla_h_u liyudeeAAa eema_nakum inna Alla_h_a bialnn_a_si laraoofun ra_h_eemun

---

2:143. And, in like manner[217], have We made you[218] an equitably balanced focal community so that you be witnesses over mankind; and the Messenger is a witness over you. And We did not but make the Qiblah, you had been facing[219], a test to distinguish one who would obey the Messenger from the one who would turn about on one's heels. And it has been indeed hard – but not for those whom Allah has guided. And Allah is not One to let your Faith go waste. Surely, Allah is kind and merciful indeed to mankind!

---

217. That is, being guided to the Straight Path by Allah's Will. Reference here is undoubtedly to the last part of the preceding Verse.

218. The corresponding pronoun in the original Arabic text is in the 2nd person plural form. And the context tells us that the first addressees were the Companions of the Prophet. The Prophet was witness to the communication of the divine Message to the Companions and to others with whom he (the Prophet) could establish contacts in his lifetime. The Companions were the ones guided by Allah's Will, and they had truly imbibed the Message. HE therefore chose them to be witnesses in their turn to the communication of the divine Message to others whom the Prophet could not contact. And, through the Companions, Allah would breed a new group of true believers, who in their turn became the torch-bearers and witnesses. And the process would and will, inshaAllah, go on till the Last Day.

219. The Qur'aan does not specify what Qiblah the Prophet and his followers had been facing before the divine designation of *Al-Masjidil Haraam* as the one. What is certain from the context is that it was different. And for the Companions of the Prophet, who from their childhood had been accustomed to considering the Kaabah as their most sacred place, it must have naturally been very hard to accept any place other than the Kaabah as the Qiblah. It was hard even for the Prophet, as is evident from the very next Verse 2:144. But Allah was merciful, kind. The Companions passed the hard test and obediently followed the Prophet in the matter of the Qiblah.

قَدْ نَرَىٰ تَقَلُّبَ وَجْهِكَ فِى ٱلسَّمَآءِ فَلَنُوَلِّيَنَّكَ قِبْلَةً تَرْضَىٰهَا فَوَلِّ وَجْهَكَ شَطْرَ ٱلْمَسْجِدِ ٱلْحَرَامِ وَحَيْثُ مَا كُنتُمْ فَوَلُّواْ وُجُوهَكُمْ شَطْرَهُۥ وَإِنَّ ٱلَّذِينَ أُوتُواْ ٱلْكِتَٰبَ لَيَعْلَمُونَ أَنَّهُ ٱلْحَقُّ مِن رَّبِّهِمْ وَمَا ٱللَّهُ بِغَٰفِلٍ عَمَّا يَعْمَلُونَ ﴿١٤٤﴾

144. Qad nara taqalluba wajhika fee alssama-i falanuwalliyannaka qiblatan tardaha fawalli wajhaka shatra almasjidi alharami wahaythu ma kuntum fawalloo wujoohakum shatrahu wa-inna allatheena ootoo alkitaba layaAAlamoona annahu alhaqqu min rabbihim wama Allahu bighafilin AAamma yaAAmaloona

2:144. WE did observe your[220] face turning towards the sky; so, We now turn you to the Qiblah you would like to have. Turn your face then towards the Sacred Place of Worship. And wherever you be, turn your[221] faces towards it. And those on whom the Book has been bestowed know it for certain that this is the Truth from their Lord.[222] And Allah is not unaware of what they do!

220. The corresponding Arabic pronoun in the original text is in the second person singular form. It therefore obviously refers to the Prophet. And it is also obvious, from what follows in this very Verse, that the Prophet had been turning his face towards the heaven in silent prayers for making Kaabah, the Qiblah.

221. Here the Arabic pronoun is in the plural form; the addressees being all the believers around the world. This is a clear divine command. But like many other divine commands, this one too is not carefully and conscientiously adhered to. In my part of the world (India), for example, many Muslims are under the impression that it is enough to face in the general direction of the West. Not so. We are not asked to face East or West. We are asked to face a tiny place in the world: the Kaabah! So as one travels from place to place, even within India or within any other country, the Qiblah direction is bound to change after every few kilometres. We are duty-bound to ascertain the direction at every place. The kind, merciful Allah may forgive us initially at a new place, but not indefinitely.

222. As we have already seen earlier in these Studies, Verse 7:157 of the Qur'aan informs us that the prophecy about the coming of the unlettered Prophet and Messenger (Muhammad, peace and Allah's blessings be upon him) was given both in the Torah and in the Gospel. And Allah is not unaware that the Jews and the Christians conceal this fact.

وَلَبِنْ أَتَيْتَ الَّذِينَ أُوتُوا الْكِتَبَ بِكُلِّ ءَايَةٍ مَّا تَبِعُوا قِبْلَتَكَ وَمَا أَنتَ بِتَابِعٍ قِبْلَتَهُمْ وَمَا بَعْضُهُم بِتَابِعٍ قِبْلَةَ بَعْضٍ وَلَبِنِ اتَّبَعْتَ أَهْوَآءَهُم مِّنْ بَعْدِ مَا جَآءَكَ مِنَ الْعِلْمِ إِنَّكَ إِذًا لَّمِنَ الظَّلِمِينَ ﴿١٤٥﴾

145. Wala-in atayta allatheena ootoo alkitaba bikulli ayatin ma tabiAAoo qiblataka wama anta bitabiAAin qiblatahum wama baAAduhum bitabiAAin qiblata baAAdin wala-ini ittabaAAta ahwaahum min baAAdi ma jaaka mina alAAilmi innaka ithan lamina alththalimeena

---

2:145. And were you[223] to confront those to whom the Book has been bestowed[224], with all the evidence[225], they would still not follow your Qiblah[226]. Nor are you going to follow their Qiblah. Nor is any section of them going to follow the Qiblah of any other[227]. And were you to follow their desires after what has come to you of the knowledge, then, surely and certainly, you would be, in that event, one among the wrongdoers![228]

---

223. The 2nd person pronoun here, in the original Arabic text, is in the singular. Obviously therefore, the original addressee of the divine statement was Prophet Muhammad.

224. Elsewhere in the Qur'aan, such people (i.e. 'those to whom the Book has been bestowed') are also described as *ahl-il kitaab* (people of the Book). For a comprehensive understanding of this Arabic term, please go back to Chapter Notes 146 and 147 of these Studies. But in the context of this Verse (2:145), 'those to whom the Book has been bestowed' connotes the Jews and the Christians, who were the ones present at the time and place of revelation of this Verse. The Muslims were there too; but the bestowal of the Book (the Qur'aan) to them was not completed then.

225. The Arabic word used in the original divine text is *aayat*. For a comprehensive Qur'aanic meaning of this term (along with its plural form *aayaat*), please refer to Chapter Notes 150 and 151 of these Studies. The term is rendered here as 'evidence' to suit the context. The Qur'aan pointed out to the Jews and the Christians that their own revealed Books contained the evidence of Muhammad (peace and Allah's blessings be upon him) being the divinely accredited Prophet of Allah (7:157). The Verse here (2:145) hints that Books revealed to other people too contained this evidence. And even if all such evidences were presented to the Jews and the Christians, they would still not accept Muhammad as Prophet and therefore not accept the Qiblah divinely appointed for the entire mankind through this last Prophet to them. The other day, I was listening to a video cassette of a talk by Brother Zakir Naik (may Allah reward him richly for his services in the way of Allah). He was reeling off evidence after evidence of the prophecy about the coming of Prophet Muhammad, contained in the ancient Hindu Scriptures!

226. For the meaning of Qiblah, please see Chapter Note 214 of these Studies.

227. Besides denoting the direction in which to face while offering formal prayers, the Qiblah has other significances for the believers. It is the designated place of pilgrimage also for them. Visiting the place

<u>and praying there, is a duty divinely ordained for those who are in a position to undertake the journey.</u> And for performing this duty, one could expect rewards from Allah, here or in the Hereafter, at Allah's Will. But various people of various religions have their own separate places of pilgrimage (qiblahs). A place of pilgrimage that is held holy by one religious sect, does not have the same significance for another sect. A polytheist does of course have many such qiblahs, which he takes the trouble to visit and to pray there, expecting worldly gains miraculously there from. And it is sad to note that some Muslims too have also gradually gravitated to such qiblahs other than the One designated for them in the Qur'aan. A careful study of this Verse (2:145) should open their eyes against following this polytheistic practice. If we *nauzubillah* follow such misguided brethren of ours, after what has come to us of the knowledge, then, surely and certainly, we would be among the wrongdoers.

228. And these rather harsh divine words were addressed, initially, to the Prophet! The phraseology does not give any definite indication that the Prophet was in fact inclined to follow the desires of the Jews and the Christians of his time. Why then were this harsh warning to the Prophet and some other such passages critical of him personally, included in the divine Book that was meant to serve as the Guidance for all mankind till the Last Day? The guidance in such warnings is two-fold. One: the All-knowing Allah has thus driven the point home that although the Prophet was divinely chosen as the best among men, he was still, after all, a man, susceptible to error. Mankind should therefore never fall into the fatal fault of *shirk*, by elevating him to the level of Allah as did the Christians do to their Prophet, Jesus. And, two: All-wise Allah has thus provided an evidence for the believers that Prophet Muhammad, peace be upon him, had honestly conveyed the divine Message <u>in its totality</u> to us. He had not suppressed any part of it, even when it was critical of him, personally!

146. Alla<u>th</u>eena <u>a</u>tayn<u>a</u>humu alkit<u>a</u>ba yaAArifoonahu kam<u>a</u> yaAArifoona abn<u>a</u>ahum wa-inna fareeqan minhum layaktumoona al<u>h</u>aqqa wahum yaAAlamoona

2:146. And those, to whom We have given the Book, recognize it[229] as they would recognize their sons! And, surely, a group of them do indeed conceal the Truth, and they know they do!![230]

229. The 3rd person sigular pronoun here obviously stands for *Al-Masjidil-haraam* (the *Kaabah)*, divinely designated as the Qiblah in Verse 2:144 and is the core subject matter of all Verses right from 2:142 to 2:150.

230. Apparently, the evidence contained in the Jewish and the Christian Scriptures was so overwhelming that it was as easy to recognize the *Kaabah* as the right choice for the Qiblah of entire mankind, as it was easy to recognize their own sons. But it was unfortunate that their pride came in their way, and they suppressed the fact – the false pride that made them think that they were the only chosen people of God and that He could not have chosen for Prophethood anyone other than from among themselves.

147. Alhaqqu min rabbika fala takoonanna mina almumtareena

2:147. The Truth[231] from your Lord! Be not then one among those who are in doubt.[232]

231. The Truth that the *Kaabah* is the right choice from Allah for the Qiblah of entire mankind.

232. This is another instance of a divine warning to the Prophet. Please see Note 228 above.

148. Walikullin wijhatun huwa muwalleeha faistabiqoo alkhayrati aynama takoonoo ya/ti bikumu Allahu jameeAAan inna Allaha AAala kulli shay-in qadeerun

2:148. And for every direction He is its Focus[233]; compete then in doing good[234]! Wherever you are, Allah will bring you all together. Surely, Allah has power over everything!

233. In other words, whatever direction one may adopt, one must go to Allah ultimately. One may do good things in one's adopted direction and one may do bad things; but one must face Allah, in the end. And there, one will be rewarded or punished in accordance with one's deeds in the direction one takes in this world. If one's deeds are in accordance with the divine commands and directions, one will be rewarded. Otherwise, one is liable to be punished.

234. Good deeds (*al-khairaat*) are obviously deeds done in accordance with divine directions and commands.

وَمِنْ حَيْثُ خَرَجْتَ فَوَلِّ وَجْهَكَ شَطْرَ ٱلْمَسْجِدِ ٱلْحَرَامِ وَإِنَّهُۥ لَلْحَقُّ مِن رَّبِّكَ وَمَا ٱللَّهُ بِغَٰفِلٍ عَمَّا تَعْمَلُونَ ۝

149. Wamin haythu kharajta fawalli wajhaka shatra almasjidi alharami wa-innahu lalhaqqu min rabbika wama Allahu bighafilin AAamma taAAamaloona

2:149.   And turn your face, whersoever you[235] hail from, towards the Sacred Place of Worship! And it is, indeed, the Truth from your Lord. And Allah is not unaware of what you do.[236]

235. In the original Arabic text, this divine command is addressed to an individual. And from the context, it is clear, that it is addressed to every individual believer located anywhere on this earth – and in any age, till the Last Day. This command is repeated and further clarified in the next Verse 2:150.

236. In the preceding Verse 2:148, the believers were urged to vie with one another in *al-khairaat* (good deeds). Obeying the divine command contained in this Verse is one such good deed. And Allah is aware whether we do obey Him faithfully. Please see Note 221 herein above also, in this context.

وَمِنْ حَيْثُ خَرَجْتَ فَوَلِّ وَجْهَكَ شَطْرَ ٱلْمَسْجِدِ ٱلْحَرَامِ وَحَيْثُ مَا كُنتُمْ فَوَلُّوا۟ وُجُوهَكُمْ شَطْرَهُۥ لِئَلَّا يَكُونَ لِلنَّاسِ عَلَيْكُمْ حُجَّةٌ إِلَّا ٱلَّذِينَ ظَلَمُوا۟ مِنْهُمْ فَلَا تَخْشَوْهُمْ وَٱخْشَوْنِى وَلِأُتِمَّ نِعْمَتِى عَلَيْكُمْ وَلَعَلَّكُمْ تَهْتَدُونَ ۝

150. Wamin haythu kharajta fawalli wajhaka shatra almasjidi alharami wahaythu ma kuntum fawalloo wujoohakum shatrahu li-alla yakoona lilnnasi AAalaykum hujjatun illa allatheena thalamoo minhum fala takhshawhum waikhshawnee wali-otimma niAAmatee AAalaykum walaAAallakum tahtadoona

2:150. And turn your face, whersoever you hail from, towards the Sacred Place of Worship! [237] And wherever you be, turn your faces towards it, so that people – except those who have been wicked among them [238]– have no grudges against you. Fear them not then, and fear Me, so that I complete My Favour upon you, and that you become guided![239]

---

237. Please see Note 235 above.

238. By meticulously determining the Qiblah direction and by scrupulously following the divine command in this regard, a believer located anywhere on this earth sends an unmistakable signal to others of the essential unity of mankind transcending all national or racial barriers. Other people, observing this symbolic act of unity, would be inspired to feel an ungrudging admiration, although the admiration may be silent and unspoken. Only those bent on being wicked among the others shall have grudges, in any event.

239. Here's a divine mantra to enable the Muslims of today to come out of the doldrums they find themselves in. Shed the fear of all worldly forces, however powerful, which would prevent you from following the divine commands and directions. And fear Allah, Who is infinitely more powerful. Follow Him at all worldly costs. And there's no reason why you shouldn't, when He, the All-Powerful, promises that if you fear Him and abide by His commands and directions, He shall complete His Favour upon you and guide you!

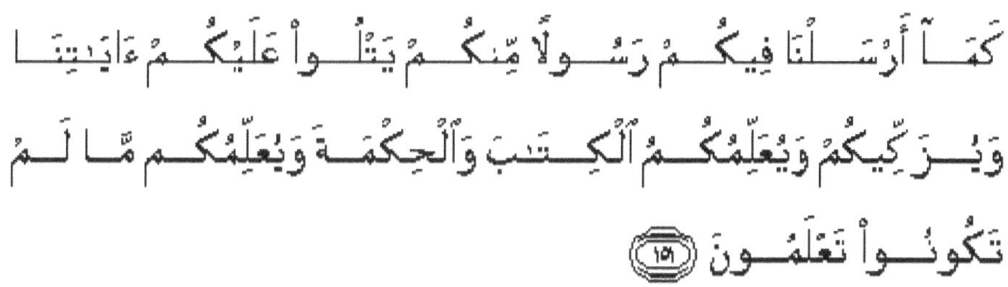

151. Kama arsalna feekum rasoolan minkum yatloo AAalaykum ayatina wayuzakkeekum wayuAAallimukumu alkitaba waalhikmata wayuAAallimukum ma lam takoonoo taAAlamoona

---

2:151. Just as[240] We sent down to you a Messenger, from among yourselves, reciting Our Verses to you, purifying you, teaching you the Book and the Wisdom[241 to 244], and teaching you what you knew not!

---

240. The Arabic conjunctive word here (*kamaaa*) connects this Verse to what is stated at the end of the preceding Verse 2:150. There, Allah directs the believers to fear Him (and not to fear wicked beings) so

that He completes His Favour upon them, and so that they become rightly guided. The sending down of the Messenger for the various tasks enumerated herein (Verse 2:151), was part of the process of completing "My Favour upon you". And the process was completed with the revelation of the last of the Qur'aanic Verses, *inter alia*, declaring, "... This day I have perfected your religion for you, <u>completed My Favour upon you</u>, and have chosen for you Islam as your religion. ..." [Q: 5:3]. And, significantly, in this last Verse (5:3) too, Allah admonishes the believers, "... fear them (the suppressors of Truth) not, but fear Me ..."

241. We have come across this word (*al-hikmata*, in Arabic), in our earlier Studies on <u>Verse 2:129</u>. Please go through Chapter Note 192 in this regard, under that Verse. We find that this word *al-hikmata* occurs in the Qur'aan more often with the word *al-kitaab* (the Book). And in Verse 17:39, where *al-hikmata* occurs unaccompanied by *al-kitaab*, the divine commands of do's and don't's given in Verses from 17:22 to 17:37, have been specifically described as *min al-hikma*, or, in other words, as some of the pearls of wisdom! Again, in Verse 43:63, where also *al-hikmata* occurs unaccompanied by *al-kitaab*, Jesus tells the Children of Israel that he has come to them, with *al-hikmati*, to explain to them some of the points in which they differed. Prophet Jesus (peace be upon him) is obviously referring here to the divine Book *Injeel* (the Gospel) bestowed upon him to sort out some differences that had cropped up among the Jews in their understanding of the provisions of the divine Book Torah revealed earlier. We can thus see that *al-kitaab*, as mentioned in the divine Book, does contain *al-hikmata*! In other words, the divine commands and directions contained in the Qur'aan are all pearls of Wisdom.

242. Why then is *al-hikmata* mentioned separately and in addition to *al-kitaab*, in the divine Book? And how come, in Verse 31:12, Allah informs us that He had granted *al-hikmata* to Luqmaan, when we know of no divine Book revealed upon him?! We thus see that although *al-kitaab* contains *al-hikmata*, the latter Arabic word is not synonymous with the former! Verse 2:269 tells us that Allah grants *al-hikmata* to whom He wills. From this Verse read with Verse 31:12, it is apparent that granting of *al-hikmata* by Allah is a continuing process, to be continued till the Last Day. But *al-kitaab* was bestowed only upon the Prophets, and Muhammad (peace be upon him) was the last of the Prophets (Verse 33:40)! From its dictionary meanings, and from the sense in which it is used in the Qur'aan, it is obvious that the word *al-hikmata* connotes the <u>Wisdom or the ability, not only to do the right things, but to do those in the right way so as to maximise the good effects of doing the right things</u>. The right things to be done, and, <u>to some extent</u>, the right way to do them, are indeed mentioned in *al-kitaab*. Therefore *al-kitaab* is *al-hikmata* too! But the right way often depends on the situation in which the right thing is to be done! And all the innumerably different situations, which can arise, cannot possibly be recorded in a written book. *Al-hikmata* is also therefore the intuition that one may get, at the spur of the moment, for the way in which to do the right thing on that particular occasion. The All-knowing Allah has therefore wisely mentioned *al-hikmata* separately and in addition to *al-kitaab*, in His Book!

244[number 243 missed by mistake]. In Verse 4:113, Allah reminds the Prophet that it is He Who has bestowed *al-kitaab* and *al-hikmata* on him and taught him what he knew not. In the present Verse 2:151, Allah reminds the believers that the Prophet, in turn, teaches them *al-kitaab* and *al-hikmata*. *Al-hikmata*, that *al-kitaab* contains within itself, got taught along with *al-kitaab*. Besides, the Prophet demonstrated, by personal example, how superbly he handled very difficult situations that arose throughout his life. He handled those situations so superbly that even a Christian writer of our present generation was obliged to rank him (Prophet Muhammad) the first among all leaders of men, of all times that the world has ever had till now! It was the use of this Allah-given intuitive part of *al-hikmata* that helped the Prophet handle those situations. It was the use of the same intuitive part that made David and Solomon, two of the other great leaders. It is this intuitive part of *al-hikmata* that Allah continues to bestow, and will continue to bestow till the Last Day, upon whom He wills, that makes some persons great as thinkers, statesmen, scientists or leaders in other fields!

152. Fao_th_kuroonee a_th_kurkum waoshkuroo lee wal_a_ takfurooni

2:152. Keep Me in your rememberance, then; so I keep guiding you. And be grateful to Me, and suppress not the Truth! [245]

245. Remember that this Verse, as the previous one, was addressed to the believers (refer Note 240 above). And remember that although the believers at the time of the revelation of the Qur'aan were the initial addressees, the Qur'aanic Message is for all times till the Last Day. The believers of the present age are, therefore, the addressees too! Looking at the Verse in this light, then, we see that Allah is drawing our attention to the fact that we generally do not remember Him (let alone being genuinely grateful to Him for completing His Favour, in the form of the completed Qur'aan, upon us) in our day-to-day worldly activities. Yes, some of us do go mechanically through our daily prayers, but while praying too, our minds are busy thinking about our worldly affairs! No wonder then that we now are bereft of divine guidance. And, doesn't such failure to remember Him, betray our lack of Faith? Save us, Allah!

153. Y_a_ ayyuh_a_ alla_th_eena _a_manoo istaAAeenoo bial_ss_abri waal_ss_al_a_ti inna All_a_ha maAAa al_ss_abireena

2:153. O you who believe! Seek help with patience and prayer. Certainly, Allah is with those who are patient! [246]

246. Allah does certainly not promise a bed of roses for the believers in this world. In order that they enjoy the Utopia in the Hereafter, they must go through a test by fire, so to say, in this life! Only two Verses later, in Verse 2:155, Allah tells us that we will be tested with fear, hunger and with losses in property, life and produce! And He asks us to seek His help with prayers, while on trial in this world, but that we shouldn't expect an immediate reward. We must wait patiently for it. Life on earth is indeed a severe test of our Faith! But happiness is a state of mind. We can be happy even in the most trying circumstances, if our Faith is so strong as to make us certain that our very Creator and Lord is with us.

وَلَا تَقُولُوا لِمَن يُقْتَلُ فِى سَبِيلِ ٱللَّهِ أَمْوَٰتٌ بَلْ أَحْيَآءٌ وَلَـٰكِن لَّا تَشْعُرُونَ

154. Wala taqooloo liman yuqtalu fee sabeeli Allahi amwatun bal ahyaon walakin la tashAAuroona

---

2:154. And say not unto those who are killed, in Allah's Path, as dead. Nay! They are alive, but you perceive not.[247 to 249]

---

247. It's one of the observed hard truths about life on this earth, that good work done in Allah's Path doesn't often get recompensed here. People have died, or have been killed, while struggling to traverse steadfastly on that Path. Seeing this happen, many of the others have fled from that Path. Should we follow suit? Allah has given us the freedom of choice. And if we follow suit, exercising that freedom, what would we get? Maybe, we would get some worldly wealth, and some worldly position. But at what cost? At the price of our abandoning good things like honesty, fair play, justice, truth et al. And even if we bid goodbye to such good things, are we sure that we would get the worldly pelf and position? Not at all! Worldly life is very uncertain. Today we set about getting the world by fair means or foul, and tomorrow (who knows?) we may die! And who knows what's on the other side of the divide? Maybe, what these religious people say will come true. What if, because of our abandoning belief in Allah and in the Hereafter, we may be put into that Hell-fire they talk about, to suffer there forever!!

248. If only we would think rationally thus, Brothers and Sisters, there is no real alternative to Allah's Path! Although Allah has given us the freedom of choice, it's a choice between certainty or uncertainty, salvation or doom. So, come! Let us be certain in our belief in Allah, and in what He tells us. HE tells us here not to consider those killed in His Path as dead. Let us have absolute belief in this, although we are not capable of understanding the divine statement. Being mere creatures, we do not understand many things. But our Lord, the absolute Creator, knows everything. So, let's believe Him, for our own good!

249. In Verse 3:169 and in Verses immediately following that Verse, we are further informed that the martyrs in Allah's Path receive provisions from Allah and that they rejoice in Allah's bounties! Allah tells us there, that He shall not let the supreme sacrifice of such believers go waste. It is thus apparent that the martyrs shall enjoy a pleasant continuity of consciousness even immediately after the end of their worldly lives. Unlike others, who shall be in a state of unconsciousness extending to even thousands of years, till they are resurrected in the Hereafter! That is an additional divine reward for the martyrs.

وَلَنَبْلُوَنَّكُم بِشَىْءٍ مِّنَ ٱلْخَوْفِ وَٱلْجُوعِ وَنَقْصٍ مِّنَ ٱلْأَمْوَٰلِ
وَٱلْأَنفُسِ وَٱلثَّمَرَٰتِ وَبَشِّرِ ٱلصَّـٰبِرِينَ

155. Walanabluwannakum bishay-in mina alkhawfi waaljooAAi wanaqsin mina al-amwali waal-anfusi waalththamarati wabashshiri alssabireena

2:155. And, certainly, We shall test you with something of the fear and the hunger, and with the loss in wealth, life and production. And gladden those who are patient, with the prophecy of good future.[250]

250. Recall Verse 2:153 and the corresponding Note 246 in this context. And let me hasten to add that the prophecy of good future need not necessarily be in the Hereafter only. It could come true in this earthly life as well. The Qur'aan says, "... seek forgiveness of your Lord, and turn to Him in repentance, that He may grant you good provision, for a term appointed, ..." [11:3, emphasis added] The phrase of the Verse, that is underlined here, doubtlessly indicates that the good future promised in the present Verse (2:155), could be in this very worldly life also.

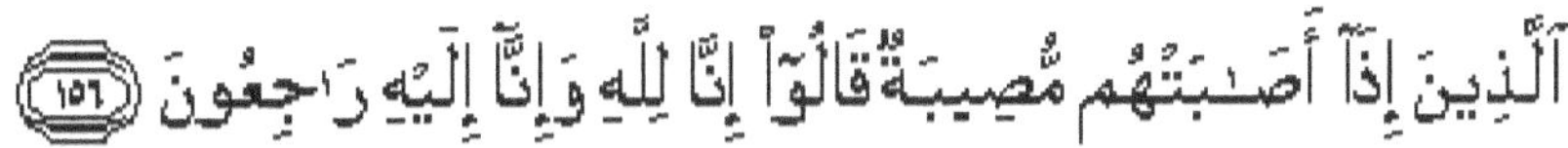

156. Allatheena itha asabat-hum museebatun qaloo inna lillahi wa-inna ilayhi rajiAAoona

2:156. Those who, when any adversity confronts them, say, "We do indeed belong to Allah; and indeed, are we to return to Him!"[251]

251. This Verse, so to say, constitutes the Qur'aanic definition of *as-saabireen* (those who are patient), mentioned in the preceding Verse 2:155. It needs no explaining that mere mechanical repetition of the quote in this Verse (2:156), as if it were a mantra, would not make people, *as-saabireen*. People, uttering the quote, must know consciously – and sincerely mean – what they say!

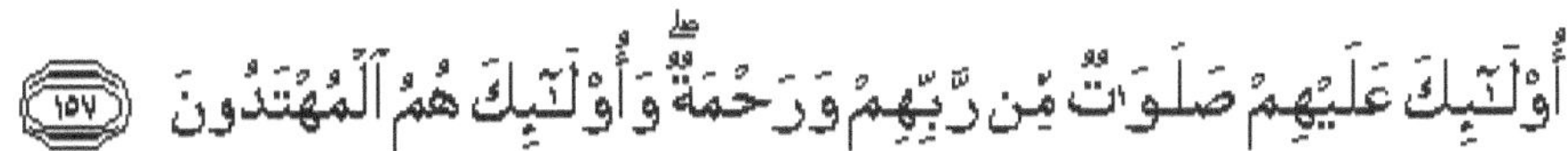

157. Ola-ika AAalayhim salawatun min rabbihim warahmatun waola-ika humu almuhtadoona

2:157. Those are the ones upon whom are blessings from their Lord and His grace; and those are the ones that are rightly guided! [252 & 253]

---

252. In the short group of four Verses, from 2:153 to 2:156 herein above, Allah Ta'ala has laid down a plain course of action – a course of action for the Muslims of today, the course of action that could lead them out of the morass of degeneration, degradation and deprivation that they find themselves in. And, in this Verse 2:157, none other than the Creator and Lord of everyone and everything guarantees the salvation of those who follow the course devoutly. But do we have the necessary faith in Him and in His Book??

253. In this context, I am reminded of a story doing the rounds on the Internet: on a pitch-dark and freezingly cold night, a mountaineer slipped and found himself hanging by the life-saving rope tied around his waist. He couldn't see anything in the darkness. In that state, he called out to God to save him. God asked him whether he would follow His instruction. When the mountaineer said he would, God asked him to cut the rope he was hanging by. But the mountaineer had doubts. How could he cut himself off the rope that provided him the slender hope of survival? A couple of days later, a rescue team found the mountaineer. His frozen hands were still clutching the rope he was hanging by. And his dead body was hardly 10 feet above a soft, level ground below!!

إِنَّ ٱلصَّفَا وَٱلْمَرْوَةَ مِن شَعَآئِرِ ٱللَّهِ فَمَنْ حَجَّ ٱلْبَيْتَ أَوِ ٱعْتَمَرَ فَلَا جُنَاحَ عَلَيْهِ أَن يَطَّوَّفَ بِهِمَا وَمَن تَطَوَّعَ خَيْرًا فَإِنَّ ٱللَّهَ شَاكِرٌ عَلِيمٌ ۝١٥٨

158. Inna alssafa waalmarwata min shaAAa-iri Allahi faman hajja albayta awi iAAtamara fala junaha AAalayhi an yattawwafa bihima waman tatawwaAAa khayran fa-inna Allaha shakirun AAaleemun

---

2:158. Indeed, the *Suafaa*[254] and the *Marwah*[254] are among Allah's Symbols[255]. So, whosoever undertakes a pilgrimage to the House[256] or does visit it, there is no sin[257] upon him/her in going to and fro between the two. And when anyone willingly follows anything good, Allah is indeed appreciative, knowing!

---

254. Muslims and others, conversant with the religious rituals performed during the pilgrimage to Makkah, know that the *Suafaa* and the *Marwah* are two spots near the *Kaabah* there.

255. Allah's Symbols (*sha'uaaair*) are symbols associated with rituals symbolising submission to His Will. It was in submission to His Will that Prophet Abraham had made some of his progeny to settle at the site (refer Verses 14:37 and 22:26). Verse 5:2 prohibits violation of Allah's *sha'uaaair*.

256. Please see <u>Chapter Note 180</u> of these Studies.

257. One may wonder, "Where's the question of a sin here?" There is indeed no question of any 'sin' here! The symbolic act (known as *Sayee*) of going to and fro between the *Suafaa* and the *Marwah* is, on the other hand, very much appreciated by Allah, as can be seen from the ending part of this Verse (2:158). A little reflection would however make it obvious that the *Sayee* was in practice, among the Arabs, even before the advent of Islam among them. And, the neo-Muslims must have initially feared that it would be a sin to continue with the practice of the *jahiliya* period. To allay that fear, Allah assured the Muslims that doing the *Sayee* was not a sin.

$$\text{إِنَّ ٱلَّذِينَ يَكْتُمُونَ مَآ أَنزَلْنَا مِنَ ٱلْبَيِّنَـٰتِ وَٱلْهُدَىٰ مِنۢ بَعْدِ مَا}$$

$$\text{بَيَّنَّـٰهُ لِلنَّاسِ فِى ٱلْكِتَـٰبِ أُو۟لَـٰٓئِكَ يَلْعَنُهُمُ ٱللَّهُ وَيَلْعَنُهُمُ ٱللَّـٰعِنُونَ ﴿١٥٩﴾}$$

159. Inna allatheena yaktumoona ma anzalna mina albayyinati waalhuda min baAAdi ma bayyannahu lilnnasi fee alkitabi ola-ika yalAAanuhumu Allahu wayalAAanuhumu allaAAinoona

---

2:159. Indeed, those who hide what We sent down of the evidences and guidance – even after the clarifications We gave thereof in the Book for mankind – those are the ones whom Allah curses and whom the curse-invokers curse.[258]

---

258. This Verse applies to all peoples on whom divine Books have been bestowed. It applies to the Jews and the Christians for what they have hidden from the divine Books – Torah and the *Injeel* (Gospel) – bestowed upon them. And it applies to the Muslims as well! The Qur'aanic Message, in original Arabic, is of course divinely protected; but the meanings of some passages therein are sought to be changed based on external sources that are man-made and man-influenced. As reiterated here in this Verse (2:159) – and as reiterated in several other passages throughout the Qur'aan – the divine Book itself contains sufficient clarifications for mankind. The divine curse is on those who ignore this oft-repeated divine reiteration. The curse on the Muslims, generally, is all too evident in today's world. As for the 'curse-invokers' mentioned in the Verse (2:159), these could be the Angels and human beings, who are adversely affected by the injustices generated by the twisting of the meanings of the divine Verses.

$$\text{إِلَّا ٱلَّذِينَ تَابُوا۟ وَأَصْلَحُوا۟ وَبَيَّنُوا۟ فَأُو۟لَـٰٓئِكَ أَتُوبُ عَلَيْهِمْ وَأَنَا ٱلتَّوَّابُ}$$

$$\text{ٱلرَّحِيمُ ﴿١٦٠﴾}$$

160. Illa allatheena taboo waaslahoo wabayyanoo faola-ika atoobu AAalayhim waana alttawwabu alrraheemu

2:160. Except for those who repent and reform and make themselves transparent. Those are the ones upon whom I bestow forgiveness. And forgiving and merciful, I am! [259]

259. But in this Verse (2:160) lies some hope for the Muslims, and others. If they could only repent and reform and make themselves transparent in all their dealings!!

$$\text{إِنَّ ٱلَّذِينَ كَفَرُواْ وَمَاتُواْ وَهُمْ كُفَّارٌ أُوْلَٰٓئِكَ عَلَيْهِمْ لَعْنَةُ ٱللَّهِ وَٱلْمَلَٰٓئِكَةِ وَٱلنَّاسِ أَجْمَعِينَ ﴿١٦١﴾}$$

161. Inna allatheena kafaroo wamatoo wahum kuffarun ola-ika AAalayhim laAAnatu Allahi waalmala-ikati waalnnasi ajmaAAeena

2:161. Indeed, those who suppressed the Truth and died while in that state of suppressing the Truth - upon those is curse of Allah, combined with that of the Angels and of mankind. [260]

260. The Almighty Allah is kind. HE gives opportunities galore to the suppressors of Truth to mend their illogical, unjust and destructive attitude. But if they maintain this attitude till the very end of their spans of life on this earth, He withdraws His grace from them. They are disgraced! *That* **is Allah's curse upon them. The Angels curse them, because they are witnesses to the suppressors' wanton rejection of divinely given opportunities. And mankind curses the suppressors, because every act of suppression of Truth, contributes to chaos and anarchy in this world.**

$$\text{خَٰلِدِينَ فِيهَا لَا يُخَفَّفُ عَنْهُمُ ٱلْعَذَابُ وَلَا هُمْ يُنظَرُونَ ﴿١٦٢﴾}$$

162. Khalideena feeha la yukhaffafu AAanhumu alAAathabu wala hum yuntharoona

2:162. [261]They shall abide therein[262]. They shall get neither relief nor respite from the punishment.

261. This Verse is in continuation from the preceding Verse, and the pronoun 'They' here stands for 'the suppressors of Truth'.

262. In the 'curse' referred to in the preceding Verse, that is. Obviously, because of this curse, the suppressors of Truth land themselves, in the Hereafter, in Hell-fire.

وَإِلَـٰهُكُمْ إِلَـٰهٌ وَاحِدٌ لَّا إِلَـٰهَ إِلَّا هُوَ ٱلرَّحْمَـٰنُ ٱلرَّحِيمُ ﴿١٦٣﴾

163. Wa-ilahukum ilahun wahidun la ilaha illa huwa alrrahmanu alrraheemu

2:163. And the Being worthy of your worship is the One, and Only! None is worthy of worship other than He, the Gracious, the Merciful.[263]

263. Allah, as we Muslims know, is the One and Only Being worthy of worship (*Ilaah*). 'Worship' connotes unquestioned obedience. We worship Allah if, and only if, we obey all His commands given in the Qur'aan. But we need to introspect, deeply and sincerely, whether we really do so. We need to introspect whether we do not have *ilaahs*, other than Allah, in the form of our own carnal desires and in the forms of other forces, human or otherwise, imagined or real, in the influence of which we often do things contrary to divine commands.

إِنَّ فِى خَلْقِ ٱلسَّمَـٰوَٰتِ وَٱلْأَرْضِ وَٱخْتِلَـٰفِ ٱلَّيْلِ وَٱلنَّهَارِ وَٱلْفُلْكِ ٱلَّتِى تَجْرِى فِى ٱلْبَحْرِ بِمَا يَنفَعُ ٱلنَّاسَ وَمَآ أَنزَلَ ٱللَّهُ مِنَ ٱلسَّمَآءِ مِن مَّآءٍ فَأَحْيَا بِهِ ٱلْأَرْضَ بَعْدَ مَوْتِهَا وَبَثَّ فِيهَا مِن كُلِّ دَآبَّةٍ وَتَصْرِيفِ ٱلرِّيَـٰحِ وَٱلسَّحَابِ ٱلْمُسَخَّرِ بَيْنَ ٱلسَّمَآءِ وَٱلْأَرْضِ لَآيَـٰتٍ لِّقَوْمٍ يَعْقِلُونَ ﴿١٦٤﴾

164. Inna fee khalqi alssamawati waal-ardi waikhtilafi allayli waalnnahari waalfulki allatee tajree fee albahri bima yanfaAAu alnnasa wama anzala Allahu mina alssama-i min ma-in faahya bihi al-arda baAAda mawtiha wabaththa feeha min kulli dabbatin watasreefi alrriyahi waalssahabi almusakhkhari bayna alssama-i waal-ardi laayatin liqawmin yaAAqiloona

---

2:164. Indeed, in the creation of the heavens and the earth, in the contrast between the day and the night, in the ship that sails on the sea with things beneficial to mankind, in what Allah sends down of water from the sky bringing the earth back to life after it was dead, in every kind of animals dispersed therein, in the winds changing their directions, and in the clouds under divine control between the sky and the earth, are compelling signs for people who make use of their intelligence.[264 to 268]

---

264. A study of the Qur'aan reveals that the Messengers, who came before Muhammad (peace be upon him and upon them all), were given some extraordinary signs to convince people of the existence of an absolute solitary Power controlling the entire Universe and to convince them of the Messengers being the really authorised ones from that Power. The earlier Messengers came when the level of general knowledge among the people was low. Their (people's) knowledge therefore needed to be supplemented by divinely given 'miracles'. But the last Messenger, Muhammad, came at the threshold of an era in which human knowledge would proliferate. The proliferation of human knowledge, combined with the divinely endowed human intelligence, became enough for people to recognise the Absolute Solitary Power. The supplement of 'miracles' was no more needed. The people are now able to recognize the Power from the signs that abound in Nature.

265. This divine exhortation made in this Verse for study of Natural phenomena, moreover, imbibed the scientific spirit, of reason and research, in the minds of the believers. Consequently, many thinkers in various fields like medicine, mathematics, physics, astronomy, literature etc. arose in the Muslim world, who were instrumental in laying the foundation of the scientific renaissance that the world is witnessing today. It was from the works of those great Muslim scientists and thinkers of the middle Ages that the Western world got the basics to develop from. And it makes one sad to think that while the Westerners built the scientific edifice of the modern world on the foundation laid by the Muslims, the Muslim world itself lost the scientific spirit with the weakening of their Faith in the Qur'aan!

266. 'The creation of the heavens and the earth' is the first *Aayat* (Sign) referred to in this divine Verse. And we have already seen in Chapter Notes 20 and 21 how the seven layers of the earth's atmosphere have been meticulously and correctly designed to act as a protective shield and a provider of sustenance for all living creatures on the earth. Only an unreasonable fool would dismiss this wonderfully exquisite arrangement as a mere accident of nature. And then we have this mind-boggling spectacle of innumerable heavenly bodies floating in their respective orbits with such mathematical precision that they never bump into one another accidentally. We cannot but marvel at the Power Who no doubt made all this possible – consciously and purposefully. It would be irrational and unscientific for anyone to think of it as a mere accident in nature.

267. About the other Signs mentioned in the Verse, the night, following the day in every 24-hour cycle in time, is an obvious provision made for rest, without which human life is impossible to be sustained. Further, had it not been for the facility of navigation by sea, transport of tonnes and tonnes of merchandise from one part of the world to another wouldn't have been easy. Had it not been for the periodic rains, there wouldn't be the recurring stock of vegetable products necessary for sustenance of any kind of life on earth. One who ponders deeply can easily detect that some Extraordinarily Intelligent Power is guiding the directions of the cloud-bearing winds to bring rains to regions, as desired by that

Manzil I: 2: Baqarah

Unseen Power. The sprouting of vegetation on dry earth after a rainfall, moreover, provides an indication that human life could likewise be resurrected even after death.

268. With my limited knowledge, I have barely touched on the immense significance of the Signs mentioned in this Verse. Persons with adequate knowledge and resources could write volumes and volumes on the significance – and on the sciences – of these Signs. All these Signs, however, unmistakably point to the Hidden Hand of the Supremely Super Power.

وَمِنَ ٱلنَّاسِ مَن يَتَّخِذُ مِن دُونِ ٱللَّهِ أَندَادًا يُحِبُّونَهُمْ كَحُبِّ ٱللَّهِ وَٱلَّذِينَ ءَامَنُوٓا۟ أَشَدُّ حُبًّا لِّلَّهِ وَلَوْ يَرَى ٱلَّذِينَ ظَلَمُوٓا۟ إِذْ يَرَوْنَ ٱلْعَذَابَ أَنَّ ٱلْقُوَّةَ لِلَّهِ جَمِيعًا وَأَنَّ ٱللَّهَ شَدِيدُ ٱلْعَذَابِ ﴿١٦٥﴾

165. Wamina alnnasi man yattakhithu min dooni Allahi andadan yuhibboonahum kahubbi Allahi waallatheena amanoo ashaddu hubban lillahi walaw yara allatheena thalamoo ith yarawna alAAathaba anna alquwwata lillahi jameeAAan waanna Allaha shadeedu alAAathabi

---

2:165. And, among humans, there are those who take to deserters, besides Allah. They love the deserters like they love Allah. And those who believe do love Allah the most. And if only the wicked persons could see – as they would, when they see the punishment – that absolute power rests with Allah, and that Allah is severe in giving punishment![269 to 271]

---

269. The word 'deserters', in the translation, is used for the Arabic *andaad* in the original. The Arabic word literally means those who run away from or desert established rule or authority. In the context here, it means those who have strayed away wantonly, from divine Authority or divine Path, *a la* the Satan.

270. And the Satan has his counterparts among human beings. And the greatest among these human counterparts could be the individual's own self. One is indeed in love with one's own self. And one's own self could well be guilty of straying away from the divine Path, under the influence of one's own carnal desires. One's own kith and kin, whom one loves, could as well be the other human 'deserters'. Allah warns us against our love for such deserters getting the better of – nay, even equal to – our love for Him.

271. The deserters, and those whose love for them is equal to or more than their love for Allah, are both called *al ladheena zhalamu* (oppressors, wrong-doers or the wicked people); for, through their deeds, they are suppressing the Truth. And the Truth is that all power rests with Allah, the Sole Creator of us all. HE has been Gracious and Kind enough to sustain us and thoroughly guide us, through divine Books, His Messengers, natural phenomena and human intelligence, to that Truth. And if we still disobey His commands and love Him not the most, we do indeed deserve to be punished – and punished severely!

إِذْ تَبَرَّأَ ٱلَّذِينَ ٱتُّبِعُوا۟ مِنَ ٱلَّذِينَ ٱتَّبَعُوا۟ وَرَأَوُا۟ ٱلْعَذَابَ وَتَقَطَّعَتْ بِهِمُ ٱلْأَسْبَابُ ﴿١٦٦﴾

166. I<u>th</u> tabarraa alla<u>th</u>eena ittubiAAoo mina alla<u>th</u>eena ittabaAAoo waraawoo alAAa<u>th</u>aba wataqatta<u>AA</u>at bihimu al-asb<u>a</u>bu

2:166. When those who were followed disown their followers, and they see the punishment, and their mutual relations are torn asunder!![272]

272. This Verse and the one succeeding (2:167) are in continuation of the preceding Verse (2:165). These two Verses (2:166 and 2:167) further describe what would happen when the wicked people would come to see the punishment as mentioned in Verse 2:165. People who <u>blindly</u> follow others in this world would realise that those whom they followed forsake them in the Hereafter. Herein is an important lesson for us: we should not blindly follow whatever our leaders, in religious or other matters, tell us. We should check whatever the leaders tell us, with the Qur'aan and our own consciences, in terms of the divine law of jurisprudence enunciated in Qr'aanic Verse 4:59. We may come to grief and fruitless regrets otherwise and find no escape from the torment of everlasting punishment, as is made clear in the next Verse 2:167.

وَقَالَ ٱلَّذِينَ ٱتَّبَعُوا۟ لَوْ أَنَّ لَنَا كَرَّةً فَنَتَبَرَّأَ مِنْهُمْ كَمَا تَبَرَّءُوا۟ مِنَّا كَذَٰلِكَ يُرِيهِمُ ٱللَّهُ أَعْمَٰلَهُمْ حَسَرَٰتٍ عَلَيْهِمْ وَمَا هُم بِخَٰرِجِينَ مِنَ ٱلنَّارِ ﴿١٦٧﴾

167. Waqala alla<u>th</u>eena ittabaAAoo law anna lan<u>a</u> karratan fanatabarraa minhum kam<u>a</u> tabarraoo minn<u>a</u> ka<u>th</u>alika yureehimu All<u>a</u>hu aAAm<u>a</u>lahum <u>h</u>asar<u>a</u>tin AAalayhim wam<u>a</u> hum bikh<u>a</u>rijeena mina alnn<u>a</u>ri

2:167. And the followers would say, "If only we would have a return, we would disown them as they have disowned us." Thus, shall Allah show them their deeds as anguishes upon them themselves. And there shall be no exit for them from the Fire!!!

$$\text{يَـٰٓأَيُّهَا ٱلنَّاسُ كُلُوا۟ مِمَّا فِى ٱلْأَرْضِ حَلَـٰلًا طَيِّبًا وَلَا تَتَّبِعُوا۟ خُطُوَٰتِ ٱلشَّيْطَـٰنِ ۚ إِنَّهُۥ لَكُمْ عَدُوٌّ مُّبِينٌ ۝}$$

168. Ya ayyuha alnnasu kuloo mimma fee al-ardi halalan tayyiban wala tattabiAAoo khutuwati alshshaytani innahu lakum AAaduwwun mubeenun

---

2:168. O mankind! Consume of that which is lawful and wholesome on the earth and follow not the Satan's footsteps. Indeed, he is to you an open enemy.[273, 274]

---

273. Further down, in Verses 2:172 and 2:173, the Qur'aan urges the believers to consume (eat) food items that are wholesome and specifies particular items that are divinely forbidden. But in this Verse (2:168), there is a general admonition for all mankind to have only lawful and wholesome things (not necessarily restricted to eatables) for their own general use. As indicated in the next Verse 2:169, indulging in evil and lewd acts and attributing, without having proper knowledge, anything to Allah, would not be among things that are lawful and wholesome.

274. About Satan and his open enmity towards mankind, please refer to Verse 2:34 and Chapter Notes 29 and 30 as well as to Verse 2:36 and the corresponding Notes 33 to 35. In Verse 4:119, the Satan is quoted as defiantly and openly declaring "...I will mislead them..." concerning some of Allah's human creatures. The Qur'aan tells us elsewhere: "And whenever your Lord has brought forth from Adam's children – from their loins – their offspring, He has asked them to testify upon the evidence of their own selves, 'Am I not your Lord?' and they have said, 'Yes, we do testify!' Lest you should say on the Day of Resurrection, 'We were indeed unaware of this.' Or, lest you should say, 'Our forefathers had indeed assigned partners to You before, and we were but the offspring following them. Would You then destroy us for what those others indulging in falsehood did?' And thus, do We explain the Verses/signs in detail, and so that they revert." [Q: 7:172 to 174] And in Verse 4:107, the Qur'aan says, "And argue not on behalf of those who deceive themselves. Allah indeed loves not those who sinfully betray their trust." From these divine Verses it should be abundantly clear that the truth about the existence of the Almighty Creator is ingrained in what we call the conscience of every human being at his/her very birth!

$$\text{إِنَّمَا يَأْمُرُكُم بِٱلسُّوٓءِ وَٱلْفَحْشَآءِ وَأَن تَقُولُوا۟ عَلَى ٱللَّهِ مَا لَا تَعْلَمُونَ}$$

169. Innama ya/murukum bialssoo-i waalfahsha-i waan taqooloo AAala Allahi ma la taAAlamoona

---

2:169. He bids you to do nothing but the evil and that which is lewd, and to attribute to Allah what you know not! [275 to 277]

---

275. There are many evil things that mankind enacts, with behind-the-scene promptings from the Satan. *Ar-Riba* is one such thing. This Qur'aanic term, in terms of Verse 30.39, may be defined as the increase in one's wealth, fraudulently sought to be made by usurping other people's properties, dues or earnings. It is this economic ill or corruption that is rampantly prevalent today, and more so among Muslims! The Muslim religious leadership generally does not tire of declaring from their housetops that *Ar-Riba* is 'haraam' 'haraam', while some of them at least may be blissfully ignorant of *Ar-Riba* growing luxuriantly in their own backyards!!

276. The Satan may not have to exert much in prompting mankind to lewdness or obscenity. The propensity thereto is inherent in its (mankind's) nature. It is by conscious effort that this propensity must be curbed. Otherwise, mankind can easily degenerate to a status lower than that of other animals. If my information is correct, it was this lure of easy and passion-pandering life in the end, that cost the Muslims their earlier centuries-old magnificent rule in Spain.

277. And the Satan employs this ruse of making man attribute falsehoods to Allah. For example, despite repeated divine assertions in the Qur'aan, that the divine commands therein, for mankind to follow, are well-explained for easy understanding, I am astonished at some of the eminent Muslim scholars even, disbelieving in this divine assertion and saying that some of the Qur'aanic terms like *Ar-Riba* are not explained in the Qur'aan! Apparently, they are unable to see the explanation inherent in Verse 30:39 (please refer Note 275 above). They have therefore come up with their own man-made explanation that *Ar-Riba* is interest charged on money lent or borrowed. And they have decreed that banking business is *haraam!* Clearly alluding to such a human decree, the Qur'aan says, in Verse 2:275, that some people declare, under satanic influence, business to be like *Ar-Riba*. The Qur'aan then asserts emphatically that Allah has made business lawful, and *Ar-Riba* unlawful.

وَإِذَا قِيلَ لَهُمُ ٱتَّبِعُوا مَآ أَنزَلَ ٱللَّهُ قَالُوا بَلْ نَتَّبِعُ مَآ أَلْفَيْنَا عَلَيْهِ ءَابَآءَنَآ أَوَلَوْ كَانَ ءَابَآؤُهُمْ لَا يَعْقِلُونَ شَيْـًٔا وَلَا يَهْتَدُونَ ﴿١٧٠﴾

170. Wa-itha qeela lahumu ittabiAAoo ma anzala Allahu qaloo bal nattabiAAu ma alfayna AAalayhi abaana awa law kana abaohum la yaAAqiloona shay-an wala yahtadoona

---

2:170. And when they are asked to follow what Allah has sent down, they say, "But we follow what we found our forefathers doing." Even if their forefathers had understood nothing, nor had they been guided!?[278]

---

278. This loaded question, divinely posed over 1400 years ago, is still valid for people today, including most Muslims! Even though the Muslims have with them the divinely protected Qur'aan, they hardly refer to this invaluable Book of guidance, and choose instead to follow what they have found their forefathers doing. So, they call dead saints to their aid in worldly matters and visit their graves, even though the Qur'aan categorically tells them that such acts of *shirk* would be unpardonable sins [Q: 4:116].

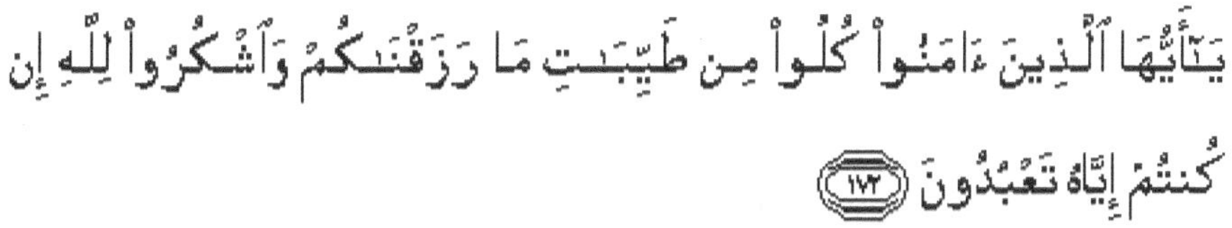

171. Wamathalu alla<u>th</u>eena kafaroo kamathali alla<u>th</u>ee yanAAiqu bim<u>a</u> l<u>a</u> yasmaAAu ill<u>a</u> duAA<u>a</u>an wanid<u>a</u>an <u>s</u>ummun bukmun AAumyun fahum l<u>a</u> yaAAqiloon<u>a</u>

2:171. And the situation of those who suppress the Truth is like the situation wherein someone gives a call to another who hears it not but as some inarticulate cry and sound. Being deaf, dumb and blind, they understand not! [279]

279. Compare this Verse 2:171 with <u>Verses 2:17 and 2:18</u>. There, the All-knowing Allah gives an example of someone kindling a fire to enlighten the environs. The obvious reference is to Prophet Muhammad (peace and Allah's blessings be upon him) through whom Allah has sent the light of His Message. But because of their wilful suppression of Truth, the wicked people had their capacity to see snatched away from them, and they could not take advantage of the divine light. Here, in Verse 2:171, the same situation is explained in a different way. Because of their suppression of Truth, the wicked people had their power of understanding snatched away. So, they could not understand the Prophet's call to them to accept Islam. The Prophet's call was a meaningless cacophony of sound beats to them.

172. Y<u>a</u> ayyuh<u>a</u> alla<u>th</u>eena <u>a</u>manoo kuloo min <u>t</u>ayyib<u>a</u>ti m<u>a</u> razaqn<u>a</u>kum waoshkuroo lill<u>a</u>hi in kuntum iyy<u>a</u>hu taAAbudoon<u>a</u>

2:172. O you who believe! Eat of good, clean and wholesome food We have provided you with. And be grateful to Allah, if Him it is you worship.[280]

---

280. Please refer in this context <u>Verse 2:168, and Note 273 thereon</u>. And, good, clean and wholesome (*tuayyibaat*) food is obviously that which promotes physical, mental and moral health. A little reflection should convince any believer that the Creator has not only created all the creatures but has also made adequate provisions for their sustenance. To name just one among countless such provisions is the wonderful phenomenon of the water cycle in Nature. But for the rains, most creatures would starve to death. And, despite all the technological progress, failure of rainfall in even a single year could ruin the economy of most countries. Believers would therefore be failing in their duty, if they do not feel sincerely grateful to their Lord for all the elaborate arrangements He has made for their sustenance.

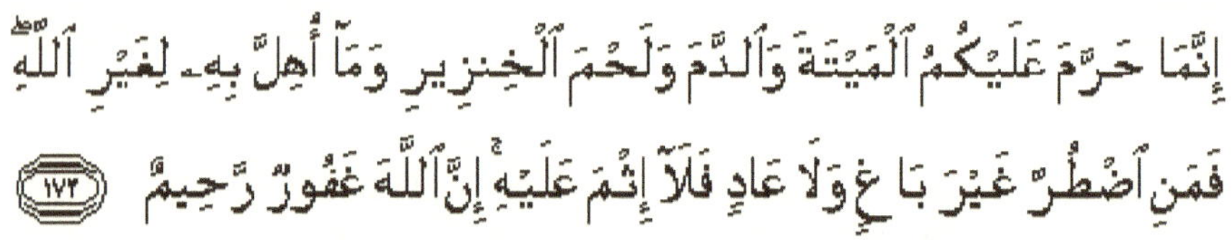

173. Innama harrama AAalaykumu almaytata waalddama walahma alkhinzeeri wama ohilla bihi lighayri Allahi famani idturra ghayra baghin wala AAadin fala ithma AAalayhi inna Allaha ghafoorun raheemun

---

2:173. HE has forbidden upon you but the carrion, the blood, the flesh of the swine, and that which is consecrated to someone other than Allah. But if one must eat such things under any constraint, and if one does this not out of wilful disobedience or transgression, no blame on such a one! Allah is indeed Forgiving, Merciful.[281 to 285]

---

281. 'Carrion' in the translation stands for *maitata* in the original Arabic. Literally, the Arabic word means 'that which is dead'. Verse 6:145 makes it further clear that what is forbidden is a living creature <u>found</u> by human beings only in a dead state. So, flesh of any found-dead living being is prohibited. It should well be remembered, in this context, that for any vegetarian or non-vegetarian source of food to be permissible, it must pass the criterion of being wholesome, and fit for human consumption. Verse 5:3 gives us further details of non-vegetarian sources of food that are forbidden.

282. About blood, the same Verse 6:145 as mentioned in the preceding Note, also clarifies that it is the blood, <u>shed or poured forth</u>, that is forbidden.

283. Swine, as we know, is an animal that lives in and breeds on filth. Eating its flesh may not therefore be conducive to physical, mental or moral health. And if my information is correct, medical opinion too confirms this view. But it is not for this reason, primarily, that the believers abstain from this food. They abstain, because Allah forbids it. Allah be praised, it is this one divine injunction that most Muslims do follow! And whatever He forbids has got to be not good for us.

284. The last in the list of forbidden items mentioned in this Verse is 'that which is consecrated to someone other than Allah'. Some commentators of the Qur'aan have interpreted this phrase to mean an animal only that is slaughtered in a name other than that of Allah. Their interpretation is because all the three preceding items in the list pertain to animals. So, they apply a man-made law applicable to human writings. Suppose, in a human script a list of 4 items is mentioned. Out of the 4, three are distinctly recognisable as belonging to the same one general class. Then as per this man-made law, the 4th item, ought to belong to the same class. This man-made law makes allowance for human weakness, because of which the human writer might have forgotten to specify or make clear to his readers, the class of the 4th item. But the human commentators have also unfortunately and unwittingly committed a human mistake of forgetting that the Qur'aan is divine and not authored by human beings. The Qur'aan is free from human errors. So, no man-made law can be made applicable to it for correcting any blasphemously supposed error therein. Every word therein is perfectly placed by the perfect Author.

285. So, the last item of forbidden foods, mentioned in this Verse, must be construed literally at its face value. And it literally means anything, vegetarian or non-vegetarian, that is consecrated or dedicated to any seen or unseen being other than Allah.

174. Inna alla_theena yaktumoona ma_ anzala Alla_hu mina alkita_bi wayashtaroona bihi thamanan qaleelan ola_-ika ma_ ya/kuloona fee bu_too_nihim illa alnna_ra wala_ yukallimuhumu Alla_hu yawma alqiya_mati wala_ yuzakkeehim walahum AAa_thabun aleem**un**

2:174. Indeed, those who conceal what Allah has sent down from the Book and earn a trifling price therefor – they, stomach not but the Fire in their bellies! And Allah will not speak to them on the Day of Resurrection, nor will He purify them. And for them will there be a painful punishment.[286 to 289]

286. The divine Books, parts of which got literally concealed by human beings, were those revealed earlier than the Qur'aan. The Qur'aan, on the other hand, cannot thus be concealed, as it is divinely guaranteed (Verse 15:9) against such concealment. But human beings, under the influence of the Satan, have resorted to other subtle and ingenious means of concealment. Since most Muslims around the world is now non-Arab, a part of the 'clergy' among them have gradually come to acquire a vested interest in creating a wrongful notion among other common Muslims. They (the commoners) are not taught the Qur'aanic Arabic as a language but are taught only to recite the Qur'aan without understanding what they recite. An impression is created that it is very difficult for the commoners to acquire the capability to understand the divine Message in original Arabic. So, they have willy-nilly to go to the 'clergy' to know what Islam is.

287. It is in such circumstances that some of the common Muslims, in different parts of the world, have come to understand that invoking dead saints for redressal of their worldly problems, and visiting their graves for the purpose, is part of Islam! The 'clergy' that is responsible for misleading the Muslims thus, are guilty of concealing the fact that the Qur'aan condemns such activity as unpardonable sin of *shirk*.

288. Let alone some ordinary Mullahs thus misleading some uneducated Muslims, but even eminent scholars of Islam do unfortunately and unwittingly fall into the satanic trap of misleading educated Muslims, when the scholars resort to their own interpolations while translating the original Arabic text into other languages. The interpolations are justified on the ground of syntactic differences between Arabic and the language into which the Qur'aan is to be translated. The interpolations are also justified claiming these are based on explanatory notes, contained in the *ahaadeeth* or given by the earlier prominent commentators of the Qur'aan. But the interpolations, often, help in changing the original divine meaning! However great in scholarship the commentator may be, it would be highly presumptuous – nay, blasphemous – on his part to assume that his interpolated word/words could explain or set right any 'complicated' part of the divine text! Such an assumption would indeed be blasphemous, particularly in the light of the oft-repeated Qur'aanic assertion that its *muhkam* Verses are clear by themselves or are well-explained in its other Verses. [Reference is invited in this context to Verse 2:99 and the corresponding Chapter Note 135 of these Studies.] And once a commentator takes a stand on the interpretation of a certain Verse, and makes an interpolation in furtherance of his stand-point, it becomes very difficult for him to change that stand, even when he gets convinced later that his stand is wrong. The Satan sees his opportunity then and gets busy in influencing the learned commentator to stick to his wrong stand, and thus unfortunately to conceal the true divine meaning of the relevant Verse from his gullible readers.

289. It is therefore necessary for every Muslim to try and get at least a working knowledge of Qur'aanic Arabic. He/she may thereby be able to find out if anything is amiss in the translation. When I wrote to one of my own readers on this need of learning Qur'aanic Arabic, he said that it was a 'tall, a very tall order' to expect every Muslim to do that. I replied that he wouldn't so dismiss the need, if he were convinced that his salvation from the Fire, in the Hereafter, very much depended on knowing the original divine Message of the Qur'aan in Arabic.

---

175. Ola-ika allatheena ishtarawoo alddalalata bialhuda waalAAathaba bialmaghfirati fama asbarahum AAala alnnari

---

2:175. Those are the ones who have exchanged right guidance for wrong guidance and error and exchanged forgiveness for punishment! How persevering then are they, in getting to the Fire!!

ذَٰلِكَ بِأَنَّ ٱللَّهَ نَزَّلَ ٱلْكِتَٰبَ بِٱلْحَقِّ وَإِنَّ ٱلَّذِينَ ٱخْتَلَفُوا۟ فِى ٱلْكِتَٰبِ لَفِى شِقَاقٍ بَعِيدٍ ﴿١٧٦﴾

176. Thalika bi-anna Allaha nazzala alkitaba bialhaqqi wa-inna allatheena ikhtalafoo fee alkitabi lafee shiqaqin baAAeedin

2:176. Thus, it is, because Allah has sent down the Book in Truth. And, indeed, those who question the Truth in the Book, those are involved in a far-fetched hostility! [290]

290. To cite just one of the many instances wherein even prominent scholars of Islam have disputed the perfection of the divine words of the Qur'aan, take the word *al-yataamaa* occurring in Verse 4:3. This Arabic word, in the form in which it occurs there, means orphans, whether male or female. But, because of a *hadeeth*, the meaning is restricted to female orphans only – converting thereby the broad meaning of the entire Verse to an illogically narrow one – by many learned scholars of Islam! The obvious implication of this man-imposed restriction is that, *nauaoozubillab*, the All-knowing Allah's word is imperfect, and needs help from an imperfect and man-influenced source to explain it!!

177. Laysa albirra an tuwalloo wujoohakum qibala almashriqi waalmaghribi walakinna albirra man amana biAllahi waalyawmi al-akhiri waalmala-ikati waalkitabi waalnnabiyyeena waata almala AAala hubbihi thawee alqurba waalyatama waalmasakeena waibna alssabeeli waalssa-ileena wafee alrriqabi waaqama alssalata waata alzzakata waalmoofoona biAAahdihim itha AAahadoo waalssabireena fee alba/sa-i waalddarra-i waheena alba/si ola-ika allatheena sadaqoo waola-ika humu almuttaqoona

2:177. It is not the righteousness that you turn your faces towards the East and the West. But the righteous is one who believes in Allah, the Hereafter, the Angels, the Book, the Prophets and who gives material assistance – despite one's love for material possessions – to the near and dear, the orphans, the impoverished, the wayfarer, the beggars and in the freeing of the bonded and who is regular and steadfast in prayers and gives to charity. And the righteous are those who keep their word when they give it and are patient in adversities and afflictions and during conflicts. Those are the true people; and those are the ones who are Allah-fearing! [291 & 292]

---

291. Read in the context of Verse 2:142, it is apparent that the divine emphasis here is on the spirit in which any duty is performed. The formal observance of facing the prescribed Qiblah in prayers would carry little significance with Allah if it is devoid of real belief in Him and of the other requirements as mentioned in this Verse 2:177. Remember also how the Allah-fearing are described in Verses 2:3 and 2:4. Here, in 2:177, we get further elaboration of that description.

292. Adherence to the letter of law is a must; for, otherwise, it would be an open defiance of authority. Similarly, the formal observance of all divine commands is a must; for, otherwise, it would be an open declaration of non-belief in Allah, in His Messenger and in the Hereafter! But we Muslims ought to reflect deeply whether our formal observance of divine commands, such as praying, fasting etc., has not degenerated into a mere show of conformity to societal norms. Do we really believe in the Qur'aan being invincible, incorruptible and divinely protected Word of Allah? Do we really believe that we all are accountable to Allah for every bit of deed in this world? Do we really believe in the Hereafter? Do we really believe that our salvation from ever-lasting suffering in the Hereafter lies in the conscious observance of not only the formal religious rites, but also of the divinely ordained etiquettes towards one another and towards society in general?

بَيَّأَيُّهَا ٱلَّذِينَ ءَامَنُوا۟ كُتِبَ عَلَيْكُمُ ٱلْقِصَاصُ فِى ٱلْقَتْلَى ٱلْحُرُّ بِٱلْحُرِّ وَٱلْعَبْدُ بِٱلْعَبْدِ وَٱلْأُنثَىٰ بِٱلْأُنثَىٰ فَمَنْ عُفِىَ لَهُۥ مِنْ أَخِيهِ شَىْءٌ فَٱتِّبَاعٌ بِٱلْمَعْرُوفِ وَأَدَآءٌ إِلَيْهِ بِإِحْسَٰنٍ ذَٰلِكَ تَخْفِيفٌ مِّن رَّبِّكُمْ وَرَحْمَةٌ فَمَنِ ٱعْتَدَىٰ بَعْدَ ذَٰلِكَ فَلَهُۥ عَذَابٌ أَلِيمٌ ﴿١٧٨﴾

178. Ya ayyuha allatheena amanoo kutiba AAalaykumu alqisasu fee alqatla alhurru bialhurri waalAAabdu bialAAabdi waalontha bialontha faman AAufiya lahu min akheehi shay-on faittibaAAun bialmaAAroofi waadaon ilayhi bi-ihsanin thalika takhfeefun min rabbikum warahmatun famani iAAtada baAAda thalika falahu AAathabun aleemun

---

2:178. O you who believe! Prescribed for you, is the capital punishment in the matter of murdered persons. If a free man, a slave/servant or a female commits the crime, this prescribed punishment would accordingly be applicable only to that free man, that slave/servant or that female, respectively. But where the guilty person's fellow citizen concerned commutes the sentence, the commutation must be adequately implemented, and the guilty person must fulfil the terms of commutation in good measure. That is a remission from your Lord, and His grace! Then whoever transgresses thereafter – for him shall there be a painful punishment.[293 to 296]

---

293. Advocates of abolition of capital punishment, beware! You cannot change what the Creator Himself has laid down. But it should well be noted that, in the light of Verse 4:92, capital punishment would be applied only to cases of <u>intentional</u> murder, and not to killing by mistake. And, of course, it is not applicable to killings in a war.

294. The Arabic *al-quisuaasu* basically means retaliation – a tit-for-tat response. In the context of an intentional murder, therefore, I have rendered the Arabic word as 'capital punishment' in the translation.

295. Literally translated, the second sentence of the Verse would look like, 'The free man, to the free man ...' In the context of the first sentence, it would obviously mean, 'If the murder is committed by a free man, the capital punishment would be meted out to that free man ...' To avoid any mistake in and consequent misconception of a literal rendering, a free renderiong is done, as in the second sentence of this English translation of the Verse.

296. In some translations, the Arabic term *min akheehi* occurring in this Verse, is so rendered as to mean 'the murdered person's brother'. But there is no justification for relating the possessive pronoun *hi* (his) here to the murdered person, as he/she (the murdered person) is not mentioned earlier in this Verse or in the immediately preceding Verses. The murderer, on the other hand, is mentioned. And it would be blasphemous to expect a mistake in a divine script. Moreover, *akhee*, in Qur'aanic terminology, does not necessarily mean only the close blood relationship of a brother. It often means (as for example in Verse 27:45) a fellow human of the same group, community or nation. *Min akheehi* would therefore mean any human being, duly authorised by the community, in which the murder is committed, to examine the case and pronounce his judgement or grant commutation of the death penalty. I have hence rendered *min akheehi* as 'the guilty person's fellow citizen concerned' in the translation. Besides, this divine provision for commutation, it may be noted, would take care of cases of murder committed, *inter alia*, under intense provocation.

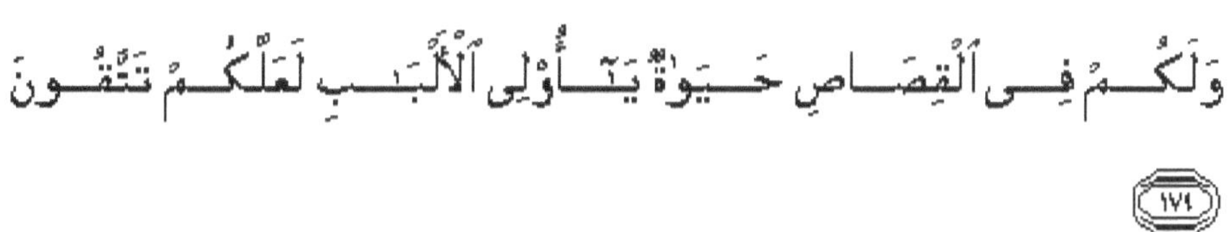

179. Walakum fee alqisasi hayatun ya olee al-albabi laAAallakum tattaqoona

---

2:179. And for you, O people endowed with insight, there is life in the capital punishment; maybe, you take heed![297]

297. The fear of capital punishment may prevent some people from committing murder. There could thus be a better security of life in this world. Perhaps, men of understanding among protagonists of abolition of capital punishment will take heed.

كُتِبَ عَلَيْكُمْ إِذَا حَضَرَ أَحَدَكُمُ الْمَوْتُ إِن تَرَكَ خَيْرًا الْوَصِيَّةُ لِلْوَالِدَيْنِ وَالْأَقْرَبِينَ بِالْمَعْرُوفِ حَقًّا عَلَى الْمُتَّقِينَ ۩

180. Kutiba AAalaykum itha hadara ahadakumu almawtu in taraka khayran alwasiyyatu lilwalidayni waal-aqrabeena bialmaAAroofi haqqan AAala almuttaqeena

2:180. It is prescribed for you that when death confronts any of you, the dying person, if he/she leaves behind any property, makes a will in favour of parents and relatives in a fair manner. Mandatory upon the pious! [298 to 302]

298. As regards 'the pious', please refer to <u>Chapter Note 2</u> of these Studies.

299. In Verses 4:11 and 4:12, the Qur'aan has given the details of the shares divinely prescribed for different relatives of the deceased. But it has also been laid down in those Verses, in clear terms, that the prescription would apply only to what remains of the deceased's property after execution of the deceased's will and repayment of his/her debts, if any. And there is no warrant in the Qur'aan for restricting the scope of the will to only third parts of the deceased's property, as most Muslims believe.

300. Making of a will is made obligatory on those who become reasonably aware of death approaching them. But death may often come suddenly, without notice. And the person may, on this account or on any other account, fail to make a will before dying. In that case, the law of inheritance as laid down in the said Verses 4:11 and 4:12 shall have to be followed, in the distribution of the deceased person's entire property.

301. But where a person does make a will, there is nothing in the Qur'aan that binds him/her to stick necessarily to rules laid down in Verses 4:11 and 4:12. He/she has of course to take heed of the divinely laid down rules overall, but the All-knowing Allah has given him/her the leeway to deviate from those rules to suit his/her circumstances. For example, the will may make better provisions for a son who is not financially well off than for a better-placed son.

302. It makes one sad to note, time and again, that we Muslims are wont to give more importance to what the *ahaadheeth* and the scholars say than to what the Qur'aan says in unambiguous and clear terms. The matter of inheritance dealt with in this Verse, read with Verses 4:11 and 4:12, is yet another instance of

how the Satan is constantly at work to deviate us from Allah's Word. No wonder our beloved Prophet (peace and Allah's blessings be upon him) would sadly say, on the Resuurection Day, "... my *Ummah* had taken this Qur'aan as a thing of no importance." [Q: 25:30]

فَمَنۢ بَدَّلَهُۥ بَعۡدَمَا سَمِعَهُۥ فَإِنَّمَآ إِثۡمُهُۥ عَلَى ٱلَّذِينَ يُبَدِّلُونَهُۥٓ إِنَّ ٱللَّهَ سَمِيعٌ عَلِيمٌ ۝

181. Faman baddalahu baAAda ma samiAAahu fa-innama ithmuhu AAala allatheena yubaddiloonahu inna Allaha sameeAAun AAaleemun

2:181. Then if anyone changes it after hearing it as one did, the sin thereof shall certainly be on those who change it. Indeed, Allah hears, He knows! [303]

303. As would commonly happen, the dying person might not have made a written will. Or, the person might wish to alter any written will previously made. The person, in such a situation, might call anyone who happens to be near that person at that critical moment, and orally express his/her will. The divine Verse here obviously alludes to such a situation.

فَمَنۡ خَافَ مِن مُّوصٍ جَنَفًا أَوۡ إِثۡمًا فَأَصۡلَحَ بَيۡنَهُمۡ فَلَآ إِثۡمَ عَلَيۡهِ إِنَّ ٱللَّهَ غَفُورٌ رَّحِيمٌ ۝

182. Faman khafa min moosin janafan aw ithman faaslaha baynahum fala ithma AAalayhi inna Allaha ghafoorun raheemun

2:182. And whoever apprehends any wrong or sin on the part of a testator and settles matters between them, then there is no sin on him/her. Indeed, Allah is Forgiving, Merciful! [304]

304. In the divine scheme of things then, there is scope for effecting a change in a testator's will, if done by mutual consent among the beneficiaries and in the interest of justice.

يَـٰٓأَيُّهَا ٱلَّذِينَ ءَامَنُواْ كُتِبَ عَلَيْكُمُ ٱلصِّيَامُ كَمَا كُتِبَ عَلَى ٱلَّذِينَ مِن قَبْلِكُمْ لَعَلَّكُمْ تَتَّقُونَ ﴿١٨٣﴾

183. Ya ayyuha allatheena amanoo kutiba AAalaykumu alssiyamu kama kutiba AAala allatheena min qablikum laAAallakum tattaqoona

2:183. O you who believe! The fasting is prescribed for you as it was prescribed for those who lived before you, so that you become pious.[305]

305. And the pious are the ones who are on the right Guidance and successful, the All-knowing Allah assures us (refer <u>Verses 2:2 to 2:5</u>)! In other words, fasting opens the door to real success in this world and to salvation in the Hereafter. To achieve success in its real sense, therefore, one has got to fast in the divinely prescribed manner.

أَيَّامًا مَّعْدُودَٰتٍ فَمَن كَانَ مِنكُم مَّرِيضًا أَوْ عَلَىٰ سَفَرٍ فَعِدَّةٌ مِّنْ أَيَّامٍ أُخَرَ وَعَلَى ٱلَّذِينَ يُطِيقُونَهُ فِدْيَةٌ طَعَامُ مِسْكِينٍ فَمَن تَطَوَّعَ خَيْرًا فَهُوَ خَيْرٌ لَّهُ وَأَن تَصُومُواْ خَيْرٌ لَّكُمْ إِن كُنتُمْ تَعْلَمُونَ ﴿١٨٤﴾

184. Ayyaman maAAdoodatin faman kana minkum mareedan aw AAala safarin faAAiddatun min ayyamin okhara waAAala allatheena yuteeqoonahu fidyatun taAAamu miskeenin faman tatawwaAAa khayran fahuwa khayrun lahu waan tasoomoo khayrun lakum in kuntum taAAalamoona

2:184. For a few numbers of days[306]. However, when any of you is ill or in journey, fasting is to be observed by him on other days to complete the number. And upon those who can afford it, a meal for a poor person is the required fee to gain exemption from a day's fasting. And he who brings himself to doing a better thing, it is all the better for him. And it is fasting that is better for you, if you but knew.[307 & 308]

---

306. This phrase is obviously a continuation of the sentence in the preceding Verse. This finishing phrase informs us that fasting is for only a few numbers of days.

307. As may be seen from the following Verse No. 185, all the days in the month of *Ramadan* are divinely appointed as the normal period for the fasting. The other days referred to in this Verse for making up the period for any missed days during the appointed period are, therefore, days of any month other than those of *Ramadan*.

308. There is a provision in this Verse, for those above the poverty line, to gain for themselves exemption from fasting. For that they must pay the price of a meal to one poor person. The exemption is obviously not available to those who cannot afford the price. A keen observer may notice that this is one small measure, among many others and bigger ones, divinely ordained for the care of the poor. But those who would be inclined to buy this exemption are reminded that observing the fast is a better thing for their own selves.

شَهْرُ رَمَضَانَ ٱلَّذِىٓ أُنزِلَ فِيهِ ٱلْقُرْءَانُ هُدًى لِّلنَّاسِ وَبَيِّنَـٰتٍ مِّنَ ٱلْهُدَىٰ وَٱلْفُرْقَانِ فَمَن شَهِدَ مِنكُمُ ٱلشَّهْرَ فَلْيَصُمْهُ وَمَن كَانَ مَرِيضًا أَوْ عَلَىٰ سَفَرٍ فَعِدَّةٌ مِّنْ أَيَّامٍ أُخَرَ يُرِيدُ ٱللَّهُ بِكُمُ ٱلْيُسْرَ وَلَا يُرِيدُ بِكُمُ ٱلْعُسْرَ وَلِتُكْمِلُواْ ٱلْعِدَّةَ وَلِتُكَبِّرُواْ ٱللَّهَ عَلَىٰ مَا هَدَىٰكُمْ وَلَعَلَّكُمْ تَشْكُرُونَ

185. Shahru ramadana allathee onzila feehi alqur-anu hudan lilnnasi wabayyinatin mina alhuda waalfurqani faman shahida minkumu alshshahra falyasumhu waman kana mareedan aw AAala safarin faAAiddatun min ayyamin okhara yureedu Allahu bikumu alyusra wala yureedu bikumu alAAusra walitukmiloo alAAiddata walitukabbiroo Allaha AAala ma hadakum walaAAallakum tashkuroona

---

2:185. Month of *Ramadan* in which was revealed the Qur'aan – Guidance for mankind with clear substantiation thereof and the Criterion. One, who gets to witness the month, observes it in fasting. And whoever is ill or in journey, for him the count of the number of days of fasting is to be made up by observing fasts on other days. Allah wants to make things easy – and not difficult – for you to complete the number of days of fasting and hymn the greatness of Allah for the guidance that He has given you, and so that you do feel grateful.[309 & 310]

---

309. The original Arabic word *al-furquaan* is rendered here as the Criterion. We have come across this Arabic word earlier in our Studies, in Verse 2:53. Please refer to Chapter Note 57 for a better understanding of the Qur'aanic term.

310. In this Verse 2:185, the provision made earlier in Verse 2:184 for postponing fastings in certain cases, is repeated. But, the provision for gaining exemption from fasting, at a price, made in the preceding Verse, is not repeated here. This has led some Muslims to believe that Verse 2:185 abrogates the provision of exemption made in Verse 2:184. It would be highly presumptuous – nay, blasphemous – on the part of any human being to consider any existing Verse, or part of it, as abrogated. Please refer to Verse 2:106 and Chapter Notes 150 to 153, 161 and 162

وَإِذَا سَأَلَكَ عِبَادِى عَنِّى فَإِنِّى قَرِيبٌ أُجِيبُ دَعْوَةَ ٱلدَّاعِ إِذَا دَعَانِ فَلْيَسْتَجِيبُوا۟ لِى وَلْيُؤْمِنُوا۟ بِى لَعَلَّهُمْ يَرْشُدُونَ ۝

186. Wa-itha saalaka AAibadee AAannee fa-innee qareebun ojeebu daAAwata alddaAAi itha daAAani falyastajeeboo lee walyu/minoo bee laAAallahum yarshudoona

---

2:186. And when my devotees ask for Me, I am indeed close to them. I respond to the call of a caller, when he calls Me. Let them then respond to Me and believe in Me, so that they tread the right path.[311]

---

311. Here's yet another prescription given by the Merciful Allah to keep mankind on the Straight Path. They have just sincerely to believe in Him and abide by all the divine Commands given in the Qur'aan! But, alas! Exercising the freedom of choice given to us, we, Muslims, just don't do that. As a result, we have fallen into ignominy in this world and face the prospect of an everlasting painful doom in the Hereafter.

أُحِلَّ لَكُمْ لَيْلَةَ ٱلصِّيَامِ ٱلرَّفَثُ إِلَىٰ نِسَآئِكُمْ هُنَّ لِبَاسٌ لَّكُمْ وَأَنتُمْ لِبَاسٌ لَّهُنَّ عَلِمَ ٱللَّهُ أَنَّكُمْ كُنتُمْ تَخْتَانُونَ أَنفُسَكُمْ فَتَابَ عَلَيْكُمْ وَعَفَا عَنكُمْ فَٱلْـَٰٔنَ بَٰشِرُوهُنَّ وَٱبْتَغُوا۟ مَا كَتَبَ ٱللَّهُ لَكُمْ وَكُلُوا۟ وَٱشْرَبُوا۟ حَتَّىٰ يَتَبَيَّنَ لَكُمُ ٱلْخَيْطُ ٱلْأَبْيَضُ مِنَ ٱلْخَيْطِ ٱلْأَسْوَدِ مِنَ ٱلْفَجْرِ ثُمَّ أَتِمُّوا۟ ٱلصِّيَامَ إِلَى ٱلَّيْلِ وَلَا تُبَٰشِرُوهُنَّ وَأَنتُمْ عَٰكِفُونَ فِى ٱلْمَسَٰجِدِ تِلْكَ حُدُودُ ٱللَّهِ فَلَا تَقْرَبُوهَا كَذَٰلِكَ يُبَيِّنُ ٱللَّهُ ءَايَٰتِهِۦ لِلنَّاسِ لَعَلَّهُمْ يَتَّقُونَ ﴿١٨٧﴾

187. Ohilla lakum laylata alssiyami alrrafathu ila nisa-ikum hunna libasun lakum waantum libasun lahunna AAalima Allahu annakum kuntum takhtanoona anfusakum fataba AAalaykum waAAafa AAankum faal-ana bashiroohunna waibtaghoo ma kataba Allahu lakum wakuloo waishraboo hatta yatabayyana lakumu alkhaytu al-abyadu mina alkhayti al-aswadi mina alfajri thumma atimmoo alssiyama ila allayli wala tubashiroohunna waantum AAakifoona fee almasajidi tilka hudoodu Allahi fala taqraboohа kathalika yubayyinu Allahu ayatihi lilnnasi laAAallahum yattaqoona

2:187. Permitted to you are sexual relations with your wives at night after a fast. They are garments for you; and you are garments for them. Allah knew you used to betray yourselves; so, He has bestowed His mercy upon you and forgiven you. Now then, enjoy sexual relationships with them and seek what Allah has ordained for you. And eat and drink until the light of dawn becomes distinct to you from the darkness preceding dawn. Then, fast till night. And have no sexual relationships with them while you are in the state of retreat, in total devotion to Allah, at the places of worship. Those are restrictions ordained by Allah; so go not near those! Thus, does Allah make His Verses/signs clear to mankind so that they become pious.[312 to 314]

312. Garments protect and hide. So, does a spouse. Protects the partner from bad influence of carnal desire and hides it from public view.

313. From the context, it is clear, that earlier to the revelation of this Verse, the believers had assumed that having sexual relations with their spouses was forbidden even in the nights during the month of *Ramadan*. The Verse allays their misconception.

314. There is a controversy among the Muslims as to the exact time when to start a day's fast. The time fixed in India, by public declaration, is about one and quarter hours before sunrise. But does this coincide with the limit divinely fixed in this Verse? Or have we abandoned the divine for the non-divine here too, as we have done in many other matters? And again, fasting is to be broken at nightfall. Why then do we break it at sunset? It is not nightfall at sunset. Nightfall comes after the dusk – that is, after the evening (maghrib) prayer.

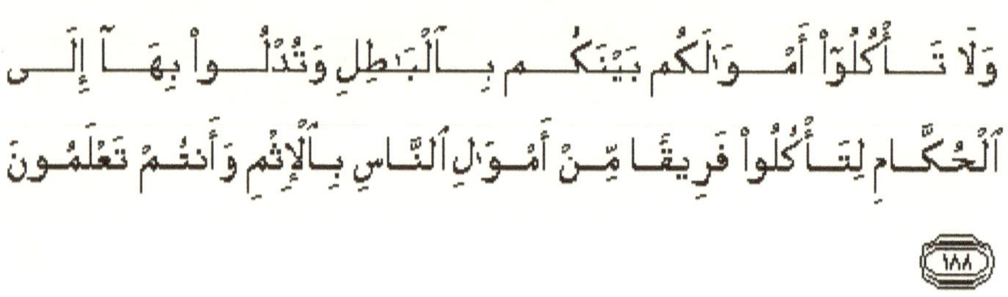

188. Wala ta/kuloo amwalakum baynakum bialbatili watudloo biha ila alhukkami lita/kuloo fareeqan min amwali alnnasi bial-ithmi waantum taAAalamoona

2:188. And usurp not property of one another among yourselves falsely and bribe the authorities therewith to knowingly misappropriate part of others' property. [315 to 317]

315. With reference to the beginning part of this Verse, the Qur'aan says, in Verse 9:60, that spending a part of one's own property on the poor, the needy etc., is an obligation. If we fail to fulfil this Allah-imposed obligation, and consume our entire property on ourselves, it would also be tantamount to consuming our property falsely. Besides, there are cases galore wherein people try to usurp others' property falsely as their own.

316. About the latter part of the Verse, people may produce false evidences to the authorities concerned or bribe them to get a favourable decision wherewith to usurp others' property.

317. As may be seen from Verse 4:161, misappropriation of others' property is a sin associated with *Ar-Riba*. And Allah has condemned *Ar-Riba* in such strong terms as calling a declaration of war from Allah against those indulging in the sin [Q: 2:279]. It's a sad fact that we, Muslims, ourselves are deeply engrossed in this sin. There are innumerable ways in which we subtly do it, and we're blissfully unaware that we're committing a grave sin! And we've mis-interpreted *Ar-Riba* to mean only interest. *Ar-Riba* covers all transactional misappropriations of others' property. To give just one example, if we pay only $10 to a labourer for a job worth $15, we're misappropriating $5 from the labourer's dues. We're indulging in *Ar-Riba*! No wonder, Allah is angry with us. HIS wrath is copiously reflected in the pitiable helplessness of Muslims in most parts of the world today. You may wonder, why only Muslims? Other communities too indulge in *Ar-Riba*! Yes, but we may be indulging in this crime more than the other communities do. Moreover, there is a ray of hope in the Muslims getting some punishment here in this world. Maybe, the Merciful Allah is thus giving a warning signal to us to mend our ways before it becomes too late! And, maybe, the other communities, indulging in *Ar-Riba*, are not similarly being warned, as they are beyond hope.

۞ يَسۡـَٔلُونَكَ عَنِ ٱلۡأَهِلَّةِ قُلۡ هِىَ مَوَٰقِيتُ لِلنَّاسِ وَٱلۡحَجِّ وَلَيۡسَ ٱلۡبِرُّ بِأَن تَأۡتُواْ ٱلۡبُيُوتَ مِن ظُهُورِهَا وَلَٰكِنَّ ٱلۡبِرَّ مَنِ ٱتَّقَىٰ وَأۡتُواْ ٱلۡبُيُوتَ مِنۡ أَبۡوَٰبِهَا وَٱتَّقُواْ ٱللَّهَ لَعَلَّكُمۡ تُفۡلِحُونَ ﴿١٨٩﴾

189. Yas-aloonaka AAani al-ahillati qul hiya maw_a_qeetu lilnn_a_si waalh_a_jji walaysa albirru bi-an ta/too albuyoota min *th*hoorih_a_ wal_a_kinna albirra mani ittaq_a_ wa/too albuyoota min abw_a_bih_a_ waittaqoo All_a_ha laAAallakum tufli_h_oona

---

2:189. They ask you about the new moons. Say, "These are fixed points in time, for mankind and the Hajj." And it is not righteousness that you enter the houses from their backsides. The righteousness, on the other hand, comes from those who fear Allah. So, enter the houses through their front doors, and fear Allah in order that you may be successful.[318 to 320]

---

318. From the first part of the Verse that refers to the new moons, it is evident that the new moon represents, for the entire mankind, a specific point of reference for measurement of time. The quantum of time between any two new moons is called a month; and 12 such months make a year.

319. It's also therefore evident from the original divine text that the fixed point in time, of the occurrence of the new moon, is commonly applicable to the entire world; and, as a matter of fact, it indeed is! It is the moment when the moon crosses the straight line between the Sun & the earth. This fixed point in time, however, is denoted by the different local times of different places. Suppose the new moon occurs at 5 pm on a Tuesday, at Makkah. The new moon is not possible to be seen anywhere in Saudi Arabia on the same Tuesday. But, in some country on the West coast of the American continent, the new moon can be seen on Tuesday itself. On this basis, it's possible for the next day (Wednesday) to be declared as the 1st date of the next lunar month, throughout the world. We can thus save ourselves from being ridiculed by other communities for observing our festivals on 2 or 3 different days in different parts of the world. We're reduced to this sorry state of affairs because of our preference for the divinely non-protected texts of the *ahaadeeth* over the divinely protected text of the Qur'aan!

320. The context reveals that at the time of the revelation of the Qur'aan, people had some sort of superstitious belief that entering houses from backsides, on certain occasions perhaps, constituted a righteous act. The latter part of the Verse denies such superstitious beliefs and educates the people that righteousness doesn't come through observance of acts of some dubious nature. It comes through being pious and Allah-fearing. And piety is the key to success.

وَقَـٰتِلُواْ فِى سَبِيلِ ٱللَّهِ ٱلَّذِينَ يُقَـٰتِلُونَكُمْ وَلَا تَعْتَدُوٓاْ إِنَّ ٱللَّهَ لَا يُحِبُّ ٱلْمُعْتَدِينَ ۝

190. Waqatiloo fee sabeeli Allahi allatheena yuqatiloonakum wala taAAtadoo inna Allaha la yuhibbu almuAAtadeena

2:190. And fight, in the way of Allah, those who fight with you. And transgress not! Indeed, Allah loves not the transgressors.[321, 322]

321. This is a divine permission, or command, for believers to take to arms in self-defence. Islam doesn't expect its adherents to be like the dumb driven cattle. But it expects them first to try and gain the capability to fight back. And until they do that, they are advised to seek Allah's help with patience & prayers. Allah assures such genuine seekers that He is with them [refer Verse 2:153]

322. Even in self-defence, Muslims are commanded to be restrained & to commit no excesses. Islam is based on justice, and to commit excesses is to be obviously unjust. Allah has made us His representatives or vicegerents (*khulafaa*) to our respective worlds, and we would be failing in our duties utterly – as representatives of the just Sovereign – if we are unjust.

وَٱقْتُلُوهُمْ حَيْثُ ثَقِفْتُمُوهُمْ وَأَخْرِجُوهُم مِّنْ حَيْثُ أَخْرَجُوكُمْ وَٱلْفِتْنَةُ أَشَدُّ مِنَ ٱلْقَتْلِ وَلَا تُقَـٰتِلُوهُمْ عِندَ ٱلْمَسْجِدِ ٱلْحَرَامِ حَتَّىٰ يُقَـٰتِلُوكُمْ فِيهِ فَإِن قَـٰتَلُوكُمْ فَٱقْتُلُوهُمْ كَذَٰلِكَ جَزَآءُ ٱلْكَـٰفِرِينَ ۝

191. Waoqtuloohum haythu thaqiftumoohum waakhrijoohum min haythu akhrajookum waalfitnatu ashaddu mina alqatli wala tuqatiloohum AAinda almasjidi alharami hatta yuqatilookum feehi fa-in qatalookum faoqtuloohum kathalika jazao alkafireena

2:191. And kill them wherever you find them and turn them out from where they turned you out. For, persecution is worse than killing. And fight with them not, near the sacred Place of Worship, unless they fight with you therein. But if they fight with you, kill them then; for, such is the 'reward' for the suppressors of Truth.[323, 324]

---

323. The word *Wa* (And) at the beginning of this Verse is significant. It connects this Verse to the preceding one, wherein permission was given to wage a war. But this permission is subject to 3 conditions. One, it must be in the way of Allah, i.e. against persecution and injustices. Two, it must be with those who fight with you, i.e. in self-defence. Three, it must be without commitment of any transgression or excesses. In the light of these conditions, it is obvious that the divine command to 'kill them wherever you find them' would be applicable only when 'you' are in a declared state of war with 'them'. And even if 'you' are in a declared state of war with 'them', 'you' are not to initiate a fight with 'them' near the Sacred Place of Worship, i.e. the *Kaabaah*. Mischievous persons desiring to depict Islam in bad light, make no mention of the context in which the Verse was revealed. They don't mention even the immediately following divine command to 'turn them out from where they turned you out'; for, this quote would reveal that the earlier command was made for the situation of a state of war waged, in Allah's path, for redressal of an injustice.

324. In any eventuality, to kill a human being is indeed an undesirable thing. And, unless it is done in carrying out capital punishment sanctioned under Verse 2:178 (also please see Note 293 thereunder) or in a state of war sanctioned under Verse 2:190 above, the perpetrator of the act would be liable to capital punishment, as we have already seen, under the Qur'aanic Law. But this very Qur'aanic Law considers, as we see in this Verse (2:191), persecution or unjustly tormenting other people, a worse crime than even killing. Persecution is rampant in our modern world. But can we find any people, collectively and sincerely guided by Qur'aanic Law, to withstand and repel the rampant persecution?

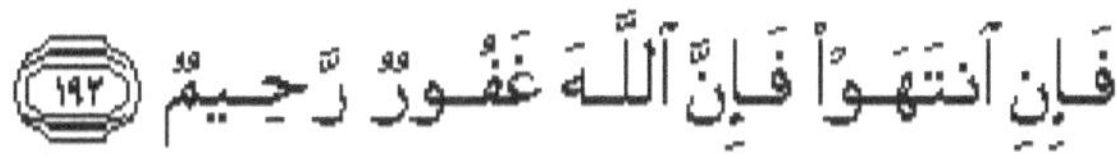

192. Fa-ini intahaw fa-inna Allaha ghafoorun raheemun

2:192. But if they refrain, then Allah is indeed Forgiving, Merciful.

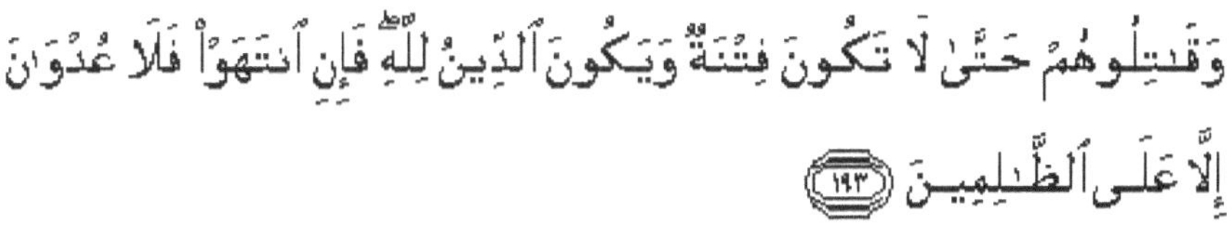

193. Waq<u>a</u>tiloohum <u>h</u>att<u>a</u> l<u>a</u> takoona fitnatun wayakoona alddeenu lill<u>a</u>hi fa-ini intahaw fal<u>a</u> AAudw<u>a</u>na ill<u>a</u> AAal<u>a</u> al<u>ththa</u>limeena

---

2:193. And fight with them until persecution exists no more, and the way of life leading to Allah is enabled. And if they refrain, no hostility shall there be, except against the persecutors.[325, 326]

---

325. This Verse (2:193) and the preceding one, both substantiate what is stated in Note 323, hereinabove.

326. Muslims are urged in this Verse (2:193) to go on fighting till persecution ends. We should well remember here that fighting is permitted against persecution and not against non-muslims as such. If the non-muslims cease to persecute, it is made abundantly clear here, there ought to be no hostility against them. It is for Allah to deal with their non-belief. Muslims cannot force anyone to believe in Islam (refer <u>Verse 2:256</u>). They can only plead. And if they force, they would themselves be guilty of persecution. And persecution is worse than killing, Allah declares.

ٱلشَّهْرُ ٱلْحَرَامُ بِٱلشَّهْرِ ٱلْحَرَامِ وَٱلْحُرُمَٰتُ قِصَاصٌ فَمَنِ ٱعْتَدَىٰ عَلَيْكُمْ فَٱعْتَدُوا۟ عَلَيْهِ بِمِثْلِ مَا ٱعْتَدَىٰ عَلَيْكُمْ وَٱتَّقُوا۟ ٱللَّهَ وَٱعْلَمُوٓا۟ أَنَّ ٱللَّهَ مَعَ ٱلْمُتَّقِينَ ۝١٩٤

194. Alshshahru al<u>h</u>ar<u>a</u>mu bialshshahri al<u>h</u>ar<u>a</u>mi waal<u>h</u>urum<u>a</u>tu qi<u>sas</u>un famani iAAtad<u>a</u> AAalaykum faiAAtadoo AAalayhi bimithli m<u>a</u> iAAtad<u>a</u> AAalaykum waittaqoo All<u>a</u>ha waiAAlamoo anna All<u>a</u>ha maAAa almuttaqeena

---

2:194. If they observe the sanctity of the prohibited month, you too observe it. And for breach of the prohibitions, there is the law of quisuaasu ('tit for tat' or 'blow for blow'). So then, whoever transgresses against you, pay him back, in like manner. And fear Allah and know for certain that Allah is with the pious.[327 to 330]

---

327. Literally, the Verse starts thus: "The prohibited month, for the prohibited month, and for the prohibitions, quisuaasu ...." This literal rendering in English, however, may fail to convey the meaning intended in the original Arabic text. Hence the free redering as resorted to, in the translation, above. The

inerpretation made therein is obvious from the context of the preceding Verses and from the latter part of this very Verse, 2:194.

328. In Verse 9:36, it is mentioned that 4 of the 12 months in a year are the prohibited (or sacred) months. To the best of my knowledge and belief, the Qur'aan has not specified the 4 sacred months. These were not specified because the Arabs, at the time of the revelation of the Qur'aan, knew, without controversy, which 4 months were sacred. And the All-Knowing Allah knew in advance that there would be no controversy ever afterwards about it. As the Arabs, since time immemorial, have been knowing, and as muslims all over the world today know, the 4 sacred months of the muslim lunar year are the first (Muharram), the seventh (Rajab), the eleventh (Zee Quad) and the twelfth (Zil-Hajj). And there has never been any cotroversy over it. The Qur'aan has not specified the 4 months because Allah, with His infinite knowledge, knew there was no need. Time has proved that there was indeed no need! And for those who ponder, there is indeed a Sign here of the Qur'aan being divine, complete and without any blemish that human writings may be prone to. Normally, fighting is prohibited during these prohibited months.

329. Earlier, in Verse 2:178, we have come across this Arabic word *quisuaasu* occurring in this Verse. There (Verse 2:178), in that context of an intentional murder unlawfully committed, we have rendered it as 'capital punishment'. It has however been clarified, in Note 294, that the Arabic word basically means retaliation. Therefore here, the context being fighting during prohibited months, it would mean that fighting is permitted against those who first breach the prohibition. What follows immediately in the Verse, after the word *quisuaasu*, makes this abundantly clear.

330. The believers however are reminded that they should fear Allah and commit no excesses. And if they do just abide by this divine admonition, Allah assures them that He would be with them in all eventualities. That's a security cover from the Almighty Creator Himself! What greater security could one ask for? If only the Muslims of today could remember this and genuinely fear Allah while doing anything in this world, they wouldn't be in the sorry plight they are in now.

وَأَنفِقُوا۟ فِى سَبِيلِ ٱللَّهِ وَلَا تُلْقُوا۟ بِأَيْدِيكُمْ إِلَى ٱلتَّهْلُكَةِ وَأَحْسِنُوٓا۟ إِنَّ ٱللَّهَ يُحِبُّ ٱلْمُحْسِنِينَ ۝١٩٥

195. Waanfiqoo fee sabeeli Allahi wala tulqoo bi-aydeekum ila alttahlukati waahsinoo inna Allaha yuhibbu almuhsineena

---

2:195. And spend, in Allah's path; and do not throw yourselves into ruin, with your own hands. And do good work. Indeed, Allah loves those who do good work.[331 to 333]

---

331. In Verse 2:190, believers are commanded to fight in Allah's path/way. And here, in Verse 2:195, they are commanded to spend in Allah's way. There, in 2:190, the context was fighting a war, and 'in Allah's way' was interpreted to mean fighting against persecution and injustices (see Chapter Note 323 herein

above). Here, in 2:195, the context being 'spending', we must generalise the interpretation. What is Allah's way? It is obviously the way shown, or the guidance given, in the Qur'aan. So, to spend in Allah's way means to spend (not just the wealth one has, but) all Allah-given resources (time, knowledge, included) in facilitating and/or furthering human life totally in accordance with the Qur'aan. It may well be remembered in this context that adequately necessary spending on one's own and on one's immediate family would of course be covered by the term 'in Allah's way'.

332. And whatever one spends otherwise, i.e. other than in Allah's way, would in effect be spending for self-destruction or for no tangible and abiding gains. That is the obvious import of throwing 'yourselves into ruin'. Frivolous spending on one's own self, as well as indiscriminate spending for others, at the cost of one's own needs, could both lead to self-destruction, in this world and/or in the next.

333. Allah directs us to do good work (*ahusinoo*). Good (*suaalihuaa*) work entails work done in accordance with divine instructions in the Qur'aan. It also entails such work done in the best possible manner. A believing carpenter, for example, would be a *muhusin* (singular of *muhusineen*) provided he does all his work, including carpentery, in a nice or beautiful manner. He wouldn't be entitled to that title (*muhusin*), if he does not attend to any of his work with all possible care and diligence. Please refer to <u>Verse 2:112 & Chapter Note 165</u> also, in this regard.

وَأَتِمُّواْ ٱلْحَجَّ وَٱلْعُمْرَةَ لِلَّهِ فَإِنْ أُحْصِرْتُمْ فَمَا ٱسْتَيْسَرَ مِنَ ٱلْهَدْيِ

وَلَا تَحْلِقُواْ رُءُوسَكُمْ حَتَّىٰ يَبْلُغَ ٱلْهَدْيُ مَحِلَّهُۥ فَمَن كَانَ مِنكُم

مَّرِيضًا أَوْ بِهِۦٓ أَذًى مِّن رَّأْسِهِۦ فَفِدْيَةٌ مِّن صِيَامٍ أَوْ صَدَقَةٍ أَوْ نُسُكٍ

فَإِذَآ أَمِنتُمْ فَمَن تَمَتَّعَ بِٱلْعُمْرَةِ إِلَى ٱلْحَجِّ فَمَا ٱسْتَيْسَرَ مِنَ ٱلْهَدْيِ

فَمَن لَّمْ يَجِدْ فَصِيَامُ ثَلَٰثَةِ أَيَّامٍ فِى ٱلْحَجِّ وَسَبْعَةٍ إِذَا رَجَعْتُمْ

تِلْكَ عَشَرَةٌ كَامِلَةٌ ذَٰلِكَ لِمَن لَّمْ يَكُنْ أَهْلُهُۥ حَاضِرِى ٱلْمَسْجِدِ ٱلْحَرَامِ

وَٱتَّقُواْ ٱللَّهَ وَٱعْلَمُوٓاْ أَنَّ ٱللَّهَ شَدِيدُ ٱلْعِقَابِ ﴿١٩٦﴾

196. Waatimmoo alhajja waalAAumrata lillahi fa-in ohsirtum fama istaysara mina alhadyi wala tahliqoo ruoosakum hatta yablugha alhadyu mahillahu faman kana minkum mareedan aw bihi athan min ra/sihi fafidyatun min siyamin aw sadaqatin aw nusukin fa-itha amintum faman tamattaAAa bialAAumrati ila alhajji fama istaysara mina alhadyi faman lam yajid fasiyamu thalathati ayyamin fee alhajji wasabAAatin itha rajaAAtum tilka AAasharatun kamilatun thalika liman lam yakun ahluhu hadiree almasjidi alharami waittaqoo Allaha waiAAlamoo anna Allaha shadeedu alAAiqabi

2:196. And complete the Hajj and the Umrah for Allah[334 to 336]. But if you are prevented, then sacrifice an animal you can afford[337]. And shave not your heads until the animal is duly sacrificed[338, 339]. But if any of you be sick or has an affliction in the head, he is exempted from this injunction provided he compensates by observing fast, spending for the needy or sacrificing. And when circumstances are favourable to you, then for the one who takes advantage of the Umrah before the Hajj, sacrificing an animal that one can afford is a must. But for the one who cannot afford, three days of fasting during the Hajj and seven after you return home. That is, ten in all. That provision is for the one whose family does not live near the Sacred Place of Worship[340, 341]. And fear Allah and beware! Allah is severe in punishment.

---

334. In Verse 28:27, the Arabic word *huijaj* (a plural form of *huajj*) has been used in the meaning of 'years'. And, as we have already seen in Verse 2:158, the Arabic term *huajjal bayta* has been used therein. In the light of Verse 2:158 read with Verse 3:97, therefore, the word *huajj* used with the Arabic definite article *al* in this Verse (2:196) obviously means the divinely ordained annual pilgrimage to the Sacred House at Makkah. As all Muslims are aware, the Hajj is performed during a specific period of the Muslim lunar calendar.

335. The Umrah, on the other hand, can be performed at any time in the year. It's a shorter visit to the holy place, with fewer rites to perform. This Arabic word, in its grammatically varied form, is also used in the same meaning in Verse 2:158. The Hajj is obligatory under certain conditions as per Verse 3:97. In Verse 2:196, the obligation is for performing both Hajj and Umrah *for Allah*, as and when the two are performed. People coming from outside for the Hajj do perform the Umrah also, separately, besides the Hajj.

336. Both the Hajj and the Umrah, however, are specifically enjoined to be performed <u>only</u> for Allah. What is the significance of this stipulation? Historically of course, it is to mark a break from the *jahiliya* past when numerous idols had been installed in the Kaabah and people used to visit to propitiate their respective gods besides Allah. But for us, now, the significance of the stipulation lies in the fact that the Kaabah, with its precincts, is the only place in the world divinely permitted for a religious visit, *for Allah alone*. Allah listens to and answers our supplications to Him, wherever we make them. But since we go to His House at His call and perform the prescribed rites there at His bidding, Allah is more likely to be pleased to grant our supplications made there. So, we do make our supplications there both for this world and for the next. There is of course no question of our making supplications there to anyone but Allah. We would thus be truly obeying Allah's command to complete or to perform the Hajj and the Umrah <u>only</u> for Him. But if we make our obeisance and supplications (even if it be to Allah only) at the grave of a saint or a prophet, thinking that Allah would more likely be pleased with supplications to Him at such places, we would be making a grave mistake! For, such visits to the graves and making such supplications there would not qualify to be termed as only for Allah. We would, invariably in such supplications, be guilty of associating the saint or the prophet with Allah. And that would be *shirk*, manifest!

337. The annually performed Hajj is ordained upon those who can afford the journey (Verse 3:97). Does this mean that if one can afford the journey every year, one has to perform it every year too? Apparently, it does. But practical considerations like those of health, money, urgent domestic or family problems do come in the way of most people. Different circumstances with different people thus prevent them from undertaking the journey. It is for such people who are not able to undertake the journey for the Hajj that the rite of sacrificing an animal is here prescribed. Maybe, the then immediate cause for revelation of this part of the Verse was an incident in the life of the Prophet; but we should always remember that the

Qur'aan was revealed for all times till the Last Day. We should therefore apply the Qur'aanic commands, given in generalised terms like this one, to our live problems and questions today.

338. The Qur'aanic injunction <u>against</u> shaving heads is applicable to men who have started the process of accomplishing their Hajj or Umrah. And it does appear from the context here that this injunction is also applicable to other believers who are required to sacrifice an animal at home during *Eidul-Adhuhuaa*. For such persons at home, the injunction ought also to start on the 8th of *Dhul-Hijj* and end when an animal is duly sacrificed, to synchronize with the period of the Hajj.

339. During Hajj, it has been the general practice to shave the head or get the hair on the head partially cut to symbolically mark the authorised end of the injunction period. But this symbolic act has assumed the sanctity of an obligatory act, which, going by the Qur'aanic text, it is certainly not! The Qur'aanic injunction is against shaving heads during Hajj up to the time the *hadyi* animal is duly sacrificed. The Qur'aan does not command us to get our heads necessarily shaved immediately after the sacrifice.

340. Please refer <u>Chapter Note 180</u> of these Studies.

341. The special provisions of this Verse are not applicable to residents of Makkah. In other words, *hadyi* (sacrificing an animal) is not obligatory on the Makkans, when they perform the Hajj.

ٱلْحَجُّ أَشْهُرٌ مَّعْلُومَٰتٌ فَمَن فَرَضَ فِيهِنَّ ٱلْحَجَّ فَلَا رَفَثَ وَلَا فُسُوقَ وَلَا جِدَالَ فِى ٱلْحَجِّ وَمَا تَفْعَلُوا۟ مِنْ خَيْرٍ يَعْلَمْهُ ٱللَّهُ وَتَزَوَّدُوا۟ فَإِنَّ خَيْرَ ٱلزَّادِ ٱلتَّقْوَىٰ وَٱتَّقُونِ يَٰٓأُو۟لِى ٱلْأَلْبَٰبِ ۝١٩٧

197. Alhajju ashhurun maAAloomatun faman farada feehinna alhajja fala rafatha wala fusooqa wala jidala fee alhajji wama tafAAaloo min khayrin yaAAlamhu Allahu watazawwadoo fa-inna khayra alzzadi alttaqwa waittaqooni ya olee al-albabi

---

2:197. The Hajj months are known ones[342]. So he, who has taken a decision to perform the Hajj during those months, should indulge in no sex, commit no transgression and have no quarrels during the Hajj[343]. And Allah is aware of whatever good you do. And take necessary provisions for the journey; but, indeed, the best provision one can take along is piety! [344] And be afraid of Me, O you, endowed with insight!

---

342. *Ash-hurunm* (months) is the word used in the original Arabic text. Since it is in the plural form, commentators of the Qur'aan have been searching for more than one month, in one lunar calendar year, in which the Hajj is performed. It has been a futile search; for, the only well-known month, in which the Hajj is performed, is *Dhul-Hajj*, the twelfth month of the Muslim calendar. Then why is the word used in

the plural form? Surely, the divine Book cannot be wrong. We can easily find the answer to this question, if we reflect a little. Suppose now we are in the first month of the Hijri calendar. The twelfth month of the last year cannot be the same as the twelfth month of the current year, although both bear the same name. The former month has already passed away, and the latter is yet to come. This simple example should make it abundantly clear to us that the time capsules represented by the common name of *Dhul-Hajj* are all different, each separated from the nearest one by the time gap of the intervening 11 months. *Ash-hurunm muaaloomaat* referred to in this Verse are the numerous different months of *Dhul-Hajj* coming year after year.

343. Along with the injunction against shaving heads imposed under <u>Verse 2:196</u>, these are the other 3 restrictions, specifically laid down in the Qur'aan, upon a person in the act of performing Hajj. Everyone is duty-bound to strictly abide by these restrictions for fear of incurring Allah's wrath, amply hinted at in the closing sentence of this Verse (2:197).

344. Piety (i.e. the character one imbibes when one fears Allah's wrath, that one would incur, on any disobedience to Him) is the human virtue that Allah is pleased with. When the Creator Himself is pleased, the creature has nothing to worry about. The creature would then get the right guidance on what provision to take for the journey, and even if the provision taken is not adequate, ways and means would divinely be opened for making additional provisions, on the way. Not only during the Hajj, but in all walks of life also, does the pious/Allah-fearing (*muttaqui*) get the right guidance and get success/salvation, as guaranteed by Allah Himself in <u>Verse 2:5</u>.

لَيۡسَ عَلَيۡكُمۡ جُنَاحٌ أَن تَبۡتَغُواْ فَضۡلًا مِّن رَّبِّكُمۡ فَإِذَآ أَفَضۡتُم مِّنۡ عَرَفَٰتٍ فَٱذۡكُرُواْ ٱللَّهَ عِندَ ٱلۡمَشۡعَرِ ٱلۡحَرَامِ وَٱذۡكُرُوهُ كَمَا هَدَىٰكُمۡ وَإِن كُنتُم مِّن قَبۡلِهِۦ لَمِنَ ٱلضَّآلِّينَ ۝١٩٨

198. Laysa AAalaykum junahun an tabtaghoo fadlan min rabbikum fa-itha afadtum min AAarafatin faothkuroo Allaha AAinda almashAAari alharami waothkuroohu kama hadakum wa-in kuntum min qablihi lamina alddalleena

---

2:198. No offence on you that you seek favour from your Lord.[345] So, as you pour into parts of *Arafaat*, remember Allah at the *Mash-uaril-huaraam*.[346] And remember Him as per guidance given to you.[347] And you were indeed among those led astray, before that.[348]

---

345. Commentators have interpreted this part of the Verse to mean that the pilgrims can have trade dealings during the Hajj. And they cite the *ahaadeeth* in support. But this interpretation would run contrary to Allah's command, in <u>Verse 2:196</u>, for us to complete the Hajj *for Allah*. In the light of Verse 2:196, therefore, seeking Allah's favour here, in this context, would obviously mean supplicating to Allah for a worldly bounty, like success in trade, cure from a long-standing disease etc.. But we ought to ask

Allah <u>also</u>, at the same time, to grant us salvation, in the Hereafter. If we ask Him for benefits for this world <u>only</u>, we are likely to go to the Fire in the Hereafter (refer <u>Verses 2:200 & 2:201</u>).

346. During the night falling between the 7th & 8th of *Dhul-Hijjah* or in the very early hours of the 8th, the pilgrims move out of Makkah to the camps in Mina and engage themselves in prayers there. In the morning of the 9th, they all move out to the farther place of *Arafaat*. Standing there for some time in absolute submission to Allah, praying to and invoking Him, is an obligatory ritual of the Hajj. At sunset, the pilgrims start moving back towards Mina. Just before entering Mina, they stop for the night at the place called *Muzdalifah*. The entire spread of land right from the borders of Mina to the farthest points, of *Arafaat*, where people go to and stand in utter submission to their One Common Lord, is described in this Verse as *Al-Mashuaril-huaraam* (the Holy/Sacred Post) – a Post of duty. The duty assigned is for them to remember Allah, wherever they move to and camp there, as per the established procedure. And how does one remember Allah? In Verse 20:14, Allah instructs us to establish proper prayers for His remembrance. We ought to remember Him also during the entire waking hours in between ritual prayers performed there. We cannot spend our time there in sport and pastime.

347. At the end of the foregoing Note, we have seen that, in Qur'aanic light, the best way to remember Allah is to offer our prayers to Him properly. Please refer to Chapter Notes <u>4</u> and <u>108</u>, of these Studies, to know more about the divine guidance given to us for the proper conduct of prayers.

348. For the people present at the time of revelation of the Qur'aan, this Qur'aanic statement obviously referred to the period of ignorance just before the revelation. In Verse 8:35, the Qur'aan informs us that the prayer of those people then was nothing but whistling and clapping of hands. Now, even though we have the divine guidance available to us through the Qur'aan, we are, sadly, still ignorant. We do not take the trouble of seriously finding out what guidance there is in the Qur'aan. And even if we come to know what the guidance is, our Faith is not strong enough to make us abide by that guidance.

ثُمَّ أَفِيضُواْ مِنْ حَيْثُ أَفَاضَ ٱلنَّاسُ وَٱسْتَغْفِرُواْ ٱللَّهَ إِنَّ ٱللَّهَ غَفُورٌ رَّحِيمٌ

199. Thumma afeedoo min haythu afada alnnasu waistaghfiroo Allaha inna Allaha ghafoorun raheemun

---

2:199. Then, pour in where the people pour in, and ask Allah for forgiveness. Allah indeed is Forgiving, Merciful.[349]

---

349. The instructions herein and in the preceding Verse (2:198), make it amply clear that the route and procedure followed (see <u>Note 346</u> above) must be the same for all, without exception. This commonality demonstrates the unity of mankind, despite their differences in colour, language, etc. And Allah asks us to seek His forgiveness; for, however pious a person, he/she is prone to mistakes, sins. Even the Prophet

(peace & Allah's blessings be upon him) was asked to seek His forgiveness at the very zenith of success in his mission (Verse 110:3).

فَإِذَا قَضَيْتُم مَّنَـٰسِكَكُمْ فَٱذْكُرُوا۟ ٱللَّهَ كَذِكْرِكُمْ ءَابَآءَكُمْ أَوْ أَشَدَّ ذِكْرًا ۗ فَمِنَ ٱلنَّاسِ مَن يَقُولُ رَبَّنَآ ءَاتِنَا فِى ٱلدُّنْيَا وَمَا لَهُۥ فِى ٱلْأَخِرَةِ مِنْ خَلَـٰقٍ ﴿٢٠٠﴾

200. Fa-itha qadaytum manasikakum faothkuroo Allaha kathikrikum abaakum aw ashadda thikran famina alnnasi man yaqoolu rabbana atina fee alddunya wama lahu fee al-akhirati min khalaqin

---

2:200. And when you complete your rituals, do remember Allah just as – or even better than how – you would remember your fathers.[350] There are then those among mankind who say, "Our Lord! Give us in this world." And they shall have no share of happiness in the Hereafter!

---

350. In the context of the immediately preceding Verses, 'rituals' mentioned here are those divinely prescribed for the Hajj. And, this Verse compares remembrance of Allah with our remembrance of our fathers. We remember our fathers with affection, with awe and with gratitude for all they did for us during our upbringing. We ought to remember Allah more intensely as it is He, in fact, Who made all the necessary provisions, behind the scenes, for our birth and subsequent upbringing. And the best way to remember Allah is to establish proper prayers (refer Verse 20:14).

وَمِنْهُم مَّن يَقُولُ رَبَّنَآ ءَاتِنَا فِى ٱلدُّنْيَا حَسَنَةً وَفِى ٱلْأَخِرَةِ حَسَنَةً وَقِنَا عَذَابَ ٱلنَّارِ ﴿٢٠١﴾

201. Waminhum man yaqoolu rabbana atina fee alddunya hasanatan wafee al-akhirati hasanatan waqina AAathaba alnnari

---

2:201. And among them are those who say, "Our Lord! Give us that which is good in this world, and that which is good in the Hereafter. And save us from punishment of the Fire!"

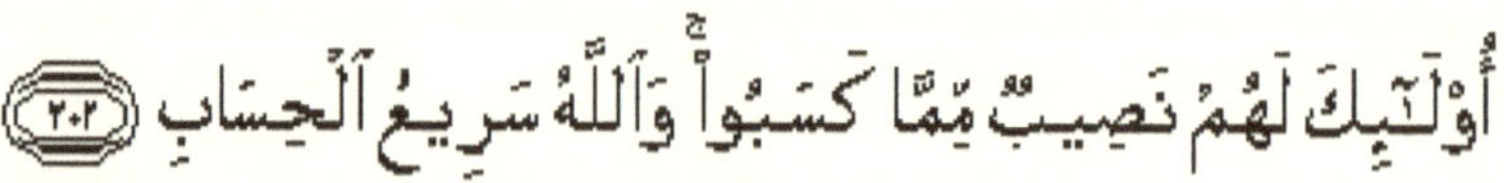

202. Ola-ika lahum naseebun mimma kasaboo waAllahu sareeAAu alhisabi

2:202. Those are the ones for whom shall there be a due share of what they earned. And Allah is quick in keeping accounts.[351, 352]

351. As you may well see, the latter part of Verse 2:200 above speaks of persons who ask Allah only for things in this world. Such persons obviously believe in Allah, but they apparently do not have any belief in the Hereafter! So, they do not ask Him for any thing in the Hereafter, and Allah debars them of any happiness there. Verse 2:201, on the other hand, speaks of persons who ask Allah for <u>good</u> things both here, in this world, and in the Hereafter. It is this latter category of persons, whom Allah promises their due share <u>of what they earned</u> – earned by their deeds here, in this life! Please note that Allah does not promise them the *huasanah* (that which is good) in the Hereafter, just because they had prayed for it. They would get it, if they had earned it by their good deeds in this world. Persons of the former category (those spoken of in Verse 2.200), however, wouldn't get it, despite any good deeds they might have done in this world.

352. I would further like to point out here, in this context, that most pilgrims, who do not know Arabic, just orally repeat *rabbanaa .... naar*, from Verse 2.201, during their *tawaafs* and prayers at the Kaabah, without understanding its implication. But when they supplicate to Him, in their own different languages, they ask only for mundane things of this life! Such people are in grave danger of losing their Hereafter; for, Allah responds to what their hearts crave for, and not to what they repeat, parrot like, what others have asked them to say.

146

203. Wao_thkuroo Alla_ha fee ayy_amin maAAdood_atin faman taAAajjala fee yawmayni fal_a ithma AAalayhi waman taakhkhara fal_a ithma AAalayhi limani ittaq_a waittaqoo Alla_ha waiAAlamoo annakum ilayhi tu_hsharoon**a**

2:203. [353]Remember Allah during those few days.[354] And no sin upon one who limits the days to two, nor upon one who extends – upon the one who fears Allah! And fear Allah and know, for sure, that you will all be brought together before Him.[355]

353. This Verse is the last one in the group of Verses, starting with Verse 2:196, about the Hajj.

354. We have seen, in Chapter Note 346, that the 10th day of *Dhul-Hijjah*, and the night immediately following the day, is spent in remembering Allah at *Al-mashuaril-huaraam*. This remembrance is in pursuance of divine instructions in Verse 2:198. Early in the morning of 11th *Dhul-Hijjah*, the pilgrims return to Mina. It is the remembrance at this place Mina that this Verse, 2:203, refers to. It is during the camp at this place, after the return from Arafaat and Muzdalifah, that most of the rituals of the Hajj are performed. And in pursuance of Verse 2:200 the pilgrims are required to remember Allah after performing the prescribed rituals.

355. This consciousness, that we will all be brought together before our One Creator one day, is the prime requisite for real success in the great Test of this worldly life. It is a sad thing to observe that most of those who do say their prayers regularly observe fasts as required and perform all their other religious duties conscientiously, fail to be governed by the same spirit of Allah-consciousness in their worldly dealings. It is in these worldly dealings, mainly, that the divine test lies!

وَمِنَ ٱلنَّاسِ مَن يُعْجِبُكَ قَوْلُهُ فِى ٱلْحَيَوٰةِ ٱلدُّنْيَا وَيُشْهِدُ ٱللَّهَ عَلَىٰ مَا فِى قَلْبِهِۦ وَهُوَ أَلَدُّ ٱلْخِصَامِ ۝

204. Wamina alnn_asi man yuAAjibuka qawluhu fee al_hay_ati aldduny_a wayushhidu Alla_ha AAal_a m_a fee qalbihi wahuwa aladdu alkhi_sami

2:204. And among mankind is one, who impresses you[356] with his utterances in this worldly life. And he cites Allah as witness to what's there in his heart. And he's very skilful in argument!

356. In the original Arabic text, the pronoun used here is in the 2nd person singular form. Initially, therefore, the Verse was obviously addressed to the Prophet (peace & Allah's blessings upon him). And as it generally happened, this Verse too could have been revealed in the background of an incidence immediately preceding the revelation. But since the Qur'aan is meant for all peoples inhabiting the earth for all times till the Last Day, its Verses are couched in general terms. The pronoun *ka* (you, or more precisely 'thou') used here has therefore to be construed to mean the person himself reading the Verse at any time till the Last Day.

وَإِذَا تَوَلَّىٰ سَعَىٰ فِى ٱلْأَرْضِ لِيُفْسِدَ فِيهَا وَيُهْلِكَ ٱلْحَرْثَ وَٱلنَّسْلَ وَٱللَّهُ لَا يُحِبُّ ٱلْفَسَادَ ﴿٢٠٥﴾

205. Wa-itha tawalla saAAa fee al-ardi liyufsida feeha wayuhlika alhartha waalnnasla waAllahu la yuhibbu alfasada

2:205. And when he turns away, he endeavours on the earth, to spread anarchy therein and destroy the field[357] and the race. And Allah doesn't like anarchy! [358 to 361]

357. In the Arabic text, the word used is *huarth*. Normally, it means a plot of land set apart for agricultural production. But in <u>Verse 2:223</u>, the same word has been beautifully and appropriately used as a simile for a man's woman. Women are obviously fields for production of human beings for the continuity of human races. In the modern scenario, *huarth* could also stand for a factory producing industrial goods. A field/factory producing agricultural/industrial goods symbolises property, and together with race (*nasl*), it would symbolise 'life & property'.

358. In these Verses, being studied here, the character depicted is that of a person who says one thing and does quite the opposite. We do come across such persons very often. And if we were to make an honest peep into our own souls, we may find that we ourselves have been guilty of such behaviour! When we declare ourselves as Muslims, we declare that we are those who abide by the Qur'aan. But do we totally abide by it? Anything we do with our own free will, in contradiction to Qur'aanic teachings, does add to anarchy in this world. We do conveniently forget this.

359. Anarchy is the catalyst that helps destroy not only life and property but also humanity. In the relatively recent past, we have had the example of Hitler who mesmerised the German people, with his speeches, into the belief that theirs is the best race that can easily conquer other peoples and rule over them. The destruction of life and property, which he wrought through his wars and his infamous concentration camps, is part of history. But Hitler also destroyed the humanity of the industrious and intelligent German people. He destroyed the character of a good human race.

360. Let us now consider the significance of taking *huarth* to mean a man's consort. Allah has made her the basic entity which can substantially influence the character of a person – her son or daughter, growing up in her lap. Some characteristics, good or bad, of the mother are liable to be subconsciously transmitted to the child in her lap. And these characteristics could form the basis of the child's character.

361. The person described in these Verses endeavours to spoil the mothers' character. In the guise of a champion of the feminists, he draws them out of their homes, and from their babes, to be equal to men in any field of worldly activity – be it politics or, even wrestling! In the name of their liberty, he entices young ladies to be socialites, wearing increasingly revealing dresses. Their semi-nakedness suits the carnal desires of the males; and apparently everybody is happy. But this social behaviour leads, imperceptibly but surely, to moral degradation that permeates the developing minds of boys and girls. They tend to copy what they see their elders doing. It is thus that the person described in Verses 2:204 & 2:205 tries to destroy the whole race by first destroying the *"huarth"*. History teaches us that moral degradation of a people leads ultimately to their annihilation as any force to reckon with, in this very world.

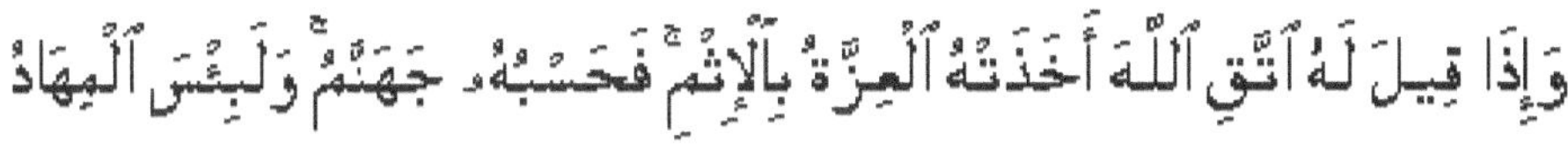

206. Wa-itha qeela lahu ittaqi Allaha akhathat-hu alAAizzatu bial-ithmi fahasbuhu jahannamu walabi/sa almihadu

---

2:206. And when he is asked to fear Allah, pride drives him to sin.[362] Hell, then, is a just retribution for him. And that, surely, is an awful resting place!

---

362. And pride it was that felled Satan from Allah's grace (peruse Chapter Note 33 of these Studies). And pride it is that distances a human being from His mercy. Pride it was that induced Satan to commit the sin of openly disobeying Allah. And pride it is that induces man to commit the sin of persisting with the wrong that he has been committing, even after realising that what he had been doing was wrong. The subject person of these Verses impresses people with his tall talks. But when people realise that his deeds lead only to destruction, they ask him to fear Allah. He however persists in his wrong-doings, just because of his false pride. He doesn't want to admit publicly that he had been wrong! Beware, my friends! Such false pride lurks in some corner of the hearts of us all. Satan is ever vigilant to exploit this lurking sense of pride to lead us astray from Allah's Straight Path.

وَمِنَ ٱلنَّاسِ مَن يَشْرِى نَفْسَهُ ٱبْتِغَآءَ مَرْضَاتِ ٱللَّهِ ۗ وَٱللَّهُ رَءُوفٌۢ بِٱلْعِبَادِ ﴿٢٠٧﴾

207. Wamina alnnasi man yashree nafsahu ibtighaa mardati Allahi waAllahu raoofun bialAAibadi

---

2:207. And among mankind are some, such as one who would sell one's own self to seek Allah's pleasure. And Allah is very kind to those who fully obey Him[363, 364].

---

363. The word *uibaad*, used in the original Arabic text, is translated here as 'those who fully obey Him'. This Arabic word literally means 'slaves'. And slaves have no alternative but to obey their masters; they do not have the right to disobedience at all. Hence, the translation as 'those who fully obey Him'. But the contextual meaning here of the word *uibaad* is well explained in the preceding sentence of this very Verse. *Uibaad* are those who would even sell their own selves to seek Allah's pleasure. Allah assures He would be kind to such persons. This assurance is not to those, mind you, who do not obey Allah on any of His commands in the Qur'aan.

364. Please also take note of the contrast in character of the person depicted in this Verse, to that of the person depicted in the preceding 3 Verses.

يَـٰٓأَيُّهَا ٱلَّذِينَ ءَامَنُوا۟ ٱدْخُلُوا۟ فِى ٱلسِّلْمِ كَآفَّةً وَلَا تَتَّبِعُوا۟ خُطُوَٰتِ ٱلشَّيْطَـٰنِ ۚ إِنَّهُۥ لَكُمْ عَدُوٌّ مُّبِينٌ ﴿٢٠٨﴾

208. Ya ayyuha allatheena amanoo odkhuloo fee alssilmi kaffatan wala tattabiAAoo khutuwati alshshaytani innahu lakum AAaduwwun mubeenun

---

2:208. O you who believe! Get into Islam thoroughly[365, 366], and follow not Satan's footsteps. He indeed is an open enemy to you.[367]

---

365. The original Arabic phrase could also be translated as 'Surrender yourselves completely to Allah'. Complete surrender to Allah would inter alia mean adherence to all applicable Qur'aanic commands.

366. Once a cyber-friend told me that it wasn't practical to do everything that the Qur'aan asks us to do. It was enough to adhere to as many Qur'aanic commands – from among those applicable – as it was practically possible. This view is a negation of this Verse we are presently studying. The Satan it is that subtly induces man to entertain such views to lead him astray. That's why the Verse further advises man not to follow the Satan's footsteps. He (the Satan) arrogantly (see Verse 7:12) thought it wasn't possible for him to follow one of Allah's commands to him – to bow before Adam!

367. In Verse 2:168 there is a similar divine instruction not to follow Satan's footsteps as 'he is to you an open enemy.' The instructions there were in the context of consuming lawful and wholesome things. One of the food items that are prohibited is 'that which is consecrated to someone other than Allah' [Verse 2:173]. This category of prohibited food could include items distributed as *tabarruk* from the shrine of a *peer* or saint. The association of the saint with the food makes the latter consecrated to 'someone other than Allah'. Consumption of such food in the belief that it specially benefits the consumer, is a manifest sin of *shirk*. It (the belief) betrays the consumer's blasphemous assumption that the *peer* or saint partners with Allah in granting special benefits in the act of eating the *tabarruk*. Satan, the avowed enemy of man, misleads the consumers in making them think that they are doing nothing wrong.

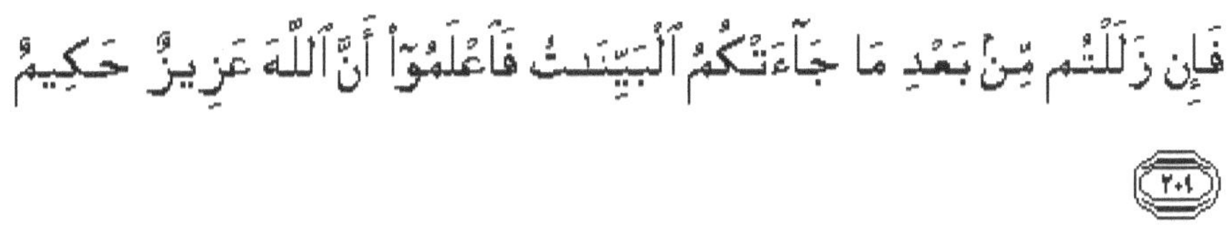

209. Fa-in zalaltum min baAAdi ma jaatkumu albayyinatu faiAAlamoo anna Allaha AAazeezun hakeemun

2:209. If then you revert to wrong-doing[368], after what has come to you of signs clear, [369] know you for certain that Allah is Omnipotent, Wise![370]

368. 'Wrong-doing' would include 'incomplete surrender to Allah'.

369. By personal experience I say that Allah does send manifest signs exclusively in a human being's life that confirm His existence and His control over everything and the truth of the Qur'aan being His Book. Verse 41:53 declares that He does show such signs in everyone's life. This is besides all the great signs of the Universe, common for everyone to see. And for us, now in this age, the Qur'aan is the greatest sign of all; it has stood the test of time. During the long period of over 14 centuries of its existence, nothing has happened that could disprove even one statement contained in the Qur'aan. Scientific discoveries, on the other hand, are continually confirming the Qur'aanic statements, one by one.

370. Allah is Almighty; anyone's failure to surrender to Him completely does not in any way impinge on His Absolute Power. Allah is wise; He knows exactly when and how anyone fails to surrender.

هَلْ يَنظُرُونَ إِلَّا أَن يَأْتِيَهُمُ ٱللَّهُ فِى ظُلَلٍ مِّنَ ٱلْغَمَامِ وَٱلْمَلَٰئِكَةُ وَقُضِىَ ٱلْأَمْرُ وَإِلَى ٱللَّهِ تُرْجَعُ ٱلْأُمُورُ ﴿٢١٠﴾

210. Hal yan*th*uroona illa an ya/tiyahumu All<u>a</u>hu fee *th*ulalin mina alghamami waalmala-ikatu waqu<u>d</u>iya al-amru wa-il<u>a</u> All<u>a</u>hi turjaAAu al-omooru

2:210. Are they waiting for nothing but Allah – and the angels – to come down to them in the shadows of the clouds, and the matter is settled once for all?[371] And to Allah are referred all matters.[372]

371. 'They' here refers to non-believers in the divine Message of the Qur'aan. In this Message, the divine purpose in the creation of mankind is explained clearly, in details and repeatedly. Arguments after arguments are presented throughout the Book to convince them that what the Message unfolds is the Truth, and nothing but the Truth. And yet they believe not! And, by way of a final argument that ought to expose the hollowness of their disbelief, they are reminded that the very purpose of their existence in this world would be defeated if Allah and the angels were to present themselves here. The purpose of mankind's existence in this world is to test them whether they come to believe in Him and in His Message without seeing Him. And when Allah presents Himself, it would be to pronounce the results of the test!

372. This divine statement is an assertion that all decisions rest with Allah, not only about the Hereafter, but also about our temporary abode in this very world. Apparently, here, <u>we</u> take decisions, individually or collectively, but these human decisions are brought to fruition if, and only if, they get the divine okay behind the scenes. So, let us remind ourselves of the reality that all our decisions and activities are under the absolute control of Allah. <u>HE is watching our every move, closely and minutely.</u>

سَلْ بَنِىٓ إِسْرَٰٓءِيلَ كَمْ ءَاتَيْنَٰهُم مِّنْ ءَايَةٍ بَيِّنَةٍ وَمَن يُبَدِّلْ نِعْمَةَ ٱللَّهِ مِنۢ بَعْدِ مَا جَآءَتْهُ فَإِنَّ ٱللَّهَ شَدِيدُ ٱلْعِقَابِ ﴿٢١١﴾

211. Sal banee isra-eela kam <u>a</u>tayn<u>a</u>hum min <u>a</u>yatin bayyinatin waman yubaddil niAAamata All<u>a</u>hi min baAAdi m<u>a</u> j<u>a</u>at-hu fa-inna All<u>a</u>ha shadeedu alAAiq<u>a</u>bi

2:211. Ask the Children of Israel[373] how many a clear Sign We gave them. And as for him who changes Allah's favour[374], after it has come to him, Allah is indeed severe then in punishment.

---

373. Refer <u>Note 39</u> of these Studies to find why Qur'aan repeatedly sites instances from Jewish history.

374. The context makes it clear that 'Allah's favour' here refers to the Torah, the devine book revealed to Prophet Moses (peace be upon him). After Moses, the Jews corrupted its Verses and thus brought upon themselves severe punishment from Allah. Their history is witness to their chastisement. Mercifully for the Muslims, the Qur'aan is divinely protected against corruption of its original Arabic text; but, nevertheless, the Muslims are suffering because of their attempts at polluting the clear meanings of Arabic Verses with human interpolations.

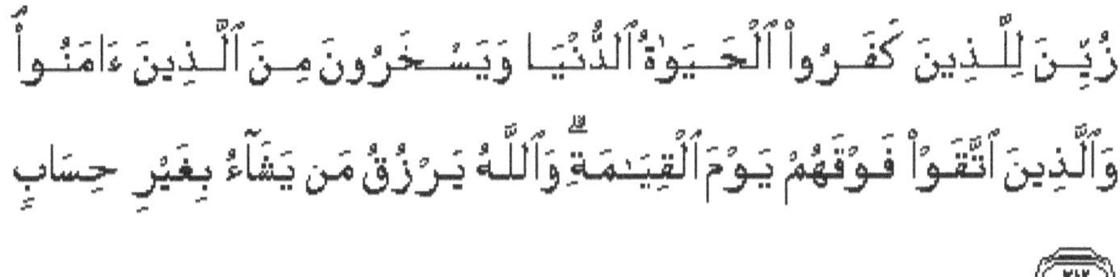

212. Zuyyina lilla<u>th</u>eena kafaroo al<u>h</u>ayatu alddun<u>ya</u> wayaskharoona mina alla<u>th</u>eena <u>a</u>manoo waalla<u>th</u>eena ittaqaw fawqahum yawma alqiy<u>a</u>mati waAll<u>a</u>hu yarzuqu man yash<u>a</u>o bighayri <u>h</u>is<u>a</u>**bin**

2:212. The life of this world is made attractive for those who suppress the Truth, and they mock at some of those who believe. And those who fear Allah shall have an upper hand over them on the Day of Resurrection.[375] And Allah provides for whomsoever He wishes, without measure![376]

---

375. One of numerous ways in which Allah tests mankind is to give a plenty in this world to some of those who disbelieve, and to give less to the believers, in comparison. In such cases, the disbelievers are wont to scoff at the believers, taunting them that despite their belief, their Allah has provided them with less wealth. The believers' test lies in whether they remain steadfast in their faith even in such seemingly unfavourable and unfair circumstances. The All-knowing and Merciful Allah however strengthens the will of the believers in such trying circumstances by promising them that they shall surely have an upper hand in the everlasting Hereafter, if they but passed the test of the temporary life of this world.

376. In the exercise of this absolute divine prerogative of our Lord, we, the creatures, have no say at all. But let us be clear in our minds that our Lord is a Just Lord. If in this world, He chooses to give undeservedly more wealth to a disbeliever than to a believer, He knows what He is doing! We should remember that He has reserved His bounty *bi ghayri huisaab* (without measure), in the Hereafter, only for the believers.

كَانَ ٱلنَّاسُ أُمَّةً وَٰحِدَةً فَبَعَثَ ٱللَّهُ ٱلنَّبِيِّـۧنَ مُبَشِّرِينَ وَمُنذِرِينَ وَأَنزَلَ مَعَهُمُ ٱلْكِتَٰبَ بِٱلْحَقِّ لِيَحْكُمَ بَيْنَ ٱلنَّاسِ فِيمَا ٱخْتَلَفُوا۟ فِيهِ وَمَا ٱخْتَلَفَ فِيهِ إِلَّا ٱلَّذِينَ أُوتُوهُ مِنۢ بَعْدِ مَا جَآءَتْهُمُ ٱلْبَيِّنَٰتُ بَغْيًۢا بَيْنَهُمْ فَهَدَى ٱللَّهُ ٱلَّذِينَ ءَامَنُوا۟ لِمَا ٱخْتَلَفُوا۟ فِيهِ مِنَ ٱلْحَقِّ بِإِذْنِهِۦ وَٱللَّهُ يَهْدِى مَن يَشَآءُ إِلَىٰ صِرَٰطٍ مُّسْتَقِيمٍ ﴿٢١٣﴾

213. Kana alnnasu ommatan wahidatan fabaAAatha Allahu alnnabiyyeena mubashshireena wamunthireena waanzala maAAahumu alkitaba bialhaqqi liyahkuma bayna alnnasi feema ikhtalafoo feehi wama ikhtalafa feehi illa allatheena ootoohu min baAAdi ma jaat-humu albayyinatu baghyan baynahum fahada Allahu allatheena amanoo lima ikhtalafoo feehi mina alhaqqi bi-ithnihi waAllahu yahdee man yashao ila siratin mustaqeemin

2:213. Mankind had once been a single community. Allah then raised the Prophets to herald news of a good future and to warn, and He sent down with them the Book with the Truth to distinguish right from wrong in matters of dispute among mankind.[377] And, differed in it not but those to whom it had been given – after clear Verses had come to them – because of rivalry amongst themselves.[378, 379, 380] Allah then guided those who believed so that what they contended in the dispute in it was based on Truth by His leave. And Allah guides whomsoever He wishes towards Straight Path.

377. In Verse 4:1, Allah informs us that creation of the entire mankind was initiated through a single pair. Initially therefore there ought to have been a single family consisting of the single original pair and their offspring. The Qur'aan recounts a quarrel among two brothers in this very first family [Verses 5:27 to 5:31]. Such other quarrels & frictions, in subsequent generations, must have caused the drifting apart of mankind to different and distant parts in this wide, wide world. In course of time, due to lack of facilities of communication and transport, people living in different parts must have lost contact with one another. In the circumstances, Allah sent different prophets at different times to people living in different parts of the world, to remind them of their duty to Allah and of the distinction between right and wrong.

378. Even though the divine messages were clear and well-explained, people indulged in voicing their personal opinions about the messages. And one person's opinion differed from another's. Thus, did the disputes arise. Although a dispassionate study of the divine messages would reveal the Truth, most people would not budge from their own contrary interpretations out of false pride. They wouldn't bear to admit that they were wrong, while some others were right.

379. And this legacy of voicing personal opinions about divine Verses continues to this day. People who consider themselves as being learned wouldn't take Qur'aanic Verses at their face value. They try to replace the plain meanings with their own opinionated meanings and to stick to the latter. Most others, who hardly take the trouble to understand the Qur'aan, go by what such 'learned' people say the Qur'aan contains. We have this way deprived ourselves of divine help, mercy and grace.

380. To regain Allah's favour, we ought therefore to stick to and abide by the plain meanings of the Qur'aanic Verses. If we encounter any difficulty in understanding any Verse, there ought to be other Verses in the Qur'aan itself that would help us understand. We just must have absolute faith in what the Qur'aan says in the rest of this very Verse. Allah is sure then to guide us to the true meanings of His Verses.

أَمْ حَسِبْتُمْ أَن تَدْخُلُواْ ٱلْجَنَّةَ

وَلَمَّا يَأْتِكُم مَّثَلُ ٱلَّذِينَ خَلَوْاْ مِن قَبْلِكُم مَّسَّتْهُمُ ٱلْبَأْسَاءُ وَٱلضَّرَّاءُ

وَزُلْزِلُواْ حَتَّىٰ يَقُولَ ٱلرَّسُولُ وَٱلَّذِينَ ءَامَنُواْ مَعَهُۥ مَتَىٰ نَصْرُ ٱللَّهِ أَلَا

إِنَّ نَصْرَ ٱللَّهِ قَرِيبٌ ﴿٢١٤﴾

214. Am ḥasibtum an tadkhuloo aljannata walammā ya/tikum mathalu allatheena khalaw min qablikum massat-humu alba/sao waalddarrao wazulziloo ḥattā yaqoola alrrasoolu waallatheena amanoo maAAahu matā naṣru Allāhi alā inna naṣra Allāhi qareebun

2:214. Do you think that you shall enter Paradise and hasn't come to you as yet the kind of what came to those who passed away before you?[381] Pain and loss afflicted them, and they were severely shaken till the Messenger and those who believed with him, cried out, "Where is Allah's help?"[382, 383] Allah's help is indeed near, isn't it? [384]

381. Life in this world is not at all a bed of roses, especially for those who expect to get Paradise in the Hereafter. Remember what Allah says in Verses 2:155 to 2:157. You may also go through the Study Notes 250 to 253 under those Verses.

382. At first sight it may appear odd that the Messenger too lost his cool at the severity of the trials and tribulations in this world. Allah didn't spare even his Messengers from it. That has been the fact as epitomised in the life of Muhammad (peace be upon him), the last of the Messengers. For 13 long years he suffered the worst kind of persecution at the hands of his own people and close relatives. If Allah wanted, He could very well have saved him from the suffering. But He wanted His Messengers to be the epitomes of suffering masses – suffering the same (or even worse) trials & tribulations that the masses were put to. Allah didn't want people to come up with the excuse that the Messengers didn't suffer as much as they (the masses) did.

383. Allah wants to drive home another important point here. HE wants to emphasise the fact that the Messengers were, after all, human beings. It was this humanness that made even a great Prophet like Jesus (peace be upon him) cry out, "Why have you forsaken me, God" or with words to that effect! And yet our Christian brothers are bent upon giving Jesus the status of divinity, and thus indulge in the unpardonable sin of *shirk*!!

384. Allah thus assures his human creatures that His help is ever so near. [Peruse also in this context, Verse 186] The benevolent Master is just testing His creature's belief in Him! HE is asking the creature to draw upon his own experience and recall how on many an occasion, his faith in Him had saved him, just on the brink of disaster – just as Jesus' faith in His Master had saved him from death on the cross, which his persecutors had so cruelly proposed for him. Just as Muhammad's ill-equipped force of just 313 men were helped to a resounding victory over a far-better equipped force of over 1000 at the famous battle of Badr, thanks to Allah and to Muhammad's unflinching faith in Him.

يَسْـَٔلُونَكَ مَاذَا يُنفِقُونَ قُلْ مَآ أَنفَقْتُم مِّنْ خَيْرٍ فَلِلْوَٰلِدَيْنِ وَٱلْأَقْرَبِينَ وَٱلْيَتَٰمَىٰ وَٱلْمَسَٰكِينِ وَٱبْنِ ٱلسَّبِيلِ وَمَا تَفْعَلُوا۟ مِنْ خَيْرٍ فَإِنَّ ٱللَّهَ بِهِۦ عَلِيمٌ ﴿٢١٥﴾

215. Yas-aloonaka matha yunfiqoona qul ma anfaqtum min khayrin falilwalidayni waal-aqrabeena waalyatama waalmasakeeni waibni alssabeeli wama tafAAaloo min khayrin fa-inna Allaha bihi AAaleemun

2:215. They ask you what is it that they should spend.[385] Say, "That which you spend of good[386] ought to be for parents[387], near ones[388], orphans, the poor and the wayfarer[389]. And whatever good you do, Allah is indeed aware of it[390]."

385. In Verse 195, Allah commands us to spend in His path. And we have discussed in Note 331, as to what Allah's path/way is. Further down in this same *surah* Al-Baqarah, we have Verse 2:219 wherein

Allah commands us, in answer to the same question from the people, to spend that which we can spare. And here in this Verse 2:215, Allah enumerates the persons on whom to spend what we can spare.

386. We spend to get something for self-consumption, or to give something to others. Allah tells us that the something we give ought to be good, and not bad. We cannot, for example, spend to serve prohibited articles like alcohol to others.

387. Parents lead the list of the beneficiaries of spendings other than for self. This is indicative of the importance given to parents in the divine scheme of things. They are to be given preferences in this regard over one's wife and children, who get included among *aqurabeena* who come next in the list.

388. The 'near ones' (*al-aqurabeena*) would include not only wife & children, but also other near and dear blood relations. It could also include close neighbours.

389. A wayfarer or a traveller could be a stranger to the place he is visiting. In such a situation, he could face problems. Allah has therefore made him also a beneficiary of a person's spare money.

390. A true believer would therefore never despair that his good work would ever go in waste.

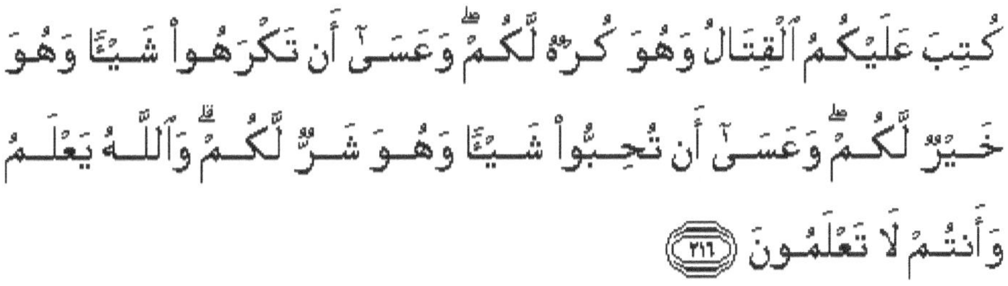

216. Kutiba AAalaykumu alqitalu wahuwa kurhun lakum waAAasa an takrahoo shay-an wahuwa khayrun lakum waAAasa an tuhibboo shay-an wahuwa sharrun lakum waAllahu yaAAlamu waantum la taAAlamoona

2:216. Conscription[391] is prescribed for you, although you are averse to it! And it may well be that you dislike a thing, although the thing is good for you. And it may well be that you like a thing, although the thing is bad for you. Allah knows, and you don't.[392 to 395]

391. The Arabic word used is *quitaal*, which has been rendered as 'fighting' by many translators. But obviously, the divine intention is not to make mankind fight and kill one another on every little pretext. Allah obviously wants us to be ever prepared to join a battle or war, when called upon to do so in Allah's path, to fight injustices and corruption. The obligation to join such a war/battle is better projected by the

English word 'conscription'. Conscription – compulsory military service, that is – is prescribed, I believe, in the USA costitution for all its citizens.

392. The thing most people are afraid of is death. It is an unknown thing for them. Of course, those who have acquired an unshakable faith in Allah, in the hereafter and in the divine scheme of things and are confident of their performance in the test of this worldly life crossing the pass mark, may be free from the fear of death.

393. And although death may come to a person even in a place considered the safest on earth, mankind traditionally considers the battlefield to be the most likely place for it (death) to come. Hence is the general reluctance to join an army. In poor countries, where getting means of livelihood is a big problem, people may join the country's army in hordes, but in affluent countries, conscription may have to be resorted to for making up the bulk of the army.

394. The abhorrence, among Muslims, to military service is depicted in Verse 4:77. The abhorrence is also there in other communities, as depicted in Verse 2:246. Allah exhorts the Muslims to get over their dislike, telling them that they may dislike fighting in a war/battle for fear, inter alia, of death. They may not die and gain a big victory. And even if they die, Allah promises them rich rewards in the Hereafter. Please peruse Verse 2:154 and Notes 247 to 249 thereon.

395. Although Allah has given this advice in the context of His command on compulsory military service, it (the advice) is couched in general terms and has general application. Man doesn't know, in certain circumstances at least, what is good or bad for him. But Allah knows, in all circumstances! It may therefore so happen that a man, with whom Allah is pleased, may find that his prayer is sometimes not answered. It may be that what he is praying for may not be good for him. Allah knows, and he does not know. A believer therefore ought to bear or be content with what Allah, in His infinite wisdom, gives him and always remember what the Qur'aan says in Verses 2:155 to 2:157.

يَسْـَٔلُونَكَ عَنِ ٱلشَّهْرِ ٱلْحَرَامِ قِتَالٍ فِيهِ قُلْ قِتَالٌ فِيهِ كَبِيرٌ

وَصَدٌّ عَن سَبِيلِ ٱللَّهِ وَكُفْرٌ بِهِ وَٱلْمَسْجِدِ ٱلْحَرَامِ وَإِخْرَاجُ أَهْلِهِ مِنْهُ

أَكْبَرُ عِندَ ٱللَّهِ وَٱلْفِتْنَةُ أَكْبَرُ مِنَ ٱلْقَتْلِ وَلَا يَزَالُونَ يُقَـٰتِلُونَكُمْ

حَتَّىٰ يَرُدُّوكُمْ عَن دِينِكُمْ إِنِ ٱسْتَطَـٰعُوا۟ وَمَن يَرْتَدِدْ مِنكُمْ

عَن دِينِهِ فَيَمُتْ وَهُوَ كَافِرٌ فَأُو۟لَـٰئِكَ حَبِطَتْ أَعْمَـٰلُهُمْ

فِى ٱلدُّنْيَا وَٱلْـَٔاخِرَةِ وَأُو۟لَـٰئِكَ أَصْحَـٰبُ ٱلنَّارِ هُمْ فِيهَا خَـٰلِدُونَ ﴿٢١٧﴾

217. Yas-aloonaka AAani alshshahri alharami qitalin feehi qul qitalun feehi kabeerun wasaddun AAan sabeeli Allahi wakufrun bihi waalmasjidi alharami wa-ikhraju ahlihi minhu akbaru AAinda Allahi waalfitnatu akbaru mina alqatli wala yazaloona yuqatiloonakum hatta yaruddookum AAan

deenikum ini istataAAoo waman yartadid minkum AAan deenihi fayamut wahuwa kafirun faola-ika habitat aAAmaluhum fee alddunya waal-akhirati waola-ika as-habu alnnari hum feeha khalidoona

---

2:217. They ask you about fighting during the sacred/prohibited month[396]. Say, "Fighting therein is a grave matter. And, to Allah, obstructing from Allah's Path and from the Sacred Place of Worship, suppressing the truth about Him and driving its residents out from the Sacred Place are matters that are graver! And, such mischievous behaviour is a more serious matter than killing.[397 to 401] They won't let up in their fighting with you till they, if they could, turn you away from your religion (way of life). And as for the one amongst you who turns back from his religion and dies whilst suppressing the truth, the deeds of such people are of no use to them – both here, and in the Hereafter. And those will be the inhabitants of the Fire. They shall be there forever."

---

396. Please peruse Chapter Note 328 of these Studies, in this context.

397. Most of the divine directives in the Qur'aan were given in the background of events that took place just before the revelations of the directives. Thus, did Allah implant the directives in the minds of the believers then. A bland directive of do's & don'ts, without the relevant background, wouldn't have made as lasting impressions on human minds as was thus made.

398. The divine directives here too had their background of events. But Qur'aanic directives weren't meant for a particular age. Those are meant for all times till the Last Day! The All-knowing Allah therefore didn't saddle the directives with the background events of those days when the directives were revealed. People of subsequent ages are thus divinely required to relate the directives (purposely made in general terms) to events of their own ages.

399. But many of our religious leaders insist on interpreting divine directives in the Qur'aan in the light of the *ahaadeeth* narrating the background events at the time of the revelations. In doing so, they do not mind even if the plain meaning of the Qur'aanic Verses has to be changed to align them with the *ahaadeeth*! And there is no guarantee that the *ahaadeeth* contain only the truth and nothing but the truth. Those were written down hundreds of years after the death of the Prophet (peace and Allah's blessings be upon him).

400. And the plain meaning of this part of the Qur'aanic Verse here is that Allah of course won't approve of Muslims initiating any fighting during a sacred month. But fighting can be resorted to even during that month if it is necessary to put down mischief/rebellion. Let us stick to this plain meaning. The *ahaadeeth* associated with this Verse may lead us astray.

401. And there is one more thing that needs to be stressed in this context. The Qur'aan has made it clear that there is no compulsion in religion (2:256). So, there is no question of Muslims ever fighting with any group of people just because that group doesn't accept Islam as its religion. Fighting is enjoined only when any group's disbelief in Islamic monotheism is coupled with mischief, aggression, transgression or rebellion.

إِنَّ ٱلَّذِينَ ءَامَنُواْ وَٱلَّذِينَ هَاجَرُواْ وَجَـٰهَدُواْ فِى سَبِيلِ ٱللَّهِ أُوْلَـٰٓئِكَ يَرْجُونَ رَحْمَتَ ٱللَّهِ وَٱللَّهُ غَفُورٌ رَّحِيمٌ ۝

218. Inna allatheena amanoo waallatheena hajaroo wajahadoo fee sabeeli Allahi ola-ika yarjoona rahmata Allahi waAllahu ghafoorun raheemun

---

2:218. Indeed, those who believed and those who migrated and struggled in Allah's Path – it is for those to expect Allah's Mercy. And Allah is Forgiving, Merciful.[402]

---

402. Obviously, this Verse is with reference to the preceding one (2:217). In that Verse, it was indicated that un-called for initiation of fighting in a prohibited month was a serious offence. Now, in this Verse, it is made clear that if the believers are guilty of committing this offence, they could <u>expect</u> mercy from their Merciful Lord. Please take note of the underlined word 'expect'. Allah doesn't promise that He would certainly forgive, but the language used indicates that He would certainly consider forgiving the offenders, if their faith is strong enough and if they had suffered migration and struggle, for the sake of their faith. The offending believers ought to take care that they do not commit the offence again.

۞ يَسْـَٔلُونَكَ عَنِ ٱلْخَمْرِ وَٱلْمَيْسِرِ قُلْ فِيهِمَآ إِثْمٌ كَبِيرٌ وَمَنَـٰفِعُ لِلنَّاسِ وَإِثْمُهُمَآ أَكْبَرُ مِن نَّفْعِهِمَا وَيَسْـَٔلُونَكَ مَاذَا يُنفِقُونَ قُلِ ٱلْعَفْوَ كَذَٰلِكَ يُبَيِّنُ ٱللَّهُ لَكُمُ ٱلْأَيَـٰتِ لَعَلَّكُمْ تَتَفَكَّرُونَ ۝

219. Yas-aloonaka AAani alkhamri waalmaysiri qul feehima ithmun kabeerun wamanafiAAu lilnnasi wa-ithmuhuma akbaru min nafAAihima wayas-aloonaka matha yunfiqoona quli alAAafwa kathalika yubayyinu Allahu lakumu al-ayati laAAallakum tatafakkaroona

---

2:219. They ask you about intoxicants and lottery. Say, "In them both, there is a great sin, and benefits, for mankind; and the sin therein is greater than the benefits thereof.[403] And they ask you what is it that they should spend. Say that which is more than your needs.[404] Thus does Allah explain to you the Verses/signs, so that you ponder

---

403. In Verses 5:90 & 5:91, it is clarified that taking intoxicants and playing lottery (any game wherein gains are made and losses suffered, purely depending on luck or chance) are disgraceful things prompted by the Satan to excite enmity and hatred amongst mankind and to hinder them from remembrance of Allah and from prayer. These (the disgraceful things) are therefore described as containing a great sin in this Verse (2:219).

404. The very same query of the people is mentioned in <u>Verse 2:215</u>. There, as a prelude to the answer proper, the categories of persons, for whom to spend, are first specified. Here, in Verse 2:219, the answer proper to the query, made by the people, is given. The prelude, in Verse 2:215, facilitates understanding the answer given here. (In this context, please take careful note of what is stated at the end of this Verse, 2:219.) Since even the closest relatives get mentioned among the recipients of one's spending, it becomes clear that what is in excess (or what one can spare) is what remains after one fulfils one's own <u>personal</u> needs.

فِى ٱلدُّنْيَا وَٱلْأَخِرَةِ وَيَسْـَٔلُونَكَ عَنِ ٱلْيَتَـٰمَىٰ قُلْ إِصْلَاحٌ لَّهُمْ خَيْرٌ وَإِن تُخَالِطُوهُمْ فَإِخْوَٰنُكُمْ وَٱللَّهُ يَعْلَمُ ٱلْمُفْسِدَ مِنَ ٱلْمُصْلِحِ وَلَوْ شَآءَ ٱللَّهُ لَأَعْنَتَكُمْ إِنَّ ٱللَّهَ عَزِيزٌ حَكِيمٌ ۞ ٢٢٠

220. Fee alddunya waal-akhirati wayas-aloonaka AAani alyatama qul islahun lahum khayrun wa-in tukhalitoohum fa-ikhwanukum waAllahu yaAAlamu almufsida mina almuslihi walaw shaa Allahu laaAAnatakum inna Allaha AAazeezun hakeemun

---

2:220. – (Ponder) over this world and the Hereafter.[406] And they ask you about the orphans. Say, "Treat and train them well. And if you mix/interact/inhabit with them, they are your brethren. And Allah does well distinguish the transgressor from the reformer.[407] Had Allah so willed, He could have made things difficult for you.[408] Indeed, Allah is Omnipotent, Wise!"

---

406. Here's the end of the sentence begun at the end of the preceding Verse. Allah makes us ponder over this world and the next through his Verses/signs. He makes us ponder why, for example, He is asking us to spend in His cause – and not accumulate – all that is more than our personal needs. He is asking us to spend because this world is transitory, illusive. He is asking us to spend so that we thereby help build our secure, comfortable and permanent abode in the Hereafter. He is asking us to spend, in fact, for our own welfare!

407. Elsewhere in the Qur'aan, Allah commands us not to cheat the orphans of/in their property (Verse 4:2). Verse 4:6 gives further directions for dealing with orphans' properties. Those who swallow orphan

property are condemned to go to Hell (Verse 4:10)! Please keep these Verses in mind in the context of what is stated here, in Verse 2:220, about the orphans.

408. But Allah desires to make things easy for us, and not difficult. [Verse 2:185].

وَلَا تَنكِحُواْ ٱلْمُشْرِكَـٰتِ حَتَّىٰ يُؤْمِنَّ وَلَأَمَةٌ مُّؤْمِنَةٌ خَيْرٌ مِّن مُّشْرِكَةٍ وَلَوْ

أَعْجَبَتْكُمْ وَلَا تُنكِحُواْ ٱلْمُشْرِكِينَ حَتَّىٰ يُؤْمِنُواْ وَلَعَبْدٌ مُّؤْمِنٌ خَيْرٌ مِّن

مُّشْرِكٍ وَلَوْ أَعْجَبَكُمْ أُوْلَـٰٓئِكَ يَدْعُونَ إِلَى ٱلنَّارِ وَٱللَّهُ يَدْعُوٓاْ إِلَى ٱلْجَنَّةِ

وَٱلْمَغْفِرَةِ بِإِذْنِهِۦ وَيُبَيِّنُ ءَايَـٰتِهِۦ لِلنَّاسِ لَعَلَّهُمْ يَتَذَكَّرُونَ ﴿٢٢١﴾

221. Wala tankihoo almushrikati hatta yu/minna walaamatun mu/minatun khayrun min mushrikatin walaw aAAjabatkum wala tunkihoo almushrikeena hatta yu/minoo walaAAabdun mu/minun khayrun min mushrikin walaw aAAjabakum ola-ika yadAAoona ila alnnari waAllahu yadAAoo ila aljannati waalmaghfirati bi-ithnihi wayubayyinu ayatihi lilnnasi laAAallahum yatathakkaroona

---

2:221. And marry not female polytheists until they believe. And a believing slave girl is better than a female polytheist, even if you like the latter. And get not married to male polytheists until they believe. And, certainly, a believing slave is better than a male polytheist even if you like the latter. They call you to the Fire, and Allah beckons you to Paradise, and to forgiveness with His permission, by His call.[409 to 410] And He explains His Verses/signs for mankind so that they remember and reflect.[411]

---

409. On the silver screen, or on TV screens, we are fed with man-coined stories glorifying man living and dying for nothing but his lady-love. As if she were the 'be-all' and the 'end-all' of human existence. Some youngsters do fall for such misleading story lines. For them, it is immaterial if their girls belong to religions other than their own. They think they would be setting good examples for others to follow in the interest of amity and goodwill among different religious groups, if they were to marry girls from other communities or religions.

410. But such amity and goodwill is bound to lead to lack of faith in religion, in Allah, and in the Hereafter. And the lack of faith is a precursor to all kinds of evil in this world, and to the Fire in the Hereafter. Allah therefore forbids believers against having spouses who do not believe. HE promises forgiveness and Paradise to all those believers who sincerely repent their past misdeeds and do not turn back to evil ways. Allah thus gives hope for even the hardest criminal unless he is on his deathbed.

411. Alas! Mankind remember and reflect but little. And they seek misleading explanations from sources other than the Qur'aanic Verses!!

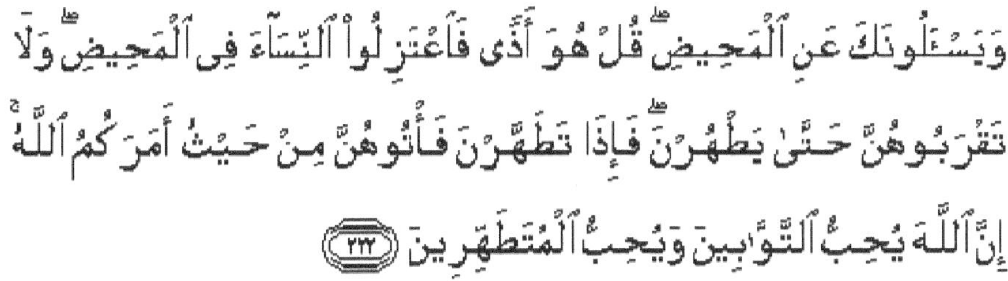

222. Wayas-aloonaka AAani almaheedi qul huwa athan faiAAtaziloo alnnisaa fee almaheedi wala taqraboohunna hatta yathurna fa-itha tatahharna fa/toohunna min haythu amarakumu Allahu inna Allaha yuhibbu alttawwabeena wayuhibbu almutatahhireena

---

2:222. And they ask you about menstruation. Tell them, "It is harmful.[412, 413] So keep away from women in menstruation, and approach them not till they're cleansed.[414] And when they are cleansed, go to them in the manner decreed for you by Allah.[415] Indeed, Allah loves those who repent and seek forgiveness, and He loves those who keep themselves clean."[416]

---

412. Every month the uterus of an adult woman, who is not already pregnant and who has not reached the age of menopause, prepares itself for pregnancy. It prepares itself to welcome, nourish and help develop an impregnated egg for over nine months to transform it into a human form ready to come out into the open world. The preparation results in a thickened lining of the inner wall of the uterus.

413. But if the pregnancy does not happen, the thickened lining of the uterus wall gets damaged and is shed out through the vagina in the form of tissues and blood. This draining of the damaged uterus lining is known as menstruation, menses or 'the monthly period' in women. A menstruating woman could be in a vulnerable state, both mentally and physically.

414. Recent studies have revealed that there is a greater risk of transmitting AIDS and other sexually transmitted diseases through sexual intercourse during menstruation. The onslaught of AIDS in recent times could be a direct consequence of the ignorance of or blatant disregard for this divine guidance/command. Man's welfare lies in the obedience of Allah's directives.

415. Aberrations in sexual behaviour like indulging in anal sex, being unnatural and therefore not as per the divine design, are obviously not as decreed by Allah.

416. The All-knowing Allah has made the sex urge strong, obviously for the procreation of mankind till the Last Day. It is so strong that even the pious may be tempted to taste the forbidden fruit, sometimes.

That is why Allah promises forgiveness for those who may commit a sin in this regard, unintentionally, and then repent and sincerely resolve not to commit the sin again. Please also take note of the importance given to maintenance of cleanliness in general.

223. Nisaokum harthun lakum fa/too harthakum anna shi/tum waqaddimoo li-anfusikum waittaqoo Allaha waiAAlamoo annakum mulaqoohu wabashshiri almu/mineena

2:223. Your women are sexual partners[417] for you. Come to your partners then how you please, [418] and make provisions beforehand for your selves[419]. And fear Allah and know that you will certainly meet Him. And give glad tidings to the believers.[420]

417. The Arabic term *harthun* literally means plot of land used for agricultural growth. Consider how beautifully, and appropriately, the divine Book has metaphorically used the term here for wives, the sexual partners for men!

418. This indicates divine sanction for foreplay before the sexual act.

419. In Qur'aanic terminology, this usually means, "Do such deeds as would please Allah to grant you a place in Paradise." But in the context here, it could also mean making provisions for added responsibilities of parenthood.

420. In other words, beware of your certain meeting with your Lord when every bit of your acts in this world will stand exposed. So, abstain from all wrongdoings, including indulging in aberrations like anal sex (see Note 415 above), while you are still in this world. And as for those who are certain of this meeting and who therefore adhere to the do's don'ts as per divine prescription in the Qur'aan, they are given here the glad tidings. Their mistakes will be forgiven, and they shall enjoy everlasting bliss in Paradise.

وَلَا تَجْعَلُوا۟ ٱللَّهَ عُرْضَةً لِّأَيْمَـٰنِكُمْ أَن تَبَرُّوا۟ وَتَتَّقُوا۟ وَتُصْلِحُوا۟ بَيْنَ ٱلنَّاسِ ۗ وَٱللَّهُ سَمِيعٌ عَلِيمٌ ﴿٢٢٤﴾

224. Wala tajAAaloo Allaha AAurdatan li-aymanikum an tabarroo watattaqoo watuslihoo bayna alnnasi waAllahu sameeAAun AAaleemun

---

2:224. And make not Allah but a front for your oaths that you're good, pious and a reformer. Allah listens, knows.[421]

---

421. This Verse discourages frequent swearing, in Allah's Name, in emphasis of one's virtues. Allah is aware of them. There is no need of the swearing for those virtuous. But we all do come across persons, who would swear by Allah, without batting an eyelid, that they're but epitomes of virtue. But, later, we come to know that they're rogues. This Verse alludes to such people as well! They should know that their Creator is aware of their perfidy. They can't escape His firm grip.

لَّا يُؤَاخِذُكُمُ ٱللَّهُ بِٱللَّغْوِ فِىٓ أَيْمَـٰنِكُمْ وَلَـٰكِن يُؤَاخِذُكُم بِمَا كَسَبَتْ قُلُوبُكُمْ ۗ وَٱللَّهُ غَفُورٌ حَلِيمٌ ﴿٢٢٥﴾

225. La yu-akhithukumu Allahu biallaghwi fee aymanikum walakin yu-akhithukum bima kasabat quloobukum waAllahu ghafoorun haleemun

---

2:225. Allah does not hold you responsible for any casual oath that you may take, but He holds you responsible for the one consciously taken. And Allah is Forgiving, Kind.[422]

---

422. Often, while in fits of anger or just in jest, we say things that we do not mean to act upon. Allah is very kind. He forgives such unintentional utterances. But we shouldn't go on repeating such casual swearing. Allah may not forgive then. It may amount to being casual in our attitude to our Lord and Creator.

لِّلَّذِينَ يُؤْلُونَ مِن نِّسَآئِهِمْ تَرَبُّصُ أَرْبَعَةِ أَشْهُرٍ فَإِن فَآءُو فَإِنَّ ٱللَّهَ غَفُورٌ رَّحِيمٌ ﴿٢٢٦﴾

226. Lillatheena yu/loona min nisa-ihim tarabbusu arbaAAati ashhurin fa-in faoo fa-inna Allaha ghafoorun raheemun

2:226. For those who vow to keep themselves away from their wives, there is a waiting period of 4 months.[423] But if they go back on their oaths meanwhile, surely Allah is forgiving, merciful.[424]

423. There is a three-fold purpose in prescribing this waiting period. One, it prevents the husband from throwing out his wife from his house, immediately upon his taking such a vow. Two, it gives the couple time for reconciliation. Three, it prevents the husband from an indefinite abstention. If the couple is not reconciled during the waiting period, the husband has to divorce the wife, who can then be free to marry another man.

424. Refer Verse 2:225 and corresponding Note 422 above, in this context. When one takes an oath for commission or omission of any act, it's a promise given to oneself. The breaking of any promise is an undesirable thing, but in the interest of reconciliation between a husband and a wife, Allah is willing to forgive.

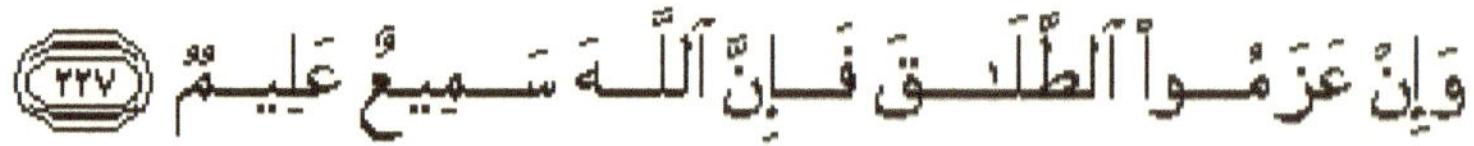

وَإِنْ عَزَمُوا۟ ٱلطَّلَـٰقَ فَإِنَّ ٱللَّهَ سَمِيعٌ عَلِيمٌ ﴿٢٢٧﴾

227. Wa-in AAazamoo alttalaqa fa-inna Allaha sameeAAun AAaleemun

2:227. And if they are firmly resolved upon divorce, then indeed Allah listens, knows.[425]

425. Allah understands the position between the husband and the wife and makes adequate provisions, in the best interest of both, for effecting the divorce. The provisions are described in Verses that immediately follow this Verse in the Qur'aan.

وَٱلْمُطَلَّقَٰتُ يَتَرَبَّصْنَ بِأَنفُسِهِنَّ ثَلَٰثَةَ قُرُوٓءٍ وَلَا يَحِلُّ لَهُنَّ
أَن يَكْتُمْنَ مَا خَلَقَ ٱللَّهُ فِىٓ أَرْحَامِهِنَّ إِن كُنَّ يُؤْمِنَّ بِٱللَّهِ وَٱلْيَوْمِ
ٱلْءَاخِرِ وَبُعُولَتُهُنَّ أَحَقُّ بِرَدِّهِنَّ فِى ذَٰلِكَ إِنْ أَرَادُوٓاْ إِصْلَٰحًا وَلَهُنَّ مِثْلُ
ٱلَّذِى عَلَيْهِنَّ بِٱلْمَعْرُوفِ وَلِلرِّجَالِ عَلَيْهِنَّ دَرَجَةٌ وَٱللَّهُ عَزِيزٌ حَكِيمٌ

228. Waalmutallaqatu yatarabbasna bi-anfusihinna thalathata quroo-in wala yahillu lahunna an yaktumna ma khalaqa Allahu fee arhamihinna in kunna yu/minna biAllahi waalyawmi al-akhiri wabuAAoolatuhunna ahaqqu biraddihinna fee thalika in aradoo islahan walahunna mithlu allathee AAalayhinna bialmaAAroofi walilrrijali AAalayhinna darajatun waAllahu AAazeezun hakeemun

2:228. And the divorced women should wait for three menstruations. And it is not proper for them to hide what Allah has created in their wombs if they do believe in Allah and in the Last Day. And their husbands have the authority to take them back during that period, if they desire reconciliation.[426] And the women have rights just as they have obligations upon them, in fair measure. And for men, a rank above them.[427 to 429] And Allah is Omnipotent, Wise.[430, 431]

426. Allah has explained here the purpose of the waiting period prescribed. It is to ascertain whether the divorced woman is pregnant, so that the parentage of the child is determined. And if the woman happens to be pregnant, it may as well be that because of the unborn child – a bond between the woman and her husband – the two may get inclined towards reconciliation. The husband has been given the authority to resume conjugal relations with the woman before the expiry of the prescribed period. And thus, the separation of the couple can be averted despite pronouncement of divorce. It may thus be observed that in the divine scheme of things, doors are kept ajar for possible reconciliation. The Merciful Allah desires that married couples do not get separated on flimsy grounds.

427. In the modern age, everyone tends to harp on equality between the sexes. Otherwise, he is likely to be branded as one prejudiced against women. But, for Allah, there is no question of hiding or evading the bare truth. So, He declares, in clear terms, that men are one rank above women.

428. So far as physical strength is concerned, even women won't deny men's superiority. Inequality in this aspect gets automatically recognized when men and women are segregated for sports events wherein success is dependent on physical strength and stamina. But Allah hasn't placed men above women just on the criterion of physical strength. The ranking given in this Verse is obviously about the comparative rights and obligations of the two sexes. If men have greater rights, they have greater obligations and responsibilities too, in fair measure, towards the other sex.

429. And if men are conscious only of their higher rights, and forget about their higher obligations, they would be disturbing the divine order. This will weaken the basic units of small families that constitute the foundation of civilization and may cause the whole edifice to come down crashing.

430. None can undo what Allah does. But He does everything wisely. And it is always in the best interests of the creatures themselves to follow what He ordains for them.

431. I think my Notes above need a clarification. Allah Ta'ala has given men only one grade above women. And He has emphasized that the women have their own rights. So, their higher status by one grade should not generate the satanic pride in men. If it does, the men concerned are likely to be doomed as the Satan has been! The All-knowing Allah has given men the higher rank, not because they are intellectually superior, but for administrative purposes. No administrative unit can have a smooth running if two equal ranking persons are appointed to head that unit. A family is an administrative unit, and, as such, it ought to have one head. Allah, in His wisdom, taking all pros and cons into consideration, has ordained that the husband should head that unit. This higher status ought to make the husband, not proud but humble. With the higher rank, come higher responsibilities. He must be ever aware that the Creator is watching him. HE is watching whether he is treating his wife with respect and care and whether he runs his house with proper consultations with her. The position of the husband is like that of a Prime Minister (PM) in a cabinet form of government. The cabinet is likely to fall if the PM treats his ministers with scant respect and as his servants.

ٱلطَّلَـٰقُ مَرَّتَانِ فَإِمْسَاكٌۢ بِمَعْرُوفٍ أَوْ تَسْرِيحٌۢ بِإِحْسَـٰنٍ وَلَا يَحِلُّ لَكُمْ أَن تَأْخُذُوا۟ مِمَّآ ءَاتَيْتُمُوهُنَّ شَيْـًٔا إِلَّآ أَن يَخَافَآ أَلَّا يُقِيمَا حُدُودَ ٱللَّهِ فَإِنْ خِفْتُمْ أَلَّا يُقِيمَا حُدُودَ ٱللَّهِ فَلَا جُنَاحَ عَلَيْهِمَا فِيمَا ٱفْتَدَتْ بِهِۦ تِلْكَ حُدُودُ ٱللَّهِ فَلَا تَعْتَدُوهَا وَمَن يَتَعَدَّ حُدُودَ ٱللَّهِ فَأُو۟لَـٰٓئِكَ هُمُ ٱلظَّـٰلِمُونَ

229. Alttalaqu marratani fa-imsakun bimaAAroofin aw tasreehun bi-ihsanin wala yahillu lakum an ta/khuthoo mimma ataytumoohunna shay-an illa an yakhafa alla yuqeema hudooda Allahi fa-in khiftum alla yuqeema hudooda Allahi fala junaha AAalayhima feema iftadat bihi tilka hudoodu Allahi fala taAAtadooha waman yataAAadda hudooda Allahi faola-ika humu alththalimoona

---

2:229. After each of the first two declarations of divorce, you may either still retain them properly as your wives or set them free in a kind and charitable manner.[432, 433] And it is not permissible to you to take back from them anything that you've given them, unless both fear that they won't be able to stick to norms set by Allah. And if you so fear, there is no sin upon them two in her giving up anything of what she had received from her husband. Those are norms set by Allah, so do not violate them.[434 to 437] And those who violate norms set by Allah, those are the ones who oppress.[438]

---

432. We have seen, in Verse 2:228 above, that there is a waiting period for divorced women. During this waiting period, the husbands are authorised, if they so wish, to take back their divorced wives and resume conjugal relations with them. They can then continue to live as husband and wife, as before. But if after some time, say a year or two, the husband again divorces his wife, it becomes a second divorce in Qur'aanic terms.

433. And if, after the first divorce, there is no reconciliation during the waiting period, the divorce takes effect and the woman is then free to marry another man. Her ex-husband is required to release her honourably, and not with any acrimony. Similar is the procedure laid down and the conduct required, during and after the second divorce, if any.

434. And we do violate Allah's laws/norms with impunity. We are impervious to His wrath that is demonstrated time and again in the form of natural calamities, like the earthquake on the 8th of October 2005. This earthquake struck Kashmir, in the Indian sub-continent, and the victims were almost exclusively Muslims. We are prone to think that such natural calamities have nothing to do with the victims being good or bad.

435. Our violation of this particular divine norm is effected by the blatant twist we give to the plain meaning of a part of this Verse. The twist given is that this Verse authorises divorce at wife's instance, provided she compensates the husband by returning to him things gifted to her as his wife. The things, as demanded, are to be returned even if the husband is monetarily well off.

436. This is a lie. First, this Verse is about women against whom their husbands have already given one or two declarations of divorce. It doesn't speak of wives seeking divorces at their (wives') initiative. Second, the primary norm set by Allah is that the husbands <u>should not</u> take back whatever has been given to the wives. It is in relaxation to this norm that the provision for the wives, willingly giving up their claims to anything, is mentioned. Obviously, the relaxation is permitted only when everyone concerned agrees that it is not possible for the couple to fulfill the primary norm.

437. The primary norm, of not taking anything back from the divorced wives, could become impossible or very difficult to be executed only if the husband's financial condition is precarious. In such a circumstance, there would be no sin on the husband taking back, for example, costly ornaments that the wife willingly surrenders.

438. By misconstruing the provisions of this Verse, the male-dominated Muslim society, particularly in my part of the world, has exploited the hapless wife seeking divorce at her initiative. The persons concerned and the clergy, aiding and abetting them in this crime, thus qualify for the Qur'aanic epithet *zuaalimoon* (oppressors) here.

فَإِن طَلَّقَهَا فَلَا تَحِلُّ لَهُۥ مِنۢ بَعْدُ حَتَّىٰ تَنكِحَ زَوْجًا غَيْرَهُۥ فَإِن طَلَّقَهَا فَلَا جُنَاحَ عَلَيْهِمَآ أَن يَتَرَاجَعَآ إِن ظَنَّآ أَن يُقِيمَا حُدُودَ ٱللَّهِ وَتِلْكَ حُدُودُ ٱللَّهِ يُبَيِّنُهَا لِقَوْمٍ يَعْلَمُونَ ۝

230. Fa-in tallaqaha fala tahillu lahu min baAAdu hatta tankiha zawjan ghayrahu fa-in tallaqaha fala junaha AAalayhima an yatarajaAAa in thanna an yuqeema hudooda Allahi watilka hudoodu Allahi yubayyinuha liqawmin yaAAlamoona

---

2:230. If he then divorces her[439], he shall thereafter have no right to conjugal relationship with her until she marries another man. Then if that other man divorces her, there is no sin upon the two to return to each other if both think that they should be able to remain within parameters laid down by Allah. And He does explain those parameters, for knowledgeable people.[440]

---

439. This obviously is with reference to the preceding Verse 229 wherein mention is made of a wife divorced twice by the same husband but retained as his wife after each of the two divorces. Now this Verse 230 deals with a situation wherein the husband divorces the wife for the third time.

440. The parameters, laws or the restrictions/limits laid down by Allah for proper conduct of either one of a married couple with the other, are duly explained in the Qur'aan. We have already seen, in Verse 228, that both husband and wife have their respective rights as they have their respective obligations. The other parameters are laid down in various other Verses – in Verse 4:19, for example – throughout the Qur'aan. Allah expects that people study the Qur'aan regularly to become knowledgeable and to imbibe those parameters.

وَإِذَا طَلَّقْتُمُ ٱلنِّسَاءَ فَبَلَغْنَ أَجَلَهُنَّ فَأَمْسِكُوهُنَّ بِمَعْرُوفٍ أَوْ سَرِّحُوهُنَّ بِمَعْرُوفٍ وَلَا تُمْسِكُوهُنَّ ضِرَارًا لِّتَعْتَدُوا۟ وَمَن يَفْعَلْ ذَٰلِكَ فَقَدْ ظَلَمَ نَفْسَهُۥ وَلَا تَتَّخِذُوٓا۟ ءَايَٰتِ ٱللَّهِ هُزُوًا۟ وَٱذْكُرُوا۟ نِعْمَتَ ٱللَّهِ عَلَيْكُمْ وَمَآ أَنزَلَ عَلَيْكُم مِّنَ ٱلْكِتَٰبِ وَٱلْحِكْمَةِ يَعِظُكُم بِهِۦ وَٱتَّقُوا۟ ٱللَّهَ وَٱعْلَمُوٓا۟ أَنَّ ٱللَّهَ بِكُلِّ شَىْءٍ عَلِيمٌ ﴿٢٣١﴾

231. Wa-itha tallaqtumu alnnisaa fabalaghna ajalahunna faamsikoohunna bimaAAroofin aw sarrihoohunna bimaAAroofin wala tumsikoohunna diraran litaAAtadoo waman yafAAal thalika faqad thalama nafsahu wala tattakhithoo ayati Allahi huzuwan waothkuroo niAAmata Allahi AAalaykum wama anzala AAalaykum mina alkitabi waalhikmati yaAAithukum bihi waittaqoo Allaha waiAAlamoo anna Allaha bikulli shay-in AAaleemun

2:231. And when you divorce women and their waiting period gets over, then retain them in honour or relieve them in honour.[441] And retain them not for harassing them wickedly; whosoever does that, does indeed wrong one's own self. And trifle not with Allah's Verses/signs, [442] and remember Allah's favours upon you and remember that which He sent down upon you – from the Book and the Wisdom – to admonish you with. Fear Allah and know that Allah is aware of each and everything.

441. Please note that while the preceding Verse 2:230 particularly deals with the situation arising out of the pronouncement of the third divorce, this Verse reverts to the situation arising from each of the first two divorces. This is apparent from the wording here, which is like that in Verse 229 above, dealing with the first two divorces.

442. If anyone had divorced his wife thrice, then arranged for the wife to be married to another man nominally and get divorced, and then gets her back as his wife, it's a clear case of trifling with Allah's Verses. The provisions of Verse 2:230, meant to limit indulgence in repeated divorces, would clearly be trifled with in that case. That apart, what do most Muslims today do? They do not care to know what Allah's Verses ask them to do. And even if they know, they neglect acting upon the guidance given in those Verses. In effect, *nauzubillah*, they treat Allah's Verses as mere jokes.

وَإِذَا طَلَّقْتُمُ ٱلنِّسَآءَ فَبَلَغْنَ أَجَلَهُنَّ فَلَا تَعْضُلُوهُنَّ أَن يَنكِحْنَ أَزْوَاجَهُنَّ إِذَا تَرَاضَوْا۟ بَيْنَهُم بِٱلْمَعْرُوفِ ذَٰلِكَ يُوعَظُ بِهِۦ مَن كَانَ مِنكُمْ يُؤْمِنُ بِٱللَّهِ وَٱلْيَوْمِ ٱلْءَاخِرِ ذَٰلِكُمْ أَزْكَىٰ لَكُمْ وَأَطْهَرُ وَٱللَّهُ يَعْلَمُ وَأَنتُمْ لَا تَعْلَمُونَ ۝٢٣٢

232. Wa-itha tallaqtumu alnnisaa fabalaghna ajalahunna fala taAAduloohunna an yankihna azwajahunna itha taradaw baynahum bialmaAAroofi thalika yooAAathu bihi man kana minkum yu/minu biAllahi waalyawmi al-akhiri thalikum azka lakum waatharu waAllahu yaAAlamu waantum la taAAlamoona

---

2:232. And when you divorce women and their waiting period gets over, come not in their way of marrying their ex-husbands with proper mutual consent.[443] Thus is admonished he who believes in Allah and in the Last Day. That is cleaner for you and purer. And Allah knows; you don't.

---

443. It does sometimes happen that a husband, estranged from his wife, marries another woman on the plea that Islam permits him to have up to 4 wives at a time. And he refuses to divorce his first wife. He himself gets married, but thus prevents her getting married to another man. His act is wicked and against the divine command given in Verse 4:19. And, sometimes, a man, even after divorcing his wife, may effectively prevent her from getting married again by indulging in backbiting and slander. Such wickedness should be eschewed. Here, in this Verse, it is clarified that the divorced couple can marry each other again, subject to the provisions of Verse 2:230 above.

233. Waalwalidatu yurdiAAna awladahunna hawlayni kamilayni liman arada an yutimma alrradaAAata waAAala almawloodi lahu rizquhunna wakiswatuhunna bialmaAAroofi la tukallafu nafsun illa wusAAaha la tudarra walidatun biwaladiha wala mawloodun lahu biwaladihi waAAala alwarithi mithlu thalika fa-in arada fisalan AAan taradin minhuma watashawurin fala junaha AAalayhima wa-in aradtum an tastardiAAoo awladakum fala junaha AAalaykum itha sallamtum ma ataytum bialmaAAroofi waittaqoo Allaha waiAAlamoo anna Allaha bima taAAmaloona baseerun

2:233. And the mothers, wishing to complete the course of breast-feeding, shall suckle their children for full two years. And upon the man who has fathered the child lies the responsibility of providing adequate food and clothing for the mother.[444] No one is burdened, but only to the extent of one's capacity. No mother shall be put to any undue difficulty because of her child, and no father, because of his child. And responsibility likewise devolves upon the heir. If then one intends weaning the child from breast-feeding with mutual consent and consultation, no sin on them both. And if you intend a foster mother to suckle your children, no sin upon you when you make the payment as agreed upon equitably. And fear Allah and know that Allah does indeed watch what you do!

444. This is a generally applicable Qur'aanic rule. But in the context of the immediately preceding Verses dealing with divorced women, this Verse also serves the purpose of reiterating the father's continued responsibility even when he divorces his wife. The later parts of this Verse clarify that this responsibility

devolves on the father's heir, if the father is dead. The responsibility has to be proportionate to the financial condition of the person bearing the responsibility.

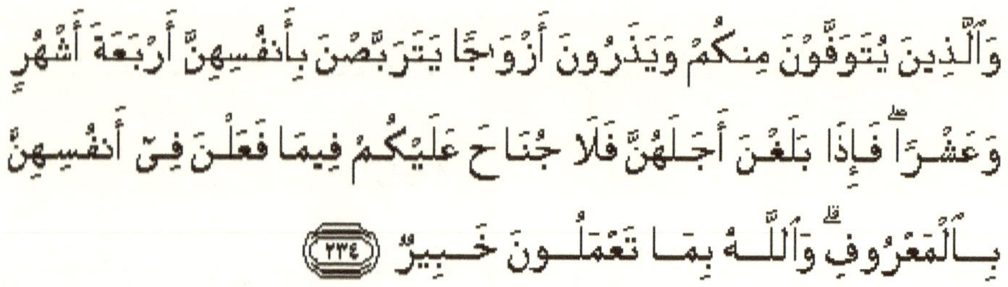

234. Waallatheena yutawaffawna minkum wayatharoona azwajan yatarabbasna bi-anfusihinna arbaAAata ashhurin waAAashran fa-itha balaghna ajalahunna fala junaha AAalaykum feema faAAalna fee anfusihinna bialmaAAroofi waAllahu bima taAAmaloona khabeerun

2:234. And about those amongst you who die and leave wives behind, their wives must restrain themselves for a period of four months and ten days. And when they complete their waiting period, no sin lies on you for anything lawful they do for themselves. And Allah is aware of what you do.[445]

445. In some societies, marrying a widow has been a taboo. If any widow remarried, it was considered a sin because of which the entire community would suffer. This Verse provides the divine negation of this superstitious belief. The waiting period prescribed, besides serving as a mark of respect for the dead husband, ensures definite knowledge of whether the widow is pregnant with her dead husband's child.

وَلَا جُنَاحَ عَلَيْكُمْ فِيمَا عَرَّضْتُم بِهِۦ مِنْ خِطْبَةِ ٱلنِّسَآءِ أَوْ أَكْنَنتُمْ فِىٓ أَنفُسِكُمْ عَلِمَ ٱللَّهُ أَنَّكُمْ سَتَذْكُرُونَهُنَّ وَلَـٰكِن لَّا تُوَاعِدُوهُنَّ سِرًّا إِلَّآ أَن تَقُولُواْ قَوْلًا مَّعْرُوفًا وَلَا تَعْزِمُواْ عُقْدَةَ ٱلنِّكَاحِ حَتَّىٰ يَبْلُغَ ٱلْكِتَـٰبُ أَجَلَهُۥ وَٱعْلَمُوٓاْ أَنَّ ٱللَّهَ يَعْلَمُ مَا فِىٓ أَنفُسِكُمْ فَٱحْذَرُوهُ وَٱعْلَمُوٓاْ أَنَّ ٱللَّهَ غَفُورٌ حَلِيمٌ ﴿٢٣٥﴾

235. Wala juna<u>h</u>a AAalaykum feema<u> </u>AAarra<u>d</u>tum bihi min khi<u>t</u>bati alnnisa<u>-</u>i aw aknantum fee anfusikum AAalima All<u>a</u>hu annakum sata<u>th</u>kuroonahunna walakin l<u>a</u> tuw<u>a</u>AAidoohunna sirran ill<u>a</u> an taqooloo qawlan maAAroofan wal<u>a</u> taAAzimoo AAuqdata alnnik<u>a</u>hi <u>h</u>atta yablugha alkitabu ajalahu waiAAlamoo anna All<u>a</u>ha yaAAlamu m<u>a</u> fee anfusikum fai<u>ht</u>haroohu waiAAlamoo anna All<u>a</u>ha ghafoorun <u>h</u>aleem<u>un</u>

2:235. And no sin upon you in that, you give hints of marriage proposals to women, or you just harbour such intentions. Allah knows you have them in your minds; but make no secret promises to them other than speaking to them in an appropriate manner. And finalise no marriage until after the prescribed period is over. And know that Allah knows what's there in your minds, so be afraid of Him. And know that Allah is indeed Forgiving, Kind.[446]

---

446. From the divine instructions given in this Verse, the importance attached to strict observation of the waiting period for widows, as also for divorced women, can be gauged. The restrictions imposed by the All-knowing and Considerate Allah are all for the welfare of human society. Ignoring the restrictions would only harm the society.

لَّا جُنَاحَ عَلَيْكُمْ إِن طَلَّقْتُمُ ٱلنِّسَآءَ مَا لَمْ تَمَسُّوهُنَّ أَوْ تَفْرِضُواْ لَهُنَّ فَرِيضَةً وَمَتِّعُوهُنَّ عَلَى ٱلْمُوسِعِ قَدَرُهُۥ وَعَلَى ٱلْمُقْتِرِ قَدَرُهُۥ مَتَـٰعًا بِٱلْمَعْرُوفِ حَقًّا عَلَى ٱلْمُحْسِنِينَ ﴿٢٣٦﴾

236. La junaha AAalaykum in tallaqtumu alnnisaa ma lam tamassoohunna aw tafridoo lahunna fareedatan wamattiAAoohunna AAala almoosiAAi qadaruhu waAAala almuqtiri qadaruhu mataAAan bialmaAAroofi haqqan AAala almuhsineena

---

2: 2:236. No blame of committing a sin will be on you if you divorce women at the stage that you have yet not touched them[447] or agreed upon the mandatory nuptial presents, to be given to wives (*Mahr*) [448], for them[449]; but do give them something reasonable, proportionate to your respectiive means. This is a duty upon good people.

---

447. In the context the words are used here, 'touched them' would mean 'had conjugal intimacies with wives'. 'Conjugal intimacies' may not necessarily mean 'sexual intercourse'.

448. It is perhaps a distinctive feature of Islam that it is the husband who must give a mandatory present to the wife, and not vice versa as is the general custom. This present is generally known as *Mahr* in the Islamic world. Its nature and quantum are, as a rule, pre-determined between the two parties to a wedding, and is mentioned in the marriage document. But in the light of this Verse, Mahr could be mutually agreed upon even after the marriage ceremony.

449. The occasion for such a divorce would arise if it is found out, immediately after the marriage ceremony, that either of the two parties to the wedding had resorted to some sort of deception. In such genuine cases, such divorce would be a justified action that could not be categorised as sin. But if this action is resorted just to harass the bride's party, it would amount to treating Allah's Verses as mere jokes, which He has specifically prohibited in <u>Verse 2:231</u>. Such divorce would then, of course, be a sin manifest.

وَإِن طَلَّقْتُمُوهُنَّ مِن قَبْلِ أَن تَمَسُّوهُنَّ وَقَدْ فَرَضْتُمْ لَهُنَّ فَرِيضَةً فَنِصْفُ مَا فَرَضْتُمْ إِلَّا أَن يَعْفُونَ أَوْ يَعْفُوَا۟ ٱلَّذِى بِيَدِهِۦ عُقْدَةُ ٱلنِّكَاحِ وَأَن تَعْفُوٓا۟ أَقْرَبُ لِلتَّقْوَىٰ وَلَا تَنسَوُا۟ ٱلْفَضْلَ بَيْنَكُمْ إِنَّ ٱللَّهَ بِمَا تَعْمَلُونَ بَصِيرٌ ﴿٢٣٧﴾

237. Wa-in tallaqtumoohunna min qabli an tamassoohunna waqad faradtum lahunna fareedatan fanisfu ma faradtum illa an yaAAfoona aw yaAAfuwa allathee biyadihi AAuqdatu alnnikahi waan taAAfoo aqrabu lilttaqwa wala tansawoo alfadla baynakum inna Allaha bima taAAmaloona baseerun

2:237. And if you divorce them before you have touched them – but had already agreed upon a *Mahr* – then give half the *Mahr* unless they (women) forgo their rights, or he, in whose hand is the marriage-tie[450], forgoes his (and agrees to give the full *Mahr*). And it would be nearer to being pious that you (men) forgo. And do not forget to be good to one another, amongst yourselves. Allah does indeed see what you do.

---

450. By so describing a husband, Allah has specifically given him the right to divorce his wife. With this right, he it is who can break the marriage-tie. But the husband must remember that with this right, he gets the added responsibility to exercise the right in a just manner. Allah may not forgive him, if he uses the right unjustly.

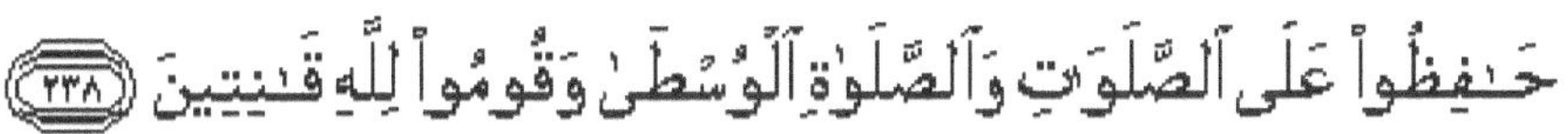

238. H̲afi*th*oo AAal̲a al*ss̲*alaw̲at̲i waal*ss̲*al̲at̲i alwus*t̲*a waqoomoo lill̲ahi qaniteena

---

2:238. Guard the prayers and the middle prayer and stand for Allah in total devotion.[451 to 455]

---

451. To guard is to be careful about. To guard the prayers would obviously mean to offer the prayers properly at proper times as divinely prescribed. It is a variation of the divine command to establish prayers (*aqueemis sualaat*) given elsewhere in the Qur'aan. Refer Chapter Notes 4 and 108, in this context.

452. And what are the prayer timings divinely prescribed in the Qur'aan? In the chronological order of revelation, the earliest revealed Verse prescribing a fixed time for prayers is 17:78. In this Verse the only time fixed is between the sunset and the deep darkness of the night – obviously the dusk, the time when we offer our *maghrib* prayers now. Then in Verse 11:114 Allah directs us to establish prayers at the ends of the day and proximities of night. This is an unambiguous description of the dawn (*fajr*) and dusk (*maghrib*) as the divinely prescribed revised timings for prayers (*sualawaat*). And now, in this Verse 2:238 we are currently studying, Allah is asking us to guard not only the prayers prescribed earlier, but also the prayer newly introduced under this very Verse 2:238 – the middle prayer. This is in keeping with the Qur'aanic practice of gradual, step by step, legislation. The timing of the middle prayer has got to be mid-way between the dawn and the dusk prayers prescribed earlier. It corresponds to the noon (*zhuhr*) prayer, or to the weekly Jumuah prayer, we now offer.

453. But where is the Qur'aanic authentication for our *uasur* and *uishaa* prayers? I do not find it anywhere. But interpreters twist the plain meanings of the above-quoted and other Verses of the Qur'aan to count the number of prayers in a day to five. They paraphrase *li dulookis shamsi ilaa ghasaquinl layli* in Verse 17:78, for example, to include therein the four prayers of *zhuhr, uasur, maghrib* and *uishaa*.

They translate *dulookis shamsi* as declination of the sun as against the clear dictionary meaning thereof as setting of the sun. As we have seen above, Verse 11:114 would corroborate with Verse 17:78 if the meaning of the phrase in the latter Verse is taken as 'setting of the sun'. There are several other Verses in the Qur'aan wherein we have been directed to praise and glorify Allah and to read the Qur'aan and ponder over it, at various times of the day and of the night. But those Verses do not specify the timings as the timings for prayers (*sualawaat*). Those Verses only ask us to glorify Allah and to read and ponder over the Qur'aan at other times also, besides doing so during the prayers.

454. How the translators have twisted the plain meanings of the Qur'aanic Verses in this regard is too vast a subject to be dealt with completely in these footnotes. A cyber-friend has done a thorough research on the subject and has recorded his findings in an e-booklet. If he permits me, I shall, *inshaAllah*, publish his work on the index page of my website. [The work, SALAAH IN THE QUR'AN, has since been published. Click https://sites.google.com/site/invitationtosalvation/salaah-in-the-quran to access it.]

455. The prayers ought to be for Allah alone. We should have no thoughts, other than of Allah, during the prayers. But the fact of the matter is that our prayers are contaminated by these other thoughts, and thus get devalued and unfruitful. The other reason for our prayers being ineffective is that we glorify and address others, besides Allah, during and after the prayers at places of worship. Places of worship should be exclusive for glorification of Allah alone. And of the Unseen, He alone should be addressed or called upon for anything.

239. Fa-in khiftum farijalan aw rukbanan fa-itha amintum faothkuroo Allaha kama AAallamakum ma lam takoonoo taAAlamoona

2:239. If you are in an insecure situation, then while walking or while riding, but if you are in a secure situation, then remember Allah in the manner He taught you, which you did not know.[456]

456. The Qur'aan teaches us to remember Allah through prayers, through reading and pondering over the Verses of the Qur'aan and through glorifying Him while doing our mundane work during the day or during the night. There should be no problem in glorifying Him while performing our worldly work. And I have seen people reading the Qur'aan while on a journey in a train. Only, they should read it, not ritualistically but understandingly. They should also ponder over what they read. But one may encounter problems while offering prayers in the right manner as prescribed in the Qur'aan, when one is on a journey in a bus, train or plane. And if one fears that by the time the transport reaches the next scheduled stop, the prescribed time for the prayer would get over, one may, under the authority of this Verse, offer prayers sitting on one's seat.

240. Waallatheena yutawaffawna minkum wayatharoona azwajan wasiyyatan li-azwajihim mataAAan ila alhawli ghayra ikhrajin fa-in kharajna fala junaha AAalaykum fee ma faAAalna fee anfusihinna min maAAroofin waAllahu AAazeezun hakeemun

2:240. And those of you who die, and leave wives behind, should make a will in favour of their wives providing for a year's worldly necessities for them, without them being turned out from their homes.[457] But if the wives leave of their own accord, no sin upon you in what they do for themselves, in a lawful and proper manner.[458] And Allah is Omnipotent, Wise.

457. In Verse 4:12, a widow has been allotted a fixed share of the deceased's property. The divine command given in this earlier revealed Verse (2:240), we are presently studying, is a precursor to the provision made in 4:12. But for that matter, 2:240 should not be considered as abrogated by 4:12, as some commentators of the Qu'aan do. (Please go through Chapter Notes 150 to 153, in this context.) The 2:240 provision is still applicable, for example, in a case where the deceased husband was a member of a joint family and had no share of property allotted to him.

458. The in-laws should not, for instance, come in the way of the widow marrying another man in a lawful manner.

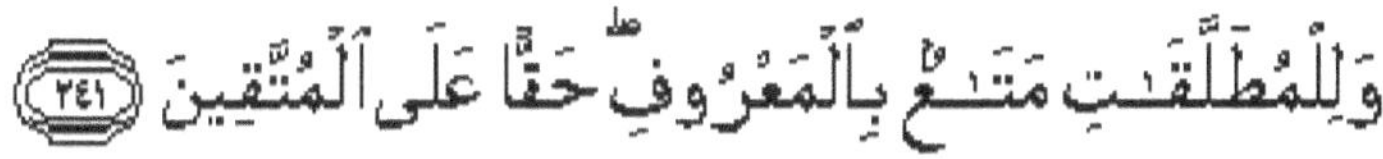

241. Walilmutallaqati mataAAun bialmaAAroofi haqqan AAala almuttaqeena

2:241. And the divorced women have a right to proper and reasonable maintenance. Providing such maintenance is an obligation upon those who fear Allah.[459]

---

459. As for the widows, so for the divorced women. The kind Lord of all has made adequate provisions for all, especially the vulnerable section of human society. It's largely because of intransigence, excesses, and generally unjust behaviour on the part of human beings themselves that bring about sufferings in this world.

كَذَلِكَ يُبَيِّنُ ٱللَّـهُ لَكُمْ ءَايَـٰتِهِۦ لَعَلَّكُمْ تَعْقِلُونَ ﴿٢٤٢﴾

242. Kathalika yubayyinu Allahu lakum ayatihi laAAallakum taAAqiloona

---

2:242. Thus, does Allah clearly explain to you His Verses so that you understand.[460]

---

460. The understanding that we have deduced in the preceding Note 459, for example, is the result of the clarity of the divine Verses. The clarity would of course be visible only to those who sincerely ponder over the Verses of the Qur'aan to understand the Truth contained therein.

أَلَمْ تَرَ إِلَى ٱلَّذِينَ خَرَجُوا۟ مِن دِيَـٰرِهِمْ وَهُمْ أُلُوفٌ حَذَرَ ٱلْمَوْتِ فَقَالَ لَهُمُ ٱللَّهُ مُوتُوا۟ ثُمَّ أَحْيَـٰهُمْ إِنَّ ٱللَّهَ لَذُو فَضْلٍ عَلَى ٱلنَّاسِ وَلَـٰكِنَّ أَكْثَرَ ٱلنَّاسِ لَا يَشْكُرُونَ ﴿٢٤٣﴾

243. Alam tara ila allatheena kharajoo min diyarihim wahum oloofun hathara almawti faqala lahumu Allahu mootoo thumma ahyahum inna Allaha lathoo fadlin AAala alnnasi walakinna akthara alnnasi la yashkuroona

2:243. Haven't you observed those who left their homes, in their thousands, fearing death? Allah then told them, "Die". He then brought them back to life.[461] Indeed, Allah showers favours after favours on mankind, but most fail to be grateful.

---

461. In the context of the immediately following Verse 2:244, it is apparent that persons referred to here were those going on a military campaign. However bravely and willingly they may be proceeding, in the way of Allah, those persons, after all, were human beings. And some of them at least might have the fear of death lurking in some corner of their minds. Some of those people must have died in action, but, having been killed in the way of Allah, they might have been immediately thereafter brought to life, in terms of Verse 2:154, and already been enjoying a utopian life in Paradise, unlike others who have to wait till Resurrection Day for being revived to life again. Allah therefore tells mankind that He always has lots of such bounties and favours for mankind. They should have full faith in Him and have no fear of anything but Allah. But most are assailed by other fears. They are thus being ungrateful to Allah.

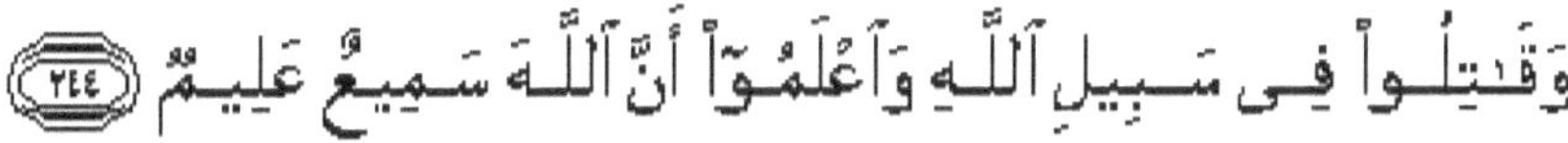

244. Waqatiloo fee sabeeli Allahi waiAAlamoo anna Allaha sameeAAun AAaleemun

---

2:244. And fight, in Allah's way, and rest assured that Allah hears, knows.[462, 463]

---

462. Allah knows whether anyone is really fighting in His way, or in some self-interest. HE does hear the fighter in Allah's way, when he calls Him for His help.

463. In today's scenario, it is pertinent to understand thoroughly whether wanton destructions like those of the WTC buildings in New York some years back, could be construed as fighting in Allah's way. Fighting in Allah's way has necessarily to be within the parameters laid down in the Qur'aan. And it is my considered view that the said destruction could not be construed as fighting in Allah's way. Please refer to my article Islam & Terrorism for details.

مَّن ذَا ٱلَّذِى يُقْرِضُ ٱللَّهَ قَرْضًا حَسَنًا فَيُضَـٰعِفَهُۥ لَهُۥٓ أَضْعَافًا كَثِيرَةً ۚ وَٱللَّهُ يَقْبِضُ وَيَبْصُۜطُ وَإِلَيْهِ تُرْجَعُونَ

245. Man <u>th</u>a alla<u>th</u>ee yuqri<u>d</u>u Alla<u>h</u>a qar<u>d</u>an <u>h</u>asanan fayu<u>d</u>aAAifahu lahu a<u>d</u>AA<u>a</u>fan kathee<u>r</u>atan waAll<u>ah</u>u yaqbi<u>d</u>u wayabsu<u>t</u>u wa-ilayhi turjaAAoon<u>a</u>

2:245. Who is there to lend a good loan to Allah, which He will repay in multiples thereof? And it is Allah Who takes possession of things and amplifies them, and to Him you shall be returned.[464]

---

464. Magnanimously thus does Allah offer a deal to His creatures, the human beings. HE wants them to sacrifice, if necessary, the pleasures of this worldly life, which are in any case temporary and unreliable. In return, He offers them everlasting rewards, many many times more in real value.

أَلَمۡ تَرَ إِلَى ٱلۡمَلَإِ مِنۢ بَنِىٓ إِسۡرَٰٓءِيلَ مِنۢ

بَعۡدِ مُوسَىٰٓ إِذۡ قَالُوا۟ لِنَبِىٍّ لَّهُمُ ٱبۡعَثۡ لَنَا مَلِكًا نُّقَٰتِلۡ فِى سَبِيلِ ٱللَّهِ

قَالَ هَلۡ عَسَيۡتُمۡ إِن كُتِبَ عَلَيۡكُمُ ٱلۡقِتَالُ أَلَّا تُقَٰتِلُوا۟ قَالُوا۟ وَمَا لَنَآ أَلَّا

نُقَٰتِلَ فِى سَبِيلِ ٱللَّهِ وَقَدۡ أُخۡرِجۡنَا مِن دِيَٰرِنَا وَأَبۡنَآئِنَا فَلَمَّا

كُتِبَ عَلَيۡهِمُ ٱلۡقِتَالُ تَوَلَّوۡا۟ إِلَّا قَلِيلًا مِّنۡهُمۡ وَٱللَّهُ عَلِيمٌۢ بِٱلظَّٰلِمِينَ

246. Alam tara il<u>a</u> almala-i min banee isr<u>a</u>-eela min baAAdi moos<u>a</u> i<u>th</u> qaloo linabiyyin lahumu ibAAath lan<u>a</u> malikan nuq<u>a</u>til fee sabeeli All<u>a</u>hi q<u>a</u>la hal AAasaytum in kutiba AAalaykumu alqit<u>a</u>lu all<u>a</u> tuq<u>a</u>tiloo q<u>a</u>loo wam<u>a</u> lan<u>a</u> all<u>a</u> nuq<u>a</u>tila fee sabeeli All<u>a</u>hi waqad okhrijn<u>a</u> min diy<u>a</u>rin<u>a</u> waabn<u>a</u>-in<u>a</u> falamm<u>a</u> kutiba AAalayhimu alqit<u>a</u>lu tawallaw ill<u>a</u> qaleelan minhum waAll<u>a</u>hu AAaleemun bial<u>ththa</u>limeen<u>a</u>

2:246. Wouldn't you like to know and deliberate[465] about the Chiefs of the Children of Israel, after Moses' time, when they spoke to their Prophet, "Appoint for us a king and we shall fight in Allah's way." The Prophet said, "What if you wouldn't fight when fighting is made obligatory upon you?" They said, "Why shouldn't we fight, when we've been driven away from our homes and from our children?" But when fighting was made obligatory upon them, they turned back on their promise, except for a few of them.[466]

465. The Arabic term used here is *Alam tara*. Literally, the term means 'Won't you see,' or 'Wouldn't you like to see'. But here, the divine words are addressed to the Prophet, peace and Allah's blessings be upon him, drawing his attention to an event that took place centuries before the time of the Prophet. This context itself therefore suggests the translation of the term as made here.

466. Human nature seldom changes. The All-knowing Allah draws attention, of the people living at the time of the Prophet and of all people living thereafter till the Last Day, to that episode that happened thousands of years ago depicting this timeless human trait or – more appropriately – human failing. This failing is the result of human fear of death – fear of the unknown, especially in those whose faith in Allah and in the Hereafter is weak. The fear of death has already been referred to in Verse 2:243 above. It was this fear of death that made the Children of Israel hesitant to proceed to the war front, in Allah's way. Centuries later, it was this same fear that made some of those who had accepted Islam, during Prophet's time, hesitant to proceed to the front, in Allah's way. And now, in this present age, Muslims are hesitant to step out in Allah's way for fear of losing something in/of this transient world.

وَقَالَ لَهُمْ نَبِيُّهُمْ إِنَّ ٱللَّهَ قَدْ بَعَثَ لَكُمْ طَالُوتَ مَلِكًا قَالُوٓاْ أَنَّىٰ يَكُونُ لَهُ ٱلْمُلْكُ عَلَيْنَا وَنَحْنُ أَحَقُّ بِٱلْمُلْكِ مِنْهُ وَلَمْ يُؤْتَ سَعَةً مِّنَ ٱلْمَالِ قَالَ إِنَّ ٱللَّهَ ٱصْطَفَىٰهُ عَلَيْكُمْ وَزَادَهُ بَسْطَةً فِى ٱلْعِلْمِ وَٱلْجِسْمِ وَٱللَّهُ يُؤْتِى مُلْكَهُ مَن يَشَآءُ وَٱللَّهُ وَٰسِعٌ عَلِيمٌ ﴿٢٤٧﴾

247. Waqala lahum nabiyyuhum inna Allaha qad baAAatha lakum taloota malikan qaloo anna yakoonu lahu almulku AAalayna wanahnu ahaqqu bialmulki minhu walam yu/ta saAAatan mina almali qala inna Allaha istafahu AAalaykum wazadahu bastatan fee alAAilmi waaljismi waAllahu yu/tee mulkahu man yashao waAllahu wasiAAun AAaleemun

2:247. And their Prophet informed them, "Allah has decreed Tuaaloot to be king for you!" They said, "How could he get precedence over us in getting the kingdom, when we were the ones more deserving? And neither is he endowed with abundance in wealth!" The Prophet said, "Allah has chosen him over you; and has given him much more knowledge and physical strength.[467, 468] And Allah grants dominion over His land to anyone He wishes. And Allah is All-encompassing, Wise!"[469]

467. Tualoot was a divinely chosen king. He was divinely appointed on the request of the people (Verse 246 above). Once such appointment was made, there was no question of the people questioning that

appointment. But the Chiefs of the Children of Israel did question the propriety of the divine appointment because of their own satanic pride.

468. In today's world, however, there can't be such direct, obviously divine appointments. Allah had made the above such appointment through one of His prophets. But Allah has ended prophethood with Prophet Muhammad, peace and Allah's blessings be upon him. What then is Allah's guidance for us now, in the matter of governance of a country? In Verse 42:38, Allah appreciates those who conduct their affairs by mutual consultations. And therein lies the divine guidance. We must conduct our public affairs by mutual consultations. In the case dealt with in these Qur'aanic Verses, the choice of Tuaaloot gives us the further guidance that there ought to be an executive head of state. The head of state must be chosen based on his abilities, and not because he belongs to a ruling dynasty or class. It is thus clear that Islam does not favour a dynastic rule. And, in view of Verse 42:38 quoted above, the chosen head of state cannot work autocratically, but by mutual consultations with an advisory council. In an Islamic state, the Qur'aan must be the Constitution; and the subsidiary rules for implementing the Constitution must be framed by a legislative body consisting of persons chosen by the people. The USA pattern appears to be in line with Islamic requirement, except of course for the Constitution.

469. Even though, in today's world, the rulers are generally chosen by the people, it is a fundamental Islamic faith that no one can become a ruler – nor, for that matter, anything happen in this world – against Allah's Will.

---

248. Waqala lahum nabiyyuhum inna ayata mulkihi an ya/tiyakumu alttabootu feehi sakeenatun min rabbikum wabaqiyyatun mimma taraka alu moosa waalu haroona tahmiluhu almala-ikatu inna fee thalika laayatan lakum in kuntum mu/mineena

---

2:248. And their Prophet told them, "Indeed, the sign of his getting the kingdom would be that a box shall come to you containing reassuring things from your Lord and the remnants of what was left behind by the families of Moses and Aaron. The box will be borne by the angels. There is indeed a sign in that for you, if you do believe."[470]

---

470. Since the Children of Israel were reluctant to believe their Prophet and accept Tuaaloot as Allah-appointed king for them, Allah sent them a sign to make them accept him. It's of no use for us now to speculate on the exact nature of that sign. Allah has thought it fit not to reveal complete details about it to us. No one else can give us more knowledge than what Allah has revealed. We should be content with what He has revealed.

فَلَمَّا فَصَلَ طَالُوتُ بِالْجُنُودِ قَالَ إِنَّ ٱللَّهَ مُبْتَلِيكُم بِنَهَرٍ فَمَن شَرِبَ مِنْهُ

فَلَيْسَ مِنِّى وَمَن لَّمْ يَطْعَمْهُ فَإِنَّهُ مِنِّى إِلَّا مَنِ ٱغْتَرَفَ غُرْفَةً بِيَدِهِ

فَشَرِبُواْ مِنْهُ إِلَّا قَلِيلًا مِّنْهُمْ فَلَمَّا جَاوَزَهُ هُوَ وَٱلَّذِينَ ءَامَنُواْ مَعَهُ قَالُواْ لَا

طَاقَةَ لَنَا ٱلْيَوْمَ بِجَالُوتَ وَجُنُودِهِ قَالَ ٱلَّذِينَ يَظُنُّونَ أَنَّهُم مُّلَٰقُواْ ٱللَّهِ

كَم مِّن فِئَةٍ قَلِيلَةٍ غَلَبَتْ فِئَةً كَثِيرَةً بِإِذْنِ ٱللَّهِ وَٱللَّهُ مَعَ ٱلصَّٰبِرِينَ ﴿٢٤١﴾

249. Falamma faṣala ṭalootu bialjunoodi qala inna Allaha mubtaleekum binaharin faman shariba minhu falaysa minnee waman lam yaṭAAamhu fa-innahu minnee illa mani ightarafa ghurfatan biyadihi fashariboo minhu illa qaleelan minhum falamma jawazahu huwa waallatheena amanoo maAAahu qaloo la ṭaqata lana alyawma bijaloota wajunoodihi qala allatheena yathunnoona annahum mulaqoo Allahi kam min fi-atin qaleelatin ghalabat fi-atan katheeratan bi-ithni Allahi waAllahu maAAa alssabireena

2:249. [471]So then, when Tuaaloot set forth with his army, he said, "Allah is certainly going to test you with a river. Whosoever quenches his thirst there from, he is not with us. And whosoever doesn't do so, but just drinks a palmful of water there from, he is indeed with us." And they did quench their thirst there from, except for a few of them. So then, as they – he and those who believed with him – crossed over, the others said, "We do not have the strength this day to confront Jaaloot and his army." Said those who were certain they would be meeting Allah, "How often, by Allah's Will, has a small party got the better of a big one! And Allah is with those who exercise patience."

471. This is a continuation of the narrative started with Verse 2:246.

وَلَمَّا بَرَزُواْ لِجَالُوتَ وَجُنُودِهِ قَالُواْ رَبَّنَآ أَفْرِغْ عَلَيْنَا صَبْرًا وَثَبِّتْ أَقْدَامَنَا وَٱنصُرْنَا عَلَى ٱلْقَوْمِ ٱلْكَـٰفِرِينَ ۝

250. Walamma barazoo lijaloota wajunoodihi qaloo rabbana afrigh AAalayna sabran wathabbit aqdamana waonsurna AAala alqawmi alkafireena

---

2:250. And when they advanced against Jaaloot and his army, they said, "Our Lord! Bestow patience on us, steady our steps and help us against the people who suppress the Truth."

فَهَزَمُوهُم بِإِذْنِ ٱللَّهِ وَقَتَلَ دَاوُۥدُ جَالُوتَ وَءَاتَىٰهُ ٱللَّهُ ٱلْمُلْكَ وَٱلْحِكْمَةَ وَعَلَّمَهُۥ مِمَّا يَشَآءُ وَلَوْلَا دَفْعُ ٱللَّهِ ٱلنَّاسَ بَعْضَهُم بِبَعْضٍ لَّفَسَدَتِ ٱلْأَرْضُ وَلَـٰكِنَّ ٱللَّهَ ذُو فَضْلٍ عَلَى ٱلْعَـٰلَمِينَ ۝

251. Fahazamoohum bi-ithni Allahi waqatala dawoodu jaloota waatahu Allahu almulka waalhikmata waAAallamahu mimma yashao walawla dafAAu Allahi alnnasa baAAdahum bibaAAdin lafasadati al-ardu walakinna Allaha thoo fadlin AAala alAAalameena

---

2:251. They then defeated them (Jaaloot and his army) by Allah's Will. And David slew Jaaloot and Allah gave him the dominion and the acumen to rule and taught him what He wished to teach him. And had Allah not subjugated some people through others, the earth would certainly have been corrupted.[472] But Allah is beneficent to the worlds.[473]

---

472. This is the moral of the story. And this moral truth has continued to come out throughout the history of mankind. In our recent past, the evil pride of Hitler, Mussolini, and the then Japanese government of subjugating the entire world with their autocratic rules, came to dust with their ultimate utter defeat at the hands of the allied forces in World War II. For a time, the evil forces may appear to be on the ascendancy, but when their evil work reaches a limit, their annihilation is certain. From this historical fact, good people should take heart. The evil forces that appear to be having an upper hand at various places in the world of today shall perish one day, *inshaAllah*. Allah promises to favour the good people ultimately, if they but exercise patience.

473. For the comprehensive divine meaning of the Arabic term *uaalameen* (worlds), please refer to Chapter 1, Note 5 of these Studies.

تِلْكَ ءَايَـٰتُ ٱللَّهِ نَتْلُوهَا عَلَيْكَ بِٱلْحَقِّ وَإِنَّكَ لَمِنَ ٱلْمُرْسَلِينَ ﴿٢٥٢﴾

252. Tilka ayatu Allahi natlooha AAalayka bialhaqqi wa-innaka lamina almursaleena

---

2:252. Those are Allah's Verses. We recite them to you in truth. And you have indeed been of those sent down as Allah's Messengers.[474]

---

474. Allah thus assures us, the present-day custodians of His imperishable Verses, that these are indeed His Verses! We should have no doubt therein. Our ultimate victory is ensured, if only we patiently abide by the divine instructions in these Verses.

تِلْكَ ٱلرُّسُلُ فَضَّلْنَا بَعْضَهُمْ عَلَىٰ بَعْضٍ مِّنْهُم مَّن كَلَّمَ ٱللَّهُ وَرَفَعَ بَعْضَهُمْ دَرَجَـٰتٍ وَءَاتَيْنَا عِيسَى ٱبْنَ مَرْيَمَ ٱلْبَيِّنَـٰتِ وَأَيَّدْنَـٰهُ بِرُوحِ ٱلْقُدُسِ وَلَوْ شَآءَ ٱللَّهُ مَا ٱقْتَتَلَ ٱلَّذِينَ مِنۢ بَعْدِهِم مِّنۢ بَعْدِ مَا جَآءَتْهُمُ ٱلْبَيِّنَـٰتُ وَلَـٰكِنِ ٱخْتَلَفُوا۟ فَمِنْهُم مَّنْ ءَامَنَ وَمِنْهُم مَّن كَفَرَ وَلَوْ شَآءَ ٱللَّهُ مَا ٱقْتَتَلُوا۟ وَلَـٰكِنَّ ٱللَّهَ يَفْعَلُ مَا يُرِيدُ ﴿٢٥٣﴾

253. Tilka alrrusulu faddalna baAAdahum AAala baAAdin minhum man kallama Allahu warafaAAa baAAdahum darajatin waatayna AAeesa ibna maryama albayyinati waayyadnahu biroohi alqudusi walaw shaa Allahu ma iqtatala allatheena min baAAdihim min baAAdi ma jaat-humu albayyinatu walakini ikhtalafoo faminhum man amana waminhum man kafara walaw shaa Allahu ma iqtataloo walakinna Allaha yafAAalu ma yureedu

---

2:253. Of those Messengers[475], We have favoured some over others. Of them is one whom Allah talked to directly[476]. And He exalted some in rank.[477] And We gave clear signs to Jesus, son of Mary, and We fortified him with the Holy Spirit.[478] Had Allah so willed, after clear signs had come to them, people of succeeding generations wouldn't have fought among themselves. But they differed. Some of them believed, and some suppressed the truth by wanton disbelief. Had Allah so willed, they wouldn't have fought. But Allah does what He wants.[479]

---

475. Reference made here is to *mursaleen* **(Messengers) mentioned at the end of the immediately preceding** Verse 2:252.

476. Verses 20:11 and 20:12 describe to us how Allah spoke to Prophet Moses directly.

477. Although the Prophets have different rankings in status with Allah, believers are required not to discriminate among them (Prophets) [Q: 4:152].

478. The very same sentence, regarding Jesus, occurs in Verse 2:87. **Please refer to Notes 113 to 116 under that Verse to get a comprehensive Qur'aanic understanding of** *roohuil quudus* **(the Holy Spirit). Some of the clear signs that the Qur'aan mentions as having been bestowed upon Jesus were speaking to people while just an infant in his cradle, bringing the dead back to life, creating a live bird out of clay, giving sight to the blind etc. [Q: 5:110].**

479. And Allah wanted to test mankind by giving them the freedom to believe, or not to believe, in Him, without seeing Him. In exercise of that freedom, some people chose not to believe, despite the clear signs given to Jesus about Divine Existence. Otherwise, had Allah so willed, every human being would have believed. But He had taken all possible measures, like giving them divine Books of guidance through His Messengers and giving them the intelligence to understand that guidance, besides giving clearly miraculous signs to some of His Messengers. HE had not just left them to fend for themselves in the dark, after giving them the freedom of choice. HE has been just and kind to mankind.

يَـٰٓأَيُّهَا ٱلَّذِينَ ءَامَنُوٓاْ أَنفِقُواْ مِمَّا رَزَقْنَـٰكُم مِّن قَبْلِ أَن يَأْتِىَ يَوْمٌ لَّا بَيْعٌ فِيهِ وَلَا خُلَّةٌ وَلَا شَفَـٰعَةٌ وَٱلْكَـٰفِرُونَ هُمُ ٱلظَّـٰلِمُونَ ﴿٢٥٤﴾

254. Ya ayyuha allatheena amanoo anfiqoo mimma razaqnakum min qabli an ya/tiya yawmun la bayAAun feehi wala khullatun wala shafaAAatun waalkafiroona humu alththalimoona

---

2:254. O you who believe! Spend[480] of what We have given you before the advent of the Day during which shall there be no trade, no friendship and no intercession. And suppressors of the Truth – those are the wrong-doers.[481]

---

480. For the Qur'aanic meaning of the Arabic term *anfiquoo* (spend) used here, please refer to Chapter Note 5 of these Studies.

481. This Verse reveals to us several things:

- Allah given things – like wealth, wisdom, time – are to be made use of and not just hoarded or wasted away.

- Every individual's position in the Hereafter inter alia depends on the way he uses those Allah-given things here.

- The proper use of those things may make him/her eligible for entry into Paradise, and their misuse may land him/her in Hell.

- Evaluation of every individual on Judgment Day shall be strictly impartial. No good man would be able to buy a better place in the Hereafter for his friend/relative.

- In the Hereafter, there is no scope for any intercession – from a friend, a relative, or even a Prophet. Beware, Muslims and Christians!

- Those who do not believe in all that the Verse implies are only deluding themselves and others. And, consequentially, they are oppressing themselves and others.

اَللّٰهُ لَاۤ اِلٰهَ اِلَّا هُوَ ۚ اَلْحَیُّ الْقَیُّوْمُ ۚ لَا تَاْخُذُهٗ سِنَةٌ وَّلَا نَوْمٌ ۚ لَهٗ مَا فِی السَّمٰوٰتِ وَمَا فِی الْاَرْضِ ۚ مَنْ ذَا الَّذِیْ یَشْفَعُ عِنْدَهٗۤ اِلَّا بِاِذْنِهٖ ۚ یَعْلَمُ مَا بَیْنَ اَیْدِیْهِمْ وَمَا خَلْفَهُمْ ۚ وَلَا یُحِیْطُوْنَ بِشَیْءٍ مِّنْ عِلْمِهٖۤ اِلَّا بِمَا شَآءَ ۚ وَسِعَ کُرْسِیُّهُ السَّمٰوٰتِ وَالْاَرْضَ ۚ وَلَا یَـُٔوْدُهٗ حِفْظُهُمَا ۚ وَهُوَ الْعَلِیُّ الْعَظِیْمُ ۝٢٥٥

255. Allahu la ilaha illa huwa alhayyu alqayyoomu la ta/khuthuhu sinatun wala nawmun lahu ma fee alssamawati wama fee al-ardi man tha allathee yashfaAAu AAindahu illa bi-ithnihi yaAAlamu ma bayna aydeehim wama khalfahum wala yuheetoona bishay-in min AAilmihi illa bima shaa wasiAAa kursiyyuhu alssamawati waal-arda wala yaooduhu hifthuhuma wahuwa alAAaliyyu alAAatheemu

2:255. Allah! None besides Him is worthy of worship. HE is for ever living, abiding. Neither slumber nor sleep overtakes Him ever. To Him belongs whatever there is in the heavens and in/on the earth. Who could intercede with Him, except by His leave? [482, 483] HE knows what is in their hands and what is behind them.[484] And none can take anything of His knowledge except for what He wills. His seat of authority encompasses the heavens and the earth, and their upkeep tires Him not. And He is the One High above anything, the One Immensely Great.[485]

---

482. In the light of the very categorical statement in the preceding Verse that there shall be no intercession on the Day of Judgment, this statement here, in the form of an interrogation, could only mean emphatic reiteration of that earlier statement. In Allah's presence, no one – not even a Prophet – can dare intercede on one's own initiative, against His Judgment or Will. That is what the interrogative statement here signifies. And if Allah gives permission for any Prophet or Angel to intercede, it means that it is, first, Allah's Own Will to pardon the person concerned.

483. It is important to understand this matter of intercession correctly. In the absence of this understanding, we're likely to fall into a satanic trap, and commit the abominable sin of *shirk*. Most Christians have already fallen into this trap. They have come to believe, absolutely, that whatever sins they commit here in this world, their Jesus is sure to intercede with God on their behalf and give them an assured entry into Paradise. See now what has happened to the Christians. They have forgotten God almost entirely and have taken to the worship of Jesus and his mother, Mary. This happening, in front of us all, has provided enough proof that if any group of persons considers any Prophet – or anyone else for that matter – as endowed with the power of intercession, that group is sure to raise that Prophet/person to divinity, and thus commit *shirk*. Most Muslims today are, I am afraid, dangerously close to following in the Christians' footsteps.

484. Verse 34:9 tells us, "Do they not then consider what is in their hands and what is behind them of the heaven and the earth? ..." This sentence in that Verse gives us a pretty good idea of the divine meaning of the Arabic term *maa bayna aydihim wa maa khalfahum*, translated literally here as 'what is in their hands and what is behind them'. The context there of the heaven and the earth indicates that 'what is in their hands' means 'what is in their knowledge' or 'what they are capable of knowing'. And 'what is behind them' means 'what is not in their knowledge' or 'what they are not capable of knowing'. The same divine meaning must be made applicable here to the very same phrase used in Verse 2:255 that we are presently studying.

485. This beautiful Verse is generally known as '*aayatul kursi*' because of the word *kursi* (seat of authority) occurring therein. Along with Chapter 112 of the Qur'aan, this Verse gives us a comprehensive divine description of Allah, our Creator, and our Lord.

لَآ إِكْرَاهَ فِى ٱلدِّينِ قَد تَّبَيَّنَ ٱلرُّشْدُ مِنَ ٱلْغَىِّ فَمَن يَكْفُرْ بِٱلطَّٰغُوتِ وَيُؤْمِنۢ بِٱللَّهِ فَقَدِ ٱسْتَمْسَكَ بِٱلْعُرْوَةِ ٱلْوُثْقَىٰ لَا ٱنفِصَامَ لَهَا وَٱللَّهُ سَمِيعٌ عَلِيمٌ 

256. La ikraha fee alddeeni qad tabayyana alrrushdu mina alghayyi faman yakfur bialttaghooti wayu/min biAllahi faqadi istamsaka bialAAurwati alwuthqa la infisama laha waAllahu sameeAAun AAaleemun

---

2:256. No compulsion in religion. Surely, the right has become distinct from the wrong. So, whoever has rejected false gods and believed in Allah, he/she has taken a firm hold of a strong link that shall never break. And Allah sees, He knows.[486]

---

486. There is no question of anyone compelling any other to become a Muslim. Becoming a Muslim requires a change in the mindset of a person. And no amount of compulsion can ever change a person's mind. Compulsion in this regard moreover implies an act against the divine plan. And the divine plan is to test a person whether he/she becomes a Muslim with his/her own free will. Most of us are Muslims by default. We call ourselves Muslims because we're born into Muslim families. But do we have Muslim mindsets? The sad fact is that an overwhelming majority of us don't. Oh, had we but sincerely believed in Allah and rejected all the false gods! The false gods come to us in many hues and colours. They come to us with enticements of the transitory benefits of this world, and we've fallen easy preys to them. Had we but rejected the satanic temptations and taken hold of that firm link to Allah, we wouldn't be in the sorry state that we find ourselves in, today.

ٱللَّهُ وَلِىُّ ٱلَّذِينَ ءَامَنُوا۟ يُخْرِجُهُم مِّنَ ٱلظُّلُمَٰتِ إِلَى ٱلنُّورِ وَٱلَّذِينَ كَفَرُوٓا۟ أَوْلِيَآؤُهُمُ ٱلطَّٰغُوتُ يُخْرِجُونَهُم مِّنَ ٱلنُّورِ إِلَى ٱلظُّلُمَٰتِ أُو۟لَٰٓئِكَ أَصْحَٰبُ ٱلنَّارِ هُمْ فِيهَا خَٰلِدُونَ

257. Allahu waliyyu allatheena amanoo yukhrijuhum mina alththulumati ila alnnoori waallatheena kafaroo awliyaohumu alttaghootu yukhrijoonahum mina alnnoori ila alththulumati ola-ika as-habu alnnari hum feeha khalidoona

2:257. Allah is *wali* of those who believe. HE takes them out of darknesses into light. And those who suppress the Truth – false gods are their *awliya*, who take them out of light into darknesses. Those shall be inhabitants of the Fire and shall remain therein forever.[487]

487. For the Qur'aanic concept of *wali* and *awliya*, please refer Notes 2:154 and 2:155 of these Studies.

أَلَمْ تَرَ إِلَى ٱلَّذِى حَاجَّ إِبْرَٰهِـۧمَ فِى رَبِّهِۦٓ أَنْ ءَاتَٮٰهُ ٱللَّهُ ٱلْمُلْكَ إِذْ قَالَ إِبْرَٰهِـۧمُ رَبِّىَ ٱلَّذِى يُحْىِۦ وَيُمِيتُ قَالَ أَنَا۠ أُحْىِۦ وَأُمِيتُ قَالَ إِبْرَٰهِـۧمُ فَإِنَّ ٱللَّهَ يَأْتِى بِٱلشَّمْسِ مِنَ ٱلْمَشْرِقِ فَأْتِ بِهَا مِنَ ٱلْمَغْرِبِ فَبُهِتَ ٱلَّذِى كَفَرَ وَٱللَّهُ لَا يَهْدِى ٱلْقَوْمَ ٱلظَّٰلِمِينَ ﴿٢٥٨﴾

258. Alam tara ila allathee hajja ibraheema fee rabbihi an atahu Allahu almulka ith qala ibraheemu rabbiya allathee yuhyee wayumeetu qala ana ohyee waomeetu qala ibraheemu fa-inna Allaha ya/tee bialshshamsi mina almashriqi fa/ti biha mina almaghribi fabuhita allathee kafara waAllahu la yahdee alqawma alththalimeena

2:258. Wouldn't you like to know and deliberate[488] about him whom Allah had given political control over a country and who quarrelled with Abraham over his Lord? When Abraham said "My Lord is One Who gives life and causes death", he retorted, "I too can give life and cause death." Abraham then said, "Allah does indeed bring the Sun from the East. You bring it from the West!" The suppressor of Truth became nonplussed then. And Allah guides not the wicked people.

488. Please refer Note 2:465 of these Studies for the rationale behind rendering *alam tara* into English thus.

أَوۡ كَالَّذِى مَرَّ عَلَىٰ قَرۡيَةٍ وَهِىَ خَاوِيَةٌ عَلَىٰ عُرُوشِهَا قَالَ أَنَّىٰ يُحۡىِۦ هَٰذِهِ ٱللَّهُ بَعۡدَ مَوۡتِهَا فَأَمَاتَهُ ٱللَّهُ مِا۟ئَةَ عَامٍ ثُمَّ بَعَثَهُۥ قَالَ كَمۡ لَبِثۡتَ قَالَ لَبِثۡتُ يَوۡمًا أَوۡ بَعۡضَ يَوۡمٍ قَالَ بَل لَّبِثۡتَ مِا۟ئَةَ عَامٍ فَٱنظُرۡ إِلَىٰ طَعَامِكَ وَشَرَابِكَ لَمۡ يَتَسَنَّهۡ وَٱنظُرۡ إِلَىٰ حِمَارِكَ وَلِنَجۡعَلَكَ ءَايَةً لِّلنَّاسِ وَٱنظُرۡ إِلَى ٱلۡعِظَامِ كَيۡفَ نُنشِزُهَا ثُمَّ نَكۡسُوهَا لَحۡمًا فَلَمَّا تَبَيَّنَ لَهُۥ قَالَ أَعۡلَمُ أَنَّ ٱللَّهَ عَلَىٰ كُلِّ شَىۡءٍ قَدِيرٌ ﴿٢٥٩﴾

259. Aw kaalla_th_ee marra AAala qaryatin wahiya _kh_awiyatun AAala AAurooshiha qala anna yu_h_yee _h_a_th_ihi Alla_h_u baAAda mawtiha faama_t_ahu Alla_h_u mi-ata AAamin thumma baAAathahu qala kam labithta qala labithtu yawman aw baAA_d_a yawmin qala bal labithta mi-ata AAamin faon_th_ur ila _t_aAAamika washara_b_ika lam yatasannah waon_th_ur ila _h_imarika walinajAAalaka ayatan lilnnasi waon_th_ur ila alAAi_th_ami kayfa nunshizuha thumma naksooha la_h_man falamma tabayyana lahu qala aAAlamu anna Alla_h_a AAala kulli shay-in qadeerun

2:259. Or[489], about a situation as the one when a man passed by a settlement which had turned upside down! He said, "How could Allah give life to it after its death?" Allah then caused him to die and to remain dead for a hundred years, and thereafter raised him alive. Asked, "How long did you remain in that condition?", he said, "I remained so for a day, or part of a day." "No! You remained so for a hundred years – look at your food and at your drink, and look at your donkey, haven't these decayed with age; and look at the bones, how We erect these together and clothe these with flesh[490] – so that We make you a sign for mankind." Then as the matter became clear to him, he said, "I realise Allah indeed has the power to do anything."

489. The conjunction 'Or' here connects this Verse to the immediately preceding one wherein Allah Almighty draws attention to the Abrahamic episode. 'Or' here therefore implies 'Or, wouldn't you like to know and deliberate'.

490. Obviously, it was the donkey's 100-year old bare skeleton lying by, that Allah was alluding to here. Allah was giving the man a lesson in anatomy as well.

وَإِذْ قَالَ إِبْرَاهِمُ رَبِّ أَرِنِى كَيْفَ تُحْىِ ٱلْمَوْتَىٰ قَالَ أَوَلَمْ تُؤْمِن قَالَ بَلَىٰ وَلَكِن لِّيَطْمَئِنَّ قَلْبِى قَالَ فَخُذْ أَرْبَعَةً مِّنَ ٱلطَّيْرِ فَصُرْهُنَّ إِلَيْكَ ثُمَّ ٱجْعَلْ عَلَىٰ كُلِّ جَبَلٍ مِّنْهُنَّ جُزْءًا ثُمَّ ٱدْعُهُنَّ يَأْتِينَكَ سَعْيًا وَٱعْلَمْ أَنَّ ٱللَّهَ عَزِيزٌ حَكِيمٌ ۝

260. Wa-ith qala ibraheemu rabbi arinee kayfa tuhyee almawta qala awa lam tu/min qala bala walakin liyatma-inna qalbee qala fakhuth arbaAAatan mina alttayri fasurhunna ilayka thumma ijAAal AAala kulli jabalin minhunna juz-an thumma odAAuhunna ya/teenaka saAAyan waiAAlam anna Allaha AAazeezun hakeemun

---

2:260. And when Abraham said, "O my Lord! Show me how You raise the dead to life", Allah asked, "Don't you believe?" Abraham said, "I do! But this I ask for, just in order that my mind may rest assured." Allah said, "Get hold then of 4 of the birds and make them familiarised with you. And place their parts on every mountain. Then call out to them: they will come post-haste to you. And know that Allah is indeed Omnipotent, Wise.[491]

---

491. In this Verse, as also in the preceding one, Allah shows how He kindly guides a believer to certainty of belief in Resurrection. While, in Verse 258 above, He tells us this divine guidance is not available to those who deliberately suppress the Truth, and thus wickedly become non-believers. The divine guidance, to the believers in this age, may not be as open and obvious as in the examples given in these Verses, but a believer, who keenly observes the course of events in his/her own life, will not fail to notice the hidden divine hand of guidance therein.

مَّثَلُ ٱلَّذِينَ يُنفِقُونَ أَمْوَالَهُمْ فِى سَبِيلِ ٱللَّهِ كَمَثَلِ حَبَّةٍ أَنْبَتَتْ سَبْعَ سَنَابِلَ فِى كُلِّ سُنْبُلَةٍ مِّائَةُ حَبَّةٍ وَٱللَّهُ يُضَاعِفُ لِمَن يَشَاءُ وَٱللَّهُ وَاسِعٌ عَلِيمٌ ۝

261. Mathalu alla<u>th</u>eena yunfiqoona amw<u>a</u>lahum fee sabeeli All<u>a</u>hi kamathali <u>h</u>abbatin anbatat sabAAa san<u>a</u>bila fee kulli sunbulatin mi-atu <u>h</u>abbatin waAll<u>a</u>hu yuda<u>A</u>Aifu liman yash<u>a</u>o waAll<u>a</u>hu w<u>a</u>siAAun AAaleem**un**

2:261. Simile of those who spend their wealth in Allah's path is like a grain that sprouts into seven ears, every ear bearing one hundred grains. And Allah gives manifold increase unto whom He wills. And Allah has boundless reach, knowledge. [492, 493]

492. By comparing it to a grain yielding 700 grains, Allah tells us that spending in Allah's path is the best investment. And for an analysis of the term *anfiquoo fee sabeelillah* **(spend in Allah's path) please refer** <u>Notes 2:331 & 2:332</u> **of these Studies.**

493. Allah says He will give multiple benefits unto whom He wills. In this Verse He has already willed that He would give such benefits to those who spend in His path. But He may also give benefits in this world to those who do not spend in His path, to test them further, or to recompense them, in this world itself, for some good deeds they might have done here.

ٱلَّـذِينَ يُنفِقُـونَ أَمۡوَٰلَهُمۡ فِى سَـبِيلِ ٱللَّهِ ثُـمَّ لَا يُتۡبِعُـونَ مَا أَنفَقُواْ مَنًّا
وَلَآ أَذًى لَّهُـمۡ أَجۡرُهُمۡ عِنـدَ رَبِّهِـمۡ وَلَا خَـوۡفٌ عَلَيۡهِـمۡ وَلَا هُمۡ يَحۡزَنُونَ

262. Alla<u>th</u>eena yunfiqoona amw<u>a</u>lahum fee sabeeli All<u>a</u>hi thumma l<u>a</u> yutbiAAoona m<u>a</u> anfaqoo mannan wal<u>a</u> a<u>th</u>an lahum ajruhum AAinda rabbihim wal<u>a</u> khawfun AAalayhim wal<u>a</u> hum ya<u>h</u>zanoon**a**

2:262. Those who spend their worldly possessions in Allah's path and follow not what they spend with boastfulness and insult – for them is their reward with their Lord; they shall have no fear, nor shall they grieve. [494, 495]

494. It is often the case with human beings that if they give something to a needy person, their behaviour with that person would be such as to make that person feel burdened with their favours. They will go on, on some pretext or the other, reminding him of their charity. They may even insult and speak harshly to him. Allah condemns such behaviour and makes their charity ineligible for any reward from Him.

495. The Qur'aanic statement *falaa khaufun ualayhim walaa hum yahuzanoon* (they shall have no fear, nor shall they grieve) has been repeated in several Verses while speaking of

- those who spend their property by night and by day, secretly and openly (2:274),
- those who believe and do good deeds and keep up prayer and give charity (2:277),
- those who believe in Allah and the last day and do good (5:69),
- the friends of Allah (10:62),
- those who say, Our Lord is Allah, then they continue the right way (46:13).

Any group of persons described by any one of the above attributes, do inherently also have all the other attributes mentioned. These are the people whose minds are at peace, whatever be their momentary situations, good or bad, in this worldly life.

263. Qawlun maAAroofun wamaghfiratun khayrun min ṣadaqatin yatbaAAuhā aṯhan waAllahu ghaniyyun ḥaleemun

2:263. Kind words and forgiveness are better than giving of poor-due that is followed by hurtful conduct. And Allah is Self-sufficient, Gentle and Kind.[496, 497]

496. Persons who help the needy in any way should not consider themselves great for having done acts of charity. And if they do so consider, their arrogance gets exposed through their bragging about it to others, or by their haughty behaviour towards recipients of their charity. They should remember that it is Allah Who has given them the means to do charitable acts. If they show arrogance on that account, Allah is not dependent on their giving the charity to the needy. HE can empower others for the purpose and condemn the arrogant to punishment for failing the test Allah had put them through. HE is kind and considerate to meet the needs of the poor, for whom He wishes to provide for, by some means or the other.

497. Allah has used the word *suadaquah* here. In terms of Verse 9.60 *suadaquah* is an obligatory charity, enjoined upon people above the poverty line.

يَـٰٓأَيُّهَا ٱلَّذِينَ ءَامَنُوا۟ لَا تُبْطِلُوا۟ صَدَقَـٰتِكُم بِٱلْمَنِّ وَٱلْأَذَىٰ كَٱلَّذِى يُنفِقُ مَالَهُۥ رِئَآءَ ٱلنَّاسِ وَلَا يُؤْمِنُ بِٱللَّهِ وَٱلْيَوْمِ ٱلْـَٔاخِرِ ۖ فَمَثَلُهُۥ كَمَثَلِ صَفْوَانٍ عَلَيْهِ تُرَابٌ فَأَصَابَهُۥ وَابِلٌ فَتَرَكَهُۥ صَلْدًا ۖ لَّا يَقْدِرُونَ عَلَىٰ شَىْءٍ مِّمَّا كَسَبُوا۟ ۗ وَٱللَّهُ لَا يَهْدِى ٱلْقَوْمَ ٱلْكَـٰفِرِينَ ﴿٢٦٤﴾

264. Ya ayyuha allatheena amanoo la tubtiloo sadaqatikum bialmanni waal-atha kaallathee yunfiqu malahu ri-aa alnnasi wala yu/minu biAllahi waalyawmi al-akhiri famathaluhu kamathali safwanin AAalayhi turabun faasabahu wabilun fatarakahu saldan la yaqdiroona AAala shay-in mimma kasaboo waAllahu la yahdee alqawma alkafireena

---

2:264. O you who believe! Make not your offerings of obligatory charity null and void with boastfulness/bragging and insult[498], like he who spends his wealth only to show off to people and who believes neither in Allah nor in the Last Day. His simile is like a barren rock covered with soil; then a heavy shower of rain lashes it and leaves it bare. Such people can do nothing with what they have earned.[499] And Allah does not guide the people who suppress the Truth!

---

498. Please also see Verse 2:262 above, in this context.

499. Offerings of such people to needy persons is compared here to soil covering a barren rock. Just like the soil getting washed away by a heavy draught of rain, leaving the barren rock useless for growing any agricultural product, the offerings of such people are useless for getting them any reward from Allah.

وَمَثَلُ ٱلَّذِينَ يُنفِقُونَ أَمْوَٰلَهُمُ ٱبْتِغَآءَ مَرْضَاتِ ٱللَّهِ وَتَثْبِيتًا مِّنْ أَنفُسِهِمْ كَمَثَلِ جَنَّةٍۭ بِرَبْوَةٍ أَصَابَهَا وَابِلٌ فَـَٔاتَتْ أُكُلَهَا ضِعْفَيْنِ فَإِن لَّمْ يُصِبْهَا وَابِلٌ فَطَلٌّ ۗ وَٱللَّهُ بِمَا تَعْمَلُونَ بَصِيرٌ ﴿٢٦٥﴾

265. Wamathalu allatheena yunfiqoona amwalahumu ibtighaa mardati Allahi watathbeetan min anfusihim kamathali jannatin birabwatin asabaha wabilun faatat okulaha diAAfayni fa-in lam yusibha wabilun fatallun waAllahu bima taAAmaloona baseerun

2:265. And simile of those who spend their worldly possessions seeking Allah's pleasure, and out of their own inner conviction, is like a garden situated on a high ground: when heavy rain falls on it, it doubles its produce; if not a heavy rain, even a drizzle would do.[500] And Allah is watching what you do.

500. A garden situated on a high ground does not get inundated with water, and thus get its yield badly affected. When heavy rain falls, the extra water flows down to lower lands around, while rainwater falling in a drizzle gets absorbed in the soil of the garden. Thus, the garden does get enough water for its needs, in either case. Likewise, in the cases of those who spend in Allah's cause, the extra wealth that they get goes to needy persons. They (those who spend) are thus spared of any chance of getting inundated with wealth and getting spoiled thereby.

أَيَوَدُّ أَحَدُكُمْ أَن تَكُونَ لَهُۥ جَنَّةٌ مِّن نَّخِيلٍ وَأَعْنَابٍ تَجْرِى مِن تَحْتِهَا الْأَنْهَـٰرُ لَهُۥ فِيهَا مِن كُلِّ الثَّمَرَٰتِ وَأَصَابَهُ الْكِبَرُ وَلَهُۥ ذُرِّيَّةٌ ضُعَفَآءُ فَأَصَابَهَآ إِعْصَارٌ فِيهِ نَارٌ فَاحْتَرَقَتْ كَذَٰلِكَ يُبَيِّنُ اللَّهُ لَكُمُ الْآيَـٰتِ لَعَلَّكُمْ تَتَفَكَّرُونَ ﴿٢٦٦﴾

266. Ayawaddu ahadukum an takoona lahu jannatun min nakheelin waaAAnabin tajree min tahtiha al-anharu lahu feeha min kulli alththamarati waasabahu alkibaru walahu thurriyyatun duAAafao faasabaha iAAsarun feehi narun faihtaraqat kathalika yubayyinu Allahu lakumu al-ayati laAAallakum tatafakkaroona

2:266. Would any of you wish to be like one in a situation as follows? He has a garden of palm trees and grape vines, underneath which run streams of water, and he gets all kinds of fruits there from. He has reached old age and his children are weak. And in these circumstances a fiery hurricane hits his garden and burns it down. Thus, Allah does make signs/Verses/messages clear to you so that you may ponder over them.[501]

501. This is a clear divine warning to those who are endowed with riches in this world. They do have to spend their wealth in Allah's Path; otherwise He could easily turn their wealth to nought any time.

267. Ya ayyuha allatheena amanoo anfiqoo min tayyibati ma kasabtum wamimma akhrajna lakum mina al-ardi wala tayammamoo alkhabeetha minhu tunfiqoona walastum bi-akhitheehi illa an tughmidoo feehi waiAAlamoo anna Allaha ghaniyyun hameedun

2:267. O you who believe! Spend[502] from the good things you have lawfully earned and from that which We have taken out for you from the earth[503], and seek not for spending, things of little worth there from, which you yourselves would not accept but scornfully. Bear in mind that Allah has everything in abundance and is Praiseworthy.[504]

502. Please go through Chapter Notes 5, 331, 385 and 404 of these Studies to get a comprehensive notion of the Qur'aanic concept of spending.

503. Agricultural products, obviously.

504. It is a general human tendency to give away only those things in charity which the giver himself would consider to be unworthy of use. Suppose, for example, I take a superior grade A rice for my personal use. Then if I intend sending some cooked rice as charity to an orphanage, I may take rice of an inferior quality. That is what Allah abhors. HE wouldn't give me any marks for charity on that score. What He expects me to do is use the same superior grade A rice for sending cooked food as charity to the orphanage. Allah allays my fears of getting impoverished by my using the superior quality rice also for charity. He reminds me that it is by His grace that I can use grade A rice for myself. And if He wants to, He can provide for the orphans with food, even better than what I use for my own consumption. By providing me with the means to give charity, He is only testing me as to how I treat the have-nots. Praise be to Him! HE can keep a simultaneous watch on everybody and everything in any part of the Universe. HE has knowledge of what goes on inside the minds and bodies of all living creatures.

$$\text{ٱلشَّيْطَـٰنُ يَعِدُكُمُ ٱلْفَقْرَ وَيَأْمُرُكُم بِٱلْفَحْشَاءِ وَٱللَّهُ يَعِدُكُم مَّغْفِرَةً مِّنْهُ وَفَضْلًا وَٱللَّهُ وَٰسِعٌ عَلِيمٌ ﴿٢٦٨﴾}$$

268. Alshshaytanu yaAAidukumu alfaqra waya/murukum bialfahsha-i waAllahu yaAAidukum maghfiratan minhu wafadlan waAllahu wasiAAun AAaleemun

---

2:268. The Satan warns you of poverty and makes you commit indecent acts. And Allah promises you forgiveness from Him and favour. And Allah is Pervasive, Knowledgeable.[505]

---

505. Refer preceding Note 504

$$\text{يُؤْتِى ٱلْحِكْمَةَ مَن يَشَاءُ وَمَن يُؤْتَ ٱلْحِكْمَةَ فَقَدْ أُوتِىَ خَيْرًا كَثِيرًا وَمَا يَذَّكَّرُ إِلَّا أُولُوا ٱلْأَلْبَـٰبِ ﴿٢٦٩﴾}$$

269. Yu/tee alhikmata man yashao waman yu/ta alhikmata faqad ootiya khayran katheeran wama yaththakkaru illa oloo al-albabi

---

2:269. He grants wisdom to whom He pleases; and whoever is granted wisdom, is indeed given a great wealth. And none remember it except those endowed with insight.[506]

---

506. A wise man has a long-term and wide-ranging perspective. A fool, on the other hand, looks only to immediate and visible gains. The latter is easily enticed by the glamour of this world that inevitably lands him into trouble. But the wise man does not get ensnared in the pomp and glitter of worldly life. He ponders over his real Creator, and over the purpose for which he is created by that Creator. He understands that this worldly life is not the be-all and end-all of his existence. His deeds are influenced and conditioned by that wider perspective, and make him eligible for the ultimate success, here and in the Hereafter.

وَمَآ أَنفَقْتُم مِّن نَّفَقَةٍ أَوْ نَذَرْتُم مِّن نَّذْرٍ فَإِنَّ ٱللَّهَ يَعْلَمُهُۥ وَمَا لِلظَّـٰلِمِينَ مِنْ أَنصَارٍ ۝

270. Wam_a anfaqtum min nafaqatin aw na_th_artum min na_th_rin fa-inna All_aha yaAAlamuhu wam_a lil_ththa_limeena min an_sa__rin

---

2:270. And whatever spending you do or whatever vow you make, surely Allah knows it then and there. And not for the wrongdoers shall there be any helpers.[507]

---

507. Allah has explained to us in details how to spend (refer Note 502 above) what He is pleased to grant to us. Allah also requires believers to keep promises/vows they make (Verses 2:177 & 76:7). HE is instantly aware if anyone does not keep any promise or obey His directions on spending. There shall be nobody to help such wrong-doers against Allah when He would punish them.

إِن تُبْدُوا۟ ٱلصَّدَقَـٰتِ فَنِعِمَّا هِىَ ۖ وَإِن تُخْفُوهَا وَتُؤْتُوهَا ٱلْفُقَرَآءَ فَهُوَ خَيْرٌ لَّكُمْ ۚ وَيُكَفِّرُ عَنكُم مِّن سَيِّـَٔاتِكُمْ ۗ وَٱللَّهُ بِمَا تَعْمَلُونَ خَبِيرٌ ۝

271. In tubdoo al_ssadaqati faniAAimm_a hiya wa-in tukhfooh_a watu/tooh_a alfuqar_a_a fahuwa khayrun lakum wayukaffiru AAankum min sayyi-_atikum waAll_ahu bim_a taAAmaloona khabee_run

---

2:271. If you give *sadaqaat* openly it is good. And if you do it in secrecy, and give it to the poor, then it is better for you. And it will atone for some of your misdeeds. And Allah is aware of what you do.[508]

---

508. In terms of Verse 9:60, *suadaquah* (singular of *sadaqaat*) is obligatory charity, which can be collected by an organization, governmental or non-governmental. There are many beneficiaries, enumerated in that Verse, of the charity fund, the main being the poor who do not openly beg. This section of society is most vulnerable, since their poor financial condition is not generally known. Allah would like persons of means to give their charities to such people secretly, so that the latter's sensibilities are not hurt. Allah assures the charity-givers that He is certainly aware of their good deeds even when done secretly, and

201

those good deeds shall not go unrewarded. Their secret good deeds will expiate some of their own misdeeds.

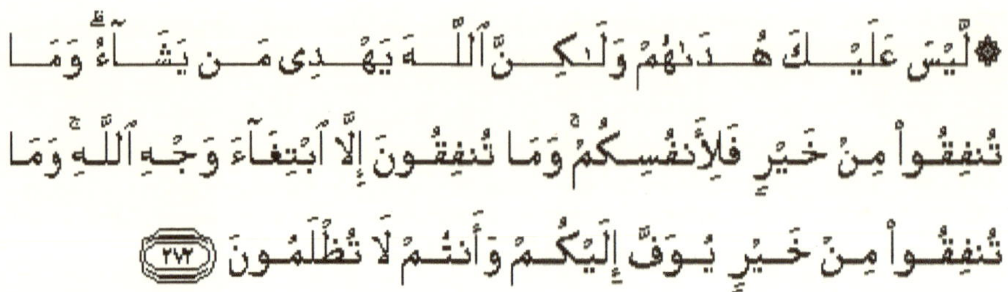

272. Laysa AAalayka hud*a*hum wal*a*kinna All*a*ha yahdee man yash*a*o wam*a* tunfiqoo min khayrin fali-anfusikum wam*a* tunfiqoona ill*a* ibtigh*a*a wajhi All*a*hi wam*a* tunfiqoo min khayrin yuwaffa ilaykum waantum l*a* tu*th*lamoon*a*

2:272. Guiding them is not your responsibility, but Allah guides whom He pleases.[509, 510] And whatever wealth you spend, it is for your own benefit. And you spend not, but to seek Allah's pleasure. And the wealth, you spend, shall be recompensed to you, and you will not be wronged.

509. Some Muslims think that even now, over 14 centuries after his death, the Prophet (peace be upon him) still somehow guides every individual of his *Ummah*. This Verse ought to correct their grievous misconception. I call it grievous because, indulging in such a conception is nothing but *shirk*. In this, we are following the footsteps of the Christians, who have taken to Jesus (peace be upon him) so much that they have forgotten their God. This Verse categorically tells us that guiding any person to the right path is the exclusive preserve of Allah Almighty. It was so even during the time when the Prophet was living in this world.

510. The Prophet taught the divine Qur'aan to his *Ummah*, under Allah's guidance. It was like a good teacher teaching indiscriminately to all pupils in his class. But some pupils learn, and some do not. Likewise, the Prophet taught the divine message for the entire mankind; some got guided by the Message, while many did not. Had it been in the power of the Prophet to guide people, he would have guided all without any distinction. It is Allah Who guides whosoever He pleases, to the Straight Path. And Allah has declared that only the pious would receive the guidance from Him. (Refer Verses 2:2 to 2:5 of these Studies.)

$$\text{لِلْفُقَرَآءِ ٱلَّذِينَ أُحْصِرُوا۟ فِى سَبِيلِ ٱللَّهِ لَا يَسْتَطِيعُونَ ضَرْبًا فِى}$$

$$\text{ٱلْأَرْضِ يَحْسَبُهُمُ ٱلْجَاهِلُ أَغْنِيَآءَ مِنَ ٱلتَّعَفُّفِ تَعْرِفُهُم بِسِيمَٰهُمْ لَا}$$

$$\text{يَسْـَٔلُونَ ٱلنَّاسَ إِلْحَافًا وَمَا تُنفِقُوا۟ مِنْ خَيْرٍ فَإِنَّ ٱللَّهَ بِهِۦ عَلِيمٌ ﴿٢٧٣﴾}$$

273. Lilfuqara-i allatheena ohsiroo fee sabeeli Allahi la yastateeAAoona darban fee al-ardi yahsabuhumu aljahilu aghniyaa mina alttaAAaffufi taAArifuhum biseemahum la yas-aloona alnnasa ilhafan wama tunfiqoo min khayrin fa-inna Allaha bihi AAaleemun

---

2:273. [511]For those needy people, confined to Allah's Path, unable to move about in the land, and whom the ignorant do not consider to be poor because of the abstinence. You recognize them by their looks. They do not ask for things from people persistently. And Allah indeed becomes instantly aware of anything you spend.

---

511. This is a continuation of the sentence at the end of the preceding Verse 2:272. Allah deals here with one category of beneficiaries of wealth spent, and He apparently recommends that this category, described in this Verse, be given the first preference.

$$\text{ٱلَّذِينَ يُنفِقُونَ أَمْوَٰلَهُم بِٱلَّيْلِ وَٱلنَّهَارِ سِرًّا وَعَلَانِيَةً فَلَهُمْ أَجْرُهُمْ}$$

$$\text{عِندَ رَبِّهِمْ وَلَا خَوْفٌ عَلَيْهِمْ وَلَا هُمْ يَحْزَنُونَ ﴿٢٧٤﴾}$$

274. Allatheena yunfiqoona amwalahum biallayli waalnnahari sirran waAAalaniyatan falahum ajruhum AAinda rabbihim wala khawfun AAalayhim wala hum yahzanoona

---

2:274. For those who spend their wealth, by night and by day, secretly and openly, their reward is with their Lord. And there shall be no fear on them, nor shall they grieve.[512, 513]

---

512. Allah thus repeatedly reassures those who spend in Allah's way that their spending shall not go in vain. They shall receive rewards from Allah much more in value than what they thus spent.

513. Right from Verse 2:261 to this Verse 2:274, Allah comprehensively deals with the subject of how to spend one's lawfully acquired wealth, in Allah's way. The emphasis in these Verses is on spending correctly what one rightfully earns. Obviously, those who do not so spend their wealth, but accumulate and hoard it, would be incurring Allah's wrath. Verses 2:261 to 2:274 thus deal with one aspect – that of Expenditure – of the Islamic Principles of Economics. The other aspect - that of Income - is dealt with in some of the Verses that follow, in this Qur'aanic Chapter of Al-Baqarah. We shall *inshaAllah* see therein how the Qur'aanic Concept of *Ar-Riba* has been grossly misunderstood.

ٱلَّذِينَ يَأْكُلُونَ ٱلرِّبَوٰاْ لَا يَقُومُونَ إِلَّا كَمَا يَقُومُ ٱلَّذِى يَتَخَبَّطُهُ ٱلشَّيْطَٰنُ

مِنَ ٱلْمَسِّ ذَٰلِكَ بِأَنَّهُمْ قَالُوٓاْ إِنَّمَا ٱلْبَيْعُ مِثْلُ ٱلرِّبَوٰاْ وَأَحَلَّ ٱللَّهُ ٱلْبَيْعَ

وَحَرَّمَ ٱلرِّبَوٰاْ فَمَن جَآءَهُۥ مَوْعِظَةٌ مِّن رَّبِّهِۦ فَٱنتَهَىٰ فَلَهُۥ مَا سَلَفَ وَأَمْرُهُۥٓ

إِلَى ٱللَّهِ وَمَنْ عَادَ فَأُوْلَٰٓئِكَ أَصْحَٰبُ ٱلنَّارِ هُمْ فِيهَا خَٰلِدُونَ ﴿٢٧٥﴾

275. Allatheena ya/kuloona alrriba la yaqoomoona illa kama yaqoomu allathee yatakhabbatuhu alshshaytanu mina almassi thalika bi-annahum qaloo innama albayAAu mithlu alrriba waahalla Allahu albayAAa waharrama alrriba faman jaahu mawAAithatun min rabbihi faintaha falahu ma salafa waamruhu ila Allahi waman AAada faola-ika as-habu alnnari hum feeha khalidoona

---

2:275. Those who consume *Ar-Riba*[514] live not but like those whom Satan makes to stumble on in life, under his spell[515]. That is because they assert, "Business is just like *Ar-Riba*.[516]" And Allah has made business lawful and *Ar-Riba* unlawful. He, then, to whom admonition has come from his Lord and has since abstained from *Ar-Riba* – to him belongs what happened in the past. And to Allah returns his deed.[517] And those who rebel – they shall be inhabitants of the hellfire, therein to remain forever.

---

514. In Verse 30:39, Allah declares, "That which you give at a premium, so that the gain accrued is on account of other people's properties, possessions or dues, such a gain has no approval of Allah ...." In that Verse, Allah has clearly expressed his disapproval of gains that are rightfully due to others, but manouvred to be usurped from them in day-to-day human dealings. An example can be given of a factory owner cheating the workers employed, in their salaries, to have a fatter profit for himself. Such gains, wrongfully usurped from others and disapproved of by Allah in Verse 30:39, are here in this Verse, 2:275, made totally unlawful. And such gains are termed as *Ar-Riba*, literally meaning the gain/increase, to distinguish it from lawfully obtained gains as through trading, giving services etc. It is unfortunate that most Muslim scholars have given a wrongly restrictive meaning of 'interest on money lent or borrowed' to the Qur'aanic term.

515. Under the satanic spell, people become reluctant to believe in any life after death. They therefore tend to believe that this worldly life is the be-all and end-all of human existence. And they try to get the most out of it. With no fear of any divine punishment, they stumble on from one wrongdoing to another and consume *Ar-Riba* to get rich quickly and enjoy all that money can buy. But the happiness and enjoyment, that they seek, ever eludes them like a mirage.

516. I have no knowledge of the people who said this at the time of revelation of this Verse. But I know people who say this now in this 21st Century (15th Century Hijri). I know people who say, 'Banking business is *Ar-Riba*', whereas Allah has categorically made business lawful and *Ar-Riba* unlawful. Business is an activity by a person or by a group of persons to make things or services conveniently available to the public. Manufacturing and trading businesses make goods conveniently available and there are firms, like those of solicitors, who provide services to the public. Likewise, banking business provides money for needful projects that an individual or a group of individuals undertake, but for which the individual, or the group, doesn't have all the necessary finance. Banking is therefore a legitimate business fulfilling a social need. Like other businesses, banking business too is legitimately entitled to a reasonable profit for itself. It is also entitled to recover expenses incurred like staff salaries, building rentals etc., on pro rata basis from its clientele. And a bank does recover its expenses plus profit and calls this recovery as interest. Such interest gets divinely sanctioned when this Verse 2:275 declares that Allah has made business lawful. But the Satan has succeeded in inducing many Muslim scholars in declaring such legitimate interest collected as *Ar-Riba*! *Ar-Riba*, I repeat, is wrongful usurpation, during transactions, of other people's properties, possessions or dues, in terms of Verse 30:39. *Ar-Riba* is <u>not</u> interest, as such.

517. Whatever *Ar-Riba* gains people had made before they became aware of the divine prohibition against it, could be retained with those people, provided they abided by the prohibition thereafter. Their matter is left for Allah Himself to deal with as He wished. Allah, in His mercy, may forgive them – but not those who consciously act against the divine prohibition.

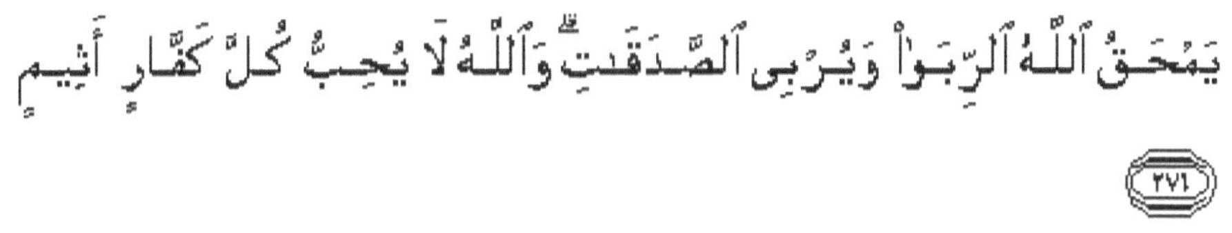

276. Yam<u>h</u>aqu All<u>a</u>hu alrrib<u>a</u> wayurbee al<u>ss</u>adaq<u>a</u>ti waAll<u>a</u>hu l<u>a</u> yu<u>h</u>ibbu kulla kaff<u>a</u>rin atheemin

2:276. Allah withdraws His blessings from *Ar-Riba* and causes prosperity in *Sadaqaat*.[518] And Allah loves not any sinful suppressor of Truth.

518. In terms of Verse 9:60, *Sadaqaat* are mandatory charities, to be compulsorily given by all those who are above the poverty line. The same Verse also indicates that arrangements for collection of these charities, and their proper distribution, may be made by the community.

إِنَّ ٱلَّذِينَ ءَامَنُواْ وَعَمِلُواْ ٱلصَّـٰلِحَـٰتِ وَأَقَامُواْ ٱلصَّلَوٰةَ وَءَاتَوُاْ ٱلزَّكَوٰةَ لَهُمْ أَجْرُهُمْ عِندَ رَبِّهِمْ وَلَا خَوْفٌ عَلَيْهِمْ وَلَا هُمْ يَحْزَنُونَ ﴿٢٧٧﴾

277. Inna allatheena amanoo waAAamiloo alssalihati waaqamoo alssalata waatawoo alzzakata lahum ajruhum AAinda rabbihim wala khawfun AAalayhim wala hum yahzanoona

2:277. Indeed, those who believe and do good deeds, establish regular prayers, and give charity – for them, their reward is with their Lord. And they shall have no fear, nor shall they grieve.

يَـٰٓأَيُّهَا ٱلَّذِينَ ءَامَنُواْ ٱتَّقُواْ ٱللَّهَ وَذَرُواْ مَا بَقِيَ مِنَ ٱلرِّبَوٰٓاْ إِن كُنتُم مُّؤْمِنِينَ ﴿٢٧٨﴾

278. Ya ayyuha allatheena amanoo ittaqoo Allaha watharoo ma baqiya mina alrriba in kuntum mu/mineena

2:278. O you who believe! Fear Allah and give up what has remained of *Ar-Riba*, if you are indeed believers.[519]

519. Recall divine Rulings, Warnings and Directions made in Verses 2:275 and 2:276. The divine admonition, here in Verse 2:278, is in pursuance thereof.

فَإِن لَّمْ تَفْعَلُواْ فَأْذَنُواْ بِحَرْبٍ مِّنَ ٱللَّهِ وَرَسُولِهِۦ ۖ وَإِن تُبْتُمْ فَلَكُمْ رُءُوسُ أَمْوَٰلِكُمْ لَا تَظْلِمُونَ وَلَا تُظْلَمُونَ ﴿٢٧٩﴾

279. Fa-in lam tafAAaloo fa/*thanoo bi*harbin mina All*a*hi warasoolihi wa-in tubtum falakum ruoosu amw*a*likum l*a* ta*th*limoona wal*a* tu*th*lamoona

---

2:279. And if you do it not, take notice of war from Allah and His Messenger.[520, 521] And if you return penitently to Allah, you are entitled to all that comes under heads of account of your property and/or dues, so that you do no wrong, nor are you wronged.[522]

---

520. "Take notice of war from Allah and His Messenger"! What warning could be more dreadful than this divine one? It clearly shows that the All-knowing Allah has given a very great importance to eradication of economic ills from human societies. *Ar-Riba* is an economic ill that corrupts human society and eats into its body polity, like cancer. It deprives people of their dues to fill the coffers of the rich, thus creating a great economic divide between the rich and the poor. On a mega scale, we have examples in history wherein the divine notice of war was put to dreadful effect in such cases. In the French Revolution, the numerically vast poor populace, for long subjected to deprivation and oppression by the obscenely rich, took to violence, took control over the land and put every rich person, they could lay their hands on, to the guillotine. A similar thing happened when the Communists, under Lenin, overthrew the Czars in Russia. On the micro individual scale also, Allah punishes most of those indulging in *Ar-Riba* in this life itself first, after giving them a long rope. A genuine believer cannot but take heed of this dreadful divine warning. But what is the ground reality? Most Muslims are unaware of what *Ar-Riba* means. I've already given earlier in these Studies the example of a factory owner cheating his employees in their salaries to fatten his profit. The factory owner may apparently be a very pious Muslim, sporting a flowing beard and offering prayers regularly. With the fat profit he is getting from the sale of goods produced in his factory, he may be buying car after car for every member of his family, and he won't touch the *haraam* interest money by putting his money in a commercial bank. But he is blissfully unaware that by paying his employees less than their rightful dues, he is guilty of committing the real *Ar-Riba*.

521. And there are examples galore of *Ar-Riba* being indulged in, in every other walk of life. Employees cheat their employers by attending to their own private affairs, during office hours, but get their full salaries. Traders hoard goods to create an artificial scarcity to sell them at higher prices and get fatter margins of profit. Taxi drivers compel passengers to pay more than what the meters indicate. Tax-payers cheat the Government by hiding part of their income. But none of our religious leaders apprise us of *Ar-Riba* masquerading in any of the forms mentioned here. They are content with declaring again and again from their housetops that interest is 'haraam' 'haraam', and they remain blissfully ignorant of the real *Ar-Riba* growing luxuriantly in their own backyards.

522. If A lends B $1000, and B repays after a year, A is entitled to get his *amwaal* back, as this Verse clearly indicates. But money, per se, is not *amwaal*. It's only the present transitory value of *amwaal*. As such, if the cost of living has appreciated by 5% during the year, A is entitled to get $1050 from B. Otherwise A stands wronged. In addition, A is also entitled to a just, mutually agreed compensation for his being deprived of using $1000 for his personal purposes, for a year. It's another matter if A & B are friends, and A waives all the additions lawfully due to him.

وَإِن كَانَ ذُو عُسْرَةٍ فَنَظِرَةٌ إِلَىٰ مَيْسَرَةٍ وَأَن تَصَدَّقُوا خَيْرٌ لَّكُمْ إِن كُنتُمْ تَعْلَمُونَ ﴿٢٨٠﴾

280. Wa-in kana thoo AAusratin fanathiratun ila maysaratin waan tasaddaqoo khayrun lakum in kuntum taAAlamoona

2:280. And if it is a case of a person in straitened circumstances, let there be a deferment to a convenient time. And to forgo, as charity, is better for you, if you do understand.[523]

523. And in the example given in Note 522 above, if B's financial condition has not improved during the year, A should give him more time to make the repayment. And if B's condition becomes precariously bad, A may waive the entire loan. Allah says it would be better for him to do so. A should have faith in Allah. And the next Verse 2.281 promises that he shall be given full compensation and shall not be wronged.

وَاتَّقُوا يَوْمًا تُرْجَعُونَ فِيهِ إِلَى اللَّهِ ثُمَّ تُوَفَّىٰ كُلُّ نَفْسٍ مَّا كَسَبَتْ وَهُمْ لَا يُظْلَمُونَ ﴿٢٨١﴾

281. Waittaqoo yawman turjaAAoona feehi ila Allahi thumma tuwaffa kullu nafsin ma kasabat wahum la yuthlamoona

2:281. Fear the Day in which you shall be taken back to Allah. Then, everyone shall be repaid in full what one earned. And they shall not be wronged.

يَـٰٓأَيُّهَا ٱلَّذِينَ ءَامَنُوٓاْ إِذَا تَدَايَنتُم بِدَيْنٍ إِلَىٰٓ أَجَلٍ مُّسَمًّى فَٱكْتُبُوهُ ۚ وَلْيَكْتُب بَّيْنَكُمْ كَاتِبٌۢ بِٱلْعَدْلِ ۚ وَلَا يَأْبَ كَاتِبٌ أَن يَكْتُبَ كَمَا عَلَّمَهُ ٱللَّهُ ۚ فَلْيَكْتُبْ وَلْيُمْلِلِ ٱلَّذِى عَلَيْهِ ٱلْحَقُّ وَلْيَتَّقِ ٱللَّهَ رَبَّهُۥ وَلَا يَبْخَسْ مِنْهُ شَيْـًٔا ۚ فَإِن كَانَ ٱلَّذِى عَلَيْهِ ٱلْحَقُّ سَفِيهًا أَوْ ضَعِيفًا أَوْ لَا يَسْتَطِيعُ أَن يُمِلَّ هُوَ فَلْيُمْلِلْ وَلِيُّهُۥ بِٱلْعَدْلِ ۚ وَٱسْتَشْهِدُواْ شَهِيدَيْنِ مِن رِّجَالِكُمْ ۖ فَإِن لَّمْ يَكُونَا رَجُلَيْنِ فَرَجُلٌ وَٱمْرَأَتَانِ مِمَّن تَرْضَوْنَ مِنَ ٱلشُّهَدَآءِ أَن تَضِلَّ إِحْدَىٰهُمَا فَتُذَكِّرَ إِحْدَىٰهُمَا ٱلْأُخْرَىٰ ۚ وَلَا يَأْبَ ٱلشُّهَدَآءُ إِذَا مَا دُعُواْ ۚ وَلَا تَسْـَٔمُوٓاْ أَن تَكْتُبُوهُ صَغِيرًا أَوْ كَبِيرًا إِلَىٰٓ أَجَلِهِۦ ۚ ذَٰلِكُمْ أَقْسَطُ عِندَ ٱللَّهِ وَأَقْوَمُ لِلشَّهَٰدَةِ وَأَدْنَىٰٓ أَلَّا تَرْتَابُوٓاْ ۖ إِلَّآ أَن تَكُونَ تِجَٰرَةً حَاضِرَةً تُدِيرُونَهَا بَيْنَكُمْ فَلَيْسَ عَلَيْكُمْ جُنَاحٌ أَلَّا تَكْتُبُوهَا ۗ وَأَشْهِدُوٓاْ إِذَا تَبَايَعْتُمْ ۚ وَلَا يُضَآرَّ كَاتِبٌ وَلَا شَهِيدٌ ۚ وَإِن تَفْعَلُواْ فَإِنَّهُۥ فُسُوقٌۢ بِكُمْ ۗ وَٱتَّقُواْ ٱللَّهَ ۖ وَيُعَلِّمُكُمُ ٱللَّهُ ۗ وَٱللَّهُ بِكُلِّ شَىْءٍ عَلِيمٌ ۝ ٢٨٢

282. Ya ayyuha allatheena amanoo itha tadayantum bidaynin ila ajalin musamman faoktuboohu walyaktub baynakum katibun bialAAadli wala ya/ba katibun an yaktuba kama AAallamahu Allahu falyaktub walyumlili allathee AAalayhi alhaqqu walyattaqi Allaha rabbahu wala yabkhas minhu shay-an fa-in kana allathee AAalayhi alhaqqu safeehan aw daAAeefan aw la yastateeAAu an yumilla huwa falyumlil waliyyuhu bialAAadli waistashhidoo shaheedayni min rijalikum fa-in lam yakoona rajulayni farajulun waimraatani mimman tardawna mina alshshuhada-i an tadilla ihdahuma fatuthakkira ihdahuma al-okhra wala ya/ba alshshuhadao itha ma duAAoo wala tas-amoo an taktuboohu sagheeran aw kabeeran ila ajalihi thalikum aqsatu AAinda Allahi waaqwamu lilshshahadati waadna alla tartaboo illa an takoona tijaratan hadiratan tudeeroonaha baynakum falaysa AAalaykum junahun alla taktubooha waashhidoo itha tabayaAAtum wala yudarra katibun wala shaheedun wa-in tafAAaloo fa-innahu fusooqun bikum waittaqoo Allaha wayuAAallimukumu Allahu waAllahu bikulli shay-in AAaleem**un**

2:282. O you who believe! When you contract a loan among yourselves for a certain period, put it down in writing. And a scribe ought to record it faithfully between you. And the scribe should not refuse to write; as Allah has taught him, so he should write.[524] And the one, upon whom lies the liability, should dictate. And he should fear Allah, his Lord, and omit nothing. Then if the one, upon whom lies the liability, is mentally unsound or weak or is himself unable to dictate, let his guardian dictate for him fairly. And two of you men should bear witness. If two men are not available, then one man and two women, you choose from among those present, should bear witness, so that if one of the women retracts, the other stands by her evidence.[525] And the witnesses must not refuse when they are called to witness. Be not weary of writing a term contract, small or big. With Allah, that's a proper thing to do for better establishment of evidence and for removal of your doubts, unless it be a hand-to-hand commercial transaction commonly done among yourselves, in which case there is no blame on you if you do not put it in writing. And keep witnesses when you do any business. And cause no harm to the scribe, or to the witnesses. And if you do so, it would indeed be wickedness on your part. And fear Allah. And Allah teaches you.[526] And Allah knows everything.

---

524. At the time of revelation of the Qur'aan, literacy among the public was low. It might have been difficult to get a person who could write. So, it was made obligatory on any literate person available to write the contract. Now, in the present age, the problem of writing down a contract may not be as acute, but still there is palpable reluctance to write. People tend to avoid it out of sheer slothfulness or undue embarrassment at the potential display of lack of faith in one another's oral promises.

525. This does not mean that women have weaker memories than men. To understand the significance of this divine provision, we must go to Verses 92:3 and 92:4. Allah declares therein that men and women have different types of work normally allotted to them. From Verse 2:282, we're presently studying here, it is apparent that the work of witnessing contracts is to be normally done by men. Women are given this duty only in the event of non-availability of two men as witnesses. Since it is not part of her normal duty, a woman may make a mistake while giving evidence as a witness. And as a precautionary measure, the divine Law of Evidence provides for two women in place of one man to witness the debt deed. This provision also makes it clear that, in times of need, women can handle jobs normally done by men.

526. As Allah taught mankind through this very Verse that it is better for everyone concerned to keep witnesses while making business deals, unless it be a hand-to-hand transaction.

۞ وَإِن كُنتُمْ عَلَىٰ سَفَرٍ وَلَمْ تَجِدُواْ كَاتِبًا فَرِهَـٰنٌ مَّقْبُوضَةٌ فَإِنْ أَمِنَ بَعْضُكُم بَعْضًا فَلْيُؤَدِّ ٱلَّذِى ٱؤْتُمِنَ أَمَـٰنَتَهُۥ وَلْيَتَّقِ ٱللَّهَ رَبَّهُۥ وَلَا تَكْتُمُواْ ٱلشَّهَـٰدَةَ وَمَن يَكْتُمْهَا فَإِنَّهُۥ ءَاثِمٌ قَلْبُهُۥ وَٱللَّهُ بِمَا تَعْمَلُونَ عَلِيمٌ

283. Wa-in kuntum AAala safarin walam tajidoo katiban farihanun maqboodatun fa-in amina baAAdukum baAAdan falyu-addi allathee_i/tumina amanatahu walyattaqi Allaha rabbahu wala taktumoo alshshahadata waman yaktumha fa-innahu athimun qalbuhu waAllahu bima taAAmaloona AAaleemun

---

2:283. And if you are on a journey and cannot find a scribe, then let a security deposit be taken over. Then if some of you entrust some others with some things, the trustee should take care of the trust, and should fear Allah, his Lord. And do not suppress evidence. And whoever suppresses it, he is sinful at heart.[527] Allah is aware of what you do.

---

527. Suppression of evidence is one of the major means of causing injustices in this world. If mankind were to abide strictly by this divine injunction against the suppression, the world would be free of many acts of injustice. And continual suppression of Allah-provided evidences it is, that makes a man an atheist. Atheism is the source of all evil.

لِّلَّهِ مَا فِى ٱلسَّمَـٰوَٰتِ وَمَا فِى ٱلْأَرْضِ وَإِن تُبْدُواْ مَا فِىٓ أَنفُسِكُمْ أَوْ تُخْفُوهُ يُحَاسِبْكُم بِهِ ٱللَّهُ فَيَغْفِرُ لِمَن يَشَآءُ وَيُعَذِّبُ مَن يَشَآءُ وَٱللَّهُ عَلَىٰ كُلِّ شَىْءٍ قَدِيرٌ

284. Lillahi ma fee alssamawati wama fee al-ardi wa-in tubdoo ma fee anfusikum aw tukhfoohu yuhasibkum bihi Allahu fayaghfiru liman yashao wayuAAaththibu man yashao waAllahu AAala kulli shay-in qadeerun

---

2:284. To Allah belong all that is in the heavens and all that is in the earth. And whether you reveal that which is in your minds or conceal it, Allah calls you to account for it. Then He pardons whom He pleases and punishes whom He pleases.[528] And Allah has complete power over everything.

---

528. This should be read with Allah's promise that none shall be dealt with unjustly (Verse 39:69).

ءَامَنَ ٱلرَّسُولُ بِمَآ أُنزِلَ إِلَيْهِ مِن رَّبِّهِۦ وَٱلْمُؤْمِنُونَ كُلٌّ ءَامَنَ بِٱللَّهِ وَمَلَٰٓئِكَتِهِۦ وَكُتُبِهِۦ وَرُسُلِهِۦ لَا نُفَرِّقُ بَيْنَ أَحَدٍ مِّن رُّسُلِهِۦ وَقَالُواْ سَمِعْنَا وَأَطَعْنَا غُفْرَانَكَ رَبَّنَا وَإِلَيْكَ ٱلْمَصِيرُ ﴿٢٨٥﴾

285. Amana alrrasoolu bima onzila ilayhi min rabbihi waalmu/minoona kullun amana biAllahi wamala-ikatihi wakutubihi warusulihi la nufarriqu bayna ahadin min rusulihi waqaloo samiAAna waataAAna ghufranaka rabbana wa-ilayka almaseeru

---

2:285. The Messenger believes in what is revealed to him from his Lord and so do the Believers. They all believe in Allah, His angels, His books and His Messengers. "We make no distinction between any of His Messengers with any other."[529] And they say: "We hear, and we obey. We seek Your forgiveness, our Lord! And to You is the final destination."

---

529. There is clear indication here that Allah doesn't want us Muslims to make any distinction between Prophet Muhammad (peace be upon him) and any of the Messengers preceding him. And yet we indulge in making the distinction. We give Prophet Muhammad the highest rank, and we have been saying that while other Messengers would be worried about their own selves on the Resurrection Day, Prophet Muhammad wouldn't be worried about his own self, but he would be the only Messenger worried about his followers. Allah doesn't want believers to entertain such parochial feelings. HE is obviously angry with the present-day Muslims for acting against His wishes/instructions/admonitions in this and in many, many other matters. Believers are expected to listen and obey, as this Verse tells us further on. But most Muslims of today do not even take the trouble of listening to the Qur'aan, let alone obeying the divine Message.

لَا يُكَلِّفُ ٱللَّهُ نَفْسًا إِلَّا وُسْعَهَا لَهَا مَا كَسَبَتْ وَعَلَيْهَا مَا ٱكْتَسَبَتْ رَبَّنَا لَا

تُؤَاخِذْنَآ إِن نَّسِينَآ أَوْ أَخْطَأْنَا رَبَّنَا وَلَا تَحْمِلْ عَلَيْنَآ إِصْرًا كَمَا حَمَلْتَهُۥ

عَلَى ٱلَّذِينَ مِن قَبْلِنَا رَبَّنَا وَلَا تُحَمِّلْنَا مَا لَا طَاقَةَ لَنَا بِهِۦ وَٱعْفُ عَنَّا وَٱغْفِرْ

لَنَا وَٱرْحَمْنَآ أَنتَ مَوْلَٰنَا فَٱنصُرْنَا عَلَى ٱلْقَوْمِ ٱلْكَٰفِرِينَ ﴿٢٨٦﴾

286. La yukallifu Allahu nafsan illa wusAAaha laha ma kasabat waAAalayha ma iktasabat rabbana la tu-akhithna in naseena aw akhta/na rabbana wala tahmil AAalayna isran kama hamaltahu AAala allatheena min qablina rabbana wala tuhammilna ma la taqata lana bihi waoAAfu AAanna waighfir lana wairhamna anta mawlana faonsurna AAala alqawmi alkafireena

---

2:286. Allah burdens not any being except with what it can bear. To it what it earns and on it befall consequences of its earnings. "Our Lord! Call us not to account if we forget or make a mistake. Our Lord! And put us not to such burden as You had put on those before us. Our Lord! And burden us not with what we have no strength to bear. And pardon us. And forgive us. And have mercy on us. You are our Protector, so help us against the people who suppress the Truth."[530]

---

530. Thus Allah does Himself teach us how to pray to Him. HE is kind and considerate and knows us much better than what we know about our own selves. HE articulates exactly what we would like to pray to Him about. We wouldn't ourselves be able to express our own thoughts so nicely. Oh! If only we had the wisdom to submit ourselves completely to the Gracious and All-knowing Lord of all of us.

Chapter 3: Aale-Imran (Family of Imran)

In the Name of Allah, the Gracious, the Merciful

1. Alif-lam-meem

3:1. Alif-lam-meem[1]

---

1. Please refer study note 2:1 about such letters occurring at the beginnings of some Qur'aanic Surahs (Chapters).

2. Allahu la ilaha illa huwa alhayyu alqayyoomu

3:2. Allah – none worthy of worship but He, the Living, the Eternal!

نَزَّلَ عَلَيْكَ ٱلْكِتَـٰبَ بِٱلْحَقِّ مُصَدِّقًا لِّمَا بَيْنَ يَدَيْهِ وَأَنزَلَ ٱلتَّوْرَىٰةَ وَٱلْإِنجِيلَ ۝

3. Nazzala AAalayka alkitaba bialhaqqi musaddiqan lima bayna yadayhi waanzala alttawrata waal-injeela

---

3:3. He has bestowed upon you[2] the Book with the Truth, confirming what came before it. And He had bestowed the Torah and the Gospel

---

2. The Arabic pronoun *ka* used here is in the 2nd person singular form. Obviously, it refers to Prophet Muhammad, peace upon him.

مِن قَبْلُ هُدًى لِّلنَّاسِ وَأَنزَلَ ٱلْفُرْقَانَ إِنَّ ٱلَّذِينَ كَفَرُوا۟ بِـَٔايَـٰتِ ٱللَّهِ لَهُمْ عَذَابٌ شَدِيدٌ وَٱللَّهُ عَزِيزٌ ذُو ٱنتِقَامٍ ۝

4. Min qablu hudan lilnnasi waanzala alfurqana inna allatheena kafaroo bi-ayati Allahi lahum AAathabun shadeedun waAllahu AAazeezun thoo intiqamin

---

3:4. Earlier, as guidance for mankind. And He bestowed the Criterion[3]. Indeed, for those who reject Allah's Verses, there shall be stern punishment. And Allah is Omnipotent and has the power to give a fitting retribution.[4]

---

3. The reference is to the divine Books: the Qur'aan, the Torah, the Gospel. The divine Books laid down the criteria for mankind to distinguish between right and wrong. Alas! Muslims of today have abandoned using the Qur'aan as the Allah-given Criterion. They have thus fallen into the morass of wrong-doing.

4. It is indeed sad that most Muslims themselves do not heed this stern divine warning. They fail to abide by Allah's Verses. Failure to conduct our lives in accordance with the directives given in the Verses is tantamount to rejection of the Verses. And rejection of Allah's Verses entails stern punishment.

إِنَّ ٱللَّهَ لَا يَخْفَىٰ عَلَيْهِ شَيْءٌ فِى ٱلْأَرْضِ وَلَا فِى ٱلسَّمَآءِ ⓢ

5. Inna Allaha la yakhfa AAalayhi shay-on fee al-ardi wala fee alssama/-i

3:5. Nothing indeed is hidden from Allah in the earth, nor in the heavens.

هُوَ ٱلَّذِى يُصَوِّرُكُمْ فِى ٱلْأَرْحَامِ كَيْفَ يَشَآءُ لَآ إِلَٰهَ إِلَّا هُوَ ٱلْعَزِيزُ ٱلْحَكِيمُ ①

6. Huwa allathee yusawwirukum fee al-arhami kayfa yashao la ilaha illa huwa alAAazeezu alhakeemu

3:6. It is He Who designs you, in the wombs, as He pleases. There is none worthy of worship besides Him, the Omnipotent, the Wise.

هُوَ ٱلَّذِىٓ أَنزَلَ عَلَيْكَ ٱلْكِتَٰبَ مِنْهُ ءَايَٰتٌ مُّحْكَمَٰتٌ هُنَّ أُمُّ ٱلْكِتَٰبِ وَأُخَرُ مُتَشَٰبِهَٰتٌ فَأَمَّا ٱلَّذِينَ فِى قُلُوبِهِمْ زَيْغٌ فَيَتَّبِعُونَ مَا تَشَٰبَهَ مِنْهُ ٱبْتِغَآءَ ٱلْفِتْنَةِ وَٱبْتِغَآءَ تَأْوِيلِهِۦ وَمَا يَعْلَمُ تَأْوِيلَهُۥٓ إِلَّا ٱللَّهُ وَٱلرَّٰسِخُونَ فِى ٱلْعِلْمِ يَقُولُونَ ءَامَنَّا بِهِۦ كُلٌّ مِّنْ عِندِ رَبِّنَا وَمَا يَذَّكَّرُ إِلَّآ أُو۟لُوا۟ ٱلْأَلْبَٰبِ

7. Huwa allat_hee anzala AAalayka alkitaba minhu a_yatun mu_hkamatun hunna ommu alkitabi waokharu mutashabihatun faamm_a allatheena fee quloobihim zayghun fayattabiAAoona m_a tash_abaha minhu ibtigh_aa alfitnati waibtigh_aa ta/weelihi wam_a yaAAlamu ta/weelahu illa All_ahu wa_alrr_asikhoona fee alAAilmi yaqooloona _amann_a bihi kullun min AAindi rabbin_a wam_a yath_thakkaru ill_a oloo al-alb_abi

---

3:7. It is He Who has sent down the Book upon you. Therein are Verses that are unambiguous and authoritative – these form the essence of the Book – and therein are other Verses, the interpretation of which is not clear to mankind[5]. Those then with dishonesty in their minds, zealously pursue what is not clear thereof, seeking mischief and seeking its interpretation; but no one knows its interpretation but Allah. And persons, deeply versed in knowledge, say, "We believe in it; it is all from our Lord." And none but those endowed with insight receive admonition.[6]

---

5. *Mutashaabihaat* are Verses, in other words, that are not clearly understood by the human mind. One example is the oft-repeated divine statement that the wicked shall be punished by putting them into Hell-fire. If any person is put into a burning fire in this world, that person is sure to die in a matter of minutes. But the Hell-fire in the Hereafter would be such as wouldn't make persons put in it to die, although they would very much wish to die. The human mind is unable to grasp the concept of such a fire. The Verses that present such concepts which are incomprehensible to the human mind, in this world, are *Mutashaabihaat*. *Muhkamaat*, on the other hand, are Verses that are well-explained in the Qur'aan itself, and therefore capable of being well-understood by the human mind, in this world. *Muhkamaat*, moreover, contain clearly worded divine commands and admonition that are required to be obeyed and acted upon by mankind to get salvation from certain doom.

6. The first Verse of this Qur'aanic Chapter, containing only Arabic letters corresponding to the English letters A L M, is another example of *mutashaabihaat*. No one knows the interpretation of those letters there, except Allah. The question then arises as to what the divine purpose is of placing such Verses in the Qur'aan, the meanings of which are not clear to the human mind! The purpose obviously is to provide for a test of a believer's faith in the divine authorship of the Qur'aan. As the Verse itself indicates, a true believer shall unquestioningly accept such Verses to be from Allah. But a deviated mind will seek mischief therein.

رَبَّنَا لَا تُزِغْ قُلُوبَنَا بَعْدَ إِذْ هَدَيْتَنَا وَهَبْ لَنَا مِن لَّدُنكَ رَحْمَةً إِنَّكَ أَنتَ الْوَهَّابُ ۝

8. Rabbana la tuzigh quloobana baAAda ith hadaytana wahab lana min ladunka rahmatan innaka anta alwahhabu

3:8. They say, "Our Lord, do not let our hearts deviate from the truth after you have guided us, and grant us mercy from You; You are the Grantor of bounties without measure.

رَبَّنَا إِنَّكَ جَامِعُ النَّاسِ لِيَوْمٍ لَّا رَيْبَ فِيهِ إِنَّ اللَّهَ لَا يُخْلِفُ الْمِيعَادَ ۝

9. Rabbana innaka jamiAAu alnnasi liyawmin la rayba feehi inna Allaha la yukhlifu almeeAAada

3:9. Our Lord, You will surely gather all mankind before You on the Day about which there is no doubt; surely Allah does not break His promise."

إِنَّ الَّذِينَ كَفَرُوا لَن تُغْنِيَ عَنْهُمْ أَمْوَالُهُمْ وَلَا أَوْلَادُهُم مِّنَ اللَّهِ شَيْئًا وَأُولَٰئِكَ هُمْ وَقُودُ النَّارِ ۝

10. Inna allatheena kafaroo lan tughniya AAanhum amwaluhum wala awladuhum mina Allahi shay-an waola-ika hum waqoodu alnnari

3:10. Neither their wealth nor their children shall be of any avail to those who suppress the Truth, against Allah. And those – those suppressors of the Truth – shall be the fuel for the Fire[7].

7. The Fire is the Hell-fire in the Hereafter. Those who deliberately deny the Reality, and die denying, shall be the fuel for that fire.

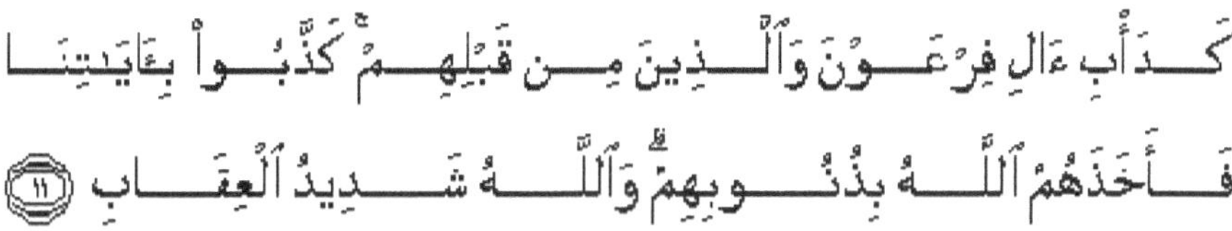

11. Kada/bi ali firAAawna waallatheena min qablihim kaththaboo bi-ayatina faakhathahumu Allahu bithunoobihim waAllahu shadeedu alAAiqabi

3:11. Like what happened to Pharaoh's people and people who lived before their time.[8] They denied Our revelations/signs. Allah then brought them to account for their sins.[9] And Allah is severe in punishment.

8. This Verse is in continuation of the immediately preceding Verse. Here, examples are given of those who will serve as fuel for the Fire of Hell.

9. Allah shall indeed make those guilty people of the past suffer in Hell fire. But He has made them – at least some of them – suffer an exemplary punishment in this world also. Like Pharaoh and his hordes, who were drowned altogether while they were in hot pursuit of Moses and his people.

12. Qul lillatheena kafaroo satughlaboona watuhsharoona ila jahannama wabi/sa almihadu

3:12. Say to those who suppress the Truth, "Vanquished shall you soon be, and driven all together shall you be to Hell! And it is a horrible place to rest."[10]

10. This is an address to those suppressors of Truth who, for the time being, may have an upper hand over others in the affairs of this world. Such people are told not to get carried away. Soon other people may have an upper hand over them. And, in any case, their death is inevitable. And then they will be raised again to be driven all together to Hell. This Verse could well be looked upon as a prophecy of the then Makkan army soon getting defeated by Muslims at the battle of Badr. Please see the next Verse.

قَـدْ كَـانَ لَكُـمْ ءَايَـةٌ فِى فِئَتَيْنِ ٱلْتَقَتَا فِئَةٌ تُقَـٰتِـلُ فِى سَـبِيلِ ٱللَّـهِ وَأُخْـرَىٰ كَافِرَةٌ يَرَوْنَهُم مِّثْلَيْهِـمْ رَأْىَ ٱلْعَيْـنِ وَٱللَّـهُ يُؤَيِّـدُ بِنَصْرِهِۦ مَن يَشَـآءُ إِنَّ فِى ذَٰلِكَ لَعِـبْرَةً لِّأُوْلِـى ٱلْأَبْصَـٰـرِ ﴿١٣﴾

13. Qad kana lakum ayatun fee fi-atayni iltaqata fi-atun tuqatilu fee sabeeli Allahi waokhra kafiratun yarawnahum mithlayhim ra/ya alAAayni waAllahu yu-ayyidu binasrihi man yashao inna fee thalika laAAibratan li-olee al-absari

3:13. Surely, there was a sign for you in the two armies that faced each other. One army was fighting in Allah's Path, and the other was an army of suppressors of Truth. The former saw the latter, by eye-estimate, to be twice in number as compared to them. And Allah strengthens, whom He pleases, with His help. Indeed, there is a lesson in that for people with vision.[11]

11. The event referred to here is, probably, that of the Battle of Badr. That battle was the first one fought by the Muslims. It was faught against the invading army of non-believers from Makkah. The name of the event is not mentioned in the Qur'aan, because the name is not important, but the event is – an event, in which a small, ill-equipped army of Muslims fighting in self-defence vanquished a far superior army – superior both in equipment and in number. The event signifies the divine help that righteous people could get against all odds.

زُيِّنَ لِلنَّاسِ حُبُّ ٱلشَّهَوَٰتِ مِنَ ٱلنِّسَآءِ وَٱلْبَنِينَ وَٱلْقَنَٰطِيرِ ٱلْمُقَنطَرَةِ مِنَ ٱلذَّهَبِ وَٱلْفِضَّةِ وَٱلْخَيْلِ ٱلْمُسَوَّمَةِ وَٱلْأَنْعَٰمِ وَٱلْحَرْثِ ۗ ذَٰلِكَ مَتَٰعُ ٱلْحَيَوٰةِ ٱلدُّنْيَا ۖ وَٱللَّهُ عِندَهُۥ حُسْنُ ٱلْمَـَٔابِ ﴿١٤﴾

14. Zuyyina lilnnasi ḥubbu alshshahawati mina alnnisa-i waalbaneena waalqanaṭeeri almuqanṭarati mina alththahabi waalfiḍḍati waalkhayli almusawwamati waal-anAAami waalḥarthi thalika mataAAu alḥayati alddunya waAllahu AAindahu ḥusnu almaabi

---

3:14. Attractive for men are the love and desire for women, children, hoarded treasures of gold and silver, branded horses, cattle and plantations. Those are possessions of the life of this world. And with Allah is the best resort.[12]

---

12. The Qur'aan draws our attention here to the transitory nature of the possessions of this world as against the far better and ever-lasting comforts that Allah-fearing persons would get in the Hereafter.

۞ قُلْ أَؤُنَبِّئُكُم بِخَيْرٍ مِّن ذَٰلِكُمْ ۚ لِلَّذِينَ ٱتَّقَوْا۟ عِندَ رَبِّهِمْ جَنَّٰتٌ تَجْرِى مِن تَحْتِهَا ٱلْأَنْهَٰرُ خَٰلِدِينَ فِيهَا وَأَزْوَٰجٌ مُّطَهَّرَةٌ وَرِضْوَٰنٌ مِّنَ ٱللَّهِ ۗ وَٱللَّهُ بَصِيرٌۢ بِٱلْعِبَادِ ﴿١٥﴾

15. Qul aonabbi-okum bikhayrin min thalikum lillatheena ittaqaw AAinda rabbihim jannatun tajree min taḥtiha al-anharu khalideena feeha waazwajun muṭahharatun wariḍwanun mina Allahi waAllahu baṣeerun bialAAibadi

---

3:15. Say[13], "Shall I tell you of better things than these[14]? For those who fear Allah, there shall be gardens beneath which rivers flow. They, and their spouses purified, shall live there forever by Allah's pleasure. And Allah takes due care of those who worship Him."

---

13. This is a divine command made to Prophet Muhammad (peace be upon him), and to every believer after him, to address mankind in general.

14. The things mentioned in the preceding Verse, that is.

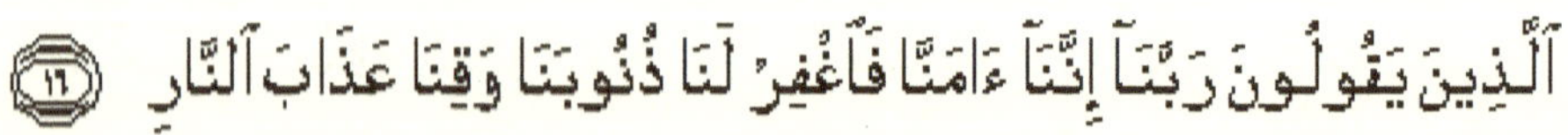

16. Alla<u>th</u>eena yaqooloona rabban<u>a</u> innan<u>a</u> <u>a</u>mann<u>a</u> fa<u>i</u>ghfir lan<u>a</u> <u>th</u>unooban<u>a</u> waqin<u>a</u> AA<u>a</u><u>th</u>aba alnn<u>a</u>ri

3:16. [15]Those who say: "Our Lord! We do believe. So, forgive our sins and save us from the torment of the Fire;"

15. This Verse and the next one (3:17) together give a detailed description of 'those who worship Him' mentioned at the end of Verse 3:15 above.

17. Al<u>ss</u>abireena waal<u>ss</u>adiqeena waalq<u>a</u>niteena waalmunfiqeena waalmustaghfireena bial-as<u>h</u>ari

3:17. Those who exercise patience, those who are truthful, sincere and honest, those who are obedient and pray to Allah, those who spend in charity, and those who pray in the wee hours before dawn for forgiveness.

شَهِدَ ٱللَّهُ أَنَّهُ لَا إِلَٰهَ إِلَّا هُوَ وَٱلْمَلَٰٓئِكَةُ وَأُو۟لُوا۟ ٱلْعِلْمِ قَآئِمًۢا بِٱلْقِسْطِ لَآ إِلَٰهَ إِلَّا هُوَ ٱلْعَزِيزُ ٱلْحَكِيمُ ﴿١٨﴾

18. Shahida All_ahu annahu l_a il_aha ill_a huwa waalmal_a-ikatu waoloo alAAilmi q_a-iman bialqis_ti l_a il_aha ill_a huwa alAAazeezu al_hakeemu

---

3:18. Allah bears witness that there indeed is none worthy of worship but He; and so, do the angels and those with right knowledge, based on truth and justice. There is none worthy of worship but He, the Omnipotent, the Wise.[16]

---

16. This fundamental article of Islamic Faith is witnessed and certified by Allah Almighty Himself and by the angels who are the first amongst His creations to know the absolute Truth of the article of Faith. And among mankind, only those endorse the fundamental article, whose acquisition of knowledge is the result of their quest and enquiry based on truth and justice. Their knowledge is not based on unverified guesswork like Darwin's Theory of Evolution. Had his theory been true, we ought to have seen at least some signs of monkeys/chimpanzees evolving into humans, during this historical period of well over a thousand years. Protagonists of the theory try to hide behind the anonymity and haziness of the pre-historic ages. There too they encounter their 'missing links'.

إِنَّ ٱلدِّينَ عِندَ ٱللَّهِ ٱلْإِسْلَٰمُ وَمَا ٱخْتَلَفَ ٱلَّذِينَ أُوتُوا۟ ٱلْكِتَٰبَ إِلَّا مِنۢ بَعْدِ مَا جَآءَهُمُ ٱلْعِلْمُ بَغْيًۢا بَيْنَهُمْ وَمَن يَكْفُرْ بِـَٔايَٰتِ ٱللَّهِ فَإِنَّ ٱللَّهَ سَرِيعُ ٱلْحِسَابِ ﴿١٩﴾

19. Inna alddeena AAinda All_ahi al-isl_amu wam_a ikhtalafa alla_theena ootoo alkit_aba ill_a min baAAdi m_a j_aahumu alAAilmu baghyan baynahum waman yakfur bi-_ay_ati All_ahi fa-inna All_aha sareeAAu al_his_abi

---

3:19. Islam is indeed the Religion sanctioned/approved by Allah.[17] And those to whom the Book was given did raise no disputes but after knowledge had come to them, thanks to competitiveness among themselves.[18] And about the one who suppresses/denies Allah's revelations/signs, Allah is certainly swift in keeping accounts.[19]

---

17. In Verse 5:3, Allah Ta'ala Himself declares, "... This day I have perfected your religion for you, completed My favour upon you, and have chosen for you Islam as your religion. ..."

18. As were the earlier divine Books, the Qur'aan is unambiguous, clear and well-explained. It warrants no disputes in interpretation. Yet, disputes are raised! These disputes are the results of human tendency to err. And once any man commits an error, it becomes difficult for him to amend it even when he comes to realise that he has committed an error. It hurts his undue sense of pride to admit it, and he thus gets himself downgraded in the esteem of other people. The Satan makes it hurtful for him to admit that the other person – and not he – is right.

19. Allah, the Creator, of course has adequate arrangements to make a debit entry in the person's accounts, for the grave sin of suppressing/denying the Truth. This entry is likely to doom that person to everlasting Hell-fire in the Hereafter!

فَإِنْ حَآجُّوكَ فَقُلْ أَسْلَمْتُ وَجْهِيَ لِلَّهِ وَمَنِ ٱتَّبَعَنِ وَقُل لِّلَّذِينَ أُوتُواْ ٱلْكِتَـٰبَ وَٱلْأُمِّيِّـۧنَ ءَأَسْلَمْتُمْ فَإِنْ أَسْلَمُواْ فَقَدِ ٱهْتَدَواْ وَّإِن تَوَلَّوْاْ فَإِنَّمَا عَلَيْكَ ٱلْبَلَـٰغُ وَٱللَّهُ بَصِيرٌ بِٱلْعِبَادِ ۝

20. Fa-in hajjooka faqul aslamtu wajhiya lillahi wamani ittabaAAani waqul lillatheena ootoo alkitaba waal-ommiyyeena aaslamtum fa-in aslamoo faqadi ihtadaw wa-in tawallaw fa-innama AAalayka albalaghu waAllahu baseerun bialAAibadi

---

3:20. So, if they argue with you, tell them, "I have submitted my being to Allah and so have those, who follow me, submitted theirs." And ask those who are given the Book and those who are unenlightened: "Have you submitted?" Then, if they have submitted they are guided, and if they have turned back, your responsibility is only to convey the Message. And Allah is ever watchful over the worshippers.[20]

---

20. This Verse was of course meant initially to guide Prophet Muhammad (peace be upon him) in his given task of propagating Islam among mankind. But, after him, the task is delegated to the Ummah. So, the guidance given in the Verse applies to members of the Ummah as well. We all must bear in mind that Islam is not to be _forced_ upon anyone. We must use only persuasion. Our responsibility is only to convey

the divine Message. We do not punish anyone just for not accepting Islam. It is for Allah to punish those who thus suppress/deny the Truth. Please also see Verse 2:256 and Note 2:486 thereunder in this context.

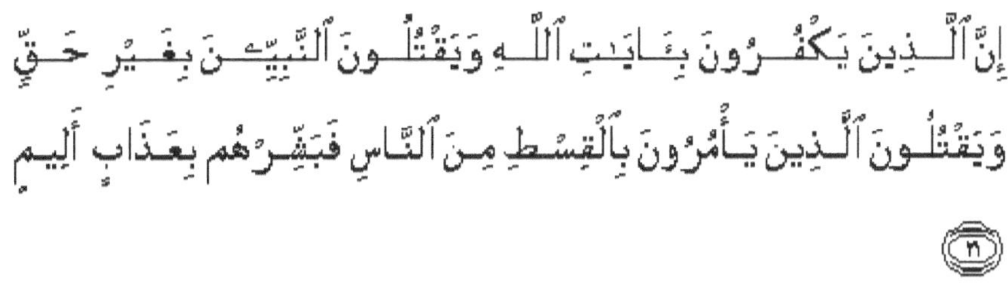

21. Inna alla*theena* yakfuroona bi-*ay*ati All*a*hi wayaqtuloona alnnabiyyeena bighayri *h*aqqin wayaqtuloona alla*theena* ya/muroona bialqis*t*i mina alnn*a*si fabashshirhum biAAa*th*abin aleem*in*

3:21. Those indeed who suppress/deny Allah's revelations/signs, and unjustly kill the Prophets, and kill from among the people those who enjoin justice – to them forebode a painful punishment.[21]

21. The Prophets are no longer there amongst us to be killed, but there are people still, who enjoin justice. And this Verse is still applicable to those who are after the blood of such people. And, of course, there are those aplenty who suppress/deny Allah's revelations/signs.

22. Ol*a*-ika alla*theena h*abi*t*at aAAm*a*luhum fee alddun*ya* waal-*a*khirati wam*a* lahum min n*a*sireen*a*

3:22. Those[22] are the ones whose deeds have become null and void, in this world and in the other. And they have none to help.[23]

22. That is, those spoken of in the immediately preceding Verse 3:21.

23. Divine punishment could come to such people in this world itself as well as in the next. All authority, in the Hereafter, would rest solely with Allah, and there would of course be no question of anyone coming to the help of those punished there. In this world, apparently, there could be some friend or relative trying to help any recipient of divine punishment out of his/her predicament. But that help would be of no use at all to the sufferer.

أَلَمْ تَرَ إِلَى ٱلَّذِينَ أُوتُواْ نَصِيبًا مِّنَ ٱلْكِتَـٰبِ يُدْعَوْنَ إِلَىٰ كِتَـٰبِ ٱللَّهِ لِيَحْكُمَ بَيْنَهُمْ ثُمَّ يَتَوَلَّىٰ فَرِيقٌ مِّنْهُمْ وَهُم مُّعْرِضُونَ ﴿٢٣﴾

23. Alam tara ila allatheena ootoo naseeban mina alkitabi yudAAawna ila kitabi Allahi liyahkuma baynahum thumma yatawalla fareequn minhum wahum muAAridoona

3:23. Have you not seen those who have been given a share from the Book? They are called upon to refer to the Book of Allah to settle things among themselves. A section of them then back out and turn hostile.[24]

24. Initially, at the time of revelation, this Verse obviously referred to the Jews or the Christians as being those given a share of the Book. But in our present times, it very well refers to Muslims who have been given the Qur'aan. The Muslims seldom refer to the Qur'aan, for settlements of disputes among themselves. At the time of writing of these comments, the Muslim Ummah is faced with the unseemly spectacle of Muslims celebrating EidulFitr on different days, not only in the different parts of the world, but also in different parts of the same country! The Muslim Ummah is not at all bothered to follow what the Qur'aan says in this regard. They would rather follow a *hadeeth*, no matter it leads them to follow a calendar, untenable and impracticable in the present circumstances when Islam has become a fast-growing world Religion. Please refer to my article The New Moon in this context.

ذَٰلِكَ بِأَنَّهُمْ قَالُوا لَن تَمَسَّنَا ٱلنَّارُ إِلَّا أَيَّامًا مَّعْدُودَٰتٍ وَغَرَّهُمْ فِى دِينِهِم مَّا كَانُوا يَفْتَرُونَ ﴿٢٤﴾

24. Thalika bi-annahum qaloo lan tamassana alnnaru illa ayyaman maAAdoodatin wagharrahum fee deenihim ma kanoo yaftaroona

---

3:24. That is indeed because they say, "The Fire shall touch us not, but for a few days." And what they fabricated in their religion, deluded their own selves.[25]

---

25. This delusion of the Jews/Christians/Muslims it is that has made them careless about their own divine Scriptures. They give scant regard to instructions therein.

فَكَيْفَ إِذَا جَمَعْنَٰهُمْ لِيَوْمٍ لَّا رَيْبَ فِيهِ وَوُفِّيَتْ كُلُّ نَفْسٍ مَّا كَسَبَتْ وَهُمْ لَا يُظْلَمُونَ ﴿٢٥﴾

25. Fakayfa itha jamaAAnahum liyawmin la rayba feehi wawuffiyat kullu nafsin ma kasabat wahum la yuthlamoona

---

3:25. What then when on that Day – in the occurrence of which there is no doubt – We will gather them together, when every soul will be given what it earned and when none of them shall be wronged?[26]

---

26. The Day referred to here is of course the Judgement Day in the Hereafter. On that Day, the Lord of us all is sure to question us closely on how we treated His Own instructions on the right conduct of our lives in this world. How would we be able to face Him then if we have fallen in the habit of giving scant regard to those divine instructions in this worldly life?

26. Quli all<u>gh</u>umma m<u>a</u>lika almulki tu/tee almulka man tash<u>a</u>o watanzi<u>AA</u>u almulka mimman tash<u>a</u>o watu<u>AA</u>izzu man tash<u>a</u>o watu<u>th</u>illu man tash<u>a</u>o biyadika alkhayru innaka <u>AA</u>al<u>a</u> kulli shay-in qadee<u>r</u>un

---

3:26. Say, "O Allah, Master of all sovereign authority! You grant the authority to whom You please and take away the authority from whom You please. And You honour whom You please and disgrace whom You please. In Your Hand[27] is all that is good. Indeed! You have power over everything."

---

27. "... There is nothing like unto Him ..." [Q: 42:11]. "And there is none comparable to Him." [Q: 112:4] In view of these clear Qur'aanic Verses, Allah's Hand cannot be like any human hand. And 'Your Hand' mentioned in this Verse, are *mutashabih* words, in terms of <u>Verse 3:7</u>. You may also go through <u>study notes 3:5 & 3:6</u> in this context. All that we humans are required to understand here is that all good things emanate from Allah.

---

27. Tooliju allayla fee alnnah<u>a</u>ri watooliju alnnah<u>a</u>ra fee allayli watukhriju al<u>h</u>ayya mina almayyiti watukhriju almayyita mina al<u>h</u>ayyi watarzuqu man tash<u>a</u>o bi<u>gh</u>ayri <u>h</u>is<u>a</u>bin

---

3:27. "You cause the night to creep into the day and You cause the day to creep into the night.[28] And You extract the living from the dead and You extract the dead from the living.[29] And You provide, without measure, for anyone You wish.[30, 31]

28. The contrast between the day and the night has been mentioned as one of the divine signs in Verse 2:164. (Readers may like to go through the study Notes on that Verse, in this context.) It has been mentioned as a sign, in that Verse (2:164), for people who make use of their Allah-given intelligence. As a further clue for such people, the fact of the darkness of the night slowly enveloping the earth is highlighted in this Verse (3:27), presently under our study here. This clue along with more clues contained in Verses 7:54, 24:44, 25:62 & 36:40, give enough indications for scientists and discoverers to become aware that the earth ought to be round and ought to be rotating around its axis to cause the observed phenomenon of the day and the night. This cause of the phenomenon was unknown to the Arabs, among whom the Qur'aan was first revealed. The Qur'aan did thus inculcate the spirit of enquiry and investigation in the minds of those early adherents of it, making them pioneers in the fields of astronomy, mathematics, physics, chemistry, medicine & art. Those pioneers gave the world that scientific base upon which is built the imposing edifice of today's technological advance. Sadly, later Muslims lost that scientific spirit as they relegated the Qur'aan to just ritual reading.

29. Recall, in this context, the divine statement in Verse 2:28. Consider also Verse 6:95 wherein our attention is drawn to the spectacle of Allah causing the dead grains and seeds sprout into living vegetation. And, by the way, the Qur'aan – revealed over 1400 years ago – is replete with such quotations, calling trees and plants as living things. It is only in the recent past that scientists have conclusively proved them to be living organisms!

30. Allah may give plenty of wealth to a non-believer, in this world, to test the believers whether it creates doubts in their minds about their belief. Allah may give plenty of wealth to believers, in this world, to test whether they succumb to the lure of worldly pleasure that their wealth can buy them. Allah may provide all good things, without measure, to the believers, in the Hereafter, as a reward from Him for their steadfast adherence to His Straight Path in this world despite innumerable satanic enducements for leaving that Path.

31. These two Verses 3:26 & 3:27, along with Verse 2:255 and Qur'aanic Chapter 112 (Surah Al-Ikhlas), which we often recite in our prayers, give important defining attributes of our Lord, Allah Almighty. A believer has necessarily to believe in all these attributes, without exception.

لَّا يَتَّخِذِ ٱلْمُؤْمِنُونَ ٱلْكَـٰفِرِينَ أَوْلِيَآءَ مِن دُونِ ٱلْمُؤْمِنِينَ وَمَن يَفْعَلْ ذَٰلِكَ

فَلَيْسَ مِنَ ٱللَّهِ فِى شَىْءٍ إِلَّآ أَن تَتَّقُوا۟ مِنْهُمْ تُقَىٰةً وَيُحَذِّرُكُمُ ٱللَّهُ نَفْسَهُۥ

وَإِلَى ٱللَّهِ ٱلْمَصِيرُ ﴿٢٨﴾

28. La yattakhithi almuminoona alkafireena awliyaa min dooni almumineena waman yafAAalthalika falaysa mina Allahi fee shayin illa an tattaqoo minhum tuqatan wayuhaththirukumu Allahu nafsahu waila Allahi almaseeru

3:28. The believers take not the unbelievers – instead of the believers – as their *awliya*[32]. And anyone who does that won't have any share in anything from Allah, except in the case that you fear persecution from them. And Allah asks you to beware of Him.[33] And to Allah is the final destination.

32. For the comprehensive Qur'aanic meaning of the word *awliya* (singular *wali*), please refer Note 2:154.

33. Here the Qur'aan tells us that Allah may condone any believer taking suppressors of Truth as his/her *awliya*, only if he/she fears persecution from them otherwise. But the Qur'aan reminds us that it is Allah that the believers should fear and not others; because, it is to Him that all must return in the end.

قُلْ إِن تُخْفُواْ مَا فِى صُدُورِكُمْ أَوْ تُبْدُوهُ يَعْلَمْهُ ٱللَّهُ وَيَعْلَمُ مَا فِى ٱلسَّمَـٰوَٰتِ وَمَا فِى ٱلْأَرْضِ وَٱللَّهُ عَلَىٰ كُلِّ شَىْءٍ قَدِيرٌ ﴿٢٩﴾

29. Qul in tukhfoo ma fee sudoorikum aw tubdoohu yaAAlamhu Allahu wayaAAlamu ma fee alssamawati wama fee al-ardi waAllahu AAala kulli shay-in qadeerun

3:29. Say, "Whether you conceal what is in your heart or reveal it, Allah knows it. And He knows all that is in the heavens, and all that is in the earth. And Allah has power over everything."

يَوْمَ تَجِدُ كُلُّ نَفْسٍ مَّا عَمِلَتْ مِنْ خَيْرٍ مُّحْضَرًا وَمَا عَمِلَتْ مِن سُوۤءٍ تَوَدُّ لَوْ أَنَّ بَيْنَهَا وَبَيْنَهُۥ أَمَدًۢا بَعِيدًا وَيُحَذِّرُكُمُ ٱللَّهُ نَفْسَهُۥ وَٱللَّهُ رَءُوفٌ بِٱلْعِبَادِ ﴿٣٠﴾

30. Yawma tajidu kullu nafsin ma AAamilat min khayrin muhdaran wama AAamilat min soo-in tawaddu law anna baynaha wabaynahu amadan baAAeedan wayuhaththirukumu Allahu nafsahu waAllahu raoofun bialAAibadi

3:30. The Day when every soul would find presented whatever good it had done! And as regards whatever evil it had committed, it (the soul) would wish there were a great distance, on that day, between it and that evil. And Allah cautions you against (disobeying) Him.[34] And Allah is kind to His devotees.

34. There is benevolence in Allah's cautioning His devotees here against disobeying Him. HE doesn't want them to commit evil deeds in this world because of which they may have to suffer in the Hereafter. The devotees wouldn't commit such deeds, if they really have Allah's fear in their hearts here.

قُلْ إِن كُنتُمْ تُحِبُّونَ ٱللَّهَ فَٱتَّبِعُونِى يُحْبِبْكُمُ ٱللَّهُ وَيَغْفِرْ لَكُمْ ذُنُوبَكُمْ وَٱللَّهُ غَفُورٌ رَّحِيمٌ ﴿٣١﴾

31. Qul in kuntum tuhibboona Allaha faittabiAAoonee yuhbibkumu Allahu wayaghfir lakum thunoobakum waAllahu ghafoorun raheemun

3:31. Say, "If you do love Allah, obey me. Allah will then love you and forgive you your sins.[35 to 37] And Allah is Forgiving, Merciful."

35. Allah loving us and forgiving our sins is apparently made conditional to our obeying His Messenger (peace upon him). At the time when the Messenger was living among mankind here in this world, this divine directive obviously meant that all directions of the Messenger, whether in matters of religion or of administration, were to be obeyed scrupulously. But what should the position be now when the Messenger is no longer living among mankind? Many Muslims believe that obeying the Messenger means following his Sunnah as described in authentic *ahaadeeth*. But who decides whether any *hadeeth* is authentic or not?

36. Allah has guaranteed the protection of the Qur'aan (Verse 15:9). There is, however, no such divine protection guaranteed for the *ahaadeeth*. And the *ahaadeeth* were floating from mouth to mouth for generations till some of them were recorded in writing, for the first time, at least 150 years after the death the Prophet (peace be upon him). There is likelihood, therefore, of the *ahaadeeth* having been contaminated and interpolated with the personal opinions and words of the narrators. The Allah-perfected Religion of Islam could not therefore be based on such an unreliable source. It is based solely on the Qur'aan now. This does not mean that the *ahaadeeth* are to be completely discarded. They are invaluable in the sense that they give us the historical perspective of the era in which our Prophet lived.

But any *hadeeth*, that is basically contradictory to the teachings of the Qur'aan, must be rejected outright. The Qur'aan is, and ought to be, the criterion.

37. Obeying the Messenger ought now, therefore, to mean following the Qur'aan.

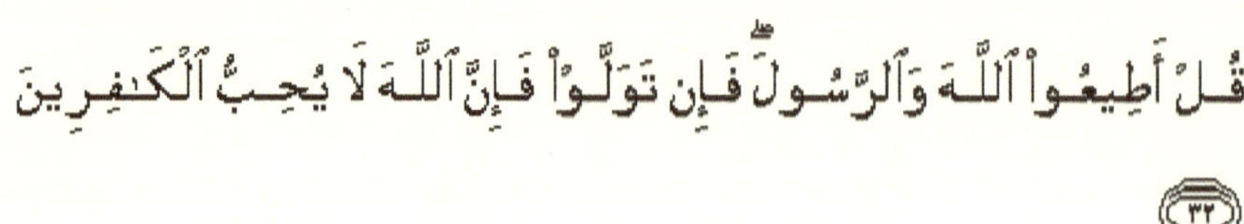

32. Qul ateeAAoo Allaha waalrrasoola fa-in tawallaw fa-inna Allaha la yuhibbu alkafireena

3:32. Say, "Obey Allah and His Messenger." Then if they turn away, surely, Allah loves not suppressors of the Truth.[38]

38. Obeying Allah and His Messenger is an act in consonance with the Reality and Truth and with one's own conscience. And disobedience to Allah and His Messenger would tantamount to suppression of the Truth. However, please see foregoing notes 35 to 37 in this context.

33. Inna Allaha istafa adama wanoohan waala ibraheema waala AAimrana AAala alAAalameena

3:33. Indeed, Allah chose Adam, Noah, family of Abraham and family of Imran above all the worlds.[39]

39. Allah chose them for leadership among mankind. Through these leaders, He gave guidance to mankind. It is the Creator's privilege to choose whom He wishes. HIS choice ought to be the best. Jesus (peace be upon him) was from the family of Imran and Moses & Muhammad (peace be upon them both) were from the family of Abraham. About *AAalameena* (worlds), please refer Note 1:5 for a comprehensive Qur'aanic meaning thereof.

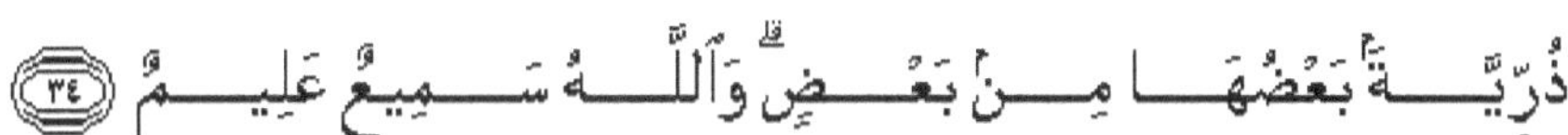

34. T̲h̲urriyyatan baAAd̲uh̲a min baAAd̲in waAllah̲u sameeAAun AAaleem**un**

3:34. They[40] were offspring of one another. And Allah is the One Who listened, the One who knew.

40. That is those mentioned in the preceding Verse.

إِذْ قَالَتِ ٱمْرَأَتُ عِمْرَٰنَ رَبِّ إِنِّى نَذَرْتُ لَكَ مَا فِى بَطْنِى مُحَرَّرًا فَتَقَبَّلْ مِنِّىٓ إِنَّكَ أَنتَ ٱلسَّمِيعُ ٱلْعَلِيمُ ﴿٣٥﴾

35. It̲h̲ qalati imraatu AAimran̲a rabbi innee nat̲h̲artu laka m̲a fee bat̲nee muh̲arraran fataqabbal minnee innaka anta alssameeAAu alAAaleem**u**

3:35. [41]When Imran's wife said, "Indeed my Lord! I do freely[42] consecrate to You that which is in my womb. So, accept it from me. You are indeed the One to listen, the One to know.[43]"

41. This is a continuation of the sentence started in the preceding Verse with the phrase, 'And Allah is the One Who listened, the One Who knew". So, the relevant sentence would read as: 'And Allah is the One Who listened, the One Who knew when Imran's wife said, "Indeed my Lord! ..." It synchronises well with what Imran's wife said at the end of her offer & plea to Allah, in this Verse.

42. That is, with her own volition, and without anyone else forcing her to do so.

43. Allah Almighty gives us here an example of how he invariably listens to invocations honestly made by any human being to Him, and to Him Alone. And He grants the humble requests of His devotees, if those are worth granting, with suitable modifications, as deemed right and appropriate by Him with His absolute knowledge. And whatever He grants would be in the best interests of the invoking devotee in prevailing circumstances. As Muslims, we must have an absolute faith in this.

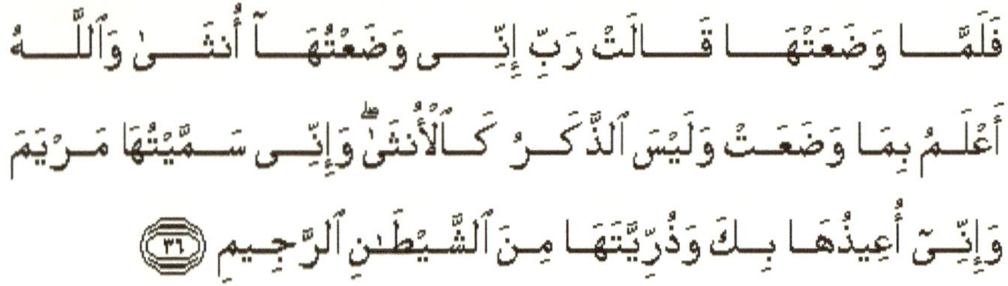

36. Falamma wadaAAat-ha qalat rabbi innee wadaAAtuha ontha waAllahu aAAlamu bima wadaAAat walaysa alththakaru kaalontha wa-innee sammaytuha maryama wa-innee oAAeethuha bika wathurriyyataha mina alshshaytani alrrajeemi

3:36. And when she delivered a female child, she exclaimed, "It's a female that I have delivered, my Lord!" – And Allah knew what she had delivered and the male is not like the female[44] – "And I do name her Mary and I entrust her protection, and her children's, to You against Satan, the accursed."

44. Imran's wife obviously expected to deliver a male child, whom she could present for Allah's service. This presumption on her part got reflected in her exclamation that it was a female that she had given birth to, as if Allah knew not what she had delivered! Allah makes this parenthetic statement to set the record right. And to bring the point home, He emphasises the fact – with a touch of good humour – that He, as the Creator, of course knew the difference between a male child and a female.

فَتَقَبَّلَهَا رَبُّهَا بِقَبُولٍ حَسَنٍ وَأَنْبَتَهَا نَبَاتًا حَسَنًا وَكَفَّلَهَا زَكَرِيَّا كُلَّمَا دَخَلَ عَلَيْهَا زَكَرِيَّا الْمِحْرَابَ وَجَدَ عِندَهَا رِزْقًا قَالَ يَمَرْيَمُ أَنَّىٰ لَكِ هَٰذَا قَالَتْ هُوَ مِنْ عِندِ اللَّهِ إِنَّ اللَّهَ يَرْزُقُ مَن يَشَاءُ بِغَيْرِ حِسَابٍ ﴿٣٧﴾

37. Fataqabbalaha rabbuha biqaboolin ḥasanin waanbataha nabatan ḥasanan wakaffalaha zakariyya kullama dakhala AAalayha zakariyya almiḥraba wajada AAindaha rizqan qala ya maryamu anna laki hatha qalat huwa min AAindi Allahi inna Allaha yarzuqu man yashao bighayri ḥisabin

---

3:37. Her Lord accepted her graciously and gave her a good upbringing. And He made Zachariah her guardian. Whenever Zachariah entered the sanctuary to visit her, he found her with food. He asked, "O Mary! How did you get this?" She replied, "It is from Allah." Allah does indeed provide for whom He wills, in an abnormal way.[45, 46]

---

45. What Allah gives to His devotees need not necessarily be through a miraculous act – although He can do it miraculously too. In the pre-historic time of Mary (Jesus' mother) and Zachariah, Allah may well have provided the food miraculously, but for the *Ummah* of His last Prophet, Allah has apparently willed that they should take cognizance of His existence through their intelligence and the surfeit of knowledge that He has now made available to them. For any person, in Mary's position now, He might induce other persons around to provide the food, turn by turn.

46. But in Mary's case, at her time, it does appear, from the term used, *bi ghayri hisaab* (translated here as "in an abnormal way"), that the food found with Mary was miraculously provided by Allah. The said Arabic term is usually translated as "without measure", but in the context here, it means "without following the normal/usual manner/course".

هُنَالِكَ دَعَا زَكَرِيَّا رَبَّهُ قَالَ رَبِّ هَبْ لِى مِن لَّدُنكَ ذُرِّيَّةً طَيِّبَةً إِنَّكَ سَمِيعُ الدُّعَاءِ ﴿٣٨﴾

235

38. Hun<u>a</u>lika daAA<u>a</u> zakariyy<u>a</u> rabbahu q<u>a</u>la rabbi hab lee min ladunka <u>th</u>urriyyatan <u>t</u>ayyibatan innaka sameeAAu aldduAA<u>a</u>/-i

3:38. Whereupon Zachariah prayed to his Lord. He said, "My Lord! Grant me a righteous child from You. You do, indeed, listen to the prayer!"[47]

47. This prayer from Zachariah was obviously prompted, on the spot, by his finding that Allah had provided food for Mary in a miraculous manner. The thought struck him that Allah could also similarly provide a child for him miraculously. From Verse 3:40 below, we learn that Zachariah himself was old and his wife barren. Normally, therefore, the couple was beyond expecting a child of their own.

فَنَادَتْهُ ٱلْمَلَـٰٓئِكَةُ وَهُوَ قَآئِمٌ يُصَلِّى فِى ٱلْمِحْرَابِ أَنَّ ٱللَّهَ يُبَشِّرُكَ بِيَحْيَىٰ مُصَدِّقًا بِكَلِمَةٍ مِّنَ ٱللَّهِ وَسَيِّدًا وَحَصُورًا وَنَبِيًّا مِّنَ ٱلصَّـٰلِحِينَ ﴿٣٩﴾

39. Fan<u>a</u>dat-hu almal<u>a</u>-ikatu wahuwa q<u>a</u>-imun yu<u>s</u>allee fee almi<u>h</u>r<u>a</u>bi anna All<u>a</u>ha yubashshiruka biya<u>h</u>y<u>a</u> mu<u>s</u>addiqan bikalimatin mina All<u>a</u>hi wasayyidan wa<u>h</u>a<u>s</u>ooran wanabiyyan mina al<u>ss</u>ali<u>h</u>eena

3:39. Then the angels, calling out to him as he stood praying in the sanctuary, said, "Allah gives you the good news of John – in confirmation of a Word from Allah[48] – honourable, chaste and a Prophet from among the righteous."

48. In fulfilment of the divine promise made to Zachariah, that is. The birth of John wouldn't be a normal one, since he would be born to old parents, the mother having been barren till the child's (John's) conception in her womb. John's birth, in other words, would be a confirmation that Allah can do and undo anything any time. And so does the very next Verse here, 3:40, say.

قَالَ رَبِّ أَنَّىٰ يَكُونُ لِى غُلَـٰمٌ وَقَدْ بَلَغَنِىَ ٱلْكِبَرُ وَٱمْرَأَتِى عَاقِرٌ قَالَ كَذَٰلِكَ ٱللَّهُ يَفْعَلُ مَا يَشَاءُ ﴿٤٠﴾

40. Qala rabbi anna yakoonu lee ghulamun waqad balaghaniya alkibaru waimraatee AAaqirun qala kathalika Allahu yafAAalu ma yasha/o

---

3:40. He said: "My Lord! How can I have a son? And I have already reached old age and my wife is barren!" One of the angels[49] said, "Thus does Allah do what He wills."

---

49. The way the reply to Zachariah is recorded here indicates that it was not Allah Himself who gave the reply. And since the verb used (*qala*) is in the 3rd person singular form, the reply was obviously given by one of the angels who had conveyed to Zachariah the prophecy of a son.

قَالَ رَبِّ ٱجْعَل لِّى ءَايَةً قَالَ ءَايَتُكَ أَلَّا تُكَلِّمَ ٱلنَّاسَ ثَلَـٰثَةَ أَيَّامٍ إِلَّا رَمْزًا وَٱذْكُر رَّبَّكَ كَثِيرًا وَسَبِّحْ بِٱلْعَشِىِّ وَٱلْإِبْكَـٰرِ ﴿٤١﴾

41. Qala rabbi ijAAal lee ayatan qala ayatuka alla tukallima alnnasa thalathata ayyamin illa ramzan waothkur rabbaka katheeran wasabbih bialAAashiyyi waal-ibkari

---

3:41. Zachariah said: "My Lord! Make a sign for me." The angel said: "Your sign is that you shall not speak to people for three days except through gestures. And remember your Lord much and glorify Him in the evening and in the morning."[50]

---

50. Zachariah had asked for a sign – and not for a command from Allah, only in compliance of which he would get the son. This fact indicates that Zachariah did not voluntarily restrain himself from speaking, but that he was physically unable to speak.

وَإِذْ قَالَتِ ٱلْمَلَٰٓئِكَةُ يَٰمَرْيَمُ إِنَّ ٱللَّهَ ٱصْطَفَىٰكِ وَطَهَّرَكِ وَٱصْطَفَىٰكِ عَلَىٰ نِسَآءِ ٱلْعَٰلَمِينَ ۝

42. Wa-ith qalati almala-ikatu ya maryamu inna Allaha istafaki watahharaki waistafaki AAala nisa-i alAAalameena

3:42. And when the angels said: "O Mary! Allah has indeed chosen you and purified you. And He has chosen you over women of the worlds[51]."

51. Refer <u>Note 1:5</u> for a comprehensive Qur'aanic meaning of the Arabic term AA<u>a</u>lameen. In the immediate context of Mary being given preference over other women here, it means that Mary was chosen among all women that lived or would live in this world from the time of Eve till the Last Day. And, in fact, the honour of giving birth to a child without insertion of sperm from a man was bestowed by Allah Almighty on Mary, uniquely. In modern days of surrogate mothers, a man's sperm is artificially inseminated asexually. Besides, a modern-day man has no reason to have his eyebrows raised at the fatherless birth of Jesus (peace upon him)! When a human modern-day scientist has been successful in cloning an animal without the male animal taking any active part in the process, it ought to have been as easy as anything could be for the Creator Himself to create Jesus without any father.

يَٰمَرْيَمُ ٱقْنُتِى لِرَبِّكِ وَٱسْجُدِى وَٱرْكَعِى مَعَ ٱلرَّٰكِعِينَ ۝

43. Y<u>a</u> maryamu oqnutee lirabbiki waosjudee wairkaAAee maAAa alrr<u>a</u>kiAAeena

3:43. [52]"O Mary! Be completely devoted to your Lord and prostrate and bow down with those who bow down."[53]

52. This is a continuation from the preceding Verse, of the angels' address to Mary.

53. And, undoubtedly, Allah would like to have the same kind of devotion from every believer hoping to be chosen for a place in Paradise, in the hereafter.

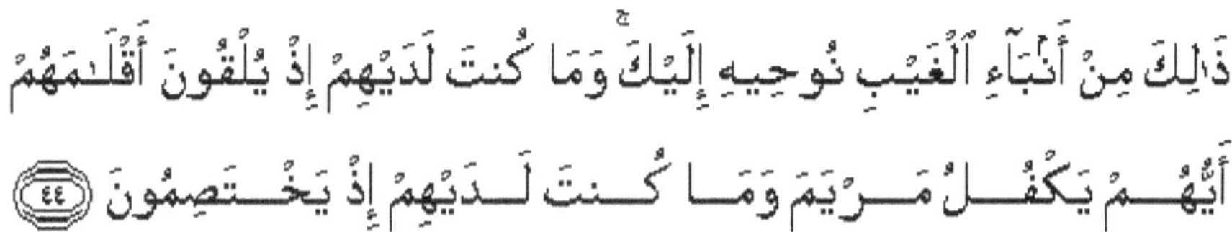

44. <u>Th</u>alika min anb<u>a</u>-i alghaybi noo<u>h</u>eehi ilayka wam<u>a</u> kunta ladayhim i<u>th</u> yulqoona aql<u>a</u>mahum ayyuhum yakfulu maryama wam<u>a</u> kunta ladayhim i<u>th</u> yakhta<u>s</u>imoon**a**

3:44. Those are narrations of events from the unknown past which We reveal to you. You were not there with them when they drew lots to decide which of them to be the guardian of Mary. Nor were you with them when they were arguing.[54]

54. This is a parenthetical note placed during the narration of events leading to the miraculous birth of Jesus. It emphasises the fact that Prophet Muhammad (peace be upon him) was unaware of those past events before those were divinely revealed to him here. It reveals that there was a dispute on who to be the guardian of Mary, in the resolution of which lots had been drawn.

45. I<u>th</u> q<u>a</u>lati almal<u>a</u>-ikatu y<u>a</u> maryamu inna All<u>a</u>ha yubashshiruki bikalimatin minhu ismuhu almasee<u>h</u>u AAees<u>a</u> ibnu maryama wajeehan fee aldduny<u>a</u> waal-<u>a</u>khirati wamina almuqarrabeen**a**

3:45. When the angels said, "O Mary! Allah does indeed give you the good news of a Word[55] from Him. His name is Jesus the Messiah, son of Mary. He is to be illustrious in this world and the Hereafter. And he is to be from among those near to Allah."

---

55. When A promises anything to B, the former gives the latter his/her word. As a human being, A may fail to, or be unable to, keep his/her word. But Allah is Almighty. None can make Him change His Word. Nor does He ever fail to keep His Word. His Word is the Truth (Verse 6:73)! "And the Word of your Lord is fulfilled in truth and in justice. None can change His Words. And He is the One Who listens, the One Who knows." [6:115] In the instant case, Allah's Word got accomplished when Mary gave birth to a son, although no man had 'touched' Mary. And the name of that accomplished Word (son) was to be Jesus.

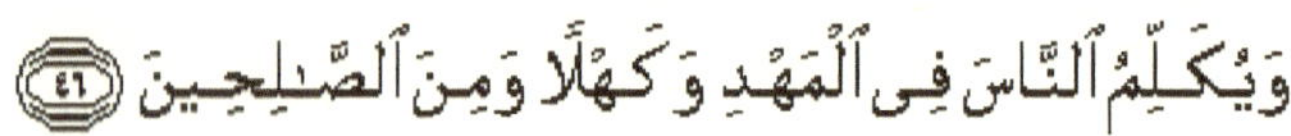

46. Wayukallimu alnnasa fee almahdi wakahlan wamina alssaliheena

---

3:46. [56]"And he would address the people while in the cradle[57] and as an adult, and he would be among the righteous."

---

56. This is in continuation of the angels' address to Mary.

57. Addressing the people even as an infant in a cradle, is one of the many miracles Allah Almighty had displayed to the people through His Messenger, Jesus. Some commentators have tried to rationalise this miracle as a metaphor for the prophetic wisdom Jesus started displaying at a very early age. But the Qur'aanic narration in Verses 19:27 to 19:37 leaves no doubt that Jesus did address the people when he was just an infant in cradle. It was indeed a miracle since such human infants can't even speak – leave alone give a prophetic address to the people! Allah showed this miracle as divine proof for the fact that Mary had committed no sin in giving miraculous birth to a child, without any male participation in the process, by Allah's Will.

قَالَتْ رَبِّ أَنَّىٰ يَكُونُ لِى وَلَدٌ وَلَمْ يَمْسَسْنِى بَشَرٌ قَالَ كَذَٰلِكِ ٱللَّهُ يَخْلُقُ مَا يَشَآءُ إِذَا قَضَىٰ أَمْرًا فَإِنَّمَا يَقُولُ لَهُۥ كُن فَيَكُونُ ﴿٤٧﴾

47. Qalat rabbi anna yakoonu lee waladun walam yamsasnee basharun qala kathaliki Allahu yakhluqu ma yashao itha qada amran fa-innama yaqoolu lahu kun fayakoonu

---

3:47. She[58] said, "My Lord! How can I have a son when no man has touched me?" One of the angels replied, "Allah does thus create whatever He wishes! When He decrees a matter, He just tells it, 'Be', and it happens!"

---

58. That is, Mary.

وَيُعَلِّمُهُ ٱلْكِتَٰبَ وَٱلْحِكْمَةَ وَٱلتَّوْرَٰةَ وَٱلْإِنجِيلَ ﴿٤٨﴾

48. WayuAAallimuhu alkitaba waalhikmata waalttawrata waal-injeela

---

3:48. "And Allah will teach him the book, the wisdom, the Torah, and the Gospel."[59]

---

59. Since both the Torah and the Gospel (*Injeel*) are mentioned here, the clause 'teach him the book' (*yuAAallimuhu alkitaba*) could mean 'teach him how to read and understand a written book.' And *Injeel* is the Book revealed to Jesus, which Book appears to have been completely lost. The New Testament part of the Bible, that we get today, is only a translated compilation of writings, the originals of which are not made publicly and openly available now. And the translations are subjected to frequent revisions, from time to time.

وَرَسُولًا إِلَىٰ بَنِىٓ إِسْرَٰٓءِيلَ أَنِّى قَدْ جِئْتُكُم بِـَٔايَةٍ مِّن رَّبِّكُمْ أَنِّىٓ أَخْلُقُ لَكُم مِّنَ ٱلطِّينِ كَهَيْـَٔةِ ٱلطَّيْرِ فَأَنفُخُ فِيهِ فَيَكُونُ طَيْرًا بِإِذْنِ ٱللَّهِ وَأُبْرِئُ ٱلْأَكْمَهَ وَٱلْأَبْرَصَ وَأُحْىِ ٱلْمَوْتَىٰ بِإِذْنِ ٱللَّهِ وَأُنَبِّئُكُم بِمَا تَأْكُلُونَ وَمَا تَدَّخِرُونَ فِى بُيُوتِكُمْ إِنَّ فِى ذَٰلِكَ لَآيَةً لَّكُمْ إِن كُنتُم مُّؤْمِنِينَ 

49. Warasoolan ila banee isra-eela annee qad ji/tukum bi-ayatin min rabbikum annee akhluqu lakum mina alttteeni kahay-ati alttayri faanfukhu feehi fayakoonu tayran bi-ithni Allahi waobri-o al-akmaha waal-abrasa waohyee almawta bi-ithni Allahi waonabbi-okum bima ta/kuloona wama taddakhiroona fee buyootikum inna fee thalika laayatan lakum in kuntum mu/mineena

---

3:49. And as a Messenger to the Children of Israel[60], he said, "I have indeed come to you with a sign from your Lord. And the sign is that I will make for you, from clay, the likeness of a bird. I will then blow into it and, with Allah's leave, it will become a living bird. And I will heal the blind and the lepers, and raise the dead to life, by Allah's leave. And, I will tell you what you eat and what you store in your houses. In that indeed is a sign for you, if you are believers."

---

60. The Qur'aan thus makes a statement here that Jesus (peace be upon him) was Allah's Messenger for the Children of Israel, and not for the entire mankind. As against this, the Qur'aan categorically states, in Verse 34:28, that Muhammad (peace be upon him) was sent for the entire mankind.

وَمُصَدِّقًا لِّمَا بَيْنَ يَدَىَّ مِنَ ٱلتَّوْرَىٰةِ وَلِأُحِلَّ لَكُم بَعْضَ ٱلَّذِى حُرِّمَ عَلَيْكُمْ وَجِئْتُكُم بِـَٔايَةٍ مِّن رَّبِّكُمْ فَٱتَّقُوا۟ ٱللَّهَ وَأَطِيعُونِ

50. Wamusaddiqan lima bayna yadayya mina alttawrati wali-ohilla lakum baAAda allathee hurrima AAalaykum waji/tukum bi-ayatin min rabbikum faittaqoo Allaha waateeAAooni

3:50. [61]"And to reaffirm that which has come before me, of the Torah, and to make lawful to you some of the things that had been forbidden to you[62]. And I have come to you with a sign from your Lord. So, fear Allah and obey me."

61. This is a continuation of Jesus' address to his people.

62. Jesus' address was to the Jews, and the food items that were specifically prohibited to the Jews are mentioned in Verse 6:146.

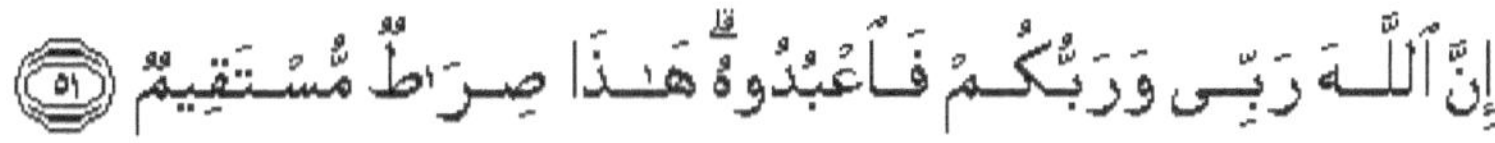

51. Inna Allaha rabbee warabbukum faoAAbudoohu hatha siratun mustaqeemun

3:51. "Indeed! Allah is my Lord and your Lord. So, worship Him! That is the Straight Path[63]."

63. The Straight Path, Allah Ta'ala taught us to pray for, in the Opening Chapter Al-Fatiha.

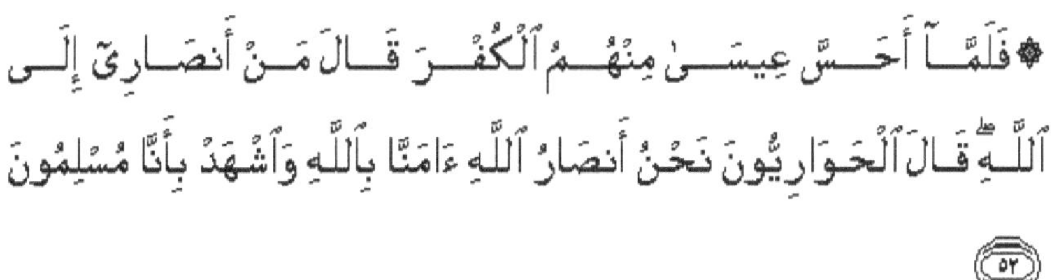

52. Falamma ahassa AAeesa minhumu alkufra qala man ansaree ila Allahi qala alhawariyyoona nahnu ansaru Allahi amanna biAllahi waishhad bi-anna muslimoona

3:52. Then when Jesus became aware of the faithlessness from them, [64] he asked, "Who will help me in Allah's cause?" The Disciples replied, "We will help you in Allah's cause. We believe in Allah. And bear witness that we indeed are those who surrender to Allah."

64. Apparently Jesus' address to his people (the Children of Israel), reproduced above in Verses 49 to 51, did not have much effect on them. He therefore sought help from the few who believed in him.

رَبَّنَآ ءَامَنَّا بِمَآ أَنزَلْتَ وَٱتَّبَعْنَا ٱلرَّسُولَ فَٱكْتُبْنَا مَعَ ٱلشَّـٰهِدِينَ ﴿٥٣﴾

53. Rabbana amanna bima anzalta waittabaAAna alrrasoola faoktubna maAAa alshshahideena

3:53. [65]"Our Lord! We have believed in what you have sent down and we have obeyed/followed the Messenger. So, mention us with the witnesses."

65. After reassuring Jesus of their solidarity with him (see preceding Verse), the disciples turn to Allah in prayer, thus, here.

وَمَكَرُواْ وَمَكَرَ ٱللَّهُ وَٱللَّهُ خَيْرُ ٱلْمَـٰكِرِينَ ﴿٥٤﴾

54. Wamakaroo wamakara Allahu waAllahu khayru almakireena

3:54. And they planned, and Allah planned. And Allah is the best of planners.[66]

66. In <u>Verse 4:157</u>, the Qur'aan tells us that the plan of the Children of Israel to kill Jesus on the Cross failed. They in fact killed someone else thus and thought it was Jesus that they killed. Jesus' death on the Cross was a mere deception, which deception later pervaded the Christians.

إِذْ قَالَ ٱللَّهُ يَـٰعِيسَىٰٓ إِنِّى مُتَوَفِّيكَ وَرَافِعُكَ إِلَىَّ وَمُطَهِّرُكَ مِنَ ٱلَّذِينَ كَفَرُواْ وَجَاعِلُ ٱلَّذِينَ ٱتَّبَعُوكَ فَوْقَ ٱلَّذِينَ كَفَرُوٓاْ إِلَىٰ يَوْمِ ٱلْقِيَـٰمَةِ ثُمَّ إِلَىَّ مَرْجِعُكُمْ فَأَحْكُمُ بَيْنَكُمْ فِيمَا كُنتُمْ فِيهِ تَخْتَلِفُونَ

55. Ith qala Allahu ya AAeesa innee mutawaffeeka warafiAAuka ilayya wamutahhiruka mina allatheena kafaroo wajaAAilu allatheena ittabaAAooka fawqa allatheena kafaroo ila yawmi alqiyamati thumma ilayya marjiAAukum faahkumu baynakum feema kuntum feehi takhtalifoona

---

3:55. When[67] Allah said: "O Jesus! I am indeed going to make you die[68] and raise you up to Me. And I will cleanse you of what those who suppress the Truth say about you.[69] And I will make those who follow you surpass those who suppress the Truth, towards the Day of Resurrection.[70] And then to Me shall be the return of you all. Then I shall judge between you on matters which you have been disputing."

---

67. That is, at the failure of the plan of the people to kill Jesus on the Cross.

68. This is the plain meaning of the Arabic term *mutawaffeeka*. But, influenced by the prevalent belief in the return of Jesus to this world at a period near its end, some translators have twisted the plain meaning to connote raising of Jesus <u>alive</u> to Allah for being sent back again to this world later. There is nothing in the Qur'aan to substantiate this belief. At death, every human soul, like Jesus', is raised to Allah.

69. The suppressors of Truth blaspheme that Jesus, was son of God – His begotten son! The uniquely divine Being of Allah is far, far above the human attribute they give Him. Through the Qur'aan, Allah has cleansed Jesus of that blasphemy.

70. This is a Qur'aanic prediction, which is, by Allah's Will, gradually but surely in the process of being fulfilled. The real followers of Jesus are those who follow the Qur'aan, and not those who suppress the Truth about him. Despite being viciously denigrated, Islam is the fastest growing Religion today.

فَأَمَّا ٱلَّذِينَ كَفَرُواْ فَأُعَذِّبُهُمْ عَذَابًا شَدِيدًا فِى ٱلدُّنْيَا وَٱلْأَخِرَةِ وَمَا لَهُم مِّن نَّـٰصِرِينَ ۝

56. Faamma allatheena kafaroo faoAAaththibuhum AAathaban shadeedan fee alddunya waal-akhirati wama lahum min nasireena

---

3:56. "So I punish, with severe punishment in this world and the Hereafter, [71] those who suppress the Truth. And they shall have none to help them."

---

71. Had the preposition *fee* (in) been used also before *akhirati* (Hereafter), then it would have meant that the severe punishment would be given <u>both</u> here and in the Hereafter. But the construction of the phrase here, – treating 'here and the hereafter' as one unit in relation to the prefix 'in' – indicates that some suppressors of the Truth may not be subjected to the severe punishment, <u>in this world</u>. Suppressors of the Truth, as the Qur'aan repeatedly says, are bound to be punished severely in the Hereafter. And incorrigible suppressors of the Truth like the people of Noah and the people of Lot are known to have suffered severe punishment in this world also.

وَأَمَّا ٱلَّذِينَ ءَامَنُواْ وَعَمِلُواْ ٱلصَّـٰلِحَـٰتِ فَيُوَفِّيهِمْ أُجُورَهُمْ وَٱللَّهُ لَا يُحِبُّ ٱلظَّـٰلِمِينَ ۝

57. Waamma allatheena amanoo waAAamiloo alssalihati fayuwaffeehim ojoorahum waAllahu la yuhibbu alththalimeena

---

3:57. "And as for those who believe and do good deeds, He will pay them their full rewards. And Allah does not love the transgressors."[72]

---

72. Those who go beyond the Allah-set limits in anything are the transgressors. Suppressors of Truth (*kafiroon*) are the obvious first claimants to being transgressors. But by placing this statement, regarding Allah's displeasure with the transgressors, just after a statement about the believers, the Qur'aan lays stress on the fact that Allah is displeased with any transgression in the deeds of the believers as well.

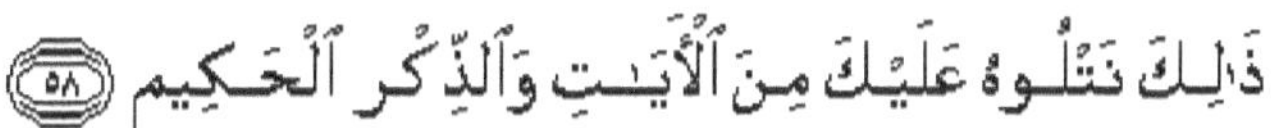

58. Thalika natloohu AAalayka mina al-ayati waalththikri alhakeemi

3:58. That We[73] recite to you from the signs of and the things about the Wise One.

73. About the use of the personal pronoun in the Qur'aan sometimes in the plural and sometimes in the singular for Allah and His divine dispensation, please refer Note 2:184.

إِنَّ مَثَلَ عِيسَىٰ عِندَ ٱللَّهِ كَمَثَلِ ءَادَمَ خَلَقَهُۥ مِن تُرَابٍ ثُمَّ قَالَ لَهُۥ كُن فَيَكُونُ ۝

59. Inna mathala AAeesa AAinda Allahi kamathali adama khalaqahu min turabin thumma qala lahu kun fayakoonu

3:59. Indeed, for Allah, the case of Jesus is like the case of Adam whom He created out of dust and then said to him "Be" and he was! [74]

74. The normal way in which any man is created is through sexual intercourse between a man and a woman. Adam and Jesus were the exceptions to this general rule. Jesus is therefore likened to Adam.

ٱلْحَقُّ مِن رَّبِّكَ فَلَا تَكُن مِّنَ ٱلْمُمْتَرِينَ ۝

60. Alhaqqu min rabbika fala takun mina almumtareena

3:60. The Truth from your[75] Lord! Be not among those, then, who doubt.

---

75. In the Arabic text, the second person pronoun (*ka*) here is in the singular form, indicating that the addressee was, primarily, Prophet Muhammad (peace be upon him). In fact, all these 3 Verses (58 to 60) were addressed to him and through him, by inference, to every believer. The Prophet and the believers were thus reassured that all the unusual facts about Jesus – his birth to Virgin Mary and the fact that Jesus was not crucified as commonly believed by the Jews and the Christians – were absolutely true!

فَمَنْ حَآجَّكَ فِيهِ مِنْ بَعْدِ مَا جَآءَكَ مِنَ ٱلْعِلْمِ فَقُلْ تَعَالَوْاْ نَدْعُ

أَبْنَآءَنَا وَأَبْنَآءَكُمْ وَنِسَآءَنَا وَنِسَآءَكُمْ وَأَنفُسَنَا وَأَنفُسَكُمْ ثُمَّ نَبْتَهِلْ

فَنَجْعَل لَّعْنَتَ ٱللَّهِ عَلَى ٱلْكَٰذِبِينَ ۝

61. Faman hajjaka feehi min baAAdi ma jaaka mina alAAilmi faqul taAAalaw nadAAu abnaana waabnaakum wanisaana wanisaakum waanfusana waanfusakum thumma nabtahil fanajAAal laAAnata Allahi AAala alkathibeena

---

3:61. So when one argues with you in this matter[76], after what knowledge has come to you, say, "Come! Let us call together our sons and your sons, our women and your women, ourselves and yourselves. Then let us pray and invoke Allah's curse on those who lie."

---

76. In the matter of the miraculous birth of Jesus to Virgin Mary and in the matter of Jesus not being crucified as alleged by the Jews and the Christians, that is.

إِنَّ هَـٰذَا لَهُوَ ٱلْقَصَصُ ٱلْحَقُّ وَمَا مِنْ إِلَـٰهٍ إِلَّا ٱللَّهُ وَإِنَّ ٱللَّهَ لَهُوَ ٱلْعَزِيزُ ٱلْحَكِيمُ ﴿٦٢﴾

62. Inna hatha lahuwa alqasasu alhaqqu wama min ilahin illa Allahu wa-inna Allaha lahuwa alAAazeezu alhakeemu

3:62. This indeed is the true account[77]. And there is none worthy of worship but Allah. And, indeed, Allah is the One Who is Omnipotent, the One Who is Wise.

77. The account about Jesus, that is. Jesus was an honourable Prophet and Messenger of Allah. But he was indeed not god or begotten son of god (I seek Allah's pardon for expressing the blasphemy), as the Christians consider him to be.

فَإِن تَوَلَّوْاْ فَإِنَّ ٱللَّهَ عَلِيمٌ بِٱلْمُفْسِدِينَ ﴿٦٣﴾

63. Fa-in tawallaw fa-inna Allaha AAaleemun bialmufsideena

3:63. And then if they turn away[78], Allah indeed knows those who are corrupted.

78. Turn away from the absolute Truth that the preceding Verse 62 revealed and emphasised.

قُلْ يَـٰٓأَهْلَ ٱلْكِتَـٰبِ تَعَالَوْاْ إِلَىٰ كَلِمَةٍ سَوَآءٍ بَيْنَنَا وَبَيْنَكُمْ أَلَّا نَعْبُدَ إِلَّا ٱللَّهَ

وَلَا نُشْرِكَ بِهِۦ شَيْـًٔا وَلَا يَتَّخِذَ بَعْضُنَا بَعْضًا أَرْبَابًا مِّن دُونِ ٱللَّهِ ۚ فَإِن تَوَلَّوْاْ

فَقُولُواْ ٱشْهَدُواْ بِأَنَّا مُسْلِمُونَ ﴿٦٤﴾

64. Qul ya ahla alkitabi taAAalaw ila kalimatin sawa-in baynana wabaynakum alla naAAbuda illa Allaha wala nushrika bihi shay-an wala yattakhitha baAAduna baAAdan arbaban min dooni Allahi fa-in tawallaw faqooloo ishhadoo bi-anna muslimoona

---

3:64. Say, "O people of the Book! Let us come together on a common ground, between us and between you, that we shall worship none but Allah, that we shall not associate any partners with Him and that some of us shall not take some others, from among ourselves, as lords besides Allah[79]." Then if they turn away, tell them, "Bear witness that we are those who have surrendered to Allah."[80]

---

79. In Verse 9:31, Allah tells us that the Jews and the Christians had taken their rabbis and their monks as lords besides Allah. The public in those communities had ceased referring their divine scriptures for solutions to their day-to-day problems. They didn't want to take the trouble. Instead, they referred their problems to their rabbis and their monks and gobbled up whatever those religious leaders told them as the gospel truth. Muslims of today are doing the same. They have stopped referring the Qur'aan for their day-to-day problems. They go to the Mullahs instead. The Muslims have thus, like the Jews and the Christians, made their religious leaders their lords besides Allah.

80. The terms mentioned in this Verse, for all religious communities to whom divine books were bestowed to come together, are valid even now. Their religious scriptures, although polluted with human writings, still contain the basic principles of monotheism that this Verse describes as the common ground (*kalimatin sawa-in*) between the communities. Efforts ought to be made in inter-religious conferences, on these lines, for world peace. And if the others turn deaf ears to the proposals, the Muslims should reiterate their basic creed of complete surrender to the Almighty Will, and stand firmly by that creed, come what may.

بَیۡتَأَهۡلَ ٱلۡکِتَـٰبِ لِمَ تُحَاۤجُّونَ فِیۤ إِبۡرَٰهِیمَ وَمَاۤ أُنزِلَتِ ٱلتَّوۡرَٮٰةُ وَٱلۡإِنجِیلُ
إِلَّا مِنۢ بَعۡدِهِۦۤ أَفَلَا تَعۡقِلُونَ ۝

65. Y<u>a</u> ahla alkit<u>a</u>bi lima tu<u>haij</u>oona fee ibr<u>a</u>heema wam<u>a</u> onzilati a<u>l</u>ttawr<u>a</u>tu wa<u>a</u>l-injeelu ill<u>a</u> min baAAdihi afal<u>a</u> taAAqiloon<u>a</u>

3:65. O people of the Book! Why do you quarrel with us over Abraham? And the Torah and the Gospel were not sent down but only after his time! Have you, then, no sense? [81]

---

81. Please see Verse 67 below in this context. Allah nails the lie here, of both the Jews and the Christians, that Abraham was a Jew or a Christian.

هَـٰۤأَنتُمۡ هَـٰۤؤُلَاۤءِ حَـٰجَجۡتُمۡ فِیمَا لَکُم بِهِۦ عِلۡمٌ فَلِمَ تُحَاۤجُّونَ
فِیمَا لَیۡسَ لَکُم بِهِۦ عِلۡمٌ وَٱللَّهُ یَعۡلَمُ وَأَنتُمۡ لَا تَعۡلَمُونَ ۝

66. H<u>a</u> antum h<u>a</u>ol<u>a</u>-i <u>haj</u>ajtum feem<u>a</u> lakum bihi AAilmun falima tu<u>haij</u>oona feem<u>a</u> laysa lakum bihi AAilmun wa<u>A</u>ll<u>a</u>hu yaAAlamu waantum l<u>a</u> taAAlamoon<u>a</u>

3:66. You have been, till now, arguing over things of which you had knowledge! Why are you now arguing over things you know nothing about? [82] Allah knows while you do not.

---

82. About Moses and Jesus, the Children of Israel had knowledge; for, those were Prophets sent to their own community. The Children of Israel had therefore some basis to argue about those Prophets. But what about Abraham, who had lived in this world much before the community came into existence? The community had its genesis in the offspring of Israel, a grandchild of Abraham! It is Allah, the All-knowing, Who knows everything about Abraham, and not they.

مَا كَانَ إِبْرَٰهِيمُ يَهُودِيًّا وَلَا نَصْرَانِيًّا وَلَٰكِن كَانَ حَنِيفًا مُّسْلِمًا وَمَا كَانَ مِنَ ٱلْمُشْرِكِينَ ۝

67. Ma kana ibraheemu yahoodiyyan wala nasraniyyan walakin kana haneefan musliman wama kana mina almushrikeena

3:67. Abraham was neither a Jew nor a Christian. But he was one who was single-minded in his devotion and submission to Allah. And he was not a polytheist.

إِنَّ أَوْلَى ٱلنَّاسِ بِإِبْرَٰهِيمَ لَلَّذِينَ ٱتَّبَعُوهُ وَهَٰذَا ٱلنَّبِيُّ وَٱلَّذِينَ ءَامَنُوا۟ وَٱللَّهُ وَلِيُّ ٱلْمُؤْمِنِينَ ۝

68. Inna awla alnnasi bi-ibraheema lallatheena ittabaAAoohu wahatha alnnabiyyu waallatheena amanoo waAllahu waliyyu almu/mineena

3:68. Those who followed him (Abraham), this Prophet, and those who believe, are indeed the people close to Abraham. And Allah is close to the believers.[83]

83. This Verse makes it clear that it is those who follow Abraham by being single-minded, like him, in their devotion and submission to Allah, who are close to him. This Prophet (Muhammad, peace be upon him) and the believers in the Qur'aan, to whom Allah is close, are included among those who are close to Abraham.

وَدَّت طَّآئِفَةٌ مِّنْ أَهْلِ ٱلْكِتَٰبِ لَوْ يُضِلُّونَكُمْ وَمَا يُضِلُّونَ إِلَّآ أَنفُسَهُمْ وَمَا يَشْعُرُونَ ۝

69. Waddat ta-ifatun min ahli alkitabi law yudilloonakum wama yudilloona illa anfusahum wama yashAAuroona

3:69. A section of the People of the Book would love to mislead you. And they mislead not but themselves! And they know not.

70. Ya ahla alkitabi lima takfuroona bi-ayati Allahi waantum tashhadoona

3:70. O People of the Book! Why do you suppress Allah's Verses/signs, and you are witnesses thereto? [84]

84. In Verse 6:20, the Qur'aan informs us that those who have been given the Book recognise it (the Qur'aan) to be divine as they would recognise their own sons. The Jews and the Christians, present near the place of revelation of the Qur'aan, had enough evidences, in their own scriptures, of the Truth of the Qur'aanic Verses being divine. But their false sense of pride, that the divine Book was not revealed to one among themselves (the Children of Israel), prevented them from giving expression to the Truth in their hearts.

71. Ya ahla alkitabi lima talbisoona alhaqqa bialbatili wataktumoona alhaqqa waantum taAAlamoona

3:71. O People of the Book! Why do you clothe the truth with falsehood and conceal the truth knowingly? [85]

85. Please see the preceding Note.

وَقَالَت طَّآئِفَةٌ مِّنْ أَهْلِ ٱلْكِتَـٰبِ ءَامِنُوا۟ بِٱلَّذِىٓ أُنزِلَ عَلَى ٱلَّذِينَ ءَامَنُوا۟ وَجْهَ ٱلنَّهَارِ وَٱكْفُرُوٓا۟ ءَاخِرَهُۥ لَعَلَّهُمْ يَرْجِعُونَ ۝

72. Waqalat ta-ifatun min ahli alkitabi aminoo biallathee onzila AAala allatheena amanoo wajha alnnahari waokfuroo akhirahu laAAallahum yarjiAAoona

---

3:72. A section of the People of the Book say, "Express belief in what is revealed to the believers early in the day, and express disbelief at the end of it; so that they may turn back."[86]

---

86. It was a ploy of the Jews and Christians thus to sow seeds of doubts in the minds of the Muslims and turn them back from Islam.

وَلَا تُؤْمِنُوٓا۟ إِلَّا لِمَن تَبِعَ دِينَكُمْ قُلْ إِنَّ ٱلْهُدَىٰ هُدَى ٱللَّهِ أَن يُؤْتَىٰٓ أَحَدٌ مِّثْلَ مَآ أُوتِيتُمْ أَوْ يُحَآجُّوكُمْ عِندَ رَبِّكُمْ قُلْ إِنَّ ٱلْفَضْلَ بِيَدِ ٱللَّهِ يُؤْتِيهِ مَن يَشَآءُ وَٱللَّهُ وَٰسِعٌ عَلِيمٌ ۝

73. Wala tu/minoo illa liman tabiAAa deenakum qul inna alhuda huda Allahi an yu/ta ahadun mithla ma ooteetum aw yuhajjookum AAinda rabbikum qul inna alfadla biyadi Allahi yu/teehi man yashao waAllahu wasiAAun AAaleemun

---

3:73. [87]"And believe not that, except to one who follows your religion," – Say, "Indeed, the (true) guidance is guidance of Allah."[88] – "anyone else could be given the like of what was given to you, or, could quarrel with you in the presence of your Lord." Say, "All favour[89] is indeed in the hand of Allah. HE grants it to whom He wills. And Allah is Pervasive, Knowledgeable."

---

87. This is a continuation of what a section of the People of the Book was quoted as saying in the preceding Verse.

88. This is a divine parenthetic interruption, in the middle of what the people of the Book were saying. The parenthetic interruption was by way of guiding and pointing out to the Prophet, and to the believers, that what the People of the Book were saying here was nothing but misguidance to their own people.

89. To make any person a Prophet or Messenger of Allah, is a special Favour from Allah. The Children of Israel wrongly assumed that Allah granted this favour only to members of their own community. They disputed the Prophethood of Muhammad (peace be upon him), since he was not one of them.

يَخْتَصُّ بِرَحْمَتِهِۦ مَن يَشَآءُ ۗ وَٱللَّهُ ذُو ٱلْفَضْلِ ٱلْعَظِيمِ ﴿٧٤﴾

74. Yakhtassu birahmatihi man yashao waAllahu thoo alfadli alAAatheemi

---

3:74. HE specifies for His Mercy whom He wills. And Allah has immense capacity to grant favours.

۞ وَمِنْ أَهْلِ ٱلْكِتَـٰبِ مَنْ إِن تَأْمَنْهُ بِقِنطَارٍ يُؤَدِّهِۦ إِلَيْكَ وَمِنْهُم مَّنْ إِن تَأْمَنْهُ بِدِينَارٍ لَّا يُؤَدِّهِۦٓ إِلَيْكَ إِلَّا مَا دُمْتَ عَلَيْهِ قَآئِمًا ۗ ذَٰلِكَ بِأَنَّهُمْ قَالُواْ لَيْسَ عَلَيْنَا فِى ٱلْأُمِّيِّـۧنَ سَبِيلٌ وَيَقُولُونَ عَلَى ٱللَّهِ ٱلْكَذِبَ وَهُمْ يَعْلَمُونَ ﴿٧٥﴾

75. Wamin ahli alkitabi man in ta/manhu biqintarin yu-addihi ilayka waminhum man in ta/manhu bideenarin la yu-addihi ilayka illa ma dumta AAalayhi qa-iman thalika bi-annahum qaloo laysa AAalayna fee al-ommiyyeena sabeelun wayaqooloona AAala Allahi alkathiba wahum yaAAlamoona

---

3:75. And among the People of the Book is one who, if you entrust him with a treasure, will return it back to you. And among them is one who, if you entrust him with a single dinar, will not return it back to you unless you constantly keep on pressing him for it. That is the position because they say, "We are not bound by any obligations to the illiterates[90]." And they knowingly ascribe a lie to Allah! [91]

---

90. The People of the Book (Jews and Christians) called others so, because the others (the native Arabs) could not lay claims to any Book previously revealed to them. And the former did not recognise the latter's claim of the Qur'aan being the Book in the process of being divinely revealed to them.

91. The lie was two-fold:

1.   that the then in-process revelation of the Qur'aan was not divine, and
2.   that any people of the Book are not bound by any obligation to anyone, literate or illiterate.

76. Bal<u>a</u> man awf<u>a</u> biAAahdihi waittaq<u>a</u> fa-inna All<u>a</u>ha yu<u>h</u>ibbu almuttaqeena

---

3:76. Yes, indeed! Allah loves the pious people, such as one who keeps one's word and fears Allah.

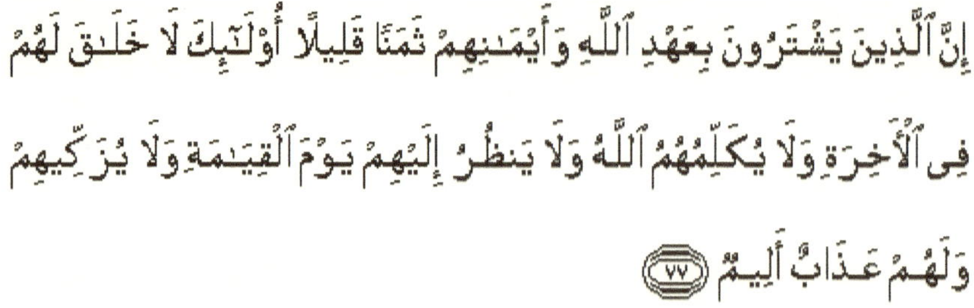

77. Inna alla<u>th</u>eena yashtaroona biAAahdi All<u>a</u>hi waaym<u>a</u>nihim thamanan qaleelan ol<u>a</u>-ika l<u>a</u> khal<u>a</u>qa lahum fee al-<u>a</u>khirati wal<u>a</u> yukallimuhumu All<u>a</u>hu wal<u>a</u> yan<u>th</u>uru ilayhim yawma alqiy<u>a</u>mati wal<u>a</u> yuzakkeehim walahum AAa<u>tha</u>bun aleemun

---

3:77. Indeed, those who trade Covenants with Allah and their pledges for a petty price[92] – those shall have nothing good for them in the Hereafter. Allah shall neither speak to them nor look at them on the Day of Resurrection. And He shall cleanse them not; and, for them, a painful punishment.

---

92. Those indicated here are, of course, the Jews and Christians living at the time and place of the revelation of the Qur'aan. But, Muslims of today are no less indicated by this Qur'aanic Verse! Like those Children Of Israel, who time and again broke their Covenants with Allah (as mentioned, for example, in Verse 2:51) and thought nothing of dishonouring their obligations (as mentioned herein above in Verse 3:75), many Muslims today are guilty of the same crimes. Although the Muslims have made a Covenant with Allah not to associate anything or anybody with Him, they visit graves of dead persons for redressal of their worldly woes. And they too, like those People of the Book mentioned in Verse 3:75 above, think nothing of breaking their pledges with non-Muslims. They should beware that they too are candidates for the humiliating punishment in the Hereafter, unless they mend their ways.

وَإِنَّ مِنْهُمْ لَفَرِيقًا يَلْوُونَ أَلْسِنَتَهُم بِالْكِتَـبِ لِتَحْسَبُوهُ مِنَ ٱلْكِتَـبِ وَمَا

هُوَ مِنَ ٱلْكِتَـبِ وَيَقُولُونَ هُوَ مِنْ عِندِ ٱللَّهِ وَمَا هُوَ مِنْ عِندِ ٱللَّهِ

وَيَقُولُونَ عَلَى ٱللَّهِ ٱلْكَذِبَ وَهُمْ يَعْلَمُونَ ﴿٧٨﴾

78. Wa-inna minhum lafareeqan yalwoona alsinatahum bialkitabi litahsaboohu mina alkitabi wama huwa mina alkitabi wayaqooloona huwa min AAindi Allahi wama huwa min AAindi Allahi wayaqooloona AAala Allahi alkathiba wahum yaAAlamoona

3:78. And, indeed, there is among them a section who so twist their tongues with the Book that you may think it is from the Book, and it is not from the Book. And they say it is from Allah and it is not from Allah. And they knowingly utter a lie about Allah.[93]

93. This Verse might well have been revealed in the perspective of the Jews and the Christians trying then to change the contents of the revealed Books with them. But, in our present-day perspective, we need not get concerned with what those people did then. The Qur'aan is valid for all times. Let us therefore look at this Verse in our own perspective. And let us first look to what we ourselves do with our own Qur'aan, before looking to what the Jews and the Christians are doing with their Books. We are fortunate, by Allah's Grace, that the Arabic text of the Qur'aan is divinely protected. But Arabic is not known to all the Muslims. In fact, a majority from among them do not know Arabic; nor are any sincere efforts made to make Arabic a compulsory subject for all Muslims to learn, all over the world. In this scenario, Satan has manoeuvred the majority Muslim mind into thinking that it is enough for them to learn just to read the Qur'aan. It is indeed a satanic handiwork to delude the intelligence of the Muslim mind against the imperative need to understand what one reads from the Qur'aan. The Moulvis and the Mullahs have, in the circumstances, become the *Arbaab* (Lords), besides the One Lord, of the common Muslims. For, they (the common Muslims) literally gulp down what their religious leaders tell them, right or wrong. And the Moulvis and Mullahs, many of them semi-literates themselves, often give the commoners a wrong picture of Islam. Besides, in the translations & commentaries of the Qur'aan in other languages, not only do human mistakes creep in inadvertently, but deviations are advertently made to cater to views promoting *shirk*.

مَا كَانَ لِبَشَرٍ أَن يُؤْتِيَهُ ٱللَّهُ ٱلْكِتَـٰبَ وَٱلْحُكْمَ وَٱلنُّبُوَّةَ ثُمَّ يَقُولَ لِلنَّاسِ كُونُوا۟ عِبَادًا لِّى مِن دُونِ ٱللَّهِ وَلَـٰكِن كُونُوا۟ رَبَّـٰنِيِّـۧنَ بِمَا كُنتُمْ تُعَلِّمُونَ ٱلْكِتَـٰبَ وَبِمَا كُنتُمْ تَدْرُسُونَ ۝

79. Ma kana libasharin an yu/tiyahu Allahu alkitaba waalhukma waalnnubuwwata thumma yaqoola lilnnasi koonoo AAibadan lee min dooni Allahi walakin koonoo rabbaniyyeena bima kuntum tuAAallimoona alkitaba wabima kuntum tadrusoona

---

3:79. A man, whom Allah has given the Book and the Command and the Prophethood, cannot say to the people, "Be worshippers of me besides Allah." But be you all faithful worshippers of your Lord in accordance with what you have been teaching from the Book and in accordance with what you have been studying/learning from it.[94]

---

94. The Verse is a direct indictment of the Christians. They worship Prophet Jesus (peace be upon him) as God Himself or as Son of God. This tendency to worship God's Messenger as God Himself is not restricted, among mankind, to the Christians alone. Worshipping of Rama and Krishna in India appears to be a result of the same tendency. Why blame other communities? There is a palpable tendency among the Muslims themselves to give their own Prophet (peace upon him) some of the divine powers. They have already 'given' him the power of intercession, as the Christians have given Jesus, to ensure their safe entry into Paradise despite their sins committed here on earth. There is nothing in the Qur'aan to show that Allah has given the power of intercession to any of His Messengers/Prophets. The Qur'aan, in fact, categorically states that there shall be no intercession on the Day of Judgement (Verse 2:254)

وَلَا يَأْمُرَكُمْ أَن تَتَّخِذُوا۟ ٱلْمَلَـٰٓئِكَةَ وَٱلنَّبِيِّـۧنَ أَرْبَابًا أَيَأْمُرُكُم بِٱلْكُفْرِ بَعْدَ إِذْ أَنتُم مُّسْلِمُونَ ۝

80. Wala ya/murakum an tattakhithoo almala-ikata waalnnabiyyeena arbaban aya/murukum bialkufri baAAda ith antum muslimoona

---

3:80. And he[95] does not ask you to take the angels and the prophets as your lords. Would he exhort you to suppression of the Truth after you have submitted to Allah!?

---

95. That is, the man whom Allah has given the Book and the Command and the Prophethood, referred to in the preceding Verse.

وَإِذْ أَخَذَ ٱللَّهُ مِيثَـٰقَ ٱلنَّبِيِّـۧنَ لَمَآ ءَاتَيْتُكُم مِّن

كِتَـٰبٍ وَحِكْمَةٍ ثُمَّ جَآءَكُمْ رَسُولٌ مُّصَدِّقٌ لِّمَا مَعَكُمْ لَتُؤْمِنُنَّ بِهِۦ

وَلَتَنصُرُنَّهُۥ قَالَ ءَأَقْرَرْتُمْ وَأَخَذْتُمْ عَلَىٰ ذَٰلِكُمْ إِصْرِى قَالُوٓاْ أَقْرَرْنَا

قَالَ فَٱشْهَدُواْ وَأَنَا۠ مَعَكُم مِّنَ ٱلشَّـٰهِدِينَ ﴿٨١﴾

81. Wa-ith akhatha Allahu meethaqa alnnabiyyeena lama ataytukum min kitabin wahikmatin thumma jaakum rasoolun musaddiqun lima maAAakum latu/minunna bihi walatansurunnahu qala aaqrartum waakhathtum AAala thalikum isree qaloo aqrarna qala faishhadoo waana maAAakum mina alshshahideena

3:81. And when Allah took the covenant of the Prophets, – "Along with what I have given you of Book and Wisdom, you would certainly believe in what a Messenger would bring to you confirming that which is with you, and you would certainly help that Messenger." – He (Allah) asked, "Do you affirm and make a contract with Me in this matter?" They said, "We do affirm." He said, "Bear witness and I am among those who bear witness with you."[96]

96. The parenthetic portion in the translation of the Verse is the Covenant proper that Allah took of the people, through their respective Prophets. The purpose of the Verse is to assure the believers that every Prophet was duly informed in advance of the coming of the final Prophet as the Messenger who would confirm the divine Message that Prophet carried. And every Prophet helped the cause of the final Messenger by specifically telling his people about him. This indicates that the religious Scriptures of the earlier people contain references to the last Prophet, Muhammad (peace be upon him). And those references are the affirmations Allah took of those earlier people. The Wise Lord and Creator of all things has thus provided unassailable proof of the genuineness of the last Prophet and the last divine Message.

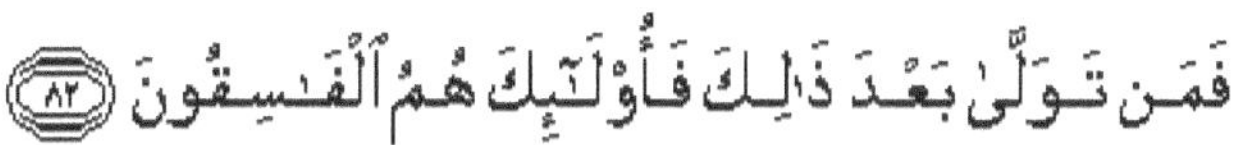

فَمَن تَوَلَّىٰ بَعْدَ ذَٰلِكَ فَأُوْلَـٰٓئِكَ هُمُ ٱلْفَـٰسِقُونَ ﴿٨٢﴾

82. Faman tawalla baAAda thalika faola-ika humu alfasiqoona

3:82. Then those, such as one who turns away after that, are the transgressors.[97]

97. The reference is to those earlier people of the Book, who despite references to the last Prophet in their own scriptures, refuse to recognise, and believe in him.

أَفَغَيْرَ دِينِ ٱللَّهِ يَبْغُونَ وَلَهُۥ أَسْلَمَ مَن فِى ٱلسَّمَٰوَٰتِ وَٱلْأَرْضِ طَوْعًا وَكَرْهًا وَإِلَيْهِ يُرْجَعُونَ ۝

83. Afaghayra deeni Allahi yabghoona walahu aslama man fee alssamawati waal-ardi tawAAan wakarhan wa-ilayhi yurjaAAoona

3:83. Are they looking for a religion other than that of Allah? [98] And to Him submits everything that is in the heavens and in the earth, willingly or unwillingly. And to Him they all return.

98. And in Verse 3:85 below it is categorically mentioned that no religion other than Islam is accepted.

قُلْ ءَامَنَّا بِٱللَّهِ وَمَآ أُنزِلَ عَلَيْنَا وَمَآ أُنزِلَ عَلَىٰٓ إِبْرَٰهِيمَ وَإِسْمَٰعِيلَ وَإِسْحَٰقَ وَيَعْقُوبَ وَٱلْأَسْبَاطِ وَمَآ أُوتِىَ مُوسَىٰ وَعِيسَىٰ وَٱلنَّبِيُّونَ مِن رَّبِّهِمْ لَا نُفَرِّقُ بَيْنَ أَحَدٍ مِّنْهُمْ وَنَحْنُ لَهُۥ مُسْلِمُونَ ۝

84. Qul amanna biAllahi wama onzila AAalayna wama onzila AAala ibraheema wa-ismaAAeela wa-ishaqa wayaAAqooba waal-asbati wama ootiya moosa waAAeesa waalnnabiyyoona min rabbihim la nufarriqu bayna ahadin minhum wanahnu lahu muslimoona

3:84. Say, "We believe in Allah and in that which is sent down upon us, in that which was sent down upon Abraham, Ishmael, Isaac, Jacob and the descendent Tribes and in that which was given to Moses, to Jesus and to the Prophets, from their Lord. We do not discriminate between any one and another of them. And to Him we do totally submit."[99]

---

99. The wordings of this Verse are almost the same as those of Verse 2:136. **Please refer study note 204 of these Studies, under that Verse.**

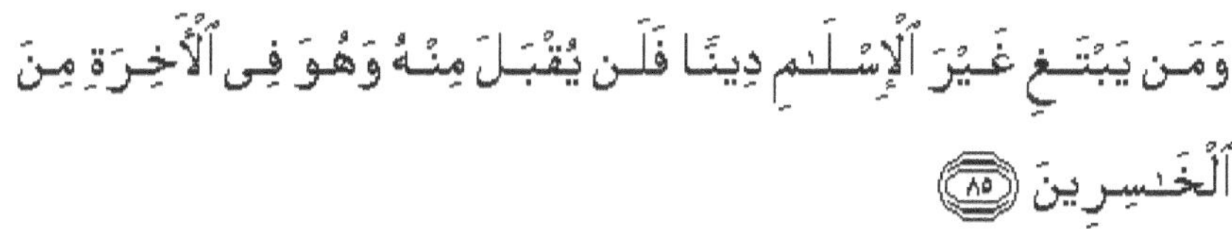

85. Waman yabtaghi ghayra al-islami deenan falan yuqbala minhu wahuwa fee al-akhirati mina alkhasireena

---

3:85. And whoever seeks a religion other than Islam, it is not accepted from him. And he, in the Hereafter, will be among the doomed.[100]

---

100. A cyber-friend of mine opines that the 'Islam' mentioned in this Verse is not the same as the perfected 'Islam' mentioned in Verse 5:3. The relevant portion of Verse 5:3 is one of the last revelations of the Qur'aan, while Verse 3:85 was revealed, before Islam was perfected. The cyber-friend says that under the 'Islam' of Verse 3:85, Christians, who do not believe in the theory of Jesus being the begotten son of God, and the Jews, could be included, because of their belief in one God. And by Verse 2:62, **such Christians and Jews could attain to salvation in the Hereafter, even though they do not believe in the Qur'aan and the last Prophet. This opinion is erroneous because, first, there are no discrepancies in the Qur'aan (Verse 4:82). Islam, mentioned in Verse 3:85, is the same as Islam mentioned in Verse 5:3. About Verse 2:62, the Qur'aan is valid for all times. The Jews and the Christians mentioned therein (Verse 2:62) are those to whom the Message of the Qur'aan had not reached, whether before or after the revelation of the Qur'aan. But for those, to whom the Message had /has reached, there is no excuse for their non-belief either in the Qur'aan or in Prophet Muhammad (peace upon him). The earlier religious scriptures, even in their present corrupted forms, contain enough evidence of the prophecy made therein about the last Prophet and the last divine Message. Please refer** Verse 3:81 **and study note 96 thereon above and study note** 2:69 **under Verse 2:62 of these Studies. The Christians and the Jews wouldn't be doing a righteous deed by ignoring the evidence in their own Scriptures. Verse 2:62 wouldn't therefore apply to them.**

كَيْفَ يَهْدِى اللَّهُ قَوْمًا كَفَرُوا بَعْدَ إِيمَـٰنِهِمْ وَشَهِدُوا أَنَّ الرَّسُولَ حَقٌّ وَجَاءَهُمُ الْبَيِّنَـٰتُ وَاللَّهُ لَا يَهْدِى الْقَوْمَ الظَّـٰلِمِينَ ﴿٨٦﴾

86. Kayfa yahdee All<u>a</u>hu qawman kafaroo baAAda eem<u>a</u>nihim washahidoo anna alrrasoola <u>h</u>aqqun waj<u>a</u>ahumu albayyin<u>a</u>tu waAll<u>a</u>hu l<u>a</u> yahdee alqawma al<u>thth</u>alimeena

---

3:86. How would Allah guide people who suppress the Truth after having accepted faith and acknowledged that the Messenger is right, and after clear signs had come to them? And Allah does not guide people who indulge in wrongdoing.[101]

---

101. The Qur'aan thus chides the People of the Book, who had already made a Covenant with their respective Prophets that they would believe in and help the Last Prophet when he comes to them (see Verse 81 herein above). This Verse too confirms that the Jews and the Christians would not attain to salvation, if they refuse to believe in Prophet Muhammad (peace be upon him) and in the Qur'aan (see preceding Note 100). This Verse applies also to the nominal Muslims of today, who do not follow Qur'aanic teachings.

أُولَـٰئِكَ جَزَآؤُهُمْ أَنَّ عَلَيْهِمْ لَعْنَةَ اللَّهِ وَالْمَلَـٰئِكَةِ وَالنَّاسِ أَجْمَعِينَ ﴿٨٧﴾

87. Ol<u>a</u>-ika jaz<u>a</u>ohum anna AAalayhim laAAnata All<u>a</u>hi waalmal<u>a</u>-ikati waalnn<u>a</u>si ajmaAAeena

---

3:87. Reward for such people[102] is that upon them is the curse of Allah, of the angels and of all mankind.

---

102. That is, those described in the preceding Verse 86. The torment, such people would suffer, is continued to be described in the next Verse 88.

خَـٰلِدِينَ فِيهَا لَا يُخَفَّفُ عَنْهُمُ ٱلْعَذَابُ وَلَا هُمْ يُنظَرُونَ ﴿٨٨﴾

88. Khalideena feeha la yukhaffafu AAanhumu alAAathabu wala hum yuntharoona

3:88. Dwellers therein[103] forever! Neither will their punishment be lightened, nor will they be given respite.

103. That is, the Hell wherein the cursed people (see Verse 87 above) are bound to land.

إِلَّا ٱلَّذِينَ تَابُوا۟ مِنۢ بَعْدِ ذَٰلِكَ وَأَصْلَحُوا۟ فَإِنَّ ٱللَّهَ غَفُورٌ رَّحِيمٌ ﴿٨٩﴾

89. Illa allatheena taboo min baAAdi thalika waaslahoo fa-inna Allaha ghafoorun raheemun

3:89. Except for those who do penitence thereafter and mend their ways. Then indeed Allah is Forgiving, Merciful.[104]

104. Allah gives every human being a long rope literally till he/she approaches death. So, for the persons covered by Verse 86 above, all is not lost. Allah may spare them from the terrible torment of Hell-fire, if they repent and mend their ways before death approaches them. But they should beware of the divine warning given to them in Verses 90 & 91 below.

إِنَّ ٱلَّذِينَ كَفَرُوا۟ بَعْدَ إِيمَـٰنِهِمْ ثُمَّ ٱزْدَادُوا۟ كُفْرًا لَّن تُقْبَلَ تَوْبَتُهُمْ وَأُو۟لَـٰٓئِكَ هُمُ ٱلضَّآلُّونَ ﴿٩٠﴾

90. Inna allatheena kafaroo baAAda eemanihim thumma izdadoo kufran lan tuqbala tawbatuhum waola-ika humu alddalloona

3:90. Those indeed who suppress the Truth after their acceptance of Faith, and then go on adding to the suppression, their penitence will not be accepted. And those are the ones who go astray.

إِنَّ ٱلَّذِينَ كَفَرُواْ وَمَاتُواْ وَهُمْ كُفَّارٌ فَلَن يُقْبَلَ مِنْ أَحَدِهِم مِّلْءُ ٱلْأَرْضِ ذَهَبًا وَلَوِ ٱفْتَدَىٰ بِهِۦٓ أُوْلَـٰٓئِكَ لَهُمْ عَذَابٌ أَلِيمٌ وَمَا لَهُم مِّن نَّـٰصِرِينَ ۝

91. Inna allatheena kafaroo wamatoo wahum kuffarun falan yuqbala min ahadihim milo al-ardi thahaban walawi iftada bihi ola-ika lahum AAathabun aleemun wama lahum min nasireena

3:91. Those indeed who suppress the Truth and die while suppressing the Truth – from none of those shall be accepted even earth full of gold if offered as ransom. Those are the ones for whom shall there be a painful punishment, and for whom shall there be no helpers.

لَن تَنَالُواْ ٱلْبِرَّ حَتَّىٰ تُنفِقُواْ مِمَّا تُحِبُّونَ وَمَا تُنفِقُواْ مِن شَىْءٍ فَإِنَّ ٱللَّهَ بِهِۦ عَلِيمٌ ۝

92. Lan tanaloo albirra hatta tunfiqoo mimma tuhibboona wama tunfiqoo min shay-in fa-inna Allaha bihi AAaleemun

3:92. Never shall you attain to righteousness unless you spend from what you love. And Allah is indeed aware of anything you spend.[105 to 107]

105. Man loves wealth. He thinks it could bring him comfort in this worldly life. His thoughts do not go beyond, to the life in the Hereafter. But Islam teaches him that this worldly life is temporary and only a

test; it is the everlasting life in the Hereafter that really matters. And the Verse 92 here tells us that unless we overcome our love of wealth by spending from it, we cannot be righteous enough to deserve comfortable lives in the Hereafter.

106. We can of course incur <u>necessary</u> expenses, from our own wealth, on our own selves. But we cannot <u>waste the wealth on our own selves beyond our genuine needs</u>. Allah would be aware of it, when we do it. And <u>Verse 2:215</u> tells us on whose genuine needs to spend our wealth that is more than our own individual needs.

107. Man loves other things also, besides wealth. He loves his spouse and children, for example. Verse 92 here could be extended in its implications to cover these other objects of love too. Our love for our own children, for instance, should not come in our way of standing firmly for justice in any matter involving them.

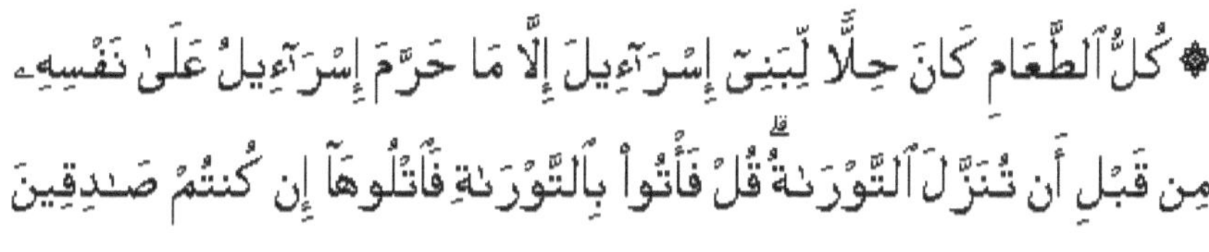

93. Kullu alttaAAami kana hillan libanee isra-eela illa ma harrama isra-eelu AAala nafsihi min qabli an tunazzala alttawratu qul fa/too bialttawrati faotlooha in kuntum sadiqeena

3:93. All food was lawful to the Children of Israel, except what Israel made unlawful for himself, before the Torah was revealed. Say, "Bring the Torah and recite it, if you are truthful."[108]

108. Even though, on the authority of this Verse, all wholesome food was lawful for the Children of Israel, Verse 6:146 informs us that certain food items were made unlawful to them <u>only</u> as punishment for their rebellious behaviour. And from <u>Verse 3:50</u>, we learn that Prophet Jesus (peace be upon him) was sent to them, inter alia, to make some of these forbidden items lawful again. But since they had rejected Jesus, they had not implemented the lifting of the ban on those items. Apparently, the thrust of this Verse 3:93 here is to tell the Jews present at the time of the revelation of the Qur'aan that they need not raise their eyebrows at the Qur'aan making lawful food items forbidden in the Torah.

$$\text{فَمَنِ افْتَرَىٰ عَلَى اللَّهِ الْكَذِبَ مِنْ بَعْدِ ذَٰلِكَ}$$
$$\text{فَأُولَٰئِكَ هُمُ الظَّالِمُونَ ۝}$$

94. Famani iftara AAala Allahi alkathiba min baAAdi thalika faola-ika humu althalimoona

---

3:94. So then, after that, people, such as one who concocts the lie upon Allah, are indeed the wrong-doers.[109]

---

109. In the context of the preceding Verse 93, it is apparent that the Jews, at the time of the revelation of the Qur'aan, were taunting the believers that the latter had made lawful the food items that Allah Himself had forbidden in the Torah. To nail that lie, the Jews were, as noted in the preceding Verse 93, asked to bring the Torah and read from it. It must have then been clear to all concerned that the forbidding of the food items in the Torah was only by way of a punishment to the Jews, for their intransigence. It wasn't a general forbiddance. Please go through the preceding Note 108 also in this connection. Those who insisted on the lie that the forbiddance in the Torah was a general divine forbiddance, even after the matter was thus clarified, were indeed insisting on their intransigence.

$$\text{قُلْ صَدَقَ اللَّهُ فَاتَّبِعُوا مِلَّةَ إِبْرَاهِيمَ حَنِيفًا وَمَا}$$
$$\text{كَانَ مِنَ الْمُشْرِكِينَ ۝}$$

95. Qul sadaqa Allahu faittabiAAoo millata ibraheema haneefan wama kana mina almushrikeena

---

3:95. Say, "Allah has told the Truth. Devoutly follow Abraham's creed then! He was not of the polytheists."[110]

---

110. In the immediate context of the preceding two Verses, 93 and 94, the truth that is referred to here in this Verse 95 as having been told by Allah is the truth about the food items forbidden to the Jews in the Torah. The forbiddance was specifically for the Jews by way of a punishment to them, and therefore not continued in the Qur'aan. The Jews are being told here to accept this truth from their Lord, and to

follow their forefather Abraham's creed devoutly. And Abraham's creed was to submit to the Lord of the Worlds. (Refer Verse 2:131 and go through study note 194 of these Studies thereunder.)

إِنَّ أَوَّلَ بَيْتٍ وُضِعَ لِلنَّاسِ لَلَّذِى بِبَكَّةَ مُبَارَكًا وَهُدًى لِّلْعَٰلَمِينَ ﴿٩٦﴾

96. Inna awwala baytin wudiAAa lilnnasi lallathee bibakkata mubarakan wahudan lilAAalameena

---

3:96. Indeed, the first House built for mankind is at Bakkah, the blessed place that has provided guidance for all the worlds.[111]

---

111. From the next Verse 97, it is apparent that the name Bakkah used here is to denote the same city we now know as Makkah. In Verse 48:24, however, Valley of Makkah is as such mentioned. This indicates that at the time of revelation of the Qur'aan, the city was known as Bakkah, while the valley in which the city is located was known as Makkah. At the same time, it may be noted that 'ba' and 'ma' are phonetically akin. This Verse also reveals that the House (Kaabah) was the first one to be built at that place. And as we all know, from this blessed place emanated the perfected religion of Islam to provide guidance for all the worlds. And about the Qur'aanic meaning of 'worlds', please refer study note 1:5 of these Studies.

فِيهِ ءَايَٰتٌۢ بَيِّنَٰتٌ مَّقَامُ إِبْرَٰهِيمَ وَمَن دَخَلَهُۥ كَانَ ءَامِنًا وَلِلَّهِ عَلَى ٱلنَّاسِ

حِجُّ ٱلْبَيْتِ مَنِ ٱسْتَطَاعَ إِلَيْهِ سَبِيلًا وَمَن كَفَرَ فَإِنَّ ٱللَّهَ غَنِىٌّ عَنِ ٱلْعَٰلَمِينَ

97. Feehi ayatun bayyinatun maqamu ibraheema waman dakhalahu kana aminan walillahi AAala alnnasi hijju albayti mani istataAAa ilayhi sabeelan waman kafara fa-inna Allaha ghaniyyun AAani alAAalameena

---

3:97. Among clear Signs therein[112] is *Maqam Ibrahim*[113]. And whoever enters it, becomes safe.[114] And for Allah is the annual Pilgrimage to the House ordained upon mankind – upon any who can afford the journey to it.[115] And as for one who suppresses the Truth, Allah is self-sufficient and stands in no need of the worlds.[116]

---

112. That is, in Bakkah referred to in the preceding Verse 96.

113. This is a stone bearing human footprints. On the authority of this Qur'aanic Verse, the footprints are those of Prophet Abraham (peace upon him). The stone was reportedly used by Abraham to build the upper portions of the walls of the Kaabah. The repeated use thus of the stone might have left impressions of his feet thereon. The preservation of the footprints is a clear sign from Allah. The stone is now kept in an enclosure in front of the Kaabah on the left side of its door.

114. The city of Makkah (Bakkah) is a no-war zone in terms of Verse 2:191.

115. The pilgrimage to Makkah is a conditional obligation. The condition is that the pilgrim can afford it – financially, physically or even otherwise. It may so happen that in a year, a person may be both physically and financially able to perform the Pilgrimage, but he may be prevented from undertaking the journey because of some other compelling business or personal circumstance. But this last reason ought not to be made an excuse for evading the Pilgrimage, year after year, particularly if the person has not gone for the pilgrimage even once.

116. A suppressor of the Truth would deny that performing the Hajj is a divinely laid down duty. And so he does not perform it. Allah Ta'ala makes it clear here to such a person that He is not in need of any pilgrimage. The non-performance of the duty will only make the human defaulter liable to punishment for disobeying his Creator.

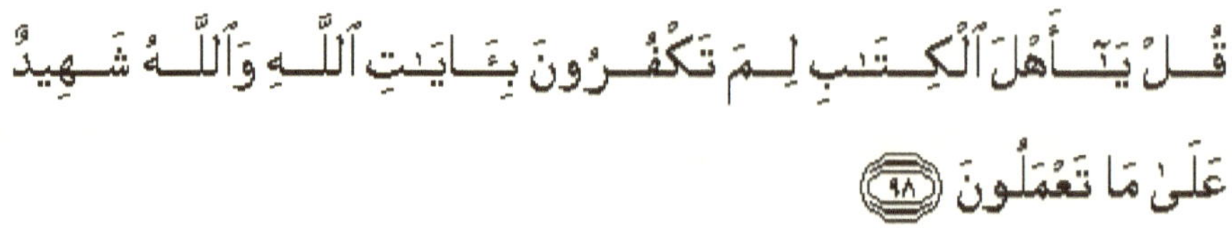

98. Qul ya ahla alkitabi lima takfuroona bi-ayati Allahi waAllahu shaheedun AAala ma taAAmaloona

---

3:98. Say, "O People of the Book! Why do you suppress Allah's signs/Verses, when Allah is Himself witness to all you do?"[117]

---

117. As we have already seen, Allah informs us in Verse 2:146 that the Jews and the Christians recognise Prophet Muhammad (peace be upon him) as they recognise their sons. That is obviously because their

own Scriptures contain the prophecy of the Prophet's coming to this world at a future time. Peruse study note 3:84 under Verse 3:70 also, in this context.

قُلْ يَـٰٓأَهْلَ ٱلْكِتَـٰبِ لِمَ تَصُدُّونَ عَن سَبِيلِ ٱللَّهِ مَنْ ءَامَنَ تَبْغُونَهَا عِوَجًا وَأَنتُمْ شُهَدَآءُ وَمَا ٱللَّهُ بِغَـٰفِلٍ عَمَّا تَعْمَلُونَ ۝

99. Qul ya ahla alkitabi lima tasuddoona AAan sabeeli Allahi man amana tabghoonaha AAiwajan waantum shuhadao wama Allahu bighafilin AAamma taAAmaloona

3:99. Say, "O People of the Book! Why do you obstruct a believer from the path of Allah, seeking crookedness in that path, while you are yourselves witnesses[118]? And Allah is not unaware of all that you do."

118. The Jews and Christians are themselves witnesses – on the authority and basis of the evidences in their own scriptures – to the fact that Allah's path, as shown in the Qur'aan, is the right path. Allah is aware of their suppression thus of the Truth. The wanton suppression may land them into irretrievable torment.

يَـٰٓأَيُّهَا ٱلَّذِينَ ءَامَنُوٓاْ إِن تُطِيعُواْ فَرِيقًا مِّنَ ٱلَّذِينَ أُوتُواْ ٱلْكِتَـٰبَ يَرُدُّوكُم بَعْدَ إِيمَـٰنِكُمْ كَـٰفِرِينَ ۝

100. Ya ayyuha allatheena amanoo in tuteeAAoo fareeqan mina allatheena ootoo alkitaba yaruddookum baAAda eemanikum kafireena

3:100. O you who believe! If you follow any faction of those upon whom the divine Book was bestowed earlier, they will turn you back to suppressing the Truth after you have come to believe!

وَكَيْفَ تَكْفُرُونَ وَأَنتُمْ تُتْلَىٰ عَلَيْكُمْ ءَايَـٰتُ ٱللَّـهِ وَفِيكُمْ رَسُولُهُۥ وَمَن يَعْتَصِم بِٱللَّهِ فَقَدْ هُدِىَ إِلَىٰ صِرَٰطٍ مُّسْتَقِيمٍ ۝

101. Wakayfa takfuroona waantum tutla AAalaykum ayatu Allahi wafeekum rasooluhu waman yaAAatasim biAllahi faqad hudiya ila siratin mustaqeemin

3:101. And how could you suppress the Truth while Allah's Verses are being recited to you, and His Messenger is amongst you? And whoever clings firmly to Allah, he/she is indeed guided to the Straight Path.[119]

119. Although Allah's Messenger is not with us now, His divinely protected and perfected Verses are with us. By meticulously adhering to the divine instructions contained in those Verses, we would be clinging firmly to Allah and thus be guided to the Straight Path.

يَـٰٓأَيُّهَا ٱلَّذِينَ ءَامَنُوا۟ ٱتَّقُوا۟ ٱللَّهَ حَقَّ تُقَاتِهِۦ وَلَا تَمُوتُنَّ إِلَّا وَأَنتُم مُّسْلِمُونَ

102. Ya ayyuha allatheena amanoo ittaqoo Allaha haqqa tuqatihi wala tamootunna illa waantum muslimoona

3:102. O you who believe! Fear Allah as He should be feared and die not but as those who have surrendered themselves completely to Allah.[120]

120. Death may come without any warning signals. Man should therefore never postpone surrendering himself to any future date. That future date may never come in his life.

وَٱعۡتَصِمُواْ بِحَبۡلِ ٱللَّهِ جَمِيعٗا وَلَا تَفَرَّقُواْۚ وَٱذۡكُرُواْ نِعۡمَتَ ٱللَّهِ عَلَيۡكُمۡ إِذۡ
كُنتُمۡ أَعۡدَآءٗ فَأَلَّفَ بَيۡنَ قُلُوبِكُمۡ فَأَصۡبَحۡتُم بِنِعۡمَتِهِۦٓ إِخۡوَٰنٗا وَكُنتُمۡ عَلَىٰ
شَفَا حُفۡرَةٖ مِّنَ ٱلنَّارِ فَأَنقَذَكُم مِّنۡهَاۗ كَذَٰلِكَ يُبَيِّنُ ٱللَّهُ لَكُمۡ ءَايَٰتِهِۦ لَعَلَّكُمۡ
تَهۡتَدُونَ ١٠٣

103. WaiAAtasimoo bihabli Allahi jameeAAan wala tafarraqoo waothkuroo niAAmata Allahi AAalaykum ith kuntum aAAdaan faallafa bayna quloobikum faasbahtum biniAAmatihi ikhwanan wakuntum AAala shafa hufratin mina alnnari faanqathakum minha kathalika yubayyinu Allahu lakum ayatihi laAAallakum tahtadoona

---

3:103. And cling together, all of you, to Allah's Rope[121], and stand not divided! And remember Allah's favour on you when you were enemies and He brought your hearts together, so that, by His Grace, you became brethren. And you were on the brink of the pit of Fire, and He rescued you from it.[122] Thus does Allah make His Signs/Verses clear to you that you may be guided.

---

121. 'Allah's Rope' is a beautiful metaphor for the Qur'aan! Mankind is, so to say, in the pit of this world, struggling for moral survival against its trials and tribulations. Only those who cling to this Rope of Hope sent down by the Lord could be saved from this pit. Only those are saved, in other words, who adhere meticulously to the instructions given in the Qur'aan.

122. What is depicted here is the state in the Arab society, just before Allah's Messenger (peace upon him) came to them with His Message.

وَلۡتَكُن مِّنكُمۡ أُمَّةٞ يَدۡعُونَ إِلَى ٱلۡخَيۡرِ وَيَأۡمُرُونَ بِٱلۡمَعۡرُوفِ وَيَنۡهَوۡنَ عَنِ
ٱلۡمُنكَرِۚ وَأُوْلَٰٓئِكَ هُمُ ٱلۡمُفۡلِحُونَ ١٠٤

104. Waltakun minkum ommatun yadAAoona ila alkhayri waya/muroona bialmaAAroofi wayanhawna AAani almunkari waola-ika humu almuflihoona

---

3:104. And there ought to come into being a community out of you, calling people to the good, enjoining what is right, and forbidding what is wrong. And they are the ones to attain salvation.[123]

---

123. There is a misconception, among the believers, about this Verse. They think that Allah wants a group of the believers – and not all of them – should devote themselves to the work entrusted here in this Verse. We should take note of what the last part of the Verse says. It says that only those who do the work entrusted shall attain to salvation. That means that those believers who do not do the work shall not attain salvation! Moreover, what is mentioned here is a community, and not just a group of that community. So, the logical understanding of this Verse is that Allah desires that the entire body of the believers should evolve into a community that does this work divinely entrusted here to them.

وَلَا تَكُونُوا كَالَّذِينَ تَفَرَّقُوا وَاخْتَلَفُوا مِنْ بَعْدِ مَا جَاءَهُمُ الْبَيِّنَاتُ وَأُولَٰئِكَ لَهُمْ عَذَابٌ عَظِيمٌ ۝

105. Wala takoonoo kaallatheena tafarraqoo waikhtalafoo min baAAdi ma jaahumu albayyinatu waola-ika lahum AAathabun AAatheemun

---

3:105. And be not like those who differ and dispute after clear signs have come to them. For them, a terrible punishment!

يَوْمَ تَبْيَضُّ وُجُوهٌ وَتَسْوَدُّ وُجُوهٌ فَأَمَّا الَّذِينَ اسْوَدَّتْ وُجُوهُهُمْ أَكَفَرْتُمْ بَعْدَ إِيمَانِكُمْ فَذُوقُوا الْعَذَابَ بِمَا كُنْتُمْ تَكْفُرُونَ ۝

106. Yawma tabyaddu wujoohun wataswaddu wujoohun faamma allatheena iswaddat wujoohuhum akafartum baAAda eemanikum fathooqoo alAAathaba bima kuntum takfuroona

---

3:106. That Day[124] some faces will brighten, and some faces will darken. Then those with darkened faces will be told, "Did you suppress the Truth after you had come to know the Truth!? Taste then the punishment since you suppressed the Truth!"

124. I.e., the Day of Judgement or the Day of Resurrection.

107. Waamma allatheena ibyaddat wujoohuhum fafee rahmati Allahi hum feeha khalidoona

3:107. And those with brightened faces will be under Allah's mercy and grace. They will dwell therein for ever.

108. Tilka ayatu Allahi natlooha AAalayka bialhaqqi wama Allahu yureedu *thu*lman lilAAalameena

3:108. Those are Allah's Verses/signs. We recite them over to you in Truth. And Allah means no oppression or injustice to the worlds[125].

125. For a comprehensive Qur'aanic meaning of the Arabic word *alAAalameen*, please see <u>study note 1:5</u> of these Studies.

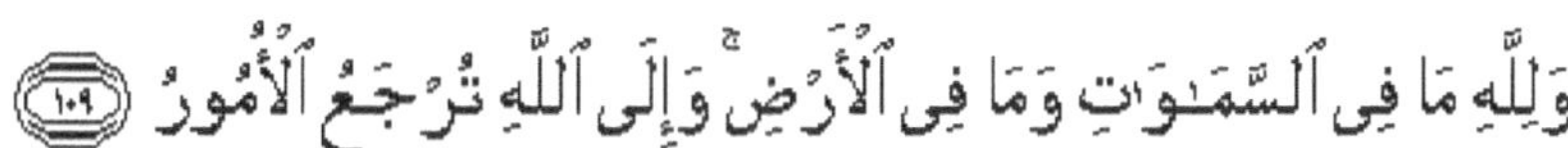

109. Walillahi ma fee alssamawati wama fee al-ardi wa-ila Allahi turjaAAu al-omooru

3:109. And to Allah belongs all that is in the heavens and in the earth. And to Allah, the matters return.[126]

126. Here's a crucial point of difference between an atheist and a believer believing in an Entity consciously creating and sustaining the entire Universe. For an atheist, this worldly life is the 'be-all' and 'end-all' of all things. To him, a man is just a superior type of animal. Nothing more. Like all other animals, he is born, he lives for an uncertain number of years, and he dies. During his span of life in this competitive world, if he uses his intelligence shrewdly in out-manoeuvring others in the games of life, he can enjoy the fruits, although temporary, thereof. Otherwise, his life would be miserable. For him, there is none to sit in judgement on the propriety or impropriety of his actions. For a believer in Allah, on the other hand, death is not the 'end-all'. Life for him here is only a test. The matters he is involved in are referred to his Creator for final adjudication. Along with the matters, he too is returned to the Creator, after death, for facing His judgement on his performance in this life. He is accountable to Allah for all his acts of omission and commission.

كُنتُمْ خَيْرَ أُمَّةٍ أُخْرِجَتْ لِلنَّاسِ تَأْمُرُونَ بِالْمَعْرُوفِ وَتَنْهَوْنَ عَنِ الْمُنكَرِ وَتُؤْمِنُونَ بِاللَّهِ ۗ وَلَوْ ءَامَنَ أَهْلُ الْكِتَبِ لَكَانَ خَيْرًا لَّهُم ۚ مِّنْهُمُ الْمُؤْمِنُونَ وَأَكْثَرُهُمُ الْفَسِقُونَ ﴿١١٠﴾

110. Kuntum khayra ommatin okhrijat lilnnasi ta/muroona bialmaAAroofi watanhawna AAani almunkari watu/minoona biAllahi walaw amana ahlu alkitabi lakana khayran lahum minhumu almu/minoona waaktharuhumu alfasiqoona

3:110. You are a better people, picked up for mankind, to enjoin what is right and to forbid what is wrong, and to believe in Allah.[127] And had the People of the Book believed, it would certainly be better for them. Among them are some who believe, but most of them are dissolute.[128]

127. This is a divine confirmation that the task of propagating Islam, the Allah-chosen and Allah-perfected Religion for mankind, has been entrusted to the followers of the Qur'aan, after the death of Prophet Muhammad (peace be upon him).

128. Although at the time of the revelation of the Qur'aan, the epithet 'people of the Book' was applied to the Jews and the Christians it is applicable now to the Muslims as well. They (the Muslims) too are given a divine Book, and among them too there are some who do believe, but most have gone astray.

لَن يَضُرُّوكُمْ إِلَّا أَذًى ۖ وَإِن يُقَـٰتِلُوكُمْ يُوَلُّوكُمُ ٱلْأَدْبَارَ ثُمَّ لَا يُنصَرُونَ ﴿١١١﴾

111. Lan yadurrookum illa athan wa-in yuqatilookum yuwallookumu al-adbara thumma la yunsaroona

3:111. They will cause you no harm, but a trifle. And if they come out to fight you, they will turn their backs to you. Then, no help shall they get.[129]

129. At the time of its revelation, the people referred to in this Verse as 'they' were the Jews and the Christians, in the light of the preceding Verse 110. But in our own context today, the 'people of the Book', as already noted in the preceding study note 128, would include Muslims too, who have strayed away from the pure Qur'aanic teachings.

ضُرِبَتْ عَلَيْهِمُ ٱلذِّلَّةُ أَيْنَ مَا ثُقِفُوٓا۟ إِلَّا بِحَبْلٍ مِّنَ ٱللَّهِ وَحَبْلٍ مِّنَ ٱلنَّاسِ وَبَآءُو بِغَضَبٍ مِّنَ ٱللَّهِ وَضُرِبَتْ عَلَيْهِمُ ٱلْمَسْكَنَةُ ذَٰلِكَ بِأَنَّهُمْ كَانُوا۟ يَكْفُرُونَ بِـَٔايَـٰتِ ٱللَّهِ وَيَقْتُلُونَ ٱلْأَنۢبِيَآءَ بِغَيْرِ حَقٍّ ذَٰلِكَ بِمَا عَصَوا۟ وَّكَانُوا۟ يَعْتَدُونَ ﴿١١٢﴾

112. Duribat AAalayhimu alththillatu ayna ma thuqifoo illa bihablin mina Allahi wahablin mina alnnasi wabaoo bighadabin mina Allahi waduribat AAalayhimu almaskanatu thalika bi-annahum kanoo yakfuroona bi-ayati Allahi wayaqtuloona al-anbiyaa bighayri haqqin thalika bima AAasaw wakanoo yaAAtadoona

3:112. Disgraced they are – bereft of rope (help) from Allah and from mankind, wherever they be found, they incurred wrath from Allah – and afflicted with poverty. That is because they wantonly ignored Allah's signs/Verses and killed the prophets unjustly. That is because they disobeyed and were transgressors.[130]

---

130. Obviously again, this Verse was revealed with reference to the Jews and the Christians living at the time of the revelation of the Qur'aan. The reference to the killing of the Prophets particularly pertained to them. But, as stated in the foregoing study notes 128 and 129 herein above, 'people of the Book' could apply to Muslims also now. And except for the killings of the Prophets, the rest of the Verse appears to be divinely applied now to Muslims, rather than to the Jews and the Christians. It is applied now to the Muslims by way of a divine warning to them. That is because, unlike the Jews and the Christians, Muslims may still be, in the eyes of Allah, amenable to leaning back to the right path as shown in the Qur'aan. The Jews and the Christians are now generally beyond guidance and warnings as communities. Allah Ta'ala has stoppped giving them the warning signals. Please also keep in mind the next two Verses 113 & 114, in this context.

۞ لَيْسُواْ سَوَآءً مِّنْ أَهْلِ ٱلْكِتَـٰبِ أُمَّةٌ قَآئِمَةٌ يَتْلُونَ ءَايَـٰتِ ٱللَّهِ ءَانَآءَ ٱلَّيْلِ وَهُمْ يَسْجُدُونَ ﴿١١٣﴾

113. Laysoo sawaan min ahli alkitabi ommatun qa-imatun yatloona ayati Allahi anaa allayli wahum yasjudoona

---

3:113. Not all of them are alike. Of the People of the Book there are some that stand for the right. They recite Allah's Verses during the night time, and they prostrate themselves.

يُؤْمِنُونَ بِٱللَّهِ وَٱلْيَوْمِ ٱلْأَخِرِ وَيَأْمُرُونَ بِٱلْمَعْرُوفِ وَيَنْهَوْنَ عَنِ ٱلْمُنكَرِ وَيُسَـٰرِعُونَ فِى ٱلْخَيْرَٰتِ وَأُوْلَـٰٓئِكَ مِنَ ٱلصَّـٰلِحِينَ ﴿١١٤﴾

114. Yu/minoona biAllahi waalyawmi al-akhiri waya/muroona bialmaAAroofi wayanhawna AAani almunkari wayusariAAoona fee alkhayrati waola-ika mina alssaliheena

3:114. They believe in Allah and in the Last Day. And they enjoin what is right and forbid what is wrong. And they hasten to do good work. They are among the righteous.

$$\text{وَمَا يَفْعَلُواْ مِنْ خَيْرٍ فَلَن يُكْفَرُوهُ وَٱللَّهُ عَلِيمٌ بِٱلْمُتَّقِينَ}$$

115. Wama yafAAaloo min khayrin falan yukfaroohu waAllahu AAaleemun bialmuttaqeena

3:115. And whatever good they do, nothing will be suppressed there from.[131] And Allah knows those who fear Him.

131. There is a general apprehension, in the minds of those who do not have a strong belief in Allah, that the good one does is not adequately appreciated and, therefore, wasted. They are thus inclined to give as much publicity as possible to their good deeds, whereby they hope to get good names and other benefits for themselves. Had their belief in Allah been strong enough, they wouldn't hanker after such mundane benefits. They would be sure that Allah, their Lord, wouldn't let their good deeds go waste.

$$\text{إِنَّ ٱلَّذِينَ كَفَرُواْ لَن تُغْنِيَ عَنْهُمْ أَمْوَٰلُهُمْ وَلَآ أَوْلَـٰدُهُم مِّنَ ٱللَّهِ شَيْـًٔا وَأُوْلَـٰٓئِكَ أَصْحَـٰبُ ٱلنَّارِ هُمْ فِيهَا خَـٰلِدُونَ}$$

116. Inna allatheena kafaroo lan tughniya AAanhum amwaluhum wala awladuhum mina Allahi shay-an waola-ika as-habu alnnari hum feeha khalidoona

3:116. Those indeed who suppress the Truth! Neither their wealth nor their progeny will be of any use to them against Allah. Those would be inhabitants of the Fire, dwelling therein for ever.

مَثَلُ مَا يُنفِقُونَ فِى هَـٰذِهِ ٱلْحَيَوٰةِ ٱلدُّنْيَا كَمَثَلِ رِيحٍ فِيهَا صِرٌّ أَصَابَتْ حَرْثَ قَوْمٍ ظَلَمُوٓاْ أَنفُسَهُمْ فَأَهْلَكَتْهُ وَمَا ظَلَمَهُمُ ٱللَّهُ وَلَـٰكِنْ أَنفُسَهُمْ يَظْلِمُونَ ۝١١٧

117. Mathalu ma yunfiqoona fee hathihi alhayati alddunya kamathali reehin feeha sirrun asabat hartha qawmin thalamoo anfusahum faahlakat-hu wama thalamahumu Allahu walakin anfusahum yathlimoona

3:117. What they spend in the life of this world is like a bitingly cold wind. It strikes the field of those people who wrong their own selves and destroys it. And Allah does not wrong them, but they wrong themselves.[132]

132. In the divine scheme of things, human life in this world is like a field. The farmer toils hard in his field in order to get a good crop. Similarly, every human being is fashioned to toil hard in the temporary life of this world to get a good crop for the permanent life in the Hereafter. And to get a good crop, the human being is required to spend his/her time and money in certain divinely laid down ways. Suppressors of the Truth suppress their consciences urging them to spend in those ways. And they spend in other ways. And those spendings in other ways generate that bitingly cold wind destined to destroy the crop that could give them a good life in the Hereafter. They thus themselves destroy their own future.

يَـٰٓأَيُّهَا ٱلَّذِينَ ءَامَنُواْ لَا تَتَّخِذُواْ بِطَانَةً مِّن دُونِكُمْ لَا يَأْلُونَكُمْ خَبَالًا وَدُّواْ مَا عَنِتُّمْ قَدْ بَدَتِ ٱلْبَغْضَآءُ مِنْ أَفْوَٰهِهِمْ وَمَا تُخْفِى صُدُورُهُمْ أَكْبَرُ قَدْ بَيَّنَّا لَكُمُ ٱلْءَايَـٰتِ إِن كُنتُمْ تَعْقِلُونَ ۝١١٨

118. Ya ayyuha allatheena amanoo la tattakhithoo bitanatan min doonikum la ya/loonakum khabalan waddoo ma AAanittum qad badati albaghdao min afwahihim wama tukhfee sudooruhum akbaru qad bayyanna lakumu al-ayati in kuntum taAAqiloona

3:118. O you who believe! Develop no intimacy with those outside your circle who leave no stone unturned to ruin you, loving to see you suffer. Hatred spews from their mouths, and what their hearts conceal is far worse. We have certainly made the Signs/Verses clear to you if you could but understand.[133]

133. This Verse, along with the next two Verses 119 and 120, clearly spells out the description of the people who should be shunned. In Verses 60:8 and 60:9, the Qur'aan makes it further clear that Allah does not forbid the believers to deal justly and kindly with those who had not fought against them because of their religion and had not driven them out of their houses.

هَـٰٓأَنتُمْ أُوْلَآءِ تُحِبُّونَهُمْ وَلَا يُحِبُّونَكُمْ وَتُؤْمِنُونَ بِٱلْكِتَٰبِ كُلِّهِۦ وَإِذَا لَقُوكُمْ قَالُوٓاْ ءَامَنَّا وَإِذَا خَلَوْاْ عَضُّواْ عَلَيْكُمُ ٱلْأَنَامِلَ مِنَ ٱلْغَيْظِ قُلْ مُوتُواْ بِغَيْظِكُمْ إِنَّ ٱللَّهَ عَلِيمٌ بِذَاتِ ٱلصُّدُورِ ﴿١١٩﴾

119. Ha antum ola-i tuhibboonahum wala yuhibboonakum watu/minoona bialkitabi kullihi wa-itha laqookum qaloo amanna wa-itha khalaw AAaddoo AAalaykumu al-anamila mina alghaythi qul mootoo bighaythikum inna Allaha AAaleemun bithati alssudoori

3:119. Behold! You are the ones who love them, but they love you not. And you do believe in every Book of His[134]! And when they meet you, they say, "We believe." And when they are alone, they bite their fingers, in their rage against you. Say, "Die in your rage. Allah does indeed know secrets of the minds[135]."

134. The believers are required to believe, not only in the Qur'aan, but also in all the Books bestowed by Allah upon earlier peoples. [Verse 2:4]

135. Please refer study note 2:117, on Verse 2:88, in this regard. In that Verse the Arabic word used was *quloob*, and in this Verse it is *sudoor*. *Sadar*, the singular form of *sudoor*, is generally translated as heart, but it also means head. And the head (governing) part of the human body is literally called the 'head', which contains the mind. And hence the translation of *sudoor* here is given as 'minds'.

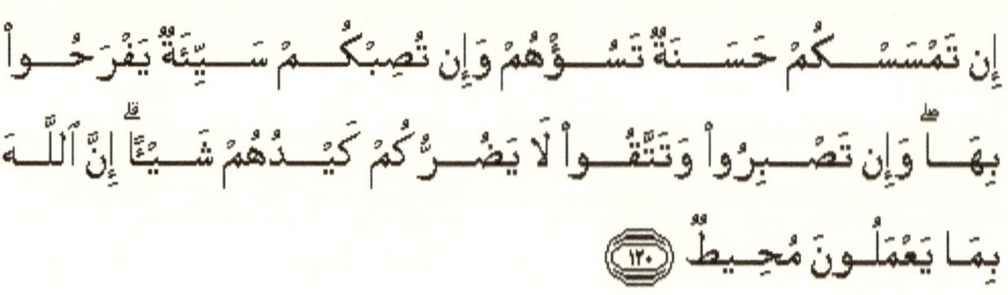

120. In tamsaskum ḥasanatun tasu/hum wa-in tuṣibkum sayyi-atun yafraḥoo biḥa wa-in taṣbiroo watattaqoo la yaḍurrukum kayduhum shay-an inna Allaha bima yaAAmaloona muḥeetun

3:120. If anything, good happens to you, it grieves them. And if anything, bad befalls you, they rejoice at it. And if you exercise patience and piety, their guile shall cause you no harm.[136] Indeed! Allah has, within His Sight, everything they do.

136. If only, the Muslims of today had unshakable belief in this!!

121. Wa-ith ghadawta min ahlika tubawwi-o almu/mineena maqaAAida lilqitali waAllahu sameeAAun AAaleemun

3:121. And when you left early from your family to set the believers in battle order.[137] And Allah hears all and He knows all.

137. This Verse and the Verses that follow, refer to a battle. And from Verse 123 below, it is clear, that this battle had taken place after the battle of Badr. This battle, details of which are given in Verses 121 to 128 and further in Verses 140 to 174 of this Chapter, is historically known as the battle of Uhud.

$$إِذْ هَمَّت طَّآئِفَتَانِ مِنكُمْ أَن تَفْشَلَا وَٱللَّهُ وَلِيُّهُمَا ۗ وَعَلَى ٱللَّهِ فَلْيَتَوَكَّلِ ٱلْمُؤْمِنُونَ ﴿١٢٢﴾$$

122. I<u>th</u> hammat <u>ta</u>-ifat<u>a</u>ni minkum an tafshal<u>a</u> wa<u>A</u>ll<u>a</u>hu waliyyuhum<u>a</u> wa<u>AAala</u> All<u>a</u>hi falyatawakkali almu/minoon<u>a</u>

3:122. When two groups from amongst you were about to lose heart! And Allah was their Guide and Patron. And upon Allah then the believers ought to put their trust.

$$وَلَقَدْ نَصَرَكُمُ ٱللَّهُ بِبَدْرٍ وَأَنتُمْ أَذِلَّةٌ ۖ فَٱتَّقُوا۟ ٱللَّهَ لَعَلَّكُمْ تَشْكُرُونَ ﴿١٢٣﴾$$

123. Walaqad na<u>s</u>arakumu All<u>a</u>hu bibadrin waantum a<u>th</u>illatun faittaqoo All<u>a</u>ha la<u>AAa</u>llakum tashkuroon<u>a</u>

3:123. And Allah had helped you at Badr, when you were very weak.[138] Fear Allah then so that you show your gratitude to Him.

138. For more details on the earlier battle at Badr, please see Verses 8:5 to 8:19.

إِذْ تَقُولُ لِلْمُؤْمِنِينَ أَلَن يَكْفِيَكُمْ أَن يُمِدَّكُمْ رَبُّكُم بِثَلَاثَةِ ءَالَافٍ مِّنَ ٱلْمَلَائِكَةِ مُنزَلِينَ ﴿١٢٤﴾

124. I_th taqoolu lilmu/mineena alan yakfiyakum an yumiddakum rabbukum bithal_athati _alafin mina almal_a-ikati munzaleena

---

3:124. When you told the believers, "Is it not enough for you that Allah would help you with three thousand of the angels sent down?"

بَلَىٰ إِن تَصْبِرُواْ وَتَتَّقُواْ وَيَأْتُوكُم مِّن فَوْرِهِمْ هَـٰذَا يُمْدِدْكُمْ رَبُّكُم بِخَمْسَةِ ءَالَافٍ مِّنَ ٱلْمَلَائِكَةِ مُسَوِّمِينَ ﴿١٢٥﴾

125. Bal_a in ta_sbiroo watattaqoo waya/tookum min fawrihim h_atha yumdidkum rabbukum bikhamsati _alafin mina almal_a-ikati musawwimeena

---

3:125. "And yes, if you be patient, and fear Allah, and they mount a sudden attack on you now, your Lord would help you with five thousand of the angels facing them."

وَمَا جَعَلَهُ ٱللَّهُ إِلَّا بُشْرَىٰ لَكُمْ وَلِتَطْمَئِنَّ قُلُوبُكُم بِهِۦ وَمَا ٱلنَّصْرُ إِلَّا مِنْ عِندِ ٱللَّهِ ٱلْعَزِيزِ ٱلْحَكِيمِ ﴿١٢٦﴾

126. Wam_a jaAAalahu All_ahu ill_a bushr_a lakum walitatma-inna quloobukum bihi wam_a al_nna_sru ill_a min AAindi All_ahi alAAazeezi al_hakeem_i

---

3:126. And Allah made it[139] not but a message of good news to reassure your minds therewith. And the help came not but from Allah, the Omnipotent, the Wise.[140]

---

139. The reference is to what the Prophet (peace be upon him) said to the believers on the battlefield, as in the preceding two Verses, regarding Allah sending down angels in thousands to help them.

140. There is a subtle indication here of the fact that Allah need not <u>physically</u> send thousands of angels down to help the believers in the battlefield. Just the Will of Allah is enough. The mention of thousands of angels was just to becalm the believers, whose human minds might not comprehend divine help without imagining the physical presence of angels preventing the enemy from attacking the believers.

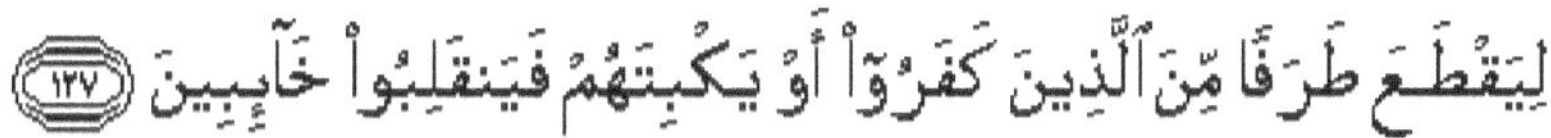

127. LiyaqtaAAa tarafan mina alla_theena_ kafaroo aw yakbitahum fayanqaliboo kh_a_-ibeena

---

3:127. [141]To cut off one side of those who suppressed the Truth or to restrain them, and they should then turn back frustrated.

---

141. This Verse is in continuation of the last part of the preceding Verse, viz., "And the help came not but from Allah, the Omnipotent, the Wise". And that was the result of that battle. Although the Muslims suffered significant casualties, they rallied around the Prophet (peace be upon him), by Allah's Grace, and fought back. The enemy retreated, and their plans to destroy the Muslims were frustrated.

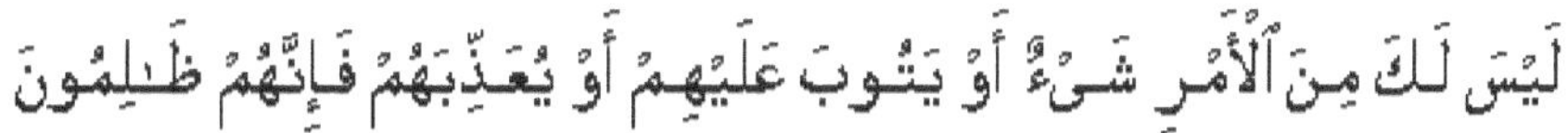

128. Laysa laka mina al-amri shay-on aw yatooba AAalayhim aw yuAAa_thth_ibahum fa-innahum _th_alimoona

3:128. It was not for you to decide whether to pardon them or punish them. But they did indeed do wrong.[142]

142. It appears that the Muslim army went in hot pursuit of the enemy, after the latter retreated from the battlefield. But they could not pursue for long. The fierce battle had taken its toll on the Muslims too. They were tired and returned to Medina after going for some distance. It was in this context that Allah tells the believers that the real decision in any matter rests with Him. In the retreating Makkan army, there were many who later became Muslims. Allah knew this beforehand and saved them for future openings of their minds to Islam.

وَلِلَّهِ مَا فِى ٱلسَّمَٰوَٰتِ وَمَا فِى ٱلْأَرْضِ يَغْفِرُ لِمَن يَشَآءُ وَيُعَذِّبُ مَن يَشَآءُ وَٱللَّهُ غَفُورٌ رَّحِيمٌ ﴿١٢٩﴾

129. Walillahi ma fee alssamawati wama fee al-ardi yaghfiru liman yashao wayuAAaththibu man yashao waAllahu ghafoorun raheemun

3:129. And to Allah belongs whatever there is in the heavens and in the earth. He forgives whom He pleases and punishes whom He pleases. And Allah is Forgiving, Merciful.

يَٰٓأَيُّهَا ٱلَّذِينَ ءَامَنُوا۟ لَا تَأْكُلُوا۟ ٱلرِّبَوٰٓا۟ أَضْعَٰفًا مُّضَٰعَفَةً وَٱتَّقُوا۟ ٱللَّهَ لَعَلَّكُمْ تُفْلِحُونَ ﴿١٣٠﴾

130. Ya ayyuha allatheena amanoo la ta/kuloo alrriba adAAafan mudaAAafatan waittaqoo Allaha laAAallakum tuflihoona

3:130. O you who believe! Consume not *Ar-Riba*[143], doubled and multiplied. And fear Allah, so that you attain salvation.

---

143. Please see study notes 2:514 to 2:516, on Verse 2:275, of these Studies for the Qur'aanic definition of this term. *Ar-Riba* got totally prohibited under Verse 2:275, and Verse 3:130, the one we are studying now, was revealed earlier in chronological order of revelation. So, at the time of revelation of Verse 3:130, *Ar-Riba* was not totally prohibited. But by this Verse, the believers were asked not to consume *Ar-Riba* at exorbitant rates. This is in line with the divine scheme of inducting prohibition of long-entrenched harmful human habits in gradual steps. Prohibition of intoxicants was also similarly done. And I recommend that the Readers review Verses 2:275 to 2:280 and all the study notes on these Verses, under these Studies, for a better understanding of what *Ar-Riba* is.

131. Waittaqoo alnnara allatee oAAiddat lilkafireena

3:131. And fear the Fire, prepared for suppressors of the Truth.

132. WaateeAAoo Allaha waalrrasoola laAAallakum turhamoona

3:132. And obey Allah and the Messenger so that Mercy is bestowed upon you.[144 to 146]

---

144. This Qur'aanic directive to obey the Messenger is grossly misunderstood. The Messenger is no longer living in this world, and there is no question of his issuing any directives now in person, which could be obeyed. The directives he had issued, while he was living, under Allah's guidance are most authentically incorporated in the Qur'aan. So when the believers obey the directives in the Qur'aan, they in effect obey both Allah and His Messenger. But most of the Muslims now say that obeying the Qur'aanic directives alone wouldn't be akin to obeying the Messenger. He (the Messenger), they insist, had issued some detailed instructions for practical implementation of the divine directives in the Qur'aan. These practical instructions, they say, are contained in the *ahaadeeth*. According to these Muslims, then, the divinely approved Religion of Islam is not complete and perfect without the *ahaadeeth*!

145. The majority contention of the present-day Muslims as above, clearly contradicts many Qur'aanic statements like those quoted below:

- "...We have missed nothing in the Book..." [Verse 6.38]
- "...It is not a concocted *hadeeth* but a confirmation of what preceded it and <u>a detailed explanation of everything</u> and a guide and a mercy for the people who believe." [Verse 12.111]

The Muslim contention in fact betrays their lack of belief in the Qur'aan.

146. It is an accepted fact that the *ahaadeeth* contain many contradictions. And in the light of the divine criterion laid down in Verse 4.82, such writings cannot be from Allah. So, by treating these non-divine writings at par with the divine Verses of the Qur'aan, the Muslims are committing the unpardonable sin of *shirk*. Nay, they are committing a sin worse than *shirk*. They are rejecting the divine Verses which say that everything is explained in the Qur'aan, and they seek the explanation instead in the error-prone, man-influenced *ahaadeeth*. They, in effect, believe in men narrating the *ahaadeeth* to the recorders, hundreds of years after the death of the Prophet. But they do not believe in Allah!! May the *GhafoorurRaheem* make them realise, before it becomes too late, that they are, by doing so, inexorably hurtling themselves into a painful doom.

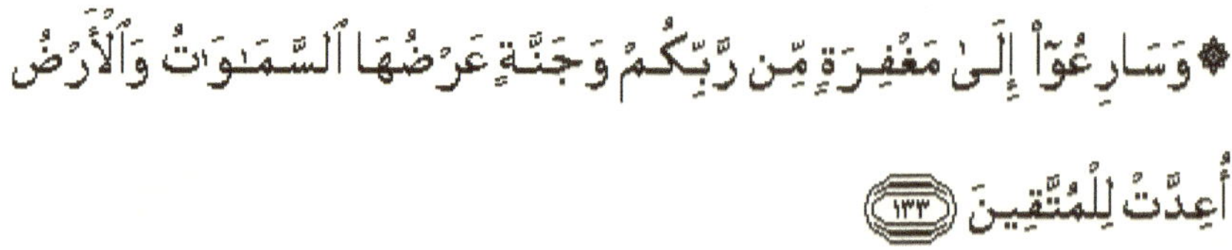

133. Was<u>a</u>riAAoo il<u>a</u> maghfiratin min rabbikum wajannatin AAard<u>u</u>h<u>a</u> alssam<u>a</u>w<u>a</u>tu waal-ar<u>d</u>u oAAiddat lilmuttaqeena

---

3:133. And strive for forgiveness from your Lord, and for a Garden, as wide as the heavens and the earth, prepared for the pious people.[147]

---

147. This ought to be the aim of every believer's life on this earth. The pious people who would get the Jannah are described in the next two Verses.

اَلَّذِينَ يُنفِقُونَ فِى ٱلسَّرَّآءِ وَٱلضَّرَّآءِ وَٱلۡكَـٰظِمِينَ ٱلۡغَيۡظَ وَٱلۡعَافِينَ عَنِ ٱلنَّاسِۗ وَٱللَّهُ يُحِبُّ ٱلۡمُحۡسِنِينَ ﴿١٣٤﴾

134. Alla_th_eena yunfiqoona fee alssarr_a_-i waal_dd_arr_a_-i waalka_th_imeena alghay_th_a waalAA_a_feena AAani alnn_a_si waAll_a_hu yu_h_ibbu almu_h_sineena

3:134. Those that spend in prosperity and in adversity, [148] those that restrain anger and those that display a forgiving attitude in their relations with people. And Allah loves those who do good deeds.

148. People tend to be miserly even when they have more than enough for their own needs. Allah loves those who eschew this human tendency. And as for those who find themselves in adverse circumstances, monetary or otherwise, wealth is not the only thing that can be spent. Allah may have bestowed upon them time and knowledge, for example, which they could spend on others. And knowledge is a thing which doesn't get diminished by spending or sharing it with others.

وَٱلَّذِينَ إِذَا فَعَلُواْ فَـٰحِشَةً أَوۡ ظَلَمُوٓاْ أَنفُسَهُمۡ ذَكَرُواْ ٱللَّهَ فَٱسۡتَغۡفَرُواْ لِذُنُوبِهِمۡ وَمَن يَغۡفِرُ ٱلذُّنُوبَ إِلَّا ٱللَّهُ وَلَمۡ يُصِرُّواْ عَلَىٰ مَا فَعَلُواْ وَهُمۡ يَعۡلَمُونَ ﴿١٣٥﴾

135. Waalla_th_eena i_th_a faAAaloo fa_h_ishatan aw _th_alamoo anfusahum _th_akaroo All_a_ha faistaghfaroo li_th_unoobihim waman yaghfiru al_thth_unooba illa All_a_hu walam yu_s_irroo AAal_a_ m_a_ faAAaloo wahum yaAAlamoona

3:135. And those who, when they do an act of indecency or wrong their own selves, remember Allah and ask for forgiveness for their sins – and who can forgive sins except Allah? – and who do not knowingly persist in doing what they had done.

أُوْلَـٰٓئِكَ جَزَآؤُهُم مَّغْفِرَةٌ مِّن رَّبِّهِمْ وَجَنَّـٰتٌ تَجْرِى مِن تَحْتِهَا ٱلْأَنْهَـٰرُ خَـٰلِدِينَ فِيهَا وَنِعْمَ أَجْرُ ٱلْعَـٰمِلِينَ ﴿١٣٦﴾

136. Ola-ika jazaohum maghfiratun min rabbihim wajannatun tajree min tahtiha al-anharu khalideena feeha waniAAma ajru alAAamileena

3:136. Those are the people for whom the reward is forgiveness from their Lord and Gardens, with rivers flowing underneath, to dwell eternally therein. An excellent reward for those who do good work!

قَدْ خَلَتْ مِن قَبْلِكُمْ سُنَنٌ فَسِيرُوا۟ فِى ٱلْأَرْضِ فَٱنظُرُوا۟ كَيْفَ كَانَ عَـٰقِبَةُ ٱلْمُكَذِّبِينَ ﴿١٣٧﴾

137. Qad khalat min qablikum sunanun faseeroo fee al-ardi faonthuroo kayfa kana AAaqibatu almukaththibeena

3:137. There indeed had been histories of people in the past before you. Travel through the earth and see what happened to those who rejected the Truth.[149]

149. The times, preceding the revelation of the Qur'aan, were prehistoric. The revealed divine Books like the Torah and the Qur'aan are the only source of written records of those people. But there are fossilised remains in the earth, which also give the then inhabitants telltale circumstances before being destroyed because of their arrogance and corruption.

هَـٰذَا بَيَانٌ لِّلنَّاسِ وَهُدًى وَمَوْعِظَةٌ لِّلْمُتَّقِينَ ﴿١٣٨﴾

138. Hatha bayanun lilnnasi wahudan wamawAAithatun lilmuttaqeena

3:138. This is a plain, well-explained, address for mankind, and a guidance and good advice to those who fear Allah.[150]

150. Obviously, what is referred to here is the Qur'aan. But alas! Most Muslims themselves have abandoned it [refer Verse 25:30]. They do only a ritualistic reading of it, without understanding what they read, as if that's all that the Religion requires them to do! And they are blissfully content therewith!! They never bother to use it as the source of divine guidance and good advice.

وَلَا تَهِنُوا وَلَا تَحْزَنُوا وَأَنتُمُ الْأَعْلَوْنَ إِن كُنتُم

مُّؤْمِنِينَ ﴿١٣٩﴾

139. Wala tahinoo wala tahzanoo waantumu al-aAAlawna in kuntum mu/mineena

3:139. Be not weak and grieve not! And you should have an upper hand if you are strong in Faith.[151]

151. And most Muslims of today are not strong in their Faith. So, they are weak as a community, and they grieve a lot.

إِن يَمْسَسْكُمْ قَرْحٌ فَقَدْ مَسَّ ٱلْقَوْمَ قَرْحٌ مِّثْلُهُۥ وَتِلْكَ ٱلْأَيَّامُ نُدَاوِلُهَا بَيْنَ ٱلنَّاسِ وَلِيَعْلَمَ ٱللَّهُ ٱلَّذِينَ ءَامَنُواْ وَيَتَّخِذَ مِنكُمْ شُهَدَآءَ وَٱللَّهُ لَا يُحِبُّ ٱلظَّٰلِمِينَ ۝

140. In yamsaskum qar<u>h</u>un faqad massa alqawma qar<u>h</u>un mithluhu watilka al-ayy<u>a</u>mu nud<u>a</u>wiluh<u>a</u> bayna alnn<u>a</u>si waliyaAAlama All<u>a</u>hu alla<u>th</u>eena <u>a</u>manoo wayattakhi<u>th</u>a minkum shuhad<u>a</u>a waAll<u>a</u>hu l<u>a</u> yu<u>h</u>ibbu al<u>thth</u>alimeena

---

3:140. If you are hurt, then surely the community is similarly hurt. And We rotate such periods (of hurt) among mankind, and We do so in order that Allah may distinguish those that believe and pick up witnesses from amongst you.[152] And Allah does not love the offenders.

---

152. So the hurt that may afflict any person is a test from Allah that would distinguish him/her as believing or non-believing. If the person recognises the hurt as the test and suffers it patiently with prayers to the Lord, employing all fair means to overcome the effects of the hurt, he/she has passed the test. Allah Ta'ala then takes him/her as a witness to the truth of the hurt being only a test. On the other hand, if the person frets and fumes at the hurt, curses his destiny and does not hesitate to employ even foul means to overcome the effects of the hurt, he/she is an offender.

وَلِيُمَحِّصَ ٱللَّهُ ٱلَّذِينَ ءَامَنُواْ وَيَمْحَقَ ٱلْكَٰفِرِينَ ۝

141. Waliyuma<u>hh</u>i<u>s</u>a All<u>a</u>hu alla<u>th</u>eena <u>a</u>manoo wayam<u>h</u>aqa alk<u>a</u>fireena

---

3:141. And in order that[153] Allah may make the believers shine and destroy suppressors of the Truth.

---

153. This connects this Verse with the preceding one to mean that Allah's further purpose of the test is to make the believers eligible for better things and the suppressors of the Truth, for punishment.

أَمۡ حَسِبۡتُمۡ أَن تَدۡخُلُواْ ٱلۡجَنَّةَ وَلَمَّا يَعۡلَمِ ٱللَّهُ ٱلَّذِينَ جَـٰهَدُواْ مِنكُمۡ وَيَعۡلَمَ ٱلصَّـٰبِرِينَ ﴿١٤٢﴾

142. Am ḥasibtum an tadkhuloo aljannata walamma yaAAlami Allahu allatheena jahadoo minkum wayaAAlama alssabireena

3:142. Did you think that you would enter the Paradise, while Allah is yet to distinguish those of you who would strive and identify those who would exercise patience? [154]

154. Although Allah in His infinite knowledge knows beforehand who would enter Paradise, He wouldn't identify them till His human creatures build a veritable record of evidences with their deeds. Justice is not only required to be done, but also seen to be done. And Allah Almighty is our Just Lord.

وَلَقَدۡ كُنتُمۡ تَمَنَّوۡنَ ٱلۡمَوۡتَ مِن قَبۡلِ أَن تَلۡقَوۡهُ فَقَدۡ رَأَيۡتُمُوهُ وَأَنتُمۡ تَنظُرُونَ ﴿١٤٣﴾

143. Walaqad kuntum tamannawna almawta min qabli an talqawhu faqad raaytumoohu waantum tanthuroona

3:143. You did indeed wish for death before you were face-to-face with it. Then you did certainly see it and you looked on. [155]

155. This Verse was revealed, as other Verses immediately preceding, and following were, in the background of the battle of Uhud. In that battle, apparently, the believers' ranks were facing a critical situation, having suffered many casualties. Allah Ta'ala here subtly censures the believers for hesitating to face death during that critical situation, while earlier, before being face-to-face with death, they had declared their readiness to face it whenever required in the Path of Allah.

وَمَا مُحَمَّدٌ إِلَّا رَسُولٌ قَدْ خَلَتْ مِن قَبْلِهِ الرُّسُلُ

أَفَإِيْن مَّاتَ أَوْ قُتِلَ انقَلَبْتُمْ عَلَىٰ أَعْقَبِكُمْ وَمَن يَنقَلِبْ عَلَىٰ عَقِبَيْهِ

فَلَن يَضُرَّ اللَّهَ شَيْئًا وَسَيَجْزِى اللَّهُ الشَّـٰكِرِينَ ۝

144. Wama muhammadun illa rasoolun qad khalat min qablihi alrrusulu afa-in mata aw qutila inqalabtum AAala aAAqabikum waman yanqalib AAala AAaqibayhi falan yadurra Allaha shay-an wasayajzee Allahu alshshakireena

3:144. And Muhammad is not but a Messenger. There were certainly Messengers before him who had passed away. If he were to die or be slain, will you then turn back? And none who turns back can do any harm to Allah. And Allah shall reward those who turn to Him in gratitude.[156]

156. Remember that these Verses were revealed in the background of a raging battle. This Verse indicates that a serious situation had developed so far as the Muslim army was concerned. And as Verse 153 below tells us, some of them had fled, leaving the Prophet (peace on him) in the thick of the battle behind. A false rumour, that the Prophet had been killed, might have triggered the flight. But Allah inspired the other believers to rally around the Prophet, so much so that the enemy had to stop the battle and retreat to Makkah with all their battle gear.

وَمَا كَانَ لِنَفْسٍ أَن تَمُوتَ إِلَّا بِإِذْنِ ٱللَّهِ كِتَٰبًا مُّؤَجَّلًا وَمَن يُرِدْ ثَوَابَ ٱلدُّنْيَا نُؤْتِهِۦ مِنْهَا وَمَن يُرِدْ ثَوَابَ ٱلْءَاخِرَةِ نُؤْتِهِۦ مِنْهَا وَسَنَجْزِى ٱلشَّٰكِرِينَ ۝

145. Wama kana linafsin an tamoota illa bi-ithni Allahi kitaban mu-ajjalan waman yurid thawaba alddunya nu/tihi minha waman yurid thawaba al-akhirati nu/tihi minha wasanajzee alshshakireena

---

3:145. None can die except by Allah's command at a recorded fixed time.[157] And as for the person who desires a reward in this world, We give it to that person there from. And as for the person who desires a reward in the Hereafter, We give it to that person there from. And We shall reward those that turn to Us in gratitude.

---

157. Allah Ta'ala thus admonishes the believers who had lost heart after believing in the false rumour of the Prophet's death in the battle. The divine admonition extends also to the next few Verses below.

وَكَأَيِّن مِّن نَّبِىٍّ قَٰتَلَ مَعَهُۥ رِبِّيُّونَ كَثِيرٌ فَمَا وَهَنُوا۟ لِمَآ أَصَابَهُمْ فِى سَبِيلِ ٱللَّهِ وَمَا ضَعُفُوا۟ وَمَا ٱسْتَكَانُوا۟ وَٱللَّهُ يُحِبُّ ٱلصَّٰبِرِينَ

146. Wakaayyin min nabiyyin qatala maAAahu ribbiyyoona katheerun fama wahanoo lima asabahum fee sabeeli Allahi wama daAAufoo wama istakanoo waAllahu yuhibbu alssabireena

---

3:146. And there were many of the prophets who had fought, and with them were many godly men. But they never lost heart because of what befell them in Allah's way, nor did they weaken or give in. And Allah loves those who exercise patience.

وَمَا كَانَ قَوْلَهُمْ إِلَّا أَن قَالُوا۟ رَبَّنَا ٱغْفِرْ لَنَا ذُنُوبَنَا وَإِسْرَافَنَا فِىٓ أَمْرِنَا وَثَبِّتْ أَقْدَامَنَا وَٱنصُرْنَا عَلَى ٱلْقَوْمِ ٱلْكَـٰفِرِينَ ۝

147. Wama kana qawlahum illa an qaloo rabbana ighfir lana thunoobana wa-israfana fee amrina wathabbit aqdamana waonsurna AAala alqawmi alkafireena

3:147. And their prayer was none other than saying, "Our Lord! Forgive us our sins and our excesses in what we do. And make us steady and steadfast in the performance of our duties and help us against suppresssors of the Truth."

فَـَٔاتَىٰهُمُ ٱللَّهُ ثَوَابَ ٱلدُّنْيَا وَحُسْنَ ثَوَابِ ٱلْأَخِرَةِ وَٱللَّهُ يُحِبُّ ٱلْمُحْسِنِينَ

148. Faatahumu Allahu thawaba alddunya wahusna thawabi al-akhirati waAllahu yuhibbu almuhsineena

3:148. Allah then gave them a reward in this world and the good reward of the Hereafter. And Allah loves those who do good deeds.

يَـٰٓأَيُّهَا ٱلَّذِينَ ءَامَنُوٓاْ إِن تُطِيعُواْ ٱلَّذِينَ كَفَرُواْ يَرُدُّوكُمْ عَلَىٰٓ أَعْقَـٰبِكُمْ فَتَنقَلِبُواْ خَـٰسِرِينَ ۝

149. Ya ayyuha allatheena amanoo in tuteeAAoo allatheena kafaroo yaruddookum AAala aAAqabikum fatanqaliboo khasireena

---

3:149. O you who believe! If you follow those who suppress the Truth, they will turn you back. Then you turn back doomed!

بَلِ ٱللَّهُ مَوْلَىٰكُمْ وَهُوَ خَيْرُ ٱلنَّـٰصِرِينَ ۝

150. Bali Allahu mawlakum wahuwa khayru alnnasireena

3:150. But Allah is your Supreme Patron, and He is the best of those who help.

سَنُلْقِى فِى قُلُوبِ ٱلَّذِينَ كَفَرُواْ ٱلرُّعْبَ بِمَآ أَشْرَكُواْ بِٱللَّهِ مَا لَمْ يُنَزِّلْ بِهِۦ سُلْطَـٰنًا وَمَأْوَىٰهُمُ ٱلنَّارُ وَبِئْسَ مَثْوَى ٱلظَّـٰلِمِينَ ۝

151. Sanulqee fee quloobi allatheena kafaroo alrruAAba bima ashrakoo biAllahi ma lam yunazzil bihi sultanan wama/wahumu alnnaru wabi/sa mathwa alththalimeena

---

3:151. Soon shall We put awe into the minds of those who suppress the Truth, because they ascribed partners to Allah, for which He had sent down no evidence. And their abode shall be the Fire. And evil is the dwelling place of the wrong-doers!

152. Walaqad ṣadaqakumu Allahu waAAdahu i<u>th</u> ta<u>h</u>ussoonahum bi-i<u>th</u>nihi <u>h</u>atta i<u>th</u>a fashiltum watana<u>z</u>aAAtum fee al-amri waAAaṣaytum min baAAdi m<u>a</u> ar<u>a</u>kum m<u>a</u> tu<u>h</u>ibboona minkum man yureedu aldduny<u>a</u> waminkum man yureedu al-<u>a</u>khirata thumma ṣarafakum AAanhum liyabtaliyakum walaqad AAaf<u>a</u> AAankum waAll<u>a</u>hu <u>th</u>oo fa<u>d</u>lin AAala almu/mineen<u>a</u>

3:152. And Allah did certainly fulfill His promise when you were routing them at His Command, until you flagged, you raised a dispute about the order and you disobeyed after He gave you some glimpse of what you love. Among you are some that desire this world and some that desire the Hereafter. Then He turned you away from them to test you. And He did forgive you. And Allah has favours to shower upon those who believe.[158]

158. Allah's promise, mentioned at the beginning of this Verse, refers to the promise, as made in <u>Verses 124 and 125</u> **above, of sending down angels to help the believers fight the enemy on the battleground. In this matter of divine help,** <u>Verse 126 and study note 140 thereon</u> **may also please be kept in mind. With this divine help, the believers did rout the enemy. But, as this Verse distinctly indicates, a part of the Muslim army disobeyed some strict orders given to them, after seeing victory, which they love, coming their way. And thus, a sure victory turned to a stalemate. The stalemate was a lesson, a test and yet, a favour from Allah. It was a lesson for the Muslims as they were deprived of a sure victory because of disobedience and worldly desire on the part of some of them. It was a test for them that they did not get a clear victory despite heavy casualties among those of the Muslims who fought bravely and steadfastly. And yet it was a favour from Allah that they did not suffer an utter defeat which they would have deserved because some of them hankered after worldly gain and disobeyed orders.**

إِذْ تُصْعِدُونَ وَلَا تَلْوُونَ عَلَىٰ أَحَدٍ وَٱلرَّسُولُ يَدْعُوكُمْ فِىٓ أُخْرَىٰكُمْ فَأَثَـٰبَكُمْ غَمًّا بِغَمٍّ لِّكَيْلَا تَحْزَنُوا۟ عَلَىٰ مَا فَاتَكُمْ وَلَا مَآ أَصَـٰبَكُمْ ۗ وَٱللَّهُ خَبِيرٌۢ بِمَا تَعْمَلُونَ ﴿١٥٣﴾

153. Ith tusAAidoona wala talwoona AAala ahadin waalrrasoolu yadAAookum fee okhrakum faathabakum ghamman bighammin likay la tahzanoo AAala ma fatakum wala ma asabakum waAllahu khabeerun bima taAAmaloona

---

3:153. That time when you were fleeing without looking back at any one, and the Messenger in your rear was calling you back! [159] HE (Allah) did then inflict you with one sorrow after another so that you do not grieve for that which you lost and for that which befell you.[160] And Allah is aware of all that you do.

---

159. Please see <u>Note 156 above</u>.

160. The sorrows for the Muslim army, coming one after another, were (1) a sure victory turning into a near total defeat, (2) heavy casualties of deaths and injuries, (3) desertion by a part of the army on seeing the turn in the battle. But Allah used these sorrows to steel the resolve of the faithful few around the Prophet (peace be upon him), and they fought with such intensity and bravery that the enemy were forced to leave the battlefield without achieving their aim of annihilating the Muslim army completely.

ثُمَّ أَنزَلَ عَلَيْكُم مِّنۢ بَعْدِ ٱلْغَمِّ أَمَنَةً نُّعَاسًا يَغْشَىٰ طَآئِفَةً مِّنكُمْ وَطَآئِفَةٌ قَدْ أَهَمَّتْهُمْ أَنفُسُهُمْ يَظُنُّونَ بِٱللَّهِ غَيْرَ ٱلْحَقِّ ظَنَّ ٱلْجَٰهِلِيَّةِ يَقُولُونَ هَل لَّنَا مِنَ ٱلْأَمْرِ مِن شَىْءٍ قُلْ إِنَّ ٱلْأَمْرَ كُلَّهُۥ لِلَّهِ يُخْفُونَ فِىٓ أَنفُسِهِم مَّا لَا يُبْدُونَ لَكَ يَقُولُونَ لَوْ كَانَ لَنَا مِنَ ٱلْأَمْرِ شَىْءٌ مَّا قُتِلْنَا هَٰهُنَا قُل لَّوْ كُنتُمْ فِى بُيُوتِكُمْ لَبَرَزَ ٱلَّذِينَ كُتِبَ عَلَيْهِمُ ٱلْقَتْلُ إِلَىٰ مَضَاجِعِهِمْ وَلِيَبْتَلِىَ ٱللَّهُ مَا فِى صُدُورِكُمْ وَلِيُمَحِّصَ مَا فِى قُلُوبِكُمْ وَٱللَّهُ عَلِيمٌۢ بِذَاتِ ٱلصُّدُورِ ﴿١٥٤﴾

154. Thumma anzala AAalaykum min baAAdi alghammi amanatan nuAAasan yaghsha ta-ifatan minkum wata-ifatun qad ahammat-hum anfusuhum yathunnoona biAllahi ghayra alhaqqi thanna aljahiliyyati yaqooloona hal lana mina al-amri min shay-in qul inna al-amra kullahu lillahi yukhfoona fee anfusihim ma la yubdoona laka yaqooloona law kana lana mina al-amri shay-on ma qutilna hahuna qul law kuntum fee buyootikum labaraza allatheena kutiba AAalayhimu alqatlu ila madajiAAihim waliyabtaliya Allahu ma fee sudoorikum waliyumahhisa ma fee quloobikum waAllahu AAaleemun bithati alssudoori

---

3:154. Then, after the sorrow, He sent down the peace of slumber covering one section of you, while another section cared about their own selves, entertaining wrong thoughts about Allah – thoughts prevalent during the times of ignorance. They said, "Have we had the authority to take decision in any matter?" Say, "The authority in taking decisions in all matters indeed rests with Allah." They hide within their own selves what they do not reveal to you. They say, "If we had anything to do with taking any decision in this affair, we would not have been slain here." Say, "Even if you had stayed in your houses, those for whom death was decreed would certainly have gone forth to their decreed places of death." And in order that[161] Allah might test that which is in your conscious minds and purge that which is in your subconscious.[162] For Allah knows well the secrets of your minds.

---

161. What follows in this sentence is the 2nd purpose of Allah Ta'ala in inflicting sorrow upon sorrow on the Muslim army. The first purpose, mentioned in the preceding Verse, was to prevent the believers from indulging in grief over what they had lost and what befell them in the battlefield. The sorrows succeeded one another so rapidly that the believers had no time for grief. And immediately after the causes for the sorrows ended, the believers were overcome with a becalming slumber.

162. The mind operates at two stages - one, conscious, and the other subconscious. It is the conscious mind that exercises the freedom of choice given to man and takes the decisions on any course of action.

The decisions may be influenced by events that are still fresh in the conscious mind, but these are also influenced by events that have got submerged into the subconscious and by feelings and emotions that have their bases in the subconscious. In this Verse, _sudoor_ (plural of _sadr_) has been used to refer to the conscious mind, whereas _quloob_ (plural of _qalb_ has been used to refer to the subconscious. Conviction on anything, good or bad, comes from the subconscious. In religious discussions, we modern-day Muslims may reiterate our faith in the Qur'aan and in all the divine directives therein. But in practical life, most of us forget those directives and do not mind resorting to falsehoods and corruption to get our worldly things done in our favour. That is because Islam has not become a matter of conviction with us. In other words, Faith has not entered our subconscious, as the Qur'aan says in Verse 49:14. The subconscious is within the conscious mind as confirmed in Verse 22:46. In the context of the battle, in the perspective of which these Verses were revealed, Allah tested the minds of those in whose subconscious still lurked wrong thoughts of the period of ignorance, before their exposure to Islam. Allah's 2nd purpose of inflicting sorrow upon sorrow on the Muslim army was to bring out into open those wrong thoughts and to purge them from the subconscious. About the translation of both _quloob_ and _sudoor_ as minds, rather than as hearts, please see study note 2:117 of these Studies and study note 3:135 herein above.

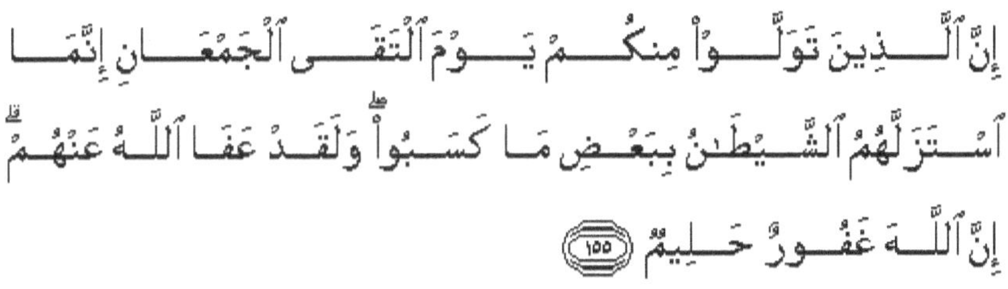

155. Inna allatheena tawallaw minkum yawma iltaqa aljamAAani innama istazallahumu alshshaytanu bibaAAdi ma kasaboo walaqad AAafa Allahu AAanhum inna Allaha ghafoorun haleemun

3:155. Indeed, those of you who turned back on the day the two armies met, it was Satan who made them slip because of something they had done.[163] And Allah did pardon them. Indeed! Allah is Forgiving, Kind.

163. The reference is to those believers who had deserted (turned back from) their posts on the battleground at sight of impending victory. The battle had turned its course, because of their disobedience (see Verse 152 above). Those were indeed believers at heart, but Satan had made them slip at that occasion. Allah tells us here that it was not primarily Satan who was responsible for the believers' deviation from their bounden duty. The primay responsibility lay on the shoulders of the believers themselves, in that they had first taken a conscious decision, in exercise of their free will, to dispute the order given to them. They thus themselves opened their minds for satanic influence in encouraging their deviation from their duty.

يَـٰٓأَيُّهَا ٱلَّذِينَ ءَامَنُوا۟ لَا تَكُونُوا۟ كَٱلَّذِينَ كَفَرُوا۟ وَقَالُوا۟ لِإِخْوَٰنِهِمْ إِذَا ضَرَبُوا۟ فِى ٱلْأَرْضِ أَوْ كَانُوا۟ غُزًّى لَّوْ كَانُوا۟ عِندَنَا مَا مَاتُوا۟ وَمَا قُتِلُوا۟ لِيَجْعَلَ ٱللَّهُ ذَٰلِكَ حَسْرَةً فِى قُلُوبِهِمْ وَٱللَّهُ يُحْىِۦ وَيُمِيتُ وَٱللَّهُ بِمَا تَعْمَلُونَ بَصِيرٌ ﴿١٥٦﴾

156. Ya ayyuha allatheena amanoo la takoonoo kaallatheena kafaroo waqaloo li-ikhwanihim itha daraboo fee al-ardi aw kanoo ghuzzan law kanoo AAindana ma matoo wama qutiloo liyajAAala Allahu thalika hasratan fee quloobihim waAllahu yuhyee wayumeetu waAllahu bima taAAmaloona baseerun

---

3:156. O you who believe! Be not like those who suppress the Truth and say of their brothers, travelling through the earth or fighting, "If they had stayed back with us, they would not have died or been slain", so that Allah makes it anguish in their subconscious.[164] And Allah it is that gives life and causes death. And Allah sees all that you do.

---

164. While the believers had come out to fight the battle, with reference to which these Verses were revealed, there were those suppressors of Truth who had preferred to remain back at Madina. It is the utterance of these latter people that is quoted here in this Verse. Allah says that the 3rd purpose for His inflicting sorrow upon sorrow on the believers in the battlefield was to make it anguish for those incorrigible people back at Madina, the casualties being those of their own ethnic brothers. About the 1st and the 2nd purposes, please see Note 161 on Verse 154 herein above. Allah's purpose in inflicting sorrow after sorrow in the battlefield was thus three-fold, for three different categories of people:

1. the believers whose Faith had entered their subconscious,
2. the believers whose Faith had not yet entered their subconscious,
3. the suppressors of Truth among the ethnic brothers of the believers.

وَلَئِن قُتِلْتُمْ فِى سَبِيلِ ٱللَّهِ أَوْ مُتُّمْ لَمَغْفِرَةٌ مِّنَ ٱللَّهِ وَرَحْمَةٌ خَيْرٌ مِّمَّا يَجْمَعُونَ ﴿١٥٧﴾

157. Wala-in qutiltum fee sabeeli Allahi aw muttum lamaghfiratun mina Allahi warahmatun khayrun mimma yajmaAAoona

3:157. And if you are killed in the way of Allah, or you die, forgiveness and mercy from Allah are far better than all they[165] could amass.

165. The pronoun refers to the suppressors of Truth mentioned in the preceding Verse as saying that the believers would not have been killed if they had stayed back. This Verse and the next are in response to that statement.

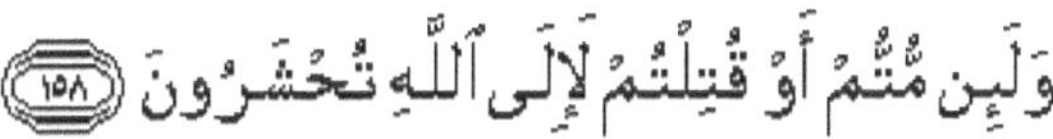

158. Wala-in muttum aw qutiltum la-ila Allahi tuhsharoona

3:158. And if you die, or are killed, you are certainly going to be brought together unto Allah.

159. Fabima rahmatin mina Allahi linta lahum walaw kunta faththan ghaleetha alqalbi lainfaddoo min hawlika faoAAfu AAanhum waistaghfir lahum washawirhum fee al-amri fa-itha AAazamta fatawakkal AAala Allahi inna Allaha yuhibbu almutawakkileena

3:159. It is Mercy from Allah, then, that you are lenient to them. And if you were harsh and hardhearted, they would have dispersed away from around you. So, pardon them, and pray for forgiveness for them, and consult them in community matters. Then, when you have taken a decision, put your trust in Allah. Indeed, Allah loves those who put their trust in Him.[166]

---

166. During the battle, in the context of which the foregoing Verses were revealed, the believers and the residents of Madina were guilty of various acts of omission and commission. The Prophet (peace upon him) still pardoned them in pursuance of divine instructions in this Verse. The pardon was also in consonance with the Prophet's natural disposition. He was never harsh or hardhearted to people around him. This Verse also imparts a lesson to rulers of men and to individuals alike, on how to conduct their affairs.

إِن يَنصُرْكُمُ ٱللَّـهُ فَلَا غَالِبَ لَكُمْ وَإِن يَخْذُلْكُمْ فَمَن ذَا ٱلَّذِى يَنصُرُكُم مِّنۢ بَعْدِهِۦ وَعَلَى ٱللَّـهِ فَلْيَتَوَكَّلِ ٱلْمُؤْمِنُونَ ﴿١٦٠﴾

160. In yansurkumu Allahu fala ghaliba lakum wa-in yakhthulkum faman tha allathee yansurukum min baAAdihi waAAala Allahi falyatawakkali almu/minoona

---

3:160. If Allah helps you, none can get the better of you. And if He forsakes you, who is there to help you thereafter? In Allah, then, believers should put their trust.

وَمَا كَانَ لِنَبِيٍّ أَن يَغُلَّ وَمَن يَغْلُلْ يَأْتِ بِمَا غَلَّ يَوْمَ ٱلْقِيَـٰمَةِ ثُمَّ تُوَفَّىٰ كُلُّ نَفْسٍ مَّا كَسَبَتْ وَهُمْ لَا يُظْلَمُونَ ﴿١١١﴾

161. Wama kana linabiyyin an yaghulla waman yaghlul ya/ti bima ghalla yawma alqiyamati thumma tuwaffa kullu nafsin ma kasabat wahum la yuthlamoona

3:161. No prophet could deceive. And if anyone deceived, he will come with what he deceived, on the Day of Resurrection. Then shall every soul be paid what it earned. And none shall be wronged.

أَفَمَنِ ٱتَّبَعَ رِضْوَٰنَ ٱللَّهِ كَمَنۢ بَآءَ بِسَخَطٍ مِّنَ ٱللَّهِ وَمَأْوَىٰهُ جَهَنَّمُ وَبِئْسَ ٱلْمَصِيرُ ﴿١٦٢﴾

162. Afamani ittabaAAa ridwana Allahi kaman baa bisakhatin mina Allahi wama/wahu jahannamu wabi/sa almaseeru

3:162. Is the one seeking Allah's pleasure like the one incurring Allah's wrath and woefully destined for an abode in Hell? And it is the worst destination!

هُمْ دَرَجَٰتٌ عِندَ ٱللَّهِ وَٱللَّهُ بَصِيرٌۢ بِمَا يَعْمَلُونَ ﴿١٦٣﴾

163. Hum darajatun AAinda Allahi waAllahu baseerun bima yaAAmaloona

3:163. There are different grades for them with Allah, and Allah does see all that they do.[167]

167. There are grades both in the Jannah and in the Hell. If the grades were not to be there, it would amount to injustice. A more pious person in Jannah may then get the same treatment and the same benefits as a person who was less pious in this world. Similarly, a person who was guilty of committing more sins in this world may get the same punishment in Hell as the one who committed fewer sins. Everything with Allah is based on justice.

لَقَـدْ مَـنَّ ٱللَّـهُ عَلَـى ٱلْمُؤْمِنِينَ إِذْ بَعَـثَ فِيهِـمْ رَسُـولًا مِّـنْ أَنفُسِـهِمْ

يَتْلُـواْ عَلَيْهِـمْ ءَايَـٰتِـهِۦ وَيُـزَكِّيهِمْ وَيُعَلِّمُهُـمُ ٱلْكِـتَـٰبَ وَٱلْحِكْمَـةَ

وَإِن كَانُواْ مِـن قَبْلُ لَفِى ضَلَـٰلٍ مُّبِينٍ ﴿١١٤﴾

---

164. Laqad manna Allahu AAala almu/mineena ith baAAatha feehim rasoolan min anfusihim yatloo AAalayhim ayatihi wayuzakkeehim wayuAAallimuhumu alkitaba waalhikmata wa-in kanoo min qablu lafee dalalin mubeenin

---

3:164. Allah did confer a great favour upon the believers when He sent among them a Messenger from among themselves, reciting to them His signs/Verses, purifying them, and instructing them in Scripture and Wisdom. And, before that, they had indeed been in manifest error.[168]

---

168. Please see study note 2:192 on Verse 2:129, in this context. It needs however to be emphasised here that the task of purifying people, and instructing them in Scripture and Wisdom, has not ended with the passing away of the Messenger (peace be upon him). The task is now passed on to those who have inherited the Qur'aan from him – his Ummah. A section of the Ummah, unfortunately, still clings to the baseless belief that the Messenger somehow still performs this task, even after his death! May Allah Subhanahu guide us away from any path that may lead us to the unpardonable sin of *shirk*.

أَوَلَمَّآ أَصَـٰبَتْكُم مُّصِيبَةٌ قَدْ أَصَبْتُم مِّثْلَيْهَا قُلْتُمْ أَنَّىٰ هَـٰذَا قُلْ هُوَ مِنْ

عِندِ أَنفُسِـكُمْ إِنَّ ٱللَّهَ عَلَىٰ كُلِّ شَىْءٍ قَدِيرٌ ﴿١١٥﴾

---

165. Awa lamma asabatkum museebatun qad asabtum mithlayha qultum anna hatha qul huwa min AAindi anfusikum inna Allaha AAala kulli shay-in qadeerun

---

3:165. When an affliction befell you – and you had certainly afflicted twice as much – did you say, "How come, we got this?"[169] Say, "You got it because of you yourselves." Allah indeed has power over all things.

---

169. This is a continuation from Verses immediately preceding, of the description of a battle, in which the believers had suffered some setbacks. Allah reminds the believers that if they had suffered, their enemies had suffered twice as much in the battle, and that the suffering the believers had to sustain was because of their own acts of omission and commission (refer study note 3:163).

وَمَآ أَصَـٰبَكُمْ يَوْمَ ٱلْتَقَى ٱلْجَمْعَانِ فَبِإِذْنِ ٱللَّهِ وَلِيَعْلَمَ ٱلْمُؤْمِنِينَ ﴿١٦٦﴾

166. Wama asabakum yawma iltaqa aljamAAani fabi-ithni Allahi waliyaAAlama almu/mineena

---

3:166. And so, what befell you, on the day when the two armies met, was with Allah's leave, and in order that He did distinguish the believers.[170]

---

170. Please see footnote 3:164 in this context.

وَلِيَعْلَمَ ٱلَّذِينَ نَافَقُواْ وَقِيلَ لَهُمْ تَعَالَوْاْ قَـٰتِلُواْ فِى سَبِيلِ ٱللَّهِ أَوِ ٱدْفَعُواْ قَالُواْ لَوْ نَعْلَمُ قِتَالًا لَّٱتَّبَعْنَـٰكُمْ هُمْ لِلْكُفْرِ يَوْمَئِذٍ أَقْرَبُ مِنْهُمْ لِلْإِيمَـٰنِ يَقُولُونَ بِأَفْوَٰهِهِم مَّا لَيْسَ فِى قُلُوبِهِمْ وَٱللَّهُ أَعْلَمُ بِمَا يَكْتُمُونَ ﴿١٦٧﴾

167. WaliyaAAlama allatheena nafaqoo waqeela lahum taAAalaw qatiloo fee sabeeli Allahi awi idfaAAoo qaloo law naAAlamu qitalan laittabaAAnakum hum lilkufri yawma-ithin aqrabu minhum lil-eemani yaqooloona bi-afwahihim ma laysa fee quloobihim waAllahu aAAlamu bima yaktumoona

3:167. And in order that He did distinguish the hypocrites. And they had been told, "Come, fight in Allah's Path, or defend." They said, "Had we been trained in fighting, we would certainly have followed you." Suppression of the Truth was nearer to them, that day, than belief. They spoke with their mouths what was not in their inner minds. And Allah knows what they conceal.

ٱلَّذِينَ قَالُواْ لِإِخْوَٰنِهِمْ وَقَعَدُواْ لَوْ أَطَاعُونَا مَا قُتِلُواْ قُلْ فَٱدْرَءُواْ عَنْ أَنفُسِكُمُ ٱلْمَوْتَ إِن كُنتُمْ صَٰدِقِينَ ۝

168. Allatheena qaloo li-ikhwanihim waqaAAadoo law ataAAoona ma qutiloo qul faidraoo AAan anfusikumu almawta in kuntum sadiqeena

3:168. Those were the ones who had said of their brethren, whilst they themselves sat back home, "Had they listened to us, they would not have been killed." Say, "Avert death, then, from your own selves, if you are truthful!"

وَلَا تَحْسَبَنَّ ٱلَّذِينَ قُتِلُواْ فِى سَبِيلِ ٱللَّهِ أَمْوَٰتًا بَلْ أَحْيَآءٌ عِندَ رَبِّهِمْ يُرْزَقُونَ ۝

169. Wala tahsabanna allatheena qutiloo fee sabeeli Allahi amwatan bal ahyaon AAinda rabbihim yurzaqoona

3:169. And think not of those who are killed in Allah's Path, as dead. Nay! They are alive, with their Lord, being well cared for.[171]

171. Please go through study notes 2:247 to 2:249 **of these Studies, on the similarly worded Verse 2:154.**

فَرِحِينَ بِمَآ ءَاتَىٰهُمُ ٱللَّهُ مِن فَضْلِهِۦ وَيَسْتَبْشِرُونَ بِٱلَّذِينَ لَمْ يَلْحَقُواْ بِهِم مِّنْ خَلْفِهِمْ أَلَّا خَوْفٌ عَلَيْهِمْ وَلَا هُمْ يَحْزَنُونَ ۞

170. Fariḥeena bima ataḥumu Allahu min faḍlihi wayastabshiroona biallatheena lam yalḥaqoo bihim min khalfihim alla khawfun AAalayhim wala hum yaḥzanoona

---

3:170. Happy with what Allah has given them, by His grace, and glad for those, who are left behind and have not yet joined them, that they shall have no fear, nor shall they grieve.[172]

---

172. This is a continuation, from the preceding Verse, of the state in which persons killed in Allah's Path will find themselves in, immediately after their being killed in this world.

۞ يَسْتَبْشِرُونَ بِنِعْمَةٍ مِّنَ ٱللَّهِ وَفَضْلٍ وَأَنَّ ٱللَّهَ لَا يُضِيعُ أَجْرَ ٱلْمُؤْمِنِينَ

171. Yastabshiroona biniAAmatin mina Allahi wafaḍlin waanna Allaha la yuḍeeAAu ajra almu/mineena

---

3:171. They[173] enjoy Favour and Grace from Allah. And Allah does indeed not waste the reward of the believers.

---

173. That is those who were killed in Allah's Path.

ٱلَّذِينَ ٱسۡتَجَابُواْ لِلَّهِ وَٱلرَّسُولِ مِنۢ بَعۡدِ مَآ أَصَابَهُمُ ٱلۡقَرۡحُۚ لِلَّذِينَ أَحۡسَنُواْ مِنۡهُمۡ وَٱتَّقَوۡاْ أَجۡرٌ عَظِيمٌ ﴿١٧٢﴾

172. Alla*th*eena istaj*a*boo lill*a*hi waalrrasooli min baAAdi m*a* a*s*abahumu alqar*h*u lilla*th*eena a*h*sanoo minhum waittaqaw ajrun AAa*th*eemun

---

3:172. Those believers who responded to Allah and the Messenger, after injuries hit them.[174] For those among them who do good and fear Allah, a great reward!

---

174. The reference is to the injuries suffered by the believers in the battle. Despite the injuries, they valiantly rallied around the Prophet who was himself injured [refer study note 3:156]. And this part of the Verse connects with the last part of the preceding Verse giving assurance to the believers that Allah won't let their sacrifices go waste.

ٱلَّذِينَ قَالَ لَهُمُ ٱلنَّاسُ إِنَّ ٱلنَّاسَ قَدۡ جَمَعُواْ لَكُمۡ فَٱخۡشَوۡهُمۡ فَزَادَهُمۡ إِيمَٰنࣰا وَقَالُواْ حَسۡبُنَا ٱللَّهُ وَنِعۡمَ ٱلۡوَكِيلُ ﴿١٧٣﴾

173. Alla*th*eena q*a*la lahumu alnn*a*su inna alnn*a*sa qad jamaAAoo lakum faikhshawhum faz*a*dahum eem*a*nan waq*a*loo *h*asbun*a* All*a*hu waniAAma alwakeelu

---

3:173. The people warned them, "Surely, there is a fearsome gathering of people against you!" And the warning only increased their faith, and they said, "Allah is sufficient for us, and the Best Guardian."[175]

---

175. The Qur'aan refers here to the scenario in Medina, just before the battle – the hypocrites trying to dissuade those true believers, preparing to go to the battlefront, by warning them against the fearsome strength of the enemy. The warning implied that the believers would be annihilated in the battle. But the believers survived and returned to Medina with their position intact. That is what the Qur'aan alludes to in the next Verse 174. And take note of what Allah tells the believers in Verse 175 below.

$$\text{فَٱنقَلَبُواْ بِنِعۡمَةٍ مِّنَ ٱللَّهِ وَفَضۡلٍ لَّمۡ يَمۡسَسۡهُمۡ سُوٓءٌ وَٱتَّبَعُواْ رِضۡوَٰنَ ٱللَّهِ وَٱللَّهُ ذُو فَضۡلٍ عَظِيمٍ ۝}$$

174. Fainqalaboo biniAAmatin mina Allahi wafadlin lam yamsas-hum soo-on waittabaAAoo ridwana Allahi waAllahu thoo fadlin AAatheemin

3:174. And the believers returned from the battleground with Favour and Grace from Allah. No evil touched them, and they followed the pleasure of Allah. And Allah has Immense Grace.

$$\text{إِنَّمَا ذَٰلِكُمُ ٱلشَّيۡطَٰنُ يُخَوِّفُ أَوۡلِيَآءَهُۥ فَلَا تَخَافُوهُمۡ وَخَافُونِ إِن كُنتُم مُّؤۡمِنِينَ ۝}$$

175. Innama thalikumu alshshaytanu yukhawwifu awliyaahu fala takhafoohum wakhafooni in kuntum mu/mineena

3:175. It is only the Satan, who frightens you of those who are close to him. Fear them not then! And fear Me, if you do believe in Me.

$$\text{وَلَا يَحۡزُنكَ ٱلَّذِينَ يُسَٰرِعُونَ فِى ٱلۡكُفۡرِ إِنَّهُمۡ لَن يَضُرُّواْ ٱللَّهَ شَيۡـًٔا يُرِيدُ ٱللَّهُ أَلَّا يَجۡعَلَ لَهُمۡ حَظًّا فِى ٱلۡأَخِرَةِ وَلَهُمۡ عَذَابٌ عَظِيمٌ ۝}$$

176. Wala yahzunka allatheena yusariAAoona fee alkufri innahum lan yadurroo Allaha shay-an yureedu Allahu alla yajAAala lahum haththan fee al-akhirati walahum AAathabun AAatheemun

3:176. And let them not grieve you, who are quick in suppressing the Truth. Surely, they can do no harm to Allah. Allah wills that He sets no share for them of the good things in the Hereafter. And a terrible punishment awaits them there!

إِنَّ ٱلَّذِينَ ٱشْتَرَوُاْ ٱلْكُفْرَ بِٱلْإِيمَـٰنِ لَن يَضُرُّواْ ٱللَّهَ شَيْئًا وَلَهُمْ عَذَابٌ أَلِيمٌ ۝

177. Inna alla<u>th</u>eena ishtarawoo alkufra bial-eem<u>a</u>ni lan ya<u>d</u>urroo All<u>a</u>ha shay-an walahum AAa<u>th</u>abun aleem**un**

3:177. Indeed! They, who have indulged in suppression of the Truth at the cost of the Faith, can do no harm to Allah.[176] And for them, a painful punishment.

176. One possible case of anyone doing such a thing is for a believer, of his/her own free will, to do something un-Islamic just to gain some temporary worldly benefit. Another case is where a believer, not acting under duress, renounces Islam openly. In no such cases can there be any question of anyone harming Allah on that, or on any, account. HE is Invincible, Almighty! On the other hand, it is that person, who does such a thing, that would have to face a painful punishment from Allah; for, he/she would be doing it by conscious suppression of his/her conscience.

وَلَا يَحْسَبَنَّ ٱلَّذِينَ كَفَرُواْ أَنَّمَا نُمْلِى لَهُمْ خَيْرٌ لِّأَنفُسِهِمْ إِنَّمَا نُمْلِى لَهُمْ لِيَزْدَادُواْ إِثْمًا وَلَهُمْ عَذَابٌ مُّهِينٌ ۝

178. Wal<u>a</u> ya<u>h</u>sabanna alla<u>th</u>eena kafaroo annam<u>a</u> numlee lahum khayrun li-anfusihim innam<u>a</u> numlee lahum liyazd<u>a</u>doo ithman walahum AAa<u>th</u>abun muheen**un**

3:178. And let not the suppressors of the Truth think that the long rein We give them is any good for them. The long rein to them is only for the purpose that they may add to their sins. And for them is a disgraceful punishment.

مَّا كَانَ ٱللَّهُ لِيَذَرَ ٱلْمُؤْمِنِينَ عَلَىٰ مَا أَنتُمْ عَلَيْهِ حَتَّىٰ يَمِيزَ ٱلْخَبِيثَ مِنَ ٱلطَّيِّبِ وَمَا كَانَ ٱللَّهُ لِيُطْلِعَكُمْ عَلَى ٱلْغَيْبِ وَلَـٰكِنَّ ٱللَّهَ يَجْتَبِى مِن رُّسُلِهِ مَن يَشَآءُ فَـَٔامِنُوا۟ بِٱللَّهِ وَرُسُلِهِ وَإِن تُؤْمِنُوا۟ وَتَتَّقُوا۟ فَلَكُمْ أَجْرٌ عَظِيمٌ ﴿١٧٩﴾

179. Ma kana Allahu liyathara almu/mineena AAala ma antum AAalayhi hatta yameeza alkhabeetha mina alttayyibi wama kana Allahu liyutliAAakum AAala alghaybi walakinna Allaha yajtabee min rusulihi man yashao faaminoo biAllahi warusulihi wa-in tu/minoo watattaqoo falakum ajrun AAatheemun

3:179. Allah will not let the believers remain in the state in which you are now, until He separates the impure from the pure. And Allah will not disclose to you the unseen/unknown, but Allah chooses whom He pleases as His Messengers. Believe then in Allah and His Messengers. And if you believe and be pious, then, for you, a great reward.[177]

177. The Qur'aan explains here the grand divine scheme for mankind. It's a matter of fact that every individual's life in this world is a test. But this fact has necessorily to be kept, for the individual, in the realm of the unseen/unknown. The test would fail its purpose, otherwise. But the Wise and Knowing Creator won't just leave the individual to grope in the dark. HE has therefore, from time to time in the past, sent His human Messengers for the guidance of the individual. Unlike the common individuals, the Messengers were made privy to a part of the vast realm of the unseen/unknown, known only to the Creator, so that they could guide with the advantage of certain knowledge. The Messengers were also sent with divine Books so that the individuals could refer to them for guidance, when the Messengers were no longer living with them. And the Creator has gauaranteed that His last such Message to mankind, the Qur'aan, is divinely protected against human pollution and corruption.

وَلَا يَحْسَبَنَّ ٱلَّذِينَ يَبْخَلُونَ بِمَآ ءَاتَىٰهُمُ ٱللَّهُ مِن فَضْلِهِۦ هُوَ خَيْرًا لَّهُم بَلْ هُوَ شَرٌّ لَّهُمْ سَيُطَوَّقُونَ مَا بَخِلُوا۟ بِهِۦ يَوْمَ ٱلْقِيَٰمَةِ وَلِلَّهِ مِيرَٰثُ ٱلسَّمَٰوَٰتِ وَٱلْأَرْضِ وَٱللَّهُ بِمَا تَعْمَلُونَ خَبِيرٌ ﴿١٨٠﴾

180. Wala yahsabanna allatheena yabkhaloona bima atahummu Allahu min fadlihi huwa khayran lahum bal huwa sharrun lahum sayutawwaqoona ma bakhiloo bihi yawma alqiyamati walillahi meerathu alssamawati waal-ardi waAllahu bima taAAmaloona khabeerun

---

3:180. And they, who are miserly in what Allah has granted them by His grace, should not think that it is good for them. Nay! It is bad for them. They shall have that with which they were miserly, hung around their necks on the Resurrection Day. And for Allah is the inheritance of the heavens and the earth. And Allah is aware of what you do.

لَّقَدْ سَمِعَ ٱللَّهُ قَوْلَ ٱلَّذِينَ قَالُوٓا۟ إِنَّ ٱللَّهَ فَقِيرٌ وَنَحْنُ أَغْنِيَآءُ سَنَكْتُبُ مَا قَالُوا۟ وَقَتْلَهُمُ ٱلْأَنۢبِيَآءَ بِغَيْرِ حَقٍّ وَنَقُولُ ذُوقُوا۟ عَذَابَ ٱلْحَرِيقِ ﴿١٨١﴾

181. Laqad samiAAa Allahu qawla allatheena qaloo inna Allaha faqeerun wanahnu aghniyaon sanaktubu ma qaloo waqatlahumu al-anbiyaa bighayri haqqin wanaqoolu thooqoo AAathaba alhareeqi

---

3:181. Allah has certainly heard the statement of those who said, "Indeed, Allah is poor and we are rich." We shall record what they said, as well as their killing of the prophets unjustly, [178] and We shall say, "Taste the punishment of burning."

---

178. On the authority of <u>Verse 2:61</u>, it was the Jews who had been guilty of killing some of their Prophets. The statement – of Allah being poor – may therefore as well be attributed to the Jews in the light of this Verse. This may be their satirical response to <u>Verse 2:245</u>.

ذَٰلِكَ بِمَا قَدَّمَتْ أَيْدِيكُمْ وَأَنَّ اللَّهَ لَيْسَ بِظَلَّامٍ لِّلْعَبِيدِ ﴿١٨٢﴾

182. Thalika bima qaddamat aydeekum waanna Allaha laysa bithallamin lilAAabeedi

3:182. "That is because of what your own hands have sent before. And, indeed, Allah is never unjust to His devotees!"[179]

179. This is the continuation, from the preceding Verse, of the divine address to those who said Allah was poor.

الَّذِينَ قَالُوٓا إِنَّ اللَّهَ عَهِدَ إِلَيْنَآ أَلَّا نُؤْمِنَ لِرَسُولٍ حَتَّىٰ يَأْتِيَنَا بِقُرْبَانٍ تَأْكُلُهُ النَّارُ قُلْ قَدْ جَآءَكُمْ رُسُلٌ مِّن قَبْلِى بِالْبَيِّنَٰتِ وَبِالَّذِى قُلْتُمْ فَلِمَ قَتَلْتُمُوهُمْ إِن كُنتُمْ صَٰدِقِينَ ﴿١٨٣﴾

183. Allatheena qaloo inna Allaha AAahida ilayna alla nu/mina lirasoolin hatta ya/tiyana biqurbanin ta/kuluhu alnnaru qul qad jaakum rusulun min qablee bialbayyinati wabiallathee qultum falima qataltumoohum in kutum sadiqeena

3:183. Those who said, "Indeed, Allah has taken a pledge from us never to believe in any Messenger until he brings us an offering which the fire consumes." Say, "There did come to you Messengers before me, with clear signs and with that which you demand. Why then did you kill them if you are truthful?"

فَإِن كَذَّبُوكَ فَقَدْ كُذِّبَ رُسُلٌ مِّن قَبْلِكَ جَآءُو بِٱلْبَيِّنَـٰتِ وَٱلزُّبُرِ وَٱلْكِتَـٰبِ ٱلْمُنِيرِ

184. Fa-in kaththabooka faqad kuththiba rusulun min qablika jaoo bialbayyinati waalzzuburi waalkitabi almuneeri

---

3:184. If they then accuse you of lying, so indeed were Messengers, who came before you with clear signs and the Psalms and the illuminating Book, accused.

كُلُّ نَفْسٍ ذَآئِقَةُ ٱلْمَوْتِ وَإِنَّمَا تُوَفَّوْنَ أُجُورَكُمْ يَوْمَ ٱلْقِيَـٰمَةِ فَمَن زُحْزِحَ عَنِ ٱلنَّارِ وَأُدْخِلَ ٱلْجَنَّةَ فَقَدْ فَازَ وَمَا ٱلْحَيَوٰةُ ٱلدُّنْيَآ إِلَّا مَتَـٰعُ ٱلْغُرُورِ

185. Kullu nafsin tha-iqatu almawti wa-innama tuwaffawna ojoorakum yawma alqiyamati faman zuhziha AAani alnnari waodkhila aljannata faqad faza wama alhayatu alddunya illa mataAAu alghuroori

---

3:185. Everyone must taste the death. And only on the Resurrection Day, shall your earnings be fully paid. So then, whoever is moved away from the Fire and admitted to the Garden, he indeed has achieved success. And the life of this world is nothing but ways and means of deception.

۞ لَتُبْلَوُنَّ فِىٓ أَمْوَٰلِكُمْ وَأَنفُسِكُمْ وَلَتَسْمَعُنَّ مِنَ ٱلَّذِينَ أُوتُوا۟ ٱلْكِتَـٰبَ مِن قَبْلِكُمْ وَمِنَ ٱلَّذِينَ أَشْرَكُوٓا۟ أَذًى كَثِيرًا وَإِن تَصْبِرُوا۟ وَتَتَّقُوا۟ فَإِنَّ ذَٰلِكَ مِنْ عَزْمِ ٱلْأُمُورِ

186. Latublawunna fee amw_alikum waanfusikum walatasmaAAunna mina alla_theena ootoo alkit_aba min qablikum wamina alla_theena ashrakoo a_than katheeran wa-in ta_sbiroo watattaqoo fa-inna _thalika min AAazmi al-omoorI

3:186. You shall certainly be put to test in your wealth and your lives, and you shall certainly hear from those who have been given the Book before you, and from the polytheists, much hurtful comments. And if you are patient and observe piety, that indeed is a determining factor in all matters.[180]

180. It is obvious that in the sight of our Creator, patience and piety play a crucial role in the determination of all matters in the life of a human being. These attributes contribute to that person's ultimate success.

وَإِذْ أَخَذَ ٱللَّهُ مِيثَـٰقَ ٱلَّذِينَ أُوتُـوا۟ ٱلْكِتَـٰبَ لَتُبَيِّنُنَّهُۥ لِلنَّاسِ وَلَا

تَكْتُمُونَهُۥ فَنَبَذُوهُ وَرَآءَ ظُهُورِهِمْ وَٱشْتَرَوْا۟ بِهِۦ ثَمَنًا قَلِيلًا فَبِئْسَ مَا

يَشْتَرُونَ ۝١٨٧

187. Wa-i_th akha_tha Allahu meetha_qa alla_theena ootoo alkit_aba latubayyinunnahu lilnn_asi wal_a taktumoonahu fanaba_thoohu war_aa _thuhoorihim waishtaraw bihi thamanan qaleelan fabi/sa m_a yashtaroon_a

3:187. And although Allah took a pledge from those who were given the Book that they would make it public and not hide it, they threw it behind their backs and traded it for a paltry gain. And evil was the trade.[181]

181. At the time of its revelation, this Verse alluded to the Jews nd the Christians. But now it alludes to the Muslims as well, since they are also the recipients of the divine Book. Although the Qur'aan is very much publicly available and can be found in every Muslim home, the Muslims generally hide its contents from themselves! They do read it but only ritualistically and without understanding. And most of those who can understand it, are influenced by the false belief that it needs to be understood only in the light of the *ahaadeeth*, although the Qur'aan repeatedly asserts it is easy to understand and self-explanatory. And such 'learned' men hide this oft-repeated Qur'aanic assertion and help spread the canard that for understanding the Qur'aan, one must be well-versed in Arabic as a language and must have studied not only the books of *ahaadeeth*, but also the works of the *fuqhaa*!!

لَا تَحْسَبَنَّ ٱلَّذِينَ يَفْرَحُونَ بِمَا أَتَوا وَّيُحِبُّونَ أَن يُحْمَدُوا بِمَا لَمْ يَفْعَلُوا فَلَا تَحْسَبَنَّهُم بِمَفَازَةٍ مِّنَ ٱلْعَذَابِ وَلَهُمْ عَذَابٌ أَلِيمٌ ۝

188. La tahsabanna allatheena yafrahoona bima ataw wayuhibboona an yuhmadoo bima lam yafAAaloo fala tahsabannahum bimafazatin mina alAAathabi walahum AAathabun aleemun

3:188. Think not of them as safe from punishment who exult in what they have got done and love to be praised for what they have not done.[182] And a painful punishment for them.

182. Relating this Verse, as also the preceding one, to the Muslims in general of the current age, those who exult in hiding the oft-repeated Qur'aanic statement that the divine Book is easy to understand and well-explained within itself and who love to be praised for thus 'guarding' Islam, should not think they will escape punishment. They are not thus guarding Islam, but are misrepresenting it to the world, and misleading the gullible Muslims.

وَلِلَّهِ مُلْكُ ٱلسَّمَٰوَٰتِ وَٱلْأَرْضِ وَٱللَّهُ عَلَىٰ كُلِّ شَيْءٍ قَدِيرٌ ۝

189. Walillahi mulku alssamawati waal-ardi waAllahu AAala kulli shay-in qadeerun

3:189. And to Allah belongs the absolute sovereignty over the heavens and the earth. And Allah can do anything.

إِنَّ فِى خَلْقِ ٱلسَّمَـٰوَٰتِ وَٱلْأَرْضِ وَٱخْتِلَـٰفِ ٱلَّيْـلِ وَٱلنَّهَـارِ

لَأَيَـٰتٍ لِّأُوْلِى ٱلْأَلْبَـٰبِ ۝

190. Inna fee khalqi alssamawati waal-ardi waikhtilafi allayli waalnnahari laayatin li-olee al-albabi

---

3:190. Indeed! In the creation of the heavens and the earth and the distinction between the night and the day there are signs for those endowed with insight.[183]

---

183. The people of this age, with the advantage of their vastly greater knowledge, are in a much better position to take cognisance of these signs. The faultless system governing the vast Universe is a standing day-to-day witness to the existence of the Almighty Creator and to His Immense Wisdom. Please also see the next Verses 191.

ٱلَّذِينَ يَذْكُرُونَ ٱللَّهَ قِيَـٰمًا وَقُعُودًا وَعَلَىٰ جُنُوبِهِمْ وَيَتَفَكَّرُونَ فِى خَلْقِ

ٱلسَّمَـٰوَٰتِ وَٱلْأَرْضِ رَبَّنَا مَا خَلَقْتَ هَـٰذَا بَـٰطِلًا سُبْحَـٰنَكَ فَقِنَا عَذَابَ

ٱلنَّارِ ۝

191. Allatheena yathkuroona Allaha qiyaman waquAAoodan waAAala junoobihim wayatafakkaroona fee khalqi alssamawati waal-ardi rabbana ma khalaqta hatha batilan subhanaka faqina AAathaba alnnari

---

3:191. Those[184], who remember Allah while standing, sitting and lying down. And, pondering over creation of the heavens and the earth, they say, "Our Lord! You haven't created this in vain. Glorious are you. Save us from punishment of the Fire."

---

184. That is, the people of understancing referred to in the preceding Verse. Their glorification and prayer to the Lord Creator is continued through, to Verse 194 below.

رَبَّنَآ إِنَّكَ مَن تُدۡخِلِ ٱلنَّارَ فَقَدۡ أَخۡزَيۡتَهُۥ وَمَا لِلظَّـٰلِمِينَ مِنۡ أَنصَارٍ ﴿١٩٢﴾

192. Rabbana innaka man tudkhili alnnara faqad akhzaytahu wama lil*ththa*limeena min an*sar*in

3:192. "Our Lord! You have indeed disgraced the one, whom You have put into the Fire. And, there is none to help those who do wrong."

رَّبَّنَآ إِنَّنَا سَمِعۡنَا مُنَادِيًا يُنَادِى لِلۡإِيمَـٰنِ أَنۡ ءَامِنُواْ بِرَبِّكُمۡ فَـَٔامَنَّا رَبَّنَا فَٱغۡفِرۡ لَنَا ذُنُوبَنَا وَكَفِّرۡ عَنَّا سَيِّـَٔاتِنَا وَتَوَفَّنَا مَعَ ٱلۡأَبۡرَارِ ﴿١٩٣﴾

193. Rabbana innana samiAAna munadiyan yunadee lil-eemani an aminoo birabbikum faamanna rabbana faighfir lana thunoobana wakaffir AAanna sayyi-atina watawaffana maAAa al-abrari

3:193. "Our Lord! We have indeed heard a call of one inviting people to Faith, 'Believe in your Lord.' And we have believed. Our Lord! Forgive us our sins and rid us of our evil spirits. And make us die among those who attained to salvation."

رَبَّنَا وَءَاتِنَا مَا وَعَدتَّنَا عَلَىٰ رُسُلِكَ وَلَا تُخۡزِنَا يَوۡمَ ٱلۡقِيَـٰمَةِ إِنَّكَ لَا تُخۡلِفُ ٱلۡمِيعَادَ ﴿١٩٤﴾

194. Rabbana waatina ma waAAadtana AAala rusulika wala tukhzina yawma alqiyamati innaka la tukhlifu almeeAAada

3:194. "And give us, our Lord, what You promised us through Your Messengers and disgrace us not on the Day of Resurrection. Indeed, You aren't the One to break promises."

فَٱسْتَجَابَ لَهُمْ رَبُّهُمْ أَنِّى لَآ أُضِيعُ عَمَلَ عَـٰمِلٍ مِّنكُم مِّن ذَكَرٍ أَوْ أُنثَىٰ بَعْضُكُم مِّنْ بَعْضٍ فَٱلَّذِينَ هَاجَرُواْ وَأُخْرِجُواْ مِن دِيَـٰرِهِمْ وَأُوذُواْ فِى سَبِيلِى وَقَـٰتَلُواْ وَقُتِلُواْ لَأُكَفِّرَنَّ عَنْهُمْ سَيِّـَٔاتِهِمْ وَلَأُدْخِلَنَّهُمْ جَنَّـٰتٍ تَجْرِى مِن تَحْتِهَا ٱلْأَنْهَـٰرُ ثَوَابًا مِّنْ عِندِ ٱللَّهِ وَٱللَّهُ عِندَهُۥ حُسْنُ ٱلثَّوَابِ ۝١٩٥

195. Faistajaba lahum rabbuhum annee la odeeAAu AAamala AAamilin minkum min thakarin aw ontha baAAdukum min baAAdin faallatheena hajaroo waokhrijoo min diyarihim waoothoo fee sabeelee waqataloo waqutiloo laokaffiranna AAanhum sayyi-atihim walaodkhilannahum jannatin tajree min tahtiha al-anharu thawaban min AAindi Allahi waAllahu AAindahu husnu alththawabi

3:195. Their Lord then responded to them, "Never shall I let any deed by anyone amongst you, male or female, go waste. You are kith and kin of one another. And those who emigrated and were forced out of their homes and were persecuted in My Path, and who fought and were killed, I shall certainly rid them of their evil spirits. And I shall certainly get them into Gardens with rivers flowing underneath" – a reward from Allah! And with Allah is the best of the rewards.

لَا يَغُرَّنَّكَ تَقَلُّبُ ٱلَّذِينَ كَفَرُواْ فِى ٱلْبِلَـٰدِ ۝١٩٦

196. La yaghurrannaka taqallubu allatheena kafaroo fee albiladi

3:196. The free movement in the lands, of those who suppress the Truth, should not beguile you.[185]

---

185. Please see the next two Verses 197 and 198.

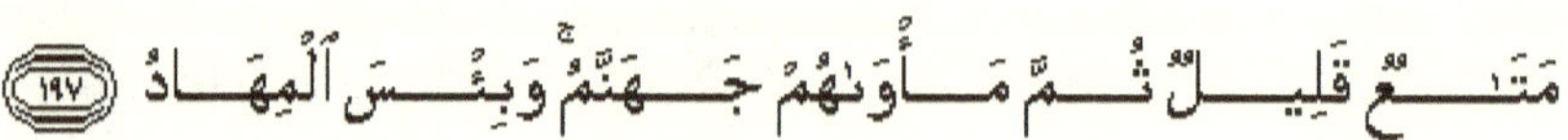

197. MataAAun qaleelun thumma ma/wahum jahannamu wabi/sa almihadu

---

3:197. Their days of ease and comfort are numbered. The Hell – the worst of the places for rest – shall then be their abode.

لَـٰكِنِ ٱلَّذِينَ ٱتَّقَوْاْ رَبَّهُمْ لَهُمْ جَنَّـٰتٌ تَجْرِى مِن تَحْتِهَا ٱلْأَنْهَـٰرُ خَـٰلِدِينَ فِيهَا نُزُلًا مِّنْ عِندِ ٱللَّهِ وَمَا عِندَ ٱللَّهِ خَـيْرٌ لِّلْأَبْرَارِ ﴿١٩٨﴾

198. Lakini allatheena ittaqaw rabbahum lahum jannatun tajree min tahtiha al-anharu khalideena feeha nuzulan min AAindi Allahi wama AAinda Allahi khayrun lil-abrari

---

3:198. But for those who fear their Lord, there shall be gardens, with rivers flowing underneath, wherein to live for ever – a bestowment from Allah. And that which is with Allah is the best for the righteous.

وَإِنَّ مِنْ أَهْلِ ٱلْكِتَـٰبِ لَمَن يُؤْمِنُ بِٱللَّهِ وَمَآ أُنزِلَ إِلَيْكُمْ وَمَآ أُنزِلَ إِلَيْهِمْ

خَـٰشِعِينَ لِلَّهِ لَا يَشْتَرُونَ بِـَٔايَـٰتِ ٱللَّهِ ثَمَنًا قَلِيلًا أُو۟لَـٰٓئِكَ لَهُمْ أَجْرُهُمْ

عِندَ رَبِّهِمْ إِنَّ ٱللَّهَ سَرِيعُ ٱلْحِسَابِ ﴿١٩٩﴾

199. Wa-inna min ahli alkit__a__bi laman yu/minu biAll__a__hi wam__a__ onzila ilaykum wam__a__ onzila ilayhim kh__a__shiAAeena lill__a__hi l__a__ yashtaroona bi-__a__y__a__ti All__a__hi thamanan qaleelan ol__a__-ika lahum ajruhum AAinda rabbihim inna All__a__ha sareeAAu al__h__is__a__bi

---

3:199. And, indeed, among the followers of the Book, there certainly are some who believe in Allah and in that which has been revealed to you and in that which has been revealed to them. Humble before Allah, they sell not Allah's Verses for a little gain. For them are their rewards with their Lord. Allah is indeed swift in keeping accounts.

يَـٰٓأَيُّهَا ٱلَّذِينَ ءَامَنُوا۟ ٱصْبِرُوا۟ وَصَابِرُوا۟ وَرَابِطُوا۟ وَٱتَّقُوا۟ ٱللَّهَ لَعَلَّكُمْ

تُفْلِحُونَ ﴿٢٠٠﴾

200. Y__a__ ayyuh__a__ alla__th__eena __a__manoo i__s__biroo wa__sa__biroo war__a__bi__t__oo wai**t**taqoo All__a__ha laAAallakum tufli__h__oona

---

3:200. O you who believe! Be patient, exhort patience, maintain good relations with one another and fear Allah, in order that you succeed.[186]

---

186. This is a veritable divine mantra for success. But, alas, there are very few Muslims in today's world with a strong enough Faith to make use of this mantra! The Muslims would not be in the doldrums, they find themselves in, otherwise.

Chapter 4: An-Nisa (The Women)

In the Name of Allah, the Gracious, the Merciful

1. Ya ayyuha alnnasu ittaqoo rabbakumu allathee khalaqakum min nafsin wahidatin wakhalaqa minha zawjaha wabaththa minhuma rijalan katheeran wanisaan waittaqoo Allaha allathee tasaaloona bihi waal-arhama inna Allaha kana AAalaykum raqeeban

---

4:1. O mankind! Fear your Lord Who created you out of a single being and created there from its mate and, from the two, created many men and women and caused them to spread out. And fear Allah about Whom, and about the wombs, you make inquiries.[1] Allah does indeed keep a close watch over you all.

---

1. People, in all ages, have wondered about their coming into existence. In due course they realise that their parents (wombs) are just instruments used. Then who is the real maker who used those instruments? Or is it that things just happen, with no real maker causing them to happen? But with their ever-increasing knowledge, the people have come to know that the universe at large and their bodies, are gems of creation, requiring a superhuman intelligence and superhuman creative abilities. Who is that superhuman creator and where is he? Is there one creator or many? And if there are many creators, how come the administration of the universe at large runs so smoothly? Questions like these arise in the human mind, and the Qur'aan gives the answers in detail. This Verse informs mankind how their One Creator and Sustainer spread them on earth, starting from one man. Although the parents are just instruments in the creation of their children, mankind is enjoined to give them, and especially the mother, due respect [Verse 31:14].

وَءَاتُواْ ٱلْيَتَـٰمَىٰٓ أَمْوَٰلَهُمْ وَلَا تَتَبَدَّلُواْ ٱلْخَبِيثَ بِٱلطَّيِّبِ وَلَا
تَأْكُلُوٓاْ أَمْوَٰلَهُمْ إِلَىٰٓ أَمْوَٰلِكُمْ إِنَّهُۥ كَانَ حُوبًا كَبِيرًا ﴿٢﴾

2. Waatoo alyatama amwalahum wala tatabaddaloo alkhabeetha bialttayyibi wala ta/kuloo amwalahum ila amwalikum innahu kana hooban kabeeran

4:2. And give the orphans their property, and do not substitute the good with the bad. And do not consume their property into yours. This indeed is a great crime.

وَإِنْ خِفْتُمْ أَلَّا تُقْسِطُواْ فِى ٱلْيَتَـٰمَىٰ فَٱنكِحُواْ مَا طَابَ لَكُم
مِّنَ ٱلنِّسَآءِ مَثْنَىٰ وَثُلَـٰثَ وَرُبَـٰعَ فَإِنْ خِفْتُمْ أَلَّا تَعْدِلُواْ فَوَٰحِدَةً أَوْ
مَا مَلَكَتْ أَيْمَـٰنُكُمْ ذَٰلِكَ أَدْنَىٰٓ أَلَّا تَعُولُواْ ﴿٣﴾

3. Wa-in khiftum alla tuqsitoo fee alyatama fainkihoo ma taba lakum mina alnnisa-i mathna wathulatha warubaAAa fa-in khiftum alla taAAdiloo fawahidatan aw ma malakat aymanukum thalika adna alla taAAooloo

4:3. And if you fear that you shall not be equitable in the matter of the orphans, then marry women suitable to you, two, three and four.[2] But if you fear that you shall not be able to do justice between the wives, then be content with only one wife,[3] or with what your right hands possess.[4, 5] That way it is more likely that you may not deviate from what is right.

2. Polygamy is allowed in Islam under certain conditions. One condition mentioned here is that a man, entrusted with the care of orphans, is not able to treat them fairly as he would treat his own children. And if the orphans have a living widowed mother, the man may marry the widow, even if he is already married to another woman. This way the orphaned children stand a better chance of being looked after well. The number of wives, a man can thus have, is limited to 4.

3. One other condition to be satisfied by a man, marrying more than one wife, is that he should do justice to all his wives, which is a very difficult thing to do, as <u>Verse 4:129</u> further down in this very Chapter tells us. It is therefore better to have only one wife. Monogamy is thus the recommended norm in Islam.

4. This is how slaves are mentioned in the Qur'aan. Slavery had been in practice at the time the Qur'aan was revealed. It had been so intricately associated with the social and economic fabric of the society then that the practice was not possible to be stopped without causing a collapse of the entire system. Islam, on the other hand, encouraged the freeing of the slaves from their bondage. And in course of time, slavery disappeared from Islamic society, without fighting a war therefor, as was done in American history.

5. There was also the custom, prevalent at the time of revelation of the Qur'aan, allowing sexual intercourse between a master and his slave-girl. It is this custom that is alluded to here, in this Verse. And the believers could continue with the custom. This custom also died with the nonsurgical elimination of slavery from the Islamic society. Muslims, in today's world, need not be apologetic about Islam allowing this custom of the period of ignorance to continue. What is a formal marriage after all? It is nothing but the society giving its permission to a man and a woman to have sexual relations with each other. When a human society can give such permission, why can't Allah Himself give the same to the master and his slave-girl? And Allah, in His infinite knowledge, knew that this custom is going to die a natural death.

وَءَاتُواْ ٱلنِّسَآءَ صَدُقَٰتِهِنَّ نِحْلَةً فَإِن طِبْنَ لَكُمْ عَن شَيْءٍ مِّنْهُ نَفْسًا فَكُلُوهُ هَنِيٓئًا مَّرِيٓئًا ۝

4. Waatoo alnnisaa saduqatihinna nihlatan fa-in tibna lakum AAan shay-in minhu nafsan fakuloohu hanee-an maree-an

---

4:4. And give the women their dues as free gifts[6]. And if they themselves give up a portion of it for you, then accept and use it with a wholesome attitude.

---

6. That is, the husband and the in-laws should never expect to get back anything out of things given to the wife (her *Mehr*, for example) for the family's use.

وَلَا تُؤْتُوا۟ ٱلسُّفَهَآءَ أَمْوَٰلَكُمُ ٱلَّتِى جَعَلَ ٱللَّهُ لَكُمْ قِيَٰمًا وَٱرْزُقُوهُمْ فِيهَا وَٱكْسُوهُمْ وَقُولُوا۟ لَهُمْ قَوْلًا مَّعْرُوفًا ۞

5. Wala tu/too alssufahaa amwalakumu allatee jaAAala Allahu lakum qiyaman waorzuqoohum feeha waoksoohum waqooloo lahum qawlan maAAroofan

---

4:5. And do not hand over to the mentally weak the property of which Allah has made you the trustee. And feed them out of that property and clothe them. And speak to them in kind words.

وَٱبْتَلُوا۟ ٱلْيَتَٰمَىٰ حَتَّىٰٓ إِذَا بَلَغُوا۟ ٱلنِّكَاحَ فَإِنْ ءَانَسْتُم مِّنْهُمْ رُشْدًا فَٱدْفَعُوٓا۟ إِلَيْهِمْ أَمْوَٰلَهُمْ وَلَا تَأْكُلُوهَآ إِسْرَافًا وَبِدَارًا أَن يَكْبَرُوا۟ وَمَن كَانَ غَنِيًّا فَلْيَسْتَعْفِفْ وَمَن كَانَ فَقِيرًا فَلْيَأْكُلْ بِٱلْمَعْرُوفِ فَإِذَا دَفَعْتُمْ إِلَيْهِمْ أَمْوَٰلَهُمْ فَأَشْهِدُوا۟ عَلَيْهِمْ وَكَفَىٰ بِٱللَّهِ حَسِيبًا ۞

6. Waibtaloo alyatama hatta itha balaghoo alnnikaha fa-in anastum minhum rushdan faidfaAAoo ilayhim amwalahum wala ta/kulooha israfan wabidaran an yakbaroo waman kana ghaniyyan falyastaAAfif waman kana faqeeran falya/kul bialmaAAroofi fa-itha dafaAAtum ilayhim amwalahum faashhidoo AAalayhim wakafa biAllahi haseeban

---

4:6. And test the orphans till they reach marriageable age. If you then find in them maturity of intellect, hand over to them their property. And do not consume it extravagantly and hastily, lest they grow up. And a rich trustee should refrain from taking anything out of the orphans' property. And a poor Trustee may take just what is proper for his own consumption. And when you hand over to them their property, the transactions should be attested by witnesses. And Allah is Self-sufficient in maintaining proper accounts.

لِّلرِّجَالِ نَصِيبٌ مِّمَّا تَرَكَ ٱلْوَٰلِدَانِ وَٱلْأَقْرَبُونَ وَلِلنِّسَآءِ نَصِيبٌ مِّمَّا تَرَكَ ٱلْوَٰلِدَانِ وَٱلْأَقْرَبُونَ مِمَّا قَلَّ مِنْهُ أَوْ كَثُرَ نَصِيبًا مَّفْرُوضًا ۝

7. Lilrrijali naseebun mimma taraka alwalidani waal-aqraboona walilnnisa-i naseebun mimma taraka alwalidani waal-aqraboona mimma qalla minhu aw kathura naseeban mafroodan

---

4:7. Men and women shall have legal shares in what the parents and the near relatives leave behind, whether little or more.

وَإِذَا حَضَرَ ٱلْقِسْمَةَ أُو۟لُوا۟ ٱلْقُرْبَىٰ وَٱلْيَتَٰمَىٰ وَٱلْمَسَٰكِينُ فَٱرْزُقُوهُم مِّنْهُ وَقُولُوا۟ لَهُمْ قَوْلًا مَّعْرُوفًا ۝

8. Wa-itha hadara alqismata oloo alqurba waalyatama waalmasakeenu faorzuqoohum minhu waqooloo lahum qawlan maAAroofan

---

4:8. And give something out of the property to the relatives, the orphans and the needy, present at the division of the property. And speak to them kind words.

وَلْيَخْشَ ٱلَّذِينَ لَوْ تَرَكُوا۟ مِنْ خَلْفِهِمْ ذُرِّيَّةً ضِعَٰفًا خَافُوا۟ عَلَيْهِمْ فَلْيَتَّقُوا۟ ٱللَّهَ وَلْيَقُولُوا۟ قَوْلًا سَدِيدًا ۝

9. Walyakhsha allatheena law tarakoo min khalfihim thurriyyatan diAAafan khafoo AAalayhim falyattaqoo Allaha walyaqooloo qawlan sadeedan

---

4:9. And let the persons concerned apprehend a situation wherein they themselves might leave weak offspring behind and fear on their account. So, let them guard against Allah's wrath, and let them speak in appropriate and straight (unambiguous and to the point) words.

10. Inna allatheena ya/kuloona amwala alyatama *th*ulman innama ya/kuloona fee butoonihim naran wasayaslawna saAAeeran

4:10. Indeed, they, who swallow the property of the orphans unjustly, swallow only fire into their bellies. And they shall burn in the flames of Hellfire.

11. Yooseekumu Allahu fee awladikum lil*th*thakari mithlu ha*thth*i alonthayayni fa-in kunna nisaan fawqa ithnatayni falahunna thulutha ma taraka wa-in kanat wahidatan falaha alnnisfu wali-abawayhi likulli wahidin minhuma alssudusu mimma taraka in kana lahu waladun fa-in lam yakun lahu waladun wawarithahu abawahu fali-ommihi alththuluthu fa-in kana lahu ikhwatun fali-ommihi alssudusu min baAAdi wasiyyatin yoosee biha aw daynin abaokum waabnaokum la tadroona ayyuhum aqrabu lakum nafAAan fareedatan mina Allahi inna Allaha kana AAaleeman hakeeman

4:11. Allah commissions you concerning your children: The male shall have the equal of the shares of two females; and if there be only females two or more, they shall have two-thirds of what is left; and if the female is only one, she shall have the half; and one sixth for each of his parents, if the deceased has any child; and if he has no child and his two parents inherit him, then his mother shall have the third; and if the deceased has brothers, his mother shall have the sixth; after making provision for any will, the deceased may have made, or for any outstanding loan. Your parents and your children – you know not which of them are nearer to you in usefulness. This is an ordinance from Allah. Indeed, Allah is Knowledgeable, Wise!

12. Walakum nisfu ma taraka azwajukum in lam yakun lahunna waladun fa-in kana lahunna waladun falakumu alrrubuAAu mimma tarakna min baAAdi wasiyyatin yooseena biha aw daynin walahunna alrrubuAAu mimma taraktum in lam yakun lakum waladun fa-in kana lakum waladun falahunna a111) alththumunu mimma taraktum min baAAdi wasiyyatin toosoona biha aw daynin wa-in kana rajulun yoorathu kalalatan awi imraatun walahu akhun aw okhtun falikulli wahidin minhuma alssudusu fa-in kanoo akthara min thalika fahum shurakao fee alththuluthi min baAAdi wasiyyatin yoosa biha aw daynin ghayra mudarrin wasiyyatan mina Allahi waAllahu AAaleemun haleemun

4:12. And, for you, half of what your wives leave behind, if they have no child; and if they have any child, then for you a quarter of what they leave behind, after making a provision for any will that they might have made, or for any outstanding loan. And for them a quarter, if you have no child; and if you have a child, then for them an eighth of what you leave behind, after making a provision for any will that you may make, or for any outstanding loan. And if the person, male or female, whose property is to be inherited, has left neither parents nor children behind, and he/she has only a brother or a sister to inherit his/her property, then for either of them a sixth; and if there are more than these, they all share a third; after making a provision for any will that the deceased might have made, or for any outstanding loan, causing thereby no harm to anyone. That is a bequest from Allah. And Allah knows, and He cares.[7 to 11]

---

7. These 2 Verses 11 and 12 here along with Verses 7, 8 and 176 of this very Qur'aanic Chapter succinctly constitute the entire Islamic Law of Inheritance.

8. One universal objection raised against this Law, particularly among non-Muslim circles, is that it is discriminatory against women. These circles conveniently forget that Islam was the first to grant legal rights to women in property matters (see Verse 7 above). And it is just and proper that a brother gets double the share of a sister among the deceased's children. In Islam – and it is the general norm in human societies – the responsibility for maintaining a family is that of the male head. If the deceased had one son and two daughters (and there are no other claimants), the brother will get half the share with the other half being shared by the two sisters. Now, if the sisters are both married, they will take their shares with no responsibility of maintaining a family. The responsibility of maintaining their respective families is their huspands'. But their brother would, on the other hand, have the responsibility to maintain his own family. Besides, if the sisters are unmarried, maintaining them would also be the responsibility of the brother. It should thus be seen that equal distribution of the property, among the three, would be an unfair proposition.

9. Some people think that there is no provision made for the wife and children of a son whose death preceded that of the father. This misgiving should vanish the moment it is realized that the son had left behind his due share in the father's property. The wife and children of the son should therefore get their dues from the son's share. Moreover, the father could make a Will, after the son's death, to provide for some additional share to the orphaned children.

10. Let us now consider a few different cases for practical implementation of the divine order on inheritance. The cases considered are of course those where the deceased have made no wills:

- If there are children, both male and female, and both parents living, father and mother get 1/6 each, and the remaining 2/3 gets so distributed among the brothers and sisters that a brother gets twice the share of a sister.
- If there are only 1 girl child and both parents living, the girl child gets half the share, each parent 1/6, and the remaining 1/6 gets disbursed in terms of Verse 4:8 above.
- If there are only girl children, two or more, and both parents living, all the sisters together get 2/3 share, the partents together getting the remaining 1/3.
- And so on – the left overs if any after distribution, as laid down, being disbursed in terms of Verse 4:8.

11. In terms of <u>Verse 2:180</u>, making a Will before one's death, is mandatory. In this context, therefore, it is incumbent on us to consider the implications of that Verse. Please refer the study notes <u>thereunder</u>, under these Studies.

تِلْكَ حُدُودُ ٱللَّهِ وَمَن يُطِعِ ٱللَّهَ وَرَسُولَهُۥ يُدْخِلْهُ جَنَّٰتٍ تَجْرِى مِن تَحْتِهَا ٱلْأَنْهَٰرُ خَٰلِدِينَ فِيهَا وَذَٰلِكَ ٱلْفَوْزُ ٱلْعَظِيمُ ۝١٣

13. Tilka hudoodu Allahi waman yutiAAi Allaha warasoolahu yudkhilhu jannatin tajree min tahtiha al-anharu khalideena feeha wathalika alfawzu alAAatheemu

---

4:13. Those are Allah's laws. And Allah will admit the one, who obeys Him and His Messenger, into Gardens with rivers flowing underneath, to dwell therein forever. And that will be the highest success.

وَمَن يَعْصِ ٱللَّهَ وَرَسُولَهُۥ وَيَتَعَدَّ حُدُودَهُۥ يُدْخِلْهُ نَارًا خَٰلِدًا فِيهَا وَلَهُۥ عَذَابٌ مُّهِينٌ ۝١٤

14. Waman yaAAsi Allaha warasoolahu wayataAAadda hudoodahu yudkhilhu naran khalidan feeha walahu AAathabun muheenun

---

4:14. And Allah will make the one who disobeys Him and His Messenger and breaks His laws enter the Fire to dwell therein forever. And for him/her will there be a disgraceful punishment.

وَٱلَّٰتِى يَأْتِينَ ٱلْفَٰحِشَةَ مِن نِّسَآئِكُمْ فَٱسْتَشْهِدُوا۟ عَلَيْهِنَّ أَرْبَعَةً مِّنكُمْ فَإِن شَهِدُوا۟ فَأَمْسِكُوهُنَّ فِى ٱلْبُيُوتِ حَتَّىٰ يَتَوَفَّىٰهُنَّ ٱلْمَوْتُ أَوْ يَجْعَلَ ٱللَّهُ لَهُنَّ سَبِيلًا ۝١٥

15. Waallatee ya/teena alfahishata min nisa-ikum faistashhidoo AAalayhinna arbaAAatan minkum fa-in shahidoo faamsikoohunna fee albuyooti hatta yatawaffahunna almawtu aw yajAAala Allahu lahunna sabeelan

---

4:15. And as for those who commit the obscene act[12] from among your women, produce 4 witnesses from amongst you, against them. Then if they bear witness, confine them to the houses until death takes them away, or Allah makes some way for them.[13]

---

12. The Arabic term *alfahishata* is used for homosexuality in Verses 7:80, 27:54 & 29:28. The term, without the prefix *al*, is used in Verse 4:22 for anyone marrying a woman whom his father had married, and in Verses 3:135, 4:19, 7:28, 17:32 etc for any other obscene behaviour or act leading or conducive to adultery.

13. The confinement is restricted only to those who do not repent and mend their ways. Please see the next Verse.

وَٱللَّذَانِ يَأْتِيَٰنِهَا مِنكُمْ فَـَٔاذُوهُمَا فَإِن تَابَا وَأَصْلَحَا فَأَعْرِضُواْ عَنْهُمَآ إِنَّ ٱللَّهَ كَانَ تَوَّابًا رَّحِيمًا ۝

16. Waallathani ya/tiyaniha minkum faathoohuma fa-in taba waaslaha faaAAridoo AAanhuma inna Allaha kana tawwaban raheeman

---

4:16. And as for the two, who commit the obscene act from among you, give them both a punishment[14]. Then if they repent and mend their ways, leave them alone. Indeed, Allah does accept repentance and is Merciful.

---

14. The punishment prescribed for adultery is hundred lashes (24:2), which has necessarily to be meted out by an Islamic government. Where there is no such government, the State criminal law will apply.

إِنَّمَا ٱلتَّوْبَةُ عَلَى ٱللَّهِ لِلَّذِينَ يَعْمَلُونَ ٱلسُّوٓءَ بِجَهَٰلَةٍ ثُمَّ يَتُوبُونَ مِن قَرِيبٍ فَأُو۟لَٰٓئِكَ يَتُوبُ ٱللَّهُ عَلَيْهِمْ وَكَانَ ٱللَّهُ عَلِيمًا حَكِيمًا ۝

17. Innama alttawbatu AAala Allahi lillatheena yaAAmaloona alssoo-a bijahalatin thumma yatooboona min qareebin faola-ika yatoobu Allahu AAalayhim wakana Allahu AAaleeman hakeeman

---

4:17. Allah's acceptance of repentance is only for those who do an evil deed in ignorance, and then turn to Allah in repentance soon thereafter. So, it is these whose repentance Allah accepts. And Allah is Knowledgeable, Wise.

وَلَيْسَتِ ٱلتَّوْبَةُ لِلَّذِينَ يَعْمَلُونَ ٱلسَّيِّئَاتِ حَتَّىٰٓ إِذَا حَضَرَ أَحَدَهُمُ ٱلْمَوْتُ قَالَ إِنِّى تُبْتُ ٱلْـَٰٔنَ وَلَا ٱلَّذِينَ يَمُوتُونَ وَهُمْ كُفَّارٌ أُو۟لَٰٓئِكَ أَعْتَدْنَا لَهُمْ عَذَابًا أَلِيمًا ۝

18. Walaysati alttawbatu lillatheena yaAAmaloona alssayyi-ati hatta itha hadara ahadahumu almawtu qala innee tubtu al-ana wala allatheena yamootoona wahum kuffarun ola-ika aAAatadna lahum AAathaban aleeman

---

4:18. And repentance is not for those who go on doing evil deeds, until when death comes to one of them, he says, "I do repent now." Nor is it for those who die while suppressing the Truth. These are the people for whom We have prepared a painful punishment.

يَـٰٓأَيُّهَا ٱلَّذِينَ ءَامَنُوا۟ لَا يَحِلُّ لَكُمْ أَن تَرِثُوا۟ ٱلنِّسَآءَ كَرْهًا ۖ وَلَا تَعْضُلُوهُنَّ لِتَذْهَبُوا۟ بِبَعْضِ مَآ ءَاتَيْتُمُوهُنَّ إِلَّآ أَن يَأْتِينَ بِفَـٰحِشَةٍ مُّبَيِّنَةٍ ۚ وَعَاشِرُوهُنَّ بِٱلْمَعْرُوفِ ۚ فَإِن كَرِهْتُمُوهُنَّ فَعَسَىٰٓ أَن تَكْرَهُوا۟ شَيْـًٔا وَيَجْعَلَ ٱللَّهُ فِيهِ خَيْرًا كَثِيرًا 

19. Y<u>a</u> ayyuh<u>a</u> alla<u>th</u>eena <u>a</u>manoo l<u>a</u> ya<u>h</u>illu lakum an tarithoo a<u>l</u>nnis<u>a</u>a karhan wal<u>a</u> taAA<u>d</u>uloohunna lita<u>th</u>haboo bibaAA<u>d</u>i m<u>a</u> <u>a</u>taytumoohunna ill<u>a</u> an ya/teena bif<u>ah</u>ishatin mubayyinatin waAA<u>a</u>shiroohunna bialmaAAroofi fa-in karihtumoohunna faAA<u>a</u>s<u>a</u> an takrahoo shay-an wayajAAala All<u>a</u>hu feehi khayran katheer<u>a</u>n

---

4:19. O you who believe! It is not lawful for you to inherit women against their will.[15] And persecute them not to usurp some of the things you have given them unless they commit something manifestly obscene. And live with them properly. And if you dislike them, it may so be that you dislike a thing while Allah has kept therein immense good.

---

15. Men may inherit mothers, sisters, or wives. Mothers and sisters are blood relations, and, therefore, there is no question of inheriting such relatives against their will. But one may inherit a woman as a wife, against her will. So, this part of the Verse is a clear divine injunction against any man forcing a woman to remain his wife against her will. It is, therefore, a divinely imposed command for any man to divorce his wife if she insists on the separation.

وَإِنْ أَرَدتُّمُ ٱسْتِبْدَالَ زَوْجٍ مَّكَانَ زَوْجٍ وَءَاتَيْتُمْ إِحْدَىٰهُنَّ قِنطَارًا فَلَا تَأْخُذُوا۟ مِنْهُ شَيْـًٔا ۚ أَتَأْخُذُونَهُۥ بُهْتَـٰنًا وَإِثْمًا مُّبِينًا 

20. Wa-in aradtumu istibdala zawjin makana zawjin waataytum ihdahunna qintaran fala ta/khuthoo minhu shay-an ata/khuthoonahu buhtanan wa-ithman mubeenan

4:20. And if you intend to change one woman for another as your wife, and you had given one of them a lot of wealth, then take not anything there from. Will you take it by resorting to a calumny and a manifest sin?

وَكَيْفَ تَأْخُذُونَهُ وَقَدْ أَفْضَىٰ بَعْضُكُمْ إِلَىٰ بَعْضٍ وَأَخَذْنَ مِنكُم مِّيثَاقًا

غَلِيظًا ﴿٢١﴾

21. Wakayfa ta/khuthoonahu waqad afda baAAdukum ila baAAdin waakhathna minkum meethaqan ghaleethan

4:21. And how could you take it when you have had enjoyed conjugal relations with one another, and they had taken a firm pledge[16] from you?

16. The marriage contract. The implication of the contract is that the man can have sexual intercourse with the woman on his paying her the *Mehr* as agreed upon in the marriage document. Once the man had the sexual intercourse with the woman, the *Mehr*, as well as all the gifts given her, are hers, and the man loses all legal rights thereto.

وَلَا تَنكِحُوا مَا نَكَحَ ءَابَآؤُكُم مِّنَ ٱلنِّسَآءِ إِلَّا مَا قَدْ سَلَفَ إِنَّهُ كَانَ فَٰحِشَةً

وَمَقْتًا وَسَآءَ سَبِيلًا ﴿٢٢﴾

22. Wala tankihoo ma nakaha abaokum mina alnnisa-i illa ma qad salafa innahu kana fahishatan wamaqtan wasaa sabeelan

4:22. And marry not those women whom your fathers married, past cases excepted. That practice was indeed an obscenity, abhorrence and an evil way of life.

حُرِّمَتْ عَلَيْكُمْ أُمَّهَٰتُكُمْ وَبَنَاتُكُمْ وَأَخَوَٰتُكُمْ وَعَمَّٰتُكُمْ وَخَٰلَٰتُكُمْ وَبَنَاتُ ٱلْأَخِ وَبَنَاتُ ٱلْأُخْتِ وَأُمَّهَٰتُكُمُ ٱلَّٰتِىٓ أَرْضَعْنَكُمْ وَأَخَوَٰتُكُم مِّنَ ٱلرَّضَٰعَةِ وَأُمَّهَٰتُ نِسَآئِكُمْ وَرَبَٰٓئِبُكُمُ ٱلَّٰتِى فِى حُجُورِكُم مِّن نِّسَآئِكُمُ ٱلَّٰتِى دَخَلْتُم بِهِنَّ فَإِن لَّمْ تَكُونُوا۟ دَخَلْتُم بِهِنَّ فَلَا جُنَاحَ عَلَيْكُمْ وَحَلَٰٓئِلُ أَبْنَآئِكُمُ ٱلَّذِينَ مِنْ أَصْلَٰبِكُمْ وَأَن تَجْمَعُوا۟ بَيْنَ ٱلْأُخْتَيْنِ إِلَّا مَا قَدْ سَلَفَ إِنَّ ٱللَّهَ كَانَ غَفُورًا رَّحِيمًا ﴿٢٣﴾

23. Hurrimat AAalaykum ommahatukum wabanatukum waakhawatukum waAAammatukum wakhalatukum wabanatu al-akhi wabanatu al-okhti waommahatukumu allatee ardaAAnakum waakhawatukum mina alrradaAAati waommahatu nisa-ikum waraba-ibukumu allatee fee hujoorikum min nisa-ikumu allatee dakhaltum bihinna fa-in lam takoonoo dakhaltum bihinna fala junaha AAalaykum wahala-ilu abna-ikumu allatheena min aslabikum waan tajmaAAoo bayna al-okhtayni illa ma qad salafa inna Allaha kana ghafooran raheeman

4:23. Forbidden to you are your mothers and your daughters and your sisters and your paternal aunts and your maternal aunts and brother's daughters and sister's daughters and your mothers that have suckled you and your foster milk suckling sisters and mothers of your wives and your step-daughters in your guardianship, born of your wives with whom you have had sexual intercourse – but if you have had no sexual intercourse, there is no sin on you marrying the step-daughters – and the wives of your begotten sons and that you should have two sisters together, past cases excepted. Allah is indeed Forgiving, Merciful.[17]

17. Mentioned in this Verse are the relatives and other women, whom a man cannot marry.

$$\text{﴿وَٱلْمُحْصَنَٰتُ مِنَ ٱلنِّسَآءِ إِلَّا مَا مَلَكَتْ أَيْمَٰنُكُمْ ۖ كِتَٰبَ ٱللَّهِ عَلَيْكُمْ ۚ}$$

$$\text{وَأُحِلَّ لَكُم مَّا وَرَآءَ ذَٰلِكُمْ أَن تَبْتَغُواْ بِأَمْوَٰلِكُم مُّحْصِنِينَ غَيْرَ}$$

$$\text{مُسَٰفِحِينَ ۚ فَمَا ٱسْتَمْتَعْتُم بِهِۦ مِنْهُنَّ فَـَٔاتُوهُنَّ أُجُورَهُنَّ فَرِيضَةً ۚ وَلَا}$$

$$\text{جُنَاحَ عَلَيْكُمْ فِيمَا تَرَٰضَيْتُم بِهِۦ مِنۢ بَعْدِ ٱلْفَرِيضَةِ ۚ إِنَّ ٱللَّهَ كَانَ عَلِيمًا}$$

$$\text{حَكِيمًا ﴿٢٤﴾}$$

24. Waalmuhsanatu mina alnnisa-i illa ma malakat aymanukum kitaba Allahi AAalaykum waohilla lakum ma waraa thalikum an tabtaghoo bi-amwalikum muhsineena ghayra musafiheena fama istamtaAAtum bihi minhunna faatoohunna ojoorahunna fareedatan wala junaha AAalaykum feema taradaytum bihi min baAAdi alfareedati inna Allaha kana AAaleeman hakeeman

---

4:24. [18]And the married among the women other than those whom your right hands possess[19]. This is Allah's ordinance for you! And permitted for you are women other than those, if you seek marriage – and not extramarital sex – with them with your own means.[20] On consummation of the marriages, then, give them their obligatory wedding gifts. And no blame on you in what you mutually agree upon, after fulfilling the obligation.[21] Indeed, Allah is Knowledgeable, Wise.

---

18. This is a continuation, from <u>the Verse</u> immediately preceding, of the list of women, that a man is forbidden to marry. By this Verse, women already married to other men, are added to that list.

19. Please refer <u>study notes 4:4 and 4:5</u> of these Studies for the Qur'aanic meaning of the term, *ma malakat aymanukum* (whom your right hands possess). The slave-girls are made exceptions here to the general divine command against marrying already-married women, who were not divorced and whose husbands were not dead. This exception was made because the slave-girls were generally those who were captured in a battle from the enemy. And before their capture, they could have been married to men still living in the enemy camp. It should be well remembered in this context that slavery is now defunct, and this Islamic sanction of sexual relationship with slave-girls should not be confused with the present-day practice of the invading forces committing rapes on women in enemy territory. During the times of the Prophet (peace be upon him), the Islamic forces did not commit such rapes. But if there were women among the war prisoners taken <u>at the scene of the battle</u>, the women were distributed among the men in the Muslim force to serve as their slave-girls. It was a nascent Islamic State then, which lacked the wherewithal of a modern-day State. Even the expenses incurred in a war were personally borne by the participating believers.

20. The restrictions/conditions mentioned in <u>Verse 4:3</u> should also be borne in mind while contracting marriages with the eligible women.

21. **From this part of the Verse, it is clear, that the *mehr* fixed must be paid by the bridegroom to the bride immediately after the marriage is consummated. Thereafter, it is the general responsibility of the husband to bear all the family expenses. But if the bride is financially rich because of her personal inheritance or other lawful means/resource, there is no blame on the husband if the wife agrees, of her own free will, to bear a part of or the entire expense.**

وَمَن لَّمْ يَسْتَطِعْ مِنكُمْ طَوْلًا أَن يَنكِحَ ٱلْمُحْصَنَٰتِ ٱلْمُؤْمِنَٰتِ فَمِن مَّا مَلَكَتْ أَيْمَٰنُكُم مِّن فَتَيَٰتِكُمُ ٱلْمُؤْمِنَٰتِ وَٱللَّهُ أَعْلَمُ بِإِيمَٰنِكُم بَعْضُكُم مِّنۢ بَعْضٍ فَٱنكِحُوهُنَّ بِإِذْنِ أَهْلِهِنَّ وَءَاتُوهُنَّ أُجُورَهُنَّ بِٱلْمَعْرُوفِ مُحْصَنَٰتٍ غَيْرَ مُسَٰفِحَٰتٍ وَلَا مُتَّخِذَٰتِ أَخْدَانٍ فَإِذَآ أُحْصِنَّ فَإِنْ أَتَيْنَ بِفَٰحِشَةٍ فَعَلَيْهِنَّ نِصْفُ مَا عَلَى ٱلْمُحْصَنَٰتِ مِنَ ٱلْعَذَابِ ذَٰلِكَ لِمَنْ خَشِىَ ٱلْعَنَتَ مِنكُمْ وَأَن تَصْبِرُوا۟ خَيْرٌ لَّكُمْ وَٱللَّهُ غَفُورٌ رَّحِيمٌ ﴿٢٥﴾

25. Waman lam yastatiAA minkum tawlan an yankiha almuhsanati almu/minati famin ma malakat aymanukum min fatayatikumu almu/minati waAllahu aAAlamu bi-eemanikum baAAdukum min baAAdin fainkihoohunna bi-ithni ahlihinna waatoohunna ojoorahunna bialmaAAroofi muhsanatin ghayra masafihatin wala muttakhithati akhdanin fa-itha ohsinna fa-in atayna bifahishatin faAAalayhinna nisfu ma AAala almuhsanati mina alAAathabi thalika liman khashiya alAAanata minkum waan tasbiroo khayrun lakum waAllahu ghafoorun raheemun

4:25. And whoever amongst you has not been able to marry free believing women then let him marry those from among slave-girls who have become believers. And Allah does know your faith. You are of one another. Marry those of them then – with the permission of their masters and giving them their wedding gifts properly – who are chaste and do not seek extramarital sex taking you as just boyfriends for the purpose. And if, after marriage, they commit fornication, their punishment is half that for free women. That is for the one amongst you who fears falling into sin otherwise. And it is better for you to be patient. And Allah is Forgiving, Merciful.

يُرِيدُ ٱللَّهُ لِيُبَيِّنَ لَكُمْ وَيَهْدِيَكُمْ سُنَنَ ٱلَّذِينَ مِن قَبْلِكُمْ وَيَتُوبَ عَلَيْكُمْ وَٱللَّهُ عَلِيمٌ حَكِيمٌ ﴿٢٦﴾

26. Yureedu Allahu liyubayyina lakum wayahdiyakum sunana allatheena min qablikum wayatooba AAalaykum waAllahu AAaleemun hakeemun

---

4:26. Allah wishes to recount to you the customs of people, who lived before you, and to guide you and forgive those of you who repent their transgressions. And Allah is Knowledgeable, Wise.

وَٱللَّهُ يُرِيدُ أَن يَتُوبَ عَلَيْكُمْ وَيُرِيدُ ٱلَّذِينَ يَتَّبِعُونَ ٱلشَّهَوَاتِ أَن تَمِيلُواْ مَيْلًا عَظِيمًا ﴿٢٧﴾

27. WaAllahu yureedu an yatooba AAalaykum wayureedu allatheena yattabiAAoona alshshahawati an tameeloo maylan AAatheeman

---

4:27. And Allah wishes that He forgives those of you who repent their transgressions, while those who follow sensual desires wish that you go far astray.

يُرِيدُ ٱللَّهُ أَن يُخَفِّفَ عَنكُمْ وَخُلِقَ ٱلْإِنسَـٰنُ ضَعِيفًا ﴿٢٨﴾

28. Yureedu Allahu an yukhaffifa AAankum wakhuliqa al-insanu daAAeefan

---

4:28. Allah wishes that He lightens your burdens, and man is created weak.

يَـٰٓأَيُّهَا ٱلَّـذِينَ ءَامَنُـواْ لَا تَـأْكُلُوٓاْ أَمْوَٰلَكُم بَيْنَكُم بِـٱلْبَـٰطِلِ إِلَّآ أَن تَكُونَ تِجَـٰرَةً عَن تَرَاضٍ مِّنكُمْ وَلَا تَقْتُلُوٓاْ أَنفُسَكُمْ إِنَّ ٱللَّهَ كَانَ بِكُمْ رَحِيمًا ﴿٢٩﴾

29. Ya ayyuha allatheena amanoo la ta/kuloo amwalakum baynakum bialbatili illa an takoona tijaratan AAan taradin minkum wala taqtuloo anfusakum inna Allaha kana bikum raheeman

4:29. O you who believe! Do not consume your property among yourselves wrongfully; except that you do it by way of trading with mutual consent. And commit no suicides, nor kill one another amongst you! Indeed, Allah is Merciful to you.

وَمَن يَفْعَلْ ذَٰلِكَ عُدْوَٰنًا وَظُلْمًا فَسَوْفَ نُصْلِيهِ نَارًا وَكَانَ ذَٰلِكَ عَلَى ٱللَّهِ يَسِيرًا ﴿٣٠﴾

30. Waman yafAAal thalika AAudwanan wathulman fasawfa nusleehi naran wakana thalika AAala Allahi yaseeran

4:30. And whoever does this[22] through animosity and injustice, We will soon cast him into Fire! And that is easy for Allah.

22. **Refer preceding Verse.**

$$\text{إِن تَجْتَنِبُواْ كَبَآئِرَ مَا تُنْهَوْنَ عَنْهُ نُكَفِّرْ عَنكُمْ سَيِّـَٔاتِكُمْ وَنُدْخِلْكُم}$$

$$\text{مُّدْخَلًا كَرِيمًا ﴿٣١﴾}$$

31. In tajtaniboo kaba-ira ma tunhawna AAanhu nukaffir AAankum sayyi-atikum wanudkhilkum mudkhalan kareeman

---

4:31. If you shun the greater of the evil things you are forbidden, We shall clear you of your evil tendencies and cause you to enter a noble entrance[23].

---

23. Obviously, of Paradise.

$$\text{وَلَا تَتَمَنَّوْاْ مَا فَضَّلَ ٱللَّهُ بِهِۦ بَعْضَكُمْ عَلَىٰ بَعْضٍ لِّلرِّجَالِ}$$

$$\text{نَصِيبٌ مِّمَّا ٱكْتَسَبُواْ وَلِلنِّسَآءِ نَصِيبٌ مِّمَّا ٱكْتَسَبْنَ وَسْـَٔلُواْ ٱللَّهَ مِن}$$

$$\text{فَضْلِهِ إِنَّ ٱللَّهَ كَانَ بِكُلِّ شَىْءٍ عَلِيمًا ﴿٣٢﴾}$$

32. Wala tatamannaw ma faddala Allahu bihi baAAdakum AAala baAAdin lilrrijali naseebun mimma iktasaboo walilnnisa-i naseebun mimma iktasabna wais-aloo Allaha min fadlihi inna Allaha kana bikulli shay-in AAaleeman

---

4:32. And covet not the things which Allah has favoured some of you with, over others. For men, the lot they earn; and for women, the lot they earn. And do ask Allah for His Favour. Indeed, Allah is conversant with everything.

وَلِكُلٍّ جَعَلْنَا مَوَالِيَ مِمَّا تَرَكَ الْوَالِدَانِ وَالْأَقْرَبُونَ وَالَّذِينَ عَقَدَتْ أَيْمَانُكُمْ فَآتُوهُمْ نَصِيبَهُمْ إِنَّ اللَّهَ كَانَ عَلَىٰ كُلِّ شَيْءٍ شَهِيدًا ﴿٣٣﴾

33. Walikullin jaAAalna mawaliya mimma taraka alwalidani waal-aqraboona waallatheena AAaqadat aymanukum faatoohum naseebahum inna Allaha kana AAala kulli shay-in shaheedan

---

4:33. And in all cases, We have appointed heirs to what parents and near relatives leave behind. And give to those to whom you have made a pledge, their portion. Indeed, Allah is witness to all things.

الرِّجَالُ قَوَّامُونَ عَلَى النِّسَاءِ بِمَا فَضَّلَ اللَّهُ بَعْضَهُمْ عَلَىٰ بَعْضٍ وَبِمَا أَنفَقُوا مِنْ أَمْوَالِهِمْ فَالصَّالِحَاتُ قَانِتَاتٌ حَافِظَاتٌ لِّلْغَيْبِ بِمَا حَفِظَ اللَّهُ وَاللَّاتِي تَخَافُونَ نُشُوزَهُنَّ فَعِظُوهُنَّ وَاهْجُرُوهُنَّ فِي الْمَضَاجِعِ وَاضْرِبُوهُنَّ فَإِنْ أَطَعْنَكُمْ فَلَا تَبْغُوا عَلَيْهِنَّ سَبِيلًا إِنَّ اللَّهَ كَانَ عَلِيًّا كَبِيرًا ﴿٣٤﴾

34. Alrrijalu qawwamoona AAala alnnisa-i bima faddala Allahu baAAdahum AAala baAAdin wabima anfaqoo min amwalihim faalssalihatu qanitatun hafithatun lilghaybi bima hafitha Allahu waallatee takhafoona nushoozahunna faAAithoohunna waohjuroohunna fee almadajiAAi waidriboohunna fa-in ataAAnakum fala tabghoo AAalayhinna sabeelan inna Allaha kana AAaliyyan kabeeran

---

4:34. Men are the supports of women, since Allah has favoured some over others in certain respects, and since men are required to bear all family expenses from their (men's) property. The righteous women then are obedient guardians of privacy[24] as Allah has guarded it. And as for those women, on whose part you fear refractoriness[25], admonish them, leave them alone in beds and turn away from them. Then if they obey you, do not resort to any punitive measure against them. Indeed, Allah is High, Great.

24. The privacy of the intimate relations between a husband and his wife. Allah does not want these relations to be exhibited in public.

25. A family consisting of the husband, wife and their children, is the basic social, cultural and economic unit of a human society. The prosperity and well-being of the entire society depends, to a large extent, on the prosperity and well-being of most of these basic units. Mal-administration of most of these units is bound to affect the administration of the entire society. For the good administration of the unit, it should have an administrative head. And, in Islam, the husband is the divinely appointed head of this basic unit. The family is expected to be run based on mutual consultations, and the husband must give due regard to his wife's views on any matter. But, it is the husband, as head of the family, who shall have the final say in that matter. Now if the wife refuses to obey her husband, the administration of the unit is bound to fall apart.

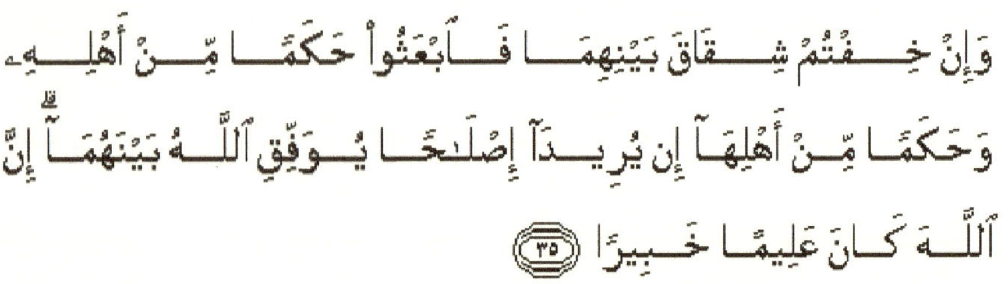

35. Wa-in khiftum shiqaqa baynihima faibAAathoo hakaman min ahlihi wahakaman min ahliha in yureeda islahan yuwaffiqi Allahu baynahuma inna Allaha kana AAaleeman khabeeran

4:35. And if you fear a breach between the two, then appoint an arbiter from his people and an arbiter from hers. If they both desire continuation of and improvement in the relationship, Allah will bring about reconciliation between the two. Indeed, Allah is Knowledgeable, Aware.

۞ وَٱعْبُدُوا۟ ٱللَّهَ وَلَا تُشْرِكُوا۟ بِهِۦ شَيْـًٔا ۖ وَبِٱلْوَٰلِدَيْنِ إِحْسَـٰنًا وَبِذِى ٱلْقُرْبَىٰ وَٱلْيَتَـٰمَىٰ وَٱلْمَسَـٰكِينِ وَٱلْجَارِ ذِى ٱلْقُرْبَىٰ وَٱلْجَارِ ٱلْجُنُبِ وَٱلصَّاحِبِ بِٱلْجَنۢبِ وَٱبْنِ ٱلسَّبِيلِ وَمَا مَلَكَتْ أَيْمَـٰنُكُمْ ۗ إِنَّ ٱللَّهَ لَا يُحِبُّ مَن كَانَ مُخْتَالًا فَخُورًا ﴿٣٦﴾

36. WaoAAbudoo Allaha wala tushrikoo bihi shay-an wabialwalidayni ihsanan wabithee alqurba waalyatama waalmasakeeni waaljari thee alqurba waaljari aljunubi waalssahibi bialjanbi waibni alssabeeli wama malakat aymanukum inna Allaha la yuhibbu man kana mukhtalan fakhooran

4:36. And worship Allah and do not associate anything with Him. And be good to parents, near of kin, orphans, the needy, the neighbour near of kin, the neighbour not of kin, the companion/colleague, the wayfarer and your slaves/servants. Indeed, Allah loves not him/her who is conceited, boastful.

ٱلَّذِينَ يَبْخَلُونَ وَيَأْمُرُونَ ٱلنَّاسَ بِٱلْبُخْلِ وَيَكْتُمُونَ مَآ ءَاتَىٰهُمُ ٱللَّهُ مِن فَضْلِهِۦ ۗ وَأَعْتَدْنَا لِلْكَـٰفِرِينَ عَذَابًا مُّهِينًا ﴿٣٧﴾

37. Allatheena yabkhaloona waya/muroona alnnasa bialbukhli wayaktumoona ma atahumu Allahu min fadlihi waaAAtadna lilkafireena AAathaban muheenan

4:37. [26]Those who are miserly and bid people to be miserly and hide what Allah has favoured them with. And We have prepared, for the suppressers of Truth, a disgraceful punishment.

26. This sentence is in continuation of the last sentence in the preceding Verse. Along with those who are conceited and boastful, Allah loves not those who are miserly and exhort people to be miserly and to hide their wealth.

وَٱلَّذِينَ يُنفِقُونَ أَمْوَٰلَهُمْ رِئَآءَ ٱلنَّاسِ وَلَا يُؤْمِنُونَ بِٱللَّهِ وَلَا بِٱلْيَوْمِ ٱلْأَخِرِ وَمَن يَكُنِ ٱلشَّيْطَٰنُ لَهُۥ قَرِينًا فَسَآءَ قَرِينًا

38. Waallatheena yunfiqoona amwalahum ri-aa alnnasi wala yu/minoona biAllahi wala bialyawmi al-akhiri waman yakuni alshshaytanu lahu qareenan fasaa qareenan

4:38. And those who spend their wealth to show off and believe not in Allah nor in the Hereafter.[27] And as for him, the Satan is an ally of whom, then he has an evil ally!

27. And Allah loves not such people too.

وَمَاذَا عَلَيْهِمْ لَوْ ءَامَنُواْ بِٱللَّهِ وَٱلْيَوْمِ ٱلْأَخِرِ وَأَنفَقُواْ مِمَّا رَزَقَهُمُ ٱللَّهُ وَكَانَ ٱللَّهُ بِهِمْ عَلِيمًا ﴿٣٩﴾

39. Wamatha AAalayhim law amanoo biAllahi waalyawmi al-akhiri waanfaqoo mimma razaqahumu Allahu wakana Allahu bihim AAaleeman

4:39. And what calamity would befall them, had they believed in Allah and the Hereafter and spent out of what Allah had given them!? And Allah does know them very well.

إِنَّ ٱللَّهَ لَا يَظۡلِمُ مِثۡقَالَ ذَرَّةٖۖ وَإِن تَكُ حَسَنَةٗ يُضَٰعِفۡهَا وَيُؤۡتِ مِن لَّدُنۡهُ أَجۡرًا عَظِيمٗا ۝

40. Inna Allaha la yathlimu mithqala tharratin wa-in taku hasanatan yudaAAifha wayu/ti min ladunhu ajran AAatheeman

4:40. Indeed, Allah wrongs not even to the infinitesimal extent of the weight of an atom. And if there is a good deed, He doubles it and bestows, from Him, a great reward.

فَكَيۡفَ إِذَا جِئۡنَا مِن كُلِّ أُمَّةِۭ بِشَهِيدٖ وَجِئۡنَا بِكَ عَلَىٰ هَٰٓؤُلَآءِ شَهِيدٗا ۝

41. Fakayfa itha ji/na min kulli ommatin bishaheedin waji/na bika AAala haola-i shaheedan

4:41. How about then, when We bring, from every people, a witness, and bring you[28] as a witness against these?

28. **Addressee here is Prophet Muhammad, peace be upon him.**

يَوۡمَئِذٖ يَوَدُّ ٱلَّذِينَ كَفَرُواْ وَعَصَوُاْ ٱلرَّسُولَ لَوۡ تُسَوَّىٰ بِهِمُ ٱلۡأَرۡضُ وَلَا يَكۡتُمُونَ ٱللَّهَ حَدِيثٗا ۝

42. Yawma-ithin yawaddu allatheena kafaroo waAAasawoo alrrasoola law tusawwa bihimu al-ardu wala yaktumoona Allaha hadeethan

4:42. That Day[29], those, who suppress the Truth and disobey the Messenger, would wish that the earth was levelled with them. And they shall not hide any event from Allah.

29. The Day of Judgement, in the Hereafter.

يَٰٓأَيُّهَا ٱلَّذِينَ ءَامَنُواْ لَا تَقْرَبُواْ ٱلصَّلَوٰةَ وَأَنتُمْ سُكَٰرَىٰ حَتَّىٰ تَعْلَمُواْ مَا تَقُولُونَ وَلَا جُنُبًا إِلَّا عَابِرِى سَبِيلٍ حَتَّىٰ تَغْتَسِلُواْ وَإِن كُنتُم مَّرْضَىٰٓ أَوْ عَلَىٰ سَفَرٍ أَوْ جَآءَ أَحَدٌ مِّنكُم مِّنَ ٱلْغَآئِطِ أَوْ لَٰمَسْتُمُ ٱلنِّسَآءَ فَلَمْ تَجِدُواْ مَآءً فَتَيَمَّمُواْ صَعِيدًا طَيِّبًا فَٱمْسَحُواْ بِوُجُوهِكُمْ وَأَيْدِيكُمْ إِنَّ ٱللَّهَ كَانَ عَفُوًّا غَفُورًا ﴿٤٣﴾

43. Ya ayyuha allatheena amanoo la taqraboo alssalata waantum sukara hatta taAAlamoo ma taqooloona wala junuban illa AAabiree sabeelin hatta taghtasiloo wa-in kuntum marda aw AAala safarin aw jaa ahadun minkum mina algha-iti aw lamastumu alnnisaa falam tajidoo maan fatayammamoo saAAeedan tayyiban faimsahoo biwujoohikum waaydeekum inna Allaha kana AAafuwwan ghafooran

4:43. O you who believe! Go not to prayer while you are under the influence of intoxication[30, 31], until you know what you say, nor while you are in an unclean state – unless on the move from one place to another – until you take a bath. And if you are ill, or on a journey, or any of you has come from the toilet or you have been in sexual contact with the women, and you cannot get water, simulate the cleaning act then with pure earth, wiping your faces and your hands therewith. Indeed, Allah is Lenient, Forgiving.

30. The human mind can be intoxicated in several ways. And the very next phrase in this Verse viz., 'until you know what you say' makes the divine meaning of the Arabic term *sukara*, used here, clear. The Arabic term obviously therefore means a state of the mind in which the person concerned does not fully understand the implications of what his/her mouth utters. Such a state of mind could be brought about

by all sorts of intoxicants, or even by drowsiness. And any person could also be in such a state when his/her mind wavers to thoughts other than that of Allah. And the person's thoughts are bound to waver particularly when he/she does not understand the meaning of the Arabic words uttered in prayers. Understanding the meanings of what we say is therefore an absolute must for our prayers to be heard, accepted and answered.

31. Total abstinence from intoxicants was ordained under Verse 5:90. Obviously, this Verse, 4:43, was revealed before 5:90. This is in keeping with divine plan of eradicating a deep-rooted evil habit in stages, and not abruptly. As a first step towards ordering total abstinence, the believers were asked not to come for prayers in an intoxicated state of mind. But, on that account, it would be wrong to say that Verse 4:43 stands abrogated by Verse 5:90. In fact, it would be wrong to say that any of the existing Verses in the Qur'aan are abrogated. Please see Verse 2:106 and study notes 150 to 154 thereunder and Verse 2:109 and study notes 161 and 162 thereunder in this context. Verse 4:43 is so construed by the All-knowing and Wise Author of the Qur'aan that its application in this regard is not negated even after the revelation of Verse 5:90. Moreover, as we have seen in the preceding note, the Arabic term *sukara*, used in Verse 4:43, implies a wider meaning than just being under the influence of drugs and alcoholic drinks.

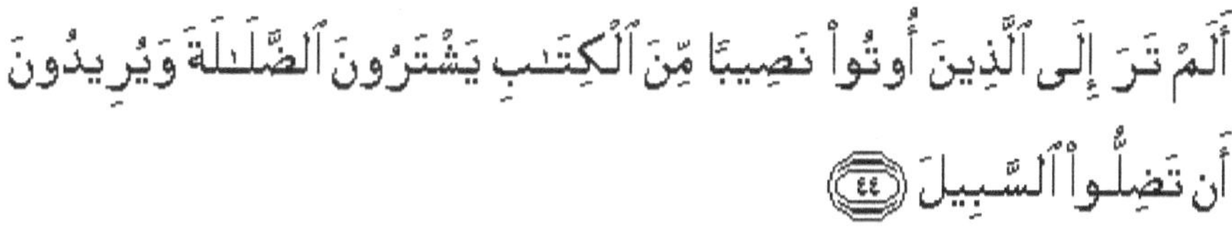

44. Alam tara ila allatheena ootoo naseeban mina alkitabi yashtaroona alddalalata wayureedoona an tadilloo alssabeela

4:44. Have you not seen those who were given an Edition of the Book[32], trading perversity and wishing that you should go off the Path?

32. The Torah and the Gospel (Injeel) were two of the earlier Editions of the Divine Book.

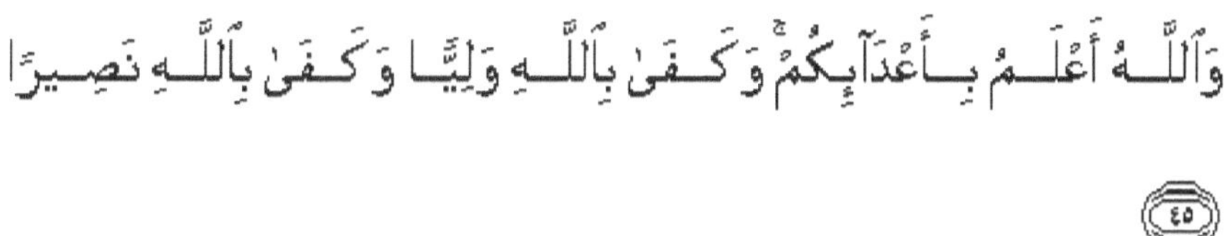

45. WaAllahu aAAlamu bi-aAAda-ikum wakafa biAllahi waliyyan wakafa biAllahi naseeran

4:45. And Allah knows your enemies. And Allah suffices as Patron, and Allah suffices as One Who helps.

مِّنَ ٱلَّذِينَ هَادُواْ يُحَرِّفُونَ ٱلْكَلِمَ عَن مَّوَاضِعِهِۦ وَيَقُولُونَ سَمِعْنَا وَعَصَيْنَا وَٱسْمَعْ غَيْرَ مُسْمَعٍ وَرَٰعِنَا لَيًّا بِأَلْسِنَتِهِمْ وَطَعْنًا فِى ٱلدِّينِ وَلَوْ أَنَّهُمْ قَالُواْ سَمِعْنَا وَأَطَعْنَا وَٱسْمَعْ وَٱنظُرْنَا لَكَانَ خَيْرًا لَّهُمْ وَأَقْوَمَ وَلَـٰكِن لَّعَنَهُمُ ٱللَّـهُ بِكُفْرِهِمْ فَلَا يُؤْمِنُونَ إِلَّا قَلِيلًا ﴿٤٦﴾

46. Mina alla_theena_ _h_adoo yu_h_arrifoona alkalima AAan maw_adi_AAihi wayaqooloona samiAAn_a_ waAAa_s_ayn_a_ waismaAA ghayra musmaAAin war_a_AAin_a_ layyan bi-alsinatihim wa_ta_AAanan fee alddeeni walaw annahum _q_aloo samiAAn_a_ waata_A_An_a_ waismaAA wa_on_t_hurn_a_ lak_a_na khayran lahum waa_q_wama wal_a_kin laAAanahumu All_a_hu bikufrihim fal_a_ yu/minoona ill_a_ _q_aleel_an_

4:46. Among the Jewish people are those who distort word from its context and say, "We have heard, and we disobey." and, "Hear, and don't make us hear! And listen to us!" twisting words with their tongues and taunting the Religion. And had they just said, "We have heard, and we obey." and "Hear, and look at us!" it would have been better and more upright for them.[33] But Allah has cursed them because of their suppression of the Truth. So, they believe not, except for a few.

33. The Jews in the audiences addressed by the Prophet (peace be upon him) used to play mischief as little children do. Apparently making a show of positively responding to the addresses, they used to twist words like _waataAAna_ (and we obey) to similar sounding words like _waAAasayna_ (and we disobey).

$$\text{يَـٰٓأَيُّهَا ٱلَّذِينَ أُوتُواْ ٱلْكِتَـٰبَ ءَامِنُواْ بِمَا نَزَّلْنَا مُصَدِّقًا لِّمَا مَعَكُم مِّن قَبْلِ أَن نَّطْمِسَ وُجُوهًا فَنَرُدَّهَا عَلَىٰٓ أَدْبَارِهَآ أَوْ نَلْعَنَهُمْ كَمَا لَعَنَّآ أَصْحَـٰبَ ٱلسَّبْتِ ۚ وَكَانَ أَمْرُ ٱللَّهِ مَفْعُولًا ۝٤٧}$$

47. Ya ayyuha allatheena ootoo alkitaba aminoo bima nazzalna musaddiqan lima maAAakum min qabli an natmisa wujoohan fanaruddaha AAala adbariha aw nalAAanahum kama laAAanna as-haba alssabti wakana amru Allahi mafAAoolan

---

4:47. O you who have been given the Book! Believe in what We have sent down, confirming that which is with you, before We efface faces and then turn them on their backs, or curse them as We cursed the Sabbath companions.[34] And Allah's command does get executed!

---

34. Refer <u>Verse 2:65 and study note 73 thereunder</u>, of these Studies, in this context. About effacing of faces, it may be noted that the human face is like the identity card of a person. Any human being is recognised by his/her face. If the facial features are obliterated, he/she cannot normally be recognised, with a certainty. That being the case, the reference here to effacing the faces may very well mean that the people referred to may not be recognised and treated as fellow human beings by other human beings. They may be despised as just other animals – or like the apes, as the Jewish people who transgressed the Sabbath restrictions were. The Muslims should not think this Verse applies only to the Jews and the Christians. Like those two communities, the Muslims too are those who have been given the divine Book. In fact, it is the Muslim community which is despised now. That is obviously because most of the Muslims now have ceased believing in and acting upon what is revealed to them in the Qur'aan.

$$\text{إِنَّ ٱللَّهَ لَا يَغْفِرُ أَن يُشْرَكَ بِهِۦ وَيَغْفِرُ مَا دُونَ ذَٰلِكَ لِمَن يَشَآءُ ۚ وَمَن يُشْرِكْ بِٱللَّهِ فَقَدِ ٱفْتَرَىٰٓ إِثْمًا عَظِيمًا ۝٤٨}$$

48. Inna Allaha la yaghfiru an yushraka bihi wayaghfiru ma doona thalika liman yashao waman yushrik biAllahi faqadi iftara ithman AAatheeman

---

4:48. Indeed, Allah forgives not that anything should be associated with Him, and He forgives whomsoever, He pleases, committing any sin other than that. And whoever associates anything with Allah, he/she is certainly guilty of concocting and committing a grave sin.

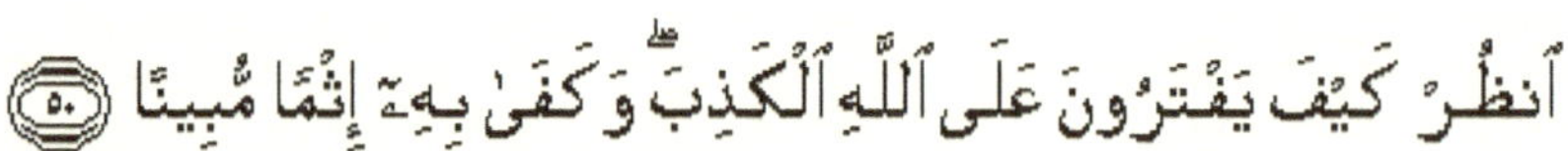

49. Alam tara ila allatheena yuzakkoona anfusahum bali Allahu yuzakkee man yashao wala yu_th_lamoona fateelan

4:49. Have you not seen those who consider themselves as pure? But Allah it is Who purifies whom He wills. And they shall not be wronged even a bit.

50. On_th_ur kayfa yaftaroona AAala Allahi alkathiba wakafa bihi ithman mubeenan

4:50. Look, how they forge the lie upon Allah! [35] And this by itself is a sin, manifest.

35. Reference here is to those, mentioned in the preceding Verse, considering themselves as pure. The Jews think that they are the only chosen people of God. The others (gentiles) are not as purified and deserving God's favours as they themselves are. This was the reason why they could not accept Muhammad (peace be upon him) as God's Messenger. He was of the gentiles – not of them! And the Christians think that only those who believe in Jesus being the son of God shall have a guaranteed entry into Paradise! And the Muslims are not far behind, in this game of one-upmanship. Most of them too are sure that their Prophet's intercession will take them to Jannah, their sins in this life notwithstanding! All these claims of the different communities are lies forged upon Allah.

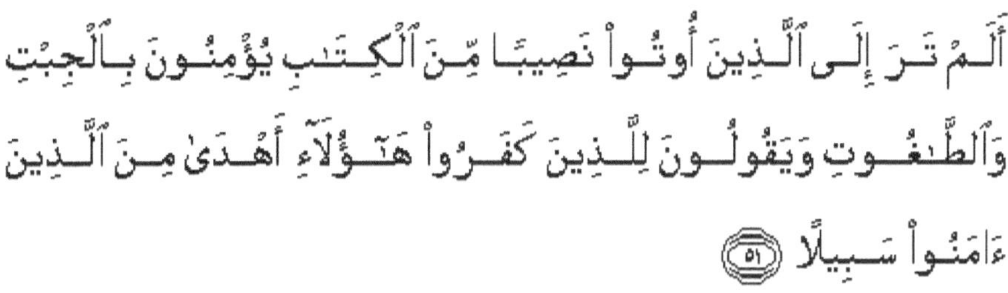

51. Alam tara ila allatheena ootoo naseeban mina alkitabi yu/minoona bialjibti waalttaghooti wayaqooloona lillatheena kafaroo haola-i ahda mina allatheena amanoo sabeelan

---

4:51. Have you not seen how those to whom has been given an Edition of the Book believe in idols and false deities[36], and say of those who suppress the Truth that the latter are better guided in the path than those who believe?

---

36. The Christians worship idols of Jesus and his mother Mary. And the Muslims worship at the graves of saints. And they condemn those who try to follow the Qur'aanic teachings as fundamentalists and Wahhabees and consider them worse than non-believers

---

52. Ola-ika allatheena laAAanahumu Allahu waman yalAAani Allahu falan tajida lahu naseeran

---

4:52. Those are the people whom Allah has cursed. And you shall find none to help whomsoever Allah curses.

أَمْ لَهُمْ نَصِيبٌ مِّنَ ٱلْمُلْكِ فَإِذًا لَّا يُؤْتُونَ ٱلنَّاسَ نَقِيرًا ﴿٥٣﴾

53. Am lahum naseebun mina almulki fa-ithan la yu/toona alnnasa naqeeran

---

4:53. Or, do they have a share in the governance? [37] Then, in that case, they would give to others, not even a little bit.

---

37. This is a reference to the Jews. Until recently they had no territory to govern. And now when they do have some territory by themselves to govern, their continual efforts at deprivation of the Arabs within and around that territory, in an on-going conflict, is a vindication of the divine statement that follows in this Verse.

أَمْ يَحْسُدُونَ ٱلنَّاسَ عَلَىٰ مَآ ءَاتَٮٰهُمُ ٱللَّهُ مِن فَضْلِهِۦ فَقَدْ ءَاتَيْنَآ ءَالَ

إِبْرَٰهِيمَ ٱلْكِتَٰبَ وَٱلْحِكْمَةَ وَءَاتَيْنَٰهُم مُّلْكًا عَظِيمًا ﴿٥٤﴾

54. Am yahsudoona alnnasa AAala ma atahumu Allahu min fadlihi faqad atayna ala ibraheema alkitaba waalhikmata waataynahum mulkan AAatheeman

---

4:54. Or do they envy the others for what Allah has given them of His Favour? [38] And, surely, We had given to children of Abraham the Book and the Wisdom, and We had given them a great territory to govern!

---

38. A reference to the Jews again. They resented the bestowal of Prophethood on Muhammad (peace be upon him), someone not of them.

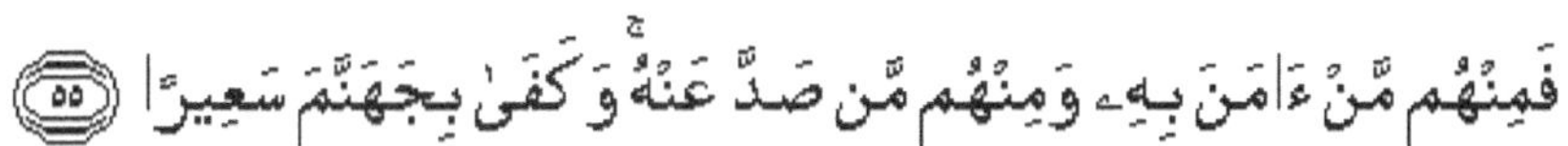

55. Faminhum man amana bihi waminhum man sadda AAanhu wakafa bijahannama saAAeeran

4:55. Then there were those among them who believed in him[39], and those among them who turned away from him. And Hell is Inferno[40] enough!

39. Muhammad (peace be on him).

40. To punish all the suppressors of Truth with, without making them die therein (please see the next Verse below).

56. Inna allatheena kafaroo bi-ayatina sawfa nusleehim naran kullama nadijat julooduhum baddalnahum juloodan ghayraha liyathooqoo alAAathaba inna Allaha kana AAazeezan hakeeman

4:56. Indeed, We shall burn those who suppress the Truth in regard to Our Verses/Signs, in fire. Whenever their skins get fully burnt, We shall replace them with other skins, so that they may go on tasting the punishment. Allah indeed is Omnipotent, Wise!

57. Waallatheena amanoo waAAamiloo alssalihati sanudkhiluhum jannatin tajree min tahtiha al-anharu khalideena feeha abadan lahum feeha azwajun mutahharatun wanudkhiluhum thillan thaleelan

4:57. And those who believe and do good deeds, We shall make them enter gardens with rivers flowing underneath, to abide therein for ever. For them shall there be mates pure, and We shall admit them into cool everlasting shade.

58. Inna Allaha ya/murukum an tu-addoo al-amanati ila ahliha wa-itha hakamtum bayna alnnasi an tahkumoo bialAAadli inna Allaha niAAimma yaAAithukum bihi inna Allaha kana sameeAAan baseeran

4:58. Allah does indeed command you to hand over the trusts to those to whom they are due, and that when you judge between people, you judge with justice. Allah does indeed give you the best of admonition. Allah does indeed hear all, see all!

$$\text{يَـٰٓأَيُّهَا ٱلَّذِينَ ءَامَنُوٓا۟ أَطِيعُوا۟ ٱللَّهَ وَأَطِيعُوا۟ ٱلرَّسُولَ وَأُو۟لِى ٱلْأَمْرِ مِنكُمْ ۖ فَإِن تَنَـٰزَعْتُمْ فِى شَىْءٍ فَرُدُّوهُ إِلَى ٱللَّهِ وَٱلرَّسُولِ إِن كُنتُمْ تُؤْمِنُونَ بِٱللَّهِ وَٱلْيَوْمِ ٱلْءَاخِرِ ۚ ذَٰلِكَ خَيْرٌ وَأَحْسَنُ تَأْوِيلًا ۝}$$

59. Ya ayyuha allatheena amanoo ateeAAoo Allaha waateeAAoo alrrasoola waolee al-amri minkum fa-in tanazaAAtum fee shay-in faruddoohu ila Allahi waalrrasooli in kuntum tu/minoona biAllahi waalyawmi al-akhiri thalika khayrun waahsanu ta/weelan

---

4:59. O you who believe! Obey Allah and obey the Messenger and those in authority from amongst you. Then if you believe in Allah and the Hereafter and quarrel on anything, refer it to Allah and the Messenger. That is better, and it is the best solution.[41]

---

41. This Verse gives the basic principle of jurisprudence in Islam. Since the Messenger is no longer living amidst mankind now, the only source for reference is Allah Himself. And the Qur'aan is His Book of Guidance especially given to mankind for the purpose. The Qur'aan therefore ought to be the final reference on any dispute. Allah assures us here that this final source for reference would provide the best solution. We have but to trust Him. About the directive to obey the Messenger, please see study notes 3:144 to 3:146 on Verse 3:132, **for further information.**

$$\text{أَلَمْ تَرَ إِلَى ٱلَّذِينَ يَزْعُمُونَ أَنَّهُمْ ءَامَنُوا۟ بِمَآ أُنزِلَ إِلَيْكَ وَمَآ أُنزِلَ مِن قَبْلِكَ يُرِيدُونَ أَن يَتَحَاكَمُوٓا۟ إِلَى ٱلطَّـٰغُوتِ وَقَدْ أُمِرُوٓا۟ أَن يَكْفُرُوا۟ بِهِۦ وَيُرِيدُ ٱلشَّيْطَـٰنُ أَن يُضِلَّهُمْ ضَلَـٰلًۢا بَعِيدًا ۝}$$

60. Alam tara ila allatheena yazAAumoona annahum amanoo bima onzila ilayka wama onzila min qablika yureedoona an yatahakamoo ila alttaghooti waqad omiroo an yakfuroo bihi wayureedu alshshaytanu an yudillahum dalalan baAAeedan

---

4:60. Have you not seen those who assert that they believe in what has been revealed to you and in what was revealed before you, and yet, they would like to go to someone who has rebelled against Allah, for judgement, although they were commanded to deny him? And the Satan desires to lead them far astray.[42]

---

42. This Verse indicates that in an Islamic State, court judges have necessarily to be those who do believe in all that the Qur'aan states. The candidates must be thoroughly grilled about their beliefs before they are appointed as judges. This requirement cannot, of course, be practically implemented in a non-Islamic State, where the Muslim minority may try to get their internal disputes settled, on Qur'aanic basis, among themselves, without resorting to the penal provisions. The Qur'aanic penal provisions are to be implemented only in an Islamic State.

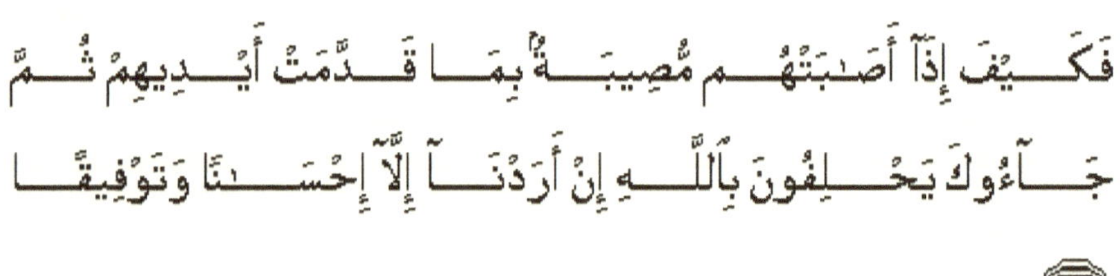

61. Wa-itha qeela lahum taAAalaw ila ma anzala Allahu wa-ila alrrasooli raayta almunafiqeena yasuddoona AAanka sudoodan

---

4:61. And when it is said to them, "Come to what Allah has revealed and to the Messenger", you see the hypocrites turning away from you in aversion.

62. Fakayfa itha asabat-hum museebatun bima qaddamat aydeehim thumma jaooka yahlifoona biAllahi in aradna illa ihsanan watawfeeqan

---

4:62. Then, how about it, when a calamity befalls them because of what they did before, and they come to you swearing by Allah, "We did not desire anything but goodwill and amity"?

أُوْلَـٰٓئِكَ ٱلَّذِينَ يَعْلَمُ ٱللَّهُ مَا فِى قُلُوبِهِمْ فَأَعْرِضْ عَنْهُمْ وَعِظْهُمْ وَقُل لَّهُمْ فِىٓ أَنفُسِهِمْ قَوْلًۢا بَلِيغًا ﴿٦٣﴾

63. Ola-ika alla<u>th</u>eena yaAAlamu All<u>a</u>hu m<u>a</u> fee quloobihim faaAAri<u>d</u> AAanhum waAAi<u>th</u>hum waqul lahum fee anfusihim qawlan baleeghan

4:63. Allah knows what is there in their inner minds. So, leave them alone, admonish them, and speak to them words that would touch their inner souls.

وَمَآ أَرْسَلْنَا مِن رَّسُولٍ إِلَّا لِيُطَاعَ بِإِذْنِ ٱللَّهِ وَلَوْ أَنَّهُمْ إِذ ظَّلَمُوٓاْ أَنفُسَهُمْ جَآءُوكَ فَٱسْتَغْفَرُواْ ٱللَّهَ وَٱسْتَغْفَرَ لَهُمُ ٱلرَّسُولُ لَوَجَدُواْ ٱللَّهَ تَوَّابًا رَّحِيمًا ﴿٦٤﴾

64. Wam<u>a</u> arsaln<u>a</u> min rasoolin ill<u>a</u> liyu<u>t</u>aAAa bi-i<u>th</u>ni All<u>a</u>hi walaw annahum i<u>th</u> <u>th</u>alamoo anfusahum j<u>a</u>ooka faistaghfaroo All<u>a</u>ha waistaghfara lahumu alrrasoolu lawajadoo All<u>a</u>ha taww<u>a</u>ban ra<u>h</u>eeman

4:64. And We did not send any Messenger but to be obeyed by Allah's command. And if only they had – when they were unjust to themselves – come to you and asked forgiveness of Allah and the Messenger asked forgiveness for them, they would have found Allah Accepting repentance, Merciful.[43]

43. The people who were unjust to themselves were told here to come to the Prophet (peace be upon him), obviously, when he was living in this world. It is unfortunate that some people take this Verse as their

licence to visit the Prophet's grave now, for the same purpose. These people assume that the Prophet, in his grave, can hear them. But they thereby deny the Truth of the Verse 35:22 declaring unequivocally, "And you are in no position to make those to hear who are in the graves."

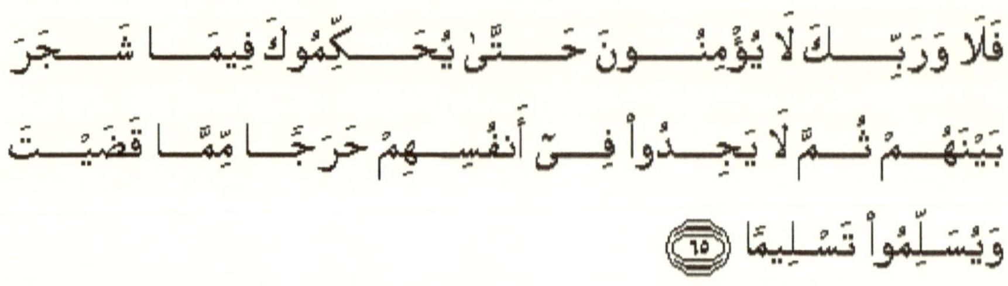

65. Fala warabbika la yu/minoona hatta yuhakkimooka feema shajara baynahum thumma la yajidoo fee anfusihim harajan mimma qadayta wayusallimoo tasleeman

4:65. No! By your Lord, no! They believe not, until they make you the arbiter in disputes among them, and then find no reservations in their minds on your decisions and submit to them entirely.

66. Walaw anna katabna AAalayhim ani oqtuloo anfusakum awi okhrujoo min diyarikum ma faAAaloohu illa qaleelun minhum walaw annahum faAAaloo ma yooAAathoona bihi lakana khayran lahum waashadda tathbeetan

4:66. And if We had passed an order for them to lay down their lives or to leave their homes, they would not have done it, except for a few of them. And had they done what they were advised to, it would have certainly been better for them and it would have very much strengthened their position.

وَإِذَا لَّأَتَيْنَـٰهُم مِّن لَّدُنَّآ أَجْرًا عَظِيمًا ﴿٦٧﴾

67. Wa-ithan laataynahum min ladunna ajran AAatheeman

4:67. And in that case, We would certainly have given them from Ourselves a great reward.

وَلَهَدَيْنَـٰهُمْ صِرَٰطًا مُّسْتَقِيمًا ﴿٦٨﴾

68. Walahadaynahum siratan mustaqeeman

4:68. And We would certainly have guided them to the Straight Path.

وَمَن يُطِعِ ٱللَّهَ وَٱلرَّسُولَ فَأُوْلَـٰئِكَ مَعَ ٱلَّذِينَ أَنْعَمَ ٱللَّهُ عَلَيْهِم مِّنَ ٱلنَّبِيِّـۧنَ وَٱلصِّدِّيقِينَ وَٱلشُّهَدَآءِ وَٱلصَّـٰلِحِينَ وَحَسُنَ أُوْلَـٰئِكَ رَفِيقًا ﴿٦٩﴾

69. Waman yutiAAi Allaha waalrrasoola faola-ika maAAa allatheena anAAama Allahu AAalayhim mina alnnabiyyeena waalssiddeeqeena waalshshuhada-i waalssaliheena wahasuna ola-ika rafeeqan

4:69. And persons like the one who obeys Allah and the Messenger, are in the company of the prophets, the truthful, the martyrs and the righteous, upon whom Allah has bestowed rewards. And how excellent are these companions!

ذَٰلِكَ ٱلْفَضْلُ مِنَ ٱللَّهِ ۚ وَكَفَىٰ بِٱللَّهِ عَلِيمًا ﴿٧٠﴾

70. Thalika alfadlu mina Allahi wakafa biAllahi AAaleeman

4:70. That is the favour from Allah, and enough is Allah, the Embodiment of all knowledge!

يَٰٓأَيُّهَا ٱلَّذِينَ ءَامَنُوا۟ خُذُوا۟ حِذْرَكُمْ فَٱنفِرُوا۟ ثُبَاتٍ أَوِ ٱنفِرُوا۟ جَمِيعًا ﴿٧١﴾

71. Ya ayyuha allatheena amanoo khuthoo hithrakum fainfiroo thubatin awi infiroo jameeAAan

---

4:71. O you who believe! Be on your guard, and then go out in strength or all together.

وَإِنَّ مِنكُمْ لَمَن لَّيُبَطِّئَنَّ فَإِنْ أَصَٰبَتْكُم مُّصِيبَةٌ قَالَ قَدْ أَنْعَمَ ٱللَّهُ عَلَىَّ إِذْ لَمْ أَكُن مَّعَهُمْ شَهِيدًا ﴿٧٢﴾

72. Wa-inna minkum laman layubatti-anna fa-in asabatkum museebatun qala qad anAAama Allahu AAalayya ith lam akun maAAahum shaheedan

---

4:72. And, indeed, among you certainly is he who would drop behind! If then a calamity befalls you, he says, "Surely Allah conferred a benefit on me that I was not present with them."

وَلَئِنْ أَصَابَكُمْ فَضْلٌ مِّنَ ٱللَّهِ لَيَقُولَنَّ كَأَن لَّمْ تَكُن بَيْنَكُمْ وَبَيْنَهُۥ مَوَدَّةٌ يَـٰلَيْتَنِى كُنتُ مَعَهُمْ فَأَفُوزَ فَوْزًا عَظِيمًا ﴿٧٣﴾

73. Wala-in asabakum fadlun mina Allahi layaqoolanna kaan lam takun baynakum wabaynahu mawaddatun ya laytanee kuntu maAAahum faafooza fawzan AAatheeman

---

4:73. And if you do get a favour from Allah, he would certainly say, as if you were not on friendly terms with him,[44] "Oh! I wish I had been with them. I would then achieve a great success."

---

44. And that was the reason why he remained behind while the believers had proceeded for the expedition. The hypocrite thus put the blame for his failure to join the expedition – and thus to get a share in the believers' success – on the lack of affection between him and the believers!

۞ فَلْيُقَـٰتِلْ فِى سَبِيلِ ٱللَّهِ ٱلَّذِينَ يَشْرُونَ ٱلْحَيَوٰةَ ٱلدُّنْيَا بِٱلْءَاخِرَةِ وَمَن يُقَـٰتِلْ فِى سَبِيلِ ٱللَّهِ فَيُقْتَلْ أَوْ يَغْلِبْ فَسَوْفَ نُؤْتِيهِ أَجْرًا عَظِيمًا ﴿٧٤﴾

74. Falyuqatil fee sabeeli Allahi allatheena yashroona alhayata alddunya bial-akhirati waman yuqatil fee sabeeli Allahi fayuqtal aw yaghlib fasawfa nu/teehi ajran AAatheeman

---

4:74. Those fight in Allah's Path, then, who are ready to exchange this life for the other (in the Hereafter)! And whoever fights in Allah's Path, and then whether he is killed, or he gets victory, We shall grant him a great reward.

وَمَا لَكُمْ لَا تُقَاتِلُونَ فِى سَبِيلِ اللَّهِ وَالْمُسْتَضْعَفِينَ مِنَ الرِّجَالِ وَالنِّسَآءِ

وَالْوِلْدَانِ الَّذِينَ يَقُولُونَ رَبَّنَآ أَخْرِجْنَا مِنْ هَـٰذِهِ الْقَرْيَةِ الظَّالِمِ أَهْلُهَا

وَاجْعَل لَّنَا مِن لَّدُنكَ وَلِيًّا وَاجْعَل لَّنَا مِن لَّدُنكَ نَصِيرًا ﴿٧٥﴾

75. Wama lakum la tuqatiloona fee sabeeli Allahi waalmustadAAafeena mina alrrijali waalnnisa-i waalwildani allatheena yaqooloona rabbana akhrijna min hathihi alqaryati alththalimi ahluha waijAAal lana min ladunka waliyyan waijAAal lana min ladunka naseeran

---

4:75. And what's the matter with you that you fight not, in Allah's Path, for the weak among the men, for the women and for the children, who say, "Our Lord! Take us out of this town, whose people are oppressors and raise for us from You a guardian and raise for us from You a helper."[45]

---

45. This Verse was revealed in the background of the believers who could not leave Makkah and were persecuted by the non-believers there. The other believers, who had established a nascent State at Medina, were thus exhorted to fight in Allah's Path for their brethren suffering at Makkah. In this present age too, the Muslims are suffering in various parts of the world. Perhaps, some Muslims now misinterpret Verses, like this one in the Qur'aan, as inspiring them to resort to suicide attacks on soft targets around the world. They choose soft targets as they don't have the means to make a direct attack on the forces that inflict the suffering on the Muslims. In such suicide attacks, it is the innocents, mostly, that sustain losses of life and property. The attacks therefore prove to be counter-productive and fail to achieve the intended objective. These cannot at all be termed as fighting in Allah's Path. The Muslims should remember that the Prophet (peace be upon him) suffered immensely at the hands of the Makkans, for thirteen long years. He did not attempt any suicide attacks on soft targets, because he did not have enough strength then to attack the mighty opposition. He bided his time, and attacked the evil forces only when he had the strength to do so. Muslims of today should take a lesson from his example. The Qur'aan exhorts the believers, in Verse 2:153, to seek Allah's help with patience and prayer. Allah is certainly with those that are patient. Let the Muslims have absolute trust in Allah, and refrain from indulging in the fruitless deeds which only boomerang on them themselves. Deeds like the suicide attacks are, moreover, exhibitions of lack of faith in Allah's promise of ultimate success. How then would Allah give them that success?

ٱلَّذِينَ ءَامَنُوا۟ يُقَٰتِلُونَ فِى سَبِيلِ ٱللَّهِ ۖ وَٱلَّذِينَ كَفَرُوا۟ يُقَٰتِلُونَ فِى سَبِيلِ ٱلطَّٰغُوتِ فَقَٰتِلُوٓا۟ أَوْلِيَآءَ ٱلشَّيْطَٰنِ ۖ إِنَّ كَيْدَ ٱلشَّيْطَٰنِ كَانَ ضَعِيفًا ﴿٧٦﴾

76. Allatheena amanoo yuqatiloona fee sabeeli Allahi waallatheena kafaroo yuqatiloona fee sabeeli alttaghooti faqatiloo awliyaa alshshaytani inna kayda alshshaytani kana daAAeefan

---

4:76. Those who believe fight in Allah's Path; and those who suppress the Truth, fight in the path of the false god. Fight then against those who are friends of the Satan[46]. The Satanic strategy is indeed weak.

---

46. The Satan has vowed to harm the believers and their interests. Hence, friends of the Satan are those who work to harm the believers and their interests.

أَلَمْ تَرَ إِلَى ٱلَّذِينَ قِيلَ لَهُمْ كُفُّوٓا۟ أَيْدِيَكُمْ وَأَقِيمُوا۟ ٱلصَّلَوٰةَ وَءَاتُوا۟ ٱلزَّكَوٰةَ فَلَمَّا كُتِبَ عَلَيْهِمُ ٱلْقِتَالُ إِذَا فَرِيقٌ مِّنْهُمْ يَخْشَوْنَ ٱلنَّاسَ كَخَشْيَةِ ٱللَّهِ أَوْ أَشَدَّ خَشْيَةً ۚ وَقَالُوا۟ رَبَّنَا لِمَ كَتَبْتَ عَلَيْنَا ٱلْقِتَالَ لَوْلَآ أَخَّرْتَنَآ إِلَىٰٓ أَجَلٍ قَرِيبٍ ۗ قُلْ مَتَٰعُ ٱلدُّنْيَا قَلِيلٌ وَٱلْءَاخِرَةُ خَيْرٌ لِّمَنِ ٱتَّقَىٰ وَلَا تُظْلَمُونَ فَتِيلًا ﴿٧٧﴾

77. Alam tara ila allatheena qeela lahum kuffoo aydiyakum waaqeemoo alssalata waatoo alzzakata falamma kutiba AAalayhimu alqitalu itha fareequn minhum yakhshawna alnnasa kakhashyati Allahi aw ashadda khashyatan waqaloo rabbana lima katabta AAalayna alqitala lawla akhkhartana ila ajalin qareebin qul mataAAu alddunya qaleelun waal-akhiratu khayrun limani ittaqa wala tuthlamoona fateelan

---

4:77. Do you see these people who were asked to withhold their hands and to establish the prayer and pay the *zakaat* (poor due)?[47] Then, when fighting was ordained for them, a section of these very people started fearing men, as they should fear Allah, or even more! And they said, "O Lord! Why have you ordained fighting for us? Had you but given us a little more time!" Say, "Short is the enjoyment of this world. And the other world is better for him who fears Allah. And you shall not be wronged, even a bit."

---

47. After the Hijrah and the establishment of the nascent Islamic State at Medina, the believers were rearing to go and fight against their oppressors at Makkah, as this part of the Verse depicts. They were advised patience. But when, finally, the permission to fight was for the first time given vide Verse 22:39, the turnaround in the attitudes of some of the believers, is depicted here, in the latter part of the Verse.

أَيْنَمَا تَكُونُواْ يُدْرِككُّمُ ٱلْمَوْتُ وَلَوْ كُنتُمْ فِى بُرُوجٍ مُّشَيَّدَةٍ وَإِن تُصِبْهُمْ حَسَنَةٌ يَقُولُواْ هَـٰذِهِۦ مِنْ عِندِ ٱللَّهِ وَإِن تُصِبْهُمْ سَيِّئَةٌ يَقُولُواْ هَـٰذِهِۦ مِنْ عِندِكَ قُلْ كُلٌّ مِّنْ عِندِ ٱللَّهِ فَمَالِ هَـٰٓؤُلَآءِ ٱلْقَوْمِ لَا يَكَادُونَ يَفْقَهُونَ حَدِيثًا ۝

78. Aynama takoonoo yudrikkumu almawtu walaw kuntum fee buroojin mushayyadatin wa-in tusibhum hasanatun yaqooloo hathihi min AAindi Allahi wa-in tusibhum sayyi-atun yaqooloo hathihi min AAindika qul kullun min AAindi Allahi famali haola-i alqawmi la yakadoona yafqahoona hadeethan

---

4:78. Wherever you are, death will overtake you even if you are within fortified fortresses. And if any good comes to them, they say, "This is from Allah." And if anything, bad afflicts them, they say, "This is from you[48]?" Say, "All things are from Allah." And what's the matter with these people that they are unable to understand the statement, [49]

---

48. That is, they put the blame therefor on someone other than themselves.

49. The statement is mentioned in the first part of the next Verse.

مَّآ أَصَابَكَ مِنْ حَسَنَةٍ فَمِنَ ٱللَّهِ وَمَآ أَصَابَكَ

مِن سَيِّئَةٍ فَمِن نَّفْسِكَ وَأَرْسَلْنَٰكَ لِلنَّاسِ رَسُولًا وَكَفَىٰ بِٱللَّهِ شَهِيدًا

79. Ma asabaka min hasanatin famina Allahi wama asabaka min sayyi-atin famin nafsika waarsalnaka lilnnasi rasoolan wakafa biAllahi shaheedan

4:79. "Whatever good comes to you, it is from Allah. And whatever bad befalls you, it is from you yourself."[50] And We have sent you as Messenger to mankind. And Allah is enough as Witness.[51]

50. **All good things that man gets are of course from Allah. And even if an apparently bad thing comes from Him, it comes by way of a test or warning. Behind the apparent badness of the test or warning, lies only good for the one who recognises it as such. And if man encounters anything bad, it is because of his own wanton acts of omission and commission against the divine law.**

51. **Allah, the Creator, Himself gives witness here that the divine Message of the Qur'aan, sent with Muhammad (peace be upon him), was for the entire mankind, and not just for the Arabs.**

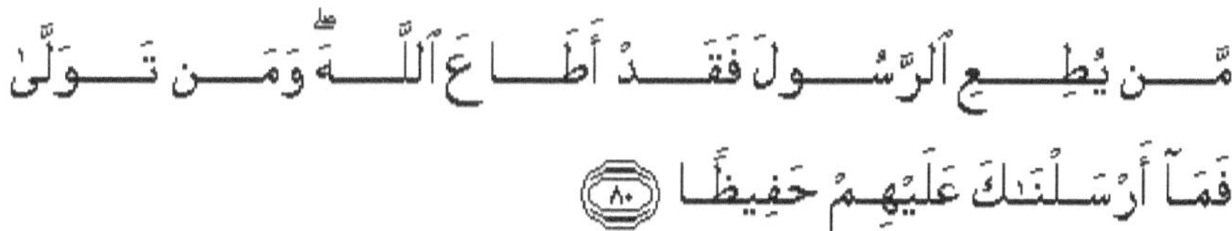

80. Man yutiAAi alrrasoola faqad ataAAa Allaha waman tawalla fama arsalnaka AAalayhim hafeethan

4:80. Whoever obeys the Messenger, does surely obey Allah. And whoever turns away, We have not sent you as guardian of such persons.[52]

52. For us today, living in this world centuries after the Messenger's passing away, obeying him (the Messenger), and thereby obeying Allah, connotes obeying the divine instructions given in the Qur'aan. Those who neglect, overlook or puposely act against these instructions, can get protection neither from the Messenger, nor from anyone else, against Allah.

وَيَقُولُونَ طَاعَةٌ فَإِذَا بَرَزُواْ مِنْ عِندِكَ بَيَّتَ طَآئِفَةٌ مِّنْهُمْ غَيْرَ ٱلَّذِى تَقُولُ وَٱللَّهُ يَكْتُبُ مَا يُبَيِّتُونَ فَأَعْرِضْ عَنْهُمْ وَتَوَكَّلْ عَلَى ٱللَّهِ وَكَفَىٰ بِٱللَّهِ وَكِيلًا ۝٨١

81. Wayaqooloona taAAatun fa-itha barazoo min AAindika bayyata ta-ifatun minhum ghayra allathee taqoolu waAllahu yaktubu ma yubayyitoona faaAArid AAanhum watawakkal AAala Allahi wakafa biAllahi wakeelan

4:81. They declare their obedience. Then, once out of your[53] presence, a section of them pass all night in doing other than what you advise them to do. And Allah records their nocturnal doings. So, leave them alone, and trust Allah! And Allah suffices as Trustee.

53. I.e., Prophet Muhammad's.

أَفَلَا يَتَدَبَّرُونَ ٱلْقُرْءَانَ وَلَوْ كَانَ مِنْ عِندِ غَيْرِ ٱللَّهِ لَوَجَدُواْ فِيهِ ٱخْتِلَٰفًا كَثِيرًا ۝٨٢

82. Afala yatadabbaroona alqur-ana walaw kana min AAindi ghayri Allahi lawajadoo feehi ikhtilafan katheeran

4:82. Do they not then ponder over the Qur'aan? And had it been from anybody other than Allah, they would certainly find in it many a contradiction.[54]

54. This Verse gives the criterion to distinguish a divine book from a non-divine one. In other words, it makes a divine statement to the effect that any book authored by a man, howsoever learned he may be, is bound to contain errors.

وَإِذَا جَآءَهُمْ أَمْرٌ مِّنَ ٱلْأَمْنِ أَوِ ٱلْخَوْفِ أَذَاعُواْ بِهِۦ وَلَوْ رَدُّوهُ إِلَى ٱلرَّسُولِ وَإِلَىٰٓ أُوْلِى ٱلْأَمْرِ مِنْهُمْ لَعَلِمَهُ ٱلَّذِينَ يَسْتَنۢبِطُونَهُۥ مِنْهُمْ وَلَوْلَا فَضْلُ ٱللَّهِ عَلَيْكُمْ وَرَحْمَتُهُۥ لَٱتَّبَعْتُمُ ٱلشَّيْطَٰنَ إِلَّا قَلِيلًا ﴿٨٣﴾

83. Wa-itha jaahum amrun mina al-amni awi alkhawfi athaAAoo bihi walaw raddoohu ila alrrasooli wa-ila olee al-amri minhum laAAalimahu allatheena yastanbitoonahu minhum walawla fadlu Allahi AAalaykum warahmatuhu laittabaAAtumu alshshaytana illa qaleelan

4:83. And when there comes to them any matter of peace or fear, they make it public. And had they referred it to the Messenger and to those in authority among them, it would have been properly scrutinized by the investigators among them. And had it not been for Allah's Favour upon you, and His Mercy, you would certainly have followed Satan, save a few of you.

فَقَٰتِلْ فِى سَبِيلِ ٱللَّهِ لَا تُكَلَّفُ إِلَّا نَفْسَكَ وَحَرِّضِ ٱلْمُؤْمِنِينَ عَسَى ٱللَّهُ أَن يَكُفَّ بَأْسَ ٱلَّذِينَ كَفَرُواْ وَٱللَّهُ أَشَدُّ بَأْسًا وَأَشَدُّ تَنكِيلًا ﴿٨٤﴾

84. Faqatil fee sabeeli Allahi la tukallafu illa nafsaka waharridi almu/mineena AAasa Allahu an yakuffa ba/sa allatheena kafaroo waAllahu ashaddu ba/san waashaddu tankeelan

4:84. Fight, then, in Allah's Path. You will be beld responsible for none but you yourself and exhort the believers. It may be that Allah will contain the power of those who suppress the Truth. And Allah is the strongest in power and the most severe in giving punishment.[55]

---

55. Although this Verse apparently addressed the Prophet while he was leading the believers on a battlefield, it continues to address every believer, in all situations of the on-going struggle in Allah's Path, till the Last Day. The struggle need not necessarily be in a field of battle. The struggle must be waged in all walks of life. The Satan is ever vigilant to see to it that his friends among mankind go on laying roadblocks on the Allah-laden Straight Path. A believer has to struggle to remove those roadblocks. And in this struggle, he is responsible for none else but his own self, although he may from time to time urge others to keep to the Straight Path come what may. The obstacles on the Path won't be insurmountable, as the believer is assured of Allah's help. He should have an unshakeable faith in Him.

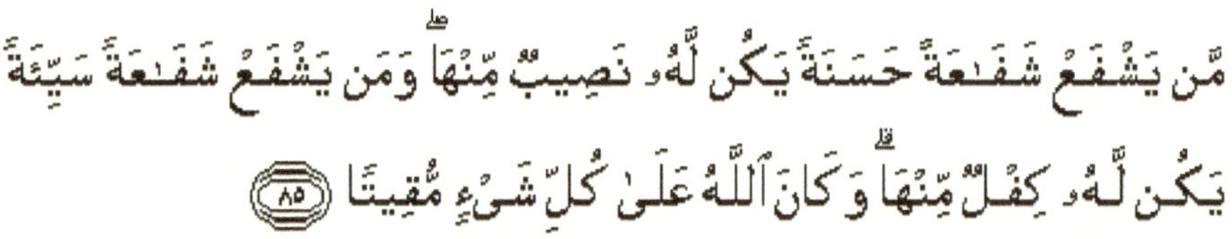

85. Man yashfaAA shafaAAatan hasanatan yakun lahu naseebun minha waman yashfaAA shafaAAatan sayyi-atan yakun lahu kiflun minha wakana Allahu AAala kulli shay-in muqeetan

---

4:85. Whoever intercedes in a good cause[56], for him a share thereof; and whoever intercedes in a bad cause, for him a part thereof. And Allah is the Controller over all things.

---

56. The Arabic word used is *shafaAAatan* (intercession). This should not be confused with intercession with Allah Ta'ala on the Day of Judgement. There won't be any intercession by anyone on that Day as reiterated in <u>Verse 2:254</u>. The intercession, referred to here in this Verse 4:85, is that made by any person with any other in any dispute/conflict arising in this life.

وَإِذَا حُيِّيتُم بِتَحِيَّةٍ فَحَيُّواْ بِأَحْسَنَ مِنْهَآ أَوْ رُدُّوهَآ إِنَّ ٱللَّهَ كَانَ عَلَىٰ كُلِّ شَىْءٍ حَسِيبًا ۝

86. Wa-itha huyyeetum bitahiyyatin fahayyoo bi-ahsana minha aw ruddooha inna Allaha kana AAala kulli shay-in haseeban

4:86. And when you are greeted with a greeting, then return the greeting in a better or similar manner. Indeed, Allah is the Comptroller over all things.

ٱللَّهُ لَآ إِلَٰهَ إِلَّا هُوَ لَيَجْمَعَنَّكُمْ إِلَىٰ يَوْمِ ٱلْقِيَٰمَةِ لَا رَيْبَ فِيهِ وَمَنْ أَصْدَقُ مِنَ ٱللَّهِ حَدِيثًا ۝

87. Allahu la ilaha illa huwa layajmaAAannakum ila yawmi alqiyamati la rayba feehi waman asdaqu mina Allahi hadeethan

4:87. Allah! None has the right to be worshipped but He. He will certainly gather you together on the Day of Resurrection about which there is no doubt. And who can be more truthful in word than Allah?

۞ فَمَا لَكُمْ فِى ٱلْمُنَٰفِقِينَ فِئَتَيْنِ وَٱللَّهُ أَرْكَسَهُم بِمَا كَسَبُوٓاْ أَتُرِيدُونَ أَن تَهْدُواْ مَنْ أَضَلَّ ٱللَّهُ وَمَن يُضْلِلِ ٱللَّهُ فَلَن تَجِدَ لَهُۥ سَبِيلًا ۝

88. Fama lakum fee almunafiqeena fi-atayni waAllahu arkasahum bima kasaboo atureedoona an tahdoo man adalla Allahu waman yudlili Allahu falan tajida lahu sabeelan

4:88. What is the matter with you, then, that, on the question of the hypocrites[57] you are divided into two opposing camps? And Allah has turned them back because of what they have earned. Do you wish to guide him whom Allah has sent astray!? And whomsoever Allah sends astray, you shall find no way for him.

57. For a detailed Qur'aanic description of 'hypocrites', please refer <u>Verses 2:8 to 2:20</u>. You may also refer <u>study note 2:10</u> in this context.

وَدُّواْ لَوْ تَكْفُرُونَ كَمَا كَفَرُواْ فَتَكُونُونَ سَوَآءً فَلَا تَتَّخِذُواْ مِنْهُمْ أَوْلِيَآءَ

حَتَّىٰ يُهَاجِرُواْ فِى سَبِيلِ ٱللَّهِ فَإِن تَوَلَّوْاْ فَخُذُوهُمْ وَٱقْتُلُوهُمْ حَيْثُ

وَجَدتُّمُوهُمْ وَلَا تَتَّخِذُواْ مِنْهُمْ وَلِيًّا وَلَا نَصِيرًا ۝

89. Waddoo law takfuroona kama kafaroo fatakoonoona sawaan fala tattakhithoo minhum awliyaa hatta yuhajiroo fee sabeeli Allahi fa-in tawallaw fakhuthoohum waoqtuloohum haythu wajadtumoohum wala tattakhithoo minhum waliyyan wala naseeran

4:89. They desire that you should suppress the Truth as they have suppressed it, so that you all become alike. Take not from among them friends, then, until they move out in Allah's Path. Then if they turn back, seize them and kill them wherever you find them.[58] And take not, from among them, anyone, either as a close friend or to help you out in any matter.

58. This should not be misunderstood as an open licence to kill anyone suspected to be a hypocrite. The divine command to kill is given in specific cases of desertions from Muslim armies set out on expeditions in Allah's Path. Deserters, during times of war, are summarily court-martialled in today's modern armies too.

إِلَّا ٱلَّذِينَ يَصِلُونَ إِلَىٰ قَوۡمٍ بَيۡنَكُمۡ وَبَيۡنَهُم مِّيثَٰقٌ أَوۡ جَآءُوكُمۡ حَصِرَتۡ صُدُورُهُمۡ أَن يُقَٰتِلُوكُمۡ أَوۡ يُقَٰتِلُوا۟ قَوۡمَهُمۡ وَلَوۡ شَآءَ ٱللَّهُ لَسَلَّطَهُمۡ عَلَيۡكُمۡ فَلَقَٰتَلُوكُمۡ فَإِنِ ٱعۡتَزَلُوكُمۡ فَلَمۡ يُقَٰتِلُوكُمۡ وَأَلۡقَوۡا۟ إِلَيۡكُمُ ٱلسَّلَمَ فَمَا جَعَلَ ٱللَّهُ لَكُمۡ عَلَيۡهِمۡ سَبِيلًا ۝

90. Illa allatheena yasiloona ila qawmin baynakum wabaynahum meethaqun aw jaookum hasirat sudooruhum an yuqatilookum aw yuqatiloo qawmahum walaw shaa Allahu lasallatahum AAalaykum falaqatalookum fa-ini iAAtazalookum falam yuqatilookum waalqaw ilaykumu alssalama fama jaAAala Allahu lakum AAalayhim sabeelan

4:90. Except those[59] who join a people between whom and you there is a treaty, or who come to you with their minds averse to fighting you or fighting their own people. And had Allah willed, He would have empowered them to fight you. So, if they withdraw from you and fight with you not, and offer you peace, then Allah has opened no way for you to act against them.

59. I.e the hypocrites. This Verse is a continuation of the previous one.

سَتَجِدُونَ ءَاخَرِينَ يُرِيدُونَ أَن يَأۡمَنُوكُمۡ وَيَأۡمَنُوا۟ قَوۡمَهُمۡ كُلَّ مَا رُدُّوٓا۟ إِلَى ٱلۡفِتۡنَةِ أُرۡكِسُوا۟ فِيهَا فَإِن لَّمۡ يَعۡتَزِلُوكُمۡ وَيُلۡقُوٓا۟ إِلَيۡكُمُ ٱلسَّلَمَ وَيَكُفُّوٓا۟ أَيۡدِيَهُمۡ فَخُذُوهُمۡ وَٱقۡتُلُوهُمۡ حَيۡثُ ثَقِفۡتُمُوهُمۡ وَأُو۟لَٰٓئِكُمۡ جَعَلۡنَا لَكُمۡ عَلَيۡهِمۡ سُلۡطَٰنًا مُّبِينًا ۝

91. Satajidoona akhareena yureedoona an ya/manookum waya/manoo qawmahum kulla ma ruddoo ila alfitnati orkisoo feeha fa-in lam yaAAtazilookum wayulqoo ilaykumu alssalama wayakuffoo aydiyahum fakhuthoohum waoqtuloohum haythu thaqiftumoohum waola-ikum jaAAalna lakum AAalayhim sultanan mubeenan

4:91. You will find others who desire that they should be safe from you and safe from their own people. Whenever they are put to the test, they readily yield to temptations therein. So, if they do not withdraw from you, offer you peace and restrain their hands, then seize them and kill them wherever you get hold of them. And against these We have given you a clear authority.

وَمَا كَانَ لِمُؤْمِنٍ أَن يَقْتُلَ مُؤْمِنًا إِلَّا خَطَـًٔا وَمَن قَتَلَ مُؤْمِنًا خَطَـًٔا فَتَحْرِيرُ رَقَبَةٍ مُّؤْمِنَةٍ وَدِيَةٌ مُّسَلَّمَةٌ إِلَىٰ أَهْلِهِ إِلَّا أَن يَصَّدَّقُوا۟ فَإِن كَانَ مِن قَوْمٍ عَدُوٍّ لَّكُمْ وَهُوَ مُؤْمِنٌ فَتَحْرِيرُ رَقَبَةٍ مُّؤْمِنَةٍ وَإِن كَانَ مِن قَوْمٍ بَيْنَكُمْ وَبَيْنَهُم مِّيثَاقٌ فَدِيَةٌ مُّسَلَّمَةٌ إِلَىٰ أَهْلِهِ وَتَحْرِيرُ رَقَبَةٍ مُّؤْمِنَةٍ فَمَن لَّمْ يَجِدْ فَصِيَامُ شَهْرَيْنِ مُتَتَابِعَيْنِ تَوْبَةً مِّنَ اللَّهِ وَكَانَ اللَّهُ عَلِيمًا حَكِيمًا ۝

92. Wama kana limu/minin an yaqtula mu/minan illa khataan waman qatala mu/minan khataan fatahreeru raqabatin mu/minatin wadiyatun musallamatun ila ahlihi illa an yassaddaqoo fa-in kana min qawmin AAaduwwin lakum wahuwa mu/minun fatahreeru raqabatin mu/minatin wa-in kana min qawmin baynakum wabaynahum meethaqun fadiyatun musallamatun ila ahlihi watahreeru raqabatin mu/minatin faman lam yajid fasiyamu shahrayni mutatabiAAayni tawbatan mina Allahi wakana Allahu AAaleeman hakeeman

4:92. And it does not behove a believer to kill a believer except by mistake. And whoever kills a believer by mistake, he should free a believing slave, and blood-money[60] should be paid to the deceased's family unless they remit it as charity. If he was from a people hostile to you and was a believer, then the freeing of a believing slave, and if he was from a people, between whom and you there is a covenant, the blood-money should be paid to the deceased's family along with the freeing of a believing slave, and he, who cannot get one (slave), should fast for two consecutive months to seek repentance from Allah. And Allah is Knowledgeable, Wise.

---

60. **Money given as compensation for the loss of life.**

وَمَن يَقْتُلْ مُؤْمِنًا مُّتَعَمِّدًا فَجَزَآؤُهُۥ جَهَنَّمُ خَـٰلِدًا فِيهَا وَغَضِبَ ٱللَّهُ عَلَيْهِ وَلَعَنَهُۥ وَأَعَدَّ لَهُۥ عَذَابًا عَظِيمًا ۝

93. Waman yaqtul mu/minan mutaAAammidan fajazaohu jahannamu khalidan feeha waghadiba Allahu AAalayhi walaAAanahu waaAAadda lahu AAathaban AAatheeman

4:93. And whoever kills a believer intentionally, his punishment is to abide forever in Hell. And Allah has sent His wrath and curse on him. And He has prepared for him a severe punishment.

يَـٰٓأَيُّهَا ٱلَّذِينَ ءَامَنُوٓا۟ إِذَا ضَرَبْتُمْ فِى سَبِيلِ ٱللَّهِ فَتَبَيَّنُوا۟ وَلَا تَقُولُوا۟ لِمَنْ أَلْقَىٰٓ إِلَيْكُمُ ٱلسَّلَـٰمَ لَسْتَ مُؤْمِنًا تَبْتَغُونَ عَرَضَ ٱلْحَيَوٰةِ ٱلدُّنْيَا فَعِندَ ٱللَّهِ مَغَانِمُ كَثِيرَةٌ كَذَٰلِكَ كُنتُم مِّن قَبْلُ فَمَنَّ ٱللَّهُ عَلَيْكُمْ فَتَبَيَّنُوٓا۟ إِنَّ ٱللَّهَ كَانَ بِمَا تَعْمَلُونَ خَبِيرًا ۝

94. Ya ayyuha allatheena amanoo itha darabtum fee sabeeli Allahi fatabayyanoo wala taqooloo liman alqa ilaykumu alssalama lasta mu/minan tabtaghoona AAarada alhayati alddunya faAAinda Allahi maghanimu katheeratun kathalika kuntum min qablu famanna Allahu AAalaykum fatabayyanoo inna Allaha kana bima taAAmaloona khabeeran

4:94. O you who believe! When you set out in Allah's way, ascertain facts, and do not say to anyone, who offers you peace, that he is not a believer, seeking benefits of this worldly life. With Allah, on the other hand, there are bounties abundant. You were like that before when Allah conferred His Grace on you! So, ascertain the facts. Allah is indeed aware of what you do.

لَّا يَسْتَوِى ٱلْقَـٰعِدُونَ مِنَ ٱلْمُؤْمِنِينَ غَيْرُ أُوْلِى ٱلضَّرَرِ وَٱلْمُجَـٰهِدُونَ فِى سَبِيلِ ٱللَّهِ بِأَمْوَٰلِهِمْ وَأَنفُسِهِمْ فَضَّلَ ٱللَّهُ ٱلْمُجَـٰهِدِينَ بِأَمْوَٰلِهِمْ وَأَنفُسِهِمْ عَلَى ٱلْقَـٰعِدِينَ دَرَجَةً وَكُلًّا وَعَدَ ٱللَّهُ ٱلْحُسْنَىٰ وَفَضَّلَ ٱللَّهُ ٱلْمُجَـٰهِدِينَ عَلَى ٱلْقَـٰعِدِينَ أَجْرًا عَظِيمًا ۝

95. La yastawee alqaAAidoona mina almu/mineena ghayru olee alddarari waalmujahidoona fee sabeeli Allahi bi-amwalihim waanfusihim faddala Allahu almujahideena bi-amwalihim waanfusihim AAala alqaAAideena darajatan wakullan waAAada Allahu alhusna wafaddala Allahu almujahideena AAala alqaAAideena ajran AAatheeman

4:95. Not equal are those among the believers who sit back at home – disabled men excepted – and those who strive in Allah's Path with their wealth and with their persons. Allah has favoured those, who strive with their wealth and with their persons, with higher rank than those who sit back. And Allah has promised the good to both, but Allah has favoured those who strive, over those who sit back, with a great reward.

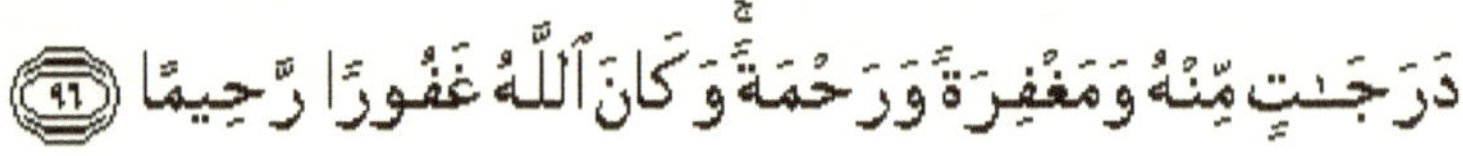

دَرَجَـٰتٍ مِّنْهُ وَمَغْفِرَةً وَرَحْمَةً وَكَانَ ٱللَّهُ غَفُورًا رَّحِيمًا ۝

96. Darajatin minhu wamaghfiratan warahmatan wakana Allahu ghafooran raheeman

4:96. Ranks from Him and forgiveness and mercy.[61] And Allah is Forgiving, Merciful.

61. This Verse is in continuation of the preceding one. Among those also who attain to salvation Allah Ta'ala has assigned ranks proprtionate to their good works here in this world.

إِنَّ ٱلَّذِينَ تَوَفَّىٰهُمُ ٱلْمَلَٰٓئِكَةُ ظَالِمِىٓ أَنفُسِهِمْ قَالُوا۟ فِيمَ كُنتُمْ قَالُوا۟ كُنَّا مُسْتَضْعَفِينَ فِى ٱلْأَرْضِ قَالُوٓا۟ أَلَمْ تَكُنْ أَرْضُ ٱللَّهِ وَٰسِعَةً فَتُهَاجِرُوا۟ فِيهَا فَأُو۟لَٰٓئِكَ مَأْوَىٰهُمْ جَهَنَّمُ وَسَآءَتْ مَصِيرًا ﴿٩٧﴾

97. Inna alla_theena tawaff_ahumu almal_a-ikatu _tha_limee anfusihim _qaloo feema kuntum _qaloo kunn_a musta_dAAafeena fee al-ar_di _qaloo alam takun ar_du All_ahi w_asiAAatan fatuh_ajiroo feeh_a faol_a-ika ma/w_ahum jahannamu was_aat ma_seera_n

4:97. While causing those persons to die who were unjust to their own souls[62], the angels did indeed ask them, "Why were you so in there?" They said, "We were in a weak position on the earth." The angels asked, "Was not Allah's earth spacious enough for you to emigrate[63] therein?" These people then would have their abode in Hell, and it is an evil destination!

---

62. Being 'unjust to their own souls' connotes going against divine dispensation. Allah, for example, has ordained that man be truthful. And when man is untruthful because of compulsions from worldly forces around him, he is unjust to his own soul as he incurs Allah's wrath upon himself thereby.

63. In today's context, emigration could mean not only moving from one geographical location to another, but also, inter alia, a change in the job one is engaged in for one's livelihood.

إِلَّا ٱلْمُسْتَضْعَفِينَ مِنَ ٱلرِّجَالِ وَٱلنِّسَآءِ وَٱلْوِلْدَٰنِ لَا يَسْتَطِيعُونَ حِيلَةً وَلَا يَهْتَدُونَ سَبِيلًا ﴿٩٨﴾

98. Ill_a almusta_dAAafeena mina alrrijali w_a_alnnis_a-i w_a_alwild_ani l_a yasta_teeAAoona _heelatan wal_a yahtadoona sabeel_an

4:98. Except the weak from among the men, women and children who neither have the means nor can they find a way.[64]

---

64. This Verse and the next one are in continuation of the last sentence in the preceding Verse, and spare the really weak from the fate awaiting those who do not emigrate, in situations warranting emigration, despite having the means to do so.

فَأُوْلَـٰٓئِكَ عَسَى ٱللَّهُ أَن يَعْفُوَ عَنْهُمْ ۚ وَكَانَ ٱللَّهُ عَفُوًّا غَفُورًا ﴿٩٩﴾

99. Faola-ika AAasa Allahu an yaAAfuwa AAanhum wakana Allahu AAafuwwan ghafooran

4:99. Allah may then pardon such people. And Allah is Lenient, Forgiving.

۞ وَمَن يُهَاجِرْ فِى سَبِيلِ ٱللَّهِ يَجِدْ فِى ٱلْأَرْضِ مُرَٰغَمًا كَثِيرًا وَسَعَةً ۚ وَمَن يَخْرُجْ مِنۢ بَيْتِهِۦ مُهَاجِرًا إِلَى ٱللَّهِ وَرَسُولِهِۦ ثُمَّ يُدْرِكْهُ ٱلْمَوْتُ فَقَدْ وَقَعَ أَجْرُهُۥ عَلَى ٱللَّهِ ۗ وَكَانَ ٱللَّهُ غَفُورًا رَّحِيمًا ﴿١٠٠﴾

100. Waman yuhajir fee sabeeli Allahi yajid fee al-ardi muraghaman katheeran wasaAAatan waman yakhruj min baytihi muhajiran ila Allahi warasoolihi thumma yudrik-hu almawtu faqad waqaAAa ajruhu AAala Allahi wakana Allahu ghafooran raheeman

4:100. And whoever emigrates in Allah's Path, he will find on the earth many places of refuge and abundance. And whoever leaves home as an emigrant unto Allah and His Messenger, and then death overtakes him, his reward falls due upon Allah. And Allah is Forgiving, Merciful.

وَإِذَا ضَرَبْتُمْ فِى ٱلْأَرْضِ فَلَيْسَ عَلَيْكُمْ جُنَاحٌ أَن تَقْصُرُوا۟ مِنَ ٱلصَّلَوٰةِ إِنْ خِفْتُمْ أَن يَفْتِنَكُمُ ٱلَّذِينَ كَفَرُوٓا۟ ۚ إِنَّ ٱلْكَـٰفِرِينَ كَانُوا۟ لَكُمْ عَدُوًّا مُّبِينًا

101. Wa-itha darabtum fee al-ardi falaysa AAalaykum junahun an taqsuroo mina alssalati in khiftum an yaftinakumu allatheena kafaroo inna alkafireena kanoo lakum AAaduwwan mubeenan

4:101. And when you are on a journey on the earth, no sin upon you if you shorten the prayer out of fear that those who suppress the truth may cause you mischief. Indeed, the suppressors of truth are your open enemy.

وَإِذَا كُنتَ فِيهِمْ فَأَقَمْتَ لَهُمُ ٱلصَّلَوٰةَ فَلْتَقُمْ طَآئِفَةٌ مِّنْهُم مَّعَكَ وَلْيَأْخُذُوٓاْ أَسْلِحَتَهُمْ فَإِذَا سَجَدُواْ فَلْيَكُونُواْ مِن وَرَآئِكُمْ وَلْتَأْتِ طَآئِفَةٌ أُخْرَىٰ لَمْ يُصَلُّواْ فَلْيُصَلُّواْ مَعَكَ وَلْيَأْخُذُواْ حِذْرَهُمْ وَأَسْلِحَتَهُمْ وَدَّ ٱلَّذِينَ كَفَرُواْ لَوْ تَغْفُلُونَ عَنْ أَسْلِحَتِكُمْ وَأَمْتِعَتِكُمْ فَيَمِيلُونَ عَلَيْكُم مَّيْلَةً وَٰحِدَةً وَلَا جُنَاحَ عَلَيْكُمْ إِن كَانَ بِكُمْ أَذًى مِّن مَّطَرٍ أَوْ كُنتُم مَّرْضَىٰٓ أَن تَضَعُوٓاْ أَسْلِحَتَكُمْ وَخُذُواْ حِذْرَكُمْ إِنَّ ٱللَّهَ أَعَدَّ لِلْكَٰفِرِينَ عَذَابًا مُّهِينًا ۝

102. Wa-itha kunta feehim faaqamta lahumu alssalata faltaqum ta-ifatun minhum maAAaka walya/khuthoo aslihatahum fa-itha sajadoo falyakoonoo min wara-ikum walta/ti ta-ifatun okhra lam yusalloo falyusalloo maAAaka walya/khuthoo hithrahum waaslihatahum wadda allatheena kafaroo law taghfuloona AAan aslihatikum waamtiAAatikum fayameeloona AAalaykum maylatan wahidatan wala junaha AAalaykum in kana bikum athan min matarin aw kuntum marda an tadaAAoo aslihatakum wakhuthoo hithrakum inna Allaha aAAadda lilkafireena AAathaban muheenan

4:102. And when you are among them and lead them in prayer, let a group of them stand up with you, taking their arms with them. Then when they have prostrated, let them go to your rear, and let another group who have not prayed come forward and pray with you, being on their guard and taking their arms. Those who suppress the Truth desire that you are off-guard about your arms and your property, so that they may then turn upon you in a single decisive swoop. And no blame on you, if you are inconvenienced by rain or if you are ill, that you put off your arms; but be on your guard. Indeed, Allah has prepared a disgraceful punishment for the suppressors of Truth.

فَإِذَا قَضَيْتُمُ ٱلصَّلَوٰةَ فَٱذْكُرُوا۟ ٱللَّهَ قِيَـٰمًا وَقُعُودًا وَعَلَىٰ جُنُوبِكُمْ فَإِذَا

ٱطْمَأْنَنتُمْ فَأَقِيمُوا۟ ٱلصَّلَوٰةَ إِنَّ ٱلصَّلَوٰةَ كَانَتْ عَلَى ٱلْمُؤْمِنِينَ كِتَـٰبًا مَّوْقُوتًا

103. Fa-itha qadaytumu alssalata faothkuroo Allaha qiyaman waquAAoodan waAAala junoobikum fa-itha itma/nantum faaqeemoo alssalata inna alssalata kanat AAala almu/mineena kitaban mawqootan

---

4:103. Then when you are due to perform the prayer, remember Allah, standing, sitting and while resting on your sides. Then when the situation for you becomes conducive, offer the prayer properly. Indeed, the prayer is ordained for the believers at fixed times.[65]

---

65. It is a war-like situation that is envisaged in Verses 101 and 102 above. But, in this Verse 103, other peace-time situations, like when one is travelling in a public transport, in a non-Islamic country, at the fixed time of the ritual prayer, are also envisaged. Stress is laid here on the performance of the _salaah_ at the time fixed even though one is travelling, say, in a public transport bus. The prayer can be performed on a notional basis, then, just by remembering Allah, without going through the normal procedure for the prayer. This Verse is also the authority for the very ill, bedridden, person to offer his/her _salah_ even while lying down.

وَلَا تَهِنُوا۟ فِى ٱبْتِغَآءِ ٱلْقَوْمِ إِن تَكُونُوا۟ تَأْلَمُونَ

فَإِنَّهُمْ يَأْلَمُونَ كَمَا تَأْلَمُونَ وَتَرْجُونَ مِنَ ٱللَّهِ مَا لَا يَرْجُونَ وَكَانَ

ٱللَّهُ عَلِيمًا حَكِيمًا

104. Wala tahinoo fee ibtigha-i alqawmi in takoonoo ta/lamoona fa-innahum ya/lamoona kama ta/lamoona watarjoona mina Allahi ma la yarjoona wakana Allahu AAaleeman hakeeman

---

4:104. And relent not in pursuing the enemy. If you have suffered, they too have suffered as you have, and you expect from Allah what they do not. And Allah is Knowledgeable, Wise.

إِنَّآ أَنزَلْنَآ إِلَيْكَ ٱلْكِتَٰبَ بِٱلْحَقِّ لِتَحْكُمَ بَيْنَ ٱلنَّاسِ بِمَآ أَرَىٰكَ ٱللَّهُ وَلَا تَكُن لِّلْخَآئِنِينَ خَصِيمًا ۝

105. Inna anzalna ilayka alkitaba bialhaqqi litahkuma bayna alnnasi bima araka Allahu wala takun lilkha-ineena khaseeman

4:105. WE have indeed sent down to you (singular) the Book with the Truth so that you decide things among mankind based on what Allah has shown you. And do not side with the treacherous.

وَٱسْتَغْفِرِ ٱللَّهَ إِنَّ ٱللَّهَ كَانَ غَفُورًا رَّحِيمًا ۝

106. Waistaghfiri Allaha inna Allaha kana ghafooran raheeman

4:106. And seek forgiveness of Allah. Indeed, Allah is Forgiving, Merciful.

وَلَا تُجَٰدِلْ عَنِ ٱلَّذِينَ يَخْتَانُونَ أَنفُسَهُمْ إِنَّ ٱللَّهَ لَا يُحِبُّ مَن كَانَ خَوَّانًا أَثِيمًا ۝

107. Wala tujadil AAani allatheena yakhtanoona anfusahum inna Allaha la yuhibbu man kana khawwanan atheeman

4:107. And argue not on behalf of those who deceive themselves. Indeed, Allah loves not one who is a sinful deceiver.

يَسْتَخْفُونَ مِنَ ٱلنَّاسِ وَلَا يَسْتَخْفُونَ مِنَ ٱللَّهِ وَهُوَ مَعَهُمْ إِذْ يُبَيِّتُونَ مَا لَا يَرْضَىٰ مِنَ ٱلْقَوْلِ وَكَانَ ٱللَّهُ بِمَا يَعْمَلُونَ مُحِيطًا ۝

108. Yastakhfoona mina alnnasi wala yastakhfoona mina Allahi wahuwa maAAahum ith yubayyitoona ma la yarda mina alqawli wakana Allahu bima yaAAmaloona muheetan

4:108. They may conceal things from people and not from Allah; for, He is with them when they draw secret schemes, which please Him not. And Allah is in complete control of what they do.

هَـٰٓأَنتُمْ هَـٰٓؤُلَاءِ جَـٰدَلْتُمْ عَنْهُمْ فِى ٱلْحَيَوٰةِ ٱلدُّنْيَا فَمَن يُجَـٰدِلُ ٱللَّهَ عَنْهُمْ يَوْمَ ٱلْقِيَـٰمَةِ أَم مَّن يَكُونُ عَلَيْهِمْ وَكِيلًا ﴿١٠٩﴾

109. Haantum haola-i jadaltum AAanhum fee alhayati alddunya faman yujadilu Allaha AAanhum yawma alqiyamati am man yakoonu AAalayhim wakeelan

4:109. Here you are those, who plead for them in this worldly life, but who will plead with Allah for them on the Day of Resurrection? Or, who will then be their advocate?

وَمَن يَعْمَلْ سُوٓءًا أَوْ يَظْلِمْ نَفْسَهُۥ ثُمَّ يَسْتَغْفِرِ ٱللَّهَ يَجِدِ ٱللَّهَ غَفُورًا رَّحِيمًا ﴿١١٠﴾

110. Waman yaAAmal soo-an aw yathlim nafsahu thumma yastaghfiri Allaha yajidi Allaha ghafooran raheeman

4:110. And he who commits an evil act or wrongs his own self and then seeks Allah's forgiveness, he will find Allah Forgiving, Merciful.

وَمَن يَكْسِبْ إِثْمًا فَإِنَّمَا يَكْسِبُهُۥ عَلَىٰ نَفْسِهِۦ وَكَانَ ٱللَّهُ عَلِيمًا حَكِيمًا ﴿١١١﴾

111. Waman yaksib ithman fa-innama yaksibuhu AAala nafsihi wakana Allahu AAaleeman hakeeman

4:111. And he, who commits a sin, commits it only against his own self. And Allah is Knowledgeable, Wise.

---

112. Waman yaksib khatee-atan aw ithman thumma yarmi bihi baree-an faqadi ihtamala buhtanan wa-ithman mubeenan

4:112. And he who commits a mistake or a sin and then throws the blame therefor on to an innocent, he has indeed burdened himself with slander and manifest sin.

---

113. Walawla fadlu Allahi AAalayka warahmatuhu lahammat ta-ifatun minhum an yudillooka wama yudilloona illa anfusahum wama yadurroonaka min shay-in waanzala Allahu AAalayka alkitaba waalhikmata waAAallamaka ma lam takun taAAlamu wakana fadlu Allahi AAalayka AAatheeman

4:113. And had it not been for Allah's Favour upon you and His mercy, a section of them[66] had certainly planned to mislead you. And they mislead not but their own selves and they can cause you no harm. And Allah has sent down upon you the Book and the Wisdom[67], and He has taught you what you did not know. And great is Allah's Favour upon you!

---

66. The reference here is to those, mentioned in <u>Verse 108</u> above.

67. The Wisdom to deal with prople, including those mentioned in Verse 108 above.

۞ لَّا خَيْرَ فِى كَثِيرٍ مِّن نَّجْوَىٰهُمْ إِلَّا مَنْ أَمَرَ بِصَدَقَةٍ أَوْ مَعْرُوفٍ أَوْ إِصْلَٰحٍ بَيْنَ ٱلنَّاسِ وَمَن يَفْعَلْ ذَٰلِكَ ٱبْتِغَآءَ مَرْضَاتِ ٱللَّهِ فَسَوْفَ نُؤْتِيهِ أَجْرًا عَظِيمًا ﴿١١٤﴾

114. La khayra fee katheerin min najwahum illa man amara bisadaqatin aw maAAroofin aw islahin bayna alnnasi waman yafAAal thalika ibtighaa mardati Allahi fasawfa nu/teehi ajran AAatheeman

4:114. No good in most of their secret talks except for one that would lead to an act of charity, propriety or reconciliation between people. And whoever does that for Allah's pleasure, We will give him a great reward.

وَمَن يُشَاقِقِ ٱلرَّسُولَ مِنۢ بَعْدِ مَا تَبَيَّنَ لَهُ ٱلْهُدَىٰ وَيَتَّبِعْ غَيْرَ سَبِيلِ ٱلْمُؤْمِنِينَ نُوَلِّهِۦ مَا تَوَلَّىٰ وَنُصْلِهِۦ جَهَنَّمَ وَسَآءَتْ مَصِيرًا ﴿١١٥﴾

115. Waman yushaqiqi alrrasoola min baAAdi ma tabayyana lahu alhuda wayattabiAA ghayra sabeeli almu/mineena nuwallihi ma tawalla wanuslihi jahannama wasaat maseeran

4:115. And whoever opposes the Messenger after what guidance has come clearly to him and follows a way other than that of the believers, We will keep him turned to what he himself has turned to and make him burn in hell. And it is an evil destination.

إِنَّ ٱللَّهَ لَا يَغْفِرُ أَن يُشْرَكَ بِهِۦ وَيَغْفِرُ مَا دُونَ ذَٰلِكَ لِمَن يَشَآءُ وَمَن يُشْرِكْ بِٱللَّهِ فَقَدْ ضَلَّ ضَلَٰلًۢا بَعِيدًا ﴿١١٦﴾

116. Inna Allaha la yaghfiru an yushraka bihi wayaghfiru ma doona thalika liman yashao waman yushrik biAllahi faqad dalla dalalan baAAeedan

4:116. Indeed, Allah forgives not that partners are set up for Him, and He forgives, whom He wills, any sin besides. And he, who sets up partners to Allah, has indeed strayed far off.

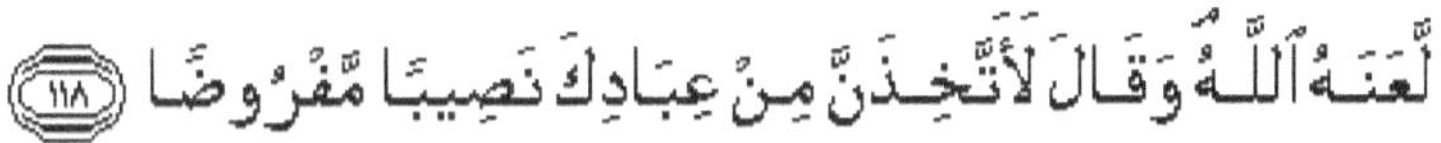

117. In yadAAoona min doonihi illa inathan wa-in yadAAoona illa shaytanan mareedan

4:117. They invoke none but women instead of Him. And they invoke none but a rebellious Satan.[68]

68. It appears that the idols that the Arab society invoked at the time of the revelation of the Qur'aan bore female names. Women are symbols of procreation among mortal creatures. They cannot, by any stretch of imagination, therefore be associated with the immortal Divinity. And, yet, the Satan had deluded the Arabs (as he has also deluded most people even in this modern world) into believing such idols as being partners of Allah. So, as a matter of fact, the Arabs were invoking none but the Satan in the name of those female deities.

118. LaAAanahu Allahu waqala laattakhithanna min AAibadika naseeban mafroodan

4:118. Allah has excommunicated him. And he had said, "I will take (influence) a certain number of Your devotees."

وَلَأُضِلَّنَّهُمْ وَلَأُمَنِّيَنَّهُمْ وَلَآمُرَنَّهُمْ فَلَيُبَتِّكُنَّ ءَاذَانَ ٱلْأَنْعَـٰمِ وَلَآمُرَنَّهُمْ فَلَيُغَيِّرُنَّ خَلْقَ ٱللَّهِ وَمَن يَتَّخِذِ ٱلشَّيْطَـٰنَ وَلِيًّا مِّن دُونِ ٱللَّهِ فَقَدْ خَسِرَ خُسْرَانًا مُّبِينًا ﴿١١٩﴾

119. Walaodillannahum walaomanniyannahum walaamurannahum falayubattikunna athana al-anAAami walaamurannahum falayughayyirunna khalqa Allahi waman yattakhithi alshshaytana waliyyan min dooni Allahi faqad khasira khusranan mubeenan

---

4:119. "And I will certainly lead them astray and arouse in them vain desires, and make them slit the ears of the cattle, and make them disfigure Allah's creation."[69] And he, who takes the Satan instead of Allah as master, shall surely suffer a manifest loss.

---

69. Apparently the Arab idol-worshippers practised cutting or slitting of animal ears to earmark the animals for sacrifice to their favourite idols. The inducement thus to disfigure Allah's creation came to them from none else than the Satan, who has vowed to mislead mankind.

﴿١٢٠﴾ يَعِدُهُمْ وَيُمَنِّيهِمْ وَمَا يَعِدُهُمُ ٱلشَّيْطَـٰنُ إِلَّا غُرُورًا

120. YaAAiduhum wayumanneehim wama yaAAiduhumu alshshaytanu illa ghurooran

---

4:120. He makes promises to them and arouses vain desires in them. And the Satan promises them nothing but vain and delusive things.

أُوْلَـٰٓئِكَ مَأْوَىٰهُمْ جَهَنَّمُ وَلَا يَجِدُونَ عَنْهَا مَحِيصًا ﴿١٢١﴾

121. Ola-ika ma/wahum jahannamu wala yajidoona AAanha maheesan

---

4:121. Abode of these people shall be Hell, and they shall find no escape from it.

وَٱلَّذِينَ ءَامَنُواْ وَعَمِلُواْ ٱلصَّٰلِحَٰتِ سَنُدْخِلُهُمْ جَنَّٰتٍ تَجْرِى مِن تَحْتِهَا ٱلْأَنْهَٰرُ خَٰلِدِينَ فِيهَآ أَبَدًا ۖ وَعْدَ ٱللَّهِ حَقًّا ۚ وَمَنْ أَصْدَقُ مِنَ ٱللَّهِ قِيلًا ۝١٢٢

122. Waallatheena amanoo waAAamiloo alssalihati sanudkhiluhum jannatin tajree min tahtiha al-anharu khalideena feeha abadan waAAda Allahi haqqan waman asdaqu mina Allahi qeelan

4:122. And as for those who believe and do good deeds, We shall admit them to gardens with rivers flowing underneath, and they will abide therein for ever. Allah's promise is the Truth. And whose statement could be truer than Allah's?

لَّيْسَ بِأَمَانِيِّكُمْ وَلَآ أَمَانِيِّ أَهْلِ ٱلْكِتَٰبِ ۗ مَن يَعْمَلْ سُوٓءًا يُجْزَ بِهِۦ وَلَا يَجِدْ لَهُۥ مِن دُونِ ٱللَّهِ وَلِيًّا وَلَا نَصِيرًا ۝١٢٣

123. Laysa bi-amaniyyikum wala amaniyyi ahli alkitabi man yaAAmal soo-an yujza bihi wala yajid lahu min dooni Allahi waliyyan wala naseeran

4:123. It will not be in accordance with your wishes and it will not be in accordance with the wishes of the people of the Book.[70] He, who does a wrong, shall be punished for it, and he will find for himself neither a guardian nor anyone to help, besides Allah.

70. The divine verdicts on the Judgement Day will not be subject to the wishes of Muslims, Jews or Christians. The verdicts would be strictly based on justice and on merits of every case.

وَمَن يَعْمَلْ مِنَ ٱلصَّٰلِحَٰتِ مِن ذَكَرٍ أَوْ أُنثَىٰ وَهُوَ مُؤْمِنٌ فَأُوْلَٰٓئِكَ يَدْخُلُونَ ٱلْجَنَّةَ وَلَا يُظْلَمُونَ نَقِيرًا ۝١٢٤

124. Waman yaAAmal mina alssalihati min thakarin aw ontha wahuwa mu/minun faola-ika yadkhuloona aljannata wala yuthlamoona naqeeran

4:124. And such people – as the one, male or female, who does good deeds and is a believer – shall enter the Garden, and they shall not be subjected to even a speck of injustice.

وَمَنْ أَحْسَنُ دِينًا مِّمَّنْ أَسْلَمَ وَجْهَهُ لِلَّهِ وَهُوَ مُحْسِنٌ وَاتَّبَعَ مِلَّةَ إِبْرَٰهِيمَ حَنِيفًا وَاتَّخَذَ اللَّهُ إِبْرَٰهِيمَ خَلِيلًا ﴿١٢٥﴾

125. Waman ahsanu deenan mimman aslama wajhahu lillahi wahuwa muhsinun waittabaAAa millata ibraheema haneefan waittakhatha Allahu ibraheema khaleelan

4:125. And who can be better in way of life than he who submits himself entirely to Allah, and is a doer of good, and devotedly follows Abraham's Creed[71]? And Allah did hold Abraham dear.

71. To learn more about Abraham's creed (lifestyle), please see <u>Verses 2:130 and 2:131</u> and the study notes thereunder of these Studies.

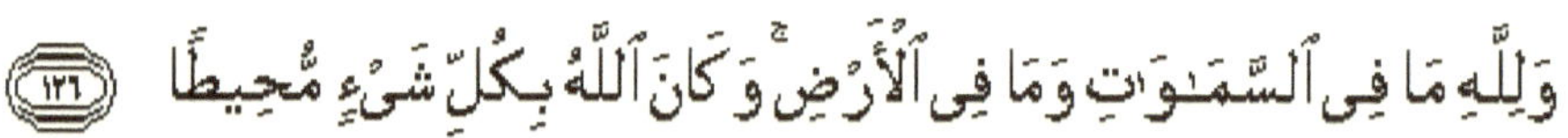

126. Walillahi ma fee alssamawati wama fee al-ardi wakana Allahu bikulli shay-in muheetan

4:126. And to Allah belongs all that is in the heavens and in the earth. And Allah is encircling each and everything.

وَيَسْتَفْتُونَكَ فِى ٱلنِّسَآءِ قُلِ ٱللَّهُ يُفْتِيكُمْ فِيهِنَّ وَمَا يُتْلَىٰ عَلَيْكُمْ فِى ٱلْكِتَـٰبِ فِى يَتَـٰمَى ٱلنِّسَآءِ ٱلَّـٰتِى لَا تُؤْتُونَهُنَّ مَا كُتِبَ لَهُنَّ وَتَرْغَبُونَ أَن تَنكِحُوهُنَّ وَٱلْمُسْتَضْعَفِينَ مِنَ ٱلْوِلْدَانِ وَأَن تَقُومُوا۟ لِلْيَتَـٰمَىٰ بِٱلْقِسْطِ وَمَا تَفْعَلُوا۟ مِنْ خَيْرٍ فَإِنَّ ٱللَّهَ كَانَ بِهِۦ عَلِيمًا ﴿١٣٧﴾

127. Wayastaftoonaka fee alnnisa-i quli Allahu yufteekum feehinna wama yutla AAalaykum fee alkitabi fee yatama alnnisa-i allatee la tu/toonahunna ma kutiba lahunna watarghaboona an tankihoohunna waalmustadAAafeena mina alwildani waan taqoomoo lilyatama bialqisti wama tafAAaloo min khayrin fa-inna Allaha kana bihi AAaleeman

4:127. And they seek decrees from you regarding the women. Tell them that Allah has decreed to you about them. And the decrees are those recited unto you, in the Book, regarding the orphaned/helpless women whom you wish to marry without paying what is ordained for them and regarding the weak and oppressed children,[72] and that you stand up for justice for the orphans. And whatever good you do, Allah would indeed be aware of it.

---

72. The decrees alluded to here are those mentioned in <u>Verses 2 to 8</u> of this Qur'aanic Chapter.

وَإِنِ ٱمْرَأَةٌ خَافَتْ مِنۢ بَعْلِهَا نُشُوزًا أَوْ إِعْرَاضًا فَلَا جُنَاحَ عَلَيْهِمَآ أَن يُصْلِحَا بَيْنَهُمَا صُلْحًا وَٱلصُّلْحُ خَيْرٌ وَأُحْضِرَتِ ٱلْأَنفُسُ ٱلشُّحَّ وَإِن تُحْسِنُوا۟ وَتَتَّقُوا۟ فَإِنَّ ٱللَّهَ كَانَ بِمَا تَعْمَلُونَ خَبِيرًا ﴿١٣٨﴾

128. Wa-ini imraatun khafat min baAAliha nushoozan aw iAAradan fala junaha AAalayhima an yusliha baynahuma sulhan waalssulhu khayrun waohdirati al-anfusu alshshuhha wa-in tuhsinoo watattaqoo fa-inna Allaha kana bima taAAmaloona khabeeran

4:128. And if a woman fears from her husband cruelty or desertion, no blame accrues on either of them, if they effect reconciliation between themselves. And reconciliation is better. And human beings are subject to greed. And if you do good deeds and fear Allah, then Allah is indeed aware of what you do.

387

وَلَن تَسْتَطِيعُوٓاْ أَن تَعْدِلُواْ بَيْنَ ٱلنِّسَآءِ وَلَوْ حَرَصْتُمْ فَلَا تَمِيلُواْ كُلَّ ٱلْمَيْلِ فَتَذَرُوهَا كَٱلْمُعَلَّقَةِ وَإِن تُصْلِحُواْ وَتَتَّقُواْ فَإِنَّ ٱللَّهَ كَانَ غَفُورًا رَّحِيمًا ﴿۱۲۹﴾

129. Walan tastateeAAoo an taAAdiloo bayna alnnisa-i walaw harastum fala tameeloo kulla almayli fatatharooha kaalmuAAallaqati wa-in tuslihoo watattaqoo fa-inna Allaha kana ghafooran raheeman

4:129. And you are unable to be just between wives, even though you may ardently wish to, but turn you not altogether away, to keep her[73], as it were, in suspense. And if you make amends and fear Allah, then Allah is indeed Forgiving, Merciful.

73. To keep one/some of the wives, that is.

وَإِن يَتَفَرَّقَا يُغْنِ ٱللَّهُ كُلًّا مِّن سَعَتِهِۦ وَكَانَ ٱللَّهُ وَٰسِعًا حَكِيمًا ﴿۱۳۰﴾

130. Wa-in yatafarraqa yughni Allahu kullan min saAAatihi wakana Allahu wasiAAan hakeeman

4:130. And if they separate, Allah will make each of them free from want out of His immense resources. And Allah is Immense in resources, Wise.

وَلِلَّهِ مَا فِى ٱلسَّمَٰوَٰتِ وَمَا فِى ٱلْأَرْضِ وَلَقَدْ وَصَّيْنَا ٱلَّذِينَ أُوتُواْ ٱلْكِتَٰبَ مِن قَبْلِكُمْ وَإِيَّاكُمْ أَنِ ٱتَّقُواْ ٱللَّهَ وَإِن تَكْفُرُواْ فَإِنَّ لِلَّهِ مَا فِى ٱلسَّمَٰوَٰتِ وَمَا فِى ٱلْأَرْضِ وَكَانَ ٱللَّهُ غَنِيًّا حَمِيدًا ﴿۱۳۱﴾

131. Walillahi ma fee alssamawati wama fee al-ardi walaqad wassayna allatheena ootoo alkitaba min qablikum wa-iyyakum ani ittaqoo Allaha wa-in takfuroo fa-inna lillahi ma fee alssamawati wama fee al-ardi wakana Allahu ghaniyyan hameedan

4:131. And for Allah it is all that is in the heavens and all that is in the earth. And We did direct the People of the Book before you, and now We do direct you, to fear Allah. And if you suppress the Truth, then, indeed, for Allah is all that is in the Heavens and all that is in the Earth. And Allah is Self-sufficient, Praiseworthy.

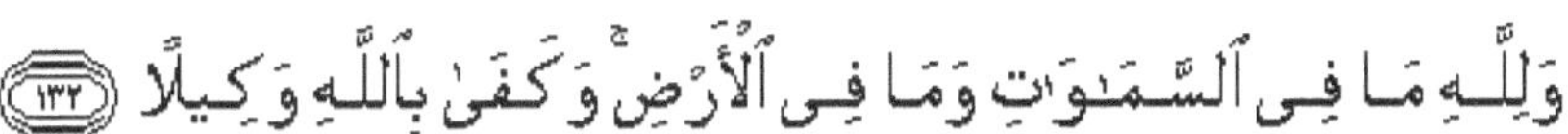

132. Walillahi ma fee alssamawati wama fee al-ardi wakafa biAllahi wakeelan

4:132. And for Allah it is all that is in the heavens and all that is in the earth. And Allah suffices as Trustee.

133. In yasha/ yuthhibkum ayyuha alnnasu waya/ti bi-akhareena wakana Allahu AAala thalika qadeeran

4:133. If He so wills, He can take you away, O people, and bring others. And Allah has the power to do that.

134. Man kana yureedu thawaba alddunya faAAinda Allahi thawabu alddunya waal-akhirati wakana Allahu sameeAAan baseeran

4:134. He, who desires the reward of this world, may know that with Allah is the reward of this world and of the Hereafter. And Allah is listening, observing.

يَـٰٓأَيُّهَا ٱلَّذِينَ ءَامَنُوا۟ كُونُوا۟ قَوَّٰمِينَ بِٱلْقِسْطِ شُهَدَآءَ لِلَّهِ وَلَوْ عَلَىٰ أَنفُسِكُمْ أَوِ ٱلْوَٰلِدَيْنِ وَٱلْأَقْرَبِينَ إِن يَكُنْ غَنِيًّا أَوْ فَقِيرًا فَٱللَّهُ أَوْلَىٰ بِهِمَا فَلَا تَتَّبِعُوا۟ ٱلْهَوَىٰٓ أَن تَعْدِلُوا۟ وَإِن تَلْوُۥٓا۟ أَوْ تُعْرِضُوا۟ فَإِنَّ ٱللَّهَ كَانَ بِمَا تَعْمَلُونَ خَبِيرًا ﴿١٣٥﴾

135. Ya ayyuha allatheena amanoo koonoo qawwameena bialqisti shuhadaa lillahi walaw AAala anfusikum awi alwalidayni waal-aqrabeena in yakun ghaniyyan aw faqeeran faAllahu awla bihima fala tattabiAAoo alhawa an taAAdiloo wa-in talwoo aw tuAAridoo fa-inna Allaha kana bima taAAmaloona khabeeran

4:135. O you who believe! Be witnesses for Allah, standing up firmly on justice, even though it may be against your own selves, parents, or relatives. Be they rich or be they poor, Allah is close to them both. So, follow not vain desires, lest you deviate. And if you swerve or turn away, then, indeed, Allah is aware of what you do.

يَـٰٓأَيُّهَا ٱلَّذِينَ ءَامَنُوٓا۟ ءَامِنُوا۟ بِٱللَّهِ وَرَسُولِهِۦ وَٱلْكِتَـٰبِ ٱلَّذِى نَزَّلَ عَلَىٰ رَسُولِهِۦ وَٱلْكِتَـٰبِ ٱلَّذِىٓ أَنزَلَ مِن قَبْلُ وَمَن يَكْفُرْ بِٱللَّهِ وَمَلَـٰٓئِكَتِهِۦ وَكُتُبِهِۦ وَرُسُلِهِۦ وَٱلْيَوْمِ ٱلْءَاخِرِ فَقَدْ ضَلَّ ضَلَـٰلًۢا بَعِيدًا ﴿١٣٦﴾

136. Ya ayyuha allatheena amanoo aminoo biAllahi warasoolihi waalkitabi allathee nazzala AAala rasoolihi waalkitabi allathee anzala min qablu waman yakfur biAllahi wamala-ikatihi wakutubihi warusulihi waalyawmi al-akhiri faqad dalla dalalan baAAeedan

4:136. O you who believe! Believe in Allah, His Messenger, the Book He has sent down to His Messenger, and the Book He had previously sent down. He, who denies Allah, His angels, His Books, His Messengers, and the Hereafter, has indeed gone far astray.

$$\text{إِنَّ ٱلَّذِينَ ءَامَنُواْ ثُمَّ كَفَرُواْ ثُمَّ ءَامَنُواْ ثُمَّ كَفَرُواْ ثُمَّ ٱزْدَادُواْ كُفْرًا لَّمْ يَكُنِ ٱللَّهُ لِيَغْفِرَ لَهُمْ وَلَا لِيَهْدِيَهُمْ سَبِيلًا ۝}$$

137. Inna alla*th*eena *a*manoo thumma kafaroo thumma *a*manoo thumma kafaroo thumma izd*a*doo kufran lam yakuni All*a*hu liyaghfira lahum wal*a* liyahdiyahum sabeel*a*n

4:137. Indeed, those who believe and then suppress the Truth, and again believe and then suppress the Truth, and then go on suppressing the Truth! Allah will neither be disposed to forgive them nor to guide them to the Right Path.

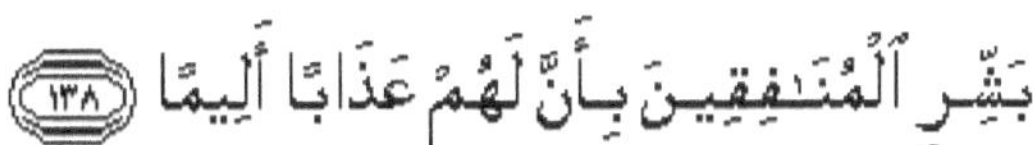

138. Bashshiri almuna*f*iqeena bi-anna lahum AAa*th*aban aleem*a*n

4:138. Let the hypocrites know that for them is a painful punishment.

$$\text{ٱلَّذِينَ يَتَّخِذُونَ ٱلْكَـٰفِرِينَ أَوْلِيَآءَ مِن دُونِ ٱلْمُؤْمِنِينَ أَيَبْتَغُونَ عِندَهُمُ ٱلْعِزَّةَ فَإِنَّ ٱلْعِزَّةَ لِلَّهِ جَمِيعًا ۝}$$

139. Alla*th*eena yattakhi*th*oona alk*a*fireena awliy*a*a min dooni almu/mineena ayabtaghoona AAindahumu alAAizzata fa-inna alAAizzata lill*a*hi jameeAA*a*n

4:139. Do they, who take the suppressors of Truth, rather than the believers, as close friends, seek honour from those suppressors of Truth? But, then, all honour does indeed rest with Allah.

وَقَدْ نَزَّلَ عَلَيْكُمْ فِى ٱلْكِتَـٰبِ أَنْ إِذَا سَمِعْتُمْ ءَايَـٰتِ ٱللَّهِ يُكْفَرُ بِهَا

وَيُسْتَهْزَأُ بِهَا فَلَا تَقْعُدُوا۟ مَعَهُمْ حَتَّىٰ يَخُوضُوا۟ فِى حَدِيثٍ غَيْرِهِۦٓ إِنَّكُمْ

إِذًا مِّثْلُهُمْ إِنَّ ٱللَّهَ جَامِعُ ٱلْمُنَـٰفِقِينَ وَٱلْكَـٰفِرِينَ فِى جَهَنَّمَ جَمِيعًا

140. Waqad nazzala AAalaykum fee alkitabi an itha samiAAtum ayati Allahi yukfaru biha wayustahzao biha fala taqAAudoo maAAahum hatta yakhoodoo fee hadeethin ghayrihi innakum ithan mithluhum inna Allaha jamiAAu almunafiqeena waalkafireena fee jahannama jameeAAan

4:140. And it is certainly laid down for you in the Book that when you hear Allah's Verses being denied or ridiculed, you should not sit with those people until they enter another topic of talk; otherwise, you shall be. like them. Indeed, Allah shall gather the hypocrites and the deniers all together in Hell.

ٱلَّذِينَ يَتَرَبَّصُونَ بِكُمْ فَإِن كَانَ لَكُمْ فَتْحٌ مِّنَ ٱللَّهِ قَالُوٓا۟ أَلَمْ نَكُن مَّعَكُمْ

وَإِن كَانَ لِلْكَـٰفِرِينَ نَصِيبٌ قَالُوٓا۟ أَلَمْ نَسْتَحْوِذْ عَلَيْكُمْ وَنَمْنَعْكُم مِّنَ

ٱلْمُؤْمِنِينَ فَٱللَّهُ يَحْكُمُ بَيْنَكُمْ يَوْمَ ٱلْقِيَـٰمَةِ وَلَن يَجْعَلَ ٱللَّهُ لِلْكَـٰفِرِينَ

عَلَى ٱلْمُؤْمِنِينَ سَبِيلًا

141. Allatheena yatarabbasoona bikum fa-in kana lakum fathun mina Allahi qaloo alam nakun maAAakum wa-in kana lilkafireena naseebun qaloo alam nastahwith AAalaykum wanamnaAAkum mina almu/mineena faAllahu yahkumu baynakum yawma alqiyamati walan yajAAala Allahu lilkafireena AAala almu/mineena sabeelan

4:141. These are they, who wait and watch to see how things shape for you. If there be a victory for you from Allah, they say: "Were we not with you?" And if the suppressors of Truth gain a share of success, they say, "Did we not guard your interests and protect you from the believers." Then Allah will judge between you and them on the Day of Resurrection. And Allah has not provided a way for the suppressors of Truth to go (triumph) over the believers.

إِنَّ ٱلْمُنَٰفِقِينَ يُخَٰدِعُونَ ٱللَّهَ وَهُوَ خَٰدِعُهُمْ وَإِذَا قَامُوٓا۟ إِلَى ٱلصَّلَوٰةِ قَامُوا۟ كُسَالَىٰ يُرَآءُونَ ٱلنَّاسَ وَلَا يَذْكُرُونَ ٱللَّهَ إِلَّا قَلِيلًا ﴿١٤٢﴾

142. Inna almunafiqeena yukhadiAAoona Allaha wahuwa khadiAAuhum wa-itha qamoo ila alssalati qamoo kusala yuraoona alnnasa wala yathkuroona Allaha illa qaleelan

4:142. Indeed, the hypocrites strive to deceive Allah, and it is He, who deceives them! And when they stand up for prayer they stand with laziness. They do it only to show off to men and remember Allah but little.[74]

---

74. This portrait of the hypocrites is continued to the next Verse.

مُّذَبْذَبِينَ بَيْنَ ذَٰلِكَ لَآ إِلَىٰ هَٰٓؤُلَآءِ وَلَآ إِلَىٰ هَٰٓؤُلَآءِ وَمَن يُضْلِلِ ٱللَّهُ فَلَن تَجِدَ لَهُۥ سَبِيلًا ﴿١٤٣﴾

143. Muthabthabeena bayna thalika la ila haola-i wala ila haola-i waman yudlili Allahu falan tajida lahu sabeelan

4:143. Wavering in between – neither here nor there. And whomsoever Allah sends astray, you shall not find a way for him.

يَٰٓأَيُّهَا ٱلَّذِينَ ءَامَنُوا۟ لَا تَتَّخِذُوا۟ ٱلْكَٰفِرِينَ أَوْلِيَآءَ مِن دُونِ ٱلْمُؤْمِنِينَ أَتُرِيدُونَ أَن تَجْعَلُوا۟ لِلَّهِ عَلَيْكُمْ سُلْطَٰنًا مُّبِينًا ﴿١٤٤﴾

144. Ya ayyuha allatheena amanoo la tattakhithoo alkafireena awliyaa min dooni almu/mineena atureedoona an tajAAaloo lillahi AAalaykum sultanan mubeenan

4:144. O you who believe! Do not take the suppressors of Truth, rather than the believers, for close friends.[75] Do you wish that you yourselves should provide for Allah a manifest proof against you?

75. The Arabic term, which is translated here as 'close friends', is *awliya*. For the comprehensive Qur'aanic meaning of *wali* (singular of *awliya*) please refer <u>study note 2:154</u>.

إِنَّ ٱلْمُنَٰفِقِينَ فِى ٱلدَّرْكِ ٱلْأَسْفَلِ مِنَ ٱلنَّارِ وَلَن تَجِدَ لَهُمْ نَصِيرًا ﴿١٤٥﴾

145. Inna almunafiqeena fee alddarki al-asfali mina alnnari walan tajida lahum naseeran

4:145. Indeed, the hypocrites will be in the lowest depth of the Fire and you shall not find anyone to help them.

إِلَّا ٱلَّذِينَ تَابُوا۟ وَأَصْلَحُوا۟ وَٱعْتَصَمُوا۟ بِٱللَّهِ وَأَخْلَصُوا۟ دِينَهُمْ لِلَّهِ فَأُو۟لَٰٓئِكَ مَعَ ٱلْمُؤْمِنِينَ وَسَوْفَ يُؤْتِ ٱللَّهُ ٱلْمُؤْمِنِينَ أَجْرًا عَظِيمًا ﴿١٤٦﴾

146. Illa allatheena taboo waaslahoo waiAAtasamoo biAllahi waakhlasoo deenahum lillahi faola-ika maAAa almu/mineena wasawfa yu/ti Allahu almu/mineena ajran AAatheeman

4:146. Except for those hypocites, who repent and make amends and hold on fast to Allah and keep their way of life purely for Allah. Then these are with the believers. And Allah will grant the believers a great reward.

مَّا يَفْعَلُ ٱللَّهُ بِعَذَابِكُمْ إِن شَكَرْتُمْ وَءَامَنتُمْ وَكَانَ ٱللَّهُ شَاكِرًا عَلِيمًا ﴿١٤٧﴾

147. Ma yafAAalu Allahu biAAathabikum in shakartum waamantum wakana Allahu shakiran AAaleeman

4:147. Why should Allah punish you if you are grateful and you do believe!? And Allah is aware as to who is grateful.

$$ \text{لَّا يُحِبُّ ٱللَّهُ ٱلْجَهْرَ بِٱلسُّوٓءِ مِنَ ٱلْقَوْلِ إِلَّا مَن ظُلِمَ ۚ وَكَانَ ٱللَّهُ سَمِيعًا عَلِيمًا ﴿١٤٨﴾} $$

148. La yuhibbu Allahu aljahra bialssoo-i mina alqawli illa man _th_ulima wakana Allahu sameeAAan AAaleeman

4:148. Allah loves not the public utterance of anything evil, except by someone who is wronged. And Allah does hear, know.[76]

76. It is human tendency to gossip about anything bad that might have happened to or done by another person. In this Verse, mankind is advised to eschew this tendency unless the publicity of an evil deed is done by a person directly affected by the evil. Pardoning of the evil by the affected party even is recommended in the next Verse, 4:149.

$$ \text{إِن تُبْدُوا۟ خَيْرًا أَوْ تُخْفُوهُ أَوْ تَعْفُوا۟ عَن سُوٓءٍ فَإِنَّ ٱللَّهَ كَانَ عَفُوًّا قَدِيرًا ﴿١٤٩﴾} $$

149. In tubdoo khayran aw tukhfoohu aw taAAfoo AAan soo-in fa-inna Allaha kana AAafuwwan qadeeran

4:149. If you disclose a good deed or conceal it, or you do pardon an evil, then, surely, Allah is Lenient, Powerful.

إِنَّ ٱلَّذِينَ يَكْفُرُونَ بِٱللَّهِ وَرُسُلِهِ وَيُرِيدُونَ أَن يُفَرِّقُواْ بَيْنَ ٱللَّهِ وَرُسُلِهِ وَيَقُولُونَ نُؤْمِنُ بِبَعْضٍ وَنَكْفُرُ بِبَعْضٍ وَيُرِيدُونَ أَن يَتَّخِذُواْ بَيْنَ ذَٰلِكَ سَبِيلًا ۝

150. Inna alla<u>th</u>eena yakfuroona biAll<u>a</u>hi warusulihi wayureedoona an yufarriqoo bayna All<u>a</u>hi warusulihi wayaqooloona nu/minu bibaAA<u>d</u>in wanakfuru bibaAA<u>d</u>in wayureedoona an yattakhi<u>th</u>oo bayna <u>th</u>alika sabeel<u>a</u>n

4:150. Indeed, those who suppress the Truth about Allah and about His Messengers and would differentiate between Allah and His Messengers and say they believe in some and deny others, and would adopt a way in between,[77]

77. This Verse, as one may obviously see, only qualifies/describes the subject 'they' of the first clause in the next Verse 4:151.

أُوْلَـٰئِكَ هُمُ ٱلْكَـٰفِرُونَ حَقًّا وَأَعْتَدْنَا لِلْكَـٰفِرِينَ عَذَابًا مُّهِينًا ۝

151. Ol<u>a</u>-ika humu alk<u>a</u>firoona <u>h</u>aqqan waaAAtadn<u>a</u> lilk<u>a</u>fireena AAa<u>tha</u>ban muheen<u>a</u>n

4:151. They, in fact, are the ones who suppress the Truth, and We have prepared a disgraceful punishment for the suppressors of Truth.

وَٱلَّذِينَ ءَامَنُواْ بِٱللَّهِ وَرُسُلِهِ وَلَمْ يُفَرِّقُواْ بَيْنَ أَحَدٍ مِّنْهُمْ أُوْلَـٰئِكَ سَوْفَ يُؤْتِيهِمْ أُجُورَهُمْ وَكَانَ ٱللَّهُ غَفُورًا رَّحِيمًا ۝

152. Waalla<u>th</u>eena <u>a</u>manoo biAll<u>a</u>hi warusulihi walam yufarriqoo bayna a<u>h</u>adin minhum ol<u>a</u>-ika sawfa yu/teehim ojoorahum wak<u>a</u>na All<u>a</u>hu ghafooran ra<u>h</u>eem<u>a</u>n

4:152. And He shall give to those their rewards that believe in Allah and His Messengers and make no distinction between any of them[78]. And Allah is Forgiving, Merciful.

78. Please refer to <u>study note 2:204</u> **in this context.**

153. Yas-aluka ahlu alkitabi an tunazzila AAalayhim kitaban mina alssama-i faqad saaloo moosa akbara min thalika faqaloo arina Allaha jahratan faakhathat-humu alssaAAiqatu bithulmihim thumma ittakhathoo alAAijla min baAAdi ma jaat-humu albayyinatu faAAafawna AAan thalika waatayna moosa sultanan mubeenan

4:153. The people of the Book ask you to bring down to them a book from the heaven. They had demanded, of Moses, a greater thing than that! They had said, "Show Allah to us openly." So, then, the thunderbolt struck them because of their transgression.[79] They then took to the calf, after clear signs had come to them.[80] We pardoned them even that! And We gave Moses a clear proof of authority.

79. Refer <u>Verse 2:55</u> **and the study note thereunder, of these Studies.**

80. This episode, of the Jews taking to the worship of the calf, is described in detail in Verses 7:148 to 7:154. Refer also <u>Verse 2:92 and study tnotes thereunder</u>, **of these Studies, in this context.**

وَرَفَعْنَا فَوْقَهُمُ ٱلطُّورَ بِمِيثَاقِهِمْ وَقُلْنَا لَهُمُ ٱدْخُلُواْ ٱلْبَابَ سُجَّدًا وَقُلْنَا لَهُمْ لَا تَعْدُواْ فِى ٱلسَّبْتِ وَأَخَذْنَا مِنْهُم مِّيثَاقًا غَلِيظًا ۝

154. WarafaAAna fawqahumu al*tt*oora bimeetha*q*ihim waqulna lahumu odkhuloo alb*a*ba sujjadan waqulna lahum l*a* taAAdoo fee alssabti waakha*th*na minhum meeth*a*qan ghalee*th*an

4:154. And We raised over them the mountain to enforce their covenant, and We asked them to prostrate while entering the gate, and We forbade to them transgression in the matter of the Sabbath, and We took from them a covenant with harsh terms.

فَبِمَا نَقْضِهِم مِّيثَاقَهُمْ وَكُفْرِهِم بِـَٔايَـٰتِ ٱللَّهِ وَقَتْلِهِمُ ٱلْأَنۢبِيَآءَ بِغَيْرِ حَقٍّ وَقَوْلِهِمْ قُلُوبُنَا غُلْفٌ بَلْ طَبَعَ ٱللَّهُ عَلَيْهَا بِكُفْرِهِمْ فَلَا يُؤْمِنُونَ إِلَّا قَلِيلًا

155. Fabim*a* naq*d*ihim meetha*q*ahum wakufrihim bi-*a*yati All*a*hi waqatlihimu al-anbiy*a*a bighayri *h*aqqin waqawlihim quloobun*a* ghulfun bal *t*abaAAa All*a*hu AAalayh*a* bikufrihim fal*a* yu/minoona ill*a* qaleel*a*n

4:155. [81]Because of their breaking of their covenant, their suppression of Allah's Verses/signs, their killing of Prophets unjustly and their saying that their minds are closed. Nay! Allah has put a seal on them, because of their suppression of the Truth. So, they believe but little.

81. Herein are given the reasons for the terms of the covenant with the Children of Israel being harsh. And the reasons for the Jews' continued sufferings till recently (World War II), are given in Verses 156 and 157 below.

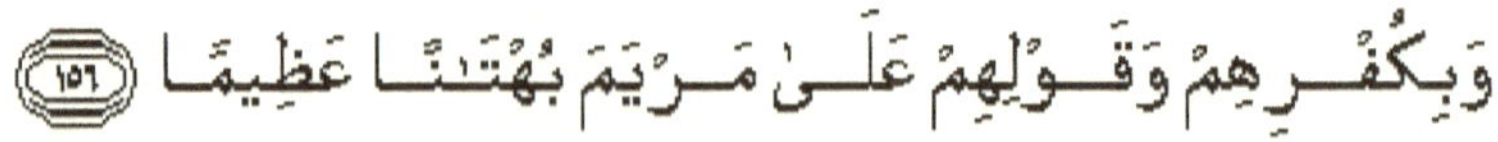

156. Wabikufrihim waqawlihim AAal*a* maryama buht*a*nan AAa*th*eem*a*n

4:156. And because of their suppression of the Truth and their having uttered against Mary a grave calumny.[82]

82. Refer Verses 19:27 and 19:28.

وَقَوْلِهِمْ إِنَّا قَتَلْنَا ٱلْمَسِيحَ عِيسَى ٱبْنَ مَرْيَمَ رَسُولَ ٱللَّهِ وَمَا قَتَلُوهُ وَمَا صَلَبُوهُ وَلَٰكِن شُبِّهَ لَهُمْ وَإِنَّ ٱلَّذِينَ ٱخْتَلَفُوا۟ فِيهِ لَفِى شَكٍّ مِّنْهُ مَا لَهُم بِهِۦ مِنْ عِلْمٍ إِلَّا ٱتِّبَاعَ ٱلظَّنِّ وَمَا قَتَلُوهُ يَقِينًۢا ﴿١٥٧﴾

157. Waqawlihim inna qatalna almaseeha AAeesa ibna maryama rasoola Allahi wama qataloohu wama salaboohu walakin shubbiha lahum wa-inna allatheena ikhtalafoo feehi lafee shakkin minhu ma lahum bihi min AAilmin illa ittibaAAa alththanni wama qataloohu yaqeenan

4:157. And their saying that they indeed killed the Messiah Jesus, son of Mary, Messenger of Allah. And they killed him not; nor did they crucify him. But it so appeared to them. And those indeed, who differ therein, are certainly in doubt. They have no knowledge about it, but follow only conjecture. And they killed him not for sure.[83]

83. Not only do the Jews have this false notion of Jesus having been killed on the Cross, but the Christians – the so-called followers of Jesus – have that notion too! The Christians have added the further falsehood that Jesus was son of God and that the son died on the Cross for atonement of the sins of the Christians, whereby every Christian now is assured of a place in Paradise, whatever sins he/she may have committed in this world!!

بَل رَّفَعَهُ ٱللَّهُ إِلَيْهِ وَكَانَ ٱللَّهُ عَزِيزًا حَكِيمًا ﴿١٥٨﴾

158. Bal rafaAAahu Allahu ilayhi wakana Allahu AAazeezan hakeeman

4:158. Nay! Allah took him up to Himself.[84] And Allah is Omnipotent, Wise.

84. Some Muslims take the divine statement here to mean that Jesus was bodily taken up to Heavens. But Verse 3:55 makes it clear that Jesus was made to die, and his soul was taken up like any other human being's. Refer study note 3:68 of these Studies under that Verse.

وَإِن مِّنْ أَهْلِ ٱلْكِتَـٰبِ إِلَّا لَيُؤْمِنَنَّ بِهِۦ قَبْلَ مَوْتِهِۦ وَيَوْمَ ٱلْقِيَـٰمَةِ يَكُونُ عَلَيْهِمْ شَهِيدًا ۝

159. Wa-in min ahli alkitabi illa layu/minanna bihi qabla mawtihi wayawma alqiyamati yakoonu AAalayhim shaheedan

---

4:159. And if there be any, of the people of the Book, who wouldn't believe in this before his/her death, he (Jesus) shall be a witness against all such persons, on the Day of Resurrection.

فَبِظُلْمٍ مِّنَ ٱلَّذِينَ هَادُواْ حَرَّمْنَا عَلَيْهِمْ طَيِّبَـٰتٍ أُحِلَّتْ لَهُمْ وَبِصَدِّهِمْ عَن سَبِيلِ ٱللَّهِ كَثِيرًا ۝

160. Fabithulmin mina allatheena hadoo harramna AAalayhim tayyibatin ohillat lahum wabisaddihim AAan sabeeli Allahi katheeran

---

4:160. And because of the transgression of the Jews and their hindering of many from Allah's Path, We prohibited to them certain good things which had been made lawful for them.[85]

---

85. Refer study note 3:108 of these Studies under Verse 3:93, in this context.

وَأَخْذِهِمُ ٱلرِّبَوٰاْ وَقَدْ نُهُواْ عَنْهُ وَأَكْلِهِمْ أَمْوَٰلَ ٱلنَّاسِ

بِٱلْبَٰطِلِ وَأَعْتَدْنَا لِلْكَٰفِرِينَ مِنْهُمْ عَذَابًا أَلِيمًا ۝

161. Waakhthihimu alrriba waqad nuhoo AAanhu waaklihim amwala alnnasi bialbatili waaAAatadna lilkafireena minhum AAathaban aleeman

4:161. [86]And because of their indulgence in *Ar-Riba*[87], though indeed they were forbidden from it, and their usurping people's property falsely. And We have prepared, for the suppressors of Truth from among them, a painful punishment.

86. This Verse, in continuation of the preceding one, gives another reason for the penal prohibition, for Jews, of certain things, otherwise permitted.

87. For a comprehensive understanding of this Qur'aanic term, please refer <u>Verses 2:275 to 2:279 and the study notes thereunder</u> of these Studies. At the time of revelation of this Verse 4:161, the complete prohibition against *Ar-Riba* was not yet imposed. It (Verse 4:161) was the second divine step towards preparing the Muslims for the final prohibition imposed under Verse 2:275. The first step was <u>Verse 3:130</u>. It (Verse 4:161) further explains the definition of *Ar-Riba*, given in Verse 30:39, by asserting that it constitutes false usurpation of people's property.

لَٰكِنِ ٱلرَّٰسِخُونَ فِى ٱلْعِلْمِ مِنْهُمْ وَٱلْمُؤْمِنُونَ يُؤْمِنُونَ بِمَآ أُنزِلَ إِلَيْكَ

وَمَآ أُنزِلَ مِن قَبْلِكَ وَٱلْمُقِيمِينَ ٱلصَّلَوٰةَ وَٱلْمُؤْتُونَ ٱلزَّكَوٰةَ وَٱلْمُؤْمِنُونَ

بِٱللَّهِ وَٱلْيَوْمِ ٱلْأَخِرِ أُوْلَٰٓئِكَ سَنُؤْتِيهِمْ أَجْرًا عَظِيمًا ۝

162. Lakini alrrasikhoona fee alAAilmi minhum waalmu/minoona yu/minoona bima onzila ilayka wama onzila min qablika waalmuqeemeena alssalata waalmu/toona alzzakata waalmu/minoona biAllahi waalyawmi al-akhiri ola-ika sanu/teehim ajran AAatheeman

4:162. But the knowledgeable among them[88], and the believers, believe in what has been sent down to you and what was sent down before you. And to those who establish prayers, give charity and believe in Allah and the last day, We will give a great reward.

88. The pronoun 'them' here stands for the Jews, referred to in Verses 160 and 161 above.

۞ إِنَّآ أَوْحَيْنَآ إِلَيْكَ كَمَآ أَوْحَيْنَآ إِلَىٰ نُوحٍ وَٱلنَّبِيِّـۧنَ مِنۢ بَعْدِهِۦ ۚ وَأَوْحَيْنَآ إِلَىٰٓ إِبْرَٰهِيمَ وَإِسْمَٰعِيلَ وَإِسْحَٰقَ وَيَعْقُوبَ وَٱلْأَسْبَاطِ وَعِيسَىٰ وَأَيُّوبَ وَيُونُسَ وَهَٰرُونَ وَسُلَيْمَٰنَ ۚ وَءَاتَيْنَا دَاوُۥدَ زَبُورًا ﴿١٦٣﴾

163. Inna awhayna ilayka kama awhayna ila noohin waalnnabiyyeena min baAAdihi waawhayna ila ibraheema wa-ismaAAeela wa-ishaqa wayaAAqooba waal-asbati waAAeesa waayyooba wayoonusa waharoona wasulaymana waatayna dawooda zabooran

4:163. We indeed have divinely inspired you[89] as We did divinely inspire Noah. And We did divinely inspire the Prophets who came after him: Abraham, Ishmael, Isaac, Jacob and the Tribes, Jesus, Job, Jonah, Aaron and Solomon. And We gave the Psalms to David.

89. The pronoun in Arabic here is in the singular, the obvious addressee being Prophet Muhammad (peace be upon him).

وَرُسُلًا قَدْ قَصَصْنَٰهُمْ عَلَيْكَ مِن قَبْلُ وَرُسُلًا لَّمْ نَقْصُصْهُمْ عَلَيْكَ ۚ وَكَلَّمَ ٱللَّهُ مُوسَىٰ تَكْلِيمًا ﴿١٦٤﴾

164. Warusulan qad qasasnahum AAalayka min qablu warusulan lam naqsushum AAalayka wakallama Allahu moosa takleeman

4:164. And Messengers We did mention to you before and Messengers we have not mentioned to you. And Allah did speak to Moses.

رُّسُلًا مُّبَشِّرِينَ وَمُنذِرِينَ لِئَلَّا يَكُونَ لِلنَّاسِ عَلَى ٱللَّهِ حُجَّةٌ بَعْدَ ٱلرُّسُلِ ۚ وَكَانَ ٱللَّهُ عَزِيزًا حَكِيمًا ﴿١١٥﴾

165. Rusulan mubashshireena wamunthireena li-alla yakoona lilnnasi AAala Allahi hujjatun baAAda alrrusuli wakana Allahu AAazeezan hakeeman

4:165. Messengers to give good news and to warn, so that there remains no argument[90] for mankind to have against Allah, after them. And Allah is Omnipotent, Wise.

90. The argument that Allah had not sent any Messenger to guide them.

لَّكِنِ ٱللَّهُ يَشْهَدُ بِمَآ أَنزَلَ إِلَيْكَ ۖ أَنزَلَهُ بِعِلْمِهِ ۖ وَٱلْمَلَـٰئِكَةُ يَشْهَدُونَ ۚ وَكَفَىٰ بِٱللَّهِ شَهِيدًا ﴿١١٦﴾

166. Lakini Allahu yashhadu bima anzala ilayka anzalahu biAAilmihi waalmala-ikatu yashhadoona wakafa biAllahi shaheedan

4:166. But Allah bears witness by what He has sent down to you. He has sent it down, with His knowledge. And the angels bear witness. And Allah is enough as a witness.

إِنَّ ٱلَّذِينَ كَفَرُوا۟ وَصَدُّوا۟ عَن سَبِيلِ ٱللَّهِ قَدْ ضَلُّوا۟ ضَلَـٰلًا بَعِيدًا ﴿١١٧﴾

167. Inna allatheena kafaroo wasaddoo AAan sabeeli Allahi qad dalloo dalalan baAAeedan

4:167. Those indeed have strayed far away, who suppress the Truth and cause hindrance in Allah's Path.

$$\text{إِنَّ ٱلَّذِينَ كَفَرُواْ وَظَلَمُواْ لَمْ يَكُنِ ٱللَّهُ لِيَغْفِرَ لَهُمْ}$$

$$\text{وَلَا لِيَهْدِيَهُمْ طَرِيقًا ﴿١٦٨﴾}$$

168. Inna allatheena kafaroo wa*th*alamoo lam yakuni All*a*hu liyaghfira lahum wal*a* liyahdiyahum *t*areeq*a*n

4:168. Allah won't indeed forgive those who suppress the Truth and do wrong, nor guide them to a way,

---

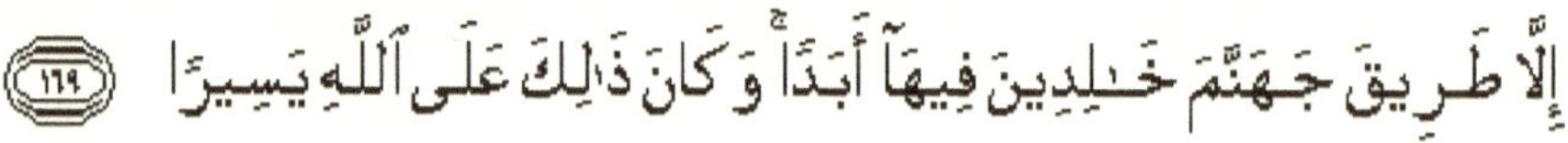

$$\text{إِلَّا طَرِيقَ جَهَنَّمَ خَـٰلِدِينَ فِيهَآ أَبَدًا ۚ وَكَانَ ذَٰلِكَ عَلَى ٱللَّهِ يَسِيرًا ﴿١٦٩﴾}$$

169. Ill*a* *t*areeqa jahannama kh*a*lideena feeh*a* abadan wak*a*na *th*alika AAal*a* All*a*hi yaseer*a*n

4:169. [91]Other than the way to Hell, for them to dwell therein forever. And that is easy for Allah.

---

91. This is in continuation of the phrase 'nor guide them to a way' occurring at the end of the preceding Verse.

$$\text{يَـٰٓأَيُّهَا ٱلنَّاسُ قَدْ جَآءَكُمُ ٱلرَّسُولُ بِٱلْحَقِّ مِن رَّبِّكُمْ فَـَٔامِنُواْ خَيْرًا}$$

$$\text{لَّكُمْ ۚ وَإِن تَكْفُرُواْ فَإِنَّ لِلَّهِ مَا فِى ٱلسَّمَـٰوَٰتِ وَٱلْأَرْضِ ۚ وَكَانَ ٱللَّهُ عَلِيمًا}$$

$$\text{حَكِيمًا ﴿١٧٠﴾}$$

170. Y*a* ayyuh*a* alnn*a*su qad j*a*akumu alrrasoolu bial*h*aqqi min rabbikum fa*a*minoo khayran lakum wa-in takfuroo fa-inna lill*a*hi m*a* fee alssam*a*w*a*ti waal-ar*d*i wak*a*na All*a*hu AAaleeman *h*akeem*a*n

4:170. O Mankind! Certainly, the Messenger has come to you with the Truth from your Lord. So, believe! It is good for you. And if you suppress the Truth, then, indeed, all that is in the heavens and the earth is Allah's! And Allah is Knowledgeable, Wise.

يَـٰٓأَهْلَ ٱلْكِـتَـٰبِ لَا تَغْلُواْ فِـى دِينِكُمْ وَلَا تَقُولُواْ عَلَى ٱللَّـهِ إِلَّا ٱلْحَقَّ إِنَّمَا ٱلْمَسِيحُ عِيسَى ٱبْنُ مَرْيَمَ رَسُولُ ٱللَّهِ وَكَلِمَتُهُۥ أَلْقَىٰهَآ إِلَىٰ مَرْيَمَ وَرُوحٌ مِّنْهُ فَـَٔامِنُواْ بِٱللَّـهِ وَرُسُلِهِۦ وَلَا تَقُولُواْ ثَلَـٰثَةٌ ٱنتَهُواْ خَـيْرًا لَّكُمْ إِنَّمَا ٱللَّهُ إِلَـٰهٌ وَٰحِدٌ سُبْحَـٰنَهُۥٓ أَن يَكُونَ لَهُۥ وَلَدٌ لَّهُۥ مَا فِـى ٱلسَّـمَـٰوَٰتِ وَمَا فِـى ٱلْأَرْضِ وَكَـفَىٰ بِٱللَّـهِ وَكِـيلًا ﴿١٧١﴾

171. Ya ahla alkitabi la taghloo fee deenikum wala taqooloo AAala Allahi illa alhaqqa innama almaseehu AAeesa ibnu maryama rasoolu Allahi wakalimatuhu alqaha ila maryama waroohun minhu faaminoo biAllahi warusulihi wala taqooloo thalathatun intahoo khayran lakum innama Allahu ilahun wahidun subhanahu an yakoona lahu waladun lahu ma fee alssamawati wama fee al-ardi wakafa biAllahi wakeelan

4:171. O People of the Book! Commit no excesses in your way of life and speak not but the truth about Allah. The Messiah Jesus, son of Mary, was only a Messenger of Allah and His Word which He communicated to Mary and a soul from Him. Believe then in Allah and His Messengers, and say not, "Trinity"! Desist. It would be better for you [to desist from uttering this abomination.] Allah is the only Entity worthy of worship. HE is too Exalted to have a son! All that is in the heavens and all that is in the earth is His. And Allah is enough as Manager of all things.

لَّن يَسْتَنكِفَ ٱلْمَسِيحُ أَن يَكُونَ عَبْدًا لِّلَّهِ وَلَا ٱلْمَلَـٰٓئِكَةُ ٱلْمُقَرَّبُونَ وَمَن يَسْتَنكِفْ عَنْ عِبَادَتِهِۦ وَيَسْتَكْبِرْ فَسَيَحْشُرُهُمْ إِلَيْهِ جَمِيعًا ﴿١٧٢﴾

172. Lan yastankifa almaseehu an yakoona AAabdan lillahi wala almala-ikatu almuqarraboona waman yastankif AAan AAibadatihi wayastakbir fasayahshuruhum ilayhi jameeAAan

4:172. The Messiah did feel no aversion to be a worshipper/devotee of Allah, nor do the angels who are near to Him. And He will gather together to Himself all those who have felt aversion to His worship and have been too proud.

فَأَمَّا ٱلَّذِينَ ءَامَنُواْ وَعَمِلُواْ ٱلصَّٰلِحَٰتِ فَيُوَفِّيهِمْ أُجُورَهُمْ وَيَزِيدُهُم مِّن

فَضْلِهِۦ ۖ وَأَمَّا ٱلَّذِينَ ٱسْتَنكَفُواْ وَٱسْتَكْبَرُواْ فَيُعَذِّبُهُمْ عَذَابًا أَلِيمًا وَلَا

يَجِدُونَ لَهُم مِّن دُونِ ٱللَّهِ وَلِيًّا وَلَا نَصِيرًا ﴿١٧٣﴾

173. Faamma allatheena amanoo waAAamiloo alssalihati fayuwaffeehim ojoorahum wayazeeduhum min fadlihi waamma allatheena istankafoo waistakbaroo fayuAAaththibuhum AAathaban aleeman wala yajidoona lahum min dooni Allahi waliyyan wala naseeran

4:173. Then as for those who believe and do good deeds, He will pay them their rewards in full and give them more, as Favour from Him. And as for those who feel aversion and are proud, He will give them a painful punishment. And they shall find for themselves, besides Allah, none to take refuge with, or to help.

يَٰٓأَيُّهَا ٱلنَّاسُ قَدْ جَآءَكُم بُرْهَٰنٌ مِّن رَّبِّكُمْ وَأَنزَلْنَآ إِلَيْكُمْ نُورًا مُّبِينًا

﴿١٧٤﴾

174. Ya ayyuha alnnasu qad jaakum burhanun min rabbikum waanzalna ilaykum nooran mubeenan

4:174. O Mankind! There has certainly come to you evidence from your Lord and We have sent to you a clear light.[92]

92. Please take note that this is an address to the entire mankind. There is evidence galore in every human body, and in all things surrounding, that an Unseen Power is in absolute control. If that human being denies the existence of that Power, he/she does so only by suppressing the overwhelming evidence before him/her. The evidence, moreover, is documented and presented to mankind in the form of the Qur'aan. The Qur'aan does not only present the evidence, but also provides the Guiding light so that mankind does not stumble astray under the influence of satanic temptations.

فَأَمَّا ٱلَّذِينَ ءَامَنُواْ بِٱللَّهِ وَٱعْتَصَمُواْ بِهِۦ فَسَيُدْخِلُهُمْ فِى رَحْمَةٍ مِّنْهُ وَفَضْلٍ وَيَهْدِيهِمْ إِلَيْهِ صِرَٰطًا مُّسْتَقِيمًا ۝١٧٥

175. Faamma allatheena amanoo biAllahi waiAAtasamoo bihi fasayudkhiluhum fee rahmatin minhu wafadlin wayahdeehim ilayhi siratan mustaqeeman

4:175. Then as for those who believed in Allah and held fast to Him, He will admit them to Mercy and Favour from Him and guide them, on the Straight Path, to Himself.

يَسْتَفْتُونَكَ قُلِ ٱللَّهُ يُفْتِيكُمْ فِى ٱلْكَلَٰلَةِ إِنِ ٱمْرُؤٌاْ هَلَكَ لَيْسَ لَهُۥ وَلَدٌ وَلَهُۥٓ أُخْتٌ فَلَهَا نِصْفُ مَا تَرَكَ وَهُوَ يَرِثُهَآ إِن لَّمْ يَكُن لَّهَا وَلَدٌ فَإِن كَانَتَا ٱثْنَتَيْنِ فَلَهُمَا ٱلثُّلُثَانِ مِمَّا تَرَكَ وَإِن كَانُوٓاْ إِخْوَةً رِّجَالًا وَنِسَآءً فَلِلذَّكَرِ مِثْلُ حَظِّ ٱلْأُنثَيَيْنِ يُبَيِّنُ ٱللَّهُ لَكُمْ أَن تَضِلُّواْ وَٱللَّهُ بِكُلِّ شَىْءٍ عَلِيمٌ ۝١٧٦

176. Yastaftoonaka quli Allahu yufteekum fee alkalalati ini imruon halaka laysa lahu waladun walahu okhtun falaha nisfu ma taraka wahuwa yarithuha in lam yakun laha waladun fa-in kanata ithnatayni falahuma alththuluthani mimma taraka wa-in kanoo ikhwatan rijalan wanisaan falilththakari mithlu haththi alonthayayni yubayyinu Allahu lakum an tadilloo waAllahu bikulli shay-in AAaleemun

4:176. They ask you for a legal decree. Say, "Allah gives you a decree concerning the person who has neither parents nor offspring. If it is a man that dies with no child, and he has a sister, she shall have half of what he leaves behind. – And he shall inherit her, if she has no child. – And if there are two sisters, they shall have two-thirds of what he leaves behind. And if there are siblings, both male and female, then the share of the male shall be equal to the shares of two females. Allah makes things clear to you, lest you err. And Allah knows all things."[93]

---

93. This Verse constitutes a sort of Supplement to the Qur'aanic Law of Inheritance enunciated in Verses 4:11 and 4:12.